THE EGO
AND ITS DEFENSES

THE EGO
AND ITS DEFENSES

H.P. LAUGHLIN, M.D., Sc.D., Sc.S.D.

Clinical Professor of Psychiatry, The George Washington University Medical School and Distinguished Visiting Professor, The University of Louisville, Practicing Psychiatrist in Frederick, Maryland, Founder, The American College of Psychiatrists, The American Society of Psysician Analysts, and Honorary Life President, The American College of Psychoanalysts.

SECOND EDITION

New York • Jason Aronson • London

DEDICATED

to Page Laughlin and to each member of our extending family...

to each of my loyal friends, colleagues and students...

and to each person who opens these pages....

Preface to the Second Edition

These concepts generate continuing clinical interest and scholarly utilization. *The Ego and Its Defenses* is a medical as well as a psychiatric best seller. It is used in colleges, universities, and graduate training programs in the U.S.A. and abroad. It assists Board Candidates. It is quoted in the literature and cited in research. Therapists, teachers, clinicians, and selected patients have found it helpful.

The National Psychiatric Endowment Fund presents this work or *The Neuroses* to recipients of its annual awards—the N.P.E.F. Fellows—from sixteen or so of our leading postgraduate training programs. Copies are awarded at the Annual Meetings of The American College of Psychoanalysts.

With *The Ego and Its Defenses* and with my other works royalties go to worthy causes of professional organizations. Supplemented by our personal contributions, award funds are thereby established to recognize contributions, dedication, and achievement. Hopefully these will be continued and enhanced via The National Psychiatric Endowment Fund.

Your kind reception of this work over the years is indeed gratifying and is very much appreciated.

Frederick, Maryland
July 1979

H. P. Laughlin

Preface to the First Edition

The Ego And Its Defenses is written for you. Students, psychiatric residents, and Board Candidates particularly, together with medical and psychiatric colleagues, have been in mind constantly throughout its preparation. Its orientation is constantly clinical, dynamic, and therapeutic. Numerous illustrations are included.

Earlier prospectively entitled the "red book" of *Mental Mechanisms,* this is the long promised supplement and successor to the earlier studies of dynamisms which were included in *The Neuroses in Clinical Practice* (1956), and the "blue book" of *Mental Mechanisms* (1963). The present title further stresses the significance and indispensibility of these defensively intended operations. They are major and universal ego functions. In addition, inasmuch as they are integral and inseparable parts of the ego, our discussion and study of either almost inevitably involves both.

Knowledge of the ego defenses is basic, and is a "must" in understanding dynamics and psychopathology, especially in the neuroses and functional psychoses. Accordingly, our present conceptions are to be integrated with those in *The Neuroses* (1967), to which some references are provided with each chapter.

Page numbers to aid in referring to this and to earlier books will accompany the appropriate entries in the *Contemporary Dictionary of Psychiatric Terms and Concepts,* which is a work now in preparation. Terms and concepts in italics in the current volume are also defined therein.

Many concepts appear in print in these pages for the first time. These plus certain labels describing clinical and psychodynamic phenomena, are offered to aid in their identification, as a convenience for the student, and when personally useful and suitable, for possible addition to your own psychiatric shorthand. I hope very much they are helpful. Should you appreciate an opportunity to check retention, sample questions follow the chapters.

The clinical work and research for *The Ego And Its Defenses* are personal endeavors, without outside help or subsidy. I am grateful to Mrs. Wyman for typing the final manuscript, and to several colleagues for case examples. Friendly comments received about conceptions are greatly appreciated, and I hope you like the present ones.

Bethesda and Mount Airy, Maryland
March 1970

H. P. Laughlin

Contents

Page

PART ONE.   THE EGO AND ITS DEFENSES

1.	MENTAL MECHANISMS	3
2.	COMPENSATION	17
3.	CONVERSION	29
4.	DENIAL	56
5.	DISPLACEMENT	86
6.	DISSOCIATION	94
7.	FANTASY	109
8.	IDEALIZATION	123
9.	IDENTIFICATION	133
10.	INCORPORATION	163
11.	INTERNALIZATION	174
12.	INTROJECTION	181
13.	INVERSION	193

PART TWO.   INTRAPSYCHIC MECHANISMS OF DEFENSE

14.	EMOTIONAL DYNAMISMS	209
15.	PROJECTION	220
16.	THE KING DAVID REACTION	236
17.	RATIONALIZATION	250
18.	REACTION FORMATION	279
19.	RECHANNELIZATION	296
20.	REGRESSION	319
21.	REPRESSION	357
22.	RESTITUTION	386

23. SUBSTITUTION 401

24. SYMBOLIZATION 412

25. UNDOING 426

PART THREE. SELECTED "LESSER" DEFENSES

26. MINOR EGO DEFENSES -I 447

27. MINOR EGO DEFENSES -II 469

PART FOUR. APPENDICES

A. GENERAL REFERENCES 499

B. BIBLIOGRAPHY FOR AUTHOR 502

C. TABLES 509

D. CASES 510

INDEX 515

THE EGO
AND ITS DEFENSES

PART 1
THE EGO
AND ITS DEFENSES

THE MENTAL MECHANISMS

*... Introduction to the Ego Defenses: Defensively-
Intended Intrapsychic Dynamisms*

A. THE RESOLUTION OF EMOTIONAL CONFLICT

1. Universality. 2. Dynamic Psychiatry: a. Distinguished from Static, Descriptive Psychiatry; b. Dynamisms. 3. Healthful and Pathologic Consequences. 4. Building Block of Psychodynamics.

B. THE MENTAL MECHANISMS: MAJOR AND MINOR

1. The Mental Mechanisms or Dynamisms Defined. 2. Major Ego Defenses: a. Concurrence Varies; b. Encouraging a Useful Trend.

C. FUNCTION SELDOM ISOLATED

1. Synergistic Operation. 2. Intended Effects.

D. VITAL ROLE IN HEALTH AND ILLNESS

1. Contributions to Adjustment, Well-Being, and Social Progress. 2. Self-defeating Consequences: a. Exaggeration and Overdevelopment; b. Concept of Pathogenic Vicious Circle; c. Exaggerated Defense Equates Pathology.

E. THE CONCEPT OF SECONDARY DEFENSE

1. The Symptom (Dynamism, Character Trait, or Neurosis) An Intended Defense Is in Turn, That Is, Secondarily, Defended. 2. Therapy and Resistance: Preservation of Symptoms Through Their Secondary Defense.

F. LOWER ORDER AND HIGHER ORDER DEFENSES

1. The More Primitive Dynamisms: a. Concept of Primitive Dynamisms: Massive, Deeply Unconscious, Lower Order, Less Developed, Magical Quality, Primordial; b. Greater Frequency in Early Years, and in the Less Mature. 2. The More Advanced, Higher Order Ego-Defensive Mechanisms: a. Highly Developed, Complex, and Less Primitive Nature; b. Greater Frequency in Later Years, and in the More Mature. 3. The Neuroses: a. Lower Order Neuroses; b. Higher Order Neuroses.

G. SUMMARY

H. REFERENCES (FROM *The Neuroses*)

I. REVIEW QUESTIONS

A. THE RESOLUTION OF EMOTIONAL CONFLICT

1. Universality

During the past few decades of scientific observation, study, and research into human behavior, a group of internal psychologic processes has become increasingly recognized. These are defensively-intended endeavors of the ego. Many of them are widely, in some instances universally, utilized by the psyche. They are rather readily identifiable and are repeatedly encountered by the observant student of human psychology. Known familiarly as the ego defenses, mental mechanisms, or dynamisms, their aims and goals are directed toward facilitating individual adaptation and defense.

Through the evolution and defensive employment of various dynamisms, the human organism unconsciously seeks to resolve *intra*psychic conflicts. These are conflicts between major internal parts of the self. Resolution of course is also sought of *extra*psychic conflicts. These are conflicts between a consciously recognized aspect or part of oneself and some demand or requirement of the external environment or society.

The mental mechanisms are defensive operations of the ego. Accordingly they are quite properly referred to as *ego defenses*. They are evolved automatically by the psyche in order to avoid psychic pain and discomfort, through the sought-after resolution of emotional conflicts. The term of ego defense may deserve preference in conveying the operation of an involved and dynamic intrapsychic process, over "mental mechanism" which might imply a rather rigid, mechanical, and stereotyped operation. The evolution of one's ego defenses occurs within the psyche as an automatic and consciously effortless process.

There are some 22 *major* ego defenses which are reasonably distinct and which we can identify and distinguish with a fair measure of facility and accuracy. We have selected 26 additional *minor* ego defenses for brief study (cf. Chapters 26 and 27). The delineation of at least the major defenses is gradually securing more professional agreement. An aim of this book is to promote further concurrence for both major and minor defenses.

Among the more familiar ego defenses are Rationalization, Compensation, and Identification. Another dozen are quite prominent and can be readily observed clinically.

2. Dynamic Psychiatry

A. DISTINGUISHED FROM STATIC, DESCRIPTIVE PSYCHIATRY.—Modern conceptions increasingly regard human personality and its various emotional, functional, and mental components as a dynamic whole. *Dynamic psychiatry* focuses interest on factors in human behavior that are active, laden with energy, and ever changing. In the older, more static *descriptive psychiatry,* study was largely directed toward clinical patterns, symptoms, life history, and classification.

The adjective *dynamic* indicates energy potential, constant change, shifting emphasis, mutual interaction, growth, evolution, and development. In psychiatry, therefore, *dynamic principles* may be defined as those which are *compelling, driving, filled with energy, and forceful. They inevitably lead to change and evolution.* From the standpoint of emotional health, *such changes may be progressive and healthful. They may also be regressive.* Dynamic psychiatry is defined in similar terms.

B. DYNAMISMS.—The ego defenses or mental mechanisms, with their development and sequelae, are an integral and major part of our concept of dynamic psychiatry. They are themselves dynamic: it is through their evolution and operation that the development, adjustment, and integration of personality becomes a dynamic process. Accordingly, *dynamism* is an appropriate alternative term for "ego defense" and for "mental mechanism" in modern dynamic psychiatry.

Like "ego defense," the term "dynamism" offers certain advantages. It is not uncommonly used, and indeed might have replaced the older term of mental mechanism were not the latter so well established. The three terms are used interchangeably in this study.

3. Both Healthful and Pathologic Consequences

It is important to bear in mind that the ego defenses or dynamisms are widely present in normal, healthy psychologic function, as well as in the unhealthy and pathologic. We find them operating in every human being; their use is by no means confined to individuals who can be regarded as emotionally ill.

Ego defenses therefore do not constitute *a priori* evidence of a psychopathologic condition. Their presence is pathologic or normal in varying degrees according to: (1) how they are employed; (2) how psychologically efficacious they prove to be as a defense; and (3) whether the net contribution they make to the total individual psychologic economy is constructive or destructive.

4. Building Blocks of Psychodynamics

This volume, like the "blue book" of *Mental Mechanisms* is devoted to the ego defenses. These defenses are basic to our current theories in psychiatry. It is essential to know these intrapsychic processes so that one's knowledge of psychiatry and indeed of human development, personality, and behavior, may rest on a solid foundation. Familiarity with them is necessary for understanding neurotic and psychotic reactions, character defenses and reactions, and the adjustment of the so-called normal, healthy personality.

An adequate conception of human motivation and psychopathology thus requires a working understanding of these vital defensively-intended endeavors. This is a *must* for the psychotherapist. The dynamisms or mental mechanisms are foundation stones of modern dynamic psychiatry. They are the building blocks of psychodynamics.

B.   THE MENTAL MECHANISMS: MAJOR AND MINOR

1. The Mental Mechanisms or Dynamisms Defined

We can now attempt a formal definition. Accordingly a mental mechanism, dynamism, or ego defense is *a specific defensive process, operating outside of and beyond conscious awareness. It is automatically and unconsciously employed in the endeavor to secure resolution of emotional conflict, relief from emotional tension, and to avert or allay anxiety. A given dynamism is evoked by the ego as an attempted means of coping with an otherwise consciously intolerable situation.*

This definition will apply throughout our study. It should be considered a preliminary part of the definition for each ego defense.

Man is able to avoid or avert painful emotions or awareness of them, through employment of the various ego defenses individually and *unconsciously*. Similar endeavors made *consciously* and deliberately are often named identically. However, for the process to be really an ego defense or mental mechanism in accord with our definition above, it must operate outside conscious awareness, that is, it must be essentially an unconscious endeavor. This distinction cannot be overstressed.

2. Major Ego Defenses

A. CONCURRENCE VARIES.—The ego defenses are listed in *Table 1*. The first group of 22 dynamisms can be more or less clearly delineated. They enjoy a fair measure of professional acceptance. I have accordingly proposed that they be referred to as the *major, senior, prime,* or *primary* ego defenses.

A number of other such defensively-intended processes are less distinctly delineated and identified. We can regard these as *minor, junior,* or *secondary* ego defenses. There is less professional acceptance and concurrence concerning these and they receive less attention and emphasis. The term "minor," however, does not imply that in a given situation, or for a given individual, their operation will not be significant indeed.

The major and minor mental mechanisms, as delineated and discussed in our present study are listed in the following tabulation:

Table 1

The Ego Defenses or Mental Mechanisms

The ego defenses comprise a group of significant patterns of psycho-logic defense which are unwittingly evolved. They are also known as *dynamisms,* or *mental mechanisms.* They may be tabulated and divided into *major* (*prime* or *primary*) and *minor* (or *secondary*) groups as follows:

I. The Major Dynamisms

We can list some 22 major ego defenses. They are also termed *prime* or *primary* dynamisms. They are discussed in alphabetical order, in Chapters 2 through 13, 15, and 17 through 25 of this book.

1. Compensation [a]	13. Projection
2. Conversion	14. Rationalization
3. Denial	15. Reaction Formation
4. Displacement	16. Rechannelization [a]
5. Dissociation	(Sublimation)
6. Fantasy	17. Regression
7. Idealization	18. Repression [a]
8. Identification [a]	19. Restitution [a]
9. Incorporation	20. Substitution
10. Internalization	21. Symbolization
11. Introjection	22. Undoing
12. Inversion [a]	

II. The Minor Dynamisms

The following are a group of internal defensive operations which have interest, and can function as ego defenses.

In view of the less distinct delineation and less professional agreement, I would propose that we refer to them as the *minor* or *secondary* ego defenses or mental mechanisms. These are briefly discussed, in alphabetical order, in Chapters 26 and 27 of this book (pp. 447–496).

1. Absolution	15. Generalization
2. Atonement and Penance	16. Intellectualization
3. Compartmentalization	17. Isolation
4. Compromise Formation	18. Overdeterminism
5. Condensation	19. Personal Invulnerability
6. Convergence	20. Replacement
7. Deferment	21. Retribution
8. Devaluation	22. Retrospective (or Retroactive) Devaluation
9. Distortion	23. Reversal
10. Diversion	24. Splitting
11. Extension	25. Unwitting Ignorance
12. Externalization	26. Withdrawal
13. Fainting	
14. Fire Drill	

III. Special Reactions and Combinations of Dynamisms

A number of complex reactions and combinations of ego defenses can be observed with sufficient frequency to warrant separate recognition, description, and study. This includes the following three examples, and doubtless others in the future.

1. The King David Reaction [b]	2. Righteous Indignation
a. Positive Type	3. Character Defenses and Character Reactions [c]
b. Negative Type	

---

[a] Covered in additional detail in the chapters so-titled in the "blue book" of *Mental Mechanisms.*

[b] Included with major ego defenses in Chapter 16, p. 236, as a matter of convenience, emphasis, and personal interest.

[c] See Chapter 5, The Character Reactions, in *The Neuroses,* pp. 227–307.

B. ENCOURAGING A USEFUL TREND.—A review of the psychiatric literature, indicates some differences of viewpoint about the delineation and classification of some ego defenses. Authorities have used different names for the same process, failed to recognize the existence of certain dynamisms, or assigned overlapping meanings and functions. The overall trend, hopefully, is toward gradual agreement on their function and meaning, and more precise definition and usage. It is hoped that this book may encourage such a useful trend, in the interest of more accuracy and clarity in professional communication and scientific progress.

To a considerable extent the above differences are more apparent than real. Some are present through personal choice, the evolution of individual terminology in a rapidly developing field, or practice and usage in a particular training center. The primary defensive operations remain the same regardless of individual preferences as to terminology, or professional variations in viewpoint. Indeed, such variations are useful to our scientific discipline through fostering continuing inquiry. Stagnation is avoided and avenues are opened for further constructive evolution, and for possible advance through new modifications of terminology, theory, thought, and view.

C. FUNCTION SELDOM ISOLATED

1. Synergistic Operation

In any thorough discussion of the ego defenses, they must be considered separately, in the interests of clarity, convenience, and simplicity. However, we should keep in mind that they are rarely to be found functioning independently. We can rarely completely isolate a given dynamism clinically, save for purposes of demonstration and study. Generally ego defenses act in concert, and thus are rather seldom encountered in practice as isolated phenomena. They often reenforce each other. Their operation is not infrequently synergistic.

There are many examples of overlapping: for examples, Idealization is often intimately associated in its operation with Identification, and Substitution with Displacement. A number of ego defenses can function in the service of Denial.

2. Intended Effects

Inversion and Reaction Formation operate similarly, are difficult to differentiate, and often enough require the drawing of a fine line of distinction. Incorporation, Introjection, and Internalization are analogous, subserve similar psychologic functions, have overlapping usage, and may be nearly impossible to clearly distinguish. (See Chapters 10 through 12.)

The observer will find that two or more ego defenses often function concurrently to produce a common defensively-intended effect: (1) to allay or prevent anxiety; (2) to resolve emotional conflict; (3) to combat emotional discomfort and pain; and/or (4) to prevent *derepression;* (defined as *the return into consciousness of ideas, thoughts, emotions, desires, fantasies, or wishes that have been earlier banished from conscious awareness because they proved too painful and intolerable*).

D.   VITAL ROLE IN HEALTH AND ILLNESS

1. Contributions to Adjustment, Well-Being, and Social Progress

The vital role which ego defenses play in emotional well-being is clear. They can contribute constructively to emotional equanimity. One's satisfactions in living may be increased and personal and professional effectiveness and efficiency may be enhanced.

It is largely exaggeration or overdevelopment of ego defenses that makes for trouble. When their operation is in proper balance it is constructively defensive and contributions are made to emotional health and to individual growth and maturity. Inevitably, the unconscious adoption and development of dynamisms and patterns of reaction based upon their operation enter into character formation. Various constellations of character traits are influenced by and influence, the individual dynamisms employed. These intrapsychic defense processes can be viewed as providing a useful emotional "safety valve." Internal pressures which are otherwise intolerable thereby can be absorbed, neutralized, or given a consciously acceptable outward expression. This can be of considerable benefit.

Finally, social benefits can accrue from the operation of ego defenses. For example, energy from the so-called instinctual drives can become both altered and redirected through their Rechannelization or Sublimation (Chapter 19) into socially useful channels. There are many examples of constructive consequences.

2. Self-defeating Consequences

A. EXAGGERATION AND OVERDEVELOPMENT.—We are especially interested in connection with the neuroses and the practice of psychotherapy, in the self-defeating, destructive, and pathologic consequences of the mental mechanisms. According to the principles of the important *Attention Hypothesis,*[1] our interest is often selectively drawn toward the difficult and troublesome aspects of a person, situation, object, or opera-

---

[1] The *Attention Hypothesis,* (*The Neuroses,* pp. 280, 349, and 586–9), points out that *one's attention tends to be selectively, automatically, and irresistibly drawn toward one's personal areas of greatest interest and concern.*

Things which trouble us, result in painful emotional feelings, or hold some special interest for us, will thus likely serve as a magnet for our attention, as distinguished from more neutral areas. There is significant attraction for our attention present in matters of concern and trouble. Such areas are likely to take priority over pleasurable ones.

tion of a dynamism. These developments can contribute to psycho-pathology.

Thus, through the exaggeration and overdevelopment of various existing ego dynamisms, or as a consequence of the evolvement of new internal psychologic defenses (in the event of the inadequacy or failure of existing ones), symptom formation can result. In this manner, the psychogenesis of all kinds of emotional illness may be facilitated. In analogous fashion, character defensive traits may evolve which become progressively more self-defeating, or existing ones may become exaggerated to an emotionally unhealthful state.

B. CONCEPT OF PATHOGENIC VICIOUS CIRCLE.—The net result of employment of a given dynamism may well be self-defeat. Hereby the dynamism may help exaggerate or ensure bringing about the very thing —conflict, dreaded contingency or situation, anxiety—which contributed to the initiating intolerable distress in the first place! What we might accordingly refer to as the *Concept of the Pathogenic Vicious Circle* can ensue.

Distress, or the threat of distress brings into play the ego defense, which increases distress, which in turn reenforces the defensive processes against it, and so on. This inimical process leads to self-defeat, psycho-pathology, and on into neurotic reactions, character reactions, and psychotic reactions. Sometimes through the operation of our *Concept of Functional-Structural Progression,* the process eventually and tragically proceeds on into fixed and irreversible structural (organic) pathology.

The use of one or more dynamisms ultimately may become so pervasive in one's life and adjustment as to this becoming literally a "way of life." This way of life may constitute a neurosis, perhaps severe, limiting, pathologic. Another possible sequela is facilitation of a serious, pathologic, regressive illness.

C. EXAGGERATED DEFENSE EQUATES PATHOLOGY.—Finally, through overdevelopment of a dynamism, insight and an accurate self-picture are likely to be clouded for the emotionally sick individual, or for one who initially is relatively healthy emotionally, as well. The defense is developed unconsciously and so maintained. In essence, an exaggerated defense equates and becomes pathology. Should its operation dawn upon one's conscious awareness, its effectiveness would probably be lost: hence the psyche of the individual will guard it well. This helps explain the resistances encountered in therapy.

Resistance is a major manifestation of the *secondary defenses:* those which in turn guard the established ego defense, character defensive trait, and neurosis. The latter have evolved as intended *primary defenses.* The foregoing states a basic and useful concept. Let us discuss this in more detail.

E. THE CONCEPT OF SECONDARY DEFENSE

1. The Symptom (Dynamism, Character Trait, or Neurosis), An Intended Defense, Is in Turn, That Is, Secondarily, Defended

One of the ego defenses is often, perhaps most often, the first unconscious endeavor which is called into play to meet psychologic conflict and danger. It is a *primary* defense. Most emotional symptoms may be also regarded as primary defenses, as may many of the character defenses (character or personality traits). Neurotic Reactions are patterns of intended defense. Now, as indicated above, once a defense is called into play and has become operative, it becomes a vital matter to the person concerned. He unconsciously seeks to maintain it, sometimes at almost all costs.

Part of this requires that its unconscious nature be maintained. Often enough it will not fully stand up under objective scrutiny, hence its effectiveness will likely be impaired if it comes into consciousness. It is therefore hardly surprising that *the primary defense becomes in turn defended*.

This is the important and useful *Concept of the Secondary Defense*. All subsequent endeavors—conscious and unconscious—which seek to maintain and preserve the operation of any dynamism, symptom, or character defense, are secondary defenses. In other words, the dynamism, or symptom, a defense itself, is in turn (i.e., secondarily) defended.

2. Therapy and Resistance: Preservation of Symptoms Through Their Secondary Defense

The nature and means of the secondary defense vary widely. For example, a patient may insist that a physical basis simply *must* be at the root of his conversion pain or paralysis, as examples, refusing even to consider the possibility of *any* emotional basis or contribution. When this most difficult state of affairs transpires we have illustrated for us a most resistant type of secondary defense. It has been termed the *Flight-to-the-Physical*.

Obviously such a flight may, for most practical purposes, block therapeutic study, preserving what are only too often the individual's tragically self-defeating, but desperately clung to, symptom defenses. Often the more handicapping, the more isolated, and the more prominent the symptom, the more grim and vigorous its (secondary) defense.

The foregoing relationship between symptom-prominence and its defense frequently tends to be one of direct proportions. This is encountered sufficiently often to lead us to formulate a *Principle of Direct Proportion of Symptom-Prominence to (its) Secondary Defense*. Devising and naming this principle may help direct attention toward and stress the underlying concept.

Secondary defenses may operate in many far more subtle ways. Much of the resistance which one inevitably encounters in psychotherapy is a secondary defensive endeavor, seeking to guard the status quo of existing psychologic defenses. This of course occurs regardless of the extent of their self-defeating consequences.

There are myriad ways in which secondary defenses operate. Some of these will be illustrated in appropriate sections as we proceed.

F. LOWER ORDER AND HIGHER ORDER DEFENSES

1. *The More Primitive Dynamisms*

A. CONCEPT OF PRIMITIVE DYNAMISMS: MASSIVE, DEEPLY UNCONSCIOUS, LOWER ORDER, LESS DEVELOPED, MAGICAL QUALITY, PRIMORDIAL. —In the study of psychologic defenses, our concept concerning the "level" of their operation is of considerable interest and value. Thus, certain defenses operate on a more primitive level than others. These can be referred to as the *Lower Order* or *more primitive* defenses. Still others are less primitive and more advanced. These latter are termed the *Higher Order* or *more advanced* defenses.

A number of the ego defenses fit rather clearly into one group or the other. Additionally, the various neurotic reactions may be so classified.

The more primitive or Lower Order dynamisms are more massive in their operation. The emotional level of the members of this major category of ego defense tends to be very deeply unconscious. They operate more automatically. Conscious efforts in the same direction are more widely disparate from the unconscious endeavors of a given dynamism. Their use is more likely to be associated with less mature individuals. Finally, they tend to be more prominent as primordial mechanisms; in infancy and in the very young.

The ego defenses of Incorporation and Repression (particularly the *primary* Repressions) are excellent examples of the Lower Order or primitive dynamism. They are quite automatic and are deeply unconscious. Conscious efforts at Incorporation are rare, as well as different from the unconscious process. Repression of consciously unacceptable material is so completely different from similar, but quite conscious, efforts at forgetting that we prefer to use a different term altogether: *suppression.*

Suppression is *the conscious attempt to subjugate unacceptable thoughts or desires, in which one is clearly aware of the attempt.* In contradistinction, Repression is automatic and unconscious. Incorporation and Repression are especially prominent as primordial mechanisms, and are most operative and significant in the very early years.

B. GREATER FREQUENCY IN EARLY YEARS, AND IN THE LESS MATURE. —Additional mental mechanisms are included in the category of Lower

Order, more primitive, or lower level defenses. These include Conversion, Denial, Displacement, Dissociation, Symbolization, and Undoing. This group of dynamisms has a more magical quality.

The more immature, impulsive, and emotionally labile person is more apt to employ ego defenses belonging to this group, although this is by no means absolute and certain. Members of the group are also encountered more often in the very early years.

2. *The More Advanced, Higher Order Ego-Defensive Mechanisms*

A. HIGHLY DEVELOPED, COMPLEX, AND LESS PRIMITIVE NATURE.— The more *advanced* and developed, or *Higher Order* group of ego-defensive mechanisms tend to operate in a more complex and involved fashion. Their emotional level of operation tends to be less deeply unconscious. They are less massive and are less automatic, seeming at times to develop more gradually. Conscious efforts in a similar direction are closely analogous and the names for both the unconscious process and the conscious effort in the same direction, are usually identical. They operate in all ages and are more frequent (than are the Lower Order group) in the older and more mature.

The mental mechanisms of Rationalization and Projection are good examples of the Higher Order, or advanced dynamisms. As with others of the more highly developed ego defenses, they are relatively more superficial and tend to operate on a more superficial level (of unconsciousness). Conscious efforts in the same direction are common, and are so identical in their aim sometimes as to result in the conscious effort merging into the unconscious endeavor. Rationalization is used to name both the conscious effort and the (unconscious) dynamism. Each may be seen to operate at any age. The same name is similarly applied to certain other ego defenses and their conscious counterparts.

Members of this group are less massive, less automatic, less primitive, and less magical in their operation than are the Lower Order type of dynamism. They also tend to be more complex and developed than the members of the more primitive group.

B. GREATER FREQUENCY IN LATER YEARS, AND IN THE MORE MATURE. —The Higher Order dynamisms operate especially in conjunction with certain types of emotional illness, and in turn contribute to the psychopathology of the more advanced or Higher Order forms of neurotic reaction. The Higher Order ego defenses will more likely be evolved by the more mature, less impulsive, and at least outwardly more emotionally stable kind of person.

Other mental mechanisms which fit into the category of Higher Order, or more advanced defenses, include those of Compensation, Intellectualization, Restitution, and Rechannelization or Sublimation.

3. *The Neuroses* [2]

A. LOWER ORDER NEUROSES.[2]—As noted, this conception also finds applicability to the neurotic reactions.

Those neuroses which fit best into the Lower Order category, or more primitive group include: (1) Conversion Reactions, with the Somatic Conversion Reactions (hysteria) most typical; (2) Dissociative Reactions; (3) Phobic Reactions; (4) Soterial Reactions; (5) some of the Neuroses-Following-Trauma; and possibly, (6) some of the Hygeiaphrontic Reactions (hypochondriasis).

B. HIGHER ORDER NEUROSES.[2]—The neurotic reactions which fit best into the Higher Order, or more advanced group include: (1) Character Reactions; (2) most of the Anxiety Reactions; (3) Depressive Reactions; (4) Fatigue Reactions; (5) most cases of Hygeiaphrontic Reactions; (6) possibly occasional cases of Neuroses-Following-Trauma; (7) the Obsessive-Compulsive Reactions; and (8) many of the Military Reactions.

G. SUMMARY

We have noted the presence of the mental mechanisms or dynamisms as comprising a group of unconscious ego defenses. They are present universally. They are the building blocks of psychodynamics and have made the term dynamic psychiatry an appropriate one. Dynamic psychiatry was distinguished from the more static type of descriptive psychiatry. The conception of a more advanced, *Higher Order* group of mechanisms was noted, as was the analogous one of the more primitive, less advanced *Lower Order* group.

The ego defense was defined, and the more distinguishable 22 major and 26 minor dynamisms were tabulated (Table 1, p. 7). The ego defenses seldom operate alone. Their action is frequently synergistic. A vital role is subserved for emotional health through their contributions to adjustment, well-being, and social progress. On the other hand, their exaggeration leads to self-defeat and to psychopathology. A vicious circle can be unwittingly established, illustrating the *Concept of a Pathogenic Vicious Circle*. The *Attention Hypothesis* received mention.

The valuable *Concept of Secondary Defenses* and their operation was introduced. Views of a *Higher Order* and a *Lower Order* level of psychologic defensive operations were also offered. Suppression was distinguished from Repression. The principle of the defensively-intended *Flight-to-the-Physical* was noted. A *Principle of Direct Proportion of Symptom-Prominence to Its Secondary Defense* was advanced.

We are now ready to briefly consider the major dynamisms alphabetically in separate chapters, beginning with Compensation. This discussion

[2] See the appropriate chapters concerning these 12 categories of neurotic reactions, as delineated, discussed, and illustrated in *The Neuroses* (London, Butterworth & Co., Ltd, 1967).

will be completed in Part II after further brief introductory material. The latter, which should be considered an extension of the present remarks, will include several additional general comments and principles, a tabulation of the functions of the ego defenses, a note on the relationship of intelligence to emotional illness, and a brief definition of emotional health. (See Chapter 14, p. 209).

H. CROSS-REFERENCES TO *THE NEUROSES* *

Mental Mechanisms (general)

as *First Line of Psychic Defense;* pp. 68–9, 343, 541, 578, 691, 731, 874, 925.
In Nature of Anxiety (Chapter 1)
    as attempted defense against anxiety; pp. 8, 16, 20, 25.
    in *King David Reaction;* p. 24.
    in patterns of reaction; p. 24.
In Illusory Gains (Chapter 2); in *endogain* of; p. 69.
In Anxiety Reactions (Chapter 3)
    in Anxiety Neuroses; p. 117.
    in childhood development; p. 233.
    in Concept of Secondary Defense: p. 97.
    in extension of existing defenses; p. 126.
    in *Precept of Inverse Anxiety-Symptom Ratio;* p. 103.
In Depressive Reactions (Chapter 4)
    in *Concept of Advanced vs. Primitive;* p. 149.
    in resistance to therapy; p. 233.
In Character Reactions (Chapter 5)
    in character trait development; p. 288.
    hypertrophy of; p. 233.
    Lower Order group, in Conversion Personality; p. 260.
In Obsessive-Compulsive Reactions (Chapter 6)
    in personality development; pp. 320–1, 374.
    in rationale for Obsessive traits; p. 319.
    in recognition and referral; p. 363.
    in therapeutic evaluation; p. 369.
    in bases for repressed data; p. 367.

I. REVIEW QUESTIONS

Sample self-check questions on Chapter 1, The Mental Mechanisms, for the student, psychiatric resident, and board candidate.

1. Describe the functions of the ego defenses? Give a definition. Name six major and six minor dynamisms.
2. What is meant by their function seldom being isolated?
3. How can the dynamisms have a vital role in both health and illness?
4. Outline the *Attention Hypothesis* and the *Pathogenic Vicious Circle Concept.* Can you offer instances from your personal and clinical experience?
5. Explain the following terms and concepts:

---

* From Laughlin, H. P. *The Neuroses,* London, Butterworth & Co., Ltd., 1967. (general references to ego defenses continued on p. 218.)

    A. *Universality of Emotional Conflict.*
    B. Intrapsychic conflict.
    C. Dynamic psychiatry.
    D. *Building blocks of psychodynamics.*
    E. Major ego defense.
    F. Synergistic operation of dynamisms.
    G. *Primary defense.*
    H. *Flight-to-the-Physical.*
    I. *Principle of Direct Proportion of Symptom-Prominence to (its) Secondary Defense.*
    J. Self-defeating consequences of the operation of dynamisms.

6. What is the psychopathologic sequence outlined in the *Concept of Functional-Structural Progression?*
7. How does the *Secondary Defense Concept* apply in relation to emotional manifestations?
8. Distinguish *Lower Order* from *Higher Order Defenses* in dynamisms and neuroses.
9. What is the relation of the ego defenses to: (1) emotional conflict, (2) anxiety, (3) repression, and (4) emotional symptoms?
10. Why is an understanding of the emotional dynamisms important to the student of psychiatry and psychology?

CHAPTER 2

COMPENSATION

. . . Making Up for Realistic and Subjectively-Evaluated Deficiencies

A. DEFINITION

B. OVERCOMPENSATION

1. Analogy to Concepts of Structural and Characterologic Hypertrophy. 2. Personal Compensation and Behavioral Compensation. 3. National Compensation. 4. Compensation and Reaction Formation; Conpensatory Character Development.

C. ADDED TYPES OF COMPENSATION

1. Don Juanism and Sexual Compensation. 2. Contributions to Vocations and Avocations. 3. The Compensatory Dream. 4. Consequence of the Deficits of Illness: Deficit-Compensation.

D. COMPENSATION AS A CONSCIOUS EFFORT

E. FURTHER COMMENTS ON THE BASES OF COMPENSATION

1. Making up for Weaknesses, Lacks, or Deficits. 2. Alfred Adler and His Contributions.

F. SUMMARY

G. REFERENCES (FROM *The Neuroses*)

H. REVIEW QUESTIONS

A. DEFINITION

The ego defense of Compensation is more readily understandable to many people than are certain other dynamisms. This is partly because it is quite common for conscious compensatory efforts to be made for one's lacks, failures, and deficiencies. Such attempts are not only widespread but are also rather readily observable.

These kinds of deliberate efforts also offer us implicit evidence as to the widespread—nearly universal—unconscious evolvement and employment of the dynamism of Compensation. It is certainly not very difficult to carry over from the concept of effortful and conscious attempts at compensation, to one of a like endeavor operating unconsciously. The latter is an intrapsychic defensive operation.

Compensation is *an ego defense or mental mechanism, operating outside of and beyond conscious awareness, through which the individual seeks to offset, to make up for, or to "compensate" for his deficiencies or defects.* These deficiencies may be actual, or may be so imagined to varying degrees. It is the subjective evaluation which is significant in deciding upon the presence of such lacks. Included are individually meaningful items in such areas as physique, appearance, and performance. Also included are lacks in various personally significant and desired skills or attributes.

Compensation represents an unconscious attempt to meet certain standards, which are likely to be self-imposed, and which generally relate to some area of actual or supposed inferiority. The major underlying bases for Compensation stem from conscious desires and inner needs to secure ego reenforcement; including the gaining of attention, securing conflict resolution, and the procurement of recognition, approval, acceptance, or love. These may be sought from internal aspects of oneself, externally in the social context from others, or from both.

With these introductory comments let us proceed to a brief discussion of several significant aspects of this major dynamism.

B. OVERCOMPENSATION

1. Analogy to Concepts of Structural and Characterologic Hypertrophy

Conscious and unconscious compensatory efforts can advance beyond an optimum point in their constructive intent, to become slowly and progressively pathologic. When they exceed a level of objective usefulness, these defensively-intended endeavors may be termed *overcompensation.*

Overcompensation leads toward and can produce emotional-psychic psychopathology. In this inimical development, one can draw a psychic analogy to the physical process which transpires in certain organic types of disease. In the latter, the progression results in the *structural* hypertrophy of an organ or part. In the area of man's emotions, an ego-defensive or character hypertrophy occurs and is in accord with what we might term the *Principle of Characterologic Hypertrophy.*

Compensation for small or large stature, or for many other kinds of real or fancied physical deficiencies, is a frequent basis for the employment of this major dynamism. At times for example, compensatory behavior for such lacks becomes developed or exaggerated sufficiently to become readily apparent.

2. Personal Compensation and Behavioral Compensation

Compensation for small stature was the prominent ego-defensive undertaking in the following instance of Behavioral Compensation. It also serves to illustrate a particular variety of what we might refer to as *Per-*

sonal Compensation, in distinction from certain other categories. There are many and varied instances of Personal Compensation.

In this example the compensatory endeavor was reflected in the person's attitude and behavior. When behavior provides the principal avenue for Compensation, the process may be classified as the subtype of *Behavioral Compensation.* When this major category of the dynamism is operative, the effects can profoundly influence the interpersonal relationships of the person concerned. Consequently many instances illustrate both Personal and Behavioral Compensation.

Case 1

Behavioral Compensation for Small Stature

A 24-year-old graduate student was the smallest member of his class. Among his associates however he was considered "a real scrapper." His general attitude and demeanor left no doubts about his outer feelings of self-confidence. He would enter a classroom with a slight swagger, greeting his classmates positively and somewhat aggressively, in a raised voice.

On occasion he might lightly (or sometimes less than lightly!) punch, push, or jostle his fellow students about. While usually done in a friendly enough manner, this was still as though to lay claim to some kind of physical dominance of the relationship. He was quick to respond to an intellectual challenge, which from his history, proved to be a similar kind of automatic response to earlier boyhood physical challenges. At times, a comment or statement would be taken by him as a challenge, where none had been intended.

His general attitude in living and the picture he presented to people were reminiscent of nothing so much as a bantam rooster. Further, he was known for his quick temper, becoming involved in fisticuffs occasionally, even after he was well along in his twenties.

Under therapeutic study his relative aggressiveness, defensiveness, and cockiness proved to be an attempted Compensation for inner and more hidden doubts and fears of inadequacy These stemmed in particular from his limited physical endowment and his pervasive inner feelings about his lacks in this area. As the needs became clarified in therapy they lessened. His demeanor became gradually less aggressive.

3. National Compensation

Sometimes the leaders of a nation, often with considerable appreciation and support from the general public, may seek or accomplish a certain measure of Compensation for their people or country. This is pursued for example, through enhancing the historical background or reputation, emphasizing various favorable aspects of the "national character," physical prowess, intellectual abilities, and so on. Such measures both wittingly or not can be sought to make up for objectively realistic, or subjectively overvalued deficiencies of the people or nation, lack of historical achievement or progress, for character-tarnishing kinds of exploits (including personal ones of present and past leaders), or for less than heroic national stature as to character or physique.

This is an interesting major type of *Group Compensation.* Encountered through both the ancient and recent history of nations, in this particular application it might be distinguished through adoption of the term of *National Compensation*.

One basis of motivation in the preservation, repetition and growth of certain folk stories, legends, and sagas may lie in seeking to undertake this kind of compensation. Enhancement may thus take place over generations in behalf of a military leader, ruler or popular figure. Statues of national heroes frequently exceed life-size. This type of endeavor is also of course quite akin to and can overlap with the analogous concept of *National Idealization* (p. 128 ff.).

Many examples are present in history and literature of Compensation for physical deficiencies. Among these Napoleon is a striking instance of *Power Compensation* for short stature. Power Compensation similarly has undoubtedly played a significant role in the emergence of other conquerors and rulers—modern and ancient. Among the latter, Alexander was also notably small of stature, in some contrast to his conquering, heroic, and later God-like roles. Also see *Case 6*, following.

4. *Compensation and Reaction Formation; Compensatory Character Development*

Instances are to be observed clinically and socially which illustrate a kind of making-up-for Compensation which is somewhat akin to the ego defenses of Inversion and Reaction Formation. As Brierley noted, Compensation and Reaction Formation can be closely allied and differ only in scope. The consequences can be particularly significant from the standpoint of the individual concerned.

In the following examples, in what we can describe as *Compensatory Character Development,* the subjectively-evaluated deficiencies were compensated for through the gradual evolvement of defensively-intended personality traits which were largely in the opposite direction. In other words, the unconscious compensation resulted in the development of outwardly opposite personality traits. Further, the Characterologic Compensation also functioned in the service of Denial of the more hidden, inner and rejected attributes.

Case 2

Compensatory Character Development by a Military Officer

An Army General was actually on the shy, sensitive, passive, introverted, and insecure side underneath. However, he had compensated for these disowned, more basic, hidden and inner attributes through the unwitting development of those traits associated with the more outward-going, extravertive, confident, and brave person. In this instance, the person described obscured (that is, obliterated or overcame) his original difficulties through their repression and replacement with the above kind of opposite characteristics. Partly, these needs had led to his seeking a military career in the first place.

These traits which he had so successfully evolved were maintained until the tremendous external stresses he was subjected to during military operations in World War II proved overwhelming. He had been a successful military officer who had volunteered for, and served well in a number of important combat assignments. Ultimately he suffered an acute emotional breakdown under severe and prolonged battle stress. Following considerable improvement during therapy, he was retired from active duty.

Case 3

Aggressive Overcompensation for Timidity

A 42-year-old lawyer, in the early course of his analytic treatment, related with pride and at length a number of stories about his physical aggressiveness. Instances had extended into his adult life. Upon relatively slight provocation he had at times physically assaulted men of greater physical stature. Several quite recent instances were reported.

As analytic study progressed, it became increasingly clear that in reality he was a timid and fearful person. He had successfully repressed these attributes and had unconsciously developed the reverse attitudes as a type of *Replacement*. This had been accompanied by considerable pride and increased self-esteem.

He had thus overcompensated for his underlying timorousness and fearfulness, which he had consciously rejected as unacceptable. Through therapy his defensively elaborated belligerence and aggressiveness gradually faded out. They were no longer important to him. As the underlying needs for them had become better understood, their significance had steadily decreased, in direct proportion.

Case 4

Compensation for Disapproved Behavior

A 35-year-old single storekeeper described himself as having "always been the black sheep of the family." He based this upon a number of episodes of drinking, sometimes accompanied by aggressive belligerent behavior and a number of arrests.

Except for these infrequent occasions, his behavior was regarded by many as most exemplary—and therefore they were all the more difficult to explain. It was an unusual paradox in behavior. He had worked continuously at his present occupation for 12 years, without missing a day's work or taking a vacation. He was "most devoted" to his mother and sisters and the majority of his earnings had gone to their support.

In therapy it was learned that he had long suffered from strong inner convictions of unworthiness and guilt, reenforced by his behavioral lapses. His exemplary conduct otherwise, and his painfully self-sacrificing attitudes toward his family proved in part to represent unconscious endeavors at Compensation. In turn, in their being so overdone, these tended to keep the entire paradoxical and self-defeating cycle going. His behavior illustrated the *Vicious Circle of Self-Defeat Concept*, sometimes quite prominent in neurotic reactions. These episodes comprised a *Behavioral Conversion* (p. 37).

C. ADDED TYPES OF COMPENSATION

1. Don Juanism and Sexual Compensation

There are many added types of Compensation which are of importance. Among these I have selected several interesting ones for our consideration. The first we can call *Sexual Compensation* or *Don Juanism*.

Interesting speculation may be undertaken as to compensatory bases underlying the legendary seductive exploits of Don Juan, after whom this type of Compensation is named. The following case illustrates one course of development along these lines.

Case 5

Don Juanism: Compensatory Success as a Lover

A 36-year-old man in intensive psychotherapy was ill-favored physically, with slight build and unprepossessing features. He had remained single, despite repeated affairs with many women, which he had pursued in a compulsive manner. Although in a number of areas his achievements often left something to be desired, as a lover, he had been a great success! As one interesting bit of confirmation, in a two-month period, *five* different women made shirts for him, as an evidence of their affection and regard!

During childhood and adolescence, he had begun to suffer psychologically from his small size and relative weakness. He admired the bigger, stronger boys who excelled in competitive athletics. This avenue of achievement was blocked to him. He gradually came to seek Compensation through his considerable successes with women. Lacking handsomeness, he became increasingly personable. He had come to invest a considerable percentage of his total energy in his compensatory endeavors of courting and seduction. This, plus the compulsive nature of his activity, conveyed correctly the impression that the sought after measure of *Sexual Compensation* was not fully achieved.

In other words, on an unconscious level his successful Don Juanism did not completley make up for his physical lacks and the significance of these to him. In analogous fashion to our *Concept of the Incomplete Symptom Defense,* this constituted an *Incomplete Dynamism Defense.* As a consequence he had been steadily driven in compulsive fashion to increase their scope and "success."

The compulsive elements in his Don Juanism stemmed from the incompleteness of the Compensation achieved. The complex had established a neurotic vicious circle (Case 4) which was quite resistant to therapeutic intervention.

2. Contributions to Vocations and Avocations

All kinds of vocations and avocations can have important roots in internal compensatory needs. These endeavors can comprise significant *Vocational* and *Avocational Compensations.* In the following case, such needs led to a major interest in automobiles. A number of elements, as apparent, lent considerable symbolic significance to aspects of this strong avocation. It represented a major *Avocational Compensation.*

Case 6

Compensation in Powerful Motors; Avocational Compensation

(1) *Powerless and Impotent Position.* A 33-year-old man had a shifting and impermanent job history. This was despite his possession of a considerable amount of mechanical ability and ingenuity. He suffered from chronic feelings of inadequacy and self-doubt, and from serious difficulties in working out constructive relationships with others.

He felt blocked and frustrated at every turn. In particular, he had experienced his position in life as being one of overwhelming impotence and powerlessness.

This man's all-absorbing hobby gradually had become that of cars—

powerful ones which he rebuilt himself. Through this vitally important activity he had unconsciously sought and secured a significant amount of psychologic compensation. This represented an *Avocational Compensation* of great personal significance.

There was considerable symbolism present. He would mount a particularly powerful motor in an old standard frame and body, adapting and building necessary drive shafts and gears. On one occasion he successfully installed a 300-horsepower Cadillac engine in a 1948 Dodge; another time an aircraft engine in an old Pontiac Even more important to his satisfaction than the building was the driving.

(2) *Power Significant.* In his words, "I get a terrific kick from the feeling of power. It makes me feel real good. I like to hear the power of the engine and to feel it go . . . Racing is not important. It's not the speed. It's the feeling of exhilaration I have about the power . . . the response to my wishes . . . my control. . . . Here I'm the one in control! I'm the boss!" This was also a significant instance of *Power Compensation* (see earlier).

The feelings of adequacy and power in controlling and handling a terrifically powerful engine at least partly compensated for his own deep feelings of powerlessness and impotence. A number of other rather interesting factors entered into the satisfactions he derived. For example, the concealed nature of the power was also important. From a casual appearance, his cars would seem run-down and disreputable, hardly capable of tremendous acceleration and performance.

(3) *Master and Successful Competitor.* He also took pride in his skill at handling his disguised behemoths of the highway. He wouldn't expose passengers to such risks, but he delighted in taking curves. On one curve several people had met death "only doing around 60!" He boasted, "I can take cars around that curve at 85 and 90, and I've done it a fair number of times! . . ."

In this dangerous and unlawful, but personally satisfying way, he "proved" he was the real master of the power, and compensated for the self-doubts and inadequacies he felt in many other areas of living. Further, he successfully competed with others (the prior losers) for the highest possible stakes—those of life and death.

As his work in treatment progressed, he did not abandon his hobby, but it lost some of its neurotic worth and compulsiveness. His perspective of it changed in constructive fashion, some of his drives gradually becoming rechanneled (Chapter 19) into personally and socially more useful avenues.

3. The Compensatory Dream

Dreams are occasionally reported in which the manifest content clearly reflects a compensatory attempt. In them, the dream undertakes a making-up-for kind of process to an ego which has suffered loss or deprivation. As instances, a man who suffered financial reverse dreamed he was again wealthy; a woman whose husband long pressed for a divorce dreamed repeatedly of being loved and wanted; a mother whose son had left home and broken his family ties, had dreams in which he was happily back in the family fold. Many similar examples are to be encountered.

These we may term for purposes of emphasis and identification, *Compensatory Dreams*. In them the dream seeks to make up or to compensate for, specific losses or hurts of one's waking life.

4. Consequence of the Deficits of Illness: Deficit Compensation

Compensation is not infrequently observed clinically in conjunction with the handicaps of both emotional and organic illnesses. Compensation in the paretic patient, for example, is at times illustrated in his grandiose delusions.

The following clinical instance is one of Korsakoff's syndrome. Herein one sees illustrated the rather typical use of confabulation as a compensatory phenomenon. Confabulation may also, of course, be regarded and serve as a type of Rationalization (p. 250 ff.). These and similar instances illustrate the major physical, emotional, or mental varieties of *Deficit Compensation*.

Case 7

The Compensatory Use of Confabulation

John M. was a 36-year-old married patient who had been admitted to a mental hospital some months before with a diagnosis of Korsakoff's psychosis. This had been the consequence of uncontrolled chronic alcoholism.

John suffered from all the typical symptoms of this condition. When asked what he had done on the preceding day, he gave a seemingly plausible and coherent account of a shopping trip to town, accompanied by a visit to the home of his sister.

His activities of a week before were likewise described in some detail. These accounts were sequential and related in a convincing manner. Actually, of course, John had not left the ward since his admission! He was compensating for his symptomatic memory defects through confabulation, defined as *the filling-in of memory gaps by imaginary experiences,* which he *related as though they were factual.*

Confabulation is a frequent development in the Korsakoff type of alcoholic psychosis. In the foregoing instance, it served as a Compensation for the deficits of illness. While it might also be regarded as a form of *Alcoholic Rationalization* (p. 271), it serves to illustrate quite well our concept of *Deficit Compensation*.

D. COMPENSATION AS A CONSCIOUS EFFORT

We must differentiate the operation of Compensation as an unconscious ego defense, from the type of compensation which takes place through clearly conscious efforts. The following are two historical examples of compensation achieved primarily through conscious efforts.

Case 8

Demosthenes Compensated for a Speech Impediment

Demosthenes, later to become a famous orator and statesman in ancient Greece, suffered in early life from a serious speech impediment. He became determined to overcome his handicap. Accordingly, he practiced speaking endlessly, often while in the hills by himself. History tells us that he placed pebbles in his mouth, to make clear enunciation doubly difficult.

This was consciously directed effort to overcome a recognized handicap. Its success was demonstrated by the lasting fame that Demosthenes later achieved as an orator.

Case 9

Theodore Roosevelt's Successful Compensation

Another example, this time from modern history, is that of Theodore Roosevelt who in early life was a rather slight person, endowed with little physical stamina. At one time he was suspected of being a victim of incipient or active tuberculosis. With great personal determination, he decided he would overcome his physical limitations. He headed west, where he undertook a vigorous physical regimen designed to compensate for his frailties.

As a result of great efforts over a period of time, he gradually developed such great physical stamina that he led the famous Rough Riders in the Spanish-American War. This achievement contributed considerably to his personal renown and his later political career.

E. FURTHER COMMENTS ON THE BASES OF COMPENSATION

1. Making up for Weaknesses, Lacks, or Deficits

Compensation finds many psychologic applications. Through our increasing understanding of the operation of the ego defense of Compensation, we come to understand how strivings for power and prestige can paradoxically arise from weakness, or from subjective self-doubts and feelings of inferiority.

Menninger pointed out that overcompensated attitudes of "super" honesty have been observed which developed in order to cover and help control more hidden counter-impulses. He also earlier noted the compensatory sexual overactivity of the male who thus attempted to overcome hidden feminine attributes. Alfred Adler (1870–1937) made organ inferiority, the Inferiority Complex, and Compensation the principal tenets of his system of *Individual Psychology*.

Compensation may be employed in response to inner needs for acceptance and love. It may lead to unconscious endeavors to secure recognition, attention, or self-esteem. As noted earlier, its employment may be the result of actual inferiorities, deficiencies, and losses, or it may follow purely subjective and even quite unrealistic feelings of this nature.

We have limited the naming of Compensation as a dynamism to instances of its unconscious employment. Compensation may be a very direct and relatively simple process. Through it the individual utilizing Compensation unconsciously seeks to make up for his feelings of loss, or of deficit, as he experiences them.

2. Alfred Adler and His Contributions

The work of Alfred Adler merits special comment in our discussion of Compensation. Adler was particularly impressed with the initial position of helplessness of the infant. Thus each individual begins life in a most helpless position vis-à-vis both the forces of nature and the (powerful) adults about him. As Adler evaluated the effects of this on the developing psyche, he viewed the defensive consequences as producing compensatory strivings for power and mastery.

One's major goal therefore would become one of seeking superiority in response to—or at the least compensation for—the infant's presumed basic feelings of inferiority. We owe to Adler the widely adopted term and concept of the Inferiority Complex. We can see how the mental mechanism of Compensation becomes an ego defense of major importance indeed, to those who accept these basic tenets of Adlerian theory.

F. SUMMARY

Compensation is a well recognized and widely employed ego defense. Compensation may be sought unconsciously for limited stature, for various deficiences of one's physical, intellectual, or emotional endowment, for poor work, for lacks in one's professional or scholastic achievement, for marital failure, and for almost any aspect of failure in one's personal attributes or experiences.

Compensation is a major dynamism or mental mechanism, operating unconsciously, through which one attempts to make up for real or fancied deficiencies. Compensation is sought because of feelings of inferiority and to secure ego reenforcement; largely through increased attention, approval, and acceptance or love from oneself and from others. The deficiencies resulting in Compensation are subjectively evaluated. Conscious efforts at compensation are likely universal. The unconscious mechanism is widely employed.

The concepts and consequences of *Overcompensation* can be viewed as analogous to those embodied in the *Concept of Structural Hypertrophy,* and to what was termed the *Principle of Characterologic Hypertrophy. Personal Compensation* was named and distinguished as were the *Behavioral Compensations.*

Concerns over physical endowment lead to frequent compensatory endeavors. Examples concerning height, weight, and physical endowment were noted. Concepts of *Power Compensation, Group Compensation,* and *National Compensation* were offered. In the process of enhancing public figures, Compensation may be undertaken on their behalf. This comprises the process of *Public-Figure Enhancement.*

Athletic skill and physical development, as well as intellectual absorption and scholastic achievement may result from compensatory endeavors. *Sexual Compensation* was illustrated in what was alternatively termed *Don Juanism.* This type of compensatory endeavor also may be employed in relation to doubts about masculinity.

Compensation may follow the deficits of any chronic illness: mental, emotional, or physical. These endeavors have been termed *Deficit Compensations.* Interesting instances are found among hospitalized psychotic patients. The intrapsychic mechanism may be difficult at times to sharply distinguish from conscious efforts in the same direction. Conscious compensation can be utilized in the development of special attributes and leadership, and in combatting the effects of aging, and feelings of inferiority. The operation of the ego defense of Compensation contributes unwittingly but substantially to characterologic development (*Characterologic Compensation*), as it also can to vocations (*Vocational Compensation*) and to avocations (*Avocational Compensation*).

Compensation follows inner needs for self-esteem, for recognition, and for acceptance. It can operate in many complex and subtle ways in seeking to combat feelings of insecurity, nonacceptance, and inferiority. Excessive (psychopathologic) strivings for power and prestige can result. The term of *overcompensation* is sometimes employed to describe the exaggerated results of compensatory endeavors which are overdone, that is, progress beyond an optimal point. Some aspects of overcompensation were illustrated. It provides an occasionally significant pathway for progression into psychopathology.

Compensation is related to other major ego defenses, including those of Rationalization, Identification, Denial, Idealization, Inversion, and Reaction Formation. The characterologic importance of Compensation has been stressed and referred to in several examples. In these areas, it may be difficult to clearly differentiate from Inversions and Reaction Formations. One may operate in the service of the other in the evolution of character and personality traits.

Compensation can play an important role in the healthy personality and also can be a contributing factor in many cases of emotional illness. It is evident in many areas of family relationships, including parental attitudes. It also is very frequently manifested through its influences on behavior (*Behavioral Compensation*). Half a dozen added case illustrations are included in Chapter 6 entitled *Compensation* in Mental Mechanism, pp. 198–223 (*Cases* 73 through 87), for those sufficiently interested.

G. CROSS-REFERENCES TO *THE NEUROSES* *

Compensation
   As a Character Reaction Defense
      in *Compensation Character;* p. 878.
      in character trait development; p. 288.
      in Compensating Personality; p. 233.
      in military correctness; p. 280.
      in Obsessive Personality; p. 253.
   As an Illusory Gain
      endogain in relation to; p. 70.
      epigain in relation to; pp. 64, 65, 878.
   Emotional Illness propagated by; p. 66.
      in *Hygeiaphrontis* (Case 94); p. 466.
      in Phobic Reaction (Case 120); p. 573.
      in *Soterial Reactions;* pp. 612, 624–5.

* From Laughlin, H. P. *The Neuroses.* London, Butterworth & Co., Ltd., 1967.

In Compensation Neuroses; pp. 64–5.

   Conversion Reaction as; pp. 703–4.

   in Neuroses Following Trauma; pp. 854, 877–85; 894.

    Bases for Management Problems in (Table 40); pp. 877–8.

H.   REVIEW QUESTIONS

Sample self-check questions on Chapter 2, Compensation, for the student, psychiatric resident, and board candidate.

1. What is the unconscious defensive intent underlying the evolution of Compensation? Cite an illustration from clinical experience.
2. The concept of *overcompensation* is analogous to that of structural hypertrophy. Explain.
3. Cite examples of: (1) *Behavioral-Compensation,* (2) *National Compensation,* and (3) *Power Compensation.*
4. How can *Compensatory Character Development* influence adjustment?
5. What is meant by, (1) *Sexual Compensation* or *Don Juanism?* and (2) *Vocational Compensation?* Can you find examples?
6. Explain the following terms and concepts:
   A. *Characterologic Hypertrophy Principle.*
   B. *Personal Compensation.*
   C. *Group Compensation.*
   D. *Vicious Circle of Self-Defeat Concept.*
   E. *Incomplete Dynamism Defense.*
   F. Effortful compensation.
   G. *Avocational Compensation.*
   H. Individual Psychology.
   I. *Replacement.*
   J. Inferiority Complex.
7. In what ways can the occurrence of a *Compensatory Dream* contribute to progress in therapy?
8. How might knowledge of the potential for *Deficit Compensation* prove useful to physicians in other specialties?
9. Why is Adler accorded a leading position in our study of Compensation?
10. What is the importance of one's subjective, vs. objective evaluation of deficiencies, in the evolution of the ego defense of Compensation?

CHAPTER 3

CONVERSION

*... Elements of Consciously Disowned Thoughts
and Urges and the Emotional Conflicts Over
Them, Transmuted so as to Secure Disguised
Symbolic External Expression*

A. TRANSMUTATION OF UNCONSCIOUS CONFLICT

    1. Emotional Conflict Converted. 2. Major Role in Symptom Formation. 3. A Broad Concept.

B. THE NATURE OF CONVERSION

    1. Symbolic Outward Expression. 2. Definition: a. Conversion a Major Ego Defense; b. Autonomic and Behavioral Conversion; c. Physiologic Conversion; d. Psychologic Conversion Concept. 3. Conversions as Communications: a. Conversion Language; b. A Primitive Preverbal Language.

C. TYPES OF CONVERSION

    1. Childhood Conversion. 2. Conversion-in-Therapy: a. Conversion Headache; b. Symptoms Convey Message. 3. Combat Conversion. 4. Behavioral Conversion: a. Behavioral Language; b. Major Types Tabulated; c. Acting out vs. the Inhibition of Acting; d. Behavioral Conversion Follows Trauma; e. Pseudo epilepsy; f. Behavioral Conversion in Behavioral Patterns.

D. SOMATIC CONVERSION

    1. Gross Motor and Sensory Changes. 2. Motor Conversion. 3. Sensory Conversion.

E. ADDITIONAL ASPECTS OF IMPORTANCE

    1. Symptom Identification; Identification in Symptom Choice. 2. Affect Equivalents. 3. The Conversion Escape. 4. The "Gain" of Conversion Symptoms: a. Endogain; b. Epigain. 5. Relations to Other Mechanisms: a. Conversion and Dissociation; b. Conversion and Displacement; c. Regression and Identification.

F. SUMMARY

    1. Defense Against Anxiety. 2. Progression of Physiologic Conversions. 3. Implied Recognition Widespread.

G. REFERENCES (FROM *The Neuroses*)

H. REVIEW QUESTIONS

A. TRANSMUTATION OF UNCONSCIOUS CONFLICT

1. Emotional Conflict Converted

Conversion is a major and basic ego defense. It belongs to the more primitive and less advanced group of ego defenses and is therefore one of the Lower Order dynamisms. Conversion is frequently employed and is clinically prominent as a defensively-intended endeavor.

Through Conversion, otherwise intolerable unconscious urges and the resulting emotional conflicts or elements of them, are transmuted (i.e., converted) into functional, emotional, behavioral, or somatic terms. This ego defense operates thus to allow some measure of symbolic expression of disowned data via these various planes of function.

2. Major Role in Symptom Formation

The process of Conversion contributes prominently to symptom formation. Through it many types of symptoms evolve. Thus, hostility may be converted into headaches. An insoluble conflict between duty and fear may result in the onset of a Somatic Conversion paralysis for a soldier in combat. Consciously intolerable sexual wishes may secure a disguised and converted outward expression as "convulsions."

Elements in the unconscious conflict over a feared uncontrollable urge to strike one's child, for example, may become transmuted, so as to result in a restrictive weakness or paralysis of the offending arm. The young bride who cannot "stomach" marital relations may develop nausea and vomiting, pain, and other gastric dysfunctions. There are many, many clinical illustrations of the role of Conversion in symptom evolvement.

People sometimes make, perhaps in very figurative terms, such comments as, "He gives me a pain in the neck." ... "It was hard to swallow." ... "That situation was certainly a headache to me." ... "Prof. James makes me sick." ... and many similar ones. It is not too far, nor too uncommon, for this kind of process to actually take place, unconsciously of course, but in far more literal fashion. Symptom formation through the mechanism of Conversion enters into many cardiovascular, gastrointestinal, genitourinary, and neuromuscular manifestations. A percentage of all headaches represent Conversions, as do a certain proportion of many otherwise nonspecific bodily aches and pains.

3. A Broad Concept

The concept of Conversion was introduced by Breuer and Freud in 1894. At this time they described a process of transmutation of the energy of the "unbearable idea" into physical terms, thereby "rendering it innocuous." Today, the employment of this very useful concept can be substantially broadened. The ego defense of Conversion and its pathologic sequelae are basic to the evolvement of the *Conversion Reactions,* a major type of *symptom neurosis.*

In its widest application, accordingly, we have proposed that the concept include not only the major physical symptoms of the *Somatic Conversion* (Conversion Hysteria), but also the often less dramatic or striking, but very numerous and most important *Physiologic Conversions* (Psychosomatic Illnesses, Somatization Reactions, Psychophysiologic Disorders, or Autonomic Conversions). In addition, there are also a large group of *Behavioral Conversions,* and the broadest group, outlined in the conception of the *Psychologic Conversions,* wherein one might include most of the remaining psychogenic symptom complexes.

In this chapter we shall briefly discuss several important aspects of the dynamisms of Conversion, with some added emphasis on those not fully covered in *The Neuroses.* Further consideration of the clinical applications of Conversion is included in Chapter 12 in *The Neuroses* (pp. 639–720).

B. THE NATURE OF CONVERSION

1. Symbolic Outward Expression

Conversion is an important internal psychologic mechanism through which the danger and anxiety which threaten from consciously intolerable thoughts, ideas, wishes, or impulses is averted or held in abeyance. In this endeavor, the otherwise unbearable thought, affect attached to it, or elements in the conflict over it are automatically and unconsciously transmuted, changed, or *converted* into other forms which then allow some measure of disguised external expression.

The resulting outward expression is a concealed and distorted one, often appearing in a symbolic guise. Through the operation of this ego defense, the primary gain for the individual includes the (continued or reenforced) Repression of the idea, belief, wish, or desire which the individual had not been able to consciously tolerate.

Conversion can result in permitting: (1) the disguised symbolic expression and partial gratification of consciously disowned impulses; (2) the symbolic simultaneous expression of factors in their control, denial, or inhibition; plus (3) elements of concomitant and resulting self-punishment or retribution for having them, as concessions to the superego or conscience, a vital party to the conflict. As we shall stress again later, the foregoing factors help comprise the endogain of the Conversion Reaction.

Emotional conflict takes place within the psyche between the demanding and urgent impulses of the id on the one hand, and the controlling and socializing forces of the superego or conscience on the other. The ego is the battleground, and also seeks to serve as the mediator. Conversion is one of the major ego defenses which may be unconsciously called into operation by the hard-pressed ego when other efforts at mediation fail, and derepression threatens.

2. Definition

A. CONVERSION A MAJOR EGO DEFENSE.—By definition, Conversion is the name for *the unconscious process through which certain elements of intrapsychic conflicts, which would otherwise give rise to anxiety if they gained consciousness, instead secure a varying measure of symbolic external expression. The ideas or impulses which are consciously disowned, plus elements of the psychologic defenses against them, are changed, transmuted, or converted usually with a greater or lesser degree of symbolism, into a variety of physical, physiologic, behavioral, and psychologic manifestations.*

Through the conversion of these consciously intolerable items, and the tension-reducing effect of the partially disguised symbolic expression and discharge thus achieved, repression can be maintained. The vital psychic defenses are thus preserved, even though this illusory "gain" is secured at great personal cost, sacrifice, handicap, and self-defeat.

B. AUTONOMIC AND BEHAVIORAL CONVERSION.—Reference has also been made to autonomic and to behavioral conversion. Autonomic Conversion is *the transmutation similarly into an "autonomic expression or language" of elements of the repressed emotional conflict.* By autonomic, we refer to the self-controlling part of the nervous system, which is independent or autonomous of central nervous system control.

Behavioral Conversion is *the expression in neurotic behavior of elements of intrapsychic conflict in the form of "acting out," as a form of behavioral language.*

C. PHYSIOLOGIC CONVERSION.—*Physiologic Conversion is an emotional illness in which the consciously disowned impulses and elements of the unconscious conflict over them are transmuted or converted into symbolic physiologic expression.*

The functional symptoms which result serve to allay anxiety through maintaining Repression and through securing some resulting measure of resolution or relief, from the pressure of the conflicts, which of course remain wholly unconscious.

D. PSYCHOLOGIC CONVERSION CONCEPT.—*Psychologic Conversion is a broad conception of the expression of elements of the unconscious conflict into a psychologic language, with the elaboration of psychologic symptoms. Psychologic Conversions are psychogenic manifestations or illnesses, in which the consciously disowned impulses and/or other elements of the unconscious conflict over them are transmuted or converted into various types of symbolic psychologic expression.*

Herein the resulting psychologic symptoms serve to allay anxiety through maintaining Repression. Some measure of resolution may be secured or relief gained from the pressure of the unconscious conflicts.

3. Conversions as Communications

A. CONVERSION LANGUAGE.—Conversion manifestations can be regarded as communications. The meaning may be obscure and difficult to fathom, but it is nonetheless there. We might say in other words, that psychologic conversion can be regarded as the expression of the unconscious conflict into a *conversion* or *psychologic language,* usually with the formation of symptoms. This language is often quite foreign to a stranger, but can become quite meaningful to the initiated.

In analogous fashion, we might on appropriate occasions equally refer to a *behavioral language,* a *physiologic language,* and a *body* or *somatic language.*

B. A PRIMITIVE PREVERBAL LANGUAGE.—Conversion symptoms thus can be thought of as the expression of a nonverbal and unwitting kind of primitive language. Therefore, through their symptoms in the Conversion Reactions, people perhaps can be regarded as unwittingly reverting to a primitive preverbal language, in which they make use of sensations, postures, gestures, and visceral processes to express their emotions and their (unconscious) wishes. The psychogenic bases of such bodily symptoms, first proven by Charcot, have been since confirmed by Breuer, Freud, Ferenczi, and many others. The work of the early pioneers provided an impetus for the psychologic phase of what has been termed the *Medical Renaissance* of the second half of the nineteenth century.

The elucidation, clarification, and resulting resolution of such symptoms comprises an important part of the therapeutic work of many psychiatrists. Each detail of the symptom turns out to have a specific meaning or meanings in expressing such communications unconsciously. In the properly conducive relationship between individual and therapist, and under optimally favorable therapeutic conditions, many of these can be elucidated. These include the necessity of self-esteem maintenance for the patient. In accord with the *Self-Esteem Maintenance Principle in therapy,* this is a requisite for the gradual relinquishing of major conversion symptoms.

C. TYPES OF CONVERSION

1. Childhood Conversion

There are many types of Conversion, several representative ones of which we can consider briefly. Among these, Conversion Reactions are not uncommon in childhood. These may be termed *Childhood Conversions.*

While still occasionally to be observed clinically, they have not received much attention in recent decades.

Not infrequently, Childhood Conversions subside spontaneously. Many are relatively minor. The bases for some are mistakenly ascribed to a physical etiology. The more noteworthy and dramatic ones, especially the *Somatic Conversions* of childhood with their major motor or sensory impairment, are likely to attract more attention than other ones. There is a tendency for many children's conversions to subside gradually and eventually, with or without psychotherapy. This is in accord with the *Concept of a Basic Trend Toward Emotional Health.*

Various kinds of Conversion Reactions of childhood are likely to be found in the experience of every pediatrician and generalist in medical practice. The following is an example of a major Somatic Conversion in early childhood in which there was a gradual remission of symptoms in approximately 2 years. See also *Cases 13* and *14* as instances of Childhood Conversion.

Case 10

Paraplegia; a Major Somatic Conversion in Childhood

(1) *Sequelae to Unwanted Pregnancy.* Susie was a little girl who arrived unwanted in a family and at an inopportune time. As a consequence, she had seemed to have more than her share of difficulties, and had had a severe feeding problem as an infant. When she was four and a half years old, she suddenly developed a complete paraplegia. This could not be explained on any organic basis by a number of specialists to whom the child was successively taken. Finally and belatedly, she was referred for psychiatric evaluation and possible treatment.

The child had a sister 4 years older than herself. The older sister was very bright, and much the favored, although at least prior to therapy this would not have been admitted. Over the course of treatment, it became clear that Susie thoroughly sensed that she was unwanted and had been relegated to a lesser position in the family. This had produced severe conflicts in her feelings toward her parents, upon whom she was, of course, completely dependent.

(2) *Childhood Conversion; Psychic Needs Subserved.* To try to secure for herself the care she desired from her parents, and to help maintain repression of the powerfully negative feelings felt by her, she had developed the paraplegia, thus unconsciously converting conflicts over her unacceptable and threatening feelings into a disguised, symbolic, and more acceptable physical handicap. Her disability resulted in the forced securing of a measure of increased care, and concern from her parents. It also served as an indirect and concealed punishment of them, as well as of herself. It cannot be overstressed that this entire process had transpired outside of any conscious awareness.

During an 18-month period of treatment Susie regained the use of her legs, and family relationships improved. Two years afterward there remained only a very slight residuum of her paraplegia. This was only apparent on certain occasions, as when walking down steps, she continued to step them off one at a time, like a young child does when learning to walk.

Not all Childhood Conversions subside completely. Sometimes a given symptom will become chronic, persist to some degree, or it may disappear, only to recur or to be replaced at a subsequent time by a different manifestation. The occurrence of the conversion pattern of symptom defense in childhood can indicate a propensity for its operation again later in life, providing the proper circumstances and initiating emotional stresses prevail.

2. Conversion-in-Therapy

A. CONVERSION HEADACHE.—Headaches are a frequent Conversion manifestation. Most headaches, likely over 90 percent, are emotionally based and certain ones of these represent Conversions. Their study is often most intriguing. On occasion a patient will develop a Conversion headache during the course of a therapeutic session. This can represent what we might term *Conversion-in-Therapy*. When this takes place, it provides an excellent opportunity for the immediate scrutiny, study, and possible resolution of the headache, providing the patient can utilize the therapeutic approach. Following their gaining an understanding of the causal relationships between emotions and headaches, occasional patients can develop considerable facility in this type of constructive self-study, analyzing fairly frequent headaches which develop in their particular situations.

This fortunate capacity had developed in the following case. During one 6-month period of an intensive therapeutic regime, this man developed and with increasing expertise therapeutically resolved a number of emotional headaches occurring during the course of sessions. The resulting insights provided a valuable contribution to the therapy.

Case 11

Headaches During Therapy

(1) *Paradox of the Neurotic Position.* A 54-year-old engineer had remained single largely because of a defensive aloofness. This he had developed and maintained through the years as a consequence of intolerable, painful emotional losses suffered in his interpersonal experiences in very early life. However, the full impact of these losses had never been allowed to enter conscious awareness as being too painful to tolerate. It should be carefully noted that the protectively-intended distance helped to perpetuate the very conditions which were early so painful. Thus often in what we might term the *Paradox of the Neurotic Position.*

As the therapy progressed, the early painful areas came closer to the surface. This was good therapeutically, but had long seemed too threatening. For months this chap struggled over the derepression of his deep inner feelings of loss, desolation, and loneliness.

(2) *Tears Suppressed.* A regular signal of these feelings approaching the conscious level was that tears would start. These were unacceptable to him and were as regularly suppressed. Usually, a headache ensued immediately. This was an instance of *Conversion-in-Therapy.*

The tears might have served as a partial release, if permissible. Their suppression denied this, increasing the inner pressure for expression. Such expression was gained in a more disguised, symbolic, and thereby acceptable form, via the headaches. Conversion into symptoms, of elements of the unconscious feelings and resulting conflicts, had taken place.

(3) *Conversion Headache a Communication.* The headaches conveyed several messages. These included one of "How tough this situation is. ... It's a real headache to me"; with the significant overtones of: (1)

control of the repressed desolation, through its partial, disguised expression and the diversion of attention away from it; (2) the implied appeal for help and dependency; (3) the exacting of a measure of retribution for the scorned tears and for deeper emotions; and (4) still deeper implications as to hostility in response to early deprivations, and the Inversion of the hostility.

These headaches continued until he became fully cognizant of their emotional linkage, meaning, and intended function. Following their repeated elucidation, they were no longer appropriate and subsided as this phase of his therapy was successfully negotiated.

B. SYMPTOMS CONVEY MESSAGE.—Illustrated in the foregoing *Case 11* is a major principle of Conversion, in that *the symptoms convey a message*. Conversion produces symptoms. It is a major mechanism for symptom formation.

Thus, we speak of symptom "language" or meaning. Since this is a necessarily disguised, symbolic, primitive, strictly individual, and nonverbal form of communication, its message is seldom readily decipherable. Its translation into conscious and meaningful terms for doctor and patient is ordinarily a long and difficult process. Such understanding is blocked by strong resistances, staunchly defended (i.e., in accord with the *Concept of the Secondary Defense,* in which emotional symptoms, a defense in themselves, are in turn defended), and influenced by various factors of conscious and unconscious (epigain) secondary gain.

Unlocking the secrets of Conversion symptoms through their therapeutic elucidation whenever feasible, leads to their dissolution. Making the unconscious conscious results in the surrender of the symptom, as it becomes more patently an inappropriate means of attempted solution. The *Transparency Theory* thus stresses the usual inability of an emotional symptom to survive its thorough elucidation through therapeutic study.

3. Combat Conversion

The following summary illustrates the development of a disability via Somatic Conversion in which conversion followed exposure to overwhelming combat stress. This patient's primary gain (endogain) lay in the anxiety-defense function of the symptom.

His unconscious secondary gain (epigain) provided an external material advantage in that, being clearly unable to perform adequately with a paralyzed leg, his removal from the dangerous situation followed. This was an example of *Combat Conversion.*

Case 12

Primary and Secondary Gain

A 38-year-old major had had considerable combat service as an enlisted man in the Korean War, in which he had performed quite well. He had again faced combat in Vietnam quite well through several operations. His emotional equanimity continued until he once more was faced with great danger during his participation in the TET offensive in Hue.

The history of his family was replete with military heroes who had received medals and citations. He himself had been originally commissioned for performance in the field. He had a strong compulsion to measure up to his personal standards and expectations, as well as to live up to the family name. He forced himself for a time to continue, although inwardly he was desperately frightened. He was caught up in an intolerable and insoluble emotional conflict.

Suddenly, under fire, he developed a paralysis of his left leg. He had suffered a *Combat Conversion Reaction.* Unable to proceed, he was evacuated. Evacuated to an army hospital in the states where neurologic studies proved negative, the emotional bases of his difficulties were recognized. Under supportive psychotherapy, the paralysis gradually disappeared and did not recur

This was the case of a person caught up in an intolerable emotional conflict. The onset of the symptom was his unconscious primary defense against anxiety. Also unconsciously, at this juncture it proved to be acceptable to become incapacitated. This was not in any way a conscious kind of operation, but the Conversion of conflict into a physical disability. The symptom contributed to the endogain; while the resulting incapacity and how this affected his environment comprised the epigain.

4. *Behavioral Conversion*

A. BEHAVIORAL LANGUAGE.—Behavioral Conversion is *the name for both the process, and for the condition or behavior which results, when consciously disowned impulses, plus elements of the conflict over them, are unconsciously converted into disguised and symbolic behavior.* As noted earlier, this mode of expression may be regarded as a nonverbal kind of *behavioral language.*

The conversion of emotional conflicts so as to secure some measure of disguised expression in one's behavior can occur in many subtle ways. If not universal, this type of operation of the intrapsychic mechanism is very close to being so. Through Behavioral Conversion, *a measure of gratification may be secured in a concealed, and thereby more consciously acceptable, form.* As with other dynamisms, *its intent is basically defensive, although very often self-defeating.*

B. MAJOR TYPES TABULATED.—Conversion behavior can take many forms, a number of which we might undertake to delineate and name. Included are at least six major types. These are (1) *Social,* or *Minimal-Conversion Behavior;* (2) and (3) *Acting Out,* on the neurotic, and the psychotic levels; (4) *Acute* Forms of *Conversion Behavior;* (5) *Conversion Delinquency;* and (6) *Antisocial* or *Criminal Behavior.*

These constitute interesting and sometimes destructive types of what we have proposed naming a *Behavioral Language,* a term useful personally and in teaching. They sometimes can provide an ample basis for the old adage that "actions speak louder than words." They are outlined further in the following *Table 2.*

Behavioral Conversion is *the automatic and unwitting translation of consciously disowned impulses, or elements of the resulting emotional conflicts over them, into a disguised form, in one's outward behavior. The resulting behavior may allow partial symbolic gratification of the repressed wishes, aid in their control, denial, or repression, and simultaneously provide for self-punishment for having had them.* Defensively-intended, the end result may be tragically self-defeating.

Conversion Behavior can extend from the nearly universal, varied but often subtle and minimal influences upon social behavior on the one hand, to the gross and rather uncontrolled motor activity of the pseudoconvulsion or the destructive antisocial acts of the murderer, on the one hand. Behavioral Conversions are analogous to the Physiologic Conversions, the Somatic Conversions, and the Psychologic Conversions. As noted, they can often be regarded as expressing a preverbal and somewhat primitive kind of Behavioral Language.

Table 2

Major Types of Behavioral Conversion

Six types of *Conversion Behavior* are delineated and tabulated below as an aid to convenience in reference, classification, and communication. While their categorization is thus undertaken, instances will be found in which the types overlap.

1. *Minimal, or Social Conversion Behavior*
   This type of marginal Behavioral Conversion includes all the numerous and varied instances which take place in social intercourse. Many are very subtle or minimal. If not universal, this form of Conversion Behavior is very nearly so.
2. *Neurotic Acting Out*
   The unconscious "acting out" of unconscious emotional conflicts with neurotic behavior of various types. Unwitting self-defeat is often more apparent with this category of Conversion Behavior.
3. *Psychotic Acting Out*
   A category which names "acting out" behavior, when it is observed in psychotic patients. The resulting behavior is often more marked and bizarre.
4. *Conversion Behavior, Acute Forms*
   In this group we would include instances of conversion convulsions, pseudoepilepsy, hysterical behavior, temporary losses of co-ordination or flailing about, astasia-abasia, and certain conversion mannerisms, tics, gesturing, and posturing, which may be encountered clinically. Some of the latter can represent *Conflict Indications* or C.I's.
5. *Conversion Delinquency*
   This category of Conversion Behavior provides many troubling and problematic instances of impulsive and sociopathic conduct. It accounts for a proportion of instances of delinquency encountered in the teen-age and young adult groups.
6. *Antisocial and Criminal Behavior*
   A significant proportion of major crimes represents a kind of criminal "acting out." This major category of Behavioral Conversion results from unconscious impulses, seething resentment, and hatred being converted so as to erupt into external violence.

C. ACTING OUT VS. THE INHIBITION OF ACTING.—Conceptions of Behavioral Conversion, a behavioral language, and acting out are useful ones and have a wide applicability in the behavioral sciences. They can help in our understanding and explanation of human behavior. This type of Conversion may at times afford an unwitting safety valve, through which some of the underlying pressure of intrapsychic conflict is released.

Acting out is a frequent phenomenon in persons with a conversion diathesis. These people often have a predilection for the operation of this process, in which unconscious external action takes place in response to internal emotions that have been disowned consciously, but that continue to be active. In this way, the patient may express significant hostile or loving feelings in some self-concealed and disguised form of outward action.

Through acting out, the individual concerned maintains conscious ignorance of his feelings or impulses; he also is ignorant of their having been acted out. In Conversion (hysterical) patients we also observe the related tendency to act impulsively, without giving adequate thought to what may be the consequences of the action.

In certain instances of Somatic Conversion, on the other hand, it is sometimes as if symptoms are defenses *against* acting. They frequently include such defensive elements. These patients seem to fear that they have *no* control, or that their emotions will be acted out, no matter how destructive such actions may be personally or socially. When present, this element represents the symbolic inhibiting component of the symptom. It often simultaneously accompanies a measure of symbolic gratification of the impulse which has been consciously disowned.

The following instance represented the Conversion of homosexual excitement into a pseudoconvulsion. The activity symbolically expressed elements of the conflict in a disguised and acceptable form, and at the same time inhibited further response. At least two major aspects of the emotional conflict were thus represented.

Case 13

Pseudoconvulsions

A 16-year-old male boarding student was referred for evaluation following what were described as repeated convulsions. This lad complained that on various occasions boys in his dormitory crawled in bed with him when the lights went out. He was afraid of a "convulsion," which followed these times, and was anxious about going to bed or to sleep.

On repeated occasions he had been about to go to sleep when he would break into heaving sobs, accompanied by spasmodic contractions of his shoulders and body. Neither consciousness nor bladder control were lost and he had not injured himself. His attacks would be precipitated by someone starting to wrestle with him, sitting on the side of his bed, or climbing in.

In therapy he became able to recognize the presence of homosexual feelings and his great conflicts over them. He became better able to cope with these and other problems. What he had termed convulsions ceased and his social and scholastic adjustments improved substantially.

D. BEHAVIORAL CONVERSION FOLLOWS TRAUMA.—An acute form of Behavioral Conversion may be precipitated by emotional or physical trauma, or by a situation which represents a combination of the two. The clinical picture may interfere with obtaining background data in helping differentiate Conversion Reaction from physical injury. However, the extent of the actual injury may be slight, and positive physical signs and symptoms absent.

The following instance illustrates an acute Conversion Reaction in which conversion (hysterical) behavior was precipitated by a rather minor physical injury. This instance is also one of *Childhood Conversion.*

Case 14

An Acute Behavioral Conversion

On February 3, 1958, a ten-year-old colored boy was brought to an emergency room by ambulance in an acutely disturbed and agitated condition. The history disclosed that he had fallen on some ice while going to school and hit his head. There was a question as to loss of consciousness. Brought home, during the day he had become irritable and agitated. He vomited several times, and his speech became partly irrational. At times he rolled about in uncontrolled fashion, flailing his arms and legs about.

Upon arrival at the hospital, restraint was required to permit an examination. He fought the examiners, muttered unintelligible phrases, and answered questions with a haphazard array of *numbers!* There were no neurologic signs and no evidence of trauma could be determined. There was none of the more typical picture of lethargy as with severe head injury. Although he vomited, it appeared forced.

Gentle handling secured no cooperation, while a firmer approach produced a noticeable lessening of the flailing movements and irrational responses. Left alone and unrestrained on the examining table, however, the rolling and flailing movements did not cause him to fall.

The patient was admitted to the hospital for observation with the diagnosis of *Conversion Reaction, Acute Behavioral* type. Over several days, his behavior gradually became more normal. Psychiatric consultation afforded an opportunity to constructively discuss some troubling family problems. He was discharged as improved, with a recommendation for clinical treatment.

E. PSEUDOEPILEPSY.—In the group which we label as acute Behavioral Conversions, there is a tendency toward the clinical overlapping with other Conversion Reactions. This is hardly surprising since the underlying diathesis for developing Conversion Reactions is not necessarily limited to one type. Thus, Physiologic Conversions or Somatic Conversions may accompany or follow Behavioral Conversions.

This is illustrated in the following case in which an acute pseudo-epileptic type of Behavioral Conversion simulated epilepsy so closely as to lead to a preadmission diagnosis of *status epilepticus.* A short time after the more acute Conversion behavior had subsided, a left-sided Conversion paralysis supervened.

Case 15

Acute Pseudoepileptic Behavioral Conversion; Followed by a Major Somatic Conversion Reaction

A 32-year-old housewife was admitted to a neurology ward by her physician with a preliminary diagnosis of *status epilepticus.* History indicated continued "convulsions" for 15 hours without control under

sedation. To the casual observer her alternating clonic and tonic movements, and bouts of frenzied gyrations were impressive. To the more
experienced observer there were distinctions from a epileptic seizure.
Some of her movements also had sexual and orgastic overtones. The
diagnosis was made of an acute pseudoepileptic form of Behavioral
Conversion.

Under adequate sedation, the "convulsions" subsided. However, a
brief time after awakening 2 days later, this young woman complained
of severe headache and an inability to move her left arm or leg. The
headache responded poorly to medication. Examination indicated normal
reflexes in the areas of paralysis. Other studies were negative.

The patient's general attitude toward her major disability rather
typically illustrated *la belle indifférence.* The Behavioral Conversion had
been superseded by a major *Somatic Conversion.* She was quite passive
in her adjustment and very resistant to psychotherapeutic efforts. In
effect she was satisfied with the compromise formation represented by
the hemiparesis.

History revealed three unsuccessful marriages. She had a 16-year-old
daughter upon whom she was emotionally dependent and who had become seriously involved with an older man. There were also serious
sexual conflicts.

The daughter's reaction fortunately later indicated she was not on
the verge of discarding her attachment to mother in favor of marriage as
the latter had dreaded. With suggestive, and supportive psychotherapy,
the mother improved sufficiently in several weeks to allow her discharge
to outpatient care.

F. BEHAVIORAL CONVERSION IN BEHAVIOR PATTERNS.—Conversion
behavior can exert influences upon a person's social life which are minor,
subtle, and of little real significance. Upon occasion, however, one can
also observe the Conversion of various internal conflictual areas result in
the gradual development of a new major overall pattern of behavior. When
this takes place, it may be difficult to make a differentiation from other
major mechanisms such as Compensation, Reaction Formation, and Sublimation. *Case 4.* (p. 21) illustrated Behavioral Conversion which formed
part of a pattern and also illustrated the *Vicious Circle of Self-Defeat* in
the neuroses.

The following instance illustrated the Conversion of conflicts into an
external pattern of behavior marked by an increase in drive, in total activity, and by the direction it took. In this case, the overall activity was
motivated by inner insecurity, and inferiority and by the need for approval
and love.

Case 16

Behavioral Conversion in Overall Activity

(1) *Personality Dynamo.* A 50-year-old schoolteacher's personality characterized her as being a veritable dynamo of activity. From
morning to night this woman simply burst with activity, part of which
was directed toward dominating people. Despite substantial accomplishments of her own, she claimed credit for various achievements of
family members and acquaintances, especially those she had aided. Her
energy while working for these persons was considerable.

The bases for this intense activity stemmed from inner anxiety
and insecurity; from a deep need for approval and love, and from
her self-doubts and feelings of inferiority. Conflicts over these had re-

sulted in their conversion and expression in a form of intense be-havioral activity.

(2) *A "Second Mother" Role.* The teacher was the only daughter and second among 11 children. Her father had a strong and dominating personality, and directed some of his own great energy into building his family into a close-knit clan, as had his Scottish ancestors. Her mother was a capable person, but immature and selfish. She had been worshipped by her husband and sons without having to try very much to obtain it.

The daughter was assigned many onorous duties and took over much of her mother's work in raising the family. Her role in the family accordingly was forced to become that of a kind of "second mother," with many of the responsibilities, but few of the rewards. She performed very well, but in compensatory fashion had come to adopt the pattern of letting everyone know about it. She was un-wittingly also forced into a pattern of self-praise in futily seeking to acquire the worshipful respect from her father and brothers that her mother received.

(3) *Conflicts Submerged.* Many times she might have preferred to rebel from this adult level of responsibility, but this was impossible. Conflicts were substantial but submerged. Combatting her role was even more impossible in the face of her father's forceful personality and his great efforts toward instilling "family union." His success in the latter was partly demonstrated in that all the children were by now married and lived within a 3-mile radius, meeting together frequently for work and play.

The patient had married and raised two children. After the latter married, she still sought to control them and their families. When not engaged in these endeavors, she was pretty much the guiding "mother" of her school. Much of her intense activity and behavior was a major kind of Conversion Reaction One might interpret the "behavioral language" thus expressed as conveying self-doubt, inner insecurity, help-less position, conscious and unconscious efforts to combat these, conflicts over hostility, and approval seeking.

D. SOMATIC CONVERSION

1. Gross Motor and Sensory Changes

We now come for brief consideration to the major and gross mani-festations of Conversion that originally attracted attention to the Conver-sion Reactions and their basic mechanism. In this group we find the major motor and sensory somatic changes, formerly diagnosed as Hysteria, and later as Conversion Hysteria. *Somatic Conversions,* as a more apt current label, refers to the symptom, to the process, and to the illness which occurs when consciously disowned impulses, and/or other elements of the unconscious conflict over them, are transmuted, or converted into symbolic somatic expression. The associated gross symptoms result in major types of physical or sensory impairment.

The Somatic Conversion (hysterical) type of neurotic reaction differs from other neuroses in that the repressed material more clearly finds a disguised kind of expression somatically in physical symptoms. Somatic Conversion results in a symbolic kind of bodily language or expression. The resulting group of symptoms includes the marked loss of sensory or motor functions. Certain disturbances of movement and activity are included, with some possible overlapping here with acute Behavioral Conversions. Conversion is the pattern of neurotic reaction in which we may see a great many gross and oftimes bizarre clinical manifestations. Symptoms are not always long term. In the *Conversion Attack,* brief and episodic attacks of conversion manifestations can be encountered clinically.

Among the marked symptoms are included instances of motor paralysis, in which the reflexes remain active (see *Case 15*) and the distribution and functioning of the nerves to the various organs can be demonstrated as remaining intact.

2. Motor Conversion

It is to be borne in mind that the symptoms appearing as a consequence to the mechanism of Conversion may represent unconscious compromises of conflicting emotional forces. Symbolically, these can express aspects of both the repressed impulses *and* the repressing forces. However, they are never without their hidden symbolic meaning. This meaning is often extremely difficult to ascertain; generally, it can be reached only through psychotherapeutic investigation. Sometimes this needs to be most extensive.

One of the principal symbolic functions of Conversion motor disturbances is to prevent or to defend against possible action. Such action it is "feared" would take place in response to forbidden and hence disowned sexual or hostile impulses, most of which are originally infantile in origin. Thus, symbolically, spasms, tics, mannerisms, and paralyses (*Case 19*) may be intended to prevent forbidden activity, to permit symbolic gratification, to secure a position of dependency, and/or effect a psychologic flight.

There may be disturbances of coordination and motor activity in structures controlled by the voluntary nervous system. Fainting can be a Conversion symptom. It also represents a dissociation and can be regarded as a minor ego defense in itself (Chapter 26). Other symptoms may be less gross and dramatic, so that instead of paralysis in a leg, we may find only weakness in it. There may be a loss of the ability to speak (aphonia). These represent instances of what we can term *Motor Conversion,* a major subtype of Somatic Conversion.

There is practically no limit to the physical symptoms that can be observed clinically as manifestations of Somatic Conversion. As already stated, we may look upon these manifold somatic expressions as a kind of body language for the disguised and symbolic representation of otherwise forbidden impulses. Actually, the variety of symptoms and their possible combinations are limited only: (1) by the variety, degree, and possible combinations of the repressed unconscious needs; (2) by the bodily structures which are available to express them; and (3) by function and structure, as these are perceived by the unconscious. Conversion can mimic almost any symptom of any disorder and has thus been termed the *Great Imitator.*

The evolvement of physical symptoms on a Conversion basis also must be viewed as a desperate psychologic effort to maintain the otherwise intolerable thought or wish or impulse in a continued state of repression. It must be kept outside of conscious awareness at all costs. Its control is otherwise feared. Conversion thus is the result of a last-ditch effort to reach some sort of solution, no matter how unrealistic or self-defeating it may turn out to be, of what is to the ego or self an otherwise insoluble conflict. It is an endeavor to avoid anxiety [1] and what appears to the ego to be an overwhelming threat. The threat is of emergence to consciousness of the intolerable impulse and a resulting irresistible impulse to act in response to it. The evolvement of the physical symptom, with its consequent surrender or interference with function, the handicap it affords the individual, and the incapacity which is occasioned, is an indication of how desperate is his underlying psychologic need.

3. Sensory Conversion

Sensory findings may include all sorts of disturbances of sensation. There may be total loss of sensation, decreased touch sensation, or sensations of skin prickling or tingling and parasthesias without an objectively apparent cause. We may find impairment or loss of function of the special senses. There may be disturbances of seeing, hearing, and sometimes, but rarely, of the sense of taste or smell. Any area may be affected, but the locations may shift, and likely more often the affected area does not correspond with the anatomic nerve distribution.

In symbolic fashion, sensory loss represents a partial unconscious giving-up or loss of this aspect of perception, a shutting-out of some aspect of awareness for defensive purposes. The loss of sensation in any area on an emotional basis may be referred to as *Sensory Conversion.*

In effect, not being able to feel says that one cannot, one must not, one dare not, or one does not wish to feel. For reasons that are hidden and unconscious, awareness must be shut out. The areas of sensory loss usually do not conform to any precise anatomic distribution of the nerve supply. Examples are the "glove" or "stocking" types of anesthesia of an extremity. The area of sensory loss in Sensory Conversion actually *corresponds* instead *to the individual's unconscious representation of the area affected,* rather than to its actual nerve supply.

The following case demonstrates a number of the foregoing points. In it, the onset of symptoms represented a final desperate defensive (but self-

---

[1] Should anxiety be experienced concurrently with a Conversion (or other emotional) manifestation, this indicates that the manifestation is what is termed an *Incomplete Symptom Defense.*

defeating) attempted psychologic resolution of her intolerable situation for a young woman who had reached an impasse in living.

Her limiting symptoms could be gradually surrendered in therapy only as it became possible to do so without loss of face, and when external changes, plus the mobilization of additional personal resources, made her situation more tolerable.

Case 17

Sensory Loss and Partial Paralysis

(1) *Organic Diagnosis Made.* A 25-year-old housewife and secretary was transferred from a small out-of-state hospital for diagnostic study, with a provisional diagnosis of poliomyelitis. The routine admission history and physical revealed that she had been in good health until 2 years earlier, when following the birth of her third child, she began to suffer from severe dysmenorrhea and bleeding, and had become very unhappy and nervous. This became so severe that she began to take off one or two days weekly from her job. Both job and marriage were going poorly.

Two months prior to admission, the patient began having occipital headaches and low back pain. Five weeks later she noted anesthesia of both legs, and one week before admission they developed significant weakness. There was no history of fever, upper respiratory infection, or other significant symptoms. Spinal fluid and a mylogram done at the previous hospital were inconclusive.

Physical examination revealed a well developed, well nourished young woman rather contentedly reading a romance magazine. The findings were negative, except for the complete subjective loss of all sensation up to the iliac crests and a paralysis which was equal in the muscles of her legs, feet, and thighs.

It was impossible for her to stand, but she was able to move easily while in bed and against no resistance. Neurologic findings were normal except for a missing plantar reflex. The patient was unconcerned when asked to move her legs against resistance; laughing as she said "I can't!" She displayed no concern about the import of her very limiting and possibly serious symptoms.

(2) *Sensory and Motor Conversion.* This young mother had a low average IQ. She had barely managed to complete high school, including the bare essentials of typing and shorthand needed for her work. Her husband had demanded that the previous hospital release his wife for a few days prior to her transfer, a marital convenience which she had sought to avoid. New and complete laboratory studies were negative. Study and observation revealed many typical character traits of the Conversion Personality. A positive diagnosis of Somatic Conversion was made, and later confirmed during psychotherapeutic study.

This patient's symptoms had developed as a last-ditch defense by an embattled and threatened ego. They expressed a considerable message symbolically.

(3) *Epigain Equates Dependent Position.* Once the symptoms were established, the unconscious secondary gain resulted in her securing a more protected position. She was safer, could renounce her adult and feminine roles, and be dependent. While hospitalized, she had little responsibility for her children and could avoid intercourse and further pregnancies, in addition to an unpleasant job situation. This "gain" was also socially acceptable in view of her illness. Of course she suffered a major disability (also a punishment), but this was a worthwhile exchange.

Other interesting features of this case included: (1) *la belle indifférence* (the striking or beautiful indifference of the patient to her major Somatic Conversion symptoms); (2) low average intelligence (IQ is more usually average or low average); (3) degree of paralysis (just sufficient to make standing and walking impossible); (4) stocking type of anesthesia (upper circular limits did not correspond to the anatomic nerve supply): (5) normal deep tendon reflexes; (6) associated "functional" symptoms of back pain, headaches, and dysmenorrhea; (7) serious problems in interpersonal relationships which added up to an intolerable position; and (8) a Conversion diathesis (typical Conversion Personality traits).

The features helped establish a positive diagnosis and also helped to determine the course of treatment. With the negative findings, they are typical of many major cases of Somatic Conversion. She was able to make substantial improvement with a supportive psychotherapeutic regime.

E. ADDITIONAL ASPECTS OF IMPORTANCE

1. Symptom Identification; Identification in Symptom Choice

Identification with another person can play an important role in the unconscious selection of the location and the type of Conversion symptom. This is hardly surprising to many clinicians in view of the characteristic suggestibility of the Conversion (hysterical) Personality, which can also contribute to the process. This development which can be individually of great consequence may be termed *Symptom Identification.*

The following case presents an illustration of this major psychic influence, which is far more apparent here than in many, more subtle and less striking instances.

Case 18

Identification and Conversion; Symptom Compathy

(1) *A Symbiotic Relationship.* A 58-year-old single retired teacher sought medical help because of a painful "tight" throat. She had trouble swallowing and could not speak above a whisper. Medical studies were negative for organic pathology; the disturbance was a functional one. As in many such cases, this fact, while reassuring from one standpoint, is often also very unwelcome for many reasons. Functional symptoms are more troubling; treatment is usually far more complex and time consuming, and any direct approach, as is usually possible in organic illness, is most often not feasible. The patient and physician alike are usually in a far more helpless and frustrating position. One cannot get medication to the basis of the trouble when this is an emotional one!

Further study from the psychologic viewpoint revealed an impoverished emotional life. In her loneliness, the teacher had earlier formed a mutually beneficial and very close relationship with another teacher. Both had subsequently retired. They had lived together, pooling their resources and sharing interests. This had served very useful and needed purposes. Their relationship proved to be an emotional symbiosis.

(2) *Life Constrictive and "Closing In."* Two years ago her companion had developed throat symptoms and careful studies indicated the presence of cancer. Her malignant condition slowly progressed to where she could only swallow with difficulty, had lost her voice, and required constant nursing care. With their personal and economic futures thus long and closely linked, the companion's illness comprised a most major psychologic blow.

Much of this, together with the conflicts so activated, was unconscious. In the Conversion process under study, unconscious conflict is converted into disguised and symbolic outward expression. This had occurred. The patient's functional throat symptoms, among other meanings, conveyed her inner feelings that life was threatening, painfully restrictive, and closing in on her. In essence this was correct.

(3) *Symptom Identification.* Through her symptoms she suffered for and with her friend. One might accordingly regard this as an instance of *symptom compathy*.[2] In her own hard-pressed position, she further expressed her own unacceptable and thereby unconscious wish for a similar dependent and cared-for position.

Through psychotherapy, which was supportive and selectively interpretive, together with some favorable situational and environmental modifications, her painful and disabling symptoms gradually subsided over a 4-month period.

2. Affect Equivalents

We have learned that many bodily aches and pains represent what we have termed *affect equivalents*. In place of a painful emotion, one experiences a bodily pain. An event or feeling which is figuratively a "heartache" may, by its conversion into bodily language, be instead experienced in more literal fashion as a chest pain, that is, as a more realistic "heartache." The conscious connection with the emotion which is replaced is lost. The painful emotion of hurt, sorrow, or loss is not experienced; the ache or pain is. All the patient knows consciously is that he hurts. He doesn't know why. He may seek medical help for diagnosis, relief, and reassurance.

We believe there is widespread implicit recognition of this process. This is partly conveyed in the many public references to a wide variety of conversions, such as a situation being a "headache," a person being a "pain in the neck," a burden, a "thorn in the side," or a prospective event giving one "cold feet."

The foregoing are usually intended figuratively—as figures of speech. However, their use and choice is not by accident. Their translation into literal terms occurs and is not too difficult nor remote. The implicit recognition that these translations can occur is indicated in the public adoption and usage of many such interesting expressions. The Broadway musical *Guys and Dolls* had an entertaining song entitled "Adelaide's Lament," in which the translation of emotional miseries (frustration and hurt over failure to be married) into physical ones (cold, cough, sinus trouble, postnasal drip, and *la grippe*) was portrayed. Appreciative audiences repeatedly indicated how widely and thoroughly such associations and relationships were understood.

Medical psychology has recognized for a long time that fears can be expressed in many more hidden and disguised forms than the simple and direct emotion of fear per se. An instance comes to mind in which their suppression was followed almost immediately by headaches. See also *Case 11*. The upper respiratory tract also provides a frequent site for various substituted, equivalent, and converted expressions of affect of various kinds.

---

[2] Compathy—the very close emotional sharing of emotional feelings with another person.

Under certain circumstances, a certain patient would become terribly unhappy and anxious. At other times, under identical circumstances, she would not so react, but instead would suffer a constrictive kind of abdominal, and/or chest pain. This was a Conversion of emotional pain into physical pain,[3] an interesting phenomenon, not infrequently illustrated. The physical pain was an *affect equivalent* symptom.

3. The Conversion-Escape

The following instance illustrates the onset of a major Somatic Conversion in a man which was precipitated by a threat of violence from the KKK, plus the painful blow of his wife becoming ill from cancer. His existing dependent position was gravely threatened. To an extent his symptoms resecured this position. His conversion symptoms also provided *an escape from reality and from intolerable threats.*

This illustrates a major type of *Motor Conversion* and also comprises what we can accordingly term the *Conversion-Escape.*

Case 19

Somatic (Motor) Conversion Follows the Threat of Injury and Wife's Illness

(1) *KKK Provided a Shattering Experience.* W. E. was a 57-year-old ex-coal miner. Several years earlier he had been involved in a mine accident in which he had sustained a serious back injury. Following prolonged hospitalization, a required support for his back helped allow his release.

Some months after his discharge from the hospital, while recovering at home, he was visited one night by members of the Klu Klux Klan. They dragged him from the house to witness the flogging of a neighbor for "failing to support his family." He was told he would get the same treatment if he didn't get back to work and soon!

(2) *Onset of Paralysis.* Shortly after this—to him a shattering experience—the patient suffered another emotional blow when he learned that his wife, upon whom he had become very dependent, was suffering from cancer, of a slowly progressive but incurable type. Shortly thereafter he found that his left arm and leg were paralyzed. He remained this way for a long time, finally returning to the hospital.

On examination, there were no neurologic abnormalities, nor was there any muscular atrophy or other changes. The patient was observed on several occasions to have movements of the affected extremities. On one occasion, while discussing his situation, he commented significantly, "I would walk out of here tomorrow if I knew that my wife was going to get well...." He was suffering from a Motor Conversion—a major paralytic type of Somatic Conversion.

(3) *Conversion-Escape Retrieves Dependent Position.* The threat of bodily injury from the secret organization, coupled with the sickness of his wife upon whom he had relied heavily for emotional support and care, had placed him in an insoluble position. His symptoms provided

---

[3] Conversion thus provides one of the major emotional routes for pain. This potential invokes a *Surgery-in-Abeyance Rule,* which stresses the Conversion Reactions as posing an emotional contraindication for other than emergency surgical procedures.

the only possible "escape," or psychologic flight, and secured a position of even more complete dependence upon others as a consequence of his physical disability. This was socially acceptable, and released him from the responsibility of caring for his wife.

His earlier retreat into a passive and dependent position had been threatened. The Conversion symptoms "retrieved" this. They also provided a *Conversion-Escape* from intolerable circumstances. He was quite resistant to psychotherapy and made only limited progress prior to his discharge from the hospital.

4. The "Gain" of Conversion Symptoms

A. ENDOGAIN.—The Conversion Reactions provide excellent illustrations of the various features of "gain" in emotional illness. This was true in *Cases 17* and *19*. While this is present in general with all Conversion symptoms, it is particularly true in the Somatic Conversions, where the gains also may be more clearly apparent. As in all emotional illnesses, the basic processes, in this instance the conversion mechanism, yields what we can term a *Primary Gain*. This is always deeply unconscious to the patient, a position emphasized by the name assigned, of *endogain*. Its function is basically anxiety-defense.

The endogain may be thought of in terms of *conflict-easing or resolution, maintenance of repression, symbolic partial gratification, ego preservation, plus various elements of denial, control and superego placation. The endogain, or the need for, or "seeking" of it, is basic to and initiates the illness and the symptoms.*

It is small wonder that, in answer to such important needs, a symptom once established (and its endogain) is often held on to quite grimly. This is to be expected regardless of the amount of self-defeat involved. It is in line with our interesting *Concept of Secondary Defense,* in which we observed that the symptom, a defense in itself, is in turn defended. The symptom thus is the intended *primary defense*. The defense of the symptom is the *secondary defense* (p. 36). The psychic gains of the various ego defenses are often the essence of the endogain, in line with regarding the dynamisms as comprising the vital *First Line of Psychic Defense.*

B. EPIGAIN.—Once established, symptoms yield other gains. These are not the primary gains, but accrue subsequently or secondarily. They are the secondary gains of the symptom or illness, which now comes to produce some external material, environmental, or interpersonal change which is to the person's advantage. These may be conscious and consciously sought. They may be unconscious, in which event the name *epigain* emphasizes their relative position of superficiality to the more basic endogain.

Epigain, therefore, is *the unconscious secondary gain, in which an illness which is already established comes to provide external and material advantage for the patient.* It is present in every emotional illness, but its extent and its importance vary considerably. In Somatic Conversion, it is likely to be especially apparent.

5. Relations to Other Mechanisms

A. CONVERSION AND DISSOCIATION.—There is a basic and close relationship between Conversion and Dissociation. Both are primitive types of mechanisms. In adulthood, they tend to follow the capacity for responses that have developed, and the patterns that have been laid down in infancy and earliest childhood. As one distinction, it may be helpful to think about the clinical manifestations which can be observed in Conversion as *Part Reactions,* while in Dissociation we are more likely to deal with a *Reaction-of-the-Whole.*

In Somatic Conversion, the conflict finds expression *somatically,* in disguised and distorted form. It is a body language which is expressed through the physical self. In Physiologic Conversion, the conflict is expressed *functionally,* in similarly disguised or distorted form. Somatic, Physiologic, and Behavioral Conversions are analogous processes.

In Dissociative Reactions on the other hand, such as amnesia or fugues, we do not find the conflict expressed through a part of the self, but rather it is expressed or acted out by a reaction of the entire self. It is the *overall activity* of the individual that expresses the conflict or parts of the conflict. This is, of course, also wholly outside of conscious awareness, and it, too, is frequently distorted or disguised. However, the Dissociative Reaction may also be looked upon as a gross overall form of symbolic expression, "acting out," or "Behavioral Language."

In the Dissociative Reactions, a person's behavior, dissociated from conscious awareness, may thus in symbolic fashion give expression to many kinds of unconscious impulses, needs, and wishes which have been the source of inner conflict and require repression.

B. CONVERSION AND DISPLACEMENT.—There is a similarity also between the near-magic of the secret (unconscious) Conversion of a hidden psychic conflict into a distorted bodily form of expression in the Conversion Reactions, and the likewise near-magic of its automatic partial Displacement externally to a symbolic external object, as occurs in the phobias. Freud early applied the name of Anxiety Hysteria to the phobias. This name is not used in psychiatry today, but dynamically it is not entirely inappropriate.

There is a psychopathologic relationship between the Conversion Reactions (hysteria) and Anxiety Hysteria (the Phobic Reactions). In both, resolution of the anxiety and threat is sought. In the Conversion Reactions, this takes place through Conversion in the shape of various physical disabilities and ailments. In the phobias, there is a displacement of the threat and dread onto external objects or situations.

C. REGRESSION AND IDENTIFICATION.—These major ego defenses are mentioned again at this point to emphasize their close relationships to the mechanism of Conversion. They have received earlier comments in our discussion.

Regression is basic to the process of Conversion. Denial is another closely related mechanism; Conversion at times acting to effect or to reenforce Denial.

F. SUMMARY

1. Defense Against Anxiety

Conversion is a major ego defense. Through it elements of unconscious emotional conflict are transposed into disguised and symbolic external expression. Major categories of Conversion Reactions are the *Physiologic, Behavioral, Somatic,* and the *Psychologic.* These are further discussed from the clinical standpoint in *The Neuroses.*

The unconscious purpose and intent of the mechanism of Conversion is to defend against anxiety and to preserve Repression. This mechanism is a major producer of psychic-emotional symptoms. These all have greater or lesser symbolic meanings. They convey a message and can be regarded as "speaking" a preverbal kind of language. The dynamic sequence of events in conversion symptom elaboration is: *first,* repression; *second,* its threatened failure; and *third,* the return to consciousness of elements of the conflict (plus possible defenses or masochistic features) in a converted and disguised form.

A number of major subtypes of Conversion were noted, including *Autonomic Conversion, Childhood Conversion, Sensory Conversion, Motor Conversion, Conversion-in-Therapy, Combat Conversion, Symptom Conversion,* and *Behavioral Conversion,* the latter with its six interesting subgroups as tabulated in *Table 2.*

Conversion was named in 1894. The study of this interesting process since has contributed greatly to the science of psychodynamics and to our understanding of human behavior. It has been largely through our early observation and study of the Conversion Reactions (hysteria) that dynamic psychiatry became established. Charcot first experimentally produced certain of the Conversion symptoms under hypnosis which had been previously regarded by many as being organic in origin. The early concepts have been widened substantially, and have been further broadened in this presentation and in *The Neuroses.*

Headaches are a common Conversion manifestation (*Conversion Headache*). Identification and Regressive forces can help to determine inadvertent symptom choice and location. Conversion Reactions are not uncommon in childhood, a fair number subsiding gradually and spontaneously.

2. Progression of Physiologic Conversions

The Physiologic Conversions are marked by functional symptoms. These can ultimately progress into more permanent, irreversible changes, in accord with our *Concept of Functional-Structural Progression. Primary* functional changes, are at times followed by *secondary* changes in structure. Both can be followed in turn by what we might term *tertiary* changes in other organs or systems. The tertiary changes are the further result of either the primary or the secondary changes continuing on, so as to become still more fixed and irreversible.

We have proposed the adoption of *Physiologic Conversion* as a convenient diagnostic term, conveying both the type of trouble (physiologic) and the mechanism (Conversion). Their incidence is large and includes many common malfunctions in every system, as well as a number of discrete and major pathologic entities. The dynamics are not terribly different in kind, but may be more subtle than in the more gross kinds of *Somatic Conversion.*

3. Implied Recognition Widespread

Many figures of speech in fairly common usage describe emotions in bodily terms. Progression from the figurative to the literal can occur, and the use of many of the related figures of speech conveys the implied and intuitive recognition of this process on the part of wide segments of the public. Pain is a common phenomenon on a Conversion basis and has been further discussed elsewhere (*The Neuroses,* pp. 639 ff.). *Affect-Equivalents* were discussed as an important concept in the psychic capacity for the carry-over from the figurative to the literal in functional manifestations.

Behavioral Conversion was considered briefly and six major varieties were tabulated for purposes of convenience. (*Table 2,* p. 38.) The *Concept of the Conversion-Escape* was offered. Several important interrelationships with other dynamisms were noted.

Somatic Conversions include gross symptoms of motor and sensory impairment. Subtypes are labeled *Motor Conversion* and *Sensory Conversion,* as appropriate. The *somatic language* of these symptoms is interesting to study and to decipher, although this process may require prolonged intensive study.

The *Concept of the Secondary Defense* finds important illustration in the Somatic Conversions, as do our conceptions of primary gain (*endogain*) and unconscious secondary gain (epigain). In accord with the *Theory of Transparency,* in the psychotherapy of the Conversion Reactions, a conversion manifestation is generally unable to survive its thorough elucidation —that is, its significances cannot become too transparent.

G.   CROSS-REFERENCES TO *THE NEUROSES* *

Conversion (pp. 639 ff.)
Endogain of; p. 690.
Epigain of; pp. 57, 64, 70–2, 671–2, 693, 716.

---

* From Laughlin, H. P. *The Neuroses.* London, Butterworth & Co., Ltd., 1967.

Fainting as; p. 687.
Language; p. 643, 742, 914–15.
Types of:
    Autonomic C.; p. 655.
    Behavioral C.; pp. 193, 258, 318, 355, 670.
    Physiologic C.; pp. 13, 14, 113, 468–9, 654–6.
    Psychologic C.; pp. 467, 643.
    Somatic C.; pp. 642, 656, 660, 676, 699, 704.
    Conversion
As an Anxiety Reaction (Chapter 3)
    in emotional illness (Table 7); p. 88.
    in *Emotional Recapitulation Sequence;* p. 116.
In reference to Depressive Reactions (Chapter 4)
    comparison to Depression; p. 181.
    Psychologic C., in Depression; pp. 138, 176.
In reference to Character Reactions (Chapter 5)
    incidence of, in clinical practice; p. 244.
    in *Conversion Personality;* pp. 232; 260, 267–8.
    in patterns of defense; pp. 238, 241–2, 261.
In reference to Obsessive-Compulsive Reactions (Chapter 6)
    Behavioral C., in acting out; p. 318.
    in analytic difficulties of Obsessive Neuroses; p. 365.
In reference to Fatigue Reactions (Chapter 7)
    emotional fatigue, a *Psychologic C.;* p. 383.
    of *Psychic Distaste* into anorexia in Fatigue Reaction (case 86); p. 418.
In reference to Hygeiaphrontic Reactions (Chapter 8)
    conversion pain, concealed expression of conflict; p. 469.
    routes of conflict expression, Somatic and *Physiologic C.;* p. 467.
In reference to Phobic Reactions (Chapter 10)
    in comparison to the phobia; p. 556.
    in the *Case of Little Hans* (Freud); p. 551.
In reference to Soterial Reactions (Chapter 11); *Physiologic C.; in Soterial Reaction*
    (Case 133); p. 627.
In reference to Conversion Reactions (Chapter 12)
    as intrapsychic process; p. 700.
    Attacks of; p. 700.
    endogain in; pp. 473, 484, 689–91, 700.
    epigain in; pp. 57, 64, 70–2, 671–2, 693, 716.
    identification, a psychic defense in; pp. 656, 692, 698, 701, 716.
    in acting out; pp. 193, 258–9, 318, 355–6, 670.
    in conversion allochiria; p. 652.
    in conversion diathesis, in diagnosis of; p. 653.
    in conversion epidemics; p. 703.
    in conversion pain; pp. 654, 667.
    in definition of Conversion Reaction; pp. 45, 115, 641–2, 717.
        origin of term, Breuer and Freud; p. 649.
    in diagnosis of *Physiologic C.* (Table 31); pp. 655–6.
    in mechanisms of Conversion Reaction; p. 691.
    in painful phantom limb; p. 704.
    in *Peg Concept,* attachment of symptoms; p. 681.
    in *Red Ink Cure* of Somatic C. (Case 147); p. 709.
    in sequence of reactions of Conversion Reaction; p. 650.
    of inadequately repressed impulses; p. 690.

oral conflict, significance in; pp. 134, 685, 700.

symbolism in; pp. 643, 662, 699–700.

symptoms of, in Conversion Reaction; pp. 691–2, 711, 716.

treatment of, pp. 706–15.

> *Self-esteem Principle* in; pp. 676, 691, 694.
> *Theory of Transparency* in; pp. 661, 691, 707.
> through *Rhazes Maneuver;* p. 678.

In reference to Dissociative Reactions (Chapter 13)

as aid in hypnotizability; p. 814.

> of young; p. 817.
> *Physiologic C.,* resulting from research in hypnosis; p. 823.

as a *Conflict Indicator;* p. 757.

as a *Part-Reaction;* p. 742.

depersonalization, a component in; p. 760.

in *Changing Trends Concept,* in relation to fainting; p. 771.

in comparison to Dissociation; p. 733.

in diagnosis of Fugue (Case 170); p. 795.

of repressed emotions into physical symptoms (Case 151); p. 735.

In reference to Neuroses-Following-Trauma (Chapter 14)

decline of gross c.; p. 845.

elements of, in Dissociative Reaction; p. 853.

incidence of, in Neuroses-Following-Trauma; p. 852.

manifestations of, Somatic and *Physiologic C.;* p. 851.

Physiologic C., in Phobic Reaction to trauma (Case 176); p. 854.

In reference to Military Reactions (Chapter 15)

incidence of Somatic and *Physiologic C.,* in World War II; pp. 907, 912–13, 945.

in diagnoses of Military Reactions (Table 40); p. 904.

in symptoms of Military Reactions (Table 46); p. 908.

Somatic C., as *body langauge;* pp. 914–15.

H.   REVIEW QUESTIONS

Sample self-check questions on Chapter 3 and Conversion, for the student, psychiatric resident, and board candidate.

1. Define *Conversion* and its principal subtypes (*Somatic, Autonomic, Behavioral, Physiologic,* and *Psychologic Conversion*).

2. How do Conversion manifestations serve as communications? What is meant by "symptom language"?

3. Cite examples and describe: (1) *Childhood Conversion* and (2) *Conversion-in-Therapy.*

4. How can the *Combat Conversion Reaction* illustrate primary gain (*endogain*) and unconscious secondary gain or *epigain?*

5. Briefly discuss *Behavioral Conversion* and list the six major types.

6. Provide a clinical application for six of the following:

   A. *Symptom neurosis.*

   B. *Autonomic language.*

   C. *Self-Esteem Maintenance Principle.*

   D. *Basic Trend Toward Emotional Health Concept.*

   E. *Paradox of the Neurotic Position.*

   F. *Theory of Transparency.*

   G. *Secondary Defense Concept.*

   H. Neurotic acting out.

   I. *Acute Conversion Behavior.*

    J. *Behavioral Langauge.*

    K. *Surgery-in-Abeyance Rule.*

    L. *Conversion Epigain.*

7. How are certain *Somatic Conversion* symptoms a defense against acting?

8. Distinguish *Motor* from *Sensory Conversion.*

9. Comment on the psychodynamics of the following:

    A. *la belle indifférence.*

    B. *Vicious Circle of Self-Defeat* in neuroses.

    C. *Conversion Attack.*

    D. Symbolic gratification in Conversion symptoms.

    E. *Incomplete Symptom Defense.*

    F. Unconscious representation of a body area in Somatic Conversion.

    G. *Symptom Compathy.*

    H. *Conversion Escape.*

    I. Conversion as a *Part Reaction.*

    J. *Reaction-of-the-Whole.*

10. Discuss Conversion symptom elaboration in relation to its representing *affect equivalents* or *Symptom Identifications.* What is the: (1) dynamic sequence of events in Conversion symptom evolvement and (2) *Concept of Functional-Structural Progression?*

CHAPTER 4

DENIAL

*...A Primitive Dynamism of Disavowal and
Disclaiming*

A. THE NATURE OF DENIAL

    1. A Primitive Kind of Psychologic Disavowal or Negation.
2. In Inverse Ratio to Maturity. 3. Definition.

B. TYPES OF DENIAL

    1. Denial-for-Confidence. 2. National and Public Denial; The
Ostrich Concept; a. An Instance of Public Denial; b. National
Denial. 3. Antitherapeutic Denial: a. Existence of Problems
or Illness Denied; b. In Drug Addiction; c. Denial of Hurt,
Loss, and Pain; d. Denial in One's Self-Picture; e. Denial-in-
Aging. f. Alcoholism. 4. Denial and Symptom Formation:
a. In Various Emotional Reactions; b. Elation and Depres-
sion. 5. In SEHC.

C. SPECIAL ASPECTS OF DENIAL

    1. Conflict Resolution; Sexual Denial. 2. The Socio-Sexual
Dilemma: The Need for the Rapid Reversal of Earlier and
Protectively-Induced Sexual Inhibitions Following Marriage.
3. Symptom Denial and Illness Denial. 4. The Denial-of-
Death: a. Unpleasant Realities; b. The Illusion-of-Continued-
Living; c. Multiple Denial; d. Grief-Stricken Denial. 5. Denial
Aids in Maintaining Destructive Patterns of Gratification. 6.
The Omission Denial.

D. DENIAL AND OTHER DYNAMISMS

E. CONSCIOUS EFFORTS AT DENIAL

F. SUMMARY

G. REFERENCES (FROM *The Neuroses*)

H. REVIEW QUESTIONS

A. THE NATURE OF DENIAL

1. A Primitive Kind of Psychologic Disavowal or Negation

    To deny is to negate or to disown. Through denial one may seek to
disavow or to disclaim awareness, knowledge, or responsibility. To deny a

claim is to reject it. To deny an act in affect is to negate the act, its occurrence, and its consequences. When this takes place as an effort, and some conscious awareness remains, it is a *conscious* endeavor and not an ego defense. When this process instead operates automatically and successfully so that one element of an emotional conflict (or a basis for it) becomes relegated to the unconscious, this becomes the dynamism of Denial.

Psychologically, Denial is a primitive and desperate unconscious method of coping with otherwise intolerable conflict, anxiety, and emotional distress or pain. As such it is closely related to Repression (p. 357), with which its operation sometimes overlaps. A painful affect or feeling may thus be denied to conscious awareness. Some or all of its effects may be denied. A fact, an event, or some aspect of reality also may be denied. In this kind of Denial, such relegation (of that which is denied) to the unconscious indicates the operation of a mental mechanism or dynamism. As such, Denial is a primitive kind of psychologic disavowal or negation.

2. In Inverse Ratio to Maturity

In the study of Denial as an ego defense it becomes increasingly clear that its operation is likely in general to be in inverse ratio to one's level of emotional maturity. It is in opposition to the vital ego functions of perception and memory. Accordingly, we might suspect, and correctly so, that Denial becomes less available as a psychic defense as the ego develops, ego functions become stronger, and this major division of the psyche becomes more healthfully integrated.

Thus Denial is a primitive and magical kind of process which is more normal and more compatible with the psychology of the infant. As memory and related ego capacities evolve during personality development, Denial normally becomes less frequent. The child may deny in play and in fantasy. Considerable stress must take place or existing defenses must be inadequate, in order to force the developing ego (or adult, later) to fall back upon this primitive kind of defense. Denial is a Lower Order dynamism.

The major instances of Denial in the adult, technically at least, represent an abnormal type of defense and are often a symptom of illness. With adults, Denial is to be observed: (1) in emotional illness (psychopathology); (2) in dreams; (3) in dissociative states; (4) in major psychotic episodes; and (5) as a desperate ego-defensive means of coping with an otherwise intolerable fact, feeling, or event. In the psychoses, Denial enters into the development of delusions, hallucinations, and other major psychotic phenomena. It is prominent in manic states, elation, manic-depressive psychoses, and the manic-depressive personality.

In adult persons with clinical neuroses, efforts at denial may be on a conscious level and are often imperfect and incomplete. The neurotic patient may *act* to himself or to others as if a painful emotion, fact, or situation were denied, i.e., he may not wish it to exist, but he really knows it does. The psychotic patient, on the other hand, is likely automatically, and seemingly effortlessly, to deny something which is emotionally painful. The ego of the neurotic patient is less successful in this unconscious endeavor. He often enough knows it is there and can't stand it, but can't fully banish it through its Denial either.

We come to recognize then that Denial tends to become less frequent, less important, and less accessible as a dynamism to the psychologically protective operations of most people as their maturity progresses. On the other hand, in individual instances its readoption upon occasion becomes most important. Thus in occasional instances, it can become most vital and most meaning ul. The operation of Denial may further indicate both the pervasiveness of the psychopathology which is present, and the desperateness of the internal psychologic need which calls forth such a basic and ofttimes irrational type of defensive operation.

Let us further undertake a definition of Denial as an ego defense, offer several further points concerning its unconscious utilization, and then proceed to some of the types of Denial, with selected clinical illustrations of its operation.

3. Definition

Denial is *a primitive, or Lower Order ego defense or mental mechanism operating outside of and beyond conscious awareness in the endeavor to resolve emotional conflict and to allay consequent anxiety, by denying one or more of the elements of the conflict.* There may be a Denial (which must be so complete as to preclude any conscious awareness) of the presence of a thought, wish, deed, or need. Likewise, conflicting standards or prohibitions may be thus negated. The consequences of one's behavior may be disclaimed through their Denial (and loss to conscious awareness). An entire area or complex may be thus disavowed. That which is consciously intolerable becomes disowned through the protectively automatic and unconscious Denial of its existence. Denial is a major mechanism.

Denial is one of the simplest and most basic and primitive forms of ego defense. As such, it is to be grouped with the Lower Order group of mechanisms. It is closely allied to the still more basic and primitive one of Repression. For a child, Denial is a way of saying, in a magical fashion, that something does not exist that the child cannot stand to have exist. Essentially, Denial is an infantile way of avoiding and resolving problems by denying one side of an emotional conflict. Begun in early infancy, this pattern of attempted defense may carry over into adulthood. Thus, the child, and later the adult, may deny, for instance, that he really cares about someone or some thing.

Later, he may deny the consequence of having cared. He may deny to himself and successfully so, that he is hurt, frustrated, furious, jealous, loving, or that he feels inadequate or inferior. When something that has been longed for and cared about is not realized, the individual, who has longed or cared, may come to consciously and sincerely deny any hurt, by denying to himself that there had been any longing or caring in the first place. Denial operates as an important intrapsychic defense in an endeavor to prevent anxiety, to ward off disapproval, to avoid hurt, to combat insecurity, and to preserve the ego. Nearly anything—any element in one's emotional life—may be denied.

B. TYPES OF DENIAL

1. Denial-for-Confidence

Denial is sometimes evolved by the ego as a means to bolster self-confidence. In these instances, the person concerned denies some or all of the basic doubts he harbors about his ability. This can thus be an unconscious endeavor, as well as a consciously attempted one. This is a very interesting type of Denial, which can be termed *Denial-for-Confidence* for purposes of delineation and inviting further attention.

In the following unusual instance of this kind of Denial, the patient (unwittingly) "used" Denial as an escape from deep-seated and overwhelming doubts about her competence in dealing with people, and more specifically as to her ability as a public speaker. The doubts were denied!

Through the Denial of basic doubts she had achieved a superficial but quite successful, albeit most shaky, position where she was all confidence, had no doubts about herself, and had been consistently able to perform as a popular speaker with considerable ability and effectiveness. The intrapsychic mechanism of Denial had achieved a fair measure of success in glossing over what was in reality a very low level of self-confidence.

Case 20

Denial-for-Confidence

(1) *Denial Facilitates Speaking Ability.* A 42-year-old woman in therapy, had taken an increasing interest in political affairs, as her children grew older and she had fewer family responsibilities. She had gained a reputation as a public speaker and, as a result, her services were in demand. She had not been consciously aware of ever feeling self-conscious. "It simply never occurred to me to doubt any of my abilities along this line. I would just get up and speak. I never gave it a second's thought. . . ."

Actually, underneath she was an inordinately timorous person who had dealt with much of her hidden fright, uneasiness, and hesitancy with people, by their Denial. It was a Denial of self-doubt; an example of *Denial-for-Confidence.*

(2) *Unstable Defensive System Collapses.* A crisis arose one day however, when some pointed questions were raised as to her ability. This came about not so much as a hostile attack, but as merely part of an objective assessment by friends and colleagues as to her possible chances as a candidate for election to a certain local public office. This was a dreadful day for her. With the questioning by others of the extent of her abilities and capacities, she began to consider these matters herself, apparently for the first time!

The immediate and devastating result was the sudden, almost total, loss of her previous "ability." She couldn't stand even to face an audience, as she became suddenly overwhelmed with the urgent flood into consciousness of long-denied doubts and fears.

The ego defense of Denial in this case illustrated the close dynamic relationship of the dynamism to Repression. It is clear that grave self-doubts had been present, but these were unconscious. Of considerable extent, they had been defensively denied with an almost "magical flight into omnipotence," and resulting complete ability in this area without question. The whole unstable defensive structure came tumbling down when recognition was forced of the existence of even slight doubt. The Denial could no longer be maintained, and there was sudden over-whelming awareness of the whole mass of doubt. Under the weight of this, her "ability" collapsed.

(3) *New Equanimity on a More Genuine Basis.* Through therapy she did not fully regain her lost ability. As she learned more and more about what made her "tick" as a person, her competence to see herself more objectively increased greatly. She became better able to perceive and to assess her real aims and desires. She learned that her speaking endeavors had been partially a neurotic kind of substitute for other satisfactions, and in part an attempted escape. She largely lost her interest in this type of activity, as it became less appropriate.

In a healthful fashion she replaced (Chapter 27) this lost avenue of libidinal investment with personally sounder ones. She again became able to appear before audiences with composure, and to speak when she wished. Now, however, her equanimity in these kinds of situations was more genuine, and was founded on a more substantial basis.

2. National and Public Denial; The Ostrich Concept

A. AN INSTANCE OF PUBLIC DENIAL.—The ego defense of Denial, as noted earlier, at times assumes a magical quality. Through denying the very possibility of the existence of disaster or danger, the individual becomes in his own eyes the all-powerful master of his fate.

This type of operation of the ego defense thus can support the *Concept of Personal Invulnerability,* outlining a major defensive endeavor which is evolved by individuals, especially in the presence of danger (*The Neuroses,* p. 919; also see resulting ego defense in Chapter 27); with the intent of self-protection. One thus dismisses threats of danger or disaster, or even death, by denying their existence. This of course can be a most shortsighted endeavor. On occasion it can be tragically self-defeating. This psychic defense can operate entirely automatically and unconsciously.

For many people possibilities of danger and destruction lie close at hand, and may appear suddenly and unexpectedly around many a corner. It is not surprising that, in order to be able to function effectively, human beings often defensively resort to putting such actual or potential dangers more or less completely out of their awareness. Hence, man frequently calls upon the protectively-intended mechanism of Denial, which in some cases can be regarded as serving a constructive end. This is hardly surprising.

During a professional world tour in 1957, the author was impressed by the widespread presence of this defense, for example in Seoul, Korea. Without it, anxiety might well have blocked some fair segment of the widespread constructive activities of the people. Through its employment the existence of the ever-present menace from the North Koreans, a mere 25 miles away, was in effect disowned by many of the people much of the time. As a consequence, they were active, busy, and could function constructively. On such a wide scale this constituted an instance of what for convenience we can term *Public Denial*.

Similar Public Denials in the face of military, natural, civil, or other major threats and/or potential catastrophes are to be noted throughout the course of history.

B. NATIONAL DENIAL.—There are instances in which Denial and its consequences have been likened to the action of the ostrich in coping with danger. The ostrich is reputed to bury his head in the sand when danger threatens. Then he cannot see or be aware of it. This is to spare himself the pain and apprehension. *It is as if his avoidance of the awareness of danger, might also magically avoid his exposure to the danger itself.*

As an ego defense, Denial also can often be likened to the ostrich in its self-defeating potential. This comprises what we refer to as the *Ostrich Concept*.

In the case of the ostrich, it is easy to see how certain consequences of the situation can make his head-burying more dangerous. In the case of human beings, the increased danger and self-defeat may be less apparent, but they can be just as psychologically uneconomic, just as potentially destructive.

There are many instances to be encountered with individuals today which illustrate the foregoing. (See *Case 35*, p. 72.) For those interested in history (e.g., see *Plutarch's Lives*), there are ample illustrations of both the *Ostrich Concept* and *Public Denial* in the reactions and the resulting destruction of peoples, their armies, cities, states, and cultures.

Upon occasion an entire nation (or its leaders or rulers) has indulged in a self-destructive and suicidal disregard of danger and imminent annihilation. Employment on such a widespread and national basis as cited, well warrants adoption and application of the term of *National Denial*.

3. Antitherapeutic Denial

A. EXISTENCE OF PROBLEMS OR ILLNESS DENIED.—In almost no area does Denial play as frequent a role and have such self-defeating and even tragic results as in certain instances of serious emotional problems, handicapping character or personality traits, and emotional illness. The observation of emotionally ill persons affords all too many sad occasions for the physician and for the observant student of human emotions and behavior to observe the intended-defense of Denial with its more unfortunate and self-destructive consequences. Many such individuals protectively deny the presence of *any* emotional problems. This constitutes a very potent secondary defense of the emotional manifestation or reaction.

One must recognize that this kind of Denial can be quite genuine and sincere indeed, since the person concerned has no conscious awareness that he has internal emotional problems. Insofar as he is thus unaware, his Denial has proven "effective" for him after a fashion, even if not so for others. As can be readily seen, however, it makes it extremely difficult for the family or physician who are trying to be of help. It can effectively block all attempts to aid him.

This desperate result is illustrated in the following case. Part of the denial was conscious and effortful while in part, it was quite unconscious.

Case 21

The Antitherapeutic Denial

(1) *Referral by Family Friend Documented Problems.* A 34-year-old married mother was referred for psychiatric evaluation by a physician who was also a close personal friend of the family. According to his carefully documented reports, based upon observations over a period of time, the patient was desperately unhappy. The marriage was a miserable failure. Her husband had been improvident in every way save financial.

On arrival the patient was red-eyed from weeping. However, she could admit only to some very mild dissatisfactions with life; slight nervousness, chronic fatigue, and occasional severe headaches. From this point onwards she had to protectively deny the existence of problems.

(2) *Antitherapeutic Denial.* First, she was not *ill*. She had *no* problems or emotional conflicts whatsoever! He husband was set forth vigorously (and defensively!) as an ideal. Her marriage, she claimed, was eminently satisfactory. She had come for consultation under protest. Her childhood had been simply wonderful, and her parents perfection. From her description alone, one might have thought her life was indeed ecstatic. She even added, "Oh, if there were only something important and deep-seated to account for my trouble. . . ."

This poor woman could not even admit the possibility of emotional conflicts or problems. How tragically blocked she was insofar as even attempting their resolution! One cannot attempt to solve difficulties that have to be defensively and protectively denied. This kind of situation can be most discouraging to the psychotherapist.

Her defenses of Denial were very potent and were maintained in a continuing desperate fashion to the point of defeating attempts to help her. From last reports, her secondary defense of Denial had continued valiantly and tragically operative, as had her unhappiness and other symptoms.

B. IN DRUG ADDICTION.—Denial can play significant and similar roles to the foregoing in regard to drug habituation and addiction.

Three marked recent instances quickly come to mind. Herein the operation of the ego defense substantially interfered with or blocked psychotherapy with physicians addicted and habituated respectively to morphine, Demerol, and Dexedrine.

C. DENIAL OF HURT, LOSS, AND PAIN.—Conscious efforts to deny hurt, loss, and psychic pain, their effects, or that one cares are common enough. The rationale for such attempts is not difficult to fathom. This kind of conscious effortful attempt is often similar to conscious efforts at Rationalization, and the latter can operate in the service of Denial. Let us carry over our concept of these conscious efforts, into similar ones operating outside of conscious awareness.

Accordingly, unconscious endeavors in the same direction become more readily understandable. Herein memories are lost; the Denial is fully achieved insofar as the conscious level is concerned. As we learned in *The Neuroses* (p. 874), Denial is operative as one of the commonly employed ego defenses against danger. It substantially contributes to the defense of *Personal Invulnerability*.

The Repression of painful data or the Denial of one aspect of an emotional conflict takes place automatically, seemingly quite effortlessly, and no conscious trace remains of that which has been denied.

Case 22

Denial of Painful Past Events

(1) *Hospitalization Leads to Inquiry into Background.* A 38-year-old businessman was hospitalized following the acute onset of a psychotic reaction. On admission, little data could be gained initially. A social service interview with his mother provided some information about his early background. He was born in Italy, the oldest of seven children. When he was 10, his father came to the United States, leaving the family behind until he could save passage money to send for them. Times were hard and there was endless work to be done on the small farm.

In the mother's blandly descriptive words, "Our goal made it easier, and working together made us all closer.... My boy did a man's work.... Sure, I had to give him a lick now and then to keep him in line.... We were all so glad when the time came to leave. It was wonderful to finally get to America! ..."

(2) *Cruel Treatment Comes to Light.* During the succeeding years, the family prospered. The children married, except the patient. He was on the serious side and was never very happy. After some years, he began to suffer with headaches; developed a marked irritability and restlessness. As he told it, this was also why he got in his car on the day of admission and "just drove off," to be picked up by the police and brought to the hospital. This sketchy information shed little light on contributing factors. The patient pictured his background in neutral terms. Nothing had been wrong, or tough, or difficult. Everything was fine. This hardly was plausible.

A younger brother finally provided important leads. It seems that the patient had been a puny and sickly child. His mother had rejected him for unknown reasons, and had treated him quite cruelly. The father's presence had been protective. After his departure, however, the mother appeared to take delight in whipping him. Sometimes this would be for no other reason than that he was "just good for nothing." Sound whippings occurred at least "five or six times a week." This was in contrast to treatment accorded the other children. The foregoing was later confirmed by other siblings. It was rather at variance with the story provided by his mother!

(3) *An Explosive Episode; Denial Maintained.* All had been well until several months prior to admission, when the patient began to have more frequent bouts of headaches and became very irritable. This progressed rapidly to where he would shout at slight noises. On the day of his arrest, he seemed to explode. He grabbed a knife and with a loud shout told his mother he was going to kill her. The brother and a sister intervened, whereupon the patient ran from the house.

Leading questions were used in an effort to secure further details. His hard life, cruel treatment, the beatings, and the attack on his mother were all denied. He maintained this euphemistic picture of these aspects of his past until eventually, an almost completely fortuitous remission allowed discharge, and subsequent contact with him was lost.

The Denial of hurt, pain, or loss can include a wide variety of situations. Sometimes Rationalization or other dynamisms reenforce the Denial. The intent is clear. If one can deny the existence of a need when fulfillment is not possible, or if he can deny a lack or handicap, then the gain is that it doesn't exist; at least in conscious awareness. He is spared experiencing the consequent discomfort.

In the following example of a childless man, the operation of Denial related to his desire for children and to sterility, the underlying handicap.

Case 23

Denial of Sterility and Desire for Children

After 12 years of marriage, a couple in their early middle age remained childless. Friends and relatives recalled their earlier eagerness to have children, followed by great disappointment, terrific frustration, endless worry and concern, and more recently by a firm denial of interest. In what some of their friends felt were rather transparent Rationalizations employed to reenforce their Denial of interest, the couple cited a little too pointedly and a bit too frequently some of the handicaps and responsibilities incidental to parenthood. "Look at all the worries, expenses, sacrifices, problems, and loss of freedom. . . ."

Circumstances later provided further confirmation of the Denial and reversal of attitudes. The couple had undertaken fertility studies after many and continued efforts to initiate pregnancy. Initial results indicated that the husband was sterile; a fact that he refused to have confirmed by further studies and which he found personally intolerable.

Through its Denial he ruled out any responsibility he may have had in the situation. He denied his sterility and gradually came to deny any interest in having children, supplementing the latter by Rationalization. At one point adoption had been ruled out. Such a step would tend to confirm the sterility.

D. DENIAL IN ONE'S SELF-PICTURE.—Denial may enter into "seeking" to maintain or to enhance one's self-picture, when certain aspects are personally unpleasant or too painful. In these instances, the effort may be deliberate and conscious, quite automatic and unconscious, or an admixture to varying extents of both. They can be difficult to separate. The following is a superficial example.

Case 24

Denial in One's Self-Picture

A young lady, several inches over 6 feet tall, of statuesque proportions, once said quite spontaneously and matter-of-factly in discussing her family: "My brother is not a very large man, I guess he is about my size."

This woman had suffered more than gained as a consequence of her height. On one occasion she had been rejected for a coveted position on this basis. She could hardly change matters. One aspect of her automatic defense was her Denial of being Junoesque, as illustrated in her description of her brother. To some extent her conscious self-picture had been altered.

In this kind of defensive operation, it is as though the person says in effect, "If I don't see or recognize it, it isn't there. It doesn't exist. No one will see it; it won't exist for them either. I will no longer suffer handicaps, disadvantages, or painful feelings about it."

The Denial of aspects of one's self-picture can readily carry over to one's image of another. This is found in the following instance. The Denial of the disowned aspects is also reenforced by their partial reversal. This case accordingly also illustrates the close relationship possible between Denial and Inversion. Also note similarities to other instances.

Case 25

Denial in the Image of Another

The husband of a middle-aged patient had suffered from moderate alcoholism for some years. At intervals he was on a binge, was intermittently improvident, and had occasionally simply "vanished" for short periods. Much of the burden of responsibility had fallen upon the wife. While her husband's deficiencies caused her endless trouble, she never complained about him, and if others offered her a lead, she denied the existence of problems.

She could not admit to herself hostile or antagonistic feelings. Instead she found minor areas to praise. These she used at times to build up an unrealistic and idealized picture of her husband which was marked by a number of Inversions. These acted to reenforce the Denial.

The Denial of impropriety is one method employed to help one's self-picture. Accordingly it may become important to see one's behavior and standards as compatible with those of society, even though such may not be the case.

In the following instance, some of our more stringent current mores were disregarded and the gains so secured were protected by Denial. This is a more striking example than one is likely to observe often; minor instances along different lines being not uncommon, and frequently supported by Rationalization.

Case 26

The Denial of Impropriety

A woman visited her son and daughter-in-law in a distant city at irregular intervals. The relationship between mother and son had always been quite close and was quite early a matter of some concern to the young wife. On the first visit the two had gone upstairs to retire early, and she discovered to her shocked surprise that she had lost her bed partner!

Thereafter this continued regularly upon the occasion of the mother-in-law's visits. When she raised any question about what they called their "bed visits" she was met with an indignant reaction. "We want to have a "proper visit," a "warm" one. . . ." "This has always been our custom. . . . " (and don't you dare as an outsider to interfere!). The attitude was flatly one of, "this is simply the way we get along together well as mother and son. . . ."

In this fashion both had denied rather effectively, to themselves at least, that there was anything improper, on the incestuous side, or sexual in their relationship. When something was so clearly "proper," how could it be "improper"—to them or to anyone else? Through Denial, any impropriety was disowned.

E. DENIAL-IN-AGING.—There are numerous varieties of Denial to be encountered in the operation of this defensively-intended endeavor. One which deserves special mention relates to the Denial of age or of the effects of aging, as is illustrated in the following instance. This type of operation of the dynamism is accordingly termed *Denial-in-Aging,* for reasons of convenience, preference, and emphasis.

Case 27

Denial-in-Aging

(1) *Age a Taboo Subject.* The Denial of "growing old" or aging has been observed with the mother of an acquaintance. For years she has refused to admit her age. Direct or indirect attempts by friends or family to discover her age have been met by violent objections. She won't discuss the ages of her siblings, fearing she might disclose her own age.

She takes pride in doing physically taxing chores, especially when younger persons complain of the strain. It became vital to her some 15 years ago to begin denying to herself in defensive fashion, that she was growing old.

(2) *Indications of Aging Denied.* That she is not as efficient or able as she once was, and tires more easily, is not attributed to aging. A suggestion to "slow down" or "let up" may be taken as an insult! Anxiety is stimulated by reminders of advancing age. Her insistence that her age not be known has precipitated several emotional upsets, so that now the members of the family avoid the issue at all costs!

The more common conflict underlying this situation relates to the fact that through aging one approaches the end of life. Aging of course is measured by the number of years of age, as well as by one's general physical fitness. To many the thought of death is unpleasant or unthinkable.

In this instance, the individual's mother and father had suffered with long, debilitating illnesses ultimately resulting in their death (cancer and stroke). Thoughts must have occurred as to the possibility of a similar end for herself. This may have been the source of conflicts, which could be dealt with, in part at least, by denying any evidence of increasing vulnerability to disability or death, i.e., of aging or growing old. Dynamics in this case were undoubtedly also influenced by other personal features that were difficult of access.

F. ALCOHOLISM.—The following case has similar elements to *Case 21,* although in this instance the patient undertook to pay a poor kind of lip service to therapeutic efforts. An added complication was his habituation to alcohol. Persons with this knotty problem frequently evolve the intended defense of Denial to preserve self-esteem, to block awareness of destructive consequences, and sometimes to retain the bottle.

Case 28

The Denial of Problems, Including Overdrinking, as an Insoluble Block to Therapy

A 36-year-old man, entered therapy at the insistence of his wife and the urging of friends. For at least 6 years he had been drinking heavily. For the past three, he had not worked, since "the right job had not come along." Infrequently applications would be made for positions which were above his abilities and experience. Rarer trials at employment inevitably led to failure, and renewed drinking. He lived on his wife's excellent business income.

He was well dressed on arriving for appointments, even though frequently on the road toward inebriation. Although he kept expressing his verbal willingness to "cooperate" in therapy, he "had no real problems." He denied that the job situation was in any way a difficulty or unusual; he merely could not find a suitable job, but this was a temporary phase. His drinking was no problem; he could control it quite easily, and it was not excessive. He certainly did not drink any more than the average man temporarily without a job!

When gentle and friendly attempts were made to discuss his wife's estimate of his drinking, its effects upon him, or the concern of his friends, he defensively and vigorously denied that it was extensive, that it was in any way a handicap to him, that he was at all abusive while drunk, or that he was ever not in complete control of himself and his behavior. There was ample evidence to the contrary.

Therapy was unsuccessful in breaching this ironclad defense in which Denial was so important, and finally efforts to help him had to be abandoned, after some 6 months of a sadly futile and frustrating endeavor. Defensively-intended, the ultimate effect of his "successful" Denial was tragically defeating. Similar more or less marked instances are likely to be encountered in the experience of every psychiatrist.

The following instance concerns more advanced alcoholism. Herein, not only was the need for the bottle denied, but another condition was substituted as the person's basis for seeking help.

Case 29

Denial and Substitution in Chronic Alcoholism

A 46-year-old patient was admitted to the medical service in the city hospital. He complained of "black-outs," memory loss and "epileptic seizures." History led to the suspicion of bouts of alcoholism, confirmed later by friends and family. His fainting spells or convulsions were unwitnessed, although there was no dearth of witnesses for his long-standing overindulgence. Physical examination was negative save for multiple spider angiomata and signs of early cerebellar deterioration—both due to prolonged alcoholism.

He had been hospitalized numerous times in Army and Veterans' hospitals with the stated complaints. Communication with them revealed thorough and exhaustive medical and neurologic workups, with no evidence of organic disease. He had also had a number of psychiatric interviews, with no therapeutic progress. It was the consensus of opinion that his problems were based on alcoholism.

This man denied having ever taken more than "an occasional drink," a denial he persisted in stoutly despite the contrary reports. Needless to say, it was impossible to help him with a problem he could not admit existed. As a consequence, it had progressed to the point of irreparable physical damage. The substitution of "epilepsy" was a psychologic convenience. It reinforced his Denial, provided a more acceptable explanation, and was an endeavor in the service of easing his disapproval. Finally, it comprised a significant *secondary defense*, i.e., the symptoms (of alcoholic habituation, character trait exaggeration, etc.), attempted defenses in themselves, were in turn *secondarily* defended.

In the preceding examples, the Denial concerns the individual's drinking. It should be noted before we proceed, that Denial may be encountered where it concerns another's alcoholism or its effects. This may take place with a spouse, prospective spouse, or children, as examples. Not infrequently, this is found to some extent in the wife of the alcoholically habituated man (or vice versa). This is at times a part of the protective role often assumed. There may be both conscious and unconscious endeavors at Denial. These may concern the drinking, its extent, various sequelae, or other aspects.

The following instance illustrates this kind of Denial, present to some extent in regard to an alcoholic husband, and more so with a son.

Case 30

Denial in Alcoholism of Husband and Son

A 56-year-old widow had suffered through a long and difficult marriage to an alcoholically habituated husband. She had exhibited endless patience and fortitude, frequently assuming more than her share of the responsibilities, financial or otherwise. She had been more of a mother than a wife, protecting her husband in many ways and in many situations. Part of this related to quite conscious efforts at protecting his reputation. However, in some areas the Denial had progressed further, to the extent of self-deception.

A great amount of her early energies had been invested in indoctrinating her two sons concerning the evils of drink. Despite her efforts, her younger son came to drink excessively. This was too much for her to face. Through Denial she treated this tragic and intolerable development as *non arrive*. It had simply not taken place.

Upon occasion she would remark to a friend how thankful she was that no one in her family drank! When he was in bed suffering from obvious aftereffects of a major binge, she once sympathetically commented to her companion as to how sick he was with "a fever and the flu."

4. Denial and Symptom Formation

A. IN VARIOUS EMOTIONAL REACTIONS.—As we know, emotional conflict can result in, or elements of it can be converted (*Chapter 3*), into symptoms which unconsciously try to resolve the conflict, in part through the symbolic gratification of an intolerable wish, or through its Denial or inhibition. There may also be a compromise. Denial also can play an important role in the evolvement of emotional symptoms.

In studies of infantile emotional development, Melanie Klein reported that Denial of psychic reality is one of the infant's earliest methods of defense against the dread of persecutors, whether they have been conceived of as existing in the external world or whether they have been internalized. This primordial Denial may result in a considerable restriction of the ego defenses of Introjection and Projection, as well as in Denial of aspects of external reality. Later remnants of these infantile defensive operations can help form the bases of severe psychotic reactions.

Denial plays a role in the delusional aspects of paranoid conditions. Denial and Projection are often the basis of delusional jealousy and belief in persecution. In these psychotic manifestations, it is often a basic sense of guilt which the person is unable to tolerate, and against which he calls into play the ego defenses of Denial and Projection.

Conversion symptoms, in disguised fashion, can serve the important psychologic purposes of denying the existence of an idea that is intolerable. They usually also provide some symbolic gratification of the wish or impulse which may have been consciously disowned. In the Somatic Conversions (*Chapter 3*), there are also symbolic elements of control and inhibition, as well as the denial of needs or impulses which are thereby disowned.

In Somatic Conversion (hysteria), we also noted a classical clinical feature that was likely first described by Charcot, and named *la belle indifférence*. This is the striking indifference, sometimes, as the name indicates, viewed as a "beautiful" or "grand" indifference of the Conversion patient to his symptoms and their consequences. The indifference is often especially striking since the symptom frequently has resulted in major incapacity. This relative unconcern over serious disability is due to a number of factors, one of which may be Denial; not only Denial of the symptom, but, further, a Denial of the presence of the manifestation, as well as the resulting disability. The Conversion Personality can make use of Denial as well as Incorporation among a number of ego defenses. Blocking or Repression of an idea (p. 96) may represent a Denial.

Denial plays a role in somnambulism (sleepwalking) and in brief memory lapses. Patients may need to deny these phenomena because of personal embarrassment or self-critical attitudes, or because of unpleasant social connotations. Such denial may be either conscious or unconscious. Confabulation, which is the filling-in of memory gaps by imaginary experiences, can be regarded as an instance of Denial. There is a relation of the foregoing to the *Concept of the Euphemistically-Intended Disguises* by both family members and authorities of (attempted or actual) suicide (*The Neuroses,* pp. 150, 196).

Denial in its most extreme form is found in major psychotic manifestations such as hallucinations, through which some degree of unrealistic gratification is achieved. Here Denial may symbolically serve the annihilation of the frustrating object or situation. It is thus bound up with feelings of omnipotence or magical powers which obtain in the early stages of life. In hallucinations, the person concerned regresses to the primitive mode of perception involving Introjection and Projection in which, through some of the primitive or Lower Order ego defenses, including magic, omnipotence, and Denial, one conjures up the image of the object which he has internalized, and projects it into the outside world. Consciously, then, for him personally the object exists in reality. (See pp. 221–225, and 369, 154, 186.)

Several cases already presented illustrate the close relation of Denial and delusion formation. In the following instance, the Denial of pregnancy approached the delusional.

Case 31

Denial of Pregnancy

A young woman became pregnant, an event which was unbearable. She could not accept the diagnosis and steadfastly denied that such an event was possible. This she continued quite determinedly through the entire course of her pregnancy! She continued to assert her nonpregnancy as her size increased and term approached.

When presented with her fine newborn son after delivery, this poor girl indignantly denied that it was her baby or that she had been pregnant. The care of the infant was taken over by a public agency for adoption. The mother was adamantly opposed to further psychiatric interviews, signed herself out of the hospital and dropped from sight.

This kind of extreme Denial is observed in an interesting inverted form, when false pregnancies are experienced. Most obstetricians have had experience with this intriguing but troubling psychologic phenomenon.

In the following instance marked by a psychotic episode, there was a Denial of painful reality. Its appearance following discharge from the hospital led to some awkward and embarrassing moments.

Case 32

A Psychotic Episode with Denial of Painful Reality

A socially minded couple discovered that their only area of compatability had been mutual interest in social events and in social climbing. Heated disagreements broke out when the husband lost these interests. This change of attitude was not understandable nor acceptable to the wife, who reacted by increasing her social drive.

More and more points of incompatability crystallized. Gradually the husband's dissatisfaction with their marriage reached an intolerable level. Ultimately, he asked for a divorce. However, to the wife this was as though she had been struck a mortal blow, from a totally unsuspected source This was the precipitating event for a psychotic episode. Hospitalization was effected and divorce proceedings were carried through.

Following return from the hospital, some close friends came by to renew their friendship and to offer their sympathy over the separation and divorce. To their embarrassment, they were met with a complete Denial that such an occurrence had transpired; and with that the subject was abruptly dropped. For a long time, she talked and acted as if the marriage were intact.

B. ELATION AND DEPRESSION.—Denial has a special relation to certain types of emotional illness. As noted, as a primitive Lower Order dynamism, it is prominent in some of the more severe ones. Denial is frequently present as a psychotic defense. It is encountered, in fact, in all of the psychogenic illness of psychotic level. Denial is often observed in association with severe regressive manifestations.

Certain individuals appear to have a capacity or predilection for the employment of Denial as a major psychologic defense. This is true of those persons subject to major mood changes including the cyclic group. Denial is therefore to be found prominently in patients who are elated. The author has observed Denial repeatedly operative in manic patients, hypomanic elations, and in patients who had newly swung over from a depressed phase.

One may outline a Manic or a Depressive Personality. These delineations help describe the personality diathesis for possible later development of increasing pathology under sufficient precipitating stresses. Again the ego defense of Denial is a significant defense employed by this group.

5. In SEHC

The following instances illustrate the Denial of loss and the effects of loss in childhood. Memory traces for an entire area and for a period of several early years can be successfully lost in this intrapsychic defensive endeavor. This type of Denial is at times encountered in relation to various ones of the SEHC—the *Specific Emotional Hazards of Childhood* [1] (See also later discussion of Denial and death).

Case 33

Denial of Loss

A young man, whose father had left his mother and taken the two small children with him when the patient was 4 years old, once said in a therapy session:

"I don't remember anything until I was six. I wasn't even aware that my mother did not live in the same house with us. After all, what difference would it make to me at that age? . . . What would I need a mother for? . . ."

Case 34

Denial in the Death of a Parent

A man reported the death of his father when he was four. In regard to his emotional reactions, he said:

"I can remember crying at the funeral. People thought it was because my father was dead, but I really was only crying because I wanted to stay at my aunt's house that day . . . I wasn't sad. I felt no loss then and never have . . . I've never missed having a father; its been no handicap to me. . . ."

C. SPECIAL ASPECTS OF DENIAL

1. Conflict Resolution; Sexual Denial

Conflict resolution can be regarded as the ultimate aim of Denial. In some instances, this can produce striking if not extreme results. The following incident is such an illustration of its attempted utilization by an extremely shy, prudish, and inhibited college student.

---

[1] Outlined in Chapter 1 of *The Neuroses.*

Case 35

Sexual Denial

An attractive college freshman had led an extremely protected and sheltered life. As part of the overprotective training imparted by her parents, she had been thoroughly indoctrinated with the great "evilness" of sex and of anything even remotely sexual in nature. Resulting attitudes had been deliberately inculcated by overanxious parents who wanted her to avoid any untoward sexual experiences at all costs. The daughter had come to regard sex as repugnant and bad, and as intolerable even of contemplation by "nice people." She had been protectively overconditioned to a pathologic degree.

In a biology class one day, shortly after the term began, the instructor was discussing reproduction in an academic and quite matter-of-fact fashion. In response to a rather naive question from another quarter, he affirmed the universality of sexual reproduction in mammals.

At this point Dorothy leaped to her feet, obviously upset, and announced in a strained voice to the class of students that this "could not possibly be true"! She found such an idea intolerable to her overly developed moralistic views. To the startled class she asserted aloud, "My parents never, never had intercourse." They simply had never done anything so nasty as that!

Her Denial was part of an attempted rejection of ideas about sex which to her, for good and sufficient reasons, had come to be consciously repugnant and intolerable. Dorothy had a difficult time emotionally during college although she managed to finish. Her subsequent history which might well be of interest, unfortunately is not available.

This preceding instance illustrates the operation of Denial in an unusually inhibited and overconditioned girl. It provides an example of *Sexual Denial* occurring through parental efforts to have their daughter reject any ideas which might lead her into difficulty.

As the consequence, the whole area of sex had been made to be consciously quite repugnant and intolerable to her and Sexual Denial had been defensively elaborated. This brings us to a major social dilemma in regard to sex.

2. *The Socio-Sexual Dilemma: The Need for the Rapid Reversal of Earlier and Protectively-Induced Sexual Inhibitions Following Marriage*

The foregoing instance of Sexual Denial illustrates in exaggerated form a frequent dilemma as to sexual adjustment in modern society. Children are not allowed to marry simply upon reaching physical maturity. It is not suitable in our culture. Economic and social factors require delays until some greater degree of emotional maturity is reached as well. This is necessary for many reasons in our present scheme of things: social, cultural, and economic.

As a consequence, the teaching of personal restraint and self-control in reference to sexual inclinations and activities is regarded almost universally as an important part of one's parental responsibilities. Sexual inhibitions are encouraged. This generally, but not necessarily, tends to find more applicability in the case of girls than with boys. Girls inevitably bear a larger share of the consequences in instances of illegitimate pregnancy. Here then arrives the paradox in our expectations.

Restraint and control of sensuality are accordingly taught, often stringently, in the early years. Upon marriage, however, it is expected that many of the earlier protectively-encouraged inhibitions against sexual activity as an avenue to pleasurable experience and/or parenthood will dissolve. Only too often it is not at all this easy!

This expectancy of an abrupt reversal of attitude contributes substantially in many instances of marital maladjustment. The successful couples get their problems ironed out. Others need expert help, though all too few receive it. This complex problem is a major current dilemma in our society. We have accordingly referred to it for convenience as the *Socio-Sexual Dilemma* of our times. Its faulty or unsatisfactory resolution can lead to all kinds of knotty problems in adjustment, marriage, and living.

Supermoralistic attitudes concerning sex are often found in the Obsessive Personality. (See *The Neuroses,* p. 231 ff.) These may have developed as part of the individual's general inhibitions. They may be present as a reenforcement of the defensive avoidance of sexual interest or as a defensive Denial of such interests. There may be, in fact, little or no conscious awareness of sexual matters. Through such measures, the individual concerned may unconsciously attempt to enhance his control over those sexual impulses which he fears, and/or which he may have consciously disowned. Denial can be an important ego defense in these characterologic developments.

3. Symptom Denial and Illness Denial

The self-defeat resulting from the hypertrophied development and overactivity of a mental mechanism is hardly more tragic than in certain extreme examples of Denial in relation to physical disease. Instances are sometimes encountered by the physician in which the Denial of symptoms, of the illness, or its effects, endangers life. Such an instance may properly be referred to as one of *Symptom Denial* or *Illness Denial,* as deemed appropriate. At times Devaluation (p. 457) is a way station on the road to Denial.

Occasionally, as in the following instance of Illness Denial, the progression in self-defeat is such that it ensures death.

Case 36

Denial of Cancer

(1) *Diagnosis Established; Operative Arrangements Pending.* A 44-year-old man was admitted to a hospital for diagnostic study because of weight loss and generalized malaise. On examination a rectal growth was found which was proven by biopsy to be a malignant type of car-

cinoma. The patient was told he had cancer, and that his physicians would immediately arrange for urgently needed surgery. The patient demurred, wishing to think it over until the next day.

In the morning he talked with the doctors at some length. He was sure that he could not have cancer, because no one in his family had had cancer. He devalued the significance or denied the existence of his admitting complaints.

(2) *Ironclad Illness Denial Prevailed.* No amount of persuasion was successful in convincing this poor man that he had cancer or that a delay could endanger his life. It seemed that the more efforts were made, the more he denied his illness! In its complete failure to respond to any kind of logic, the Denial came to appear akin to delusion formation.

This unhappy man signed himself out of the hospital the following day against medical advice. By chance one of the physicians met him some months later. In appearance he was pale, drawn, appeared to have lost substantial weight, and looked sick. His attitude was unchanged. He laughed openly at the doctor's concern. The Illness Denial was ironclad.

This man's defensive endeavor to shield himself from the recognition of cancer and its potential consequences made certain that a dreaded train of events would occur. One might well wonder what unconscious needs may have existed to thus help ensure his death, which transpired within the year.

The foregoing is a marked and extreme example. Its seriousness is of a rarely so pointedly encountered life-and-death level. Its consideration, together with the two next instances of *Illness Denial,* leads us to the related topic to follow, concerning the Denial-of-Death.

The following instance illustrates the kind of Illness Denial sometimes to be encountered in terminal illness. The Denial supports of the patient's apparent lack of concern and his seeming unrealistic appraisal of the situation.

Case 37

Illness Denial in Terminal Illness

A 33-year-old painter was hospitalized and a diagnosis of cancer established. He had developed a scrotal mass of 10 months duration, found to be a malignant embryonal cell tumor. His clinical course was steadily downhill. Operation (orchectomy) afforded little benefit. He experienced pain in his right leg, and a rapidly enlarging mass developed in right supraclavicular region. X-ray of the chest revealed metastatic lesions. There was progressive weight loss, low grade fever, and anorexia. He experienced bowel difficulties, lost bladder control, and a retention catheter became necessary. As a last resort, experimental chemotherapeutic agents were employed. He was examined frequently by many doctors.

This man was endowed with above average intelligence. However, despite the multiple procedures and a rapidly progressive downhill course, he didn't inquire about his condition and seemed concerned only about the leg pain. Although obviously a terminal patient, he expected to return to work after his release from the hospital. When told he had a "very bad tumor," and that the outlook was not good at all, he was apparently unconcerned. He had no interest in further information.

Although the exact nature of his difficulties, or the anticipated end result, had not been spelled out to him in so many words, it was felt that he very well *knew* on some level the inevitable course of his disease. His actions and attitudes in other ways were those of an individual with an intractable disease. Nevertheless, he did not display interest in the course of his disease, ask questions about it, or inquire as to when he would leave the hospital and return to work. He did not consider time important.

This man sensed on a deeper level that his time was limited and that he was going to die, but this was consciously intolerable and he denied its existence even in the face of "undeniable" evidence. His death transpired as anticipated, with no change in the Illness Denial.

The operation of Denial has many important applications in various types of physical ills and in their sequelae. Resulting handicaps may be denied. This may likewise transpire with defects, limitations, and with various deficits which can follow illness.

Denial in serious illness also can operate in relation to threatened terminal results in the physical illnesses of those near and dear. This is illustrated in the following example of Illness Denial by a mother.

Case 38

Illness Denial and Its Mortal Prognosis

A mother was devoted to her chronically ill infant son. A year after birth the child had began to show signs of leucoencephalopathy, a rare and fatal disease, necessitating thorough diagnostic procedures. The diagnosis was confirmed at a research center.

Death could be expected within 5 years from onset. People connected with the case, including the father, recognized and accepted this sad certainty. The mother, however, insisted that the difficulties were not those of a terminal disease process. She firmly believed the symptoms to be those of an obscure but curable disease. She took offense when the child was viewed as a medically interesting case. Greater than normal love was lavished on this unfortunate child. She overprotected him and did not leave the hospital after his admission, slept in the room, and gave him constant care.

She could not accept the painful facts of the case. She had denied to herself the nature of the illness and its inevitable sad prognosis. On another level, the tremendous love and care given the infant could indicate an underlying recognition of his limited days.

4. The Denial-of-Death

A. UNPLEASANT REALITIES.—Denial enters into the psychic defenses of many people in their endeavors to cope with death and whatever death means to them personally. For many, the threat of death is completely intolerable. It cannot be allowed thought or consideration; a quiet and detached contemplation of its consequences is impossible. The roots of Denial in relation to death are in infancy, when nebulous and primordial defenses gradually evolve into the patterns of psychologic defenses to be employed in later life.

In infancy, a wish-fulfilling denial of various aspects of unpleasant realities is common. This might help us recognize how effectively the "pleasure principle" can operate. Denial often succeeds best as a defense against certain internal perceptions of a painful nature, that the individual finds impossible to accept, including for the adult, doubts as to his competence and the dread of death.

In the later phases of personality or character development, of course, attempts at denial may be defeated, as they come into direct opposition to the ego's increasing functions of perception and memory. In very early childhood, as long as the ego is weak, however, the tendency toward Denial may get the upper hand over these functions. Into later childhood, the characteristic solution is more likely to be that the objectionable truth or painful data comes to be denied instead through fantasy and in play (also see p. 111). This is *Denial-in-Fantasy*. The reasonable part of the ego may at the same time recognize the truth as well as the playful or fantastic character of the Denial.

Denial-in-Fantasy may continue in the normal adult; he recognizes an unpleasant truth, but nonetheless, or perhaps for that very reason, he indulges in daydreams that deny this truth. Fenichel advanced a view that what can be observed in neurotic patients is a splitting of the ego, into a superficial part that knows and recognizes the truth, and a deeper part that denies it. To some degree, perhaps, this can be found in all.

B. THE ILLUSION-OF-CONTINUED-LIVING.—In the following example it was not clear what part was conscious and what part was unconscious. Shortly after it was reported this man accepted a position in another city and further data was unobtainable.

Case 39

An Illusion-of-Continued-Living

A 26-year-old salesman worked at a business machine company for 2 years. Other employees had come to notice the strong attachment of this young man for his mother. Hardly a day would pass wherein he did not mention some kind thing his mother had done for him on that particular morning, or the evening before. These instances would be quite specific. It had been noteworthy enough to have become an occasional topic of office discussion.

During this period he cultivated a friendship of sorts with a fellow employee. The latter was understandably surprised when he chanced to learn that this man's mother had been dead for the past 5 years! Seemingly, his friend had found the death of his mother too painful to accept and in his endeavors at Denial, he had continued behaving and talking as if she were still alive.

He was thus seeking to maintain what we can term an *Illusion-of-Continued-Living*. To the extent this might prove successful, the intolerable event of his mother's death was denied. In various less prominent or unrealistic ways, this kind of illusory aim is pursued by many persons.

There are, of course, outside of clinical practice, many partial, subtle, and less obvious ways in which human beings actively or inadvertently pursue a Denial of death. Sometimes otherwise unnecessary possessions of the departed member are kept in view, or things are left in the exact state they were in when the person died. This is done with an evident intent to help support just such an *Illusion-of-Continued-Living,* and helps constitute a Denial-of-Death. Often aspects of such endeavors are, at least in part, unconscious.

Examples are also found in literature. In the song "Grandfather's Clock," the clock stood in the hall having "stopped short, never to go again, when the old man died. . . ." The clock was not repaired if repairable, nor, if not repairable, did anyone care to remove it as a useless object. Its sentimental attachment and maintenance undisturbed were perhaps due to its relation to the grandfather, as well as to the eerie coincidence of its time of stopping. Eugene Field, in his well known poem " Little Boy Blue," wrote of the beloved little boy's plaything remaining in the places he had last put them:

> "Aye, faithful to Little Boy Blue they stand,
> Each in the same old place,
> Awaiting the touch of a little hand,
> The smile of a little face."

Many examples of Denial relating to death are observed in medical practice. We observed how terminal patients may attitudinally deny the prospect of approaching death. Some of our cultural patterns in funeral arrangements also tend to deny death. Death is regarded as sleep. Caskets are arranged as beds. The dead one is "sleeping." The body may be in a "slumber room."

The many subtle ways in which this type of Denial appears are quite pervasive. To become aware of them personally can sometimes require perceptiveness. The following is an example.

Case 40

Denial-of-Death

In illustration of this important aspect of Denial, Dr. Marjorie Brierley sent along an interesting personal instance. Several years ago the analyst carried out long-standing plans to retire in the beautiful country area near Keswick, Cumberland, in the north of England. The change was achieved with considerable joy and satisfaction.

As she aptly analyzed her feelings for us later, with particular reference to this aspect of Denial, ". . . after the commotion and fatigue of moving and settling in, I was consciously much relieved to think we should never have to move again. My way of expressing this was by saying that we had come here to live forever! . . ."

C. MULTIPLE DENIAL.—Sometimes the Denial-of-Death goes so far as to overstep the bounds of reality, and ends in delusion formation. Intended as a protective measure, yet wholly unrealistic, something is denied which a person is consciously unable to tolerate.

In the following instance, the Denial of the death of a son was in similar fashion followed by the neglect (ignoring, Denial) of a cancerous lesion, to the point of its reaching a state of inoperability. This illustrates the *Multiple Denial Concept,* including as it does the Denial of at least two major areas of reality.

Case 41

Denial of Death and Neglect of Cancer

A middle-aged woman appearing older than her stated age was admitted to the public ward of a general hospital. She had a large inoperable cancer of the right breast. A family member reported a long history of emotional lability much worse following her son's death 3 years ago. When asked about her son, she asserted that he was living in another city. His death was denied.

History and examination revealed that she had ignored an open lesion in her breast for at least 18 months, during which time it had progressed to massive size and inoperability. Only because of hemorrhage and family insistence had hospitalization been effected. She had denied its existence, its effects, and thereby any danger from it. This represented an extreme case of *Multiple Denial:* the son's death and the cancer.

While on the ward she continued to deny the seriousness of her lesion, its inevitable consequences, and at times even its presence. Daily she had to be humored to undertake change of dressings. Treatment was palliative and supportive until her death ensued some weeks later.

The following instance illustrates Denial in the loss of a child. Here the area of Denial becomes an isolated and discrete kind of delusion, which however seemed to interfere little in other areas of living. It blocked out conscious recognition of a disaster which had been intolerable to the mother. Herein we again see illustrated the Illusion-of-Continued-Living.

Case 42

Denial in the Death of a Child

A 39-year-old woman long yearned for motherhood and had finally become pregnant. Following her child's birth, she centered her existence around the long-awaited little girl.

When the child was nine, she was struck and killed instantly by a truck. This sudden tremendous loss was more than the mother could bear. It was consciously inadmissible.

Her intended defense was through a Denial-of-Death. To family and friends she spoke constantly of her little girl as one who was "away on a visit" and would "soon return." She would allow no one to speak of the child as dead. A place was regularly set at the table, and the child's bed was made and remade daily. Her room and playthings were all maintained as if the child would walk in momentarily. This continued for years.

D. GRIEF-STRICKEN DENIAL.—The following instance illustrates a more marked example of the distraught attempted Denial sometimes temporarily present following the death of a loved one. This may be termed *Grief-Stricken Denial.* There are similarities to prior instances.

Case 43

Denial-of-Death in the Grief-Stricken

A young man was critically injured in a highway accident and was admitted to the surgical service. Emergency surgery was undertaken, but almost from the outset his condition was clearly hopeless. His devoted mother remained at the bedside constantly for 72 hours. Shortly thereafter he succumbed. The mother was not immediately present, but was in the building and promptly informed, after which she abruptly left the hospital in an emotionally disturbed state.

The following morning she returned. She was very distraught and demanded to see her son. When so reminded, she denied that he was dead. She sought to deny the consciously intolerable event in her grief-stricken state. A sympathetic and understanding husband responded to a call and took her home. The Denial and its consequences, so marked by pathos, were resolved under the kindly care of her family physician.

5. Denial Aids in Maintaining Destructive Patterns of Gratification

Denial is a primitive type of mechanism. Denial magically says that something does not exist that one cannot stand. Denial also is a way of avoidance, through which one attempts the resolution of conflict by denying one side of it. As noted, this mode of attempted ego defense can be carried over into adult life. Thus the child (and the adult) may deny that he cares or is hurt. Consequences of having cared can be denied. When one works toward something unsuccessfully or loses something meaningful, the loss may be denied.

Denial is an important dynamism in the rejection of something consciously intolerable. As in the following case, through its Denial, one may maintain a protective nonawareness of destructive aspects of his behavior. Denial was an aid in retaining a fiercely guarded pattern of gratification.

Case 44

Denial of the Destructive Consequences of Extramarital Sexual Experience

A 32-year-old patient in psychotherapy led a sexually promiscuous life, in which his partners (and he) suffered various indignities and potential injury. His behavior was such as to seriously jeopardize his reputation, social standing, and marital happiness. This patient denied the possibility of untoward results to himself or to the others involved. This Denial allowed him to continue the neurotic satisfactions which resulted from his blatant and unrestrained sexual behavior.

Through the process of Denial, he pushed any possible awareness or censorship by a critical and painful superego out of consciousness. When analysis had progressed to a point where he became able to recognize and accept the consequences of his behavior in terms of the injuries done himself and his partners, his behavior modified considerably. He became willing to sacrifice the immediate fulfillment of his sexual impulses.

6. The Omission Denial

Denial is a dynamism which does not always require something to be done or changed. Often an omission acts in the service of Denial. This can be found in the various ways in which people seek to deny death personally, i.e., in relation to themselves—their own death. When observable, this comprises what we might refer to as the *Omission Denial*.

In this area the Denial-of-Death can be found *implicit in the acts* ❧ *which people fail to perform in preparation to meet it*. Thus a significant number of individuals do not make burial or funeral service plans. Despite clear advantages in so doing and the efforts of attorneys and courts, many will not (or cannot?) have wills drawn. For others, the Omission Denial interferes with an adequate insurance program.

A more active kind of approach to the Denial-of-Death may be found via certain items of humor. Many examples are to be found in jokes and cartoons, in which the content makes light of death, as though to deny its "sting"—for those who fear it.

D. DENIAL AND OTHER DYNAMISMS

Denial is an important mental mechanism of ego defense which can be illustrated to operate in many diverse situations, some of which have been outlined in the foregoing comments. Denial also makes use of other ego defenses to achieve its results. Some of these have been noted.

The Denial of reality occurs through the use of Fantasy as noted earlier. A similar Denial of reality often is an underlying motive in children's games. We have noted the early struggles between Denial and memory. Denial has a close kinship to Repression. From this viewpoint, Denial may be regarded as an adjunct or auxiliary to Repression. We observed its importance in the endogain of Conversion (p. 49 ff.) and that it may be effected or reenforced through Conversion (p. 51).

Noyes described how Projection can be used as an adjunct to Denial. Unable to tolerate the anxiety aroused by his hatred for "B", "A" unconsciously reversed this to what he then subjectively experienced as "B hates me." Thus his own hatred is Denied. In this fashion, Denial is usually associated with Projection when the latter dynamism is operative. Denial as an ego defense or mental mechanism becomes an unconscious wiping-out of a segment of the perceptive powers.

Denial can operate in the service of Idealization. This is illustrated in the following example (also see Case 61, p. 114).

Case 45

Denial Supports Idealization

An airline pilot was married, with two children. His work necessitated his being away from home frequently. His wife had a reputation for overdrinking, was flagrantly flirtatious, and led a promiscuous life. Nevertheless, an acquaintance could have pictured her as a paragon of virtue and a model mother from the husband's comments. Seemingly, he would be blind not to have been aware of her conduct.

This man's reaction, however, was considered to reflect Denial because of the obvious sincerity of his comments and his attitude. He had idealized his wife. His inability to see what others saw so clearly, and to deny any such recognition, contributed to and maintained the Idealization.

E. CONSCIOUS EFFORTS AT DENIAL

Denial can also be consciously attempted, as has been indicated. This is most common. Many persons turn away from unpleasant or frightening scenes, as if to deny their existence. They may reject unpleasant topics.

Criticism may be ignored and its underlying truth denied, as a defensively-intended effort.

Responsibility is often denied, even when secretly admitted. As illustrated, it is not an uncommon experience for older people to attempt to deny certain losses in their physical or mental capacities. Parents, and perhaps more often grandparents, tend to deny faults or failures on the part of the children or grandchildren, of which they nonetheless may be fully aware. It is not always easy or possible to determine how much of the denial is conscious and how much is unconscious.

There are many instances in which jealousy must be denied because of other forces; pride, self-respect, or unworthiness. The following is a superficial example.

Case 46

Jealousy is Denied

An attractive young woman had been brought up by strict and religious parents. When she went away to college, she became a roommate to a very attractive and popular girl who had many dates. Due to Susan's coldness and prudishness, more than because of her physical attributes, she did not have many dates or much of a social life.

Susan objected strenuously to her roommate's many dates. Once she phoned the latter's parents to tell them that their daughter was "running around." When the roommate found out about the phone call, an argument ensued. She accused Susan of being jealous.

This was vigorously and indignantly denied. Susan said she "would not go out with boys like that." It was later learned that she really liked one of the boys and very much wished she would be asked out. She was indeed jealous, but this emotion had had to be strongly and vocally denied.

F. SUMMARY

Denial is a major and basic ego defense which is automatically and unconsciously employed to preserve and defend the ego, through the elimination (banishment) of intolerable data from conscious awareness. Denial is a primitive dynamism of disavowal and disclaiming. Through Denial, an individual seeks to resolve conflict and to avert anxiety. A certain amount of Denial is almost universal and in many instances is to be considered normal. Its defensive evolvement is likely to be in inverse ratio to maturity. We have offered illustrations as to how its overemployment can lead to seriously self-defeating consequences, and in extreme instances endanger life. Denial is an unconscious type of negation.

Through the operation of this dynamism, self-confidence may be bolstered by the Denial of doubts. This is *Denial-for-Confidence*. The interesting *Ostrich Concept* was presented and its rationale outlined. Denial in emotional illness is a frequent block to therapy, in the *Antitherapeutic Denial*, and at times tragically defeats all efforts to interest the patient in a need for, or in tackling, constructive self-study. In this employment of the ego defense, the person denies the existence of problems or denies their effects.

Severely self-defeating forms of Denial are commonly met with in cases of alcoholic habituation and drug addiction, the use of this *Lower Order,* primitive mechanism suggesting the deep-seated nature of these problems. Denial can constitute an effective *secondary defense* of emotional symptoms, in which the symptom—a defense in itself—is in turn defended. The destructive consequences historically, of certain instances of *National Denial* were noted.

People unwittingly seek to cope with psychic hurt, loss and pain through Denial. Major areas of painful experience may be repressed and denied in this kind of operation, as well illustrated in *Case 22.* The accuracy of one's self-picture or of one's views of another may be distorted through Denial. This dynamism is commonly encountered in efforts to cope with the sequelae of aging. This type of operation of the defense was labeled *Denial-in-Aging.*

Denial may be employed rather specifically to resolve an emotional conflict in a specific area. Conflict resolution may be regarded as its ultimate aim. It may also be employed to allow retention of destructive sexual or other gratifications. Our modern *Socio-Sexual Dilemma* was mentioned, in regard to culturally necessary and protectively-induced sexual inhibitions and restraints prior to marriage, and the expectation that these will easily dissolve in the newly married state. Some serious aspects of Denial were noted in reference to grief (*Grief-Stricken Denial*), to death (*Denial-of-Death*), to the lack of preparations to meet it (*Omission Denial*) and to physical illness. Added important types include *Symptom Denial* and *Illness Denial.* The *Denial-of-Death* merited special attention, with its many pervasive ramifications in individual living and in society. The *Illusion-of-Continued-Living* is related, or can be employed in its support. The *Multiple Denial* is a concept of two or more major areas being concurrently denied.

Denial plays an important role in symptom formation and a few of its aspects herein were noted. Denial can enter into major manifestations of the psychoses, including hallucinations and delusions. Conscious efforts at Denial are universal and enter into many areas. These include or contribute to certain *Mass* and *Public Denials,* as well as in myriad individual instances. Denial operates at various times in conjunction with or is supported in its function by many other ego defenses.

G.   CROSS-REFERENCES TO *THE NEUROSES* *

Denial
In Nature of Anxiety (Chapter 1); of hostility; p. 15.
In Illusory Gains (Chapter 2)
   in emotional symptom formation: p. 56.

---

* From Laughlin, H. P. *The Neuroses.* London, Butterworth & Co., Ltd., 1967.

in *endogain* of emotional illness, in primary gain; p. 78.
  Table 5; p. 69.
in *King David Reaction;* p. 76.
In Anxiety Reactions (Chapter 3)
defensive d., of emotional bases; p. 91.
of emotional problems; p. 126.
of hostility, in *Anxiety Tension State* (ATS), (Case 22); p. 103.
In Depressive Reactions (Chapter 4)
of destructive drives; p. 182.
of emotional bases, in Depression; p. 144.
of grief; p. 166.
of hostility, in depressive *endogain* (Table 14); pp. 178–9.
of infantile needs, in evolvement of Depression; pp. 169, 172, 174.
In Character Reactions (Chapter 5)
as a personality type; p. 233.
in character patterns of defense; p. 238.
in defenses of *Convérsion Personality* (Table 19); p. 260.
in defenses of *Depressive Personality;* p. 271.
of hostility, in *Depressive Personality* (Case 58); p. 276.
of sexual interests, in *Obsessive Personality;* p. 296.
In Obsessive-Compulsive Reactions (Chapter 6)
attempted d., of obsessive thoughts; p. 310
encouraged, in inhibition of emotions; p. 323.
in *First Line of Psychic Defense;* p. 343.
of hostility; p. 341.
  Case 65; p. 325.
  Case 71; p. 347.
In Fatigue Reactions (Chapter 7)
in *endogain* of Fatigue Reaction; p. 408.
of adult role (Case 82); p. 405.
of hostility; p. 411.
of unconscious drives and needs; p. 383.
In Hygeiaphrontic Reactions (Chapter 8)
consequences of d., in *Hygeiaphrontis;* p. 475.
in Hygeiaphrontic *endogain* and *epigain* (Table 26); p. 511.
in primal patterns of reaction and response; p. 493.
of emotional conflicts (Case 97); p. 474.
of emotional relationship to physical symptoms; p. 462.
of hostility (Case 102); p. 500.
of murderous rage (Case 100); p. 486.
of parental hostility, in symptom formation; p. 479.
of repressed conflicts; p. 481.
of unconsciously sought dependency goals; pp. 494–5.
In Fear and Its Avoidance (Chapter 9)
of inner drives; p. 520.
of sexual interests (Case 104); p. 523.
In Phobic Reactions (Chapter 10)
of hostility (Case 125); p. 598.
of rejection by significant adult (Case 117); p. 567.
of unconscious basis of phobia; p. 562.
of unconscious desire for dependent position;
  Case 115; p. 561.
  Case 119; p. 572.

resulting from *Dependency-Dilemma of Infancy;* p. 579.

In Soterial Reactions (Chapter 11); a factor, in comparison of phobia to *soteria* (Table 30); p. 628.

In Conversion Reactions (Chapter 12)

in *endogain* of Conversion Reactions (Table 36); pp. 691, 700.

in *la belle indifférence,* in lobotomies; p. 685.
in mechanisms of Conversion Reaction; p. 692.

of dependency needs (Case 137); p. 668.

of disowned impulses; p. 682.

of hidden bases of symptoms; p. 685.

of intolerable unconscious impulses; pp. 663, 693.

in Somatic Conversion; p. 690.

In Dissociative Reactions (Chapter 13)

in relation to fainting; p. 772.

of memory gaps; p. 725.

in spotty amnesia; p. 775.

of painful stimulus, in Automatic Writing; p. 810.

of responsibility in Fugue; p. 798.

reinforced d., of hypnotic experience; p. 820.

representations of d., expressed in dreams; p. 746.

In Neuroses-Following-Trauma (Chapter 14)

a psychic retreat to d., in *Compliant-Resignation-Response* to death; p. 859.

of responsibility (Case 174); p. 853.

of threat and danger; pp. 874, 894.

In Military Reactions (Chapter 15); of futility in part-surrender, in *Prisoner Processing;* p. 939.

H.   REVIEW QUESTIONS

Sample self-check questions on Chapter 4 and Denial, for the student, psychiatric resident, and board candidate.

1. Briefly discuss the nature of *Denial.* Comment on its operation in childhood and adulthood. When is it more likely to be observed in adults?

2. How does the dynamism of Denial operate in the following:
    A. *Denial-for-confidence.*
    B. *Public Denial.*
    C. *Personality Invulnerability.*
    D. *The Ostrich Concept.*
    E. Denial of Impropriety.
    F. *Denial-in-Aging.*
    G. Alcoholism.
    H. *La belle indifférence.*
    I. *Multiple Denial.*
    J. *National Denial.*

3. Discuss the significance of the *Antitherapeutic Denial* in psychiatry.

4. How can Denial contribute to various types of symptom formation in emotional illness?

5. What is the self-defeat inherent in the operation of *Symptom Denial* and *Illness Denial?* Comment on its significance (1) in psychotherapy, (2) for the internist.

6. Outline the defensive intent in the *Denial-of-Death* and the related *Illusion-of-Continued-Living* and *Grief-Stricken Denial.*

7. Explain the *Socio-Sexual Dilemma* and resulting inimical consequences.
8. What is meant by *Omission Denial?*
9. Illustrate how Denial can operate in the service of other dynamisms.
10. How can Denial contribute to the *secondary defense* of emotional symptoms?

CHAPTER 5

DISPLACEMENT

...Intrapsychic Transference and Redirection Externally

A. DEFINITION

B. TYPES OF DISPLACEMENT
   1. Personal-Feeling Displacement. 2. The Scapegoat Reaction and the Convenient Target. 3. Sexual-Object Displacement.

C. DISPLACEMENT AND SUBSTITUTION
   1. Emotional Symbiosis. 2. The Displaced Complex.

D. DISPLACEMENT FUNDAMENTAL AND PRIMITIVE
   1. Primal Displacement. 2. Summary.

E. REFERENCES (FROM *The Neuroses*)

F. REVIEW QUESTIONS

A. DEFINITION

Displacement *is a primitive, Lower Order ego defense operating outside of and beyond conscious awareness, through which an emotional feeling is transferred, deflected, and redirected from its internal object to a substitute external one. The emotional feeling, fear, anxiety, drive, or complex is thus displaced to a new person, situation, or object.* Displacement is the basic and most prominent dynamism in the evolution of the phobic pattern of neurotic defense.

In the Phobic Reactions through the mechanism of Displacement, there is an automatic transfer of fear and threat from its original hidden and internal (unconscious) source, to another one which is external and apparently unrelated. This important intrapsychic mechanism is observable to be repeatedly operative in the phobias.

Through Displacement the phobic endogain largely lies in sparing the individual painful awareness of the basic and internal source of the conflict. The effects of such conflicts have conscious influences, but their underlying nature and source remains concealed. Repression is maintained.

Utilization of the dynamism in the Phobic Reaction can be termed *Phobic Displacement*. Illustrations of this prominent type of Displacement

are to be found in some dozen clinical cases cited in *The Neuroses,* pp. 515–638.

B. TYPES OF DISPLACEMENT

1. *Personal-Feeling Displacement*

There are a number of additional important types of Displacement which can be delineated currently and occasionally observed. Several of these are chosen for inclusion in our discussion as being representative of their potential influence in people's reactions and lives.

Among these is the Displacement of painful feelings toward or about the self, to external people or situations. The latter objects for the Displacement may be real or fictional. A certain amount of emotional Deferment (p. 456) is usually also present. The protective intent of the operation becomes quite clear. This comprises what we might refer to as *Personal-Feeling Displacement.*

Instances similar to the following may be occasionally observed.

Case 47

Personal-Feeling Displacement and Deferment

A 33-year-old married high school science teacher reported in therapy rather matter-of-factly her emotionally painful and copiously tearful reactions while attending movies. It did not take long to learn that this represented a protectively-intended Displacement of her own strong inner emotional feelings.

The tears, crying and sadness were thus deflected and redirected, or displaced, to the people and events of the screen. Through the Displacement of her personal feelings, concealment and reduced awareness were inadvertently sought of her great sadness and major personal problems, including a tragic marital situation.

This was an instance of *Personal-Feeling Displacement* which had become personally significant. It is hardly surprising therefore and not really contradictory, that despite her seeming misery at the cinema, she attended regularly.

It is clear that the accompanying capacity for the deferred expression of emotional feelings is required to maintain this kind of defensively-intended reaction pattern. It was gradually surrendered as inappropriate and no longer necessary, but only after it became thoroughly elucidated in her therapeutic work.

2. *The Scapegoat Reaction and the Convenient Target*

Angry feelings are not uncommonly displaced. Indeed, one of the more frequent employments of the dynamism of Displacement is the reassignment of anger, hostility, or resentment toward a different object, situation, or person. Usually this different object is safer and therefore less threatening or dangerous. The substituted object (p. 403) becomes the scapegoat. Accordingly, we would term this the *Scapegoat Reaction.*

The intent of this intrapsychic operation is self-protection and defense. Through the Scapegoat Reaction, for example, a parent may displace anger from his spouse to one of their children. A wife may unwittingly bear the brunt of anger and frustrations deflected from her husband's employer or from some other aspect of his work situation. An animal may well become the hapless victim of displaced hostility and frustration.

There are many examples of this reaction to be encountered in day-to-day living. See also *Case 50*. The new object for Displacement comprises what can be labeled the Convenient Target.

The following is an instance of the *Scapegoat Reaction*. The pattern of response evolved is illustrated by a verbatim extract from the analytic work of a housewife-editor, well along in intensive psychotherapy. The Displacement herein was from self to children, who became the safer and more *convenient target*.

Case 48

The Scapegoat Reaction

(1) *Pattern of Anger Evident.* "Until recently I used to get mad at the children every Sunday morning. Now I think I understand why. I've really been angry with myself. It's about the house and efficiency and getting things done. . . .

"The house and everything in it has been so disorganized. It is so big and always such a mess! Clothes scattered. Can't find anything. . . . Children at loose ends. I've had the whole journal (the entire editorial responsibility for a small magazine) now for over 2 years. I was always working on it, writing, doing letters, editing, visiting people, or having people in. I loved it. . . . It was exciting. . . .

(2) *Sunday a Culmination.* "People said it didn't bother me if things didn't get done. I guess that's the impression I gave. . . . It wasn't the kids' fault that I'm running the journal. All the phone calls, all the visitors in. Everything was a rat race. Terrible. . . .

"All week no help. When Sunday came I was always way behind. No ironing done. No help. No clean clothes. . . . I wanted the children to go to church. Actually the whole family should go, and I just couldn't manage it. . . . I would really be so angry with myself for these failures and my inefficiency. . . . It was also the culmination of the week! [*Note* also the operation here of Convergence (p. 456); probably Overdetermination, (p. 477), and Deferment (p. 476).)]

(3) *Children Comprise Convenient Target.* "So I would lose patience with the children. . . . I was really disgusted with myself, but I would get demanding, and the children would be all upset. . . . Things would go from bad to worse.

"I was really taking out on them my anger with myself. (They became the *Convenient Target.*) My anger was shifted over to them. They became the objects instead of me. . . . I hadn't begun to realize this until recently. . . . Since then things have been getting better . . ."

3. Sexual-Object Displacement

One means of attempted resolution of serious emotional conflict over sexual matters is through the Displacement of otherwise unacceptable and thereby consciously repressed urges, toward a more acceptable object. This can occur when marital, personal, or social barriers prohibit the outward expression and the conscious recognition of strong sexual feelings.

This type of Displacement is a consequence of sexual conflict, which it seeks to resolve. In the interests of its delineation, ease of reference, and as a part of our convenient psychiatric shorthand, we might refer to it as *Sexual-Object Displacement*.

In the following example the original object of the deeply buried and consciously intolerable sexual drive had been the young woman's father. The Displacement to substitute male objects was understandably defensive and sought to subserve a number of vital psychologic purposes. Anything in the nature of incest even as to thoughts, was most abhorrent and for years had been absolutely inadmissible.

Case 49

Sexual-Object Displacement

(1) *Father Relationship Strained.* A 29-year-old, single college graduate lived with her parents. Her relationships with other people especially men, were difficult and troubling. Resulting problems led her to seek therapy.

Relations with her father had become decidedly strained. She could barely speak to him, despite frequent attempts on his part to be friendly. When she found herself alone with him she became anxious, so that she would either leave or get her mother to join them. This was puzzling to her, the more so since she had always been his favorite. She had been quite close to him until she was 14.

(2) *Series of Brief Torrid Affairs.* Her relations with men had been characterized for 10 years by a long series of brief but passionate love affairs. These had routinely involved older men, usually in their forties. They were quite intense until sexual relations were established, after which her attraction would rapidly fade. She would come to feel dissatisfied—this man was not the one she was looking for.

The affair would be broken off. Soon afterwards she would start another one. This had become a compulsive repetitive pattern of behavior. Her resulting dissatisfactions helped her decide to embark upon treatment.

(3) *A Protectively-Intended Sexual-Object Displacement.* During the course of therapy, it eventually became apparent that she had long harbored strong but hidden sexual feelings toward her father. These had been absolutely intolerable to her and had been successfully repressed. However, the repression of these feelings was not really complete. Further, they were being unconsciously displaced onto other men. Each of these substitute objects for her affection had to some extent resembled her father physically and in personality.

This *Sexual-Object Displacement* represented a further unconscious reenforcement of repression, plus allowing a certain amount of disguised outward expression and symbolic gratification of her consciously disowned feelings. As more and more data accumulated in support of this thesis, she became slowly able to understand her reactions.

She gained increasing understanding of her compulsive sexual behavior concurrently with the ability to more constructively cope with her previously deeply unconscious conflicts. She was eventually able to relinquish the fruitless and defeating pattern of relationships. A little over 3 years subsequently she married and has made an excellent adjustment since.

C. DISPLACEMENT AND SUBSTITUTION

1. Emotional Symbiosis

Displacement is an unconscious, protectively-intended process through which the individual concerned unconsciously attempts to prevent awareness of an internal threat, or of one element of an emotional conflict. The associated feelings are thereby "automatically and effortlessly" transferred (i.e., displaced) externally to another object. The effects of Displacement can be similar to Conversion (p. 50).

Displacement frequently if not universally operates in conjunction with Substitution (*Chapter 23*). Herein a new object is *substituted* for the original one, and the original emotional feelings are then *displaced* to the substitute object. The dynamisms comprise what we can refer to as an *emotional symbiosis.* (See also pp. 125 and 131.) The following instance is illustrative.

Case 50

Substitution and Displacement

A 28-year-old single school teacher was having serious difficulties with her principal, an older woman. These were apparently unaccountable. Both women were popular and were well liked by their associates. The younger woman found herself frequently enraged at her supervisor without an adequate cause, or upon an extremely minor pretext, at least as assessed by her friends.

Briefly, history revealed that the teacher lived with her invalid mother, who had long made constant and inordinate demands upon her for attention, services, and affection. Relationships with other young people had been almost impossible. On a conscious level the teacher was very devoted to her mother. She was overly defensive of critical comments directed toward her mother or their relationship.

Her feelings eventually proved to be not so purely one-sided as she had long maintained. She was really quite strongly ambivalent, the negative side of the ambivalence having been repressed as intolerable. Certain minor similarities between the mother and the principal had not only made *Substitution* of the latter possible, but had facilitated the development of the entire defensively-intended complex. The principal became a more acceptable and safer object, to whom the negative feelings were *displaced.* Also illustrated is the Scapegoat Reaction, p. 87, through which a *convenient target* was provided.

2. The Displaced Complex

In the following example there was also Displacement to another person, who had come to serve as a less dangerous formidable object-target for emotional feelings. This instance illustrates the *Displaced Complex.*

Case 51

The Displaced Complex

Two teen-age sisters were in love with the same man. Following an intense competitive struggle, one of them married him, while the other sister remained single. Two children, a boy and a girl, resulted from the union, but their mother soon died.

The care of the children fell to their aunt. She was quite fond of the boy, but developed a strong dislike for the girl and grossly mistreated her. This progressed to the point where the aunt alleged that the girl was insane and once sought to have her committed to an institution. For various cogent reasons the foster-mother entered psychotherapy.

In this instance, a greatly condensed summary of the results of analytic study revealed that a great amount of unacceptable and consciously disowned envy and hatred had been long harbored by the foster mother toward her sister, who had successfully married the man both girls had loved. The repressed hatred was unconsciously displaced to the niece, who became the innocent victim (and more *convenient target*) of the *Displaced Complex*.

In another instance of the operation of Displacement, the elements bear a resemblance to the foregoing cases. Herein, however, the operation of the ego defense was on a more conscious level.

Case 52

The Convenient Target

A 31-year-old, mild-mannered male patient frequently became furious with his superiors at work. Particularly impotent to express his emotional feelings in any direct way, he would partly unconsciously "take out" his anger and frustration on his wife. He was *displacing* angry feelings which he could not express toward those in authority, toward his wife as a safer object; a more *convenient target*.

Mild-mannered and retiring in other relationships, in striking contrast he was often hostile, sadistic, overbearing, and cruel to his wife. As increasing awareness of his Displacement was gradually forced through therapy, this pattern of reaction became substantially modified.

D. DISPLACEMENT FUNDAMENTAL AND PRIMITIVE

1. Primal Displacement

Displacement is another basic and primitive mechanism. In view of its fundamental position, we might include it with the *Lower Order* dynamisms.

What we can term *Primal Displacement* occurs very early in life. In some instances, its early position developmentally is perhaps comparable to that of Repression. As Brierley commented, "We do not think so much in terms of conflict between impulses, as in terms of tension or conflict between id, ego, and superego," i.e., between the primary impulses or infantile interests, and reality self and conscience. But, since the reality self, from the angle of motivation, is an organization of the channels of instinct discharge, such processes as Displacement are almost more primitive than Repression.

Thumb sucking in infants thus need not mean Denial or Repression, but instead the Displacement of "missing breast by thumb." This would of course comprise an instance of Primal Displacement.

2. Summary

Displacement commonly, if not routinely, operates in the Phobic Reactions as the *Phobic Displacement* of the original and internal anxious threat and danger to a new and safer external object. The emotions are assigned a *convenient target*. This comprises one of the most important clinical roles of the dynamism. Further study of this major type of Dis-

placement has been included in the appropriate chapters of *The Neuroses.*
Reference was made to the defense of emotional deferment operating with
Displacement.

Displacement and Substitution function together in what we have
termed an *emotional symbiosis.* This is also true in other patterns of neurotic reaction. *Case 70,* p. 344 in *The Neuroses* illustrates the conjoint
operation of these dynamisms in the Obsessive-Compulsive Reactions. Displacement is essential in the evolvement of the *Scapegoat Reaction,* with
its provision of a *convenient target.*

Among a number of additional types of Displacement, we noted in
this brief chapter those of *Personal-Feeling Displacement* and *Sexual-
Object Displacement. Primal-Displacements* are often major operations
of this dynamism in infancy and early childhood. The ego defense can
result in producing what is called the *displaced complex,* which was also
illustrated.

E.   CROSS-REFERENCES TO *THE NEUROSES* *

Displacement
In Illusory Gains (Chapter 2); in *King David Reaction;* p. 76.
In Anxiety Reactions (Chapter 3); in dynamics of the phobia; p. 120.
In Character Reactions (Chapter 5)
   as a personality type; p. 233.
   to trifles, by obsessive persons, in therapy; p. 301.
In Obsessive-Compulsive Reactions (Chapter 6)
   as defense against anxiety; p. 344.
   encouraged, by parents, toward inhibition of emotions; p. 323.
   in *First Line of Defense;* pp. 343–5, 374.
   in obsessions, related to repressed conflict; p. 345.
   of sexual affect; p. 314.
   of disowned impulse; p. 311.
   of murderous impulses; p. 326.
   of repressed data; p. 367.
In Hygeiaphrontic Reactions (Chapter 8)
   of anxiety and frustration, to Somatic Conversion; p. 466.
   of fantasied views to external object, in *Soterial Reaction;* p. 491.
   of physician's feelings, to patient; p. 445.
In Fear and Its Avoidance (Chapter 9)
   in external *Peg Concept;* p. 529.
   in phobic evolvement; pp. 518–19, 541.
   in *psychologic flight;* p. 524.
In Phobic Reactions (Chapter 10)
   in *Critical Attack of Anxiety;* p. 582.
   in *Critical Displacement* type of *Phobia;* pp. 548, 566, 578, 588, 601.
      Case 117; p. 567.
   in dynamics of phobia (*Gradually Evolving Phobia*); p. 575.
   in *endogain* of phobia; p. 548.
      secondarily defended; p. 549.
   in evolvement of *Emotional-Object-Amalgam* (EOA); pp. 571, 578, 582, 584–5.

---

* From Laughlin, H. P. *The Neuroses.* London, Butterworth & Co., Ltd., 1967.

in *Phobic Attacks;* childhood phobias; p. 565.
> Case 111. Little Hans (Freud); p. 551.
in selection of Phobic Object (Table 28); p. 583.
in *Situational* type of *Phobia;* pp. 547, 601.
of affect, to external (manifest) source; pp. 547–8, 556–7, 601.
of anxiety, to phobia of flowers (Case 119); p. 572.
of dangerous hostility
> to phobia of cats (Case 120); p. 573.
> to phobia of people (Case 114); p. 557.
of sexual desires; p. 580.
In Soterial Reactions (Chapter 11)
in *Peg Concept;* p. 635.
in principal mechanisms of *Soterial Reaction;* p. 627.
in *Soteria a*nd Phobia (Table 30), a comparison; pp. 628–9.
of danger in phobia, compared to dynamics of *soteria;* p. 608.
of security, associated with mother-ideal; p. 626.
to external source, in psychodynamics of *soteria;* p. 627.
In Conversion Reactions (Chapter 12)
in mechanisms of Conversion Reaction; pp. 691, 716.
of sexuality, to oral region (Case 146); p. 696.
In Dissociative Reactions (Chapter 13); in dreams; p. 748.
In Neuroses-Following-Trauma (Chapter 14)
as a defense against danger; p. 874.
of concerns, in obsessive persons; p. 854.

F. REVIEW QUESTIONS

Sample self-check questions on Chapter 5 and Displacement, for the student, psychiatric resident, and board candidate.

1. Write a definition for Displacement.
2. What is the role of Displacement in the phobic pattern of defense?
3. What are the new objects for otherwise intolerable feelings toward or about the self when these become defensivly transferred and redirected? To what type of Displacement do we refer?
4. The *Scapegoat Reaction* is an important and frequently evolved psychic operation. What is the defensive intent? Explain its inner motivation and operation. Illustrate from your personal or clinical experience.
5. What has been termed the *Convenient Target* is an essential component for many if not all instances of Displacement operation. Explain.
6. What happens to sexual conflict in *Sexual-Object Displacement?*
7. How can *Emotional Symbiosis* contribute to conflict resolution? Illustrate in reference to Displacement; to another dynamism.
8. What advantages can you envisage for your clinical practice through awareness of the potential for the *Displaced Complex?*
9. A. Why are *Phobic Displacement* and *Primal Displacement* so termed?
   B. Reference was made to *Convergence, Emotional Deferment,* and *Overdetermination.* How can these concepts relate to the operation of Displacement?
10. What are the bases for referring to Displacement as a Lower Order dynamisms? Would you agree?

CHAPTER 6

DISSOCIATION

...Detachment of Affect

A. DEFINITION
: 1. Dynamism and Neurotic Reaction. 2. The Amorphous Dissociation.

B. PERSONALITY DISSOCIATION
: 1. Opposed to Integration and Synthesis. The Janet Concept. 2. Side-by-Side Dissociation Concept. 3. The Self-Defense Concept in Dynamism Elaboration. 4. The Dissociative Reactions.

C. AFFECT DISSOCIATION
: 1. Painful Emotional Feelings Detached. 2. Dissociation and Psychosis: a. Concept of Dissociated Psychotic-Survival; b. Schizophrenic, or Bleuler's Dissociation. 3. Depersonalization.

D. MENTAL FUNCTION DISSOCIATION

E. SUMMARY

F. REFERENCES (FROM *The Neuroses*)

A. DEFINITION

1. Dynamism and Neurotic Reaction

Dissociation as a scientific term has two major uses in medical psychology: *first,* as the name for the ego defense or mental mechanism of Dissociation; and *secondly,* to describe a number of intriguing psychologic phenomena, the *Dissociative Reactions.* We are primarily interested in *Dissociation* as a dynamism, although the two are closely related and can function together.

In the first sense, Dissociation may be defined *as an ego defense or dynamism operating outside of and beyond conscious awareness through which the affect and emotional significance is separated and detached (i.e., dissociated) from an idea, situation, object, or relationship.* Essentially this is what we have also termed *affect dissociation.*

In the second category and from a psychopathologic viewpoint, the process of Dissociation leads to and produces a partial or total kind of personality disorganization. This is illustrated by several of the clinically identifiable Dissociative Reactions, which we have studied elsewhere (*The Neuroses*, pp. 721–830). They comprise a major division of the neuroses. The Dissociative Reactions include Dissociation per se, Double Personality, Depersonalization, the psychologic Amnesias, Somnambulism (p. 69), the Fugue States, and hypnotic phenomena. Their level of pathology varies substantially.

These neurotic reactions occur clinically when the personality, usually under intolerably great pressure and strain, divides and splits off or dissociates a segment. Usually major components are disunited and behave for a time as though they were unrelated. One of them may tend to function independently in a detached fashion. In this sense, a group of mental processes or functions is regarded as separated or dissociated from consciousness and from the rest of the personality. They may continue to operate more or less autonomously, and for a longer or shorter period of time. Dissociation is the converse of association and is in opposition to personality synthesis as usually maintained.

2. The Amorphous Dissociation

Dissociation and the Dissociative Reactions can occur in response to intense diffuse anxiety. At such times for example, a housewife reported experiencing episodes of frightening, unreal, . . . "floating feelings . . . like the induction of an anesthetic. . . ." These were terribly disturbing.

The unreal floating feelings ultimately proved to represent a seeking to run away or flee; an attempted *psychologic flight*. This was her desperate and unwitting response to overwhelming responsibilities as a wife, as a mother, and to living generally.

This illustrates what we might term the undifferentiated or *Amorphous Dissociation*. She further described her reaction as, "a partial floating into oblivion." The accompanying intense fear was associated with the threat of losing her mind, the danger of loss of control, and an accompanying urge to wildly "run out and call for help. . . ."

Instances similar to the foregoing illustrate the Amorphous Dissociation, although there are a fair number of variations possible in the clinical picture. This type of dissociation is a less developed and organized predecessor to the more distinct neurotic Dissociative Reactions. There is nonetheless a close kinship between the Amorphous Dissociation and such more readily delineated clinical reactions as the *Fugue State, Amnesia, Fainting, Depersonalization*, and *Alternating Personality*, each of which represents a defensively-intended pattern of psychologic flight.

We shall briefly consider dissociative phenomena under the headings of *Personality Dissociation*, concerning clinical patterns; and *Affect Dissociation*, concerning the operation of the dynamism per se. They are of course interrelated.

B. PERSONALITY DISSOCIATION

1. Opposed to Integration and Synthesis. The Janet Concept

In the Dissociative Reactions, we can observe that certain aspects of the personality are detached or dissociated from the balance. A dissociation of affect, memory, function, or activity can occur. This is *Personality Dissociation*. As a term, it is most frequently reserved diagnostically and clinically for use in reference to obviously pathologic states, as noted.

It is important at this juncture for us to recognize that *all psychic defenses and dynamisms*, as indeed *all events and influences, tend to have either an integrative* (that is, a synthesis-promoting) *effect, or a dissociative and disjunctive effect upon the personality.* Thus, in general, they either *promote synthesis and integration, or have the reverse effect.* Ego defenses in proper balance are at times described as being ego-synthetic or ego-integrative. Hypertrophied, their effects can be ego-destructive and dissociative. This is an important psychologic conception which perhaps most appropriately should be named after Janet. Accordingly it comprises and summarizes the basic and important *Janet Concept* in psychiatry. Personality Dissociation is opposed to integration and synthesis.

The blocking or Repression of an idea or striving, may represent the *Deferment* (p. 456) or *Denial* (p. 69 ff.) of something otherwise painful. The detachment of such an item from the mainstream of conscious awareness in effect constitutes a dissociation. This viewpoint would stress that *Repression* (p. 357), thus can tend to be dissociative. In contrast, on the other hand *Identification* (p. 133) with a loved object is more likely to be ego-synthetic.

2. Side-by-Side Dissociation Concept

Dissociation of mental functions takes place, in which two or more parts of the mind operate independently, albeit concurrently. Each may function, following its own course for a time, and in a reasonably satisfactory fashion. For a fair number of people, this facility allows or facilitates the carrying-out of concurrent activities. This is the *Side-by-Side Dissociation Concept* and type of Dissociation. See *Case 59,* p. 105 as an illustration.

Today we recognize the wide usefulness of concepts of dissociation. Pierre Janet assigned this process a prominent if not dominant, role in his early pioneering studies of psychopathologic processes around the turn of the century; similarly as Alfred Adler did later with the *Inferiority Complex* and Compensation. Other pioneers have also assigned a preeminent role to a given complex, mechanism, system, or viewpoint.

3. The Self-Defense Concept in Dynamism Elaboration

Dissociation, in its detachment of affect, may be compared to the physical cutaneous dissociation of sensory perception, in which the physician occasionally finds that there is a loss of the pain and temperature senses, with preservation of the tactile sense.

In a more technical sense, Dissociation sometimes splits off a portion of the ego for the purpose of isolating a corresponding portion of the punitive superego. This then serves as a means of subverting the superego through the splitting-off process, thereby perhaps "clearing the way" for certain "painless" impulsive, or otherwise personally intolerable external expressions of ideas or behavior.

Every defensive psychologic operation is ultimately an intended defense of the self or ego against painful affects. This must be ultimately regarded also as the responsible underlying motivation for Dissociation. This comprises the *Self-Defense Concept,* essential to our understanding the forces responsible for the unconscious elaboration of each of the various dynamisms. It is a most basic concept in human motivation, behavior, and psychology. In order to further emphasize, invite continuing attention, and properly distinguish its operation in the context of the ego defenses, we would postulate a narrower *Self-Defense Concept in Dynamism Elaboration.*

4. The Dissociative Reactions

The following tabulation (*Table 3*) affords some comparative data covering the various clinical Dissociative Reactions. It is included for convenience and as a ready reference source for the interested student.

C. AFFECT DISSOCIATION

1. Painful Emotional Feelings Detached

The splitting-off of emotional feeling or affect from an idea, situation, object, or relationship is to be observed clinically with moderate frequency. We refer to this as *Affect Dissociation.* It serves as an alternate term for the ego defense of Dissociation. It helps delineate the function of the dynamism. Its relative frequency is hardly surprising, especially in view of the universal attachment of affect to objects. This latter is a statement of the important principle which is embodied in the *Law of Universal Affect.* It will be referred to again when we discuss Repression, ·p. 366.

Affect Dissociation is more commonly encountered as a partial devaluation, than as the total splitting away of affect, as usually implied by the term "dissociation," although this too can occur. Affect Dissociation is almost always in regard to detachment of the painful variety of

Table 3

The Dissociative Reactions; Comparative Data

	Clinical Entity or Symptom	Type of Dissociation	State of Consciousness	Memory
1. *Alternating* (or *Multiple Personality*)	C.E.	Alternating D.	No change apparent; as though the conscious is double or multiple, and the parts completely alternative, to *replace* each other completely	Little or no memory by the dominant personality present for the suppressed one
2. *Amnesias*	C.E. or S.	Fragmental D.; rarely Alternating	May or may not appear impaired	Blank area the distinctive feature
3. *Automatic Behavior* and *Writing*	S., or neither; a phenomenon which is sometimes useful. Indicates dissociative capacity	D. of Automaticity; occasionally Fragmental D.	No apparent change	May not consciously recall
4. *Depersonalization* (including *Deja Vu*)	Nearly always S	Fragmental D.	No apparent change	Unaffected
5. *Dreams*	Normal, S., or nonassociated with a C.E.	Fragmental D.	Sleeping state	Ability to recall varies; almost never total
6. *Fainting*	S.	Fragmental D.	Unconscious	No recall for duration (period) of attack
7. *Fugue States*	C.E.	Alternating D.	From no apparent change to confusion and poor synthesis	Recall absent or spotty
8. *Hypnosis*	Neither	B.B.C. or Induced D.	Neither waking nor sleeping, with aspects of both. May appear close to either	Quite variable
9. *Memory Loss* (Repression)	S., or neither	Affect D.; none	No effect	Nil
10. *Side-by-Side Dissociation*	S.; possibly neither	Side-by-Side D.	No effect	Partial, variable
11. *Somnambulism*	S.; very rarely C.E.; or nonassociated with a C.E. or S.	Fragmental D.	Dissociated activity while asleep	Nil

Table 3 (Cont.)

Historically Associated With	Response to Therapy	Ease of Diagnosis	Incidence	Significant Clinical Features
James	Potential excellent	Fair, to difficult	Terribly rare	A previously submerged major area of the personality alternates, to become dominant for a variable period of time from weeks to years.
———	Poor, to excellent	Ranges from readily made, to impossible	Not infrequent	A blank space of memory loss. Psychologic or physical initiation.
———	Rarely required. Occasional use as adjunct to treatment	Usually evident	Moderately rare	A dissociated area directs the behavior or writing automatically (outside of consciousness).
Krishaber; Dugas; Janet	Very good	Easy	Common, if not universal	Subjective; person must report. Sometimes accompanies or prodromal to more serious problems.
Freud	interpretation an excellent adjunct to therapy	One is dependent upon person's reporting	Universal and nightly	Probably vital to health and well-being. Meanings usually distorted, symbolized, hidden, and so on.
———	Fair	Usually few problems	Gradually becoming more rare	Lack of injury usual. A significant person or persons likely to witness. Epigain tends to be more apparent.
———	Poor to fair, Occasionally good	Problems can be major	Rare	A figurative and literal flight from unbearable conflict. Confusion at times.
Mesmer; Braid; Liebault; Bernheim; Charcot; Breuer	Judiciously employed as an adjunct to treatment	Occasionally uncertain	5–10 % or more of people are hypnotizable	See definitions. Contacts limited to operator. Capacity to dissociate; suggestibility.
Breuer; Freud	Good	Only recall establishes	Universal	Important in treatment. Associative recall possible.
———	Seldom needed	Depends upon history	Fairly common	Useful simultaneous activities may be carried on
———	Fair	Person or family reports	Moderately common especially in childhood	Self-preservation maintained. An unconscious "acting" or "seeking."

Table 3 (Cont.)

	Clinical Entity or Symptom	Type of Dissocia- tion	State of Consciousness	Memory
12. *Traumatic Encepha- lopathy of Boxers*	S. or C.E.	Usually none	Scattered effects upon cerebral activity, not on consciousness	Scattered defects
13. *Pharma- cologic Dissocia- tions* (Esp. L.S.D.)	S. or syndrome	Drug- Induced (Under- lying Per- sonality Diathesis Contrib- utes)	Usually dulled ob- jectively. Greater input subjectively	Usually good

affect, or of a perception or relationship which would likely lead to painful affects. (*Case 113*, p. 304, *The Neuroses.*)

Many situations illustrate the defensive operation of the dynamism of Dissociation. The following two instances are rather striking examples of the defensive detachment of emotional significance or *Affect Dissociation*. The first was observed in therapy over a 2- to 3-month period, and the person's observations and recognition of the process follow.

Case 53

Dissociation of Feelings in Therapy

"I've certainly become aware how very often tears well up when I'm on the couch! I have no feelings, no emotions, no thoughts at these times.... Nothing troubles me, at least as far as I am consciously concerned. The tears just come. I *feel* nothing! ...

"It makes me angry. I don't like tears and I can't understand the reasons for them. You would think I felt terrible!—sad or lonely or deprived ... I don't...."

Actually she did, as we well learned over the succeeding months of analysis. The dissociative mechanism was protectively intended. As the need for it lessened, it became gradually more permissible for her to consciously experience these feelings and to work them through therapeutically.

Case 54

Dissociation of Responsibility

A 22-year-old California student attended college on the east coast. At Christmastime he decided to drive across the country and spend the holidays at home. To help with expenses he took along three other students. Due to the shortness of time and the long distance, he de- termined to make the trip nonstop. He had a reputation as a fast and somewhat reckless driver.

On the second night of the trip, speeding through fog on slippery roads, he lost control of the car and it went off the road. Seeking fran-

Table 3 (Cont.)

Historically Associated With	Response to Therapy	Ease of Diagnosis	Incidence	Significant Clinical Features
Hartland	Nil	Can be difficult; progression is insidious	Occupational hazard for boxers	Major preventative is early retirement from the ring.
———	Little interest	Variable	Variable, currently a cultural phenomenon	Lack of concern and fear for many. Hazards of spontaneous trips and ppt. of psychoses

tically to regain control, he jerked the wheel. The car lurched back onto the highway, but crossed the center lane and collided head-on with a car coming in the opposite direction. Two of his passengers were killed and the other seriously injured. Both occupants of the other car were killed. He escaped with a broken wrist and minor injuries. He was charged with negligent homicide, but these charges were dropped.

A rather surprising circumstance was the apparent lack of effect emotionally on this young man. He was quite cold; devoid of emotional feelings. In response to a query, he blandly said, "It must have been time for those people to die," adding almost nonchalantly there was nothing he could have done to prevent it, it was fate. His defensive dissociation of affect consciously disclaimed responsibility and guilt.

It would have been most interesting had it proved feasible to follow this young man psychologically in some depth over several years. One might well anticipate that some psychologic sequela could eventuate sooner or later. Despite his Affect Dissociation and resulting ironclad denial of responsibility, it is doubtful if he could emerge completely unscathed emotionally.

2. Dissociation and Psychosis

A. CONCEPT OF DISSOCIATED PSYCHOTIC-SURVIVAL.—Dissociation as a psychopathologic sequence is encountered in its more handicapping and self-defeating forms in the psychotic reactions. Many of these comprise or contribute to Affect Dissociations. The desperately unhappy and intolerably disturbed person may thus secure a measure of conscious detachment from life and its otherwise unendurable misery and psychic pain. In fact, from one viewpoint we can regard the emotional withdrawal and retreat into psychosis as one of nature's methods of protection (p. 490). It thus comprises a "last ditch" desperate means of psychologic defense.

This outlines the *Concept of Dissociated Psychotic-Survival*. Via this conception one might better appreciate that the psychotic dissociation affords a means of survival, even though on the plane of a psychotic level of adjustment.

In what can be thus termed *Psychotic Dissociation,* there is the desperate psychologic detachment or dissociation of the self from reality and the environment which has become no longer tolerable. This is secured through a process resulting in one's perceptions being seemingly limited or absent, so that painful aspects of living no longer impinge for the person concerned.

Various individual psychotic manifestations also can be regarded as being dissociative in character. For instance, hallucinations would thus be interpreted as the dissociated and projected segments or reflections of a person's ego, superego, or id (cf. Psychotic Projections, p. 230). Delusions might be similarly regarded.

B. SCHIZOPHRENIA, OR BLEULER'S DISSOCIATION.—In schizophrenia, one characteristically encounters the defensively-intended dissociation of appropriate affect from ideation. This is the splitting-off or dissociative process which is the basis for the common but often publicly misunderstood term of "split personality." We have earlier suggested that this significant process be referred to as *Bleuler's Dissociation,* after Bleuler who introduced the term of schizophrenia.

In schizophrenic, the affect is split-off and thereby absent or inappropriate to the event, thought, or relationship. This is Bleuler's Dissociation, in the schizophrenic type of psychotic process.

Case 55

Dissociation of Affect in a Schizophrenic Patient

A 22-year-old, single male patient was admitted to a hospital for study following increasing emotional difficulties at home and at work. He appeared detached, and it was difficult to secure his attention or to hold it. His conversation was quite restricted and at times inappropriate.

One day his sister was seriously injured in an automobile accident. She was the person to whom he was most attached. When the news of the accident was relayed to him, he accepted it with less show of emotion than might have been ordinarily displayed by someone who has just learned what is to be served at dinner.

The news seemingly had no real emotional import to him! While ordinarily it would have been very painful and disturbing, he automatically and unconsciously dissociated the affect from the event.

The foregoing instance prominently illustrates the somewhat typical Schizophrenic Affect Dissociation, or Bleuler's Dissociation. The affect was defensively split-off and was inappropriate to the situation and ideation. The effect is to spare the conscious emotional impact of an otherwise troubling and painful happening.

Dissociation is to be observed in many psychotic patients. It enters into delusion formation, as noted. Affect Dissociation is encountered in emotionally disturbed persons in connection with various kinds of abnormal mental content. A schizophrenic patient may discuss various bizarre ideas about himself or his fate, without evidencing any measure of appropriate affect. As an example, one patient alternately laughed and grimaced while relating that part of his insides were missing.

A young schizophrenic woman talked volubly about the involved torments which were planned for her. She explained how she was to be shipped down the Potomac River the following week "to be burned in big furnaces," furnishing further horrifying details. Instead of appearing frightened or terrified as would be ordinarily appropriate with the certainty of such a fate, the emotional feelings were dissociated and detached. She smiled gently, talking rapidly but quietly during her recital of arrangements for her forthcoming tortures.

Another person with paranoid ideation sat calmly and was inappropriately moved while he related the involved and complex plans already in motion to destroy him. This is the type of relative unconcern which we can term the *Paranoid Indifference* to subjectively actual or impending disastrous events (p. 230) planned against the person concerned. It is reminiscent of the phenomenon of *la belle indifférence* in the Conversion Reactions. A relation to Conversion was earlier noted (p. 43), and the two dynamisms were distinguished, p. 50.

3. Depersonalization

The defensively-intended purposes and function of the symptom of depersonalization are often poorly understood. In this emotional manifestation one feels unreal or the world about him seems unreal or strange. Many times the effects of Depersonalization approximate or secure Affect Dissociation, i.e., the aims of Dissociation as an ego defense. Depersonalization has been discussed more fully in *The Neuroses* (pp. 758–770).

In supplement thereto, the following instances illustrate its support of the mental mechanism function of Dissociation which it can assist or evolve, and from which a clear distinction may be difficult.

Case 56

Dissociation: "Someone Else's Children"

A mother of three small children came into therapy because of difficulties in her marriage. She also suffered from intense feelings of resentment and rejection of the children. The latter feelings evoked a great deal of guilt and self-condemnation. She was often caught in an intolerable crosscurrent of conflicting feelings.

A major psychic defense automatically evoked upon some of these occasions would be the dissociation of herself from her children as the objects of conflict. As she described it, "I have a feeling I'm standing on the side watching *someone else's* children! I have no feeling that they belong to me. . . . They're not mine at all; they must belong to someone else! . . ."

The reaction was a dissociative depersonalization. The psychologic advantage was one of Affect Dissociation.

If the troubled young mother could effect a temporary psychic transfer of her responsibilities, some of her conflicts would be allayed and anxiety averted. The intended function of her Depersonalization was in accord with the *Self-Defense Concept,* seeking to afford her a protective relief or respite, from her conflicts over her children and her overly burdensome responsibilities of parenthood.

Case 57

Dissociation: Depersonalization as a Defense Against Impact of Painful News

(1) *Angry Accusation.* A physician had a 13-year-old son of whom he was very proud. One evening the father received a call from an attorney in the neighborhood. The latter was enraged and described how the doctor's son threatened his boy with a switchblade knife. The attorney angrily denounced the boy as a "hoodlum" and "juvenile delinquent . . . not fit to live in the neighborhood." He would devote his legal talent, . . . every ounce of his energy, . . . every bit of influence . . ." to ensure his punishment.

(2) *Depersonalization Defense Evoked.* The tirade was concluded with an ultimatum that the alternative was for the boy to be sent to a correctional institution forthwith. The father was quite overwhelmed on one level. Consciously, however as he listened, he found himself calm. It was "something that just couldn't happen. . . ."

He reported, "I never thought it possible that I would ever hear anyone say such things about my boy. . . . It was as though all this was happening to someone else . . . as though I were some kind of a detached observer, watching a play . . . an onlooker, not a participant. . . . It was just too much of a shock! I couldn't believe it. . . . This just can't happen! . . ."

He had emotionally dissociated himself from the painful situation. Through the automatic and unconscious employment of the psychic defensive process of dissociative depersonalization, he had blocked, or at least deferred (p. 456), the impact of the painful accusation, threats, and ultimatum. The depersonalization was in the service of Affect Dissociation. Aided by time, the situation was resolved more amicably.

Case 58

Depersonalization Dissociates Affect

A cattle dealer of some integrity took several truckloads of beef cattle to Florida. He felt safe enough in writing a number of local checks to cover his expenses, wages, and minor purchases, on the promise of his receiving dealer friend to deposit his check in turn for the cattle on Monday. The "friend" failed him. The checks bounced and resoundingly! To his shock and dismay he suddenly found himself in the county jail, where he spent three days before restitution was effected from Maryland.

In his words, "It could have been horrible, but I developed the ability to completely detach myself. It was as though it wasn't real. It was as though the jail wasn't there, and this wasn't me it was happening to. . . ." A protective kind of dissociative depersonalization took over to make the situation bearable. Affect Dissociation was effective as a protection.

D. MENTAL FUNCTION DISSOCIATION

The Dissociation of mental components transpires so that a major segment comes to operate more or less independently. This situation is encountered rather commonly and does not need to be pathologic. Many women can sew or type efficiently, and listen to the radio or watch television at the same time. What we can call *Mental Function Dissociation* is often featured by more conscious control and direction, as well as awareness. Other instances have been cited in *The Neuroses*.

In the following example, two types of mental activity were simultaneously carried on with little loss of efficiency. This illustrates the *Side-by-Side* type of *Dissociation* as outlined earlier (p. 96).

Case 59

Authorship and Cabdriving

The young author of a best seller earned his living by driving a cab while he was writing what turned out to be a successful novel. Much of his composition and facets of the plot were worked out while he was busily piloting fares around the downtown section of a major metropolis. He earned a high proficiency rating with his taxi company. His earnings, on a percentage basis, were among those of the top drivers. His safety record was unsurpassed.

Although he was engaged much of the time in two widely separated types of activity, he was able to divide his attention efficiently. Neither activity suffered. Each was successful.

Often the secret of such successfully dissociated mental operations follows the relegation of one of the activities to a semiautomatic type of operation. The author did this with his driving, although from the various indications of success, one can hardly conclude that it lacked very much as a result.

Dissociation in this instance is often a more consciously directed kind of process. Most people can utilize this to some extent. As a mental mechanism, Dissociation takes place fully automatically and beyond conscious awareness. In its more marked forms it is a primitive kind of intrapsychic process which can operate in massive fashion with the onset of one of the rather uncommon gross Dissociative Reactions. Elsewhere as noted, the various types of dissociation and the resulting clinical reactions have been delineated and classified with more precision, and in more detail.

E. SUMMARY

Dissociation is an ego defense through which emotion and emotional significance is detached from its object. In the Dissociative Reactions, parts of the ego are split off or dissociated and the part (or balance) functions more or less independently. Dissociation in its fragmentation of the ego is the converse of association and of ego synthetic influences.

The *Amorphous Dissociation* is a poorly developed, variable and less differentiated type of reaction which occurs in response to emotional conflict and anxiety. It may be regarded as an incomplete progression or way station in the psychopathologic sequence toward the more marked clinical dissociative states. The latter include Amnesia, Fugue States, and Alternating Personality as major clinical patterns of defensively elaborated *psychologic flight*.

Personality Dissociation is opposed to ego integration and synthesis. It describes the dissociative separation of portions of the ego and is generally reserved to the clinical reactions. The *Janet Concept* notes that all influences and events have either an integrative or a dissociative effect upon the ego. Ego defenses may be *ego synthetic* or *ego disjunctive* in their net consequences.

The capacity for *Side-by-Side Dissociation* allows concurrent activities to be pursued. The *Self-Defense Concept* outlined the basic motivation of ego preservation and defense in the elaboration of psychologic manifestations. In the context of the ego defenses, it is the *Self-Defense Concept in Dynamism Elaboration.*

Affect Dissociation is an alternate term for the ego defense of Dissociation, and has the advantage of pointing out its function. Affect Dissociation is often partial. It can also contribute to *Deferment*.

Psychotic Dissociation is the dissociation and withdrawal from reality as encountered in the psychotic reactions. The *Concept of Dissociated Psychotic-Survival* concerns the psychotic dissociation affording a desperately sought means of survival, albeit on the plane of a psychotic adjustment. Hallucinations and delusions can be regarded as dissociative in character. *Bleuler's Dissociation* is the detachment of appropriate affect from ideation, as observed in schizophrenia. It can defend against the impact of painful emotional feelings.

The defensively-intended function of Depersonalization was noted and illustrated. Depersonalization is a dissociative phenomenon and supports or effects Affect Dissociation.

Mental Function Dissociation is often a more consciously directed process. It enters into the Side-by-Side Dissociation. As an ego defense, Dissociation (or Affect Dissociation) is quite widespread and offers many variations. There are close interrelationships with the clinical Dissociative Reactions.

F.   CROSS-REFERENCES TO *THE NEUROSES* *

Dissociation
Major types of:
  Affect D., pp. 25, 343, 517, 729, 731.
  Alternating D., pp. 729, 732, 792, 795, 796, 806–9.
  B.B.C. (Braid, Bernheim and Charcot) *D.,* pp. 647, 730, 733, 812–13.
  Breuer's D., pp. 648, 730, 733.
  Fragmental D., pp. 730, 734.
  Janet's D., pp. 648, 653, 674, 693.
  Physiologic D., 730, 734–5.
  Schizonphrenic (Bleuler's) *D.,* 682, 730, 735–6.
  Side-by-Side D., pp. 730, 736–7.
    Dissociation
In Nature of Anxiety (Chapter 1); as a major mental mechanism; p. 25.

---

* From Laughlin, H. P. *The Neuroses.* London, Butterworth & Co., Ltd., 1967.

In Character Reactions (Chapter 5)
  as a personality type; pp. 73, 228–9 232, 251, 283, 286, 785.
  capacity for, in Conversion Personality; pp. 268–9.
    Table 15; p. 239.
    Table 18; p. 260.
In Hygeiaphrontic Reactions (Chapter 8)
  as depersonalization, in *Hygeiaphrontic* preoccupation (Case 96); p. 472.
  of birth process in infant; p. 492.
In Phobic Reactions (Chapter 10); in psychodynamics of
  Conversion compared to Displacement in phobic evolvement; p. 556.
In Conversion Reactions (Chapter 12)
  as avoidance, in mechanisms of Conversion Reactions; p. 691.
  a factor in Conversion Epidemics; p. 703.
  Breuer's D., pp. 648, 730, 733.
  emergency therapy for, in Dissociative Reaction, (*Emergency Analytic Bridge*);
    pp. 678–80.
  in compartmentalization of self; p. 682.
  in Conversion diathesis, in *Unconscious Simulation Concept;* p. 662.
  induced D., (hypnosis), *B.B.C. Dissociation;* p. 647.
  in suggestibility of Conversion Reaction; p. 692.
  of a major personality component, *Janet's D.,* pp. 648, 653, 674, 693.
    in convulsions; p. 685.
  of particular sensation (in anesthesia); p. 700.
In Dissociative Reactions (Chapter 13); pp. 723 ff.
  Affect D.; p. 729, 731.
  analogous to Repression; p. 741.
  as a mental mechanism; p. 731.
  as part of *Total Reaction to Crisis* (TRC); p. 740.
  as *Reaction-of-the-Whole;* p. 742.
  defined, as important concept in psychiatry; pp. 726–7.
  in psychodynamics of Alternating Personality; pp. 806–9.
  in psychodynamics of Amnesia; pp. 773–91.
    Types of Amnesia (Table 41); p. 777.
  in psychodynamics of Automatic Behavior (*Dissociation of Automaticity*); pp.
    732, 809.
    Automatic Writing; pp. 809–10.
  in depersonalization, a symptom language of; p. 758.
    as part of *Total Reaction to Crisis* (TRC); p. 762.
  in dream function; p. 744.
    within the dream; p. 752.
  in dynamics of hypnosis; pp. 810–16.
    an induced dissociation; p. 810.
    B.B.C. Dissociation; pp. 812–13.
  in psychodynamics of the Fugue, a major personality D.; pp. 791–806.
  in Janet's theories in the etiology of the neuroses; pp. 728–9.
  in somnambulism; p. 755.
  symptoms of; p. 732.
  types of D. defined (Table 34); p. 729–30.
In Neuroses-Following-Trauma (Chapter 14)
  as defense against danger; p. 874.
  following traumatic event (case 174); p. 853.
  incidence of, in Neuroses Following Trauma; p. 852.
In Military Reactions (Chapter 15)

as depersonalization
> as *Conflict Indicator* (C.I.); p. 916.
> as *Prognostic Signal Flag* (P.S.F.); p. 922.
> during wartime; p. 914.
> induced D., in *Prisoner Processing;* p. 943.

induced D., in narcosynthesis for catharsis); p. 931.
in *Janet's D.,* p. 915.
of homosexual conflict (Case 142); p. 914.

G. REVIEW QUESTIONS

Sample self-check questions on Chapter 6 and Dissociation for the student, psychiatric resident, and board candidate.

1. Differentiate the employment of the term *Dissociation* in describing an emotional dynamism and a neurotic reaction.
2. The clinical phenomenon of *Amorphous Dissociation* was described. Why is this term suitable?
3. What is meant by *Personality Dissociation?* How can Regression contribute?
4. Outline the *Janet Concept.* What is its significance in evaluating the consequences of operation of a given dynamism? Do you know why it is suitable to name this concept for Janet?
5. Explain the conception of *Side-by-Side Dissociation.* Can you find both beneficial and self-defeating illustrations of its witting and unwitting utlilization? How does the subtype of *Mental Function Dissociation* relate to this conception?
6. What is conveyed by the following terms and concepts?
   A. *Psychologic flight.*
   B. Ego-synthetic effect.
   C. *Hypertrophied defense.*
   D. Dynamism elaboration.
   E. *Self-Defense Concept in Dynamism Elaboration.*
   F. *Affect Dissociation.*
   G. *Psychotic Dissociation.*
   H. Ego disjunctive defense. *Bleuler's Dissociation.*
   I. *Traumatic Encephalopathy.*
7. The *Self-Defense Concept* was described as "most basic in human motivation, behavior, and psychology." Why accord it this significance?
8. What are the Dissociative Reactions? Name six of them with the type of Dissociation involved, incidence, and effects on memory. Cite clinical illustrations for four from your experience.
9. How does the *Concept of Dissociated Psychotic-Survival* support a view of the psychoses comprising defensively-intended reactions?
10. What is Depersonalization? How can it be considered as an emotional-psychic defense?

CHAPTER 7

FANTASY

. . . Retreat to a Dream World

A. THE NATURE OF FANTASY

> 1. Unconscious Motivation and Direction. 2. Definition. 3. Unconscious Fantasy. 4. Fantasy in Childhood and Adolescence: a. Fantasy Content Secret; b. Adolescent Fantasy-Life.

B. CONSTRUCTIVE AND NONCONSTRUCTIVE FANTASIES

> 1. The Constructive Fantasy. Imagination and Mental Pictures in Adulthood. 2. The Unhealthful Fantasy: a. Major Characteristics; b. The Fantasy-Pattern; c. The Sexual Fantasy-System. Gratification-Enhancements (GEs); d. Fantasy and Aggression; the Fantasy Lesson-Function Concept. 3. Fantasy and Dreams. Fantasy-Pattern and Fantasy-System. 4. Manifest and Latent Content of the Fantasy.

C. FANTASY AND CONFLICT

D. SUMMARY

E. REFERENCES (FROM *The Neuroses*)

F. REVIEW QUESTIONS

A. THE NATURE OF FANTASY

1. Unconscious Motivation and Direction

In its widest usage the Fantasy or phantasy includes a broad spectrum of mental and emotional activity. From providing an avenue for constructive planning, it varies all the way to its becoming a deeply regressive and unrealistic manifestation of emotional illness. It comprises an ego aid which can inimically progress into becoming an hypertrophied and pathologic process of self absorption.

The amount of conscious direction and control of Fantasy is quite variable. Ordinarily people tend to think of daydreams and Fantasies as mental activity which is fully self-directed. However, like so many things we do or feel, the influence of unconscious forces is strong. The *Iceberg Analogy* helps point out the large hidden bulk of unconscious material in one's psyche. This concept can be similarly applied to the hidden aspects and control of one's Fantasies. Thus the Fantasy has more of the unconscious in its motivation and direction than can be readily perceived. This together with its ego-defensive intent and functions, is why it qualifies as a mental mechanism.

2. Definition

The elaboration of Fantasy is dependent upon man's essential and differentiating capacity for imagination and upon his unconscious. Fantasies tend to be pictorial with series of mental images. They can be constructive or nonconstructive, and realistic or nonrealistic. They may serve as substitutes for action, be preparatory to action, or accompany action. The harried and frustrated person may take refuge in his fantasies; the acutely anxious or troubled person may take flight into them; and the emotionally sick person can regress and withdraw (p. 489) into an unrealistic and substitutive Fantasy-life. The employment and experiencing of Fantasies is a universal phenomenon.

A Fantasy is *an imaginary sequence of events or mental images which seek to resolve emotional conflict. This is through such avenues as: (1) affording unreal, substitutive satisfactions, (2) serving as a substitute for inappropriate or dangerous actions, (3) affording partial, secret discharge of otherwise unacceptable inner urges and impulses, especially of a sexual or aggressive nature, (4) prefacing action so that it will become more effective, more reflective, and less impulsive; and (5) the embellishment of activity which may be otherwise distasteful, so as to make it more acceptable or pleasurable.*

A Fantasy is *a vivid kind of daydream possessing unconscious components, which is emotionally significant* to the individual. It is often to be regarded as nonconstructive and psychologically unhealthy. The use of the term Fantasy usually implies more than the ordinary imagining of future plans, painting mental pictures of anticipated events, or exploration of the consequences of an action.

As an ego defense or mental mechanism, a Fantasy is in part an unconscious endeavor toward partial fulfillment or gratification of otherwise difficult or impossible goals or wishes. Fantasy occurs at any time of the day or night during consciousness. Fantasies are both consciously and unconsciously directed. Purely consciously directed Fantasies are daydreams.

3. Unconscious Fantasy

Certain Fantasies are completely unconscious. Certain other Fantasies are fleeting ones and are rapidly and automatically repressed so that for all practical purposes they are not only unconscious, but may be considered as never having entered conscious awareness.

The nearly instantaneous process of Fantasy repression is particularly active in infancy and childhood. Unconscious Fantasies comprise the major portion of what have been classified as the *Primary Repressions* (p. 363).

4. *Fantasy in Childhood and Adolescence*

A. FANTASY CONTENT SECRET.—Childhood Fantasies reported in therapy provide an important source of information about unconscious mental content. Such content is more readily reflected in these early Fantasies. Earlier we noted the concept of *Denial-in-Fantasy* (p. 76). Klein rather extensively studied the Fantasies of children and many of her contributions to analytic theory were based upon this important source of data. She pointed out a principle observed by others about childhood Fantasies. Thus their Fantasies reported in the treatment situation are a very much kept secret elsewhere. Allowing parents or other significant and inevitably emotionally involved, people to become aware of these secret areas would be unsafe. Revealing them becomes possible to the child therapist who is emotionally detached, and nonjudgmental.

This principle, of course, has considerable application also to the reporting of Fantasies by adults in treatment. Adults are likely to have even greater reluctances in discussing their Fantasies, having erected more formidable barriers of defense and reserve. Fantasy content is private, secret, and accordingly is safeguarded.

B. ADOLESCENT FANTASY-LIFE.—Adolescence with its many emotional conflicts, stresses, and impact is a rich era for Fantasies. Adolescents at times spend hours on end indulging in Fantasy. Seldom is their content readily or fully divulged. However, our discussion of this interesting subject would hardly be complete without an illustration. The following instance is somewhat exaggerated from the experiences of many teen-agers.

Case 60

Fantasy in Adolescence

(1) *Dream World Available.* A girl in her early teens was troubled by not being part of a certain desirable clique of girls in her class. She was unhappy because of her lack of nice clothes, money to go places and buy things, poise, and inability to be attractive to boys.

Increasingly worried about her awkwardness, shyness and unhappiness, she found that she could retreat into a "dream world." Here, quite opposite from the realities of her situation, she *was* everything she desired to be, and did everything she wished.

(2) *Varied and Colorful Content.* In her daydreams she had a different name, was pretty, gay, generous, and poised. She wore beautiful clothes. She designed some of the creations, aspiring for a while to be a fashion designer. Whereas the boy on whom she had a crush paid no attention, in her Fantasies he was devoted. In one of her productions she won him by brilliant piano artistry

In another, the young man rescued her from kidnappers. In still another, as a softball star, performing outstandingly in a crucial game, she broke her leg and he came to call upon her during her hospital stay; her bravery-in-suffering and sweet patience then had won him over, as well as her fellow patients.

(3) *Fantasy-Patterns.* These daydreams as sampled above, were vivid ones and occupied much of her time. At one juncture she attempted to write them down in book form, although this project was shortly abandoned. Unknown in school, in her daydreams she was the most popular girl. In one of her Fantasies she was world-famous as a circus acrobat. Having "run away to the circus" because her parents were cruel to her, she won their love, appreciation, and better treatment.

There were other favorite Fantasies, some of them were systemized and repeated sufficiently to warrant the designation of *Fantasy-Patterns* (see later).

This was a period of active Fantasy-life which gradually subsided. It served its function in helping to take her, in a way bearable for her, through some of the trying conflicts and emotional storms of her early teenage years. By the time she was a senior in high school, she had entered into many activities—sports, dramatics, poster committee, chorus, and reporter for the school paper, and become a leader in the young people's group at her church. Though she had no really close friends, she was friendlier and had become well accepted by her peers.

The use of Fantasy is probably a universal process in childhood. It may be regarded as closely akin to imagination, a variant thereof, an exaggeration or caricature. In view of this relationship, within reasonable limits this kind of activity during the course of life may be constructive and useful. However, children commonly engage in a great deal of daydreaming or Fantasy, some of which may not be healthful. Serving as a means of substitute gratification or wish fulfillment, it can become too engrossing, too replacing of reality, or too satisfying. One would not wish to see this type of major Fantasy pathway established for one's satisfactions. Extensive Fantasy in the mature adult is less frequent, and is to be more readily regarded as pathologic.

While superficially the Fantasy appears to be under conscious control and direction, what we might term the outward or *manifest content* is a cover for the more hidden *latent content,* which is unconscious.

B.   CONSTRUCTIVE AND NONCONSTRUCTIVE FANTASIES

1. The Constructive Fantasy. Imagination and Mental Pictures in Adulthood

There are closely related aspects or variations of Fantasy which are a useful adjunct to adult living. The mature adult may well learn to employ these processes as useful and constructive faculties. They are closer to consciousness and are goal-directed. They are utilized in visualizing situations before they take place, in anticipating the consequences of behavior, and in planning for the future.

Through these faculties the architect or engineer "sees in his mind's eye" the finished product; the inventor irons out mechanical details before the construction of a working model. The mathematician or physicist may be better able to solve difficult problems; and perhaps a doctor may make a diagnosis. A type of imaginative-fantasy is required for the patient in the desensitization method of Behavior Therapy of phobias, as described by Dengrove.

From these examples we see how these more consciously directed processes, which are tangentially but nonetheless definitely related to the more pathologic types of Fantasy can serve useful purposes. Here they are constructive and goal-directed. As instances of what we have termed the *Constructive Fantasy*, they are an asset and are beneficial.

2. The Unhealthful Fantasy

A. MAJOR CHARACTERISTICS.—The major characteristics of what might be referred to as the *Unhealthful Fantasy* include one or more of the following aspects tabulated below (Table 4).

Table 4

Features of the Unhealthful Fantasy

The Unhealthful Fantasy contributes or leads to psychopathology. Dynamically it represents an hypertrophy, exaggeration or overdependence upon an intended ego defense which can be otherwise useful.

This unreal and nonconstructive utilization of the Fantasy would include several of the following characteristics:

1. The Unhealthful Fantasy is essentially nonconstructive.
2. Contact with reality is lessened or even minimal.
3. Imaginary gratifications replace real ones. The latter have come to be regarded as too difficult, or otherwise impossible to achieve save through Fantasy.
4. Fantasy attempts the avoidance and resolution of emotional conflict (and thereby the prevention of anxiety) through providing sought-after satisfactions, although in an illusory fashion. To meet the criteria for the ego defenses, in some measure this must be an unwitting process.
5. In Fantasy the unreal wish-fulfilling needs are ascendant over the sterner appearing requirements of reality.
6. Increasing retreat, withdrawal (p. 489), or regression (p. 319) into fantastic satisfactions lessens the motivation to meet and to secure satisfactions from the external world. The *Unhealthful Fantasy* offers an illusory and self-defeating pathway away from reality.
7. Dynamically, the Unhealthful Fantasy represents an exaggeration, distortion or psychic hypertrophy of an intended ego-defensive process.
8. The *Fantasy-Pattern* or *Fantasy-System* can evolve, often equating neurotic symptom formation and indicating actual or potential psychopathology.

B. THE FANTASY-PATTERN.—The Fantasy-Pattern serves an analogous role dynamically to emotional symptoms. The role of Fantasy has a closer relation to emotional symptom formation than is commonly recognized. Its purposes, its defensive intent, and factors in its evolvement can be analogous. Thus, for example, the Somatic Conversion symptom may act out the secret forbidden wish, take its place, and/or serve to forestall feared or dangerous action (pp. 42–3). The Fantasy can subserve similar functions.

In the following instance what can be termed the *Fantasy-Pattern* "sought" to: (1) forestall potential action; (2) block awareness of complex underlying emotional needs; (3) unwittingly allow their partial gratification; and (4) through the ensuing limitation and suffering, provide self-punishment for having had them.

Case 61

Fantasy-Pattern in Dependency and Hostility

(1) *Emotional Fatigue State.* A 29-year-old mother presented a picture of emotional fatigue, weakness, and was nearly narcoleptic. She had absolutely no energy: the slightest effort was tiring. She slept 14 hours a day and felt worn out when she awoke. She was the victim of a severe Fatigue State.

It was learned through psychotherapeutic study that she basically suffered from an overwhelming, diffuse, unconscious rage. This was evoked by nearly everyone in her environment. Essentially it was in response to terrific frustration, as her strong underlying needs to be cared-for were not met.

(2) *A Fantasy-Pattern.* Although she realized she was "irritable," the true extent of this was not experienced consciously. Rather, she found herself preoccupied by long, involved and repeated Fantasies in which the death of her husband or her child were visualized in great detail. These would begin automatically and involuntarily, and at times proceeded despite her efforts to stifle them.

Typically, she would go to the door (in Fantasy) and be met by a delegation from her husband's office telling her that her husband had been killed in an accident. The Fantasy would then proceed in organized detail up to and after the funeral.

(3) *Compulsive and Repetitive Nature Indicates Import.* These Fantasies literally took up hours of her time. They were so real and vivid that they approached the quality of hallucinations, although she knew at all times that they were not real. When one was finished and she reflected on what she had been doing, she would feel guilty and distressed. Still they were almost compulsive in character, an indication of their psychologic import to her.

The resolution of this system of fantasy-substitutive defense and succeeding guilt, was a measure of the therapeutic results achieved. Her more specific *Fantasy-Pattern* gradually became less important and rare, finally being abandoned altogether.

This patient's retreat into Fantasy constituted a major psychologic defense. Her absorption in her Fantasies aided in blocking awareness of her dependency needs, frustration, and rage; at the same time allowing partial expression of the latter, as indicated in the Fantasy content.

The Fantasy aids in maintaining Repression (p. 357). Its vital importance to the above young woman was reflected in: (1) the compulsory nature of the activity; (2) her level of absorption in it; (3) the largely unwitting determination of the content and (4) the evolvement and maintenance of a repeated *Fantasy-Pattern*. This is an illustration of fantasy employed as an unwitting defensive endeavor in a rather malignant form, by a sick person.

C. THE SEXUAL FANTASY-SYSTEM. GRATIFICATION-ENHANCEMENTS (GEs).—Love and romance are favorite subjects for daydreams. The romantic Fantasy provides a roseate, albeit unrealistic emotional aura. Substitutive satisfactions are thereby sometimes quite readily available. Gustave Flaubert's Madame Bovary was portrayed as indulging in idyllic romantic fantasies to such an extent as to lead to her later inability to adjust to reality. Fantasies widely accompany romance and courtship.

The Fantasy likewise can play a substantial role in sexual activity and gratification. As an accompanying part of the sexual process they can provide more or less important individual embellishments. This is a concept which can be individually significant. For further emphasis and readier identification, we would label these as *Gratification-Enhancements*. For many, *GEs* comprise a regular part of the routine accompanying sexual activities of all kinds. The Gratification-Enhancement can enter significantly into various impulsions and perversions.

The following instance illustrates the evolution and employment of what can be termed a *Sexual Fantasy-System*. Evolved so as to enjoy sexual relations, the underlying need also points out the kind of serious problem which can stem from our *Socio-Sexual Dilemma*. Noted earlier (p. 72), this conception concerns the cultural pattern of antisexual indoctrination for intended early protection, *vs.* expected later participation and enjoyment of sex with marriage.

Case 62

Fantasy Allows Sexual Gratification

(1) *Sexual Fantasy-System Evolved.* A young married woman entered therapy because of emotional conflicts which handicapped her in several areas of living. An additional problem concerning her sexual life became more prominent after a period of successful therapeutic work. This concerned her inability to enjoy sexual relations, unless she simultaneously engaged in a particular *Fantasy-Pattern.*

The pervasiveness of variations of this pattern and their accessory role in sexual relations in our culture, warrant its more specific recognition as comprising a *Sexual Fantasy-System*. Attention was initially invited to its operation in the present instance from a letter to her mother. She had made considerable progress and pleased with this, she had intended to report, "I no longer feel like a *worth* (less person) ..." In a significant error she had instead mistyped the word *whore*.

As part of her protectively-intended indoctrination about sex, her mother had all too effectively stressed the doctrine that "nice girls have nothing to do with sex! ... respectable and worthwhile girls couldn't enjoy this kind of thing! ..." As a consequence she had been unable to enjoy sexual relations until the evolution of a particular *Sexual Fantasy- Pattern.*

(2) *Fantasy Permits Dissociative Splitting.* Having felt intolerable guilt over having sexual interests, these had been renounced, that is, as herself. Through Fantasy however, she could become a low class woman, depraved and disgraceful ... "drunk and a whore." For this kind of woman sexual activity was quite acceptable and expected. Enjoyment and gratification were consistent and quite all right.

Through Fantasy it was no longer she who was involved! Instead, it was this "evil, bad, and vile" person. While in part successful, this device had not really spared her guilt, but had rather increased it in indirect fashion. Bad enough to become involved in sex; to become thus (in Fantasy) the evil person who could do so, was worse. She bore a large measure of unconscious guilt.

Unwittingly her self-esteem had also suffered. The error in typing helped invite attention to this and to how pervasive it had become. The elucidation of this pattern allowed its subsequent resolution through therapy. Her self-esteem was enhanced. The once requisite *Fantasy-System* became no longer necessary. This instance also illustrates *Splitting-Through-Fantasy* (see p. 488).

D. FANTASY AND AGGRESSION; THE FANTASY LESSON-FUNCTION CONCEPT. Fantasies are sometimes employed to prove a point, to restrain action, and to serve as caution or brake to oneself. In these purposes the operation sometimes serves what we would call the *Fantasy Lesson-Function*. Herein the Fantasy endeavors to bring home a lesson.

In one type of *Fantasy Lesson,* anger and revenge are held in check. This is illustrated in the following instance from a therapy session. The businessman in this example was overly threatened by the pressure for expression of his inner angry and be-put-upon feelings. He doubted his continued ability to adequately restrain and control them. His Fantasies, as with the one reported, strove to reenforce suppression and control. They illustrate our Concept of the *Fantasy Lesson-Function*.

Case 63

The Fantasy Lesson-Function

" . . . So I take my car in to the dealer for repairs. Like other times, they won't do the work right, or will do something I didn't want, or will overcharge me. I will ask to see the manager, and then the owner (unsuccessfully), and get in an argument and leave angry, and feeling badly treated. . . .

"Then I plan retaliation; like throwing bricks through their plate glass windows. Then I'll be caught, because someone will see the car and report it; or else I'm anxious to get away. I run across the street through the rain and am hit by a car and killed! . . .

"Why this type of Fantasy?

"It's to control anger and behavior . . . Maybe it's a lesson to me not to try and seek revenge in view of possible consequences. . . . I shouldn't hold on to and nurture animosity so much. . . . It points out to me the retaliatory dangers inherent in angry acts. . . See, in my daydream I'm punished; by myself, or by Providence, or by God. The point is that if I hadn't been there for that reason (revenge) I wouldn't have been killed. . . . If I hadn't gotten angry in the first place, it wouldn't have happened

"It's a caution to me; proves that resentment and violence (and revenge, or acting upon anger) don't pay. . . . It's a real lesson! . . ."

3. *Fantasy and Dreams. Fantasy-Pattern and Fantasy-System*

The Fantasy of consciousness often takes place in daytime, retains contact with reality, and is more consciously directed. Fantasies are usually wish-oriented and fulfilling. Dreams are usually nocturnal and are far less realistic. They are more or less disguised representations of unconscious material and ordinarily cannot be consciously directed. There is nearly always a wish-fulfillment element, which may, however, be deeply concealed from recognition. Fantasies are more coherent, and their manifest content when reported is usually more readily intelligible.

Dream-like Fantasy at the time of awakening, or of drifting off into slumber, is common for some people. At times when the content is not too far from reality, or when the subject matter for Fantasy or dreams is repetitive, there may be some trouble in distinguishing them from remembered or dimly remembered actual events, as well as from dreams.

The Fantasy is an integrated flow of more or less directed associations. It includes ideas, feelings, interpretations, and draws freely on past experiences. Other people move in and out at will as controlled puppets, obeying the dictates and needs of the individual, who is usually the dominant central figure in his own play.

Fantasies are sometimes repetitive, occurring over and over again, perhaps with added embellishments upon each "performance," as with the *Fantasy-Pattern* outlined above. These repetitions indicate the continuing inner needs, of which the Fantasy-Pattern is an outward reflection. Its continuation indicates a persisting unresolved inner conflict and disturbance, in analogous fashion to the repeated dream. In the Fantasy-Pattern, as with an old, treasured, oft-read book, the devotee may come to treasure his private Fantasy increasingly, as it becomes more a part of him.

The *Fantasy-System* is a further evolvement and elaboration. Upon it some significant activity, gratification or performance will devolve. This was illustrated in one major area—the sexual—as the *Sexual Fantasy-System*. Needless to say, it can likewise play a major role in other significant aspects of one's life.

4. Manifest and Latent Content of the Fantasy

Fantasies have two major elements which were referred to earlier, and which we have found convenient to distinguish by adopting the terms of manifest and latent content. The *Manifest Content* of the fantasy attempts to satisfy the more acceptable *conscious* wishes and needs. However, the manifest part of the Fantasy may perhaps more accurately be viewed as the outward shadowy reflection of more potent and meaningful underlying *unconscious* material. This is in accord with the earlier noted *Iceberg Analogy* in which the smaller conscious and much larger unconscious portions of the psyche are compared to the smaller visible and much larger invisible (submerged) portion of the iceberg.

Important unconscious contributions to the Fantasy are made by its *Latent Content*. The latent content, of course, is not really accessible to the ordinary means of perception, since it is unconscious. However, as with the manifest content of dreams, the study of the manifest content of the Fantasy and the Fantasy-life can help lead to an understanding of the latent significance of the important underlying (unconscious) areas, through the cooperative working together by the experienced self-knowing therapist and his patient.

In the following instance, the value of Fantasy in therapy is well illustrated. Herein the manifest content is more superficial and deals with the locale of fantasied intercourse. The latent content is nuclear and concerns long-standing (unconscious) competitiveness.

Case 64

Fantasy Useful in Psychotherapy

(1) *Self-Defeating Pattern.* A 26-year-old single woman lived with her parents. She entered therapy because of a weight problem. The psychologic problems underlying this proved to be serious.

Her masochism was crippling her life. Six years earlier she had "accidentally" become pregnant and refused to marry. She insisted on keeping her newborn son and continuing to live with her parents. She turned down several offers of marriage.

Although she had a good job as a medical secretary, she did not move into an apartment by herself. Rather, she lived in cramped quarters with her parents, provoking them inadvertently but constantly to abuse of her, and bravely suffering.

(2) *Center of Parental Conflict.* The nuclear emotional conflict behind her masochism stemmed from her early childhood, when her father had openly competed with her mother for her love, and won. Because of his type of employment, he was home much of the day, and insisted upon caring for the child entirely, while he was there. He bathed her till she was 10, and in many ways indicated his attention and favoritism.

Very early the patient thought of and referred to herself as "Daddy's little girl." Her father repeatedly threw this in her mother's face. Her mother responded by intermittent overt hostility toward the child. The family setting was one of smoldering and poorly suppressed hostility and competitiveness.

(3) *Fantasy Leads to Insight.* In therapy this young woman was unable for some time to recognize any of her life-long competitiveness with her mother; nor her anger, guilt, or self-punitive behavior. One day in the course of therapy, during a period of quite slow progress, she was able to report a detailed Fantasy. This had taken place the previous evening when she was alone in the house (an unusual situation), and while expecting a date to pick her up.

She had been having an affair with him, and anticipated they would return to the house later and have intercourse. The Fantasy particularly concerned the *place* for the affair. She successively pictured their having intercourse in the living room, then in turn visualized this as transpiring on her son's bed, and on her father's bed. Each of these locations repelled her! When the Fantasy turned to her mother's bed, with a great wave of satisfaction she knew that this was "the right place"!

This Fantasy led directly into the topic of competition with mother, and eventuated in producing substantial therapeutic progress.

In the following example there is again evidence of manifest and latent content. While useful in therapy, as in the foregoing instance, this man's Fantasies for a time also comprised an effective resistance.

Case 65

Fantasy, a Resistance in Psychotherapy

A young man in intensive psychotherapy with intense unconscious hostility to his father (see *Cases 147* and *149*, pp. 283 and 286) began having more and more difficulty in talking to his therapist. There were long pauses between associations, and he became more tense and anxious. He was unable to account for this.

As time went on, he gained ability to report certain Fantasies he had been having, usually on the way to his sessions. Among his Fantasies were ones in which: (1) he Fantasied running into the therapist's car; (2) being very wealthy so that he might enter treatment with the "nation's best psychiatrist"; and (3) defiantly telling the therapist that something had happened which he didn't feel like talking about; he'd be damned if he would!

These Fantasies were used by this young man to help him partially satisfy his hostile and destructive feelings toward the therapist, without the feared risk of taking more direct action. Their intent was defensive. As he gained understanding of this, he became able to express these feelings more directly. His tension decreased and his ability to communicate increased.

As would be expected, there were important transference implications in this reaction. The self-knowledge gained herein helped lay the foundation for further important insights in this direction.

The Fantasies were a block to the patient's working out his problems and hence constituted a resistance to therapy. The manifest direction of hostility was toward the therapist; the latent object was the young man's father.

C. FANTASY AND CONFLICT

Fantasy is a potent means for the avoidance of conflict. Through Fantasy there is almost no limit to the difficult situations from which one can at least temporarily escape. It can comprise a means of *psychologic flight*. The addict may be seeking to promote pleasurable Fantasies by means of his drug; so, too, the alcoholically habituated person. Fantasies characterize the marijuana and LSD user. When the use of Fantasy becomes marked enough to interfere with productive effort, it becomes a matter for concern. When indulgence in Fantasy gets "out of control," or the person involved has difficulty in distinguishing the realities of life about him from the roseate, wish-fulfilling and unreal life of Fantasy, then we have stepped over the borderline of normality into serious psychopathology.

For our final illustration, one is chosen in which the retreat into Fantasy was nonconstructive and self-defeating.

Case 66

Retreat into Fantasy

A young business executive was faced with serious problems involving the usurping of his authority by some of the people he supervised. Under the leadership of a personable subordinate, the usurpers in various devious ways were increasingly circumventing and undermining his policies and his authority. It was an extremely difficult situation.

He was unable to find solutions and felt increasingly helpless to cope with his problems. He found himself indulging in an increasingly unrealistic series of Fantasies in which he was the central figure of a management success story. In fact, he indulged in these to such a degree that the mental activity and effort which became invested in Fantasy in itself came to absorb more and more time and energy. There was accordingly less available for problems confronting him. This led into a self-defeating vicious circle in which things became worse.

Overwhelmed by his difficulties, he tended to regress to a more childlike and infantile level. The wish-fulfillment method of attempted solution of conflict utilized by the child had begun to replace the more adult and mature process of facing directly and dealing constructively with the problems at hand.

Through therapy he slowly developed additional resources. As his ability to cope with his problems increased, his Fantasies decreased in frequency, vividness, and significance.

D. SUMMARY

The Fantasy is a vivid daydream with an imaginary sequence of events. It is often pictorial. As an ego defense, there are unconscious elements directed toward satisfaction of difficult or impossible goals and in seeking the resolution of emotional conflicts. *Unconscious Fantasies* are those which have never entered awareness or which have been repressed. Fantasies are important in childhood, offer a source for unconscious mental content and are guarded. Adolescent Fantasy-life can be active, with decreasing prominence into maturity, where Fantasies are still less accessible.

The *manifest content* of the Fantasy is conscious and covers over the hidden and unconscious *latent content*. The Fantasy which is an asset and beneficial is called the *Constructive Fantasy*. Characteristics of the *Unhealthful Fantasy* were outlined in Table 4. The Fantasy can serve functions which are analogous to those of more specific emotional symptoms. It is an ally to Repression.

The *Fantasy-Pattern* often represents a progression psychopathologically of the Fantasy. It usually reflects its level of significance via its underlying compulsion, its repetition, unconscious contributions to its content, and the individual's absorption. *Gratification-Enhancements,* or *GEs,* aid or permit satisfactions and gratification of various kinds, especially including those associated with sex. The *Sexual Fantasy-System* can be evolved in this service, as was illustrated in *Case 61.*

Restraining, behavioral modifications, and lesson-functions are embodied in the *Fantasy Lesson-Function Concept.* The *Fantasy-System* is a further evolvement and elaboration of the Fantasy-Pattern. Fantasies can aid therapy and the gaining of insight when constructively utilized. They can also contribute to the forces of resistance.

Fantasy can be a means of escape, a refuge, withdrawal, and Regression. The user of LSD. and marijuana is subject to accompanying Fantasies, some of which can be disturbing. Fantasies run the gamut from the useful and constructive, to comprising a pathway of retreat from reality, on into the deeply pathologic and the psychotic.

`E. CROSS-REFERENCES TO *THE NEUROSES* *

Fantasy
In Depressive Reactions (Chapter 4)
    of aggressive acts (Case 37); p. 183.
    of replaced authority figure; p. 187.
In Character Reactions (Chapter 5); of dishonesty, in *Obsessive Personality;* p. 255.

---

* From Laughlin, H. P. *The Neuroses.* London, Butterworth & Co., Ltd., 1967.

In Obsessive Compulsive Reactions (Chapter 6)
helpful, in *Tracing-Technique* in therapy; p. 366.
in outline of obsessive symptomatology; p. 327.
of hostility, toward siblings (Case 65); 325.
In Fatigue Reactions (Chapter 7); as an escape from boredom; p. 416.
In Hygeiaphrontic Reactions (Chapter 8)
of infantile retaliatory attacks on "bad" breasts; p. 491.
in preoccupation with cancer (Case 101); p. 488.
of physical threat and punishment (*Primal Threat*); p. 493.
Unhealthy F., of somatic concerns in onset of psychosis; p. 472.
In Soterial Reactions (Chapter 11)
in *soteria* compared to phobia (Table 30); p. 628.
of gratifying mother-ideal, represented by *soteria;* p. 626.
In Conversion Reactions (Chapter 12)
in acting out (Case 144); p. 684.
in conversion pain (Fenichel); p. 703.
in "too intense" experience, predisposing factor in Conversion Reaction; p. 695.
of sex reported in Conversion therapy (Freud); p. 650.
overdetermined, in diathesis of Conversion Reaction; p. 703.
Unconscious F., in symptom choice (Table 37); pp. 698–9.
In Dissociative Reactions (Chapter 13)
in somnambulism (*Activated-Nocturnal-Fantasy Concept*); p. 754.
Nocturnal F., dream as; p. 752.
Unconscious F., in psychodynamics of Fugue; p. 806.
In Military Reactions (Chapter 15); somnambulism as *Nocturnal F.;* p. 917.

F.   REVIEW QUESTIONS

Sample self-check questions on Chapter 7 and Fantasy for the student, psychiatric resident, and board candidate.

1. What is the *Fantasy?* What are its contributions to emotional conflict resolution?
2. Comment on the role of Fantasy in childhood. Illustrate the content and scope of adolescent Fantasy-life from your own observations.
3. How does Fantasy relate to: (1) The *Iceberg Analogy* and (2) *Primary Repression?* Can you recall *Denial-in-Fantasy* from Chapter 4?
4. Fantasies generally can be classified as *Constructive Fantasies* or *Nonconstructive Fantasies.* Explain.
5. List five characteristics denoting the *Unhealthful Fantasy.*
6. What is the *Fantasy-Pattern?* Comment on its intended functions and consequences.
7. How can *Gratification-Enhancements* or GSs influence sexual relations? Can the elaboration of a *Sexual Fantasy-System* contribute?
8. Comment briefly on the following:
   A. The *Socio-Sexual Dilemma.*
   B. *Splitting-Through-Fantasy.*
   C. A comparison and contrast of dreams *versus* Fantasy.
   D. *Manifest* and *Latent Content* in Fantasy.
   E. Fantasy as a route for *psychologic flight.*
   F. *Unconscious Fantasies.*

   G. The priminence and frequency of Fantasies in relation to maturity.

   H. "The *Unhealthful Fantasy* represents . . . psychic hypertrophy . . ."

 9. Hypothecate the value of the *Fantasy Lesson-Function* in relation to an emotional complex other than one based upon aggression and hostility.

 10. Discuss the role of Fantasy in psychotherapy including its utilization and resistance functions.

CHAPTER 8

IDEALIZATION

. . . Emotional Overestimation Sets Up an Ideal

A. PROCESS OF OVERVALUATION

    1. Definition. 2. Literary, Oedipal, and Parental Idealization. 3. Idealization and Unconscious Needs.

B. SELF-DEFEAT OF IDEALIZATION

    1. Relating to a Fantastic Person. 2. The Impossible Standard and The Unobtainable Ideal. 3. The Shattered Ideal.

C. FURTHER TYPES OF IDEALIZATION

    1. Object-Ideals. 2. Relationship-Ideals. 3. Social Idealization and National Idealization. 4. Marital Idealization. 5. The Substitute-Idealization. 6. Characterologic Idealization.

D. SUMMARY

E. REFERENCES (FROM *The Neuroses*)

F. REVIEW QUESTIONS

A. A PROCESS OF OVERVALUATION

1. Definition

Idealization is *an ego defense or mental mechanism operating outside of and beyond conscious awareness through which a person, group, nation, family, or some other object is overvalued and emotionally aggrandized.* This dynamism is *often marked by an attachment of attention, interest, and significance to a particular love-object which has become exalted, overestimated, and overvalued.* Idealization is *the process through which one sets up or creates an ideal. Persons, positions, situations, possessions, and goals can thus become regarded as ideals or as idealistic.* Idealization can be employed to block awareness of painful and perhaps otherwise unacceptable aspects of a significant object or relationship.

Idealization can also be a conscious or partly conscious endeavor in which the individual purposely "builds up" and enhances his evaluation of another person, his attributes, a principle, or a political or religious system, so as to make them into an ideal. The position and value thus assigned has a varying degree of unreality when judged objectively. To the person concerned, his idealized object may appear or to all intents and purposes become, the standard of excellence; the ultimate.

Most people have established ideals at one time or another. They are intended to subserve various needs. Freud's early career, for instance, was marked by a series of relationships with idealized colleagues. These included in turn Meynert, Fleischl, Charcot, Breuer, and Fliess. While not so apparent at the time perhaps, nor to the persons involved, they are readily enough so delineated in retrospect.

2. Literary, Oedipal, and Parental Idealization

The process of Idealization has been widely recognized, empirically and intuitively, for a long time. This is evidenced in literature, although usually not so identified. We might refer to such examples as *Literary Idealizations*. The following instance is from Shakespeare.

Case 67

A Literary Idealization; Hamlet's Father

In Shakespeare's *Hamlet* (Act III, Scene iv, 55–62), Hamlet's exalted description of his father suggests an Idealization serving some important inner needs. Hamlet speaks thus:

"See, what a grace was seated on this brow,
Hyperion's curls, the front of Jove himself,
An eye like Mars, to threaten and command;
A station like the herald Mercury
New-lighted on a heaven-kissing hill;
A combination and a form indeed,
Where every god did seem to set his seal
To give the world assurance of a man . . ."

In these lines Hamlet's idealized father is compared with the gods. Through this process one might speculate that Hamlet combats Oedipal aggression toward his father, and possibly takes a step toward identifying with him.

Idealization is an ego defensive-mechanism not uncommonly evolved unconsciously and utilized by sons as an aid in the resolution of their Oedipal conflicts. When this type of Idealization is operative, for purposes of identification we might term it *Oedipal Idealization*. In its frequent operation in relation to parents when an anti-Oedipal basis is absent or minimal, this significant operation of the dynamism is *Parental Idealization*.

3. Idealization and Unconscious Needs

Idealization as an intrapsychic mechanism can seek to subserve many vital needs and goals. Some of the more important intended functions are listed as follows, in Table 5.

Table 5

Idealization
The Internal Psychologic Intended Functions of
a Major Dynamism

The ego defense of Idealization can serve, attempt to serve, or contribute to several important, deeply unconscious psychologic needs and functions. These might be referred to collectively as the *endogain* of Idealization. The vital intrapsychic functions of Idealization include:

1. Idealization is often an important *preliminary to Identification.* Both of these mechanisms play a vital role in superego (conscience) development, and in character formation. Their conjoint operation represents an emotional symbiosis, as with Displacement, p. 89, and Substitution, p. 402.

2. Hidden dissatisfaction with one's own ego may be dealt with in part through the *transfer of libidinal attachment to the (new) ideal.* From the standpoint of the vicissitudes of the instincts, the emphasis thus has become placed upon the *object* rather than upon the aim.

3. As a method of or aid to, Denial (*Chapter 4*):

     a. One's *sexual or aggressive urges* toward an individual may be *more readily denied,* disowned, held in check, or regarded as less unworthy or "base," when the person concerned becomes an idealized object and is thereby placed on his special pedestal.

     b. *Unacceptable aspects of one's ideal* are also *denied* in the process of Idealization, through which the person concerned becomes increasingly acceptable and looked up to.

4. Various unconscious internal needs are satisfied through the *"external emotional supplies"* secured from the idealized object. These gratifications are, of course, unrealistic and illusory. They are sought as a means of lessening conflict, for example, through increased satisfaction of dependency needs, and the unrealistic but subjectively experienced receipt of emotional supplies from the object which has been idealized.

     This process can progress into psychopathology, with an unrealistic and neurotic (external) source of supply increasingly established in response to the internal needs. In effect also, the individual may create a *soteria*—the converse of a phobia—as an external neurotic source of security, protection, and gratification. (See Soterial Reactions, *The Neuroses,* p. 607.)

5. *Self-punishment* may be provided in a devious neurotic fashion. When the pedestal is broken, the person who has built it suffers the loss (the Shattered-Ideal). In other instances, an obviously (to others) poor object is tremendously overvalued. An unreal, fantastic person may be created. The self-defeat lies in the consequences of self-deception, increased vulnerability, and the potential for dissillusionment and loss.

     Other masochistic avenues exist: (a) in the creation of an unobtainable ego-ideal; and in that (b) when the idealized loved one or lover is so created, he becomes never obtainable as such.

6. A *replacement for a lost object* or former source. A gap may be thus filled, for example, following the loss by death of a loved person. A rapid process or transfer of Idealization may also facilitate the emotional phenomenon of "rebound" to a new love object, as commonly observed following a broken love affair.

7. In combatting internal aggression, as an aid to resolution of the Oedipal situation (*Oedipal Idealization*), and in fostering identification with parents through *Parental Idealization.*

B. SELF-DEFEAT OF IDEALIZATION

1. Relating to a Fantastic Person

Idealization inevitably results in an unrealistic view of another person, parts of him, or the relationship. The disadvantages inherent in such a situation are many. One begins to relate to and to deal with what we can refer to as a *Fantastic Person,* instead of a real one.

The process of Idealization takes place in such commonly recognized situations as "hero worship" and "falling in love." When this process has been sufficiently operative, one then tends to accept everything as "good" about the person. A *Fantastic Person* is created. He comes to be seen in a very favorable light—a "rosy glow." Equally operative is the tendency for the automatic rejection of everything which might be considered to be unfavorable, or "bad," about the idealized person.

2. The Impossible Standard and The Unobtainable Ideal

On occasion an idealized relationship establishes what could be termed the *Impossible Standard.* Since the process of Idealization sets up criteria which can hardly be met, the establishment of new meaningful and significant relationships may be hampered or prove not possible. Such was the situation in the following instance. The potential for self-defeat inherent in this kind of situation is apparent and can be considerable.

Case 68

The Impossible Standard

A bachelor veterinarian had friends who had tried unsuccessfully over the course of some years to promote a match with several attractive young ladies, whom they considered well suited. He was interested in meeting new girls, and typically would have a series of dates with each. Eventually, however, he would stop seeing them, for such general reasons as, "We don't agree on certain things . . ."; "I just don't feel at ease with her . . ."; or "I like her a lot but that's as far as it goes . . ."

While in school he had been very much in love with a girl. He couldn't do enough for her in the way of gifts and dates. When she and her family moved to the West Coast soon after graduation, the romance continued to flourish for a time through correspondence. After a year however, it ended, through the attenuation of time and distance, plus a new boy friend. He had dated a number of girls, but became serious with none. Here then was the mechanism of Idealization operating with unfortunate, continuing, and self-defeating consequences.

His earlier sweetheart had been idealized to such an extent that in comparison all other girls must fall far short. Further, the hurt had been too great to risk its reputation. Thus, while he consciously sought a replacement, the extent of his earlier Idealization established criteria which could not be realistically met. No one could measure up. This tragic and defeating complex provided an excellent illustration of what we would term the *Impossible Standard,* following a significant Idealization.

The establishment of an *Impossible Standard* is illustrated in other situations. At times a young person loses a fiancé through death, or a young wife a husband. Although a new mate is sought more or less seriously, no one ever seems good enough. The lost person may become increasingly idealized as time passes, perhaps so much so that no one new is ever really acceptable.

The aim in this kind of situation can be very defensive, to guard against hurt and loss. One comes to evolve a person or goal as what we might term the *Unobtainable Ideal*. Its maintenance aids in the preservation of defensively-intended distance. This concept is closely related to the foregoing one. The Unobtainable Ideal similarly guards against renewed vulnerability or loss and hurt. There are also possible masochistic elements.

3. The Shattered Ideal

We can readily see that emotional satisfactions can accrue from the consequences of Idealization. Through the creation of an ideal, one is then blind or partially blind to the unpleasant side or qualities of the love-object. It becomes more acceptable and more satisfying. As noted, there are disadvantages inherent in this mechanism, a major one being its interference with judgment and objectivity.

When a person has been idealized, one is unable to see the real person objectively. A second major disadvantage lies in the constant potential for the Idealization as a protective process to fall apart. The psyche cares naught about this hazard! However, when the idealized image comes crashing down in fragments because of major defects or growing discrepancies that can no longer be ignored, or for more hidden reasons, serious disappointment and disillusionment can result. The agent of such a personal tragedy might be referred to as the *Shattered Ideal*.

Neither the Ideal nor the Shattered Ideal is always readily surrendered. The following instance portrays an intense example of the rather commonly observed Teen-age Idealization or *Hero Worship* of a movie star. Her idol rapidly lost much of his public appeal and glamor, but not so for her.

Case 69

Reluctant Surrender of an Idealized Image

Corinne was not too different from a number of teen-agers but perhaps more intense in her Idealization of a young movie star, Tab Young. She helped organize and was president of a fan club at school, and went to see each of his pictures repeatedly. Her room was plastered with pictures and magazine cutouts of Tab and she wrote him weekly.

Sadly, it happened one day that the newspapers headlined a narcotics scandal involving her hero. Corinne could not believe this disclosure. As the papers reported unfolding legal events and confirmed Young's involvement by his conviction, Corinne's friends turned their attention from Tab to new movie idols.

Corinne refused to accept the verdict of the court, the public, or her friends. She could not so readily surrender her ideal or transfer her feelings. For a long time she maintained his innocence. Eventually her emotional allegiance was transferred. Tab had been a reluctantly recognized *Shattered Ideal*.

C. FURTHER TYPES OF IDEALIZATION

1. Object-Ideals

There are additional types of Idealization and many social and personal situations in which this ego defense is operative. Some brief reference to several representative ones is in order. Among these, one which we might call *Object-Idealization* is not uncommon. Herein an Object-Ideal is established of a personal possession. This becomes overvalued in an endeavor which greatly increases its significance. This can sometimes bear a relationship to Rationalization (*Chapter 17*) and to Soterial formation.

In one instance a man had idealized his ancient car. He made comparisons with newer autos, in which their more modern features were regarded as quite inferior. A collector-philatelist came to so regard his stamp collection, assigning it a completely unrealistic value and worth; a musician displayed inordinate personal pride in a musical instrument which was little better than average. The intent of such endeavors can be apparent as can their degree of success. The possession of something great is ego enhancing.

Object-Idealization can carry over to include persons. They thus come to be sometimes regarded and perhaps also treated as though they were indeed personal possessions, and thus subject to this kind of idealized overvaluation.

2. Relationship-Ideals

There are few kinds of human relationships which are not subject to the process of Idealization. The process of what might be named *Relationship-Idealization* is common enough. Careful observation will indicate its entering subtly or more apparently, into relationships in many families. It often plays a role in love, romance, and marriage.

Idealization also relates to, and can contribute to or augment the strength of positive transference in therapy. As noted, it sometimes assists in or can be akin to soterial development.

3. Social-Idealization and National Idealization

Social-Idealization is a broader operation involving groups of people, parties, or nations. Political ideologies can reflect such a broader overvaluation of a particular body of political thought or party.

Idealization can enter into preserving fanatical religious beliefs and systems. For their adherents, the ensuing strength of their commitment can help justify, permit, or encourage sadistic cruelties and the oppression of opponents and nonbelievers.

National Idealization can transpire in concert or overlap (emotional symbiosis) with *National Compensation* (p. 20). It can also occur independently.

4. Marital Idealization

In the following instance Idealization was prominent in a marriage. The prospects of its continuation were thereby enhanced. See also *Case 45* (p.

129), in which Idealization was supported by Denial. Marital Idealization, in greater or lesser measure, is far from rare. Its function is that of making a marriage more tolerable.

Case 70

Marital Idealization

A young college graduate became romantically involved with a nurse who had a reputation for promiscuity. They had been dating only a short time when she found she was pregnant. This led to great emotional stress for the young man whose strong religious background and rigid standards demanded that he marry the girl. This was accomplished, but not before he had expressed some grave doubts to friends about the girl and her potential as a wife and mother. Her lack of moral fiber caused him deep concern.

The marriage progressed shakily, and another child was born. The wife was unkempt and slovenly. Rumors circulated about her infidelities. However, he had gradually become reconciled to the situation.

A process of Marital Idealization had been active. After some years the doubts gave way to praise. He felt "fortunate to have found her . . ." He went to some lengths to support this. The Idealization helped make a once doubtfully tolerable situation more acceptable. It aided in justifying the early relationship, the unwanted pregnancy, and counteracted earlier criticisms.

His emotional conflicts were seemingly at least consciously resolved. Furthermore, it helped immunize him against criticisms of his wife from others. Stemming from his Marital Idealization, his views of his wife were shared by few.

5. The Substitute-Idealization

It is occasionally possible for one idealized relationship to replace or to succeed another. At times this can transpire rather smoothly and uneventfully, as well as unwittingly. When this occurs it comprises what could be referred to for convenience as the *Substitute-Idealization*.

Psychodynamic relationships of this process exist and can help to support our theories concerning the Recapitulation of Antecedent Patterns, Impression Priority, and the frequent vital psychic-emotional need for rapid Replacement (*Chapter 27, p. 479*) and Substitution (*Chapter 23, p. 401*) when an emotional hiatus develops. The following is an illustration.

Case 71

Substitute-Idealization

A 23-year-old man had an older brother who was intelligent, popular, handsome, and athletic. He strongly admired and looked up to him. Although he had long walked in his brother's shadow, he seemingly had never minded. The older brother was no doubt a superior type of person, but Eddie had further idealized him. To him he was indeed peerless. Tragically, he was killed in an auto accident.

The process of replacement began almost immediately. Eddie became fast friends with a local boy of similar age, but of substantially lower caliber than his brother. The new relationship was a recapitulation, although the process of *Substitute-Idealization* had to be a more active one. Although not to others, to Eddie the new friend became a paragon; unequalled, and an ideal.

The sudden and tragic loss had required a transfer of the Idealization to an available substitute. The hiatus was quickly filled; the devastating loss was thereby to this extent assuaged. The defensively-intended purpose in this instance of *Substitute-Idealization* was achieved.

6. Characterologic Idealization

One function of the dynamism of Idealization is of such a level of import as to warrant our assigning it the distinguishing name of *Characterologic Idealization*. Through this particular function of the mechanism, major contributions are made to personality development and character formation. The attributes of an idealized person are likely to be attractive and appealing, and thus are far more readily emulated or taken over. The emulation or adoption can be sought through conscious efforts, can evolve as an unconscious endeavor, or both.

One can hardly overstress the importance of Idealization in characterologic evolvement. Characterologic Idealization and the following dynamism of Identification, often operate conjointly in their influences upon character formation, representing another instance of emotional symbiosis (p. 89).

D. SUMMARY

Idealization is the ego-defensive process of emotional overestimation through which a person, object, or relationship is assigned undue value and significance. Conscious efforts may precede or accompany the dynamism, or be made independently.

Instances of Idealization from contemporary or classic literature are termed *Literary Idealization,* illustrating the long-standing, intuitive, and empiric recognition of the process. An *Oedipal Idealization* of the parent of the same sex is evolved as an intended aid in resolving Oedipal conflicts. *Parental Idealization* is a variable but frequent process through which a parental figure is idealizd.

Idealization leads the individual concerned to deal with an unrealistic *Fantastic Person*. Hero Worship and falling in love commonly involve an emotional overestimation. *Teen-Age Idealization* is commonly encountered.

Table 5 outlined the intended functions of the dynamism. Sometimes through the prior Idealization of a lost object, the presence of an *Impossible Standard* ensures that a new relationship is most unlikely to measure up. A person or goal may, in analogous fashion be set up as an *Unobtainable Ideal*. This is a defense which guards in part against a new hurt or loss, as distance is protectively maintained.

The *Shattered Ideal* is the former object of Idealization when the process falls apart. A once *Idealized Image* however may not be easily surrendered, as illustrated in *Case 69*.

Object-Ideals include possessions, personal items, and pet beliefs or ideas, which are assigned undue significance and value and presumably are thus ego-enhancing for their possessor. Persons can be so treated. *Relationship-Ideals* refer to and can occur in all types of human relationships; the family is rare without this process being operative to some extent. *Social Idealization* and *National Idealization* expand the concept to include broader groups of people, the latter at times observed in concert with *National Compensation* as an example of *emotional symbiosis*.

Marital Idealization is not uncommonly operative as an aid to enhancing one's partner and the relationship of an otherwise poorly tolerable marriage. On occasion one idealized relationship can rapidly succeed a lost one in the *Substitute-Idealization*. Idealization can operate in conjunction with other dynamisms, including those of Denial, Substitution, Replacement, Compensation, Repression, and Identification. *Characterologic Idealization* is the significant type of function of this ego defense, when it enters into personality development and character formation.

E.   CROSS-REFERENCES TO *THE NEUROSES* *

Idealization
In Character Reactions (Chapter 5)
  in character patterns of defense (Character Neuroses); p. 238.
    of *Conversion Personality* (Table 19); p. 260.
In Hygeiaphrontic Reactions (Chapter 8); of good breast, in *soteria* evolvement; p. 491.
In Phobic Reactions (Chapter 10)
  of mother, in *Faulty Identification Concept* (Case 115); p. 561
    in phobia of travel (Case 121); p. 576.
In Soterial Reactions (Chapter 11)
  in principal mechanisms of defense in *Soterial Reaction;* p. 627.
    Object Idealization (Case 133); p. 627.
  of dependency object, projected externally; p. 626.
In Conversion Reactions (Chapter 12); in the development of Conversion diathesis; p. 695.
In Dissociative Reactions (Chapter 13); of World War I hero, in interest in aviation (Case 173); p. 803.

F.   REVIEW QUESTIONS

Sample self check question on Chapter 8 and Idealization for the student, psychiatric resident, and board candidate.

    1. *Idealization* is described as a process of emotional overestimation or overevaluation. Explain.
    2. Can you recall or find an example of *Literary Idealization?*
    3. A form of Idealization evolves at times as an intended aid in resolving the Oedipal situation. What is it called? How might its successful operation contribute?
    4. Summarize the unconscious needs and functions which the evolution of Idealization seeks to subserve (from *Table 5*).

---

* From Laughlin, H. P. *The Neuroses*. London, Butterworth & Co., Ltd., 1967.

5. What is the significance of the following terms and concepts?
   A. *Parental Idealization.*
   B. *Endogain of Idealization.*
   C. *External emotional supplies.*
   D. *Fantastic Person.*
   E. *The Unobtainable Ideal.*
   F. *Teen-age Idealization.*
   G. Love-object.
   H. *Object-Idealization.*
   I. *Relationship-Ideals* in friendships and families.
   J. The type of Idealization through which attributes are taken over.
6. How is self-defeat implicit to maintaining an *Impossible Standard?*
7. "When the idealized image comes crashing down in fragments . . . ," the consequence is the *Shattered Ideal.* Can you account for its emotional impact?
8. The overestimation of a body of political or religious thought may be categorized as what type of Idealization?
9. How can *Marital Idealization* contribute to the continuation of a marriage?
10. The evolvement of a Substitute-Idealization in filling an urgent need and void can be regarded as a matter of psychologic expedience. What is the advantage to the ego when the process is "successful"? Can you fit the situation of falling in love "on the rebound" into this concept?

CHAPTER 9

IDENTIFICATION

. . . An Emotional Alliance [1]

A. IMPORTANT DEFENSIVELY AND IN CHARACTER DEVELOPMENT

1. Attributes Acquired. 2. Definition: a. Making Oneself Like Another; b. Unconscious Taking Over Desired Traits.

B. PLACING ONESELF IN ANOTHER PERSON'S SHOES

1. Central Identification. 2. Actor Identification.

C. SYMPATHY, EMPATHY, AND COMPATHY

1. Projective and Affective Types of Identification. 2. Rapport and Sympatico. 3. Sympathy. 4. Empathy. 5. Compathy or Emotional Identification a. An Affective Identification; b. Definition; c. Compathy Facilitated Through Close Relationships; Individual Compathy and Group Compathy; d. Compathic Identification and Central Identification.

D. CONTRIBUTING TO PERSONALITY AND TO CHARACTER

1. Predecessor Identification. 2. Mannerism Identification and Trait Identification: a. Trait Adoption Merging into Characterologic Change; b. Admiration Leads to Attribute Adoption. 3. Characterologic Identification: a. Influencing The Course of Life; b. Basking in Reflected-Glory Concept. The Celebrity-Seeker. 4. Public-Figure Identification; Mass Identification: a. Prominence Invites Identification; b. Entertainment Figures and Mass Identification. 5. Major Influence in Learning. Vocational Identification. 6. Seeking to Be Like an Admired or Envied Person.

E. ADDITIONAL SIGNIFICANT ASPECTS OF IDENTIFICATION

1. Criminal Identification: a. The Spurious Confession; b. With the Wrongdoer. 2. Bad Identifications: a. Socially Nonconstructive: The Bad Influence; b. Parental Identification. Adoption of What One Disapproves. 3. In Advertising: The Secondary Appeal: a. The Primary Appeal: Toward the Direct Satisfaction of a Need; b. The Secondary Appeal. 4. Identification in Military Life; Military-Unit Identification (MUI): a. Necessary for Morale; b. Military-Unit Identification. 5. Group Identification: a. Gregariousness and Belonging to Organizations; b. Group Identification: Seeking Ac-

---

[1] "And then I'll . . . be like him, and he will then love me." William Blake, 1757–1827. In *The Little Black Boy,* Blake poetically stated the *raison d'être,* the basis and goal of Identification.

ceptance, Security, Support, and Belonging. 6. Vicarious Satisfactions: a. Seeking Satisfactions Not Otherwise Available; b. Substitutive Gratification.

F. The Personal Yardstick in New Relationships

1. Identification of a New Acquaintance with Someone from Earlier Experience: a. Conditioning Effect of Earlier Relationships; b. The Rule of Impression Priority; c. Applying the "Personal Yardstick" to New Acquaintances; d. Great Personal Value in Their Elucidation. 2. Major Effects on Interpersonal Relations. Interpersonal Identification: a. Why is "Personal Yardstick" Applied? What Advantages Sought? b. Fostering Recapitulation With Inherent Potential for Major and Minor Inaccuracies and Distortions.

G. Identification Encouraged by Parents

1. Holding Forth Example or Standard. 2. Pressure and Requirement.

H. Identification Influences Manifestations in Neurotic and Psychotic Reactions. (Symptom Identification)

I. Underdog Identification

J. Summary

K. References (from *The Neuroses*)

L. Review Questions

A. IMPORTANT DEFENSIVELY AND IN CHARACTER DEVELOPMENT

1. Attributes Acquired

Identification is a major ego defense or dynamism. It plays a most important role in character development. It is frequently employed as a vital psychologic defensive endeavor. Through the unconscious operation of Characterologic Identification one "takes over" or develops attributes, traits, or attitudes which are in various degrees like those of another significant person.

Through Identification, acceptance, love, recognition, security, and ego-enhancement unwittingly can be sought or secured. Identification with a loved object is likely to have ego-synthetic and constructive effects (p. 96). In its many applications, it would be difficult to overstress its importance. It should certainly be noted that Identification is a universally employed intrapsychic operation. It belongs to the more advanced and developed group of dynamisms.

2. Definition

A. MAKING ONESELF LIKE ANOTHER.—Identification may be defined as *an ego defense or mental mechanism operating outside of and beyond conscious awareness through which an individual, in varying degree, makes himself like someone else; he identifies with another person. This results in the unconscious taking over of various elements of another.* Such elements may include thoughts, goals, behavior, mannerisms, reactions, attributes, or character traits and emotional feelings. Identification is an *emotional alliance.*

The process of Identification may be conscious or unconscious. When it is conscious, it is often accompanied by a simple form of imitation, and the modeling of oneself after (some aspect or aspects of) another, perhaps most often after one who has become in this area, an ideal. What we are primarily considering in this discussion, however, is a deeper kind of unconscious molding of oneself. It is an intrapsychic Identification *with* someone, or with a given aspect of someone—as for examples a parent, an authority, a prominent figure, a group, a movement, an admired, idealized or famous personage, an actor or character, an organization, or even a criminal, and so on.

More often Identification is with a "good" figure, someone to whom one looks up, or a respected group. One unwittingly endeavors to conform to the image of the ideal, as it is perceived. Accordingly, there frequently must be Idealization (Chapter 8) before Identification can occur. Most instances of Identification may be viewed as being motivated by deep basic needs for acceptance, approval, and love. It can have a relation to Conversion (p. 46 ff.)

Identification, however, may be made with "good" or with "bad" objects. The latter may include as examples, an aggressor, one's captors, an unfair or oppressive authority, or in occasional instances, a murderer.

B. UNCONSCIOUS TAKING OVER OF DESIRED TRAITS.—This ego-defensive mechanism plays a major role in emotional health. Early childhood Identifications with loved objects are necessary to sound personality development, and to emotional integration. On the other hand, faulty Identification, its failure or absence, tend to produce what we might term *misidentifications* which can play a significant role in the onset of emotional illness and its treatment.

An understanding of this major intrapsychic process accordingly is vital to the psychotherapist and to all who are interested in human motivation and behavior. Identification is a major mental mechanism. As noted, it is a less primitive, and more advanced type of internal defensive operation. Accordingly, it belongs with the *Higher Order* group of dynamisms.

B.   PLACING ONESELF IN ANOTHER PERSON'S SHOES

1. Central Identification

The important position of Identification in our day-to-day living can be readily illustrated. In our use of books, novels, plays, radio and television programs, Identification is common. Often made with a central figure, it plays a continuing and useful role. The level of consciousness of its operation varies. This is a universal and most important type of Identification. In an effort to further delineate and emphasize it we would propose terming it *Central Identification,* (1) after the prominent position of its more usual object, and (2) in view of its central position in these phases of living.

Usually the reader, listener, or observer tends to identify with the *central* character; the hero or heroine of a story, drama, or movie. Through such Identification he may immerse himself further and more enjoyably. This increases its significance and adds to his pleasure. He may to a varying extent share the emotions and experiences of a given character or characters. This may approach compathy (see later) in level.

Feelings of success, happiness, sadness, and other affects can be vicariously experienced. What occurs in this common type of Identification can be an emotional feeling of likeness or sharing with a character, or with the stage or screen actor making the portrayal. A reasonable capacity for Central Identification can greatly add to one's level of satisfaction in reading and enjoyment of the dramatic arts.

2. Actor Identification

A capacity for Identification is quite vital in turn for the would-be actor. Thorough Identification with the character he undertakes to portray, can result in an actor being far more convincing in his role. In fact, his relative ability to so identify himself will often largely determine not only his ability in a given role, but also his entire career success.

Such a capacity and ability may be termed *Actor Identification.* This may be an effortful and conscious process, an automatic and intuitive one, or probably more often with the successful actor, a combination of both. Professional casting tries to facilitate this empirically by matching actor and role. Implied recognition of Actor Identification is also perhaps sometimes indicated through the expressions "in character" and "out of character."

C.   SYMPATHY, EMPATHY, AND COMPATHY

1. Projective and Affective Types of Identification

The individual ability to adequately appreciate, and further to share the emotional feelings of others varies among people. These kinds of capacities are a distinguishing feature of man. Their genuineness and depth can be a measure of his relative maturity. Identification is basic to their evolvement.

A number of terms are useful in expressing varying degrees and types of those useful capacities. These include *rapport, sympatico, sympathy,* and *empathy.* Another term *compathy,* we have proposed and utilized for some years. The use of compathy has been a convenience in referring to and describing a related useful concept and situation. It expresses a further degree or progression of such emotional feelings. This is a conception of the occasional intriguing phenomenon in certain relationships in which one person literally feels with another.

These five terms can be employed to help distinguish and label the important forms of the projective or intellectual types of Identification, and its affective form. Rapport, sympatico, sympathy, and empathy are forms of *Projective Identification.* Another type of *Projective Identification* is also discussed later in Chapter 15. Compathy is a closer, sharing, affective form (or level) of *Emotional Identification.* Thus compathy is *Affective Identification,* as distinguished from Projective Identification. Emotional Identification is an alternate term for both compathy and Affective Identification.

2. Rapport and Sympatico

When two people are in rapport, they are *thinking alike or together.* Rapport is an intellectual kind of Identification, although there can be some emotional overtones.

Sympatico differs somewhat in its connotations. This term has been more or less widely adopted for usage in the United States from its Spanish and Latin American origins. Sympatico connotes *a state of mutual felicity,* or *a harmony of viewpoints.* It is more likely to have emotional overtones. Sympatico denotes a measure of Projective Identification.

3. Sympathy

In sympathy, *one has compassion for another person, especially in view of his trials, tribulations, pain, suffering, and misery.* Accompanying feelings of pity or commiseration are common. Sympathetic feelings are widely held for those in trouble, need, or sickness. They account for many of our social good works.

Sympathy is an important type of Projective Identification, but more superficial than empathy. It entails the experiencing of sorrow and compassion *for* another's grief, loss, hurt, or misfortune.

4. Empathy

Another significant form of Identification is that of empathy. Of relatively recent origin, this is the label for the useful concept of an important and deeper type of Intellectual and Projective Identification.

Empathy may be defined as *the objective, detached, and intellectual awareness of the feelings, emotions, and behavior of another person, and/or their meaning and significance.* In empathy one has *the capacity to feel for another person; to thus appreciate more fully his feelings and his situation.*

Through this form of Identification one has an increased capacity for, and comes to more adequately understand the emotional feelings of the other person; their extent and significance. This is (ideally insofar as the therapist is concerned) without regard to the kind of emotional feeling. The capacity for empathy is often present to a more or less parallel degree or extent, insofar as appreciating the level of the emotional feelings of the particular other person is concerned.

Emotional overtones can be strong in empathy but are not a requisite. Further, objectivity, as so necessary for the psychotherapist for instance, would rather require them to be of limited extent. Sharing the other person's feeling in kind or extent is not only not required, but is probably undesirable, in distinction from our concept of compathy, which represents not only a further step in progression, but is also of a different and tangential order.

The capacity for empathy is valuable to anyone. It is very useful for work in the humanities. It is a necessary quality for the physician. Finally, in his joint roles of participant and observer in the process of intensive psychotherapy, such a capacity is a "must" for the psychotherapist. To a large extent, empathy is consciously directed and is subject to a considerable measure of voluntary control, again in some contrast to compathy.

The individual capacity for the empathic understanding of another person is widely variable. Empathy is to be distinguished from sympathy, and from compathy. Empathy is a major form of *Projective Identification.*

5. Compathy or Emotional Identification

A. AN AFFECTIVE IDENTIFICATION.—A number of types of Identification have been discussed thus far. Mention has been made of the conscious placing of oneself in another's shoes. The term and concept of *empathy* has been presented above, in which there is a *Projective* type of Identification which allows and helps secure an objective awareness and understanding of another's emotional feelings and their meaning, and a more adequate appreciation of their extent.

There is a closer kind of emotional sharing. It is an *affective* type of Identification as distinguished from the foregoing projective forms. Also known as *Emotional Identification,* this is the psychic reaction in which an emotional feeling is literally shared with another. It is not so much a feeling *for,* as a feeling *with.* It operates on a deeper level. This close kind of emotional sharing we have termed *compathy.*

Compathy thus is stronger, deeper, closer, and of a different order than sympathy. It is to be distinguished from empathy, as noted above.

B. DEFINITION.—We can define compathy accordingly as *the close sharing of emotional feelings with another person. Compathy is an affective kind of Identification through which one subjectively experiences the emotions of another. It is semiautomatic and thus practically independent of voluntary control or direction.* Certain distinctions are to be noted between this kind of emotional sharing, and both empathy and sympathy, *to which it is akin tangentially but of a different order. It operates on a deeper emotional level of significance.*

In compathy, then, one literally feels with another person. Feelings of the other person are closely, if not exactly, shared. This is in *kind,* and also often in *extent.* Compathic feelings therefore are those which are emotionally communicated between people, so as to result in an actual sharing of the feeling. This is without regard to the variety of feeling; any emotional feeling may be so shared. As noted, compathy is automatic and beyond conscious control. Thus efforts at its conscious direction or control are likely to have little effect.

Compathy makes possible deep bonds of emotional attachment between people. Such bonds accordingly can be increased, strengthened, or gain more significance through the psychic reaction of compathy. Compathy represents the deepest and strongest type of Affective Identification. It often helps to establish the emotional bases through which mannerisms, traits, tastes, and characteristics are taken over by one person from another. A capacity for compathy can be an asset.

C. COMPATHY FACILITATED THROUGH CLOSE RELATIONSHIPS; INDIVIDUAL COMPATHY AND GROUP COMPATHY.—The closeness of a relationship can facilitate compathy and *vice versa.* Compathy thus is far more likely to occur with persons who share a close interpersonal relationship, although this is not a requisite. While the feelings shared in compathic experience do not have to be present to an equal extent, they must be the same in kind. However, their level is often fairly close. Most compathic experiences available for clinical or social observation are those of *Individual Compathy.* Compathy is prominent in successful sexual experiences.

The presence of compathy as well as its effects can be most subtle. The persons concerned are often quite unaware of its operation or of their personal compathic capacity. It may well escape the detection of the casual observer. Compathy is most frequent individually, as noted. Instances of *Group Compathy* however, are sometimes to be encountered as well. *Case 18* (p. 46) illustrated the interesting phenomenon of *Symptom Compathy.*

The following example is a brief illustration of Group Compathy. Through this interesting, warm, human capacity there was the compathic communication and sharing of the sadness over parting in a small neighborhood gathering.

Case 72

Group Compathy; Emotional Feelings of Sadness Shared

> A 48-year-old attorney died unexpectedly, leaving a widow and two children. After the funeral and necessary business arrangement were completed (a period of several months) it was decided that the wisest course of action would be for the family to join relatives on the West Coast. This represented quite an emotional wrench, since they had lived in their home for years and had many long-standing friendships. Although difficult, the discussions about it and the final reaching of the decision were made with outward calm.
>
> On the day they drove away, a small group of neighbors gathered to wish them a good trip and farewell. Several were very close friends, and several were not. Suddenly, as if in response to a signal, everyone began to weep, in a sudden contagion of their sadness over parting. The objective basis of loss varied considerably.
>
> This was a striking instance of *Group Compathy*. There was an emotional close sharing of strong feelings with those departing. To an observer, the level of shared feelings seemed approximately equal.

The above is a rather dramatic example. Compathy operates widely and far less obviously, in a great variety of interpersonal situations. Parents, for example, may sometimes literally experience themselves the pleasures and successes, or the difficulties and rebuffs of their children. Vicarious experience may become more possible through a measure of compathy. Mobs and riots can illustrate a destructive type of Group Compathy, as well as emotional contagion.

D. COMPATHIC IDENTIFICATION AND CENTRAL IDENTIFICATION.—The compathic kind of Affective Identification occasionally may be present for the reader of a novel or the viewer of a play, TV drama, or movie. Herein a measure of compathy increases the significance of Central Identification, as outlined earlier. Also see p. 47.

A live, "real" person or an actual relationship with him is not an absolute requirement for compathy. One may share closely the actor's feelings. Indeed, some persons have such strong capacity for this kind of *Compathic Identification* that they literally can stand to see few movies, or even none at all. Coming thus to compathically share too closely the emotional feelings of the persons portrayed is too great a strain.

D. CONTRIBUTING TO PERSONALITY AND TO CHARACTER

1. Predecessor Identification

The ego defense of Identification is particularly significant because of its vital role in personality development. Its useful functions thereby are not surpassed. Accordingly, the personal value of this mechanism can hardly be overestimated. This is true for most, if not all, individuals.

The social values of Identification are likewise most important. Most of the social virtues involve the operation of some form of Identification. Warm interest in other people, concern for their concerns, kindly empathic understanding, and the empathic sharing of their attitudes and feelings involve its conscious and/or unconscious operation. Some capacity for Projective Identification is required to secure a real measure of appreciation of the other person's position.

From a social viewpoint, the dynamism of Identification can have a wide variety of valuable consequences. The following is an interesting example of one of the socially useful purposes occasionally aided or made possible through the operation of what might be termed *Predecessor Identification.*

Case 73

Predecessor Identification; Social Purpose Subserved

A single man fell in love with an older woman, a widow, whom he married. The new wife had earlier borne several children. The foster father became greatly interested in the children, and increasingly identified with their father. He gradually assumed many of the real father's characteristics and behaved like him in many ways. This came to comprise a major characterologic instance of *Predecessor Identification.*

Consciously and unconsciously, he strongly desired to be like him and to take his place. As a consequence, he succeeded most admirably in his role as a foster parent. He thus came far nearer to actually replacing the real father.

2. Mannerism Identification and Trait Identification

A. TRAIT ADOPTION MERGING INTO CHARACTEROLOGIC CHANGE.—In the foregoing example, the foster father unconsciously assumed some of the behavior of his predecessor through the mechanism of Identification. This included several of the latter's mannerisms and traits. The unconscious adoption of traits and mannerisms can be secondary to Identification and/or contribute to it.

The small boy more consciously, may "ape" an adult, especially one whom he admires or who for some reason makes an impression. The grown-up walk or facial expressions may be copied, this being a very deliberate imitative kind of activity. Often this is to be observed as an outward behavioral expression of *I want to be like him!* This is not invariably the basis, however. At times, for example, it can be a way of poking fun, or may constitute a form of hostile mockery.

Imitative conscious Identification differs mainly in the quality of voluntary control, assumption, and discard, as well as degree, from the Identification which takes place outside of conscious awareness. The latter may be thought of as a kind of progression in complexity, depth, and completeness of the process. Indeed, instances exist in which the conscious and effortful type of endeavor can lead to the actual adoption of traits. In sequence, these are continued sufficiently to become first semiautomatic, and thence what transpires is the gradual loss of awareness that the trait has been so adopted! In other words, what was deliberate adoption in the first place at times can gradually progress, so as to merge over a period of time into characterologic change. This is Characterologic Identification.

B. ADMIRATION LEADS TO ATTRIBUTE ADOPTION.—Admiration and envy of status or position can contribute to mannerism and attribute adoption through Identification. This took place in the following instance,

Case 74

Mannerism Identification

Carol M. was a short, stocky, and somewhat awkward 13-year-old, a schoolteacher's daughter, whose parents frequently were critical and reprimanded her for the appearance of a nasal twang in her speech. She defended herself against these criticisms by denying its presence, or that she couldn't help the way she talked.

Carol's best friend, whom she greatly admired and whose position she envied immensely. was her opposite. She was the tall, slender, poised, and considerably pampered daughter of a leading business man. Her home, clothing, and other possessions were smarter and more expensive than those of Carol. The friend sometimes jibed Carol about her contrasting physical appearance. She possessed a marked nasal speech component.

Carol, in an attempt to win her friend's admiration, but more importantly in this instance to be like her. had unconsciously "borrowed" from her the one thing which could be duplicated—the nasal twang. After the girls began attending different high schools, this adopted mannerism was gradually lost. This was a significant, albeit transient, instance of *Mannerism Identification*.

Variations in kind and in extent of the foregoing example are encountered frequently in social and professional experience. In marked instances, mannerisms and traits can be reproduced singly or in multiple fashion. Such *Mannerism Identifications* may be continued temporarily, semipermanently, or permanently. Identification can lead to the development of such close ties with another person that an individual may act thus in various ways as if he *were* the other. The other's characteristics become reproduced consciously or unconsciously.

The kind of development illustrated in *Case 74* can in more marked fashion sometimes contribute to the choice of and the development of symptoms of emotional illness (Symptom Identification, see later). Several instances warranted illustration, particularly in relation to the Conversion Reactions in *The Neuroses* (Chapter 12: pp. 639–721).

3. Characterologic Identification

A. INFLUENCING THE COURSE OF LIFE.—It is an expected progression that Identification can lead to further characterologic development and change. This we would term *Characterologic Identification,* to help emphasize this important function of the dynamism. Thus, it can play quite a major role in one's overall personality development. Included can be the origins of one's interests and ambitions, as well as the adoption of major character traits.

The following is the summary of an instance of this sequence of development. The entire direction and course of this young woman's life was profoundly influenced through her Characterologic Identification with a stable and admired college professor.

Case 75

Identification in Personality Development

(1) *Home Life Disrupted and Unstable.* Helen, a young married woman, had been an only child in a home disrupted by violent disagreements, excessive drinking, and divorce. Her mother, after divorcing the girl's father, soon married a second alcoholically-habituated man. From an early juncture, the second husband mostly ignored both Helen and her mother, whether in drunken aloofness, or in a state of depressed sobriety.

Helen's mother was an aggressive kind of pseudointellectual woman who associated with persons in the less disciplined or successful fringes of the art and theatrical worlds. Preoccupied with her own frustrations, and often motivated by the ideas of her Bohemian friends, her usual attitudes concerning her daughter resulted in her viewing her as a boring and encumbering obligation.

(2) *Suitable Object for Identification Lacking.* Rejected by her mother, ignored by her stepfather, and confused by the behavior of her mother's acquaintances, Helen found no one with whom she could identify in her shifting and unstable environment. By the time her mother and stepfather separated in turn, she was of college age.

In college, Helen hesitantly began an art curriculum, which she found had pleased her mother. Gradually she began to have an increasing interest in the abstract art forms emphasized by a certain professor in the art department, who also happened to be greatly admired by her mother.

(3) *Characterologic Identification Profoundly Influential.* The professor represented the first stable, well-established person with whom Helen had been able to maintain contact for any length of time. He took a considerable friendly interest in her, and she found herself admiring and being drawn to him. Quite consciously and deliberately she copied his artistic style, but unconsciously and more significantly she also came to adopt many of his social opinions, verbal expressions, vocal inflections, and physical gesticulations. Gradually she had identified herself with him quite thoroughly.

Helen longed for her mother's love, acceptance, and recognition, but she also felt extremely hostile toward her for her rejection, and in turn had rejected much about her. Instead of identifying herself with her mother's actual personality and life-role, Helen unconsciously identified herself with an admired person who was quite different from mother, but one whom her mother "happened" to also admire and respect.

There are a number of interesting elements here, among which it is clear that Helen still unconsciously sought to gain to her mother's acceptance. This helped to determine this particular man as her object for Characterologic Identification.

Through this young lady's Identification with her professor, her personality development was profoundly influenced, the direction of her interests and ambitions was more definitely established, and major character traits were unconsciously adopted. Hers was an instance of a major Characterologic Identification.

B. BASKING IN REFLECTED-GLORY CONCEPT. THE CELEBRITY-SEEKER.
—Many kinds of emotional needs may enhance or lead to the development
of Identification. Among these is the interesting one which we like to refer
to as *Basking in Reflected Glory*. This phenomenon can frequently be
observed among certain of the persons who choose to or "must" live in
the shadow of "important" people. Some of these persons justly warrant
the label of *Celebrity-Seeker*. When encountered, the "importance" of
course is a matter of the subjective evaluation and assessment by the
basker. Thus the glory as assessed can be strictly a matter of personal
significance; actual position and prominence; or some combination of
these.

Hereby people seek and may secure a certain measure of prestige
through association and Identification. Basking in Reflected-Glory at times
may be observed among those associated with leading political figures,
artists, orators, the President, a senator, premier, king or queen, successful
professionals in many fields, and indeed any personage regarded as successful, prominent, or renowned. The adoption of traits, mannerisms, or
behavioral features by those who seek or maintain such associations is
not uncommon. A variation of this phenomenon will be mentioned as we
proceed, following an illustration of our theme.

The Celebrity-Seeker and others who pursue reflected glory together
with their motivations, sometimes find illustration in dreams. This is
reflected in the following interesting dream descriptions from a therapy
session, with an analysis of their bases.

Case 76

Basking in Reflected Glory, in Dreams

". . . I often dream of contacts with famous people or public figures.
Last night there was a long sequence in which the President and one of
his Cabinet members were present. . . . I seem to be a celebrity-hunter
in my dreams. . . . It's a matter of basking in reflected glory; a reflected
kind of recognition. . . .

"I am never dynamic myself or influential; never a manager of men,
or able to control or direct a group . . . I've always thought I had a
good mind though, so my best future would be to associate myself with
leaders and prominent people. Then I would direct and aid in this control
sub rosa. This is a secondary means of control. It's a way to secure some
behind-the-scenes influence. . .

"I've always had the secret desire for power—if nothing else, for
self-preservation. The more power the better you are able to take care
of yourself This is better than just being a feather blown around. . . .

"Fame and fortune are always intriguing, even if for someone else.
I guess I turn to this in others since it's impossible for me alone. . . ."

4. Public-Figure Identification; Mass Identification

A. PROMINENCE INVITES IDENTIFICATION.—As indicated, Identifications may be made with people of prominence in almost any field. These
have evolved on an individual basis and comprise a type of reaction to
which we might invite more notice by attaching the label of *Public-Figure*

Identification. In relation to certain prominent people however, who possess a widespread public appeal and interest, the process can come to affect groups of people, or even a fair segment of the population. The result can be a large-scale mass reaction which might be regarded from one standpoint as a psychologic kind of epidemic.

While not confined to our culture, this wider scale Identification with public figures is perhaps more prominent as an occasional feature of the American scene. When this social phenomenon is in evidence, it may warrant our terming it *Mass Identification.* It is greatly facilitated of course in the U.S.A. by the modern mass communication media of radio, TV, and movies. Like a tide, it ebbs and flows.

Mass Identification is well illustrated through the influence of successful figures in the entertainment world. For a time they can exert a powerful influence on the tastes, dress, and behavior of their followers and beyond. Teen-age groups are particularly responsive to this type of Mass Identification, although such influences are by no means limited to them.

B. ENTERTAINMENT FIGURES AND MASS IDENTIFICATION.—Through entertainment media, at intervals the American public "adopts" and tends to identify with a forceful personality who for a time serves as the archetype for a particular mode of expression. There has been a long series of such actors, popular singers, and movie stars.

Mass Identifications have contributed thus to numerous fashion changes, fads, hair-do styles, and public attitudes. To a lesser extent and more subtly, the long-range development and evolution of the public's philosophy, morals, religion, and legal concepts have been similarly influenced by prominent figures and leaders.

5. Major Influence in Learning. Vocational Identification

It is hardly possible to overstress the many influences which the operation of Identification can have on learning. Admiration and liking for a teacher can lead in this way to an increased and sometimes paramount and lasting interest in his subject. Learning can be facilitated tremendously through such constructive kinds of Identification. As illustrated in *Case 74,* this can progress to the point of influencing or even determining definitively one's choice of life work. Conversely, a person can completely and tragically reject what might otherwise offer a promising and productive career avenue through his negative response to, and rejection of an instructor. Our *Rule of Impression Priority* [1] applies here.

Thus, Identification with a liked and admired person can enhance the chances for or even lead to, a major commitment in his particular field

---

[1] According to which, other things being equal, the earlier impression tends to be more significant and thereby to take a position of emotional priority. (See later, p. 152.)

of endeavor. This type of Vocational Identification can have an important bearing on one's "choice" of interests. It can have a tremendous effect on one's facility and level of learning, and indeed on the course of one's entire life. Through Identification, a pathway for learning can be greatly facilitated. Through its reverse, it can be handicapped or discarded.

6. *Seeking to Be Like an Admired or Envied Person*

The following instance illustrates what used to be a more common phenomenon in the taking over of the qualities of an intensely admired movie star. TV personalities can stimulate similar reactions.

Case 77

Identification with a Movie Star

A housewife became intensely interested in a certain glamorous movie star. A considerable portion of her time and energy was spent in gathering all kinds of information about the star's life. It became gradually apparent to her friends (but not to her!) that certain movements, gestures, and responses of the star had been "taken over" by their friend.

She had identified with her idealized actress-figure to such an extent that she had unwittingly adopted certain attributes, which she associated with her.

Approval, acceptance, and love are common basic goals sought through the operation of this dynamism. Identification differs from Projection (through which intolerable qualities of oneself are disowned through assigning or imputing them to another) in that, as a consequence, admired and desired elements of another's personality are reproduced within oneself. The motivation originates, as indicated earlier, in the wish to be like (and often *to be liked by*) the other person.

The sought-after result is greater approval from the self, and increased acceptance or love from the object. Others will approve, respect, or love more also. (In application of the Personal Yardstick Concept, must they not also like and admire the person and his attributes, even as does the identifier?) Self-approval may come to supplement, to equate, or to replace approval from others.

One might for example in this light, ponder the rationale underlying the ancient proverb, "When in Rome, do as the Romans do." Other motives have also been noted.

E.   ADDITIONAL SIGNIFICANT ASPECTS OF IDENTIFICATION

1. *Criminal Identification*

A. THE SPURIOUS CONFESSION.—The phenomenon of *Multiple Confessions* is sometimes encountered in murder. When there has been a particularly newsworthy and violent crime, which remains unsolved, a number of people may eventually come forward "to confess." This may well have been a crime they could not possibly have committed! An unconscious process of Identification frequently contributes to or is responsible for a particular variety of what we might term the *Spurious Confession*.

The foregoing Spurious Confession eventuates as a consequence of what could be described as *Criminal Identification*. Repressed aggression, hostility and violent impulses together with other possible unconscious factors, help account for such Identification with the criminal. This interesting phenomenon was illustrated in a famous West Coast murder case still remembered from some years ago.

Case 78

Criminal Identification and the Spurious Confession

Subsequent to the wide publicity afforded the notorious "Black Dahlia" murder case on the West Coast some years ago, a number of persons came forward and "confessed" the crime. Multiple Confessions were forthcoming for the murder. Thorough investigation proved the confessed "murderers" to be completely innocent.

In response to powerful unconscious needs, these unfortunate persons had so thoroughly identified with the actual but unknown murderer that they had come to believe that they had committed the crime. These are instances of *Criminal Identification*.

The lurid facts of the murder presumably had sufficiently corresponded with secret (unconscious) motivations or needs of those who confessed. Through the process of Identification, they had come to place themselves in the murderer's role. Occasional new *Spurious Confessions* in this case are still forthcoming, years after the crime.

The Criminal Identification which can contribute to producing the Spurious Confession, can also represent in part an unconscious seeking of punishment for disowned inner aggressiveness, or a neurotic seeking of attention and notoriety. Trained law enforcement officials are aware at least empirically of the possibility of such admissions of guilt being totally in error. As a consequence, they may question a suspicious confession today as thoroughly as a suspicious alibi! They have learned that both can be counterfeit and phony.

B. WITH THE WRONGDOER.—The phenomenon of Multiple Confession can lead sometimes to rather bizarre circumstances, as illustrated further in *Mental Mechanisms*, pp. 118–168. However, these instances often may be regarded as more an extension or an exaggeration of occasions which are not too different nor too uncommon in the average human experience.

The following excerpt from a therapy session illustrates the not infrequent tendency to identify with the wrongdoer in far milder circumstances, and some of the bases for this reaction.

Case 79

Identifying with the Wrongdoer

". . . In a fair number of instances I have subconsciously identified myself with another person who would not be acceptable or attractive

for some reason or other. . . . The first instance of this which I can
remember was one time in school when the entire class was called together to find out who had stolen a dime off the teacher's desk. I knew
that I was not the thief, but I became terribly anxious and uncomfortable. . . . In this situation I was identifying myself with the child who
had taken the dime. . . .

"At Christmastime this year my wife and I did a feature article for
the newspaper on shoplifting. I began to feel mighty uncomfortable on
going into a store, and whenever I thought of the possibility of any of
the shopkeepers thinking that I might be a shoplifter. In this case I was
identifying myself with that sort of an unacceptable person. . . . Lots of
people would like to swipe things from stores. A whole group of children
used to swipe candy bars from the drugstore when we were 14 or 15. I
wanted to, but was always too frightened to. I was afraid of being
caught. . . ."

In this instance the Identification and resulting discomfort conforms
to the rejected secret wishes and doubtless his self-estimation. Further, it
allows a measure of gratification of the disowned (similar) interests.
Finally, it punishes him, through the ensuing anxious feelings, guilt, and
uneasiness. This is a superficial instance of identifying with the wrongdoer,
contributed to by an overzealous superego.

2. Bad Identifications

A. SOCIALLY NONCONSTRUCTIVE. THE BAD INFLUENCE.—Most instances of Identification operating together with learning processes are
constructive, that is, they lead to individual progress in a socially approved
fashion. However, this is not always so. It would be a mistake to assume
that all Identifications are "good" in this sense. Many are bad ones or
nonuseful. The socially nonconstructive Identification and its consequences
may be termed for our purposes the *Bad Identification*.

Such nonconstructive or Bad Identifications are made in a great many
ways. These may be superficial and of little importance. They may be
major, lead to personally and/or socially destructive consequences, and
can be a symptom of, or contribute in a major way to emotional illness.
Indentifications are sometimes made with an aggressor, a bad leader,
or a criminal, as described and as illustrated elsewhere.

Bad Identifications also can influence learning in a converse and
negative way, as noted. The person sometimes spoken of as a "bad influence" for children or teen-agers may become thus because of a propensity of the child or teen-ager to identify with him and thence "take after
him." Not unrelated to our present study is the observation that recent
state campaigns have been urging parents to "set a good example" in their
driving practices, for their children to follow.

B. PARENTAL IDENTIFICATION. ADOPTION OF WHAT ONE DISAPPROVES.
—The unconscious adoption of parental traits, attitudes, emotional responses, or behavior through Identification is by no means confined to "good"
ones, those which are approved of by the identifying child. *Some of the*

"bad," personally disapproved ones are also almost inevitably taken over, and from each parent. However, because of one's personal disapproval of them, these latter consequences of *Parental Identification* are likely to be even more inaccessible to conscious awareness and recognition.

This is a further indication of the unconscious operation and automaticity of the process of Parental Identification. Hereby one adopts what he consciously disapproves of, and would reject. He is usually also defensively loath or unable to admit and to recognize its existence should someone seek to point it out. Most therapists are thoroughly familiar with this in the patient-colleague who learns for the first time that he possesses attributes he thoroughly dislikes in his parents and has heretofore not at all recognized in himself.

3. In Advertising: The Secondary Appeal

A. THE PRIMARY APPEAL: TOWARD THE DIRECT SATISFACTION OF A NEED.—Advertising men in the last several decades have well learned the value of cultivating what the author likes to call the *Secondary Appeal*.

Wanting to purchase a drink to satisfy thirst, food to satisfy hunger, or a tool to use for a specific purpose, is the basic reason for buying a given product. This may be referred to accordingly as the *Primary Appeal* of the given item or service, and of the advertising promoting it. The Primary Appeal is concerned with selling a product to a prospective user in ways related to the direct satisfaction of the basic or primary need.

B. THE SECONDARY APPEAL.—Seeking to stimulate sales by encouraging less direct and tangential interests or needs comprises what has been called the *Secondary Appeal* of the product and of the advertising efforts in its behalf. Many sales result from this type of advertising. In this endeavor, Identification or the desire for Identification is promoted. This of course is with admired people or persons of envied status of one kind or another who use, or who by implication are users of the product or service.

By buying or owning the product himself, the user hopes to secure, or is urged to thus seek Identification with the publicized, admired, or prominent user. He may thus come to feel a bit like him. Masculinity, femininity, sex appeal, athletic prowess, social status, and gracious living, among others, are held up for admiration and emulation in this Secondary Appeal for Identification through advertising.

4. Identification in Military Life; Military-Unit Identification (MUI)

A. NECESSARY FOR MORALE.—Many forms of Identification are to be encountered in military service. Some of these serve vital personal needs. Some have a very important function for the service. Identification with one's outfit is widely recognized as necessary for morale. For example, one may have heard the proud statement, "I belong to the best damn outfit in the whole army!" This is *Military-Unit Identification.*

Identification with the military unit promotes individual security, loyalty, a useful feeling of belonging, and a sense of personal value and worth. As a consequence, working together for the mutual good and success of the unit is enhanced, as are mutual confidence, comradeship, and pride. The individual benefits; the unit benefits; the service benefits; and the campaign and country benefit.

B. MILITARY-UNIT IDENTIFICATION.—In the following instance, which has a light overtone, a young airman-to-be began his *Military-Unit Identification* a little prematurely. This process can assist in one's military adjustment. For this man it was on a somewhat superficial level.

While largely, and especially at first, his MUI was a matter of conscious effort, part of it was unwitting and was consciously denied. Its vehemence at times also was surprising, and reflected its heightened emotional significance and a measure of unconscious operation.

Case 80

Military-Unit Identification Begins Before the Fact

A 22-year-old college graduate was called into the Air Force through the AFROTC. He had been of a retiring nature, shying away from most social engagements, while maintaining an excellent academic standing. At the time of activation he hoped to enter graduate school, a plan which had to be deferred pending completion of his tour of duty.

From before the receipt of notice, in a newly acquired aggressive style, he began to use the slang and profanity he anticipated would be common to his new associates. On beginning duty, he was outdoing them, both in extent and occasion.

"We" came to be used in reference to anything done by the Air Force; even tremendous world-wide accomplishments were "ours," or accomplished by "us"! He had identified rather thoroughly, with his new surroundings and with the Air Force.

The defensive intent of this operation lies in gaining strength through identifying with this large, established, and powerful group. Hereby one combats anxiety and insecurity. The requirement to defer graduate work became less disturbing. His identity and role became more certain and established. By "fitting in" as he viewed it, he also conformed to the military pattern and was better accepted and assimilated. His personal adjustment internally and to the new situation was facilitated.

5. Group Identification

A. GREGARIOUSNESS AND BELONGING TO ORGANIZATIONS.—Many people seek Identification with a group. People join churches, lodges, fraternities, civic groups, social and professional organizations, unions, alumni groups, classes, patriotic groups, political bodies, and many others. There usually are several contributing factors. These include man's gregariousness and, possibly on a deeper level, the so-called herd instinct. There are also social reasons; finding friends, status seeking, mates, or promoting a worthy cause.

Affiliation with a group, however, can also be an important security operation which is often pursued unwittingly. Indeed, all kinds of plausible explanations and Rationalizations (Chapter 17) may be advanced to obscure from oneself, as well as others, the real underlying defensive bases for one's Group Identifications. One gains allies, supporters, and friends. He is less alone. When the ego defense is operative as described we can refer to it as *Group Identification*.

B. GROUP IDENTIFICATION: SEEKING ACCEPTANCE, SECURITY, SUPPORT, STRENGTH, AND BELONGING.—"In union there is strength" is a principle which applies to the individual and to his joining an organization, as well as to states and to the nation. Thus, Group Identification can offer a person in varying degree a feeling of strength.

Perhaps a satisfying sense of common endeavor may be conveyed, as well as brotherhood, acceptance, and belonging. One identifies thus with something bigger and stronger, some of which strength, support, and supply of dependency needs emotionally accrues to him.

6. Vicarious Satisfactions

A. SEEKING SATISFACTIONS NOT OTHERWISE AVAILABLE.—To some extent, everyone secures satisfactions vicariously. These can vary from a superficial Identification and experiencing with, to a point where one becomes literally immersed in a vicarious role. In the most extreme cases of the latter, a parent, for example, can come to live *through* a child. This can progress into an interpersonal situation which is markedly psychopathological.

Much of our foregoing discussion bears on this subject. Such satisfactions and the unconscious seeking of them are an important part of the endogain (the unconscious primary gain); the very basis, or *raison d'étre* of the major ego defense of Identification.

The needs and gratifications which are sought in vicarious fashion may be personally forbidden and disapproved. As a consequence, they may only be possible in these guises. They may also be unobtainable otherwise. It is hardly surprising that one's conscious awareness of this very interesting kind of substitutive experiencing and living may be most limited. *Vicarious Identification,* as this complex operation can be termed, can subserve vital intrapsychic needs, constituting an important internal defensive operation.

B. SUBSTITUTIVE GRATIFICATION.—The following instance illustrates an interesting type of important *Substitutive Gratification* which can be sought through the operation of Vicarious Identification. As in this case, this endeavor and its consequences, can have a major influence on one's interests and activities, and in one's entire life.

Case 81

Substitutive Gratification Through Vicarious Identification

A 52-year-old bachelor had developed an increasing interest in the theater as the years progressed. Attempts at courtship had been unsuccessful and he had never found a wife. Although he professed great satisfaction with the advantages and freedom of remaining single, there were strong secret desires for married life and family. His interest in the theater was partially rationalized on a conscious level, as being simply on the basis of his interest in the art per se.

The plays, however, which he never missed and which he in fact, would see repeatedly, were ones in which a happy married life was portrayed. Through a *Vicarious Identification* with the head of the family in the theatrical production, he secured considerable Substitutive Gratification and satisfaction.

Later he joined an amateur theatrical group in which he was never happier than when allowed occasionally to play the bit part of a family head. He had had very little conscious awareness of what motivated him, and much of the underlying need for the gratification which he secured had long been unconscious.

F.   THE "PERSONAL YARDSTICK" IN NEW RELATIONSHIPS

1. Identification of a New Acquaintance with Someone from Earlier Experience

A. CONDITIONING EFFECT OF EARLIER RELATIONSHIPS.—The concept of relationship conditioning is of major importance in the science of interpersonal relations. Early relationships often have an important conditioning effect in their antecedent position for subsequent ones. There is a strong tendency to evaluate and to "see" a new person, in the light of the relationship with an earlier (and usually important) person from the past.

Generally, some similarities are present which stimulate such a subjective Identification between the new person and the antecedent one. These can be relatively gross ones, such as age, size, build, or coloring. They also can be personality and characterologic ones, sometimes of a quite minor or subtle nature, yet still helping to trigger such a reaction. The "repeated relationship" or "recapitulation" can often be anticipated. Experienced in various degrees, it is often enough a caricature or distorted. One can be led unwittingly into all kinds of false expectations, judgments, and evaluations of the new person and relationship.

B. THE RULE OF IMPRESSION PRIORITY.—The foregoing views are in accord with the *Rule of Impression Priority* (see also p. 145). According to this concept, with other factors being equal, the earlier impression tends to take a position of emotional priority. This rule is also applicable to one's interpersonal relationships.

The earlier relationship has an important prior position, emotionally. A pattern for the establishment of new relationships tends to be set up.

C. APPLYING THE "PERSONAL YARDSTICK" TO NEW ACQUAINTANCES.—The conscious and deliberate, as well as the automatic and unwitting use of one's own past experiences and reactions (as well as one's own personal reactions and emotional patterns of response) as a measuring device for anticipating and judging future ones of other people, and their emotional responses, is most understandable. This is the important *Concept of the Personal Yardstick*. Although obviously subject to all kinds of inaccuracies, which however are not readily accessible to the awareness of the person concerned, the Personal Yardstick is a necessary and vital measuring device. We all use it. It is, especially early in life, the only one available. We are accordingly hardly surprised to find it operating rather automatically in the realm of one's interpersonal relations.

Identifications in relationships are by no means always present in conscious awareness. They can exist completely outside of awareness, to account for all kinds of otherwise "unaccountable" emotional responses toward other people. They can help to determine initial reactions, love and affection, prejudices, (degree of) acceptance or rejection, and so on, toward and for another person.

D. GREAT PERSONAL VALUE IN THEIR ELUCIDATION.—A patient talked interminably about his harsh, distant, and unapproachable boss. Eventually, after much hard work, he came to recognize (and to appreciate the important consequences to him in living) that: (1) he had made an unconscious Identification of his boss with his father; and (2) he had in error "assigned" to the boss, or magnified several times certain of the boss' (existing) traits, which in actuality were those of his father.

These kinds of hidden, self-defeating, and often destructive effects are far more common in human relations than most people imagine. One can hardly overstate their importance. There is indeed great personal value to an individual in learning about their unwitting operation within himself.

2. Major Effects on Interpersonal Relations. Interpersonal Identification

A. WHY IS "PERSONAL YARDSTICK" APPLIED? WHAT ADVANTAGES SOUGHT?—There are various bases for one's utilization of his Personal Yardstick in making assessments of relationships and people's emotional reactions. These can apply in many situations (see Table 6), as well as those in which Interpersonal Identification is prominent. This is a vital, albeit often inaccurate, personal standard for making emotional estimations.

Table 6

Bases for Application of the Personal Yardstick

Bases for the operation of the Personal Yardstick in conjunction with Identifications of new persons with people (especially significant ones) from the past, can be outlined in several ways. These include:

1. The defensively vital need for making assessments of people and hav-

ing some idea about what to expect from them in any given circumstance.
2. A matter of psychologic convenience and familiarity.
3. The utilization of experience.
4. The conditioning effect of the earlier relationship.
5. An instance of a type of "repetition compulsion."
6. The following of "habits" or patterns in one's interpersonal relations.
7. Employment of the only standard available for use in making comparisons, judgments, and in anticipating possible responses and reactions.

In accord with the bases for application of the Personal Yardstick as outlined in the foregoing table, earlier relationships set up a representation which is more easily matched in later experiences; a shadow which lingers and which is more readily filled; more easily given substance anew at a later date. Relationships also follow our rule about the priority ordinarily assigned to a first or earlier impression, or relationship (i.e., the *Impression Priority Rule*).

In summary, the Identification of a new acquaintance with a person from one's earlier experience is a frequent phenomenon in interpersonal relationships. This is an example of additional important types of Identification which do not clearly fit into our earlier definition. Through this major type of *Interpersonal Identification,* a person may be "perceived" and reacted to almost as though he were the other person known earlier. This may be stimulated or reenforced at times through (major or minor) items of physical or of characterologic similarity. As a consequence of this important type of Identification, the new person may be seen, judged, reacted to, and dealt with (unwittingly), as was the earlier one. Similar views, attitudes, judgments, reactions, and behavior may be anticipated.

The wide room for inaccuracy, distortion, and subsequent disappointment or hurt through this operation of the ego defense is apparent. Interpersonal Identifications can have widespread repercussions personally and socially. These may be constructive, destructive, or both.

B. FOSTERING RECAPITULATION, WITH INHERENT POTENTIAL FOR MAJOR AND MINOR INACCURACIES AND DISTORTIONS.—The degree of utilization of Interpersonal Identification has considerable individual variation. However, *this tendency to set up inaccurate representations of new relationships, on the basis of prior experience with earlier figures is much more widely prevalent than is commonly recognized.* It accounts for many, many problems in interpersonal relationships. It also leads to benefits. Later relationships tend to recapitulate the earlier one in the subjective experience and expectations of the person who has unconsciously made the Identification.

The clarification of this Interpersonal operation of the dynamism of Identification together with its very important implications and consequences, is an important part of the therapeutic learning process is every analysis and course of intensive psychotherapy.

G. IDENTIFICATION ENCOURAGED BY PARENTS

1. Holding Forth Example or Standard

We have discussed briefly the important position which is often occupied by Identification in learning and education. This is certainly not confined to formal education by any means. One finds it likely to operate in many kinds of learning experiences.

Parents sometimes consciously promote efforts to identify on the part of their children. A worthy person or a successful one, as they assess him, may be deliberately held out as an example which the child is encouraged or admonished to emulate.

Sometimes such an attempt is made by an adult to encourage self-discipline or to influence behavior, as in the following interesting and poignant incident. Herein one again sees a stimulation of an effort to please and the desire for approval. In this instance, the need to please was directed primarily toward the physician as a parent-surrogate, but also of course, toward the father as well.

Case 82

A Standard is Held Up

An 11-year-old boy injured his wrist while swinging out and jumping from a rope high on the bank of a stream where he liked to swim. X-rays revealed a dislocation of the navicular bone.

His family physician said to the boy, in tears with pain, "Clench your teeth like a good soldier. This will only hurt for a minute or so." The boy gritted his teeth, stopped crying, and did not make a sound while the physician manipulated his wrist to reduce the dislocation.

As he was leaving the office, his arm in a cast, the doctor overheard the boy ask his father, "Was I a good soldier, Daddy?"

2. Pressure and Requirement

Children are not always free to pursue their own choice as to Identification. Various kinds of pressure can be exerted by a determined parent. The following quote from a woman in therapy indicates some of the possible strength and pervasive influence of parental pressures.

Case 83

Parental Identification Succeeded by Interpersonal Identification

" ... It occurs to me that I have been thinking of the way I identify myself with other people in a positive sense. I feel that I am beginning to understand why, for one reason or another, I have often in manners of speech, gestures, dress, and other ways, developed subconsciously a true imitation of women whom I feel are accepted, or are popular. ... They are attractive and charming in some way that I want to be. ... Without thinking, I, after a short while, sometimes may pick up an idiosyncrasy of speech, or an attitude which I subconsciously feel that if I possessed it, would make me acceptable, popular, and attractive. ...

"I'm nobody by myself.... I had to do this in order to be somebody, to be a real person, an individual. I was never allowed to be a
person by my parents.... I was always expected to be and tried desperately to be someone I wasn't.... The easiest way to get along was to
be exactly as Mommy wished, identifying with her standards, and so
on.... As long as I was just like Mommy, I was all right!...."

H.   IDENTIFICATION INFLUENCES MANIFESTATIONS IN NEUROTIC AND PSYCHOTIC REACTIONS. SYMPTOM IDENTIFICATION

Upon occasion, Identification can play a prominent role in the
"choice" of symptoms of hygeiaphrontis (hypochondriasis). This applies
to patients with all types of neurotic reactions. Earlier we discussed
Identification in symptom "choice" (p. 46). This was termed accordingly
Symptom Identification and comprises an important concept.

Identification can also exert an influence in many of the anxiety,
conversion, dissociation, and phobic manifestations. This also applies in
the more transient hygeiaphrontic concerns, such as the frequent and
troubling but interesting ones, developed by medical students and young
physicians through their early contacts with many varieties of pathology
and with patients suffering from various illnesses.

Symptom Identification can also sometimes be important during the
onset of an acute episode of Overconcern-With-Health. Certain of these
relationships between Hygeiaphrontis and Identification are illustrated in
the following case, in which the neurotic reaction followed a hygeiaphrontic
pattern.

Case 84

Symptom Identification in Hygeiaphrontis (Overconcern-with-Health)

A 32-year-old housewife began to have increasingly severe conflicts
over her role as a wife and mother. Her illness took the form of a
neurosis in which the most prominent feature was the rather rapid onset
of increasingly troubling and preoccupying hygeiaphrontic concerns. In
studying the onset of her symptoms, the part in this unfortunate sequence
of events played by the ego defense of Identification gradually unfolded.

Several years earlier she had begun to read the obituary columns,
with an increasing interest and concern about the deaths of persons her
own age and younger. The causes of death were significant for her, and
partly through Identification, she began to look for, to worry about, and
finally to experience various uncomfortable and at times painful sensations. For her, these equated the symptoms which she believed to characterize certain of these illnesses.

The process of *Symptom Identification* as with the foregoing description, had soon extended so as to include her friends who became ill, and
certain of their manifestations. Gradually she came to worry almost
constantly over illness, symptoms, and bodily function. In this fashion,
she "found" important sources of worry and concern. Among other
unconscious purposes, they served as a diversionary focus of attention
and interest, away from her unconscious, more basic, and intolerably
painful emotional conflicts. On a number of occasions, through Symptom
Identification, she developed subjectively almost identical emotional
symptoms to the physical ones of friends or family members.

Case 85

Identification in Psychotic Reactions

A psychotic patient developed a delusional system in which he believed himself to be Christ. The process of Identification was complete and quite beyond reality.

This patient accordingly sought to live and to act the part. This he did in many ways and most of the time, although some almost characteristic inconsistencies were also present in his attitudes, thought content, and behavior.

As in the foregoing case, there are likely to be found, or to have been present, "Napoleons," "Julius Caesars," and "Jesus Christs," among the psychotic patients of many large mental hospitals. The completeness of these instances of unconscious *Psychotic Identification* vary greatly. At times, there are also evident (to others) as noted, glaring inconsistencies and incongruities in his behavior or role, of which the patient is seemingly unaware. The presence of some of these is almost characteristically present in such psychotic delusional systems.

I.   UNDERDOG IDENTIFICATION

Many individuals find themselves quite upset when they observe a person being unfairly picked on, maligned, abused, badly treated, or physically beaten. This is likely to be especially marked when the person is in a helpless position. Thus, some people tend to be fervent sympathizers with, or ardent defenders of the underdog. Indeed, the American people are somewhat noted for these sympathetic tendencies, a feature of the national character which could have some interesting historical roots in the events of the late eighteenth century.

The ego defense of Identification plays a prominent role in many of these reactions. Often enough the defender is unconsciously identifying with the victim or underdog, and thus in unwitting fashion is really defending himself. This can help account for the strength of the feelings and the vigor of the defense.

Identification in a number of variations of this theme is not infrequently encountered in psychotherapy. The following instance is a condensed illustration of one form of Underdog Identification.

Case 86

Underdog Identification

In January 1956, a patient entered her therapeutic session incensed over the Russian double cross of the Hungarians, after promises of withdrawal and self-determination had been made to them. They had been oppressed, betrayed, and many killed. She spent the session in a powerful emotional attack upon the Russians, concurrently expressing fervent sympathy for the abused, deceived, and slaughtered Hungarians.

It was suggested that although her reaction seemed to have some justification, its intensity appeared to indicate deeper feeling and personal significance. She gradually became able to see the Identification she had made with the Hungarians.

The intensity of her feeling ultimately proved to be due to her own intense but more hidden feelings of resentment toward her parents for their partly real, and partly fancied betrayal and ill-treatment of her, through a long series of incidents in earlier years.

J. SUMMARY

Identification is a major ego defense or mental mechanism through which an individual comes to take over feelings, traits, attitudes, or various aspects of another person. It often contributes to or is motivated by, the unconscious desire for an *emotional alliance.* Imitation is a conscious form of Identification, and bears somewhat the same relative relation to it as does fear to anxiety, and grief to depression. Identification may be made with "good" or "bad" objects, but is more likely to be motivated by love and respect or the desire and need for them. *Central Identification* is an important factor in enjoying books, movies, and TV. *Actor Identification* was noted, together with its role in actor career success.

Forms of *Projective Identification* include: (1) *Sympathy,* through which one feels sorrow, pity, or compassion for another's loss, hurt, grief, or misfortune; and (2) *Empathy,* in which one has a keen objective awareness of another's emotional feelings and can understand them and adequately appreciate their extent, as well as (3) rapport and (4) sympatico. The *Affective* (form of) *Identification* is compathy, which represents a progression, and is stronger, closer, and deeper. *Compathy* is the close sharing of emotional feelings *with* another person. Through it one subjectively experiences in kind and often in extent the emotions of another person. *Individual Compathy* and *Group Compathy* were discussed. The concept of *Symptom Compathy* was offered. *Emotional Identification* is an alternate term for both compathy and Affective Identification. *Compathic Identification* is a strong reaction, at times operating in conjunction with Central Identification.

Through Identification one can place oneself "in the other person's shoes." It is vital to personality development and has important personal and social values. Its extent can vary widely, from the temporary taking over of a small mannerism (*Mannerism Identification*) to the assumption of much of the role of another. Through this mechanism a child may identify with a parent, or a parent with a child. *Predecessor Identification* was delineated. *Characterologic Identification* can influence the entire course of one's life. An envied person, such as a more socially successful figure, may be chosen as the object for Identification.

The *Concept of Basking in Reflected Glory* was outlined. This can take place in conjunction with this dynamism, in the shadow of "important" people. Some of these baskers are *Celebrity Seekers.* This concept was also illustrated in dreams.

The *Characterologic Identification* is that which leads to personality development and change. *Public-Figure Identification* received comment. Identification can play a very important role in the development of character traits. *Mass Identification* is to be observed when a large group identifies in varying degrees with a nationally prominent figure. Identification can play a major role in educational and learning processes. As in *Vocational Identification* it can influence one's life work and goals. *Criminal Identification* can lead to and help explain the phenomenon of *Multiple Confessions* in crimes. Many of these are examples of the *Spurious Confession*. *Bad Identifications* were noted as including all instances in which the results are socially nonconstructive. The so-called "bad influence" received comment, as did identifying with a "wrongdoer." Both desired (admired) and disapproved attributes and traits are likely to be unwittingly "taken over" from parents in *Parental Identification*.

In advertising, the *Primary Appeal* is toward the basic need for the article itself. The *Secondary Appeal* refers to the efforts on the part of the advertisers to stimulate a desire for Identification with the people who actually, or by implication, use the product.

In combination with other ego defenses, Identification has many important uses. In the Inversion of hostility in Depression, Introjection followed by Identification with the introjected person results in outward self-depreciation and punishment.

Identification in military life was noted, as was MUI—*Military-Unit Identification*. *Vicarious Identifications* lead to *Substitutive Gratifications*, take place rather widely, and can serve useful and constructive purposes, as well as other less personally or socially valuable ones.

The *Concept of the Personal Yardstick* in basing one's assessment, expectations, and reactions to a new person upon one's experience in a past relationship is important. The margin for inaccuracy, distortion, and subsequent disappointment or hurt is quite large. Some bases for operation of the Personal Yardstick were tabulated (*Table 6*). *Interpersonal Identifications* are numerous and can be quite significant.

Identifications in childhood are very important. These are particularly made with significant adults—especially with parents and parent-surrogates. "Like father—like son" has considerable validity. *Emotional contagion* is the compathic communication of attitudes and emotional feelings. The earliest Identifications form important precedents for later ones and for later relationships, in accordance with the *Rule of Impression Priority*. For various reasons, childhood Identifications may be deliberately encouraged by parents. In addition to the many purposes in seeking acceptance, one may also identify with an aggressor, as a figurative means of pulling his teeth. This is another defensive operation. It helps provide a basis for certain children's games.

Instances of Identification with the harsh enemy captors are reported from prisoner-of-war camps. Identification influences the occurrence and form of many neurotic and psychotic manifestations. *Parental Identification* is a universal process in which both approved and disapproved parental aspects are adopted.

Misidentifications refer to the adoption of conflicting aspects or traits, which lead to an uncertainty about one's role or identity. Depersonalization may follow and the background may be laid for later vulnerability to Dissociative Reactions. Identification with parents whose attitudes mirror their Overconcern-With-Health may lead to similar problems for the child. The Conversion Personality has a considerable capacity for imitativeness and for Identification with others. This can help determine the directions and progress of his personality development. *Symptom Identification* can play a major role in determining the location and type of symptoms in neuroses and in psychoses. *Psychotic Identification* can aid in the delusional assumption of a new identity and role.

The therapist needs to be aware both of long-established and of new and developing Identifications, and to help his patient secure their clarification and understanding. Interesting Identifications are to be noted with the underdog, as illustrated in *Case 86. Compathic Identification* was noted. *Group Identification* seeks the acceptance, security, support, and strength through belonging to (and identifying with) an organization or group. For some and perhaps especially for many Americans, *Underdog Identification* is not infrequent.

For those sufficiently interested, some added data and instances may be found in the corresponding Chapter 6, entitled *Identification,* pp. 118–168, in *Mental Mechanisms.**

K.   CROSS-REFERENCES TO *THE NEUROSES* **

Identification
In Concept of Faulty I.; pp. 559, 560, 563, 681–2, 764, 769–70.
Identification
In Nature of Anxiety (Chapter 1)
   in childhood development (in *First Tenet of Parental Role*); p. 23.
   in *emotional contagion* of anxiety; p. 32
      in military life; p. 37.
   source of anxiety (Table 2); p. 30.
In Illusory Gains (Chapter 2); in *endogain* of *King David Reaction;* p. 76.
In Anxiety Reactions (Chapter 3); in *emotional contagion* of anxiety; p. 85.
In Character Reactions (Chapter 5)
   in character defenses of *Conversion Personality* (Table 19); p. 260.
   in determination of character structure; p. 288.
In Obsessive-Compulsive Reactions (Chapter 6); of obsessive symptoms, to repressed
   data; p. 345.

---

* From Laughlin, H. P. *Mental Mechanisms.* London, Butterworth & Co., Ltd., 1963.
    ** From Laughlin, H. P. *The Neuroses.* London, Butterworth & Co., Ltd., 1967.

In Hygeiaphrontic Reactions Chapter 8)
 of ego, with suffering good objects (Klein); p. 491.
 of physician with patient; p. 496.
 with mother, in somatic and physiologic concerns (Case 90); p. 455.
 with parents, in *Interpersonal Perpetuation Cycle Concept;* pp. 464, 479.
 in patterns of reaction; p. 477.
In Phobic Reactions (Chapter 10); in *Faulty Identification Concept;* p. 560.
  Case 115; p. 563.
In Conversion Reactions (Chapter 12)
 capacity for I., in mechanisms of Conversion Reaction; pp. 646, 656, 692, 716.
   Hostile Identification in; pp. 701, 716.
   The Great Imitator; p. 652.
 in bases of Conversion pain (Fenichel); p. 703.
 in conversion epidemics; p. 703.
 in *Faulty Identification Concept* (Case 143); pp. 681–2.
 in *predisposing factors of Conversion diathesis;* p. 695.
 in symptom choice (Table 37); p. 698.
 in *Unconscious Simulation Concept;* p. 662.
 of pain with phantom limb; p. 706.
 with *emotional prototype* (Case 145); p. 694.
 with envied friend (Case 146); p. 696.
 with stepfather, in onset of symptoms (Case 144); p. 684.
In Dissociative Reactions (Chapter 13)
 in *Identification Fugue* (Table 42); p. 796.
 in sources of depersonalization (*Unwanted Identifications Concept*); pp. 769–70.
   Table 40 (in *Faulty Identification Concept*); p. 764.
 with World War I hero (Case 173); p. 803.
 with victim, in inducing confessions (Table 43); p. 818.
In Neuroses-Following-Trauma (Chapter 14); with mother (Case 182); p. 872.
In Military Reactions (Chapter 15)
 absence of capacity for, in traits of processor (*Prisoner Processing*); p. 938.
 Unit I., in concealment of emotional problems; p. 926.

L.   REVIEW QUESTIONS

Sample self-check questions on Chapter 9 and Identification for the student, psychiatric resident, and board candidate.

 1. *Identification* is described as an *emotional alliance*. Explain.
 2. Illustrate the following types of Identification:
     A. *Central Identification.*
     B. *Actor Identification.*
     C. Forms of *Projective Identification.*
     D. *Predecessor Identification.*
     E. *Public-Figure Identification.*
     F. *Affective Identification.*
     G. *Symptom Compathy.*
     H. *Basking in Reflected-Glory.*
     I. *Mass Identification.*
     J. *Vocational Identification.*
     K. *Vicarious Identification.*
     L. *Interpersonal Identification.*
 3. Define, and if possible, find an instance to illustrate *compathy.* What is *Group Compathy?, Compathic Identification?*

4. *Mannerism Identification* and *Trait Identification* are described as steps toward or merging into *Characterologic Identification*. How would you support this concept?
5. What do the following terms and concepts convey?
   A. *Misidentification.*
   B. Empathy.
   C. Rapport.
   D. *Emotional Identification.*
   E. *Individual Compathy.*
   F. *Impression-Priority Rule.*
   G. *Personal Yardstick Concept.*
   H. *Bad Identifications.*
   I. *Parental Identification.*
   J. *Vicarious Satisfactions* through a child.
   K. *Underdog Identification* in the American scene.
   L. *Celebrity Seekers.*
6. How does the concept of *Criminal Identification* aid in understanding the *Spurious Confession* and the phenomenon of *Multiple Confessions?*
7. Why is the *Secondary Appeal* sometimes effective in promoting commercial ventures? Distinguish from *Primary Appeal.*
8. A. What are the implications for service morale in *Military-Unit Identification* or MUI?
   B. How can *Group Identification enhance one's level of security?*
   C. Give an example of *Psychotic Identification.*
   D. Outline the significance in child development of *Parental Identification;* of parentally promoted Identifications.
9. Why is the *Personal Yardstick* inaccurate? Why universally employed? Cite bases for its application, and instances from personal or clinical experience.
10. What is the significance of *Symptom Identification* in emotional illness? *Misidentifications?*

CHAPTER 10

INCORPORATION

...Psychic Ingestion and Assimilation

A. SYMBOLIC ASSIMILATION

    1. Definition. 2. Literal Incorporation, in Primitive Societies. 3. Physical and Literal Ingestion Succeeded by the Psychic, Figurative, and Symbolic: a. Relation to and Distinction from Identification; b. Implied Recognition in Figures of Speech.

B. RELATION TO PERSONALITY DEVELOPMENT

    1. Orally Incorporative Attitudes: a. Normal for Infant; b. Inadvertent Direct Expression. 2. Nutrition Plus ... 3. Superego Development. 4. Parental Incorporation.

C. ADDITIONAL ASPECTS

    1. Psychotic Incorporation. 2. The Engulfment Concept. Incorporation in Interpersonal Relations: a. Parental Engulfment and Marital Engulfment; b. Defensive Operation. 3. Incorporation of Knowledge; Incorporative Learning.

D. SUMMARY

E. REFERENCES (FROM *The Neuroses*)

F. REVIEW QUESTIONS

A. SYMBOLIC ASSIMILATION

1. Definition

Incorporation is *a primitive ego defense or mental mechanism operating outside of and beyond conscious awareness through which another person, certain of his attributes, aspects, reactions, attitudes or standards; or various possibly significant nonmaterial elements from one's life situation are in symbolic fashion taken within oneself, to be symbolically ingested and assimilated.* Incorporation is a basic, fundamental, less developed, magical, Lower Order mechanism. As such it is likely to be a more massive process in which something is "swallowed whole." Loved *or* hated objects or portions of them can be incorporated.

Incorporation as a dynamism is associated principally with the primary and massive kinds of emotional processes, especially those from the oral stage of personality development. The prototype of Incorporation is

to be found in certain of the infantile fantasies (Chapter 7) dating back
into the oral stage of psychosexual development, (p. 329). Orality may
be thus regarded as the earliest primordial type of interpersonal relatedness.

The baby suckles for nourishment and for satisfaction. He needs to
and has to. It is hardly surprising that the roots of powerful emotional
reactions are laid down in this era. Suckling is the literal incorporation of
food from mother. In the operation of the ego defense, this process evolves
psychologically, as as to eventually become figurative and symbolic in
nature.

Incorporation is very similar to but not entirely identical with both
Introjection and with Internalization. These three dynamisms are intimately related, their usage has varied, their meanings have at times over-
lapped, and the distinction between them is often rather academic. This
makes the delineation of each of them substantially more difficult, the
task of attempting to write a definitive statement problematic indeed, and
ensures that our attempts in this direction will occasion some disagreement.

Incorporation is a more "devouring" type of intrapsychic process, in
which this ego defense may be regarded as equating a psychic swallowing
and assimilation. Fairbairn noted that the inherent aim of the oral impulse
is Incorporation. This Incorporation must evolve of course, originally as
a more physical incorporation. However, the emotional mood accompanying these incorporative strivings has itself an incorporative coloring. Hence,
when a fixation in the early oral phase of personality development occurs,
an incorporative attitude inevitably becomes a feature of the developing
structure of the psyche. The oral aspects are often emphasized in the
literature through our combination of the two terms, as *oral incorporation*.

2. *Literal Incorporation, in Primitive Societies*

There is another area which suggests some of the meaning of the
incorporative process. We speak of Incorporation as a primitive mechanism
and this is correct. Interestingly, this is correct also from the *racial* primitive level, as well as from the standpoint of the *individual* primitive oral
era in individual personality development. Anthropologists are cognizant
of the presence of analogous beliefs, rites, and customs among various
primitive groups. Some of these are connected with the past and history.
A few however still survive in isolated areas today. The primitive beliefs
and rites of certain peoples thus can illustrate some of the incorporative
"magic" having carried over directly into adult life.

We refer particularly to cannibalism and to certain associated practices and myths. These are fortunately more frequent in historical perspective than extant. Certain primitive people actually incorporated their
vanquished enemies. They ate them!

In cannibalism, one fairly commonly held belief is that eating a
person or some particular part of him will give the eater his strength,

attributes, position, or cunning, or other value of the assimilated part. This is not too far removed from infantile oral fantasies. To continue, the eating of a part of another person's body has been long believed in various quarters to confer the quality symbolized by that part. Thus, the ingestion of a hand would make one skillful or dextrous, his heart courageous, or his tongue, well spoken. This would convey still more significance if there had been some special individual faculty or talent present in relation to a given part. Cannibalism is a primordial practice of literal incorporation, expressed directly and overtly.

Similar beliefs have been held in eating animals. The Masai partake of an animal's strength by drinking its blood. Others have sought cunning through eating the great cats, ferocity and strength through the bear or bull, craftiness through the fox, or power and longevity by eating elephant meat.

The assimilation of special powers has been long ascribed to ingesting certain special animal parts. The desire for rhinocerous horn as an aphrodisiac has been so great that it now threatens the extinction of this animal. A physician traveling companion of the author in Java and Bali had to most carefully guard the whiskers of his Sumatra trophy tiger, believed by some to be unequalled in promoting sexual prowess. Beliefs in the taking over of attributes through their literal assimilation have been widespread, and continue for some peoples today.

3. Physical and Literal Ingestion Succeeded by the Psychic, Figurative, and Symbolic

A. RELATION TO AND DISTINCTION FROM IDENTIFICATION.—Incorporation can be closely related to Identification, which it may precede, and from which its consequences may be difficult to distinguish (*Case 89*). The earliest Identifications are at the oral level and are more likely made with the mother (Chapter 9). She also has been likely subject and model for a figurative kind of Incorporation, which may directly accompany and/or succeed the more literal incorporative pattern already established through nursing and the resulting relatedness of the oral period.

The original physical oral incorporative processes, having been succeeded by the figurative, establishes a psychic pattern. This is one of symbolically or in fantasy ingesting and assimilating human and other objects from the environment. This is a more or less continuing process, or if discontinued, at the least establishes a potential primitive avenue to which the sufficiently hard-pressed individual later can perhaps revert or regress, (Chapter 20, p. 333), if this pattern proves the proper one for the embattled psyche. The mature personality largely foregoes the use of this primitive mechanism or its particular availability as a defensively-intended resource.

If we attempt to set up criteria, the major distinctions between

Incorporation and Identification (Chapter 9) in the taking over of traits or other aspects of another person, relate mainly to its degree, completeness, massivity, and "swallowing whole." Added criteria for Incorporation are in its primitiveness, its Lower Order nature, and its depth of unconsciousness. Incorporation is more profound and is ordinarily associated with an earlier level of development, or is marked by deeper and more pathologic regression.

B. IMPLIED RECOGNITION IN FIGURES OF SPEECH.—Occasionally, common parlance includes an expression which conveys some implicit recognition of this process of psychic ingestion and assimilation. Such references while not numerous do occur and are of interest. Thus one may hear of a person, a problem, a difficult lesson, a conflictual situation or an attitude, as being hard to digest.

A student may assimilate or digest a book, an article, a subject, or a lecture. The scholar drinks up knowledge. One laps up everything he hears, or whatever his hero or ideal may say. A parent fondly relates that her child is so sweet, she could eat him up. A lover may speak of devouring his love, or comment; "I was lost, absorbed in her . . ." A teacher admonishes her class to study the subject, "until it becomes part of you."

On the other hand, of course, one may not be able to stomach a person, one of his traits, an exam, the professor, or a situation. Something is too tough, too raw, or too lame an excuse to swallow. Still a credulous person may swallow something preposterous. Actual swallowing and assimilation and that which is psychic and figurative tend to overlap and to be confused in the unconscious. However the psyche does not have to submit to the boundaries of reality, nor is consistency in any way a requisite for the unconscious.

B.   RELATION TO PERSONALITY DEVELOPMENT

1. Orally Incorporative Attitudes

A. NORMAL FOR INFANT.—The infant normally has an orally incorporative attitude. As his personality first evolves, parts or whole areas are "taken over" from another person and "incorporated" into the new personality. Infantile Incorporation is primitive, gross, and massive.

The developing child later incorporates certain fundamental qualities from one or the other or both parents as they appear to him, usually more from one than the other. Incorporation is an analytic term which has important connotations in symbolic language, fantasy, dreams, and emotional symptoms. Incorporation of objects in the broad sense can take place, which have many and varied emotional associations.

B. INADVERTENT DIRECT EXPRESSION.—Incorporative ideas are not infrequently encountered in contacts with small children. They may be the subject of fantasies (Chapter 7), and are also occasionally expressed directly. Small children are closer to the appropriate stage of psychosexual development, less inhibited, and upon adequate occasion can give forth with a direct comment reflecting the concept of oral incorporation.

At times an unexpected spontaneous remark gives inadvertant expression to underlying feelings of deeper significance. The following two instances reflect secret (unconscious) rivalry and hostility. Each was proffered lightly enough, and passed off with some amusement by the largely adult audiences.

Case 87

Sibling Rivalry and Incorporation

A young family, including a 5-year-old boy with strong feelings of sibling rivalry toward his 3-year-old sister, were spending the summer at a tiny cottage by the lake. One day unexpected guests stopped by and there was talk about having them stay overnight. Actually the house was too small to provide the necessary number of beds.

"That's okay," declared young Charlie, "We'll manage. Before we go to bed, I'll just swallow Susie up!..." As an after thought then, he added, "Maybe in the morning I'll spit her out again!..."

This was the spontaneous, unwitting outward expression in light enough terms of a hostile feeling and partial secret destructive wish on the boy's part toward his little sister, for whom he had displayed intense jealousy. The presence of ambivalence is illustrated, plus other features of his reactions, in his succeeding Undoing (Chapter 25) addendum.

The primordial aim of devouring is not infrequently expressed in conjunction with hostility. Even in anger it is likely to approach the surface only in the severely regressed patient, or the very young. The following instance is also a good illustration, in which the punished and angry child expressed his wish for literal incorporation to secure the reversal of his parent-child role.

Case 88

Incorporation Expressed by a 4-Year-Old

A colleague reported a personal instance to help illustrate this aspect of Incorporation. His 4-year-old son had damaged his high-fidelity turntable, in an excessive burst of childish anger. He had been admonished about the need for caution around the Hi-Fi on several previous occasions. His father punished him with several sharp smacks on the seat.

The little boy's immediate and, needless to say, hostile response was to yell, "Daddy, I'm going to eat you up!... Then I'll be a daddy, and you'll be a little boy!..."

2. Nutrition Plus . . .

It is not surprising that the events and vicissitudes of the earliest phases of development, those of the Oral Stage, comprise the significant foundation for much of what later evolves in one's character and personality structure. Masserman aptly pointed this out:

> "From the circumstances of early mammalian development, obviously the most important single source of satisfaction for the human child is its mother, who furnishes the nutriment and the tender protection indispensable to the child's very existence. Even before the infant is able to distinguish other parts of its body, it must become aware, however dimly, that its lips, mouth, and tongue, through direct or substitutive contact with mother, are the organs by which it obtains satisfaction of its needs. In addition there is good evidence from animal experiments and clinical observation that the adequate stimulation and exercises of the oral region of infants satisfies needs other than those of simple nutrition.[1]
>
> "However, whether or not the infant's 'oral needs' are adequately satisfied, the functions of the oral region become forever linked with the regressive dependent longings that lie not far beneath the apparent self-sufficiency of human beings of every age. Certainly when, through weaning, the child is deprived of the maternal breast, it may also begin to seek substitutively symbolic satisfaction of its 'oral erotic' desires through the medium of the pacifier or the thumb. Later substitutes may include such seemingly unrelated activities as chewing gum, pipe stems, or the unlit cigar. Mixed with subsequent sexual activity, oral erotism may express itself in various behavior patterns ranging from kissing—acceptable in many societies—to various 'oral perversions'—acceptable in relatively few places."

3. Superego Development

Early incorporated objects form the beginnings of the superego or conscience. The incorporation of parental attitudes begins most early and it is through them that foundations of the conscience are created. According to the relative stringency of parental standards, many aspects of the child's outlook and attitudes may be thereby influenced. When thoroughly incorporated by the child, strict attitudes which were originally the parental ones toward him, can help evolve a punishing and burdening conscience.

When these attitudes and standards are more reasonable and are accompanied by a secure, relaxed attitude, relations between mother and child progress constructively, as does the child's psychic development. The young child develops a kinder attitude towards himself and towards others. He is freer of fears. Figuratively speaking, he is more able to go into a dark room without uneasiness.

One might describe such abilities as resulting from the Incorporation of his good kind mother; as she has become part of his personality, he has nothing to fear. As this is written, the writer recalls a little girl who has had the good fortune to have an unusually cheerful, happy mother. This child has literally incorporated this rather considerable aspect of her mother's personality, laughing and singing all day long.

There are many related facets. As a consequence of Parental Incorporation which is constructive, a new experience may be faced with confidence and equanimity, as distinguished from consternation. Among many

---

[1] As Spock wrote about infant sucking: "A baby nurses eagerly for two separate reasons. First, because he's hungry. Second, because he *loves* to suck."

experiences one may need to face, the 5- and 6-year-old's possible apprehensions and fear on going off to school for instance, may be viewed in this light. He needs the incorporated (aspects, memory, mental pictures, and equanimity of) kind and loving parents to accompany him into this new, unfamiliar, and otherwise threatening setting.

Incorporated parental attitudes and beliefs can be strong indeed. When strong ones are concerned with religion, for example, the person may not be able to discuss religious convictions with others. He may be unable even to listen to others argue among themselves or discuss differing views. A hidden fear of danger to his own perhaps less certain beliefs can also of course contribute to this kind of reaction.

4. Parental Incorporation

As noted in the foregoing discussion, various aspects of parents are subject to symbolic ingestion and psychic assimilation. What we would distinguish and invite attention to by the term of *Parental Incorporation* include many varied and significant ones.

Repressed urges which result in guilt feelings usually earlier led to parental disapproval, criticism, punishment, or contempt. Fears of parents and of their reactions, as well as many of their views are incorporated into the conscience. These become personal standards which are utilized by the individual, in his self-regard and judgments, just as earlier did his parents or other significant adults. Their image has been incorporated. There has been a massive kind of psychologic ingestion and assimilation.

Case 89

Parental Incorporation, Mother's Patterns of Reaction

(1) *Emotional Crippling.* F.I. was an attractive 23-year-old girl. When she was able to work (from an emotional standpoint), she earned her living as a chorus girl in musical shows. She had a great deal of talent, but found herself unable to take adequate advantage of this. For instance, because of her intense fear of auditions, she found herself most reluctant to try out for a better role. She had periods in which she was so depressed that she was unable to work.

After she entered therapy, it quickly became apparent that she was seriously disturbed. The youngest of three children, her early life had been filled with every conceivable psychologic trauma. Her mother appeared to have been psychotic, although never hospitalized. The mother's behavior was characterized by what might best be called "predictable unpredictability." It was impossible for the child to determine what the mother's attitude would be to anything! At one moment quite loving, the mother might suddenly turn into a raging, vindictive person, seemingly with no provocation.

(2) *Ambivalence and Parental Incorporation.* The patient's memories were filled with painful incidents in which her mother inexplicably locked her out of the house, tore her clothes, beat her, berated her, and accused her of sexual promiscuity. These traumatic episodes alternated with love and tenderness. The patient thus developed an intense ambivalence to her mother. This carried over in self-defeating fashion to subsequent relationships.

Early in her unconscious endeavors to survive, the ego defense of Incorporation had been called into play. In seeking to preserve the mother whom she both loved and hated, the patient early incorporated many aspects of her mother and her seemingly irrational patterns of reaction. As a consequence of the Incorporation, she experienced many of the same impulses, feelings, thoughts, and behavioral responses, which eventually she came to recognize in therapy as being those of her mother!

(3) *Recognition Difficult; Clarification Beneficial.* Because of the intense hate she harbored, she couldn't recognize or accept these for a long time. She condemned and hated herself for possessing these consciously rejected aspects of mother. The Incorporation was unconsciously accomplished in part as a primitive attempt to maintain the feeling of being loved by her mother. This became increasingly apparent in this very sick patient, who described her mother and her hated self in almost the same terms. A relationship in aim to that of Identification (Chapter 9) is to be noted.

Employment of this dynamism had undoubtedly begun very early. Its operation was typically primitive, automatic, and deeply unconscious. Its unearthing and clarification in therapy added immeasurably to this patient's level of self-understanding, and subsequent improvement.

Incorporation of parental aspects can have wide implications in the various neurotic reactions. In Hygeiaphrontic Reactions (hypochondriasis), parental attitudes toward himself as well as those toward his child may be assimilated by the latter. So may parental attitudes about rest, sleep, digestion, health, and fatigue. The Conversion Personality may utilize a number of the more primitive ego defenses including Incorporation, as well as Denial, Symbolization, Idealization, and Reaction Formation.

Nail-biting, frequently a significant Conflict-Indicator, may express incorporative trends, when the symbolism present is appropriate. Incorporation when operative within the transference-countertransference relationship of therapy may contribute to the occasional long-standing stalemate which can occur in analysis and intensive psychotherapy.

C.   ADDITIONAL ASPECTS

1. Psychotic Incorporations

Incorporation may be sometimes observed to be operative in the delusional content of psychotic individuals. These are instances of what we might refer to as *Psychotic Incorporations.* Such persons for example, have directly and verbally reported on occasion their (supposedly literal) ingestion of people or their attributes. Sometimes groups of people are reported as being inside of the patient.

Incorporation is a primitive oral mechanism. When manifested in adult psychopathology, it is usually quite regressive in character. In such massive and obvious form, Incorporation is associated only with very sick persons.

2. The Engulfment Concept. Incorporation in Interpersonal Relations

A. PARENTAL ENGULFMENT AND MARITAL ENGULFMENT.—Recently our attention has been directed toward the subtle operation of the incorporative process in relationships between people. Interpersonal relatedness may be subconsciously experienced by an individual to a greater or lesser extent as what we might term an *Emotional Engulfment*. One may feel or in effect be, overwhelmed or assimilated, or perhaps and more rarely, the reverse—assimilating and overwhelming. This is the *Concept of Engulfment*.[2]

The parent-child relationship occasionally illustrates our *Concept of Engulfment*. So does the sibling one, as do others. Actually, emotional engulfment may occasionally occur in any type of relationship. It can be marked and apparent, or operate far more subtly. It can be transient or long-standing.

The *Parental Engulfment* can be relatively benign. However, the consequences are not always so felicitous. When such an Emotional Engulfment is rough-shod and malignant, powerful emotional conflicts are stoked. These can burn fiercely out of sight, buried in the unconscious. Their eventual eruption, should it occur, can result in major psychic illness. In one such destructive instance of a mother-daughter relationship, the latter came to suffer repeated severe cyclic depressions.

At times one marital partner thus may figuratively come to so overshadow, direct, control, and take over his spouse, and to such an overwhelming extent as to constitute what we have termed a *Marital Engulfment*. This phenomenon as a specific subtype of our foregoing concept, may be marked by kindness and benevolence at the one end of the emotional spectrum, extending all the way to sadism, extreme cruelty, destructiveness, and resulting severe psychopathology at the other end. Rarely there may be overtones of a masochistic-sadistic combination of the two people involved.

Marital Engulfment, Parental Engulfment, and other types may receive an impetus from such factors as marked discrepancies in education, age, sophistication, or extroversion *vs.* introversion. The following is a brief illustration.

Case 90

Marital Engulfment

A tough, experienced, and successful bachelor lawyer finally married. He was one who relished courtroom battles and was typically extrovertive in character. To the surprise of some of his colleagues, his bride turned out to be 13 years his junior, was shy and retiring in nature, with a semirural background and a bare high school education. He had battled his way up from the slums. Hers had been a sheltered family life. While on superficial view the match was astonishing, a closer look revealed many interesting ways in which their attributes complemented each other; at the outset clearly illustrating the *Hand-in-Glove Concept* in relationships. However, he was the dominant member of the partnership from the start.

During the early years he came to direct her activities, her choice of friends, hair style, and clothes. Passively and dependently accepting his

---

[2] See also later *Concept of Emotional Exploitation* (p. 258).

judgments, this was quite fine to her. As time advanced, the control and direction increased. Her opinions and thinking were a carbon copy of his. Even minor decisions were deferred to him. The couple was quite satisfied and happy, however. This was an instance of Marital Engulfment, but one which was primarily voluntary, quite kindly, and acceptable to both persons.

B. DEFENSIVE OPERATION.—Searles regarded Incorporation as subserving certain important defensive needs, including defense against: (1) painful awareness of reality of the external world, (2) accession of hostile feelings into awareness (derepression), and (3) awareness of feelings of rejection.

The alert therapist should be aware of the existence of incorporative processes within the interpersonal situation of treatment. These can be of some consequence and influence in the results of therapy, and in the facility with which they may be achieved.

3. Incorporation of Knowledge; Incorporative Learning

The ease and the level of learning show great variation. Some things are learned with a rather superficial approach. Some are the consequence of effortful rote memory. For some, the results of cramming are transient; for others more lasting. However, learning takes place at other, far deeper levels.

At this other extreme, material that is learned is *absorbed*. Often enough it is as though there was little conscious effort or teaching involved. This is not so much the ordinary learning process of school, teachers, and books; it is what we would term *Incorporative Learning*.

The subject matter of such learning often relates to broad and deep areas. These include attitudes as well as the ways in which one judges and evaluates. Incorporative Learning may be reflected in the accumulated wisdom of the dedicated professional. It can contribute to knowledge, discrimination, judgment, and wisdom.

In discussing qualification in his subject (anthropology), a young professor commented in significant fashion on the need "to really get it under your belt; one must thoroughly absorb it. . . . If you really have learned it, it will become part of you. . . ." If it is really a part of oneself, one *really* knows it and can use it; it is really absorbed.

D. SUMMARY

To recapitulate, Incorporation is a massive primitive type of ego defense with prominent roots extending into the oral stage of development. It is a devouring kind of ingestion and can be regarded as a symbolic swallowing up of whatever is incorporated. Our principal utilization of concepts of this dynamism and term is in analytic, psychologic, and behavioral theories in psychodynamics, and in the therapeutic process.

E. CROSS-REFERENCES TO *THE NEUROSES* *

Incorporation

In Nature of Anxiety (Chapter 1); of outside world, in superego development; p. 21.

In Illusory Gains (Chapter 2); of symptom by ego, in function of secondary gain (Freud); p. 62.

In Depressive Reactions (Chapter 4); of loved object, in dynamics of Depression; p. 186.

    Case 39; p. 186.

In Character Reactions (Chapter 5)

  in character defenses of *Conversion Personality* (Table 19); p. 260.

  in character trait formation of Obsessive person (English); p. 295.

  of judgmental parent, in Obsessive self-condemnation (*Concept of Personal Yardstick*); p. 249.

In Obsessive-Compulsive Reactions (Chapter 6); of harsh parental attitudes, in superego development; p. 331–2.

In Fatigue Reactions (Chapter 7); of parental admiration, in superego development; p. 404.

In Hygeiaphrontic Reactions (Chapter 8); of dangerous parental figures, in pattern of distrust of *Hygeiaphrontic* person; p. 503.

In Conversion Reactions (Chapter 12); a factor in Conversion diathesis; p. 695.

F. REVIEW QUESTIONS

Sample self-check questions on Chapter 10 and Incorporation for the student, psychiatric resident, and board candidate.

1. Define *Incorporation*. Why is it regarded as a *Lower Order* dynamism? A senior ego defense?
2. Comment on the relation of orality to the process of Incorporation.
3. Give examples from common parlance reflecting incorporative thinking. Can you add to the figures of speech cited?
4. What is meant by an orally incorporative attitude?
5. *Parental Incorporation* is described as symbolic or psychic ingestion and assimilation. Please explain. What is the significance in personality development?
6. In line with the *Engulfment* Concept a process of *Emotional Engulfment* can transpire in a relationship. What are your thoughts about the potential for self-defeat implicit to this evolvement for each party?
7. Describe the operation of *Marital Engulfment; Parental Engulfment.*
8. How does *Incorporative Learning* vary from other types?
9. When the operation of this dynamism is reflected in delusional thought content, what is the term used? Can you cite examples from your clinical observations of psychotic persons?
10. As with dynamisms generally, we regard Incorporation as defensively motivated. How would you support this view?

---

* From Laughlin, H. P. *The Neuroses.* London, Butterworth & Co., Ltd., 1967.

CHAPTER 11

INTERNALIZATION

... Attitudes and Standards Taken In

A. THE NATURE OF INTERNALIZATION
1. Definition and Types. 2. Values Internalized. 3. Kinship to Incorporation and to Introjection.

B. APPLICATIONS IN PERSONALITY DEVELOPMENT
1. The Ego. 2. The Superego. 3. Identification, Internalization and Projection. 4. Internalization of Attitudes and Views.

C. SUMMARY

D. REFERENCES (FROM *The Neuroses*)

E. REVIEW QUESTIONS

A. THE NATURE OF INTERNALIZATION

1. Definition and Types

Internalization is an ego defense which is closely akin to both Incorporation and Introjection. It too refers to the symbolic "taking in" of external objects or parts of objects. Of these three similar dynamisms, Internalization is the more advanced and less primitive.

Incorporation mainly and more prominently, occurs in the very early years, or when operative in later life, is in evidence during the course of deep regression (Chapter 20) and with certain psychotic reactions. Introjection (Chapter 12) is particularly associated with emotional depression. Internalization can operate in relation to less powerful and disruptive internal forces and in less desperate situations. We would prefer to largely reserve the concept and term for use in conjunction with its operation in attitudinal, personality, and character evolvement. It is a *major* or *senior* dynamism.

We may define Internalization as *an ego defense or mental mechanism operating outside of and beyond conscious awareness through which external attributes, attitudes, or standards are, or have been, taken within oneself, that is, internalized.* The two major subtypes are *Attitudinal Internalization* and *Characterologic Internalization.* Accordingly, Internalization is a dynamism through which the attitudes, views, or prejudices of another person may be taken over. The delineation and attempted distinguishing of Internalization propounds similar problems to those outlined in beginning our discussion of Incorporation, in the preceding Chapter 10.

One's tastes in art, literature, music, food, and attitudes toward people, can be in large measure internalized from parents, friends, intimates, and other significant associates. This is likely to apply especially to those whom one admires, and is a process which occurs particularly during childhood and adolescence. Internalized attitudes may be adopted defensively. At times they may have a relationship to a form of Rationalization, Chapter 17.

The hardened delinquent may have an internalized facade, taken over from another and adopted so as to appear and hopefully to be, outwardly nonvulnerable, tough, and unafraid. Maintaining a hard exterior may more or less effectively cover over actual or potential weaker, more tender, and susceptible inner reactions. Various facades may be thus adopted through contacts with parents or associates.

2. Values Internalized

Internalized attitudes and views may be useful or handicapping, or a combination of both. The following example concerning the taking-over through Characterologic Internalization of a set of attitudes about money is illustrative. Early useful, in their continuation they became superfluous.

Case 91

Views About Money Internalized

Sarah's parents had had a hard time of it during the depression of the early thirties. The struggle had left its mark on them in their concern about monetary matters, although they had been able to make a go of it. Their daughter had been reminded constantly how hard money was to come by. Many decisions were made affecting her education, the kind of dates she could go on, where she ought to go and what she ought to do, on the basis of "Can we or can't we afford this?"

Although the family was not rich, neither were they paupers. However, what had come to be an excessive preoccupation with money together with the resulting concerns and attitudes towards life and society, were passed on to Sarah.

She had internalized them. They came to color her life as they had that of her parents. At a museum, all she could say was "What is it worth?" Beauty was immaterial. Money was reserved for necessities and was not to be used for fun, pleasure, or small luxuries. Concerning expenses and money, her phraseology was often the same as that earlier of her parents.

Her attitudes were advantageous, during the early days of marriage, and the young couple got by quite well on her husband's small income. Her internalized set of views were a useful contribution at a time when frugality was a boon to the slim budget of the couple. Her attitudes about the value and importance of money have remained however, beyond the point of necessity and usefulness. They are likely to be taken over by her children in turn, to some extent. Thus as their financial situation improved, her views did not relax. After a time they too came to be excessive, as had those of her parents before her!

3. Kinship to Incorporation and to Introjection

Although Internalization may be used loosely as interchangeable with Incorporation, the meanings are not identical. Incorporation is also an internalizing process but is one which is more massive, more primitive, and assimilating. See prior discussion (p. 164, also p. 68).

The professional usage of the adjective "internalized" is often properly employed to refer to the object *after* it has been taken in. An incorporated object has been psychologically ingested usually earlier, massively, and has been more or less assimilated. Introjection and Incorporation are more often used to describe the psychologic process of "taking in." Usage of these three terms in any event tends to be imprecise and overlapping.

Some attempt little distinction between the terms and processes and the differences lie perhaps more in subtle individual variations in connotation and usage, than in marked differences in meaning. Thus, an introjected object is also an internalized one. However, the introjected object is likely to be one toward which there have been intolerably strong feelings present. An object may also become internalized through incorporation.

We may regard Internalization as a more general term for that which has been psychologically and in symbolic fashion "taken in." The internalized object thus tends to be regarded as a distinct object, while the incorporated object tends to be regarded as something which has been swallowed and assimilated—a process which is more primitive and regressive. The introjected object may be both; it may be treated either as a foreign body and/or as a part of the self. The terms, as noted, are similar, and express overlapping concepts, yet the connotations they convey to us offer different shadings of meaning.

B.   APPLICATION IN PERSONALITY DEVELOPMENT

1. The Ego

The importance of internalized objects is a basic consideration in theories of ego development. Fairbairn writes that any theory of ego development that is to be satisfactory must be conceived in terms of relationships with objects. In particular, this includes objects which have been internalized during early life, usually under the pressures of deprivation and frustration.

The following instance illustrates the taking-over of postural attitudes, in distinction from psychologic ones. One might speculate as to the presence of possible psychic contributions to the ensuing pain.

Case 92

Postural Attitudes Taken Over

A 25-year-old woman was having difficulty with back pain. She consulted an orthopedic specialist and postural expert. This began a chain reaction which eventuated in her learning that the more immediate cause of her discomfort was strictly postural and positional. She undertook to try and correct her faulty walking habits and posture; eventually entering psychotherapy when major emotional blocks interfered with her endeavors, plus her recognition of additional emotional conflicts.

Much to her surprise, in therapy she came to realize that her postural habits, including the ways she sat and walked, followed closely those of her mother. From the emotional standpoint, the two of them were quite different. Unwittingly the daughter had internalized and taken over the "postural attitudes" of her mother, but not her emotional or intellectual ones. Recognition was followed by her relinquishing of these and the easing of her pain.

2. The Superego

The superego, or conscience, is substantially influenced through the acceptance and Internalization of the standards of significant persons during the early life of the individual. This process receives considerable impetus during the so-called Latent Period of personality development (p. 329). As the conscience develops, it takes on the functions of approval and/or disapproval which previously were exerted by important parental or parent-surrogate figures. These acted as *external* censors. With the evolvement of the conscience one has an *internal* censor.

In other words, there is now an internalized authority, the conscience. An individual's conscience develops as a direct consequence of his early relations with his parents and with other significant figures in his early years. He has internalized various attitudes and standards of these parents or parent-figures; he has taken them within himself.

Klein observed and described the incredible and fantastic type of superego which one can encounter in the small child.

"... We get to look upon the child's fear of being devoured, or cut up, or torn to pieces, or its terror of being surrounded and pursued by menacing figures, as a regular component of its mental life ... The evil monsters out of myths and fairy-tales flourish and exert their unconscious influence in the fantasy of each individual child (who is all too likely to feel) itself persecuted and threatened by those evil shapes ..."

Klein has no doubt "that the (real, hidden) identities behind those imaginary, terrifying figures "represented" the child's own parents . . ." The dreadful shapes from fiction and fantasy (Chapter 7) thus in one way or another reflect the attributes or behavior of his father and mother, however distorted, one-sided, and fantastic the resemblance may be.

Klein feels that the acceptance of these findings of early analytic observation and study of infants, and our recognition that the things the child fears are these internalized wild beasts and monsters which it equates with its parents, lead us to conclude that the superego of the child is created out of such imaginary pictures or images of the parents, which it has taken up into itself, that is, internalized. The process of Internalization which begins in the early stages of infancy, is instrumental in the development of potential later psychotic positions when and if they should appear.

3. Identification, Internalization, and Projection

In their complex development, these three dynamisms often operate in similar ways. One may have understandable difficulty in drawing clear lines of distinction between them. One mechanism is often defined in terms of another. In the development of conscience, as noted, the child internalizes other people's criticisms of his own behavior. In one analysis the child criticized the analyst for her own fault. With the criticism internalized, the child succeeded in externalizing the offense. In essence this becomes Projection (Chapter 15).

One can recognize how Identification with the aggressor (q.v., Chapter 9) can be supplemented by another defense mechanism, in which guilt for example, becomes projected. Fenichel holding to the view that Identification is the first of all object relations, points out that a later Regression (Chapter 20) toward its renewed operation may be used in fighting off object relations of all kinds.

4. Internalization of Attitudes and Views

The Internalization of attitudes may be sometimes dated as to their major initiating influence or period of onset. This would appear to have been possible in our final two brief instances. Outlining the earliest antecedents may not prove feasible. However, the final determining factors do not have to extend into early childhood.

In the following example, the Internalization of prejudicial attitudes illustrates the *Rule of Impression Priority,* as referred to earlier (p. 145).

Case 93

Internalization of Prejudicial Attitudes

A group of college students working in a service unit with the AFSC in a midwestern state, were discussing their endeavors toward integrating white and Negro patients in a state hospital. One of the boys, from a New England community, noted his feelings against the program. His friends asked him about his experience with Negroes. This it seems was limited to several Negro students he had met and become friendly with at college. He was unable to explain his opposition.

Following a good deal of reflection, he was able to recall some background from a vacation at a summer camp when he was 10. One of the counselors had taken a special interest in him. He recalled several discussions in which the counselor had participated and had derided Negroes in general, accusing them of degradation, incompetence, immorality, and slovenliness.

Largely because of his admiration and attachment to the counselor, the boy had internalized some of the latter's attitudes in an area about which he had no prior experience or knowledge. Being influenced in this way, with the adoption and internalization of the older chap's views is in accord with the *Impression-Priority Rule* (p. 152).

Case 94

Internalization

". . . When I was a young and impressionable lad of 12 years, my parents and I left the small farming community in which we lived, for a visit to the big city—San Francisco. This was my first exposure to some of the "lower" types; our small town life being quite stereotyped as regards social strata.... I had never been aware of the impoverishment and self-prostitution which many of the less fortunate endure....

"During our sightseeing, I was surprised when a typical character from skid row approached Dad and made the usual request. Dad's reaction was one of sincere pity, and he responded with some coins, expressing his feelings to us, 'Poor devil! We certainly are lucky.'

"His sympathy for this unfortunate chap, and his gratitude for his position were internalized into my system of attitudes and standards. What happened made a deep inmpression on me.... I usually respond with similar feelings for these social outcasts, and feel grateful for my advantages...."

C. SUMMARY

Internalization belongs to an interesting triad of similar ego defenses, thereby however, posing difficulties in its delineation. Through this defensively-intended process, attitudes and standards are taken in, or a facade adopted. We would restrict application of the term and concept to the major types of *Attitudinal Internalization* and *Characterologic Internalization*. There are many applications in personality development.

Internalized values can be constructive, or exaggerated, prolonged, and self-defeating, or can include elements of both. The kinship of Internalization to Incorporation and to Introjection and the often subtle distinctions in their connotations were discussed. Internalized objects contribute to the ego and, via the Internalization of parental standards and censorship functions, to the conscience. The superego is the internalized authority.

Relationships with and contributions to Identification and Projection received comment. The Internalization of prejudicial attitudes can transpire in ways that are in accord with the *Impression-Priority Rule*. Four examples illustrated various aspects of the ego defense.

D. CROSS-REFERENCES TO *THE NEUROSES* *

Internalization

In Nature of Anxiety (Chapter 1); of attitudes of significant persons, in superego development; p. 35.

In Depressive Reactions (Chapter 4)
of enemy, and its symbolic destruction through suicide; pp. 206, 220.
of lost love object, in concealed hostility (Case 29); p. 160.
of parental authority, in masochism of Depressive Reaction; p. 177.

In Character Reactions (Chapter 5); of parental authority in Depressive diathesis; p. 282.

In Obsessive-Compulsive Reactions (Chapter 6); of rejection by parents, in obsessive cleanliness (Case 68); p. 336.

In Hygeiaphrontic Reactions (Chapter 8)
of bad objects, as bases in hypochondriasis (Klein); p. 491.
of disappointing object, in concern over cancer (Case 101); p. 488.
of loved/feared object, in Primal Threat (Heimann); p. 493.
of parent, in symptom formation (*Concept of Interpersonal Perpetuation*); p. 371.

---

* From Laughlin, H. P. *The Neuroses.* London, Butterworth & Co., Ltd., 1967.

E.   REVIEW QUESTIONS

Sample self-check questions on Chapter 11 and Internalization for the student, psychiatric resident, and board candidate.

1. What is the ego defense of *Internalization?*
2. Two major subtypes were named. These are?
3. Our concepts of Incorporation and Introjection admittedly are overlapping and not always possible to distinguish clinically from Internalization. Note theoretical points of similarity and difference. Why refer to them as a "triad"?
4. *Characterologic Internalization* leads to the taking over of attitudes and views. Can you provide examples from text and experience?
5. Internalization is important in theories of psychic interaction and personality development. What are some consequences of its operation in turn for the ego, id, and superego?
6. How is the *Impression-Priority Rule* illustrated in *Case 93?* Please cite further instances of the application of this rule from personal and professional experience.
7. "Internalized values can be constructive (or) ... self-defeating." Explain.
8. A. How can the operation of Internalization relate or contribute to Projection?
   B. What is *Attitudinal Internalization?*
9. Why is it next to impossible to recognize the operation of a given dynamism in one's personal psychology? What are the routes to insight?
10. A. Briefly discuss the concepts of overlapping and *emotional symbiosis* in the operation of ego defenses.
    B. List the 10 dynamisms thus far considered as belonging to the advanced Higher Order group, versus the more primitive Lower Order group.

CHAPTER 12

INTROJECTION

*...Feelings More Safely Directed Toward the
Self Through the Introjection of the Loved
or Hated Object-Person*

A. LOVED OR HATED OBJECTS TAKEN IN

    1. Definition: a. Distinguishing Features; b. Safer Substitute
Target Provided. 2. Prominence in Depressive Reactions. The
Depressive-Introject. 3. Introjection and Suicide.

B. MAJOR TYPES OF INTROJECTION

    1. Symptom-Introjects. 2. Psychotic Introjection. 3. Pregnancy
an Oral Introject. 4. Behavior and Attributes. The Incomplete
or Partial Introjection.

C. ADDITIONAL ASPECTS

    1. Implied Recognition. 2. Psychodynamics: a. Primordial In-
trojects; b. Contributions to Superego Development; c. Regression and Psychopathology.

D. SUMMARY

E. REFERENCES (FROM *The Neuroses*)

F. REVIEW QUESTIONS

A. LOVED OR HATED OBJECTS TAKEN IN

1. Definition

    A. DISTINGUISHING FEATURES.—Introjection is a major ego defense
or dynamism through which objects are symbolically taken in by the individual. As noted earlier, it is closely allied but not identical with both
Internalization and Incorporation. The potential value in more precise
scientific terminology leads us to make technical distinctions in their
respective meanings and connotations.

    The members of this interesting and related triad of dynamisms are
correctly discussed in their employment as individual mechanisms in the
specific psychodynamics of certain of the emotional reactions. Table 7
outlines the major distinguishing features of Introjection.

Table 7

Introjection
Major Distinguishing Features of the Ego Defense

In distinguishing Introjection at least seven major features are worthy of attention.

1. The object so treated symbolically often is another person or some aspect of another person. This object-person can be properly referred to as the *introject* when appropriate, helping to denote its non-assimilation.
2. There usually have been terribly strong emotional feelings present toward the object which is introjected. Love and hate, with their variations and combinations, serve frequently as responsible affects. These may be conscious in part or deeply unconscious.
3. Such feelings *appear* to be directed toward the self, since this is indeed their direction, insofar as conscious recognition is concerned.
4. The process and the presence of the object remains unconscious to the person concerned, albeit taken in, and thus closely identified with the self.
5. The introject, despite its close affiliation and alliance with the ego, remains essentially discrete. Thus, it retains its identity from the psychologic point of view. It is not assimilated as occurs with the object psychologically ingested in the process of Incorporation (Chapter 10).
6. In the complete or successful Introjection the ego or self in turn becomes treated as though it *were* the introject.
7. Finally, one might regard the entire defensively-intended process of Introjection as a major variation of the *Scapegoat Reaction* (see Chapter 5), in which the self or ego becomes the less hazardous substitute-object and the Scapegoat.

B. SAFER SUBSTITUTE TARGET PROVIDED.—Introjection is a more advanced, developed, and less primitive mechanism. As a *Higher Order* dynamism, it is usually associated with emotional reactions and neuroses of corresponding level. Its operation is particularly characteristic in states of emotional depression. As shortly discussed, it is the reverse of Projection. Through Introjection, otherwise unacceptable emotions become redirected toward a safer substitute target.

Introjection is *a Higher Order ego defense or mental mechanism operating outside of and beyond conscious awareness, through which loved or hated objects are symbolically taken into oneself.* Introjection usually involves another person or persons, who have been greatly (but intolerably) loved and cherished, or hated and punished. Unconsciously and figuratively these feelings continue, however being consciously directed toward the ego or self. *Strong and otherwise unacceptable emotional feelings thereby secure expression toward and are experienced by the self. The ego becomes a safer and consciously acceptable substitute target, through the Introjection of the loved or hated object-person, who is thus unwittingly loved or punished.*

The introject is the object which has been figuratively taken in. It remains more or less discrete psychologically, and is not assimilated as in Incorporation. Feelings and actions which are not tolerable consciously are thus able to secure a disguised expression in which oneself becomes so associated and identified with the introject as to become a substitute, and a more acceptable and safer target. Study of the psychodynamics reveals that the defensive process of Introjection is approximately the converse of Projection (Chapter 15). Accordingly, one's love or hate for another can be redirected inwardly toward self, through the Introjection of the object-person. Conversely, one's love or hate can be experienced as coming from an external source—another person—through their Projection outwardly to him. Each process is evolved in defensive intent.

It is sometimes lost sight of that the operation and consequences of each of these dynamisms can be normal, that is, nonpathogenic, as well as pathogenic. Their end results can be constructive and ego synthetic, or self-defeating and ego disruptive. It is their exaggeration, imbalance, hypertrophy, or misapplication which contributes to the onset of psychopathology, which is often of a serious degree.

2. Prominence in Depressive Reactions. The Depressive Introject

Introjection in general is to be regarded as less primitive, less massive, and less regressive than Incorporation. Parts of a person or the entire person may become a symbolically introjected object. Introjection rather commonly seeks to provide a major and ironclad defense against the conscious recognition of intolerable hostile aggressive impulses. We observed this illustrated repeatedly in discussing the Depressive Reactions (*The Neuroses,* Chapter 4).

Essentially, the dynamics in Emotional Depression are based upon the unconscious Introjection and punishment of the disappointing or lost object. The negative feelings become in effect *inverted* (Chapter 12) through this dynamism process, so that in punishing the introjected object the depressed patient actually and outwardly is judgmentally and unduly harsh and critical toward himself. This accounts for his self-punitive and self-deprecatory attitudes and expressions. He has identified himself for all conscious purposes with the introject. In the interests of emphasis and clarity, we might term this object-person the *depressive-introject.* It is an essential feature in the psychodynamics of every Depressive Reaction.

This process, as summarized above, is the essence of the pathogenesis of depression. It may appear complex to the student in the foregoing condensation, but it will become clearer following a study of the dynamics and the clinical illustrations in the foregoing reference. Introjection finds its most typical and prominent illustrations in relation to emotional depression. Cases cited in *The Neuroses* should be consulted for additional illustration of various points in our present discussion.

The following instance illustrates the onset of a Depressive Reaction marked by a gradual process of Introjection.

Case 95

Introjection in Onset of Depressive Reaction

(1) *Bitterness and Resentment Generated.* A 55-year-old minor executive had been repeatedly passed over when annual promotions were made in his firm. With a single large industry in town, promotions were everyone's business. The social repercussions magnified his conflicts.

With each succeeding year, he became progressively more angry, bitter, and filled with resentment toward his company and its officials. In his struggles to cope with and to contain this, much was repressed. After a time the storehouse for repression became overfull and in danger of bursting.

(2) *Introjection Eases Pressures.* As an unwittingly employed measure of defense, his objects (for resentment and negative feelings) were introjected. The intolerable pressures and danger of derepression were eased. In effect, it became safer to hate and to punish (this introject within) himself. Signs of emotional depression gradually appeared. The man's behavior reflected this. He began to shy away from social functions, beginning with those sponsored by the firm and his business colleagues.

He developed inability to sleep, a decrease in appetite, and annoying headaches. Careful history later elicited additional signs of depression, with a lack of interest in his job, hobbies, and family affairs. His friends noticed that he had lost his sense of humor, and that his speech had become slower and sparser.

This reaction progressed to the point where he no longer could work. He spent his days sitting around the house in low-spirited and self-recriminating moodiness. His physician successfully encouraged him to seek psychiatric help, which eventually proved most beneficial.

The self-critical comments in the above instance reflected operation of the Introjection. As is at times quite typical of this process, although specifically directed toward himself, these recriminations and harsh criticisms could be directly transposed as to apply to the company and his superiors. As expected in depressions, the individual concerned was unaware of this, and of course it would not be at all meet to so suggest.

Generally, however, the experienced observer can find a person (or persons) in the immediate environment toward whom the self-recriminations are actually, but thus in secret fashion, directed. When identifiable, this person is the *depressive-introject*. Needless to say, there were other important dynamic features present in the above example, including significant antecedents.

3. Introjection and Suicide

Introjection can play a role in the psychodynamics of suicide. Hereby murderous impulses become directed within or toward (the introjected object in) oneself, to the extreme level of self-destruction. Intolerable hatred for another person may in effect thus become turned against the self, as an unconscious endeavor to destroy the introjected and hated enemy. Herein the process which is defensively motivated makes an ultimate contribution to misdirection and the extreme of self-defeat.

Thus, through the process of Introjection, the patient can unconsciously secure the redirection toward himself of the unacceptable and consciously disowned hostility and aggressiveness which was originally directed toward another.

B. MAJOR TYPES OF INTROJECTION

1. Symptom-Introjects

Introjection can contribute to the formation of various emotional symptoms. The consequence of this type of the psychic process are termed *symptom-introjects,* and the process is that of *Symptom-Introjection.* This conception can be significant in individual instances of psychopathology.

Operation of the process of Introjection upon occasion accordingly can help to explain certain otherwise obscure somatic complaints. At times these may be ascribed to a functional basis, hygeiaphrontis (hypochondriasis), physiologic conversion, suggestion, or even to imagination or growing pains. Introjection can lead to visceral masochism. An accompanying depressed mood is not required.

The major aims and consequences of Introjection include conflict resolution, ego defense, maintenance of repression, psychologic symptoms and self-punishment. Symptom-Introjection thus contributes to the evolvement of certain emotional symptoms. The following is illustrative.

Case 96

Introjection and Abdominal Pain

An 11-year-old boy had been the youngest of five children and had long enjoyed a special position in the family. At this juncture a new baby sister arrived. A major realignment in the family constellation ensued, as much of the extra attention and affection in which he had basked was suddenly redirected. Not only the greatest loser and most affected, he was nonetheless expected to regard the newcomer as did the others.

This was the background, unbeknownst at the time, when his pediatrician was consulted because of severe abdominal pains. Medical studies were negative for organic findings. There was moderate hyperperistalsis on a functional basis. Medication afforded little relief. The physician was interested in emotional factors and in kindly fashion elicited the above background, suspecting a causal relationship to the symptoms. Psychiatric referral followed. The physician proved to be correct, as was borne out by confirmatory findings and the results of therapy.

The boy intensely hated and resented his baby sister. She had been responsible for his loss of parental love, position, and family attention. To admit or to evidence his hate openly was intolerable. His position with regard to his parents in any way would have been further jeopardized. Repression and nonawareness aided containment. The process of Symptom-Introjection reenforced this endeavor. As an unconscious defensive operation his sister had been introjected. Consequently his otherwise unbearable hatred was turned upon himself. His self-punishment for having it was also insured through the pain of the symptoms. These say symbolically not only, "My little sister is a pain to me," but also, "I shouldn't have these feelings, so it's right that I'm the one to suffer." Through Introjection the consciously intolerable feelings secretly secured a measure of expression and discharge.

Sound psychotherapy in this instance required an understanding of the contributory background and the psychodynamics. Any attempted direct explanation to this lad would have been most defeating. Therapy included rather the more general discussion of family relationships and the gradual elucidation of their implications for him, together with his emotional reactions to them. After several months of decreasing frequency, the abdominal pains finally disappeared permanently.

In the above instance we observe Introjection operating less primitively than Incorporation. It commonly serves as a defense against the conscious recognition of intolerable hostile and aggressive impulses. The object is introjected, the person identifies with the object, and emotions, self-depreciation and discomfort become self-punitive as in the foregoing instance. Important implications are present in our discussion of *Symptom-Introjection* for the dynamics and pathogenesis of the Hygeiaphrontic (hypochondriacal) Reactions.

2. *Psychotic Introjection*

Introjection is encountered in its most bizarre forms in emotional reactions of psychotic depth. Herein, what we may term Psychotic Introjections, are often also more transparent to the objective observer. The introject may be only partially concealed or poorly so. Delusions are encountered in which the individual describes the existence of another person, or part of another person, within him. There is a relation of Psychotic Introjection to Denial and to other dynamisms encountered in certain hallucinations (pp. 69 and 176).

Partial, or more complete Identification with the introject is a frequent, though not invariable, sequel to the Psychotic Introjection. However this is not a requisite, and there was little Identification in the following instance.

Case 97

Psychotic Introjection

A severely ill psychotic patient believed he had swallowed a mouse. To a selected listener he would relate how the mouse was eating his stomach. As such, the delusional mouse represented the Introjection of a bad object. This man did not identify himself with it, although it was probable that he had projected a part of his own sadistic impulses onto the mouse (also a fantasy-object; Chapter 7).

There is an interesting type of psychologic alternation possible between Projection (that is, as the converse of Introjection) and Introjection. As with the mouse, the reintrojection of objects rendered "bad" through Projection can occur.

The presence of the mouse in the delusion subserved self-punitive, masochistic purposes. This instance also illustrates the Incomplete Introjection as discussed shortly (p. 187).

3. *Pregnancy an Oral Introject*

In the emotional reaction to pregnancy the prospective mother may unconsciously regard the product of conception as an introject and in part as a foreign body. As such, symbolically it may be both punished and punishing. Its expulsion may be sought orally, in certain instances of pernicious vomiting of pregnancy, in accord with a fantasied view of conception as an oral process.

This not uncommon fantasy (Chapter 7) leads us to the guilt and fear at times associated with kissing by the adolescent girl. Here again there may be conscious or unconscious fears of oral pregnancy. In the following instance the (conscious) explanation to herself of subsequent mouth-washing efforts were on the basis of the presumed presence of germs or dirt. On a deeper level however, it was as though she were endeavoring to rid herself of an oral introject.

Case 98

Adolescent Fears of Kissing

The parents of a sensitive 15-year-old high school student were very strict and authoritative, and did not allow her to date. They had told her that she was too young, and that dating would lead to not clearly specified "bad things."

The daughter was attracted to a senior basketball player. Although she liked him very much, her parents of course would not hear of her dating him. During a "sneak" date, he kissed her passionately. She became very upset and went directly home.

For a week after this episode, she rinsed her mouth out as often as she could reach the bathroom without being too conspicuous. Thus, she sought to wash away the guilt and fear she experienced as a result of the incident. The kiss had led to her feeling that something bad remained in her mouth. The mouth-washing efforts continued, but with gradually decreasing frequency for several weeks. The deeper implications were uncovered in therapy several years later. The incident had been a significant one for her.

4. Behavior and Attributes. The Incomplete or Partial Introjection

Undoubtedly the dynamism of Introjection plays a role in influencing behavior and attitudes. Sometimes this can be substantial. Such effects are more frequent than ordinarily recognized, perhaps at least partially so because of their concealed nature and the subtleties of their operation. Primordial Denial may considerably restrict Introjection (p. 68). In the Depressive Reaction, the influences are major and often quite apparent to the clinician. In other, nonclinical situations it can be quite pervasive also, but far less apparent.

Following the death of a loved one, the survivor may in effect retain the person lost through his Introjection, via the (often unconscious) fantasy (Chapter 7) that the lost one is "forever within me." The survivor's behavior gradually may come to display some of the lost one's attributes. At times a lover or a lost lover may also become in effect an introject and be so treated.

A major source of emotional difficulty can be encountered in the course of what we might term the *Incomplete* or *Partial Introjection*. There are many applications of this concept in emotional illness. In the following case, the process of Introjection was only partially successful, as in *Case 97*. This instance also helps illustrate some of the untoward consequences which can result from the incomplete operation of ego defenses.

Case 99

Idealization, Identification, and Partial Introjection

A young woman complained of an inexplicably poor handwriting. Eventually it was learned this attribute was psychologically regarded, treated, and functioned as a foreign object, an introject.

Study disclosed that she had written well until the age of 16. For some months there was no explanation for the subsequent change. Under intensive psychotherapy, a significant and relevant relationship was finally uncovered. She had become excessively fond of an aunt, whom she had idealized, and with whom she had identified. This antedated and had influenced the change in handwriting.

The patient unconsciously endeavored to pattern herself after the aunt. She had partially introjected the aunt's style of writing. Whereas certain other attributes had been taken over more successfully, the process of Partial Introjection with regard to the aunt's handwriting had led to conflict with her own way of writing.

The net result of this confusion had been the deterioration of her writing to an almost illegible scrawl. Therapy eventually led to the elucidation and resolution of the untoward consequences of the Partial-Introjection and resulted in other major gains as well.

One must remember, of course, that in the foregoing instances the operation of such a mechanism is an unconscious process. The young woman earlier would have had no conscious recognition of such a development and would have been astonished and quite unbelieving to have had the bases of her behavior pointed out to her. This is likewise true for the young woman above. Note the close relationship also to the widow in *Case 73* (p. 141).

C.   ADDITIONAL ASPECTS

1. Implied Recognition

The operation of Introjection is occasionally implied in common parlance. Such usage suggests some general recognition of this process. The theme of Introjection is also illustrated sometimes in popular songs or poetry. Recall the song, "I've got you under my skin." Brown pointed out that "in normal life we tend to introject admired and loved objects."

Through this process one tends to strengthen the love instinct. "I shall carry you forever in my heart," "You are always with me," and similar statements from popular usage serve as examples. Introjection can take place in the marital relationship. After years of marriage, husband and wife may come to act alike, to think alike, and even to look alike. Introjection can contribute to these developments. The introject is loved and cherished with mutual benefit.

Bychowski called attention to the following lines from Walt Whitman's *Leaves of Grass:*

"There was a child went forth every day;
And the first object he looked upon, that object he became;
And that object became part of him for the day,
  or a certain part of the day, or for many years,
  or stretching cycles of years . . ."

2. Psychodynamics

A. PRIMORDIAL INTROJECTS.—The earliest antecedent introjects can be traced to the oral era of personality development (Chapter 20). A pattern of utilizing the defense of Introjection can begin here. When this occurs these are *Primordial Introjects,* as we might name them. Of course these PIs or the process involved may become dormant, with the potential for later reactivation under appropriate conditions of psychic stress.

Melanie Klein wrote that the first objects, that is, the primordial objects, which the infant introjects are the good mother and the bad mother, as the infant unwittingly envisages her. In the earliest or oral phase of development, the bad objects and the good objects are represented by the mother's breast, which the infant takes in, or spits out. Swallowing an object is for the infant accordingly first an expression of affirmation. Thus it is first more likely to be a prototype for (instinctual) satisfaction, rather than of a defense.

The earliest pleasant objects are subject to incorporation by the infant. Incorporation, however, although thus an expression of love, objectively destroys the existence of an object as such. Becoming aware of this, the ego learns to employ both Incorporation and Introjection for hostile purposes. These to an extent satisfy hostile and destructive impulses. An antecedent defensive pattern may be established.

B. CONTRIBUTIONS TO SUPEREGO DEVELOPMENT.—With regard to his environment, the young child gradually learns through deprivation, frustration, and various types of psychic and physical punishment, that he must accept and follow certain precepts of good social and moral behavior. Failure to do so leads to more pain, suffering, restriction, and handicap. This sequence in turn ensures the elaboration of an individual and personal superego. Accordingly the individual gradually establishes the resources to take over himself the educative, restraining, and punitive functions, which significant persons outside himself had previously undertaken.

In other words, the child comes to take over appropriate segments of outside reality and transplant them psychologically into his own personality. An important route is through the Introjection of (parts of) parents, teachers, and other significant adults.

C. REGRESSION AND PSYCHOPATHOLOGY.—One must recognize that Introjection can: (1) be an effective defense; (2) contribute to emotional adjustment; (3) serve as a vital reinforcement to repression (Chapter 21); (4) contribute to symptoms of several types (via Symptom-Introjects); (5) provide a basis for the psychopathology of various emotional reactions; and (6) for the small child it can serve as an important defensive mechanism for the safer redirection of otherwise intolerable hostility against the self, in place of mother.

The development of Introjection can be contributed to through unconscious masochistic needs. Feelings of guilt and the need of punishment may be in part so satisfied. The husband of an unfaithful, worthless wife may long tolerate her cruelty and thoughtlessness, expressing in words his feeling (the result of Introjection): "If I had been a better husband, she would have done far better." In line with our earlier comments, this might more accurately be transposed to: "If she had been a better *wife, I* would have done far better"—which in essence is correct.

Regression can lead to the readoption or reemployment of introjective defenses of earlier years. Fenichel notes another distinction from Incorporation, the latter being the most archaic aim directed *at* an object. Identification, performed by means of Introjection, is the most primitive type of relationship *to* objects. Therefore, any later type of object relationship, upon meeting with sufficient stress and problems, may regress to Identification; and any later "instinctual" aim may regress to Introjection. The evolving of Primordial Introjects as an ego defense can provide an example of the operation of the early archaic mechanisms, which may also be later employed by the ego.

D. SUMMARY

Introjection is the third member of the interesting triad of dynamisms concerning the symbolic taking in of objects. Through it the object-person remains discrete, and Identification with it thence provides a new and safer target for otherwise unacceptable feelings in the guise of the self. Hated and resented or loved and cherished objects can become *introjects. Table* 7 summarized the major distinguishing features of Introjection.

The converse relationship between Introjection and Projection * was noted. Introjection is a very prominent dynamism in the Depressive Reactions, which are generally characterized by the presence of the *Depressive-Introject.* The psychodynamic sequence in emotional depression was summarized and several clinical facets received comment. Attention was invited to supplementary data in *The Neuroses.* The extreme of self-defeat through Introjection occurs through its occasional contribution to the psychodynamics of suicide, in which one extracts the supreme penalty from the self (as identified with the introject).

Major types of Introjection include one marked by its contributions to the evolvement of emotional manifestations (*Symptom-Introjection*). The internal consequences, i.e., the object-person taken in via this process, is

---

* See p. 227.

the *symptom-introject*. In the psychoses, *Psychotic Introjection* contributes to the bases for certain delusions, hallucinations, and other abnormal mental content. Pregnancy is at times regarded as an *oral introject,* with implications for certain instances of pernicious vomiting in pregnancy, and for adolescent fears of impregnation via kissing. The *Partial Introjection* as with instances of its exaggeration, incompleteness, hypertrophy, and mis-application, contribute to psychopathology. As in *Case 99,* the consequence can be conflict, confusion, and the gross handicapping or distortion of a prior faculty.

Certain indications of implied recognition of the function of the dynamism can be found in song, poem, and common parlance. *Primordial Introjects* date to the oral era, and can establish a prototype for later readoption of this mode of psychic defense. Contributions to superego development were noted, as were further relationships to regression and psychopathology.

E.   CROSS-REFERENCES TO *THE NEUROSES* *

Introjection
In Illusory Gain (Chapter 2); of disappointing object,
   In *Endogain* (Table 5); p. 70.
In Depressive Reactions (Chapter 4)
   in psychodynamics of Depression; p. 220. Table 14; p. 179.
   of frustrating object, symbolically punished; p. 184.
In Character Reactions (Chapter 5); utilization of I.,
   in guilt feelings of *Depressed Personality;* p. 270.
In Obsessive-Compulsive Reactions (Chapter 6); of rejecting object, in Displacement and Substitution (Case 70); p. 344.
In Hygeiaphrontic Reactions (Chapter 8)
   as important mechanism, in symptom formation of *Hygeiaphrontic Reaction;* p. 479.
   in transformation of infantile anxiety, in antecedents for emotional patterns; p. 493.
   of disappointing mother, in *visceral masochism;* p. 491.
   of hated object, bases for *Hygeiaphrontic Attacks,* (Case 99); p. 483.

F.   REVIEW QUESTIONS

Sample self-check questions on Chapter 12 and Introjection for the student, psychiatric resident, and board candidate.

1. How would you define *Introjection?* Can you cite an instance of its operation from clinical experience?
2. List five distinguishing features of this major ego defense.
3. What is an *introject?* What does it represent and what can happen to it?
4. How can Introjection be regarded as illustrating the *Scapegoat Reaction?*
5. Discuss the role of the dynamism in the Depressive Reactions. What is meant by the *depressive-introject?*
6. How can Introjection contribute in a consideration of the psychodynamics of suicide?

* From Laughlin, H. P. *The Neuroses.* London, Butterworth & Co., Ltd., 1967.

7. The process of *Symptom-Introjection* is occasionally significant in psychopathology. Please discuss in relation to two types of emotional reaction. What are *symptom-introjects?; Primordial Introjects?* Do you know what is meant by *"visceral masochism"?*

8. Through the operation of *Psychotic Introjection* what groups of psychotic manifestations can be influenced?

9. Briefly discuss,

   A. The concept of pregnancy as occasionally representing an *oral introject* and

   B. The psychopathologic implications of the *Incomplete* or *Partial Introjection.*

10. *Object-introjects* are spoken of as being "loved or hated" and thus would be examples of the *emotional-object amalgam* or EOA. Do you consider an affective charge essential to the operation of the process of Introjection? If so, why? What if any other types of affect might be encountered?

CHAPTER 13

INVERSION

. . . An Emotional Reversal

A. NATURE OF INVERSION

    1. In Psychiatric Terminology. 2. The Intrapsychic Dynamism. 3. Definition. 4. Social Inversion.

B. TYPES OF INVERSION

    1. Hostility-Inversion and Positive Affect Inversion: a. Negative or Positive Affect Transposed; b. Secondary Elaboration. 2. Attraction-Inversion. 3. Memory-Inversion. The White-Washing Operation. 4. Standards-Inversion. 5. Characterologic Inversion.

C. ADDITIONAL ASPECTS

    1. Resistance-Inversion. 2. Ego-Enhancing Inversion. 3. In Character Trait Development: a. The Depressive Personality; b. Goal-Inversion and Attitude-Inversion.

D. MOOD-INVERSION

    1. Cyclic Swing in Spirits. 2. Depression into Elation. 3. Deficient Insight; A Danger Signal.

E. INVERSION AND OTHER EGO DEFENSES

    1. Inversion and Reaction Formation: a. Emotional Reversal; b. Criteria in Delineation. 2. Repression Reenforced; Progression Beyond Denial.

F. SUMMARY

G. REFERENCES (FROM *The Neuroses*)

H. REVIEW QUESTIONS

A. NATURE OF INVERSION

1. In Psychiatric Terminology

To invert is to turn upside down or inside out. Inversion has been adopted in psychiatry to describe a number of situations. We may speak for example of the *inversion of sleep* habits. This usage refers to the reversal of the more usual nocturnal pattern of sleeping into a diurnal, i.e., day-time pattern.

Sexual inversion has been used in reference to homosexuality; whereby heterosexual drives are regarded as being inverted into homosexual ones. Freud used the term of inversion to describe the dissimulation of hostile affect. Finally, inversion has been used to describe the turning of outwardly directed affect or emotion inwards towards the self.

2. The Intrapsychic Dynamism

Through Inversion something is turned around or reversed. We have adopted and used the term Inversion for an ego defense which operates in this way. This concept has proven useful and a convenience in communication, teaching, and psychotherapy.

The operation of Inversion as an intrapsychic dynamism, while not common, can be observed with some frequency by the interested and observant student of human behavior. Let us proceed with a definition.

3. Definition

For the purposes of our study, we may define Inversion as *an ego defense or mental mechanism operating outside of conscious awareness. Through this process, a specific wish, affect, or drive which has been repressed from conscious awareness as otherwise intolerable, becomes inverted and thus acceptably gains subjective awareness or can be expressed in attitudes or behavior which are directly opposite.*

In other words, through the process of Inversion an unacceptable and disowned (unconscious) impulse or emotion becomes directly reversed in one's conscious awareness and in its outward expression.

4. Social Inversion

Inversion as noted has been used in a social context to describe a conscious and deliberate type of operation. Herein there is a reversal of the tenor of attitudes which one outwardly expresses towards another person.

This attitudinal inversion is made through conscious effort. This represents one major type of social dissimulation which is employed fairly frequently. To varying degrees in social situations people both conceal and/or invert their true feelings, in whole or in part.

Freud early noted in this regard, "If I am conversing with a person to whom I must show consideration while I should like to address him as an enemy, it is almost more important that I should conceal the expression of my affect from him than that I should modify the verbal expression of my thoughts." In social intercourse, this comes close to being an understatement.

At times in this conscious endeavor of concealment and denial, the outward expression is a complete inversion of what is genuinely felt. Distaste or dislike thus may be masked by a superficial and feigned friendliness. More rarely perhaps, affection and fondness may be disguised by a display of aloofness, coolness, or even hostility.

It is not difficult for us to understand that similar developments can take place which are completely unconscious. The differences may be ones of awareness or complexity, rather than kind. The operation of inversion as a conscious, effortful concealment progresses in sequence gradually, to merge on into an unconscious endeavor. This utilization of the ego defense evolves in protective intent. When present and observable it is termed *Social Inversion.*

B.   TYPES OF INVERSION

1. Hostility-Inversion and Positive Affect Inversion

A. NEGATIVE OR POSITIVE AFFECT TRANSPOSED.—As an ego defense, Inversion operates automatically and unconsciously to transpose repressed impulses, desires, and emotions into their opposites, thereby permitting them to have an outward expression which is, however, most well-disguised. Thus, through Inversion, a personally intolerable impulse toward destruction, aggression, or hostility, can become consciously experienced and expressed in its reversed form. Social Inversion as above, more commonly operates in conjunction with negative affect.

Consciously unacceptable hostility may give rise through its Inversion to outward expressions of positive affect, including friendliness, love, or protectiveness. This operation comprises the *Hostility-Inversion.*

The reverse process to Hostility-Inversion may also occur as we have illustrated elsewhere. (*Mental Mechanisms.* See also *Case 11,* p. 35.) An interesting Inversion of the pregnancy denial syndrome (p. 70) describes the false pregnancy.

Inversion sometimes operates in the attitudes of a child toward a long-domineering and overly demanding parent. The operation of this ego defense can help bring about the lifelong type of relationship in which a child has come to devote himself more or less completely to a parent, in place of living his own life. (See also *Engulfment Concept* in Chapter 10.)

B. SECONDARY ELABORATION.—As indicated, a warm and tender emotional feeling which one does not dare experience may similarly through its Inversion come to be subjectively experienced as a feeling at once milder, or even reversed so as to become a hostile and antagonistic one. This of course is also a defensively-intended endeavor, and was earlier illustrated in the "blue book" of *Mental Mechanisms.*

Unconsciously, the intent of the dynamism in either Hostility-Inversion or in Positive Affect Inversion is to defend and protect. In the case of destructive impulses, these are feared because of one's superego and because of the dreaded potential of retaliation.

The intolerable impulse is denied and repressed but beyond that, is reversed or inverted into its opposite—a further process of defense. Herein Inversion becomes a *secondary elaboration* or reenforcement of the dynamisms or Repression and Denial. In secondary elaboration, one or more dynamisms are evolved to support the operation of an existing defense.

2. *Attraction-Inversion*

Inversion of positive into negative feelings is not observed as readily nor as frequently as the Inversion of negative into positive ones. We are reminded of the gruff old fellow who proverbially, "has a heart of gold." The defensive intent is not too difficult to fathom. Various instances including characterologic ones, are encountered and also have been illustrated. The Positive Affect Inversion however is not a commonly encountered phenomenon in clinical practice.

The following instance offers some similarities. Herein are the kinds of defensive patterns which can be automatically called into play in the endeavor to control intolerable sexual urges. It is an *Attraction-Inversion*. The Inversion endeavored to protect against consciously unacceptable homosexual attraction.

Case 100

Attraction-Inversion in Homosexuality

A young, homosexually-oriented male suffered with powerful emotional conflicts. He employed every resource at his command in trying to suppress his unacceptable urges and to ensure their control. Over a period of time in therapy we learned that similar unconscious forces were also at work.

Upon several occasions he had noted the growth of dislike toward a male acquaintance. While these reactions were seemingly unaccountable, his interest in exploring them further in his therapeutic work was most apathetic. This was sufficiently marked to arouse interest about his apathy equating resistance, and as to whether this represented a secondary defense of some existing significant psychologic defensive endeavor. Such eventually proved to be the case.

One day he was discussing a troublesome attraction toward a new friend. As he talked about how this troubled him and of his efforts at control, he suddenly cried, "I know what will happen now. I will gradually find things to dislike and to disapprove about him. I'll gradually come to dislike; to hate him! ... This has happened before! This is why I've had such revulsion for Gordon, and for Horace before that! ... With them I had 'forgotten' what went before—only could recall my intense feelings of revulsion. ... Now it all becomes clear ... This has been another defense. I didn't dare recognize these feelings before! ..."

This patient had developed a pattern of defense which operated to repress and deny his intense attraction toward certain male friends, and by a further defensive progression secured its Inversion into the opposite affect and attitude of an active distaste or revulsion. This was an instance of a major variety of the *Attraction-Inversion*.

The foregoing case illustrates in more striking fashion what can happen more frequently in less noteworthy instances. Herein the Inversion was evolved as a secondary elaboration of prior defense. Inversion also can operate in partial fashion; in segments of relationships.

3. Memory-Inversion. The White-Washing Operation

One of the defensive operations which we can sometimes observe taking place in regard to memories is the Inversion of certain distasteful or troubling ones. Through this means a source of possible distress instead can become one which is in various ways satisfying or ego building. In this kind of operation, Inversion can perform a function akin to that of the ego defense of Retrospective Devaluation (Chapter 27), in which service it can be viewed as a further progression.

The following instance is one in which memories have been inverted into their reverse. It is one type of what we term the *White-Washing Operation*. The WWO occurs not infrequently and is to be encountered in many areas of living in less striking examples.

Case 101

The White-Washing Operation; Retrospective Denial and Memory-Inversion

We have known a woman of 87 for many years. For over 20 years she has been widowed. During many decades of married life, Tom had not been what one would call a good husband. Far from it, he was a miserable failure at holding up anywhere near his end of the marital partnership. His wife had not been particularly secretive or timorous about remarking on his failures. He had done "a poor job as a father," given up good positions to the detriment of the family, was abusive with little objective basis, and often "drank too much."

For some years however, all unpleasant memories have been denied. Many memories have become inverted. She has now come to remember her husband quite sincerely as ". . . the best husband one could possibly have had . . ." He is remembered as a thoughtful and kind man. Her recollections having been inverted, serve as a significant source of pleasure and satisfaction.

4. Standards-Inversion

Occasionally one may encounter instances of the Inversion of individual standards in some major area. The following is a striking and major example of what might be termed *Standards-Inversion*, through which an underlying stringent attitude about morals and sexuality became inverted into its outward reverse, with a resulting series of flagrant love affairs.

Case 102

Standards-Inversion in Sexual Behavior

An attractive and well-to-do divorcée was referred for psychotherapy by her physician because of handicapping personality traits and general dissatisfaction with her life. A pattern of promiscuous sexual behavior soon came to light. She asserted that her repeated alliances caused no problems. She ruled out the presence of resulting emotional conflicts, and vetoed further discussion.

Nonetheless we gradually secured more data about this particular area of her living, while concentrating more specifically upon others. Her love affairs were conducted with little circumspection. She exhibited a flagrant disregard of her friends' criticisms on repeated occasions, and practically invited their attention to her sexual adventures. Her flaunting attitude conveyed contempt for their "prudishness" and "narrow viewpoints." Still it appeared clear that 15 years earlier, prior to her marriage and divorce, her own views had, if anything, been considerably more stringent than those of her friends.

During these emotionally stormy years her standards of sexual behavior gradually had become completely inverted. This had been a major instance of *Standards-Inversion*. Entering into the dynamics were elements of defiance, hostility, and disillusionment, plus contributing assists from the dynamisms of Denial and Rationalization (p. 269). The Inversion allowed her certain neurotic gratifications for which, however, she also paid in other ways. The effects of an underlying strict superego while no longer effective in controlling her behavior, exacted a substantial though more devious toll.

During the course of therapy the elucidation of the psychologic endeavors of Repression, Denial, and Inversion gradually led to a reinstatement of personally and socially more approved standards of behavior. These came to be based on sounder, objective and more rational bases, however, than were extant in her earlier years.

5. Characterologic Inversion

Inversions may operate in various aspects of living. Character and personality changes result which may be major or minor. The new and inverted trait or characteristic is intended as a defense against that which it replaces. The Inversion in the preceding case was in part also an attempted defense against the patient's stringent and overinhibiting conscience.

The person who is overly cautious in money management may have defensively inverted feared and disowned spendthrift tendencies as a rigorous endeavor in their control. Conversely, through Inversion a person who was originally miserly may become overgenerous, as a defense against disowned and overdeveloped needs to hoard. Suspiciousness may develop as an attempted defense against naiveté and vice versa. When sufficiently marked and individually influential in trait evolvement, the process is *Characterologic Inversion*. (Also see later.)

C.   ADDITIONAL ASPECTS

1. Resistance-Inversion

We observe Inversion operate in a number of areas. These include the Inversion of specific disowned thoughts, intent, attitudes, aims, and goals. Another important area is that involved in one's interpretation of the attitudes and behavior of another person. The automatic operation of Inversion can color one's perception of what takes place so as to provide a completely false picture. This may serve to reenforce preexisting misconceptions or needs.

In this type of operation, Inversion produces major Distortions (Chapter 26) of one's evaluation. This proved to be the case in the following instance of what we call *Resistance-Inversion*, in therapy.

Case 103

Inversion of Therapist's Role; A Distortion in Therapy

A patient with severely handicapping obsessive character traits entered treatment because of his desire to secure constructive change. From time to time in therapy sessions there would be an incoming phone call. The therapist's usual response was to indicate that he was not free to talk and arrange to call back.

The patient just as regularly inverted the doctor's role in these instances from a passive to an active one. He greatly resented the calls. He complained about them often and at great length. He also thought and spoke of the calls repeatedly as having been initiated by the therapist. Thus, he would say, "When you made that call...." "The phone call you just made..." "That call you made on Tuesday..."

To him the physician was the active party. Pointing out a distinction made little difference. He could recognize it on an intellectual level but any reference to the calls made the therapist the caller. This Inversion of his role continued for *years*.

To have made such calls while he was relating important events and during a period set aside for him would have been a gross disregard of his interests. It would have constituted contemptuous treatment of him, of his seeking help and efforts to communicate. Eventually, seeing the doctor in an unfavorable light proved to have been the major aim of this entire unconscious operation. This was an antitherapeutic maneuver reflecting negative aspects of his transference. As an important element in his resistance it helped guard his *neurotic status quo*. It was also urgently required to help him maintain distance; the dangers inherent in a close relationship were too threatening. This was an instance of *Resistance-Inversion*, in therapy.

He preserved his defensively-intended distance and emotional isolation through various distortions about his therapist and about his presumed attitudes and behavior toward him. Among these unconsciously motivated endeavors, the Inversion of the doctor's role in the phone calls, from being a passive recipient to that of the person initiating the calls, was an interesting and significant facet.

The importance of the foregoing Resistance-Inversion as a psychologic defense is amply demonstrated in the persistence and tenacity with which it was maintained and in its duration. This is often the situation. In the above case it did not give way to logic or reason. It was an emotionally determined part of his unconscious defenses. It constituted another facet of the many entering into his resistance; his unconscious efforts to maintain his *neurotic status quo*. It provided another strong, but unwitting *secondary defense* of his (primary, defensive) character structure.

Thus, pointing out to him on more suitable occasions the Inversion —literally over several years—plus after a time, his conscious recognition that he was thus tricking himself, made only a very gradual inroad upon this particular defensive operation. Long after his attitudes had undergone considerable modification, an occasional slip of the tongue betrayed lingering tenacious subconscious remnants.

2. Ego-Enhancing Inversion

The maintenance or enhancement of an acceptable self-picture is a vital endeavor. Sometimes it is referred to as preserving one's ego or self-esteem. Related is the Orient-originated reference to "saving-face." Rationalization (Chapter 17) is another important ego defense which is frequently evolved to maintain one's self-picture. At times the defensive endeavor progresses so that a complete Inversion takes place. When such an instance occurs it constitutes what we term an *Ego-Enhancing Inversion*.

In the following instance the patient had come to believe that he was behaving nobly, doing good, and that he was a benefactor, while conducting a damaging and self-defeating affair with his best friend's wife. It was absolutely intolerable in the face of his high personal standards, to consciously recognize the destructive implications through a more objective appraisal of the situation and his role.

Case 104

The Ego-Enhancing Inversion

A young engineer in therapy became involved in an affair with the wife of his best friend. Consciously he saw himself as "doing good." He maintained that his motivation was in providing (selflessly) necessary warmth and affection. This his friend couldn't or wouldn't provide, and therefore he was "holding the marriage together."

He had to see himself in a favorable light in every situation, especially in this affair. This was more necessary in this situation since he was farther from meeting his standards. He was the "benefactor" of the family. Several instances of pedophiliac sex play with their 6-year-old daughter were also rationalized, on the superficial basis that of course the child "couldn't possibly know what was going on anyway."

Unconsciously his judgments were of quite a different order. Ultimately, his Rationalizations lost their potency and his overly strict moral judgments became more apparent. These had to be kept submerged in order to permit the neurotic gratifications he sought.

The Inversion of what was destructive into something noble had allowed him to continue his otherwise personally intolerable behavior. His strict moralistic and judgmental self-assessments of criminal, detestable, immoral, and deceitful had been shunted aside. We eventually learned of these through a gradual process of therapeutic working out and derepression. As his supportive Rationalizations (Chapter 17) collapsed, his real standards became reestablished. He surrendered this affair and, more importantly, a pattern of similar destructive behavior, into which this fit. Other more personally acceptable and constructive avenues of gratification were developed.

3. In Character Trait Development

A. THE DEPRESSIVE PERSONALITY.—Character (personality) traits may be influenced through Inversion, as noted earlier in the process of *Characterologic Inversion*. This can be observed in various personality constellations.

Among these, such influences can be demonstrated at times in the Depressive Personality. In this group, the character traits often result at least in part from an Inversion of hostile and aggressive impulses. This has been illustrated elsewhere (*The Neuroses,* Chapters 4 and 5, and *Case 127,* p. 247).

B. GOAL-INVERSION AND ATTITUDE-INVERSION.—Blocking of a goal can lead to its Inversion. When the motivation is sufficiently powerful, even the personally-intolerable underlying need will demand some measure of expression. This may sometimes be satisfied through the Inversion of the goal, comprising a defensively-intended reaction named *Goal-Inversion.*

Attitudes may become inverted for a number of reasons. An important basis for the Inversion of an attitude may be found in frustration; for example when a sustained drive or aim fails. When such an event occurs, other things which had not seemed important heretofore may rapidly become so, while interest is similarly lost in the area which has proven unobtainable. The new area may be an opposite or reversed one, representing a Goal-Inversion and/or one of attitudes, an *Attitude-Inversion.*

The new goal also quite likely represents a Compensation (Chapter 2). Instances in which compensatory character development were akin to our conception of the Characterologic Inversion were summarized in *Cases 2, 3,* and *4* (pp. 20–21). (See also *Goal Devaluation* and *Sour-Grapes Rationalization,* pp. 259–60.)

D. MOOD-INVERSION

1. Cyclic Swing in Spirits

An interesting and important application of the principles of Inversion is encountered occasionally in the area of mood and mood swings. As with an emotion in *Affect Inversion,* the reversal of a mood can sometimes take place quickly; rarely even dramatically, in the absence of an apparently sufficient external basis. The more this is reflected in demeanor and behavior, the more noteworthy it will be. (See *Reversal,* pp. 486–8.)

The most marked examples of what is called *Mood-Inversion,* however, are to be found clinically in those emotional illnesses which are characterized by major cyclic swings in spirits. Our discussion requires an illustration and the following example is offered accordingly. It should be noted that only by having known this person over a fair span of time could one have been aware of the Mood-Inversion, even though it was so major in extent.

2. Depression into Elation

To have observed this patient at one pole (elation) of the emotional spectrum, or the other (depression)—with each being sustained over a period of time—would provide little hint of the marked change possible, or of the potential for the other. These changes transpired gradually but effected a complete transition in the individual, as we shall see.

Case 105

A Major Mood-Inversion

(1) *Depressive Mood Prevalent.* A 24-year-old teacher was in treatment because of the onset of a severe Depressive Reaction which had first restricted and then ended her effectiveness at work. In October, after 4 months of therapy, she was still quite ill. She was dejected, sad, and morose. She had abandoned most of her social life, and suffered from terrible self-consciousness.

To escape contacts with people she went to movies or roamed about on long solitary walks, often at night. She was molested several times, and perhaps narrowly escaped more serious consequences. Hiking along the banks of the C. and O. canal and the Potomac river she ruminated about suicide. Her being in therapy was not very reassuring in this regard, since her commitment to it was quite tenuous.

(2) *Mood-Inversion Transpires.* She shared an apartment with her sister, where her desperate shyness required her to avoid meeting callers. On one occasion she retreated to the bedroom and used chinaware as a urinary receptable to keep from going to the bathroom. Her appearance and manner were such as to repel most people. Only a faithful friend or so managed occasionally to seek her out in the face of her marked unresponsiveness and withdrawal (pp. 488–91).

By April, all this had changed completely! In the space of a few months she had undergone a complete metamorphosis. The transformation was nearly unbelievable. If not observed during this period, it would have been difficult to have recognized the radiant, vivacious, and attractive butterfly who had by now emerged from her cocoon of depression.

(3) *Pervasive Influences on Life.* In mood, appearance, and behavior everything was opposite. She had reversed moroseness into gaiety; somberness into lightheartedness; shyness into confidence and boldness; dull and ponderous mental activity into that which was facile and witty. The once so backward, unattractive, frightened, and sad little mouse had blossomed so, that she hardly gave a thought to flirting mischievously with an older married man. From dowdy she had become beautiful; from friendless, to having a host of friends who grew steadily and rapidly in number. Depression was inverted and transposed into elation.

Her relations with her parents were also reversed. Previously she complained about them constantly and bitterly, and avoided them. Now everything was rosy—too much so. Her glossing over points of conflict was another evidence of a new defense, one of superficiality. From depressed she had become elated in mood; a major Mood-Inversion.

It was fascinating to observe the change. This took place gradually, unwittingly, unconsciously, inexorably; brought about by powerful intrapsychic forces.

Was the changed girl still ill? By many of our social standards her adjustment would have been rated as superior. Her elation was far more marked in a relative sense to her prior state, rather than as a symptom-complex of such apparentness, and as one which might set her apart as different or strange. Socially, it was within bounds. Still, given the opportunity, the careful clinician might have found a number of indications which would have led him to consider her still very much in need of therapy.

3. Deficient Insight A Danger Signal

First, there was the considerable likelihood of another clinical episode of depression. She had suffered another one earlier. *Secondly,* her insight now was, if anything, more defective than previously. *Finally*, there were other personality features, including, as examples, her superficiality, glossing-over of problems, relative nonawareness of others' feelings or sensitivities, and impatience. Her rapid sequence of thoughts tended to prevent sufficiently thorough attention to most items, and her usually high spirits were quite brittle.

Everything was "fine," she believed. What need was there to continue therapy? "I don't want to even remember how things were 6 months ago!" (nor when she had earlier been depressed). In many respects, she was still less a willing and promising candidate for therapy following the major Mood-Inversion. Actually, her need for treatment if anything, might have been considered to be greater.

E.   INVERSION AND OTHER EGO DEFENSES

1. Inversion and Reaction Formation.

A. EMOTIONAL REVERSALS.—The defensively-intended dynamisms of Inversion and Reaction Formation (Chapter 18) are related, although distinctions can be made. Most important is that the end results of these unconscious psychologic endeavors are similar. Both represent emotional reversals which are automatic, unconscious, and without any conscious effort on the part of the individual.

Drawing lines of demarcation between the dynamisms of Inversion, Reaction Formation, and Reversal (Chapter 27) can be a difficult matter. Their separate delineation clinically may require an arbitrary decision.

B. CRITERIA IN DELINEATION.—We can note certain general criteria in delineating Inversion from Reaction Formation. Inversion differs from Reaction Formation in that: (1) it is relatively specific; (2) it is more immediate; (3) it usually functions within narrower limits; and (4) there are less frequent involvements of ego machinations over any considerable period of time in its development. Generally, Reaction Formation involves a series of related attributes or attitudes, while Inversion is more likely to have a more limited application to a specific idea, feeling, trait, standard, or mood.

Inversion does not usually reflect as much of the long-term characterologic development process which is more implicit to the operation of Reaction Formation, although this is variable as we have noted with the Characterologic Inversion. Reaction Formation is known as a "reaction of the opposite." It is likely to involve large areas of the personality. Inversion is frequently confined to being a direct and more isolated "turning around" or reversal, of the specific discrete original impulse, wish, or mood. Inversion by definition is nearly 100 percent effective in its more narrow area; Reaction Formation is effective in varying degrees and seldom is so completely effective in the degree of direct reversal which transpires.

2. *Repression Reenforced; Progression Beyond Denial*

Inversion, like other ego-defensive mechanisms, technically cannot stand by itself. For a feeling or a wish or complex to be inverted, it must first be repressed. In consequence, there exists a consciously disowned feeling. For example, feelings of disgust, perhaps vociferously expressed, may come to replace disowned feelings of pleasure. Through Inversion as a secondary elaboration, the Repression is reenforced. The original feeling has not only become disowned (repressed), but it remains further hidden from conscious awareness.

This progression of events goes beyond Denial, as discussed earlier in Chapter 4, through which the disowned feeling is denied. Through the operation of Inversion, Denial not only takes place, but the feelings are further disguised so that the concealment from conscious awareness (and the sought-after escape from the anxiety which this would occasion) is reenforced. What is finally allowed conscious expression has been inverted into the exact opposite of the intolerable affect, which remains unconscious. (See reference, p. 64.)

F.   SUMMARY

Inversion is employed for several concepts in psychiatry. These include the inversion of: heterosexual orientation, sleep habits, expression of feelings, and aggressive impulses in depression. In our discussion, its operation as an ego defense has been stressed. Herein the term and concept of Inversion finds its most important utilization. The concept of *Social Inversion* was outlined.

A dynamism which operates outside of conscious awareness, Inversion acts automatically and with defensive intent to specifically and directly reverse an intolerable impulse or wish so that it becomes consciously experienced as its opposite. It is an important intrapsychic defensive endeavor. In *secondary elaboration,* Inversion (or other dynamisms) are evolved to support the operation of an existing defense.

We observed how hostility may be inverted into affection (*Hostility-Inversion*) and the less frequently observed process of love into hate (*Positive Affect Inversion*). The *Attraction-Inversion* defense in homosexuality was noted. Patterns of Inversion may begin in childhood which may continue or be reactivated in later years. Inversion can play a role in the development of many symptoms of the neuroses including the phobias, obsessions, and hygeiaphrontis or overconcern-with-health (hypochondriasis). Memories may become inverted, in *Memory-Inversion*. The *White-Washing Operation* was cited as one way in which this can operate. *Standards-Inversion* was noted and illustrated (*Case 102*) in sexual areas.

Inversion operates in conjunction with other ego defenses, especially Repression, and sometimes with Introjection, Identification, Projection, Distortion, and Rationalization. It can represent a further step beyond Denial.

Inversion and Reaction Formation are major kinds of emotional Reversal. Inversion can also represent an overcompensation (Chapter 2). The end results of the operation of Inversion are similar to Reaction Formation (Chapter 18), from which distinctions have been made. Resistance-Inversion of its defensively-intended role in therapy was described.

The role of Inversion has been noted in maintaining or enhancing an acceptable self-picture (*Ego-Enhancing Inversion*), as has been a similar contribution to influencing one's evaluation of others. The important and useful concept of the *Secondary Defense* has been cited. *Goal-Inversion* and *Attitude-Inversion* were described.

Inversion enters into the impotrant area of character trait development in major or minor ways in the *Characterologic Inversion*. Finally, the potential for *Affect Inversion* and *Mood-Inversion* was noted. The latter is most marked in cases of emotional illness characterized by major cyclic mood swings. An illustration was cited from clinical experience. The important concept of the treatment resisting *neurotic status quo* received mention. Additional significant illustrations of the ego defense of Inversion are to be found in *Cases 58* through *71* in Chapter 5 (pp. 168–198) of the Blue Book of Mental Mechanisms.

G. CROSS-REFERENCES TO *THE NEUROSES* *

Inversion
In Depressive Reactions (Chapter 4)
　of aggression, in "infantile prototype" (Abraham); p. 170.
　of destructive impulses
　　in *Accident-Prone* persons; p. 198.
　　in *Final Straw* (Case 30); p. 162.
　of grief, in Depression; p. 167.
　of hostility
　　in melancholiacs (Freud); p. 177.
　　in relation to Depressive manifestations; pp. 161, (Fig. 1), 219.
　　satisfied, in electroshock therapy; p. 218.
　　toward self, in onset of Depression; p. 159.
　of unconscious sadism
　　in Anxious Depression (Case 40); p. 190.
　　in suicide (symbolic expression of); pp. 205–6.
In Character Reactions (Chapter 5)
　of aggressive drives, in *Obsessive Personality* (Case 62); p. 290.
　of hostility, overdeveloped in *Depressive Personality* (Case 58); p. 276.
In Obsessive-Compulsive Reactions (Chapter 6); of hostility, in genesis of obsessive thoughts (Case 70); p. 344.
In Fatigue Reactions (Chapter 7)
　of aggression, comparison of Depression to Fatigue; p. 411.
　of prohibited impulses, Fatigue into Depression; p. 405. Case 83; p. 406.
In Hygeiaphrontic Reactions (Chapter 8)
　of aggressive-hostile feelings, toward ego
　　in *Hygeiaphrontic Attacks* (Case 99), p. 483.

---

* From Laughlin, H. P. *The Neuroses*. London, Butterworth & Co., Ltd., 1967.

in loss of dependent position (Case 102); p. 500.
of frustrating object, in *visceral masochism;* p. 491.
of infantile anxiety, in antecedents for emotional problems; p. 493.
In Phobic Reactions (Chapter 10); of unconscious wish
  in phobic ambivalence; pp. 569–70, 601.
In Dissociative Reactions (Chapter 13); of prior attitude, in evolvement of Fugue
  (Case 173); p. 803.

H. REVIEW QUESTIONS

Sample self-check questions on Chapter 13 and Inversion for the
student, psychiatric resident, and board candidate.

1. A. Define *Inversion* as an ego defense.
   B. What is meant by Inversion in reference to sleep, affect dis-
      simulation, and sexual orientation (sexual inversion)? How
      does *Social Inversion* differ?
2. What is the ego's defensive intent in:
   A. the *Attraction-Inversion?*
   B. the *White-Washing Operation* or WWO? How does *Memory-
      Inversion* operate in its service?
3. Discuss the influence of *Standards-Inversion* in sexual behavior.
   Can you cite its influence in relation to another major area of
   living?
4. Explain the following and illustrate when you can:
   A. *Hostility-Inversion.*
   B. *Positive Affect Inversion.*
   C. Inversion as a *secondary elaboration.*
   D. Apathy and disinterest comprising a *secondary defense.*
   E. *Retrospective Denial.*
   F. *Characterologic Inversion.*
   G. *Neurotic status quo.*
   H. *Ego-enhancing Inversion.*
   I. *Goal-Inversion.*
   J. *Attitude-Inversion.*
5. Illustrate the role of *Resistance-Inversion* in therapy.
6. What diagnoses fit into the concept of the *Mood-Inversion?*
7. Both Inversion and Reaction Formation are referred to as *emotional
   reversals.* What points can you recall in attempting their delineation?
8. Inversion is described as a progression beyond Denial. Do you
   agree? Explain.
9. What other dynamisms operate in conjunction with Inversion? How
   can operation of this dynamism represent Overcompensation?
10. Can you find three clinical illustrations of the defensively intended
    operation of this major dynamism?

PART 2
INTRAPSYCHIC MECHANISMS OF DEFENSE

CHAPTER 14

EMOTIONAL DYNAMISMS

... Further Conceptions Concerning Ego Defenses

A. IMPROVING ADAPTATION

1. Resolution of Internal Conflicts. 2. Defending Against Psychic Pain and Anxiety.

B. RESPONSES TO DANGER

1. Internal Dangers. 2. Psychopathologic Sequence: Anxiety; Dynamism; Hypertrophy or Failure; Emotional Illness. 3. Automatic and Unconscious.

C. UNDERSTANDING VITAL IN PSYCHOTHERAPY

D. INTENDED FUNCTIONS OF DYNAMISMS

1. Potential, Aim, and Goal. 2. Bolstering Intrapsychic Defenses. Maintaining Ego Integrity.

E. INTELLIGENCE AND EMOTIONAL PROBLEMS

1. Evolving Conceptions: a. Prejudice Melts; b. Correlations of Intelligence with Defense or Illness. 2. Superior Intelligence No Protection: a. Emotional Illness Preferred Term; b. Differences Between People Quantitative; c. Successful Persons Neurotic. 3. No Place for Prejudice: a. Need for Respect and Understanding; b. Normal Relative; c. Psychic Defenses Similar.

F. EMOTIONAL HEALTH DEFINED

G. SUMMARY

H. REFERENCES (FROM *The Neuroses*)

I. REVIEW QUESTIONS

A. IMPROVING ADAPTATION

1. Resolution of Internal Conflicts

In Part I the ego and its defenses were introduced as a group of more or less specific emotional dynamisms which are widely utilized. Twelve major mechanisms were discussed in chapter form in alphabetical order, and certain important general principles were outlined. In essence, these dynamisms or mental mechanisms are defensive operations. They are evolved unwittingly within the psyche for the intended purposes of helping the individual improve his adaptations to life and bolster his psychologic defenses.

We humans make use of these devices in our unconscious endeavors to resolve conflicts. The ego thus seeks in particular to resolve emotional conflicts which are intrapsychic. These are internal conflicts taking place between major parts of one's personality, for example, the conflict between a strong drive and one's conscience, which forbids its gratification.

Significant conflicts also arise between a need or urge and requirements of the environment. In these, the desires of the individual come into conflict with the restrictions and limitations posed by society.

2. Defending Against Psychic Pain and Anxiety

The aim and intent of an ego defense is the avoidance of psychic discomfort and pain. Its operation is an important function of the major part of one's personality called the ego. Dynamisms or mental mechanisms are accordingly termed ego defenses.

Various ego defenses are evolved and employed unwittingly by everyone as part of their individual defensive operations. Conflict avoidance and resolution are major goals. The ego defenses aim to defend against psychic pain and anxiety.

B.   RESPONSES TO DANGER

1. Internal Dangers

As we have learned, it is helpful to regard the dynamisms as evolving psychologically in response to the more internal kinds of threat and danger. This is analogous to preparations for fight or flight, which take place physically and physiologically in response to the more external kinds of threat and danger. These physical and physiologic preparations are made particularly in response to dangers which are external, or extrapsychic. The accompanying emotional response is one of *fear*.

In turn, the ego defenses are psychologic endeavors through which one unconsciously attempts to cope with danger which is primarily internal, or intrapsychic. This type of threat or danger is not in conscious awareness. The accompanying emotional response is one of *anxiety*. In other words, external dangers may be met by a physical and actual fight or flight. Internal dangers are met by the psychic equivalents of flight or fight. The ego defenses are called into play as part of this psychic fight or flight response to unconscious dangers.

2. Psychopathologic Sequence: Anxiety; Dynamism; Hypertrophy or Failure; Emotional Illness

Man seeks to avoid anxiety in every possible way. One major avenue for this defensively-intended avoidance is via the unconscious evolution of various of the ego defenses. Their hypertrophy, misdirection, inadequacy or failure contributes to psychopathology. This is a central formulation in our conceptions of the origin of the emotional illnesses, whether these are neuroses, character neuroses, or functional psychoses.

In our discussion we seek to portray and to emphasize the potential for the operation of this major psychopathologic sequence. Conflict and derepression threatens or produces anxiety, which leads to the evolvement of ego defenses. Their operation can be successful and constructive, partly successful, or at least not self-defeating, or pathogenic, and they can contribute to adjustment, stability, and emotional health. On the other hand their failure and/or hypertrophy contributes to emotional illness.

Internal dangers arise from the threats to the self or ego which are incident to serious emotional conflicts. The ego defenses evolved represent attempts at solutions when the individual is faced with conflicts which would otherwise prove intolerable. As defenses which are intended against anxiety, they seek to provide acceptable kinds of internal compromise or resolution. The consequences may be very self-defeating to the individual concerned. Nevertheless, they are vital operations and are likely to be held on to grimly and defended vigorously. Often elaborated as a primary defense they are in turn (secondarily) defended, in accord with the *Concept of Secondary Defense* (Chapter 1).

3. Automatic and Unconscious

One can hardly overstress that ego defenses are utilized by everyone, and that they are processes which are employed automatically and outside of conscious awareness. Thus, it is far easier for an observer to recognize their operation than the person himself. The particular ones which may be uncovered in the psychologic operations of a given person are strictly individual as to their type, possible combination with others, and relative prominence.

An ego defense may evolve to cope with some narrow aspect of living. On the other hand its operation may become so significant as to be the major influence in one's adjustment; or sufficiently pervasive to dominate one's way of life. To whatever extent this takes place, the development and operation of the genuine ego defense is automatic and unconscious. Deliberate efforts with an identical aim and name may be undertaken in full conscious awareness. When this is true, however, the process is not a true dynamism. These points are perhaps clearer in the light of the preceding chapters and case illustrations.

Chapters 1 and 14 serve as an introduction to the ego defenses or mental mechanisms. Every student of human behavior should have a vital interest in these internal psychologic operations; what they are, how they arise, the forms they take, and the possible consequences of their operations.

C.   UNDERSTANDING VITAL IN PSYCHOTHERAPY

It should be quite apparent from the material thus far, that a working familiarity with the ego defenses is a basic requirement for working with those who suffer from emotional illnesses. This is particularly true for anyone interested in psychotherapy.

A most important goal in modern psychotherapy is the increase of self-understanding. More insight is sought. The patient needs to learn more about what makes him "tick" as a person. With the help of the self-knowing therapist, the patient undertakes the working out of the important "whys" and "hows" of his psychologic defenses. Inevitably, the therapeutic process will include a fair amount of *de*repression; the bringing of previously unconscious material into conscious awareness. Following its recall to consciousness, its existence must be accepted; it must be reconciled with material which is already conscious, and it must be studied and understood. In the course of all this, it will undergo modification as to its emotional import. Inconsistencies, discrepancies, and unclear aspects of one's emotional reactions require elucidation. Work in these areas can prove most beneficial to the patient.

Successful treatment will lead to greater understanding by patient and physician of the former's intrapsychic defense operations; his ego defenses. The more knowledge the therapist possesses concerning the general principles of their operation as well as of his own, the better are his chances for therapeutic success in a given case, and the speedier will be the progress of therapy. While patients with specific emotional symptoms, or those having handicapping personality traits, are usually thought of in connection with therapy, it should be carefully noted that the therapeutic process of self-study has a universally useful potential. Psychotherapy is essentially an educational process; a very personal one and one of considerable depth.

D.   INTENDED FUNCTIONS OF DYNAMISMS

1. Potential, Aim, and Goal

We observe repeatedly that the potential for serious emotional illness can be a consequence of the operation or failure of certain dynamisms. This, of course, is certainly far from the underlying intent! It is also interesting to note that their operation unconsciously constitutes both an advantage and a disadvantage. It is an advantage, indeed a necessity, since if maintained as an unconscious operation, it is not then subject to rationality. Its existence is not then threatened by the possibility of objective evaluation and judgment. On the other hand, the unconscious status of the process places the person concerned in a helpless position in regard to its modification. How can he influence something he is unable to recognize? He is at a decided disadvantage. An inability to make constructive changes is an inevitable accompaniment. He is indeed impotent.

As has been illustrated, what is (unconsicously) sought is an adjustment to life. Each individual seeks to adapt himself satisfactorily to his environment. The most important aspects of one's environment generally are the interpersonal ones. One aims to avoid psychic discomfort and pain; to secure a measure of psychologic homeostasis. Emotional stability and equanimity are goals.

We have referred to the need for conflict resolution. There are a number of major ways in which ego defenses undertake this goal. Through a dynamism, an alternate more consciously acceptable solution may be pursued. Through Displacement (Chapter 5) and Substitution (Chapter 23), for example, an emotionally and psychically tolerable aim may replace one which the person concerned finds consciously intolerable. Anxiety is exceedingly unpleasant. Its control, prevention, or avoidance is an ever-present goal. To whatever extent this can be achieved contributes to increasing equanimity and security.

The ego defenses attempt to secure acceptable compromises. These are sought when personal drives, goals, needs, or wishes are present which are intolerable and/or impossible to satisfy, frequently because of opposing personal or social standards. The maintenance and reenforcement of Repression (Chapter 21) can also be an important function of ego defenses. In this type of service, the process represents a *secondary elaboration* (Chapter 13) which can fit into the important *Concept of Secondary Defense, as referred to earlier* (p. 11; see also Index, references).

2. Bolstering Intrapsychic Defenses. Maintaining Ego Integrity

The dynamism and its intended goals essentially comprise an ego function; its vital service being the maintaining of ego integrity. Bolstering internal psychologic defenses helps to combat the disruptive effects of anxiety, conflict, and stress, and thereby fosters ego integration.

Instinctual drives which are intolerable have an ego dissociative and disintegrating effect. Their impact is blunted and their energy absorbed or deflected through the operation of various dynamisms. Herein the development of the ego defense is a major emotional and psychologic response to this internal danger; especially the danger that the consciously intolerable wish or drive might not be kept in control. As noted earlier, this process may be regarded as psychologically analogous to the physical and physiologic preparations for "fight" or "flight" which occur in response to danger or a threat that is essentially external in origin.

The following is a tabulation of the principal defensively-intended goals of the ego defenses, and some of the beneficial and the injurious consequences of their employment (*Table 8*).

Table 8

The Ego Defenses
Aims, Functions, and Consequences

The *ego defenses* are alternately referred to as *dynamisms* and *mental mechanisms*. As a group, they comprise a score or more of vital, specific, intrapsychic processes which operate outside of and beyond conscious awareness. They attempt to subserve important defensive aims and purposes, in the service of the ego. Resolution of emotional conflict and freedom from anxiety are sought.

Following is a list of their principal defensively-intended aims and functions, together with certain vital consequences to their elaboration by the psyche. As outlined, some of these inevitably are overlapping. The effectiveness of a given ego defense is highly variable.

A. *Defensively-Intended Aims and Functions*
   1. The increase of personal security.
   2. Contributions to one's defenses against the subjective experiencing of anxiety.
   3. The preservation and enhancement of self-esteem.
   4. The maintenance of emotional stability (reasonable psychologic homeostasis, or equanimity). The promotion of emotional health and well-being.
   5. The maintenance or reinforcement of *repression* through *secondary elaborations*.
   6. Ego synthetic and integrating influences and effects.
   7. The securing of acceptable compromise between one's individually intolerable or impossible urges, needs or goals, versus personal standards and social requirements.
   8. The resolution of emotional (intrapsychic) conflict.
   9. As an aid in securing:
      a. control,
      b. denial, and/or
      c. secret gratification of otherwise (consciously) intolerable impulses or needs.
B. *The Potential for Certain Possible Vital Consequences to Their Elaboration and Utilization by the Psyche*
   1. Constructive contributions to efficiency and satisfactions in living, and to one's emotional equanimity.
   2. Helping to determine the important individual personality structure, and the personal constellation of defensively-intended character traits which are evolved.
   3. The misdirection, confusion, overdevelopment (hypertrophy); improper or antagonistic action, or exaggeration of a given ego defense or group of dynamisms. The consequences of these untoward results or failure of the ego defense can contribute to numbers 5, 6, and 7 following.
   4. Satisfaction of masochistic needs for having the unacceptable drive, and for whatever measure of its unconscious gratification (A.:9, c, *above*) that has been secured.
   5. The untoward consequences of ego dissociation and disruption (the converse of A.:6, *above*).
   6. Contributions to the unhealthy exaggeration of existing character defensive traits.
   7. Symptom formation, contributing to all kinds of emotional illnesses. Includes contributions to any type of psychopathologic and self-defeating emotional manifestation.

E.   INTELLIGENCE AND EMOTIONAL PROBLEMS

1. Evolving Conceptions

A. PREJUDICE MELTS.—Not too many decades ago, it was fashionable to believe that emotional illness was far more likely to occur where intelligence was limited; or that it was perhaps restricted to such persons. With the prevalence of this kind of belief, of course, prejudice toward sick people, workers, and indeed the entire field of emotional illness flourished. Currently, few continue to subscribe to this myth. The presence of emotional problems is universal and relative. Their level has little correlation with the level of intelligence. What correlations we can determine are of a different nature than that implied above.

The person who is emotionally ill is not stupid. He is ill. He has not become sick through the lack of intelligence or through stupidity, nor does he remain so for any such reason. Nor is he ill through a lack of will power. His illness has come about as a consequence of the ineffective operation of unconscious defenses which were developed automatically, in response to unconscious conflicts, danger, and anxiety. He may become ill because the defenses unwittingly elaborated are overwhelmed by powerful internal or external stresses. He may also become ill because the defenses themselves become hypertrophied or exaggerated; a development which can occur to the point of handicap, self-defeat, or even gross pathology. Defenses are automatically erected, and the person concerned generally has little or no voluntary control over them.

B. CORRELATIONS OF INTELLIGENCE WITH DEFENSE OR ILLNESS.— With certain types of emotional illness, as in the Depressive Reactions, for example, there is an increased incidence among the better educated and more intellectually favored people. The development of certain kinds of emotional conflicts, and the utilization of particular ego defenses are more likely to be associated with persons who happen to be endowed with superior intelligence.

Other correlations which we may suggest are between the types of defense evolved and the individual and general: (1) levels of education; (2) intellectual capacities; and (3) sophistication. (See *Changing Trends,* pp. 658 ff., and *Cultural Vogue Concepts,* pp. 244, 316, 844, in *The Neuroses.*) Herein we may note a more frequent tendency toward the evolution and utilization of the more primitive or Lower Order defenses by those less favored. However, these correlations are subject to fairly frequent exceptions. See also Concepts of Unwitting Ignorance, p. 489.

2. Superior Intelligence No Protection

A. EMOTIONAL ILLNESS PREFERRED TERM.—It becomes clear from the foregoing that superior intelligence is by no means a protection against emotional illness. We have worked with many patients in psychotherapy whose intellectual endowments were considerably above the average, including some whose I.Q.'s quite clearly indicated the genius level. Through the author's experience as a therapist, this point has been amply and repeatedly brought home. Others in the field have reported parallel experiences.

The bases of the illness thus lie in the sphere of the emotions, and not in the sphere of the intellect. The term "emotional illness" in contradistinction to that of "mental illness" is of importance therefore in indicating the origin of the problems and in directing the main focus of attention away from mental function and the intellect. We would accordingly find the term "emotional illness" preferable to "mental illness." This is further indicated since the latter can convey a mistaken impression concerning the origins of the difficulty. The finding that emotional problems when present can impede or interfere with intellectual functioning, is in a different sphere.

B. DIFFERENCES BETWEEN PEOPLE QUANTITATIVE.—Everyone has emotions, and some share of painful feelings. It is part of being human. Everyone experiences anxiety. Everyone has problems.

People's problems vary in extent and degree. They vary from time to time and from one period of life to another, as well as from person to person. However, no one remains constantly calm and untroubled. The differences between people in these respects is more one of quantity than of quality.

C. SUCCESSFUL PERSONS NEUROTIC.—Psychologic defenses which are evoked in response to one's problems are individual ones. Certain correlations with background and capacity are possible, as noted. Just as certain defenses and types of illness are likely to evolve with the more favored, it is also true that certain ones can interfere with the application of one's intellectual faculties, and can restrict judgment.

The overall process of maturation may be impeded by neurotic processes. However, we must note that many brilliant, sociably valuable, and successful people are highly neurotic. Indeed their neurotic drives may have contributed or been responsible for their achievements and success.

3. No Place For Prejudice

A. NEED FOR RESPECT AND UNDERSTANDING.—In view of the foregoing comments and for many additional reasons, the reader should have an adequate and kindly respect for the emotionally sick person. Such respect is enhanced through increased understanding of the ways in which such illnesses develop. In emotional illness, the patient is powerless to extricate himself. His character defenses and neurotic symptoms constitute a steel trap in which he is inexorably and rather helplessly held.

The sound approach to emotional problems, defenses, and illness is through securing more knowledge about the purposes, nature, and operation of human psychologic defenses in general, and about one's own in particular. Sufficient knowledge leaves no room for prejudice. Our present survey of the dynamisms is intended to help in this regard, as have been earlier works.

B. NORMAL RELATIVE.—Several increasingly recognized findings stand out as more or less counter to some of the continuing bias surrounding emotional illness, which lingers on stubbornly in a few scattered quarters. *First,* in the field of emotional or mental health, the so-called normal is a relative matter. Normality, problems, and illness are all relative. The normal therefore is somewhat difficult to define. *Second,* the normal gradually merges into the borderline, which in turn merges on into illness.

Third, the evolution of ego defenses can contribute to health. *Finally,* and on the other hand, their exaggerated development, hypertrophy, or misdirection may gradually and imperceptibly progress into the manifestations of a neurosis, character neurosis, or functional psychosis.

C. PSYCHIC DEFENSE SIMILAR.—From the standpoint of their emotional reactions, people are not really very different. They use the same psychologic defenses; the identical ego defenses. The differences are in amount, extent, and the combination of those which are evolved. These differences are far more ones of degree rather than of kind. This of course does not deny that such differences can be most important individually as to their effects and results. Finally, emotional problems are universal, as earlier noted.

In modern science, in medicine, and among the more sophisticated laity, there is truly no longer any place for uninformed prejudice about emotional or mental health. As we view the patient who suffers with cancer; it is more a matter of "There, but for the grace of God, go I."

F.   EMOTIONAL HEALTH DEFINED

It would seem incomplete to conclude the introduction of Part II of our text and our further study of additional interesting ego defenses without undertaking a definition of emotional health.

We may therefore define emotional health as *a state of being which is relative, rather than absolute. In general, the person who is emotionally healthy has effected a reasonably satisfactory integration of his instinctual drives.* He has worked out psychologically harmonious solutions for them which are acceptable to himself, and to his social milieu. Some 30 additional criteria for emotional health are listed in *Mental Mechanisms* pp. 25–26.

Let us continue on then to our next dynamism, following in alphabetical sequence the remainder of the *Major Mechanisms,* after which the *Minor Ego Defenses* will be briefly considered alphabetically in our two final chapters.

G.   SUMMARY

As a continuation of the comments in Chapter 1, further conceptions were offered concerning the ego defenses, 12 major ones having received consideration thus far. These emotional dynamisms evolve to improve individual adaptation, particularly through resolving intrapsychic conflicts and defending against psychic-emotional pain and anxiety. The ego defenses evolve individually as responses to stress and danger, somewhat as one consciously mobilizes his resources to meet physical threats.

The significant conception of a *sequence of psychopathology* was noted, in which conflict and depression produce anxiety, leading to defenses, whose failure or hypertrophy in turn contribute to emotional illness. Ego defenses can represent *secondary elaborations* (of existing defenses), or as primary defenses can be themselves (secondarily) defended, in accord with the *Secondary Defense Concept*. Their operation is automatic and unconscious.

Knowledge of the ego defenses and understanding the principles in their operation is vital in undertaking psychotherapy. Succesful treatment inevitably will lead to their elucidation. Psychotherapy is an educational process of considerable depth and one which is highly personal.

The intended functions of the dynamisms were discussed, including their aims and goals. They are essentially an ego operation, aiming to maintain and preserve its integrity and synthesis in the face of conflict and stress. *Table 8* outlined the aims, functions, and goals of the ego defenses and certain of their potentially constructive and destructive consequences.

Recognition that emotional problems occur universally, are not a reflection of intellectual deficit, and that resulting illness is no respecter of person or position should lay to rest lingering prejudices toward the field and about persons so affected. Differences between people are more quantitative than qualitative as to the presence of emotional factors. Many successful persons are highly neurotic. Normality is relative and people evolve similar psychic defenses.

H.   CROSS-REFERENCES TO *THE NEUROSES* *

Mental Mechanisms (general references, continued from 21)
In Hygeiaphrontic Reactions (Chapter 8)
    as equivalent to Depression; p. 499.
    as *Higher Order vs. Lower Order;* pp. 497, 511.
    in neurosis resolution; p. 507.
    in preexisting pattern of; p. 498.
In Fear and Its Avoidance (Chapter 9)
    in avoidance of anxiety; pp. 516–17, 525.
    in bases of phobia evolvement; p. 529.
    in psychologic pain avoidance; p. 530.
In Phobic Reactions (Chapter 10); in psychodynamics of phobia evolvement; pp. 574, 602.
In Soterial Reactions (Chapter 11); in psychodynamics of *soteria* evolvement; p. 633.
In Conversion Reactions (Chapter 12); in Conversion character defenses; p. 675.
In Dissociative Reactions (Chapter 13)

---

* From Laughlin, H. P. *The Neuroses*. London, Butterworth & Co., Ltd., 1967.

Dissociation as (Table 38); p. 729.
in *Affective Escape Route* (in depersonalization); p. 762.
in psychodynamics of hypnosis; p. 813.
investigation of, in hypnosis; p. 825.
In Neuroses-Following-Trauma (Chapter 14)
    as defense against anxiety; p. 874.
    failure of, in genesis of neuroses; p. 869.
    in conjunction with Repression; p. 873.
    use of, in reaction to stress; p. 894.
In Military Reactions (Chapter 15)
    collapse of; p. 922.
    in military man's defensive pattern; p. 925.

I.   REVIEW QUESTIONS

Sample self-check questions on Chapter 14 and the Emotional Dynamisms for the student, psychiatric resident, and board candidate.

1. Discuss the role of ego defenses in facilitating adaptation.
2. Trace how the psychopathologic sequence progresses from emotional conflict to illness.
3. Outline the unconscious aims, functions, and consequences of the psychic-emotional dynamisms.
4. Discuss the relationship between emotional problems and intelligence.
5. Define emotional health.
6. What is:
    A. *secondary elaboration?*
    B. *concept of Secondary Defense?*
    C. psychic pain?
    D. ego integrity?
    E. derepression?
7. Why is an understanding of the ego defenses vital in doing psychotherapy?
8. How can dynamisms contribute to emotional health? To psychopathology?
9. Discuss the concept of normalcy being relative.
10. Define and describe an illustration from your clinical experience of each of the 12 *major* or *senior dynamisms* discussed.
    A. Compensation.
    B. Conversion.
    C. Denial.
    D. Displacement.
    E. Dissociation.
    F. Fantasy.
    G. Idealization.
    H. Identification.
    I. Incorporation.
    J. Internalization.
    K. Introjection.
    L. Inversion.

CHAPTER 15

PROJECTION

*. . . The Unacceptable Ascribed to Others; A
Mirror-Defense*

A. THE NATURE OF PROJECTION

    1. Definition. 2. Projection and Other Dynamisms. 3. Defensive Motivation; Self-Defeat. 4. Antecedents. 5. Psychologic Blind-Spots: a. Perception Lacking; b. Value of Analysis; c. Criticized in Others, Unrecognized in Self. 6. Literary Recognition.

B. THE PERSONAL YARDSTICK

    1. Universal Measuring Device. 2. Mirror-Defense Concept.

C. ADDED TYPES AND PURPOSES OF PROJECTION

    1. Repression Maintained: a. Guarding Against Depression; b. The Vicious Circle of Projection or PVC. Interpersonal Projection. 2. Minor Projections. 3 Psychotic Projections: a. The Diffuse Projection. Paranoid Indifference; b. The Negative Projection; c. The Grandiose Projection. 4. Reality Distortion.

D. SUMMARY

    1. Handicaps Imposed. 2. Ascribing to Another; Personal Yardstick Allows Distortion.

E. REFERENCES (FROM *The Neuroses*)

F. REVIEW QUESTIONS

A. THE NATURE OF PROJECTION

1. Definition

From one viewpoint Projection can be regarded as a further progression of elaboration of psychologic avoidance. It avoids conflict, through ascribing that which is personally intolerable, to others. Through Projection one imputes to others motives and emotional feelings which are consciously unacceptable and disowned. Psychic pain, anxiety, shame, anger, resentment, hostility, burdensome responsibility, and guilt each can comprise the unwelcome harvest of internal emotional conflict and can provide ample motivation for Projection. When this ego defense operates successfully the feelings so ascribed are reflected back toward oneself. Accordingly, one also responds more or less appropriately for example, to the resulting hostility and aggression directed toward him, through its unwitting Projection to what becomes the "hostile" person.

From a broad viewpoint, Projection is the throwing of something forward and outward. In psychiatry, Projection is *an ego defense or mental mechanism operating outside of and beyond conscious awareness through which consciously disowned aspects of the self are rejected or disowned and thrown outward, to become imputed to others.*

Projection as an emotional dynamism provides a *Mirror-Defense;* furnishing us with a useful description, and one which can serve as an alternative term. Through the operation of this very important and widely evolved intrapsychic process, an individual may attribute his own intolerable wishes, emotional feelings, or motivations to another person.

Through their Projection, the attributes which are unwittingly assigned to others appear real enough to the person concerned. Indeed they become factual. His reactions and behavior are influenced accordingly in his responses to this fantastic person [1] whom he has thus created. The PVC or *Projective Vicious Circle* is the conception which outlines the self-defeat inherent in the reactions to such unreal people, as created through Projection. As such consequences progress, a vicious spiral may become established, contributing in circular fashion to exaggerating the very situation one may be defending against and seeking to avoid.

Projection is also used less exactly in referring to the outward direction of emotion from internal conflicts, a process more properly referred to as Externalization [2] (Chapter 26). Projection is, of course, similar in that the disowned attribute, feeling, or complex is directed outwardly. However, in Projection as more strictly defined above, the process carries a significant step further, through the imputation to another of the consciously disowned material.

2. Projection and Other Dynamisms

Projection is closely associated with Repression (Chapter 21), in which the Repression is reinforced by Projection. Projection is roughly the converse of Introjection, as noted earlier in Chapter 12. These dynamisms and their effects can be constructive and normal as well as pathologic. As with the ego defenses generally, it is: (1) the method of their employment, (2) the extent of their use, and (3) their exaggeration or imbalance, which results in their becoming pathogenic.

Projection in its widest usage may be said to refer to any kind of

[1] See earlier reference in Chapter 8 to another type of fantastic person, created through the operation of the process of Idealization.

[2] In the psychogenesis of the phobia for example, the emotional feeling associated with the internal conflict is redirected outward, that is, it becomes displaced and externalized. This is Externalization, and not Projection (pp. 462–4).

active emotional extrusion from the body. Like Introjection, it can have constructive and healthy uses. The projected material and its effects do not have to be inimical. One may project kindly feelings and motives to another. A type of Projection together with Identification, may also better aid one in temporarily occupying another person's shoes, as referred to in Chapter 9. Most of the social virtues, kindly attitudes toward others, and interest in their concerns, involve some degree of what is referred to as *Projective Identification*. (See also earlier types of *PI,* as discussed in Chapter 9.)

Through Introjection and Projection either love or hate as well as many other types of affect, can be unconsciously turned inward the self in the first instance, or outward to another person in the second. Projection operates in concert with Repression, Identification, and Rationalization in the interesting *King David Reaction* which we shall shortly discuss (p. 236). Projection also enters significantly into the evolvement of serious psychopathologic formations, such as delusions and hallucinations.

3. Defensive Motivation; Self-Defeat

The following instance illustrates the defensively-intended but self-defeating results from the Projection of personally disowned affect. An underlying defensive motivation and self-defeating consequences, are rather typically associated with the operation of the dynamism of Projection.

Case 106

Projection of Affect: "I dislike them" becomes "They dislike me"

(1) *A Social Pattern.* A 19-year-old college student, was in psychotherapy because of difficulty in concentration, which was greatly handicapping his work. Although his intelligence was quite above average, in several subjects his work was barely passing, and there was danger of his failing the semester.

He was also greatly troubled by his certainty that many people regarded him as self-centered, boorish, and generally unlikable. This belief was underscored by a pattern of behavior which would occur at social gatherings. Early in the evening the student (who could be quite personable) would enter into the spirit of things, and soon become the center of attention. As the evening progressed, however, he increasingly felt disliked. As this feeling grew, he became quiet and withdrawn. Almost invariably he would leave the party feeling that he was disliked by all.

(2) *Competitiveness and Hostility.* In therapy, the student's underlying intense competitiveness and hostility soon became apparent. Accompanying his desire to be the center of attention socially were strong angry feelings toward the others present together with the need to prove that he was better than they. As the evening progressed, these feelings came closer to the surface. The threat of their breaking through into awareness brought on anxiety. To help repress his consciously disowned competitiveness and hostile feelings, to avert anxiety, he projected the hostility onto his companions, coming to feel instead that they disliked him.

In other words, this young man maintained his defensive nonawareness of his hostile and competitive feelings partly through their Projection and assignment to others. "I dislike them" became experienced by him instead as "they dislike me."

(3) *Self-Defeat: Actual Creation of the Disowned and Projected Feelings. Therapeutic Elucidation.* It should be emphasized that he was not disliked at the parties as he believed; his angry feelings were not apparent in his behavior. Nonetheless the dislike he experienced was genuine to him, and he reacted accordingly; feeling disliked and rejected, he became resentful, antagonistic, and withdrew in turn. In other words, reactions to the attitudes imputed to the others, in turn influenced their acceptance of him, with the effect of eventually creating the very kind of unfriendly atmosphere which he experienced. The potential for self-defeat in this pattern is evident. It illustrates the PVC (p. 228).

The repeated elucidation in therapy of this defensively motivated but self-defeating pattern fortunately led to its gradual dissolution.

4. *Antecedents*

The earliest determination of the infant relates to his distinguishing between edible and nonedible objects. His earliest acceptance · is through ingestion and swallowing. His earliest rejection similarly is through refusal or spitting out.

Projection might be regarded as ultimately deriving from this first, primordial rejection. It expresses the meaning of a rejecting throwing out or away. In his earliest reactions, the emotions or excitations which the infant tries to get rid of, to escape from, or to ward off are figuratively spit out, on the model of the antecedent and more literal spitting out. When the process of Projection is successful they are psychologically expelled and hence are experienced as being outside the ego.

In the evolution of the intended defense of Projection, primordial reactions are later adopted by the ego for its own purposes. In general, the organism prefers to feel dangers as threats coming from without rather than from within. Certain mechanisms of protection against unwelcome or overly intense stimuli can be set in motion only against external stimuli. Primordial Denial can considerably restrict Projection (p. 68).

The externalization of (internal) danger situations is one of the ego's earliest methods of defense against anxiety, and plays an important role in psychologic development. What happens is that the child projects his own impulses on to his objects.

In effect this can comprise the earliest *Personal Yardstick* (p. 226) application. Thus, the infant expects in fantasy that his objects (significant adults) will do to him what he has done, or that which he fantasies he has done or might wish to do, to them. His fear of retaliation is both con-scious and unconscious. For the child, the dynamisms of Introjection and Projection often are methods of mastering feelings which he has fantasied as actual dealings with significant persons. See also earlier references in relation to Denial (pp. 68 and 69).

5. *Psychologic Blind-Spots*

A. PERCEPTION LACKING.—The term psychologic blind-spot is an interesting descriptive label. It can be aptly applied to *those aspects most frequently involving oneself, or those aspects of one's relationships with others for which one lacks conscious perceptive ability.* The perceptive ability is blocked. This, of course, is often despite clear recognition by another person. An alternative term is *emotional block.*

The presence of psychologic blind-spots is universal. They often concern significant defects in our awareness of unpleasant things about ourselves. Their existence and the resulting personal handicap can be a potent reason for intensive personality study.

B. VALUE OF ANALYSIS.—The invariable presence of psychologic blind-spots is alone an important justification for young psychiatrists undertaking a personal analysis. This kind of study leads to more self-knowledge, and is likely to be personally invaluable. Further, it can be a most important adjunct to the improvement of ability to help one's patients through intensive psychotherapy. It is essential that each person in analysis have a trained and competent objective observer to help uncover his psychologic blind-spots.

Robert Burns poetically expressed the wish that people have felt over the course of history to have an increased ability to see themselves more clearly, in the oft-quoted lines:

> "O wad some power the giftie gie us
> To see oursels as ithers see us!"

He continued, noting some benefits in the less known lines, which follow:

> "It wad frae monie a blunder free us,
> An' foolish notion;
> What airs in dress and gait wad lea'e us,
> And ev'n devotion!"

C. CRITICIZED IN OTHERS, UNRECOGNIZED IN SELF.—Often psychologic blind-spots or emotional blocks make is impossible to recognize traits about ourselves that have personally and socially handicapping consequences. This is true even though we may be easily aware and often highly critical of the same things in other people.

The following examples are illustrative of this frequently encountered phenomenon. In each of them, the person is critical of an attribute in others which he is unable to recognize in himself.

Case 107

Psychologic Blindness to Child's Behavior

An indignant mother called the police to report a young "criminal" who had taken some pennies from the sidewalk flower stand set up as a juvenile business venture by her daughter. The mother bitterly and repeatedly condemned the boy to anyone who would listen. However, in a tolerantly amused fashion, she would describe, almost in the same breath, how the flowers were taken from a neighbor's garden.

There was little difference in the "taking" which had been done by either child. The mother, however, was blind to the implications of what her child had done, while bitterly indignant and condemning about what essentially amounted to the same thing in the other child.

Case 108

Profanity: External versus Personal

A hospitalized man had gained notoriety among patients and staff because of his proclivity for profanity. One day when another person was overheard swearing, this man was the first to criticize.

His condemnations were more outspoken and critical than others. He had become incensed at an aspect of another, corresponding with something consciously unrecognized in himself. Herein are elements of a more simple variety of the negative type of *King David Reaction* (Chapter 16, p. 236 ff.).

Case 109

Debt Payment

A business man was being vociferous in denouncing those whom he found slow to pay bills.

A listener recollected wryly about a hundred-dollar loan made to this business man. Done as a personal favor some time back, the debt was long past the promised date of repayment.

This short presentation of the interesting and significant phenomenon of *Psychologic Blind-Spots* can serve as a useful introduction to our continuing discussion of the important ego defense of Projection.

There are many social and clinical examples of the projective type of protectively-intended psychologic operation. Through its evolution, one unwittingly seeks to "have his cake and eat it too." Personal attitudes or attributes are consciously intolerable and disowned. Internal needs and satisfactions, however, are not surrendered. The person represses awareness. The not infrequent next step in the defensively-motivated sequence is that of their unconscious Projection.

6. Literary Recognition

In Webster's play, *The Duchess of Malfi* we find indications of early recognition of the principles of Projection. Herein Julia expressing her doubts of the Cardinal's constancy was cautioned that this stemmed from herself. " . . .You fear my constancy, because (of) those giddy and wild turnips in yourself. . . ."

The playwright indicated through his character his appreciation of the unwitting assignment to another of what is present but disowned in oneself. John Webster (1580–1625) wrote this play sometime between 1611 and its publication in 1623.

There are doubtless many literary examples which might contribute to a historical validation of our present-day concepts of the ego defense of

Projection. We might well so expect, in accord with the *Concept of Historical Validation* (pp. 240 and 301).

B. THE PERSONAL YARDSTICK

1. Universal Measuring Device

There is another important consideration in the evolution of Projection. We refer to the very useful and necessary use of the self as a "yardstick" in the estimation, and evaluation of other people's feelings and attitudes, and in one's efforts to predict their responses and behavior. The more or less automatic employment of this type of what is termed the *Personal Yardstick* begins early with the child. This is true for everyone. It becomes a universally employed measuring device. One's dependence upon his Personal Yardstick, however, varies greatly.

The relative accuracy and usefulness on one hand, *versus* resulting distortions and self-defeat from the employment of the Personal Yardstick likewise have tremendous individual variations. There are all kinds of handicaps inherent in employing this standard of comparison and basis of estimation. The picture as it is perceived will inevitably reflect to some extent what is present in the self.

As emotional maturity progresses, experiences gained through relationships with many other people will ordinarily tend to reduce the dependence upon the Personal Yardstick. Immature reactions earlier present in the self will also diminish, tending to increase its accuracy as a guide. These developments are in accord with an *Hypothesis of a Basic Trend Toward Emotional Health.*

One can perhaps see however how neurotic overreliance upon the Personal Yardstick can lead to serious distortions in one's perceptions of others. Among these are the erroneous attributing of one's own qualities or reactions to another. The dynamism of Projection can play an important role. The child early learns that disapproval and blame from others as well as from himself, can be mitigated if responsibility can be successfully assigned to another. This leads us to the *Concept of Projection as a Mirror-Defense.*

2. Mirror-Defense Concept

One normally seeks to anticipate the attitudes and behavior of others towards himself. This is invaluable, the value being directly proportional to the level of validity. Projection is a major source of error. Through its operation the other person unknowingly has had ascribed to him attitudes, feelings, and reactions which were not consciously recognized by the attributor as being his own. This other person thereby becomes a *mirror*, in thus unwittingly reflecting back the consciously disowned emotional feelings. This is why we have found it useful and explanatory to refer to

Projection as the *Mirror-Defense,* and to employ it as an alternative term. The foregoing outlines the useful *Concept of Projection as a Mirror-Defense.*

In some instances of its operation the Mirror-Defense Concept becomes more apparent, as in the following example. Herein it can approach and gradually merge with the King David Reaction in character and in consequence, as we shall observe in the following chapter. Also illustrated is the transposition of emotions and attitudes. Thus, the hatred ascribed to and experienced as coming from another is really one's own. Even the words employed can be transposed, and often they fit rather well. This is analogous to the similar direct but reversed transposition which was earlier noted as possible in Introjection (p. 190).

Case 110

The Mirror-Defense

A 36-year-old elementary school teacher was perhaps best known by her colleagues for her bitter condemnations of anyone in whom she observed signs of poor organization, lack of orderliness and meticulousness, or inability to cope with difficult situations. Becoming easily emotional or unnerved was an anathema to her. Many times her severe criticisms magnified trifles.

It had been long and painfully obvious to her friends that she possessed herself the attributes so readily ascribed to others, and so much the cause for censure. Her appearance was unkempt; her desk was generally in disarray; and she readily "flew off the handle" when things did not go smoothly.

Her fellow teachers recognized implicitly that she was projecting her inadequacies and shortcomings to others. This endeavored to spare her the anxiety and intolerable burden of self-censure which otherwise would result were she to consciously recognize them in herself.

The teacher's Projection prevented her from seeing herself more clearly. Operation of the ego defense led to excessive criticism of her colleagues, sarcasm, cynicism, and intolerance. While seemingly a vital gain, the many effects upon her relationships were destructive and most self-defeating. Much of the exact phraseology which she employed in criticizing others in her Mirror-Defense could have been directly, and perhaps more accurately transposed to herself.

Case 111

Projection of Responsibility

A middle-aged man was admitted to the orthopedic service because of advanced cellulitis and gangrene of his right foot. Amputation was necessary, but conservative treatment first was instituted in order to save as much of the extremity as possible.

This serious situation had arisen because of neglect of a puncture wound, and its subsequent seriousness. Originally, he appeared to understand his own contributions and responsibility for the tragic progression of pathology. Soon enough, however, this position had shifted completely.

This poor man became the most difficult person to manage on the service. He was uncooperative, mean, antagonistic, and at times belligerent to the point of combativeness. He openly expressed diffuse hostility toward doctors, nurses, aids, and orderlies.

During occasional outbursts, with shouting and obscenity he maintained that everyone was neglecting and mistreating him. He blamed everyone for his misfortune. He called his lawyer to sue the hospital, although the attorney dissuaded him.

Through Projection, this man had come to direct his feelings of self-condemnation and anger outwardly toward others. In condemning them for their "neglect" of him as a patient, he secured a substitute and more tolerable target for his resentment, accusations, and recriminations. His abuse of others could have been directly transposed so as to apply, and more accurately, to himself.

C.   ADDED TYPE AND PURPOSES OF PROJECTION

1. Repression Maintained

A. GUARDING AGAINST DEREPRESSION.—Projection is defensively intended to help maintain lack of awareness of one's rejected and disowned ideas, wishes, impulses, and motives. This is referred to as the maintenance or reinforcement of Repression (Chapter 21). The feared danger is derepression.

The threat of derepression in turn threatens the ego with anxiety and often with a loss of self-esteem. Conflict annd consequent anxiety are avoided through maintaining Repression. Projection directs outwardly and attributes to others aspects of one's own disclaimed and personally objectionable character traits, attitudes, motives, and desires. The dynamism of Projection thus helps enable one to remain blind to important personal factors, while at the same time being potentially self-defeating, through distorting his picture of the world around him.

B. THE VICIOUS CIRCLE OF PROJECTION OR PVC. INTERPERSONAL PROJECTION.—Self-critical feelings are frequently projected. The consequences may comprise a vital gain and nonetheless prove quite self-defeating. The discomfort often is not substantially diminished. This type of Projection often offers little advantage.

Let us cite the following superficial instance. This also illustrates the vicious circle which can become established through Projection, as what is termed the *Projective Vicious Circle* or PVC. The PVC is responsible for a great deal of self-defeat.

Case 112

Self-Critical Feelings Projected; PVC Evolved

A resident physician reported nervousness and feeling ill at ease. He believed himself regarded in an unfriendly light by his colleagues.

With some reflection he attributed this to having reported late for duty on frequent occasions.

The young doctor was a conscientious, rigid person, with high standards for himself and others. He strongly disapproved of his laxity on a deeper level. His tardiness had been most difficult to face in view of highly self-critical attitudes.

His consciously rejected judgmental feelings had been projected to his associates. In his eyes they strongly disapproved of him for his tardiness. He was convinced that this was displayed in various ways. As a result, the young physician began to suffer in more complex fashion. Feeling disapproved, criticized, and rejected, he tended to withdraw and to feel bitter and antagonistic. The projected attitudes he experienced, in illusory fashion, from his colleagues helped to account for his feeling ill at ease and for his nervousness.

In point of fact, his associates had taken little notice of the tardiness. They were not critical about this. They had in fact become somewhat critical and unfriendly toward him, however, but only in response to his antagonism and withdrawal. In other words, they were responding to the resident physician's behavior, which in turn had resulted from his misinterpretations (a consequence of Projection) of their behavior toward him. (See also *Case 106*). From the foregoing, one can see how a Projective Vicious Circle may begin through what is called *Interpersonal Projection*.

The potential destructive consequences upon one's relationships are clearly evident from the above clinical vignette. It illustrates the operation of Interpersonal Projection and its resulting evolution of a PVC.

2. *Minor Projections*

Although Projection frequently contributes to psychopathology, this is by no means invariable. The observer can discern its frequent operation in everyday life far more readily of course in others. The following incidents are examples of what we refer to as *Minor Projections*.

Case 113

Intended Defense Against Recognizing Resentment; Gives it Away

Two brothers got along very well together. One day, however, the younger felt his older sibling had done something unfair. He complained about this in a mild manner and voice. The older brother felt this to have some merit, was stated most reasonably, and he experienced no particular emotional response.

The grievance concluded with a denial of any rancor being present. Surprisingly this was directly followed by forceful comments about "recognizing" his brother's resentment, anger, and antagonistic feelings toward him.

The younger brother had more negative feelings than he had recognized or expressed. Their attribution through Projection to his brother (who had not experienced them) was an intended defense against their recognition. His comments and reaction however, proved to be a giveaway as to their presence.

In the following instance an observant student came to suspect the operation of a Minor Projection in his own psychology. Taking place during the course of his usual activities, he was able to secure some corroborative evidence.

Case 114

A Minor Projection

"... The following incident occurred during our last Wednesday evening seminar on psychopathology. Having been up late the previous night, I was tired and restless during the entire evening. ..."

... Although the subject should have been of interest, I had the compelling impression that the lecturer was not at all interested in speaking to the group, his attitude was condescending, and his enthusiasm lacking. ... Indeed I felt at the time that I could have given a more stimulating lecture myself, that the instructor was compensating for his lack of knowledge on the subject by throwing out questions to the class and that he was repeating obvious material. ... There was no doubt in my mind that his real concern was to run out the allotted time as effortlessly as possible. ..."

"In reflecting later on my dearth of notes, it occurred that it was I who was concerned with getting through the evening 'as effortlessly as possible!' I was in fact the disinterested and unenthusiastic one, who wanted the seminar over with! ..."

"On checking with my colleagues later, they felt the presentation had been a good one, that our instructor was up to his best form, and two or three were surprised that I even raised the question. ... On further analysis there is no doubt that I had projected my own attitudes to the teacher and reacted accordingly. ... I ascribed the evil to him. '*Honi soit qui mal y pense!* ...'"

3. Psychotic Projection

A. THE DIFFUSE PROJECTION. PARANOID INDIFFERENCE.—The employment of Projection usually reaches its most malignant form in the psychotic reactions. Herein it contributes to the development of major and fixed delusions, in which the prognostic outlook is often poor. There are patients in every mental hospital, in whom Projection has contributed to the development of paranoid states. Projection is prominent in hallucinations (p. 69), which can represent projections of intrapsychic elements of the superego or id (pp. 102–3).

Illustrations of what we identify as *Psychotic Projections* are sometimes bizarre, often intriguing, and always tragic. The following three brief excerpts are illustrative. They illustrate in turn three major subtypes of Psychotic Projection: namely the *Diffuse Projection,* which can include many areas and persons—at times shifting in turn from one to the next— the *Negative Projection,* and the *Grandiose Projection.*

Case 115

Diffuse Paranoid Projection

A very ill young man suffered from an obviously paranoid type of Schizophrenic Reaction. He was antagonistic, belligerent, suspicious, and repeatedly accused those with whom he came in contact of being "out to get" him. His was a paranoid type of *Diffuse Projection.* He was treated kindly, with little evident response. It seemed that the kinder his treatment, the more it was met in perverse fashion with more suspicion and hostility.

One day an intercurrent infection and fever led to the need for laboratory tests, and two medical students undertook to obtain blood samples. The patient stated pointedly and specifically that they were seeking to injure him.

He voiced his certainty that the students were "injecting materials into him" which would "harm" or "kill" him. Although the syringes were obviously empty and were so demonstrated, together with all the means of attempted reasoning which they could muster, he continued to maintain that they had injected things that would kill him, even as blood was being withdrawn into the empty syringe.

These beliefs were stated and held, until other "evidences" of his supposed "maltreatment" were forthcoming, to serve as replacements and a new focus of attention. His calmness of speech and manner while relating his suspicions reflected the interesting clinical phenomenon of *Paranoid Indifference*, at times encountered in this form of illness.

The foregoing instance illustrates several prominent features in the paranoid reaction. Supplying evidence or what may be interpreted (or perhaps rather *mis*interpreted) as such by the individual concerned, is eagerly seized upon in support of his self-appraisal, prejudiced beliefs, Projections, and paranoid system. Each such bit of data serves to reinforce the projected image of hostility and persecution and the Projection. Increasing weight and support are thus added to the person's unrealistic conclusions.

Another important clinical facet illustrated is one which was earlier termed *Paranoid Indifference* (p. 103). This concept and term were introduced to invite attention to inappropriate or dissociated affect in the paranoid situation. A patient, as in our illustrations, thus may talk quite calmly in detailing the plans which are underway to persecute, injure, or destroy him.

B. THE NEGATIVE PROJECTION.—In Projection there is the unconscious relegation of an otherwise unacceptable thought or idea to another individual, with the individual's reaction to this. As noted, a PVC can become established. As encountered within the context of the paranoid pattern of psychosis, the consequences frequently lead to delusions of persecution.

The following comprises a variety of employment of this dynamism which we term the *Negative Projection*. Most paranoid individuals feel that they are being persecuted for something they have done. In this case, however, a delusional system was established on a negative basis, in that the patient instead felt that he was being persecuted for things he had failed to do. This occurred in a clinical example of the grandiose paranoid reaction.

Case 116

Negative Projection

A 34-year-old engineer was admitted to the hospital disturbed by his beliefs that truck drivers had been trying to kill him on the highway. Further, he anticipated that the F.B.I. was about to arrest him on serious charges. An employee in the design division of a small aircraft factory, he was convinced that he had failed to perform adequately or competently. This, he had believed, had caused so much consternation among the other people working with him, that they also were unable to perform effectively. As he viewed it, he therefore had been responsible for many resulting aviation accidents.

He believed grandiosely that others were so preoccupied and disturbed over his problems that the then current steel strike had followed. As part of this unfortunate patient's grandiose delusions, physical violence would be done him for his lack of performance; for the things he had failed to do. This was in part an instance of *Negative Projection.*

In therapy, it eventually developed that the patient had fallen far short of achieving the goals set for him by his parents, to become a physician or priest. Part of his resulting self-condemnation as well as his hostility had been projected. He was the product of a very rigid and orthodox religious upbringing. Any thought with sexual connotations, for example, was unthinkable. There were many contributory antecedents and ramifications entering into his emotional breakdown.

Following 18 months of hospitalization and psychotherapy, his illness had modified sufficiently favorably to allow his discharge to an outpatient status with continued intensive therapy. He was shortly able to resume part time work in a less demanding milieu.

C. THE GRANDIOSE PROJECTION.—Elements of grandiosity were also present in the following instance. The lack of insight and failure to recognize the presence of illness is typical. This chap's statements about the anger of others toward him being responsible for his hospitalization is of interest, as it was of course, really his own (projected) anger which was responsible.

Case 117

Projected Anger

A young psychotic patient reported periods of dejection. He related how he painted a self-portrait which "has broken many hearts," and "has been the cause of death of various people. . . ." On admission he had identified himself flatly and with conviction as God!

During an interview later held for teaching purposes, this unfortunate young man was asked if he should be in the hospital. He answered that he was not sick and that of course he should not be in the hospital. Next he was asked why he was there.

He responded, "There is nothing wrong with me. I am here because certain people have become terribly angry with me. Their anger has been so great that it has driven them crazy. . . . It is because these people are crazy that they keep me here. Their anger is responsible. . . ."

4. Reality Distortion

Many complex illustrations of Projection are observed clinically. Projection has a potential for more psychogenic hazards, trouble, and pathogenicity than have many of the other ego defenses. The potential for self-defeat in a spiraling PVC has been noted. In its further pathogenic progression, Projection can contribute to emotional illness of a most serious nature, as we have also observed. Ultimately the morbid operation of Projection can serve as the basis for most of the paranoid delusions in schizophrenia, and in certain hallucinations. These represent its most extreme forms of reality distortion. One particular subtype of paranoid mechanism results in the individual feeling hated and plotted against.

Through a complex, hidden, and involved route, homosexual feelings may be dealt with unconsciously through their Projection. Through this pathway: "I love him" may become "he hates me." This can progress to the point where the patient believes that people regard him unfavorably or with hatred as a homosexual. Men may appear to be making advances toward him. Voices might be heard accusing him of homosexual interests. His disowned and unconscious homosexual drives, and/or his disapproval of himself for having them are projected to others. In more extreme instances, a physical assault may be made on the supposed accuser.

D. SUMMARY

1. Handicaps Imposed

The effects upon emotional health of the more pathogenic operations of Projection are clearly inimical and most unfortunate. The less obviously morbid effects of Projection, however, are also considerable. The handicaps, limitations, inhibitions, discomfort, and self-defeat suffered by persons diversely affected through its operation are substantial. Projection represents a type of psychic avoidance as approximately the converse of Introjection; and is to be distinguished from Externalization. The motivation is defensive.

The untoward results of Projection mainly stem from the inevitably distorted and fantastic people one inadvertently has helped to create for himself. Through the unhealthful operation of the intended ego defense of Projection, the overall net results are widespread psychologic inefficiency, socially wasted effort, and personal loss. Self-defeat may be further engendered through the development of a spiraling PVC, or *Projective Vicious Circle*. Concepts of Antecedents and primordial Projections were offered. *Psychologic Blind-Spots* were discussed and *Minor* and *Major* Projections were noted. An instance of early literary recognition was cited.

2. Ascribing to Another; Personal Yardstick Allows Distortion

Projection is the ego defense through which one assigns disowned ideas, thoughts, or feelings to someone else. One's original *Personal Yardstick,* evolved to measure the feelings and reactions of other people, derives from awareness of his personal feelings and reactions. Thus, very early of necessity we form the pattern of judging others on the basis of how we ourselves feel, think, and react. This can be useful. It is, however, subject to the potential for considerable error and distortion. The value of *therapeutic elucidation* was illustrated in *Case 106.*

Intellectually, one is generally well aware that his own emotional reactions to experiences may be widely divergent from those of others. In judging others' feelings by our own, there is great likelihood for error in whole or in degree. Reality distortion can result. Yet we often tend to accept as fact such estimates of the feelings of other people, in the absence of more objective knowledge and/or more adequate checking.

From our recognition of the almost universal presence of psychologic blind-spots, the frequency of our judging others by ourselves, and widespread human desires to escape responsibility, we can better appreciate the facility with which Projection can take place. When displeasure or anger with oneself is consciously rejected by the individual as untenable for whatever cause, these feelings may be disowned and projected. The interesting clinical phenomenon of *Paranoid Indifference* may accompany the discussion of impending dire events and was illustrated (*Case 115*). The P.I. is analogous to *la belle indifférence,* or frequently encountered in major Somatic Conversions.

What are termed *Psychotic Projections* account for or contribute to many significant symptoms (including delusions and hallucinations) in the psychotic reactions. Reference was made to the subtypes of *Diffuse Projection, Negative Projection,* and *Grandiose Projection.* The potential for reality distortion through Projection was noted. Additional types of operation of the dynamism were mentioned and illustrated.

The *PVC* can become individually significant and this was illustrated. The *Interpersonal Projection* was noted, with its potential for substantial consequences upon a given relationship or upon one's entire circle of relationships. At times, as illustrated in *Case 113,* an evident Projection can give away the feelings it intends to conceal.

Projection is an unconscious device through which disapproved wishes, motives, or feelings are disowned and ascribed to someone else. Since one can well react to these in others as to a mirror, Projection has been termed the *Mirror-Defense.* This dynamic view of the basis and operation of the dynamism, is the *Mirror Concept.* There are many examples of Projection in daily living as well as in emotional pathology.

Let us proceed at this juncture to the *King David Reaction* in which we can observe another interesting employment of Projection, operating in conjunction with other important dynamisms.

E.   CROSS-REFERENCES TO *THE NEUROSES* *

Projection

In Nature of Anxiety (Chapter 1)
  as a possible factor
      in loss of speech (Case 6); p. 17.
      in sources of anxiety; p. 37.
  employment of, in self-appraisal; p. 14.
In Illusory Gains (Chapter 2); in the service of primary gain (*King David Reaction*); p. 76.
In Depressive Reactions (Chapter 4); of negative aspects of self, in *King David's Anger;* p. 205.

---

* From Laughlin, H. P. *The Neuroses.* London, Butterworth & Co., Ltd., 1967.

In Character Reactions (Chapter 5); overutilized, in *Paranoid Personality;* pp. 233, 284.

in patterns of defense; p. 238.

In Obsessive-Compulsive Reactions (Chapter 6)

in *First Line of Defense* of obsessive patient; pp. 343, 374.

in obsessive symptoms and *King David Reaction;* p. 345.

of judgmental attitudes, in distance maintenance of *Obsessive Personality;* p. 331.

of unconscious hostility (Case 71); p. 347.

In Hygeiaphrontic Reactions (Chapter 8); of destructive infantile fantasies, in bases of *Hygeiaphrontis;* p. 491.

In Fear and Its Avoidance (Chapter 9); of hostility, as a source of fear; p. 541

In Phobic Reactions (Chapter 10)

of competitive feelings, in phobia of women (Case 125); p. 598.

of hidden homosexual desires, in phobia of hirsutism (Case 115); p. 560.

of hostile feelings, in phobia of cats (Case 120); p. 573.

in phobia of people (Case 114); pp. 557–8.

previously ascribed to phobias (Freud); p. 551.

In Soterial Reactions (Chapter 11); of idealized dependency object, in psychodynamics of *soteria;* pp. 626, 627, 636.

In Neuroses-Following-Trauma (Chapter 14); in *First Line of Psychic Defense;* p. 874.

F.   REVIEW QUESTIONS

Sample self-check questions on Chapter 15 and Projection for the student, psychiatric resident, and board candidate.

1. Define and illustrate *Projection*. Why have we alternatively termed it a *Mirror-Defense?* What is the *PVC* (projective vicious circle)? *Projective Identification?*
2. Discuss the antecedents of projection.
3. Define:
   A. *psychologic blind-spot.*
   B. *emotional block.*
   C. *Historical Validation Concept.*
   D. *Interpersonal Projection.*
   E. *Paranoid Indifference.*
   F. projected anger.
   G. reality distortion.
   H. *therapeutic elucidation.*
   I. *Psychotic Projection.*
4. Discuss the significance of the *Personal Yardstick.*
5. Cite an example of *Minor Projection* from your own experience.
6. Discuss the role of Projection in the psychotic reactions. Give a clinical instance of the *Diffuse, Negative,* or *Grandiose Projection.*
7. How can Projection operate defensively in relation to homosexual conflicts? In hallucinations?
8. Discuss relationships of Projection with other dynamisms.
9. How is Projection intended to function as a defense?
10. Discuss the self-defeating consequences possible in the defensively motivated evolution of Projection by the ego.

CHAPTER 16

THE KING DAVID REACTION

...Unrecognized Personal Attributes
Reacted to in Others

A. INEXPLICABLE ATTRACTIONS AND REPULSIONS

1. Projected Aspects of One's Self-Appraisal: a. Nathan's Parable; b. Circumstances Objectively Insufficient; c. Expressed Toward Disguised Substitute. 2. Definitions: a. Cooperative Interaction of Dynamisms; b. Unrecognized Similarities Initiate.

B. KING DAVID'S ANGER

1. More Readily Observed than Positive Counterpart. 2. Literary Examples. 3. Physical Resemblance Facilitates: a. Negative Reaction Toward Entertainer; b. Therapeutic Utilization. 4. Further Illustrations: a. Fear, Guilt, Compensation, Projection, Identification, Anger; b. Rejection on Minimal Acquaintance; c. Behavior Influenced.

C. POSITIVE KING DAVID REACTION

1. Less Prominent. 2. Latent Homosexuality. The Narcissus Reaction. 3. Additional Instances: a. Masochistic-Like Reaction; Personal Yardstick Misleads; b. Disowned Drives Provide Bases.

D. SUMMARY

E. REFERENCES (FROM *The Neuroses*)

F. REVIEW QUESTIONS

A. INEXPLICABLE ATTRACTIONS AND REPULSIONS

1. Projected Aspects of One's Self-Appraisal

A. NATHAN'S PARABLE.—The biblical story of David and Bathsheba is familiar to many. From his palace rooftop the king spied the beautiful Bathsheba bathing. Her husband Uriah was away at war in David's service. David took Bathsheba for himself. He arranged matters so that the helpless and hapless Uriah was killed in battle.

The prophet Nathan forcibly pointed out to the king his cruelty and destructiveness by telling him the following story. It is called the *Parable of the Ewe Lamb.*

"... *There were two men in one city; the one rich and the other poor. The rich man had exceeding many flocks and herds: But the poor man had nothing, save one little ewe lamb.... it grew up together with him ... it did eat of his own meat, and drank of his own cup, and lay in his bosom, and was unto him as a daughter....*"

"*A traveller came to visit the rich man, who would not prepare an animal from his own large herds. Instead he took the poor man's lamb.*

The reaction of the king to the parable was immediate and strong:

"... *David's anger was greatly kindled against the man; and he said to Nathan, 'As the Lord liveth, the man that hath done this thing shall surely die: And he shall restore the lamb fourfold, because he did this thing, and because he had no pity!*"

"*And Nathan said to David, 'Thou art the man'....*"

B. CIRCUMSTANCES OBJECTIVELY INSUFFICIENT.—The student of human behavior may occasionally encounter the situation in which seemingly untoward feelings develop in one person toward another. These may be positive or negative ones. On occasion the emotional reaction can be quite strong, but its basis being unclear, it seemingly is inexplicable. At times the reaction is prominent. Likely far more often however, this kind of reaction and its influences are subtle and unobserved.

In instances of either positive or negative feelings they can be pervasive and of considerable moment. The entire future course of a relationship can be determined at its outset. This is in accord with, and can illustrate the *Rule of Impression Priority* [1] outlined elsewhere (*The Neuroses,* Chapter 9). However we are not speaking here of the influences of unwitting prototypes or emotional antecedents. In other words, the reaction we are seeking to delineate is not primarily based on hidden influences from earlier significant relationships. It has other bases.

On the surface at least, these reactions are unexplained, and the person concerned often has a poor acquaintance or none at all with the second. Thus the relationship has been insufficient to have fostered the development of such strong feelings. Other apparent circumstances are also not sufficient. Many of the reactions to which we refer reflect the operation of the *King David Reaction.* Powerful unconscious forces are influential in this process.

C. EXPRESSED TOWARD DISGUISED SUBSTITUTE.—These seemingly inexplicable positive and negative feelings develop through the mutual interaction of several dynamisms. This is a special combination of Repression (Chapter 21), Projection (Chapter 15), and Identification (Chapter 9), frequently supported by Rationalization (Chapter 17), and sometimes by Denial (Chapter 4). There is a close relationship to the quality of one's self-estimation or self-appraisal. In the King David Reaction, approved or disapproved aspects of the self which are not con-

---

[1] The Rule of Impression Priority points out the emotional priority ordinarily gained by an earlier impression over later ones. Accordingly, one's initial impression can be extremely important in determining his future attitude toward a type of experience, activity, or friend.

sciously recognized, are reacted to in the second person. These in reality may be present in the second person, minimally or invisibly present, or completely absent. They may be totally experienced or contributed to in part, through their Projection to him.

This interesting complex has been named the *King David Reaction* after the king who became enraged at the rich man in the parable. Overreacting due to greater significance than otherwise might have been anticipated from an uninformed evaluation, he had decreed the man's death. The strength of the king's anger becomes more understandable since it was in reality directed at this concealed image of himself as held out by Nathan. His feelings thus secured a more tolerable substitute object (see *Scapegoat Reaction*, p. 87) and achieved a measure of expression.

The negative King David Reaction marked by anger, is called *King David's Anger*, or *Royal Anger*. The positive King David Reaction is alternatively *Royal Affection* or *Love*. These reactions are included in our text because of their interest, to help stress their occurrence and occasional significance clinically, as a matter of personal preference, and because of the challenge offered in working out the dynamics of a complex reaction which involves the cooperative interaction of several of our major ego defenses (p. 222; *Case 108*, p. 225).

The KDR is accordingly included and appropriately follows that of Projection (Chapter 15). Its relation to Projection is very close and can be regarded as that of an auxiliary, reenforcement, extension, or secondary elaboration. Let us attempt a definition of the King David Reaction.

2. Definitions

A. COOPERATIVE INTERACTION OF DYNAMISMS.—The King David Reaction is *a complex intrapsychic defensive operation. Involving the cooperative and mutual interaction of Repression, Projection, and Identification; it is usually supported in some measure by Rationalization and at times relates to Denial and other dynamisms. Through this reaction, consciously unrecognized and disowned elements of the self-appraisal which were often originally present to some extent in the other person, are also further ascribed to him through Projection, and reacted to accordingly. This process has evoked the otherwise unexplained feelings which are experienced toward the other person. The King David Reaction may be negative or positive in subjective experience and in direction.*

The resulting feelings can show wide variation in strength and in kind. Needless to say, this interesting complex operation takes place unconsciously. Its presence may be reflected outwardly in affect and behavior, clinically and socially. In the awareness of the person concerned, there is only his experiencing certain emotional feelings toward and about another person, whom he may scarcely know or not know at all. He may find explanations for them which satisfy him and they are quite real. Often they appear out of keeping only to an alert observer.

Variations of the King David Reaction help influence in subtle but often significant ways one's initial responses to a new acquaintance. The acceptance or rejection of a friend may be thus determined, or even predetermined perhaps before a relationship can begin.

In the *negative* KDR, the reaction to the other person is a negative, critical, and rejecting one. One may accordingly feel disgust, anger, revulsion, distaste, criticism, disapproval, and condemnation toward him. In the *positive* KDR the feelings toward the other person are warm, positive, and accepting. One may experience feelings of warmth, affection, approval, love, and admiration toward the other person.

B. UNRECOGNIZED SIMILARITIES INITIATE.—The negative King David Reaction may be defined as *an intrapsychic defensively-intended process, through which condemnation and hatred of consciously disowned aspects of the self become experienced as rejection, dislike, or anger for another person.* When appropriate, the resulting feelings as noted are alternatively referred to as *King David's Anger,* or the *Royal Anger.*

In the positive King David Reaction, this complex process operates in like manner, with approved portions of the self-appraisal similarly coming to be consciously experienced as affection or love for the second person. This important intrapsychic process may thus be the basis for otherwise unexplained positive *or* negative feelings for another person.

The King David Reaction is initiated or facilitated in some instances by consciously unrecognized physical, behavioral, psychical, or characterologic resemblances. This can be an important aspect of the reaction. The important ego defenses operative are Repression, Identification, Projection, and Rationalization as noted. The entire positive or negative type of King David Reaction occurs unwittingly; unconsciously. The individual has no awareness of the process and is only cognizant of his feelings toward the other person, which may seem unduly strong and out of keeping.

B.   KING DAVID'S ANGER

1. More Readily Observed Than Positive Counterpart

When feelings of dislike, distaste, or hatred are more marked than might be originally anticipated; when they are out of keeping with the objectively judged facets of the situation, the explanation in some instances is to be found in the reaction of King David's Anger. This is the negative type of King David Reaction.

Herein, as noted, the disliked self-picture is to some extent projected to another, and negative feelings towards him are experienced consciously —often intensely. King David's Anger is more readily uncovered and more likely to be observed than is its positive counterpart. A number of explanations for this variation in relative frequency may be surmised without too great difficulty.

2. Literary Examples

The classic literary instance is the biblical one for which we have named the reaction. Other examples exist and perhaps a reader will invite attention to further literary or clinical instances. These contribute to our *Concept of Historical Validation* (pp. 226, 240, and 301).

The following brief excerpts from Shakespeare's *Hamlet* contribute to the development of our theme. Shakespeare's greatness stems in large measure from his understanding of human motivation, and many illustrations of psychic processes are to be found in his works.

Case 118

Shakespeare Uses the Nathan Device

In the following lines (*Hamlet*, Act III, ii) one notes the excessive aversion with which the Player-Queen regards the possibility of a second marriage, although a secret desire for such a marriage is already present in her mind. Is the aversion an attempt to deny, to project, or to reenforce her defenses against awareness or possible action?

This is a complex interplay. Shakespeare has devised a play within a play, in which the action is deliberately similar and is thus designed to secure recognition of the import of their behavior and motivation to two viewers; Hamlet's mother and uncle. Note the similarity of intent to Nathan's telling the "Parable of the Ewe Lamb" to King David.

"O Confound the rest!
Such love must needs be treason in my breast.
In second husband let me be accurst;
None wed the second but who kill'd the first.

The instances that second marriage move
Are base respects of thrift, but none of love;
A second time I kill my husband dead,
When second husband kisses me in bed.

Nor earth do me give food nor heaven light!
Sport and repose lock me from day and night!
"To desperation turn my trust and hope!
An anchor's cheer in prison by my scope!"
Each opposite that blanks the face of joy
Meet what I would have well, and it destroy!
Both here and hence pursue me lasting strife,
If, once a widow, ever I be wife!"

Shakespeare's acquaintance with the psychologic reaction is evidenced by the subsequent comment of the real Queen. She has been a viewer and a somewhat suspicious one, of the underlying motivation of the Player-Queen; this through a reflection of her own psychology. She comments, "The lady doth protest too much, methinks."

The *Nathan Device* has been successfully employed by Shakespeare to hold up a self-image.

Case 119

King David's Anger in Hamlet's Reaction

Another example of the negative phase of this interesting defense pattern is also observed in *Hamlet*. Hamlet's fury at Claudius was magnified because of his disowned Oedipal aggression toward his father and attraction for his mother. Thus, when Claudius came to possess the feelings toward them that Hamlet had consciously disowned, the latter's anger was evoked, to become consciously experienced as hatred of Claudius. Claudius was responsible for the death of Hamlet's father, afterwards marrying the widow.

In other words, Hamlet hated vehemently in Claudius that which was perhaps unconsciously present in himself. He had found this unacceptable and it had been repressed. The strength of his feelings toward Claudius was multiplied because of the presence of his own similar but repressed emotions. The *King David's Anger* as consciously experienced by Hamlet, allowed partial outward expression of his inner feelings in disguised and more acceptable form, since they were directed toward a substitute and thereby more tolerable object (Claudius). This helped to maintain the nonawareness (repression). The endeavor is a vitally defensive one; complex and intrapsychic. His hatred drove Hamlet to murder.

3. Physical Resemblance Facilitates

A. NEGATIVE REACTION TOWARD ENTERTAINER.—In some interesting instances of the negative kind of King David Reaction, there is a physical or psychical resemblance which facilitates and contributes to the (unconscious) Identification. This may be observed by others, but strongly and angrily denied by the person concerned. An instance of this was observed during a social occasion, as follows:

Case 120

The Negative King David Reaction: Unrecognized Resemblance Stimulates Identification and Projection, with Production of "Royal Anger"

A group of friends were together at a Saturday evening social gathering some years ago. In a corner of the room the TV was tuned to a currently popular program which occupied the attention of a few of the guests. Of the latter, an attorney was enjoying the show. It was announced that a number would be sung by the Billy Williams quartet. The response of our friend to this information and their appearance shortly thereafter was startling. His face became flushed, and he clenched his fists.

Turning his back to the TV and the performer, he stated in angry tones that he simply could not tolerate Billy Williams. Something about him was intensely repugnant. As he was expressing his strong feelings, his friends were simultaneously struck by the closely similar appearance of the two men. The same wide mouth and fixed facial expression were accompanied by a pleading, ingratiating and yet rather arrogant manner. The features and attitude of the quartet leader were quite individual but they were nearly duplicated in the lawyer.

The latter complained that his dislike had grown until he could no longer stand the sight of the man. He found the sound of his voice very disturbing. His listening friends were startled by the strength and bitterness of his feelings, accompanied as they were by the marked resemblance. The speaker was oblivious of the latter. The observers of this incident checked with each other later to confirm the correspondence of their observations. It is significant that no one dared venture to point out the resemblance.

In this instance, the similar appearance appeared to have unwittingly stimulated Identification. Projection of disowned portions of the self-appraisal took place and helped magnify the strongly negative reaction to the entertainer which was experienced.

B. THERAPEUTIC UTILIZATION.—Occasionally the elucidation of this reaction is helpful in treatment. This is illustrated in the following instance.

Case 121

King David's Anger

A 35-year-old chemist brought an alumni bulletin to a treatment session. Displaying a picture of a man of about his age, he expressed a great repugnance toward the man pictured—hitherto unknown to him. The picture was of a rather pleasant but determined-appearing person, with strong features, and a prominent high-bridged nose. He was commended for noteworthy work in directing a fund-raising campaign for the college. There was a distinct physical resemblance to the patient, of which the latter was not aware.

Speculating about his repugnance, the patient described the man as too aggressive, contemptuous of others, too much interested in money, and one who would bear watching as a sharp dealer. Perhaps his success in the campaign was due to chicanery.

After a time the therapist ventured to tell his patient of the similarity in appearance; an observation which was met with an indignant denial. Fortunately the initial strong resistance to recognizing the likeness gradually gave way to a surprised and somewhat sheepish recognition. Only after some time, however, did he come to understand how he had projected certain aspects of his own self-disapproval to the man pictured. The characteristics ascribed in this manner to the campaign head may or may not have fitted. However to a greater or lesser extent, they were indeed his own!

Unconscious recognition of the physical resemblance had possibly contributed to Identification. The patient's attributing his own disowned characteristics (as subjectively assessed) to the unknown man, seemingly occurred as an after-the-fact and unwitting effort at Rationalization, and contributed to the strength of his otherwise unexplained feelings. The elucidation of this complex was an important milestone in his therapy.

4. Further Illustrations

A. FEAR, GUILT, COMPENSATION, PROJECTION, IDENTIFICATION, ANGER.

Case 122

King David's Anger in a Combat Hero

(1) *Entertainer's Arrival Disturbing.* It was shortly after the end of the second World War. A certain entertainer had secured a degree of notoriety for attempting to use influence to obtain states-side duty. Sometime after the foregoing episode, he was to entertain troops in the European theater. A regimental commander who had been through months of strenuous combat, became infuriated on learning about this. He went to the division commander and gave vent to an emotional diatribe against the performer. He threatened to refuse permission for his troops to attend.

His level of overreaction and threatened insubordination in the face of a decision by higher authorities was out of character. He had received several decorations for meritorious service, and was considered an extremely able leader. The division commander realized something was amiss. Judiciously he was able to arrange psychiatric consultation.

(2) *Negative KDR Initiated.* Several interviews provided background data concerning contributory sources for his reaction. Interestingly enough, the officer once sought in not very dissimilar fashion to

avoid combat service. His efforts were unsuccessful and of course not the sort of thing for a career officer to try and do. They were not publicized as with the entertainer. However, he had personally suffered a great deal of guilt, shame, and self-condemnation over this. These feelings subsequently forced him both consciously and unconsciously to overcompensate for his self-protective needs.

He plunged headlong into the most difficult and threatening combat situations, from which he had emerged as quite a hero, and fortunately a living one. The advent of the entertainer led to the initiation of a negative King David Reaction. There were some physical similarities between the two men. A hesitant reference to these once by a fellow officer had elicited a vigorous denial and an angry outburst!

(3) *Low Self-Esteem Contributes.* Learning of the entertainer's coming was a cogent reminder. His old unconscious guilty fears and damaged self-esteem were rekindled and forced closer to the surface. Although some realistic bases were already present as a stimulus in the entertainer-object for his anger, these were substantially enhanced through the Projection of his low self-esteem, and Identification.

In terms which he might have applied to himself as a part of his (unconscious) poor level of self-esteem and self-evaluation, the entertainer was ". . . beneath contempt, cowardly, and disgraceful. . . ." Actually the officer had overcompensated through outstanding combat performance and becoming a hero. This was not enough retribution, however, for his punitive superego. An added facet was a measure of subconscious rage over the fact that the entertainer had succeeded in escaping danger in the final analysis, while he had not.

B. REJECTION ON MINIMAL ACQUAINTANCE.—The following instance points out how a strong immediate reaction, in this instance negative, can develop on the basis of little or no real acquaintance. Through the spontaneous and automatic operation of the King David Reaction what occurs between two people can be significantly influenced.

The whole tone and future of a possible relationship can be thus determined and delineated before there is a chance for any mutual interchange.

Case 123

The Negative King David Reaction: A Physician feels Disgust toward Certain "Strangers"

A 40-year-old physician, undertook psychotherapy initially because of recurrent attacks of spastic colitis. His therapy met with considerable success and led him into the recognition of many interesting ramifications of his character defenses.

One day the doctor reported a puzzling pattern of emotional reaction he had observed in himself, which he could not explain. These instances took place when he passed a newsstand and noticed someone thumbing through the magazines. His emotional reaction was routinely negative toward the person concerned. It was quite marked if the magazines involved were even mildly lurid in nature. In the latter instances he felt acute disgust, irritation, and abhorrence toward the otherwise unknown person concerned. None of them would have had much chance subsequently to become a friend or acquaintance. Their rejection was immediate and certain.

The patient outlined his childhood as a lonely and unhappy one, full of feelings of guilt and inadequacy. A main source of pleasure in adolescence was a voyeuristic type of sexual activity, which took the form of looking at pictures of nude women in magazines and books. Since his upbringing and parents were puritanical, this activity aroused a great deal of guilt and had to be furtively pursued. As he grew older the guilt became far greater than the pleasure derived; the activity had to be given up, and the entire area was discarded from recollection, until its later recall in therapy, during the study of the aforementioned pattern of reaction.

It became apparent that his previously unexplained reactions of irritation and disgust were actually about his own long repressed voyeuristic impulses. These and his self-condemnation about them he unconsciously projected onto the newsstand-stranger, with whom he unconsciously identified.

The foregoing example illustrates the operation of the special combination of the ego defenses of Projection and Identification, accompanied by the strongly antagonistic affective feelings toward another person, which mark the negative King David Reaction. In this instance, Rationalization was not particularly prominent in regard to the feelings, which were clearly negative and therefore represent the King David's Anger phase of the reaction.

C. BEHAVIOR INFLUENCED.—Lest one regard the negative King David Reaction as being restricted to emotional responses, let us note that behavior can be influenced. Occasionally where the emotions reach a sufficient crescendo, controls are weak, or both, this reaction can help foster violence, as in the literary example (*Case 119*), and the following instance.

Case 124

Violence Fostered

A 22-year-old secretary was referred for therapy following a rage reaction against her roommate. She had attacked her with a pair of scissors and had to be forcibly restrained from doing her serious harm.

History disclosed that the two girls had gone through college together. They had been together enough so that people sometimes referred to them as a unit. Their relationship generally had been friendly, although somewhat on the casual and distant side. However, there was a great deal of difference in their social backgrounds and in their personality make up including conscience and standards.

Sarah, the one who was referred for therapy had been brought up with a super strict socio-cultural and religious orientation, and her views of conduct and morality were extremely strict and rigid. Her roommate, Joan on the other hand, was raised with more leniency and had considerable more flexibility in her outlook and personal standards.

A young engineer had taken Sarah out a number of times but had been unable to establish emotional rapport, largely due to her tremendous need to deny any sensual or sexual feelings. He stopped seeing her (which seemed at the time of little moment to Sarah) and later began courting Joan.

After several dates with him, Joan returned to their room one evening with her hair in disarray and lipstick smeared. Sarah accused her of sexual intimacy in detailed terms and began to berate her furiously. The accusation was conjectural at best, and unrealistic in terms of the circumstances under which this might have occurred. The attack had rapidly progressed to violence, at which point Sarah attacked her roommate with the scissors.

During subsequent study, the dynamisms of Denial and Projection proved to have been operative for the attacker, in relation to her own condemned, disowned, and unconscious sexual drives. Identification subsequently evolved with the disowned and projected aspects of herself in her roommate. Her conscious feelings toward Joan were of intense condemnation and rage, augmented by subconscious jealousy.

The intensity and extreme nature of her reaction was considerably out of keeping with the outward facts of the situation or with her prior indifferent level of interest in the young man. Sarah's harsh, archaic, and punitive superego had thus been allowed expression toward her bottled-up and consciously disowned sexual strivings—part of her own hidden condemning self-estimation projected thus to her roommate. The ensuing reaction was a violent one.

C. POSITIVE KING DAVID REACTION

1. Less Prominent

It is important to observe that positive (that is, warm, friendly, and loving) feelings evolving on a similar but reversed basis to the negative ones of Royal Anger can occur, as noted earlier. This is the positive side of the King David Reaction. Automatically favorable reactions to new people can develop along this intriguing pathway. Examples often are more difficult to delineate than are those illustrating the negative side.

This may relate in part to their usually being far less a matter of conflict, anxiety, distress, discomfort, or concern. Thus it is considerably less likely that they are a subject for complaint, that they will appear untoward to others, or that they become as readily submerged as unacceptable aspects of the self. Elements of self-defeat also are usually less apparent.

These four factors enter into making the positive type of KDR less prominent in personal observation and in clinical experience. One might well anticipate, however, that many varying and less noteworthy instances are to be encountered than the following ones selected for purposes of illustration.

2. Latent Homosexuality. The Narcissus Reaction

An individual with repressed (and thereby latent) homosexual drives through the King David Reaction can come to like and admire someone with a similar orientation. The liked person may be more or less overtly homosexual with this remaining unrecognized by the first person, although apparent to others. In reversed fashion, of course, the negative King David Reaction may operate in this type of situation, particularly where Repression, Projection and Identification have been associated with and follow negative feelings, guilt, self-condemnation, and rejection, rather than positive feelings and self-approval.

The positive King David Reaction appeared to have been operative in the following instance, with the attraction rationalized on the grounds of personal and social graces.

Case 125

A Positive King David Reaction

A young attorney who had graduated with honors from a leading law school was referred for therapy at his request because of lack of success at work and unhappiness and general dissatisfaction with life.

In the course of therapy, a strong personal attraction was disclosed toward another lawyer with whom he was associated. His fondness and liking were explained as due to the other attorney being handsome, intelligent, considerate, and having a great deal of social poise. The patient had become somewhat preoccupied with his interest in his friend. He was doing increasingly poorly at work and came overly to depend upon the friend.

The latter helped him over rough spots in conferences, reviewed his briefs, and was called on for frequent council in instances which the patient should easily have been able to handle unaided. Eventually latent homosexual components were uncovered. By chance, the therapist later met the second lawyer and was struck by a physical resemblance between the two and a correspondence in their intellectual outlook. These factors likely helped stimulate the positive KDR which evolved.

Through therapy, the first man gradually came to realize that he admired in his colleague mainly attributes that he himself possessed in some measure. Superficially these included his intellectual endowment, views of life, acceptance by colleagues, considerateness, and social poise. These, however, were considerably overvalued in his friend as an attempted Rationalization for his fondness and admiration, and as a cover for deeper and projected homosexual drives.

He had become preoccupied with admiration and love for the friend, when the object was at least in part, his projected and idealized self-image. There had been several earlier relationships on this basis. He was able to work this complex defensively-intended operation through in therapy. Awareness led to dissolution of this phase of his problems. Before long he increased his efficiency, independence, and productivity. Life became more meaningful and satisfying.

The foregoing instance points out the close parallel of the positive KDR and that of Narcissus. The term *narcissism* in psychiatry has come to mean *an unhealthful and exaggerated reaction of self-absorption, preoccupation, and self-love.* In the original Greek myth Narcissus fell in love with his image in a pool. However he did not know the reflected image was that of himself. This is what we term the *Narcissus Reaction.*

Unwittingness is likewise a requirement in Royal Love. The person concerned lacks conscious recognition that he responds with fondness, affection, friendship, or love to projected favorable and positive aspects of himself, and about which he may have little or no conscious awareness. This is another facet of the *Mirror-Defense Concept* (see Chapter 15). He is attracted to the other person but really does not know why. Since fondness and positive feelings are far less a source of conflict, concern, and problems than are their reverse, he often does not care.

3. Additional Instances

A. MASOCHISTIC-LIKE REACTION; PERSONAL YARDSTICK MISLEADS.—One ordinarily might not think of the potential for masochistic and self-defeating consequences in conjunction with the positive King David Reaction. However, masochistic needs can occasionally be subserved and self-defeat engendered. Honesty, reliability, lack of guile, trustworthiness, and high personal and social values, through their projection and through one's anticipation of their presence in another—via application of the Personal Yardstick (see reference in Chapter 15), can result in naiveté, hurt and self-defeat. One's exploitation can follow as an inimical consequence.

Case 126

Positive King David Reaction Self-Defeating

A 34-year-old widow became a real estate salesman. She was shy and retiring, although these qualities, as well as an inability to speak up for herself were not apparent, being concealed from superficial observation by a reversed outer facade. She possessed a stringent and quite idealistic set of ethical and moral values.

Not only did she anticipate that her standards would be present in everyone with whom she dealt; she literally assigned them to each new person. Through Projection, Identification, and Idealization, she overly liked and trusted nearly everyone. The untoward consequences included her being taken advantage of and at times seriously hurt. She lost sales repeatedly. Men occasionally took advantage of her sexually, because of her overtrusting nature and kindness.

Reacting to the projected (often in error) kindly aspects of herself, she was certain that others would look out for her best interests, as she did for theirs. There were repeated instances of her ill treatment, sufficiently so to establish a masochistic-like pattern. Elements of the positive King David Reaction contributed unwittingly. She had ensured her continuing self-defeat. Only following extensive therapy did she become able to elucidate and favorably modify this complex and self-defeating pattern.

B. DISOWNED DRIVES PROVIDE BASES.—The roots of King David Reactions are often found to extend into early life. An emotion or drive has to be earlier repressed in order for its Projection to be effected or for subsequent Identification to take place. Such drives may take various guises. They are often hostile or sexual ones or variants of these.

Case 127

Inversion of Exhibitionism Sets Stage

The strong exhibitionistic drives of a certain little girl had been repressed in response to powerful parental pressures. Ultimately she had further inverted these drives to become instead retiring in nature and behavior. This was reflected in her demeanor and dress, which developed into the demure and prim. Later in life by profession she became a fashion designer and was quite successful.

For some years she was strongly drawn toward a succession of her younger clients. These young ladies often had more than a trace of the same exhibitionistic trends which she had long since disowned. This hidden characterologic similarity seemed to have provided an initial basis for the further Projection of these disowned aspects of herself which she, thereby, viewed in exaggerated form and liked in them.

As a stimulus for fond feelings toward her clients along the lines of the positive King David Reaction, the presence of basically conflicting attitudes about the exhibitionism was suggested. She could approve and be drawn to aspects in the girls which were consciously disowned in herself, but which at the same time also comprised an aspect of her hidden positive (and projected) self-appraisal.

D. SUMMARY

In the King David Reaction we encounter the operation in special combination of the ego defenses of Projection, Repression, Identification, and Rationalization. It is named after a classical example from Biblical History. Through the KDR projected aspects of the self-appraisal can lead to seemingly inexplicable attractions and repulsions.

The negative phase of the *King David Reaction* is an intrapsychic defensive process through which the condemnation and hatred of consciously disowned aspects of the self become experienced as dislike for another person. The resulting negative feelings are also referred to as *King David's Anger,* or *Royal Anger.* Literary instances from the Bible and *Hamlet* were cited, bearing out the *Concept of Historical Validation.* As with positive feelings on a similar basis, external circumstances are insufficient to explain them or their strength.

This complex process can work conversely, with approved portions of the self-appraisal similarly coming to be consciously experienced as friendship, affection, or love for the second person. Thus this important process may be the basis for otherwise unexplained positive or negative feelings for another person. The positive KDR is less prominent than its negative counterpart for several reasons. The KDR can be initiated or facilitated in some instances (*Cases 120* and *121*) by consciously unrecognized physical, behavioral, or characterologic resemblances. The important unconscious mechanisms which are cooperatively interacting as noted are primarily those of Repression, Identification, Projection, and Rationalization. The *Rule of Impression Priority* received reference.

The KDR provides a disguised substitute target for emotional feelings, offering another route in the evolution of the *Scapegoat Reaction.* Through operation of the KDR, the entire course of a relationship can be substantially influenced at the outset. The effects on behavior of the negative KDR can potentially progress to violence, as illustrated in *Case 124.* The potential for operation of the positive KDR in latent homosexuality was cited, and the *Narcissus Reaction* noted. The positive type of KDR (as with the negative) can prove inimical and self-defeating (*Case 126*). Therapeutic value is occasionally present in working through the King David Reaction.

In the Biblical Parable of the Ewe Lamb, the prophet Nathan told a story to David the King in which the King's own conduct was pictured but in a disguised fashion. David was so angered toward the person (actually a projected self-image) as described, that he decreed death for him. This is the prototype for King David's Anger, and the technique for producing it is the *Nathan Device.*

This type of interesting complex process takes place automatically and unconsciously. The conscious feelings are those of dislike, hatred, or anger toward the person to whom Projection has been made in the negative instances, or of affection, fondness, or friendship in the positive instances.

E.   CROSS-REFERENCES TO *THE NEUROSES* *

King David Reaction
  as a factor, in low self-esteem of Depressed person; p. 205.
  awareness of, resulting in strong emotional reactions; p. 362.
  evidenced, in harsh superego of Obsessive person; p. 345.
  in neurotic gain of, pp. 75–6.

F.   REVIEW QUESTIONS

Sample self-check questions on Chapter 16 and the King David Reaction for the student, psychiatric resident, and board candidate.

1. Explain the *King David Reaction*. Which dynamisms are operative?
2. How can the *KDR* contribute to certain otherwise inexplicable attractions and repulsions to people?
3. Discuss: (1) the *Concept of Historical Validation* in relation to the King David Reaction; (2) instances from literature.
4. Briefly explain six of the following:
   A. *Royal Anger*.
   B. *Impression Priority Rule*.
   C. The role of physical or characterologic resemblance in *KDRs*.
   D. *Positive KDR*.
   E. How can application of the *Personal Yardstick* contribute?
   F. *The Nathan Device*.
   G. Latent homosexuality.
   H. The KDR in evolving a *Scapegoat Reaction*.
   I. The Ewe Lamb Parable as a KDR prototype.
   J. Projection of the negative self-appraisal.
5. List factors in the positive KDR being less prominent clinically.
6. What is the *Narcissus Reaction?*
7. Discuss the significance of the self-appraisal in: (1) the King David Reaction; (2) the *Mirror-Defense Concept*.
8. How can elucidation of the KDR contribute to progress in psychotherapy?
9. Cite ways in which *Royal Anger* and *Love* can influence behavior.
10. Briefly discuss ways in which the KDR can contribute to: (1) emotional equilibrium, ego synthesis, adjustment, and health, *versus* (2) self-defeat, increased emotional conflict, and psychopathology.

---

* From Laughlin, H. P. *The Neuroses*. London, Butterworth & Co., Ltd., 1967.

CHAPTER 17

RATIONALIZATION

... Self-Deceptive Adoption of the More Acceptable and Creditable

A. PLAUSIBLE EXPLANATIONS FOR THE CONSCIOUSLY REPUGNANT

    1. Step Beyond Justification. 2. Definition. 3. Compromise and Reconciliation.

B. WIDESPREAD UTILIZATION

    1. Posthypnotic Rationalization. 2. Frequent Bases. 3. Contributing to Mediation. Types Listed.

C. MAJOR FUNCTIONS

    1. Block to Conscious Recognition: a. Recognition-Deferment Rationalization; b. Complex-Supportive Rationalization. 2. Goal Devaluation: a. Easing Disappointment, Loss, and Frustration; b. Sour-Grapes Rationalization. 3. Motive-Rationalization. 4. Protection Against Anxiety.

D. ELEEMOSYNARY RATIONALIZATION

    1. On Behalf Of . . . 2. Modifications of Usual Codes. 3. Absence of Gain Illusory. 4. Historical Perspective.

E. SOCIAL OR COLLECTIVE RATIONALIZATION

    1. Social Phenomenon. 2. Supporting Extermination. 3. Car Purchase; Sexual Rationalization.

F. FAMILIAL RATIONALIZATION

    1. Equitable regard. 2. Equality an Ideal.

G. IN SYMPTOMS AND EMOTIONAL ILLNESS

    1. Ubiquitous Role. 2. The Supporting, or Secondary Delusion. 3. Concept of Secondary Defense; Symptom-Defensive Rationalization. 4. Alcoholic Rationalization.

H. DYNAMICS

    1. Nonconformity with Ego Ideal. 2. More Creditable Alternatives. Characterologic Rationalization. 3. Relation to Other Ego Defenses

I. SUMMARY

      1. Making the Unacceptable Acceptable. 2. Major Functions.
      3. Special Types. 4. Final Points.

J. REFERENCES (FROM *The Neuroses*)

K. REVIEW QUESTIONS

A. PLAUSIBLE EXPLANATIONS FOR THE CONSCIOUSLY REPUGNANT

1. Step Beyond Justification

In common parlance, Rationalization is the conscious attempt to explain away or to justify something which is unacceptable. One seeks to make it more tolerable and more creditable. This kind of conscious effort, or its counterpart as an unconscious endeavor, is frequently encountered clinically, in relation to one's motives, behavior, personally and socially, and for disapproved or unobtainable desires.

Rationalization may be attempted on either level in relation to aspects of other persons, sometimes, for instance, in support of the dynamism of Idealization. It may be called into play as a secondary elaboration bolstering other ego defenses. Rationalization is an attempt at justification or finding reasons or bases which are plausible and personally more acceptable.

The term Rationalization is often used in a way which makes its meaning almost synonymous with justification, but perhaps a step further. The person employing Rationalization, in lay language, is kidding himself.

2. Definition

For this discussion, we are primarily concerned with the evolvement of this process as an unconscious, intrapsychic, defensively-intended endeavor. Accordingly, we have defined Rationalization as *an ego defense or mental mechanism operating outside of and beyond conscious awareness through which the ego justifies, or attempts to modify otherwise unacceptable impulses, needs, feelings, behavior, and motives into ones which are consciously tolerable and acceptable. It is employed in the ego's endeavor to reconciliate and to mediate. A certain measure of self-deception is present in seeking to make the consciously repugnant more tolerable or more creditable, and the incompatible, compatible.* Rationalization is one of the most universally and frequently employed of the ego defenses. It is one of the less primitive major dynamisms. It is a more advanced, Higher Order defense.

What are the intended purposes of Rationalization? Basically, its defensive aims are to: (1) lessen emotional conflict, and (2) secure equanimity through increased acceptance, primarily from oneself, but also by others. It is an unconscious process through which people try to have their cake and eat it too. Through the mental mechanism of Rationalization, more tolerable, but incorrect bases or motives are devised. These are more or less plausible substitutes for the real ones, which are replaced because they are consciously repugnant and unacceptable.

Rationalization is one of the most commonly employed of the various interesting ego defenses. It is an important adjuvant or auxiliary to Repression, in that it supplies an acceptable for an unacceptable motive or wish. Through its use as an unconscious mental mechanism, the Repression of consciously intolerable motives or needs is facilitated. Something irrational is made to appear more reasonable to the person concerned, through its Rationalization. The nonrational but more acceptable and creditable thus may be made to seem accurate and rational.

3. Compromise and Reconciliation

Through Rationalization, the ego endeavors to effect compromises between one's conscience or superego, and one's unconscious, more basic so-called instinctual drives and wishes. This dynamism serves as a major intrapsychic reconciliator. Reconciliation is sought between one's needs on the one hand, and personal or social standards on the other, where these are in conflict. As such, it can operate constructively and promote ego synthesis and integration. Often, however, Rationalization results in a destructive kind of self-deception, with the potential for significant self-defeat.

Instances in which this ego defense is operative are to be observed in a great many well-adjusted people. Instances are invariably uncovered in intensive psychotherapy. When evolved as a major attempted psychic defense in emotional illness, Rationalization can prove stubbornly resistant to insight and understanding. The strength, level, and persistence of this resistance is usually in direct proportion to its importance as a defense to the person concerned. Rationalization has many and widespread uses.

In the following instance, Rationalization endeavored to deny and conceal from recognition the injurious consequences of a destructive love affair. Through this dynamism the neurotic gains were preserved and the injury and self-defeat obscured.

Case 128

Protection of Neurotic Gains Through Rationalization and Denial

A 30-year-old man in intensive treatment had been conducting a destructive extra-marital love affair. This relationship he justified to himself (i.e., rationalized) on the superficial basis that he was "being helpful." He would dwell (to an extent that invited attention to his underlying defensiveness) on the satisfactions he brought to his partner, which he claimed she could not obtain in her own marriage. He described how his relationship had contributed to the stability of their marriage. In self-righteous fashion, he believed himself responsible for holding the marriage together, through his essential contributions sexually. He had been doing the greatest of good for husband, wife, and children.

Actually, in this particular situation this individual was not only actually injuring himself in a number of ways and potentially still more so, but was also greatly injuring his partner, her husband, and their family. With his great need to maintain a favorable picture of himself however, he had ruled out the possibility of any injurious effects from the alliance. Through Rationalization he had managed further to explain and justify the situation with resulting satisfaction and enhancement of his self-image over a considerable period of time.

B. WIDESPREAD UTILIZATION

1. Posthypnotic Rationalization

The tendency toward Rationalization is present with many people. It is possible through hypnosis to experimentally demonstrate its operation. Hereby we secure interesting examples of Rationalization operating entirely unconsciously. This process is found to be almost invariably evolved when the question "why?" is asked in regard to their behavior, of the individuals acting in response to posthypnotic suggestions.

This major type of operation of the dynamism is *Posthypnotic Rationalization*. Several generations ago this phenomenon was used as a classic demonstration to illustrate the existence of the unconscious and to prove the presence of unconscious mental-emotional activity.

When posthypnotic suggestions are later carried out by the once hypnotized subject, he of course has no conscious awareness of why he had performed the act. However, he has a strong need to explain his response to the suggestion made earlier while he was under hypnosis. Accordingly, he will give more or less plausible, but perhaps only under the circumstances and to observers, what are transparently insufficient or inaccurate explanations, for his behavior.

Through the Posthypnotic type of Rationalization one endeavors to justify his behavior, especially to himself and to others. His ego provides explanatory motives. This type of operation of the dynamism is illustrated in the following instance.

Case 129

Rationalization Justifies Behavior of Posthypnotic Suggestion

In a demonstration to a group of medical students, a volunteer was given the following suggestion while under hypnosis. "Shortly after you return to a nontrance state I will light a cigarette. This will be a signal for you to remove your shirt, fold it neatly, and place it on the podium. . . . You will not remember having received this suggestion. . . ."

After the student had been awakened from the hypnotic state and the predetermined signal given, the events occurred as suggested. He had no conscious memory that the suggestion had been made, nor that his behavior had been so directed. At this juncture, he was asked for an explanation of his actions.

In response to the query, the student explained easily and spontaneously how he had ". . . been interested for a long time in the various ways that people react to unexpected situations. . . ." As a result of this interest, it had occurred to him that ". . . it would be quite interesting to observe the class' reaction. . . ." to his unusual behavior. Since he had been willing to be a subject for hypnosis for their benefit, he saw no reason why he should not use his classmates as subjects so as to observe their reactions in turn.

This explanation, invented unconsciously and with facility to explain to himself (and to others) his bizarre behavior, was an instance of the Posthypnotic type of Rationalization. It illustrates the readiness and automaticity with which this ego defense can be called into play.

2. Frequent Bases

Many of our emotions can become disapproved of in kind or in extent. As one example, among many kinds and variations of emotional feelings, envy as the basis for one's dislike of another is often personally and socially disapproved and therefore must be "covered over" or concealed. In general, people tend to look down on feelings of envy. There are often considerable pressures toward disowning this feeling (consciously as well as unconsciously) through various Rationalizations, which may be much more acceptable. This is similarly true of many varied feelings or reactions. They can be socially or personally intolerable in kind, according to their level or extent, or when present inappropriately, in some particular situation (see *Motive-Rationalization,* p. 260).

A person may ascribe his lateness for an appointment, or similar lack of performance, to working overtime, extra duties or work emergencies. This may constitute a Rationalization; the underlying explanation may lie in his reluctance, fear, unwillingness, or any number of motives which he does not wish to, or cannot admit to himself, or reveal to others. Work as an explanation is likely more socially and personally acceptable. Accordingly, such an explanation may be readily adopted through the process of Rationalization. Its utilization may be conscious and deliberate; it may provide a convenient peg for an unwitting process—an illustration of the *Peg Concept* (*The Neuroses,* pp. 545 ff.); or it may represent a combination of the two. (See *Ego-Enhancing Inversion,* p. 200.)

The reformer may be drawn into his work because it brings him into contact with vice. He may be wholly unaware of this. The inner needs must be kept secret, especially from himself. His ability to point out the social usefulness of his work can provide him with excellent Rationalizations.

Frequently Rationalization attempts to maintain self-esteem, through what is termed the *Ego-Maintaining Rationalization.* A teenager who is a failure at school may ascribe this to his having been ill, as a more creditable explanation than that he has been remiss in not getting around to completing his assignments. He may regard a low grade in an examination as the consequence of the teacher's unfairness, instead of his poor preparation. This process can extend. As an extreme progression, he may develop a contempt for all learning, as a major *Characterologic Rationalization* (see later Section H) for his lack of success in educational fields.

Often excuses are made to oneself and to others for forgetting something. Frequently the real reasons for a loss of memory are concealed, or partially so, from conscious recognition through the use of Rationalization. It requires considerable training in self-observation and a keen perceptiveness to be able to grasp the underlying basis for many of these minor lapses. The situations and examples cited in this section can offer us only a sampling of the myriad bases and ubiquitous operation of this major ego defense.

In fairly frequent instances, Rationalizations are employed to gloss over one's conduct and to explain away one's failures. Sometimes these are more or less conscious and represent little more than superficial excuses. They can sometimes, as in the following case, hold potentially serious consequences for the individual concerned. Their intent for this individual was to provide acceptable bases for her serious failure to follow medical instructions.

Case 130

Rationalization for Failure in Weight Reduction

(1) *Diabetes Suspected.* A 35-year-old housewife was referred to a hospital clinic following a mass health screening.

Symptoms of polyuria, polydypsia, and polyphagia had begun 6 months earlier. Two weeks prior to referral, a blood test indicated a high sugar level and she received a letter from the Health Department in which further studies were recommended. Diabetes was strongly suspected.

(2) *Weight Loss Essential.* Physical examination revealed an obese female, weighing some 220 pounds. Other physical findings were negative. A random urine specimen showed 2 plus sugar. The fasting blood sugar was 160 mg percent, and the glucose tolerance curve was typically that of diabetes mellitus. The diagnosis was established.

She was placed on a carefully planned diabetic diet of 1,500 calories with 25 units per day of NPH. It was strongly emphasized that reduction of her weight with the diabetic diet was essential in order to secure the desired improvement of her diabetic condition. She was instructed to return at weekly intervals for follow-up treatment.

(3) *Failures Lead to Superficial Rationalizations.* Of more than average intelligence, she understood the advice and the urgent reasons for it. Upon the ensuing visit, she was found to have gained over 5 pounds, instead of the desired reduction. When asked about this, she rationalized as follows: "I just couldn't reduce because when I do I get irritable. My husband so much prefers me pleasant . . . I just didn't dare cut down on food this week. . . ."

The following week she gained again, and again the third week, accompanying her failures with similarly superficial Rationalizations on each occasion. In this fashion, she sought to avert self-condemnation or disapprobation from clinic personnel. After all, if it were impossible, or not feasible to lose weight, then she couldn't be blamed for her failure to do so. This unhappy woman ran an up and down course with her weight for more than a year while she was followed in the clinic. At no time could she get below 205 pounds.

Obesity can result from vital emotional needs. These can be powerful enough to defeat most efforts to reduce, thoroughly frustrating doctor and patient alike. It is small wonder the obese patient's psyche will bring into

operation various ego defenses, among which Rationalization can be prominent. These are called into play to rationalize resulting social handicap,
self-disapproval, that one cares, the failure to reduce, or as in the foregoing instance, the importance of reducing. ("After all, isn't it more important that my husband is contented and happy?")

3. Contributing to Mediation. Types Listed

As a widely used mechanism, the capacity for Rationalization seems
almost "built in." As humans, we are heirs of anxiety and humanly we
seek to avoid it, and to minimize its effects. Some control over one's anxieties
is essential to successfully secure and maintain personality integration.
One's superego makes demands, sets standards, and requires conformance.
The id in turn seeks satisfaction and pleasure through the gratification of
inner needs which are often unacceptable to the self (the ego) and to
society.

In seeking to resolve these conflicting forces, the ego serves as the
mediator. Rationalization is an important dynamism which the ego calls
into play in this endeavor. It is a mediating and reconciliating mechanism.
Through it, the incompatible becomes compatible. It is a Higher Order
ego defense, a more advanced and developed one.

It is to be expected that this major mental mechanism will have many
and diverse functions. Among these at this point we can identify four
additional major functions and briefly outline a number of special types of
Rationalization.

The major intrapsychic functions of Rationalization, in addition to the
foregoing, include: (1) a block to conscious recognition; (2) devaluation
of an unobtained or unobtainable goal; (3) unconscious justification and
self-deception; and (4) an intended defense against anxiety.

Six types of *Major Rationalization* are: (1) *Complex-Supportive Rationalization;* (2) *Eleemosynary Rationalization;* (3) *Collective or Social
Rationalization;* (4) *Familial Rationalization;* (5) *Symptom-Defensive Rationalization;* and (6) *Characterologic Rationalization.*

Types of *Minor Rationalization* include: (1) *Posthypnotic Rationalization;* (2) *Recognition-Deferment Rationalization;* (3) *Ego-Maintaining
Rationalization;* (4) *Motive-Rationalization;* (5) *Sour-Grapes Rationalization;* (6) *Material Rationalization;* (7) *Alcoholic Rationalization;* (8)
Sexual Rationalization; and (9) *Behavioral Rationalization.* We shall
briefly consider these in turn, followed by comments about the operation
of this ego defense in emotional illness and its psychodynamics.

C. MAJOR FUNCTIONS

1. Block to Conscious Recognition

A. RECOGNITION-DEFERMENT RATIONALIZATION.—Rationalization can
act as a further block to conscious awareness, or aid in the deferment

of recognition, of ideas, thoughts, feelings, impulses, or needs that are
personally unacceptable and intolerable. When encountered, this operation
of the dynamism is *Recognition-Deferment Rationalization*. Such postpone-
ments of painful recognition can prove very self-defeating (pp. 456–7).

Through the utilization of Rationalization, a more effective wall can
be maintained against the conscious recognition of certain aspects of one's
self-image which are objectionable. When operative, this is a type of
Ego-Maintaining Rationalization. It will be illustrated in *Case 132*. The
Rationalization of physical or characterologic features of one's self-picture
which one cannot consciously tolerate is a frequent function of this operation of the dynamism.

Rationalization is also employed in preventing the recognition of aspects about one's relationships with others which would be disappointing
or painful. As an example, this type of defensively-intended operation is
sometimes evolved in maintaining an illusory preservation of the existence
of affection, after the warmth has faded. This is illustrated in the following
case, which is an instance of the *Recognition-Deferment* type of Rationalization.

Case 131

Loss of Affection Rationalized

A 46-year-old professional man was in therapy because of a series
of problems in his interpersonal relationships. In several major instances he had blocked conscious recognition of the deterioration of a
relationship, until all possible chances for its salvage were lost. This
had happened in an earlier marriage.

He had been on a foreign assignment for his firm, living in Copen-
hagen when his wife ". . . took off suddenly and without a word of
warning. . . ." with their three children for America. The event was true
enough, but the circumstances proved to be quite different. Actually,
she had told him on many occasions that she no longer loved him, and
that she merely awaited a propitious moment for separation.

Following its thorough analysis, as he later put it, "I just couldn't
believe she didn't love me, despite all the warnings. I just couldn't believe anything like this could happen. . . . I told myself that her statements were idle thoughts, that she didn't really mean them. . . . I reas-
sured myself that it was just her way of blowing off steam, or that this
was part of her unrealistic reaction to living abroad. . . . I just completely
rationalized myself out of even any chance of a clear picture of what was
going on. . . . I didn't see it coming. . . ."

"I guess I couldn't face the possibility; felt I couldn't cope with it.
So I would tell myself that of course she really loved me; that it could
never happen to me. . . . I guess this was another awful instance of how
very good I've been at kidding myself all my life. . . . The next thing I
knew, she was gone, bag, baggage, and children, and I was absolutely
stunned! You would have thought the possibility hadn't even existed.
. . ." Through his Rationalization of course, it had not.

This patient had successfully shielded himself from the recognition of
data which would have been psychically painful. It was a protection of the
present at the cost of the future, and illustrates the *Recognition-Deferment
Rationalization*. Through thus "kidding himself," he had surrendered any

possible chance to retrieve an increasingly hopeless situation. This was part of the self-defeat he engendered and which he had exchanged for what proved to be an illusory and temporary respite from painful recognition.

B. COMPLEX-SUPPORTIVE RATIONALIZATION.—In the following case, conscious recognition was blocked through Rationalization of the destructive domination and parental overcontrol of a child. This instance is also in accord with and illustrates the *Concept of Emotional Exploitation* of the child by his parent. See also p. 172 ff., in *The Neuroses,* and our earlier *Concept of Engulfment,* p. 171.

Through potent Rationalizations, the mother in this instance shielded from conscious awareness certain unadmirable aspects of herself and her role in a destructive relationship. This is an instance of a major type of operation of this ego defense which we call the *Complex-Supportive Rationalization.* Through this operation of the dynamism, a given emotional complex which is conflictual and self-defeating is maintained and protected. The complex can be an extremely significant one.

Case 132

Ego-Maintaining and Complex-Supportive Rationalization

A 40-year-old mother in psychiatric treatment had a 22-year-old daughter whom she controlled with an iron hand. Her arbitrary decisions and rigid supervision of every detail of the young woman's life left the latter little freedom of action or even thinking in her own behalf. The mother was demanding in a way that relegated the daughter to a slave-like position of giving constant service and "devotion." She described all that the daughter did for her as merely being "what any loyal child would do for her mother. . . ." The overall consequence was a destructive relationship which left a great deal to be desired.

During 18 months of intensive treatment, efforts to interest the mother in recognizing and analyzing this major phase of living were rather fruitless. When material relating to this significant relationship came up for discussion, the mother would veer away, or launch into what had become standard Rationalizations. Questions were met by indignant, self-righteous protestations concerning her deep devotion and love for her daughter and vice versa.

In short, the mother had been able to conceal from herself conscious awareness of her destructive overcontrol of her daughter's life. This was possible through her being able to rationalize her conception of the relationship. She ascribed every aspect of her own behavior and that of her daughter as being in response to mutual deep devotion and love. She preserved a self-picture more in keeping with her standards and desires through a powerful *Ego-Maintaining Rationalization.*

The entire complex of the mother-daughter relationship was thus maintained and protected, despite its destructive nature and substantial self-defeat. Also illustrated is the *Complex-Supportive* type of *Rationalization.*

In the foregoing situation, the mother accounted to herself, for her feelings and behavior by justifying them with "made up" but socially acceptable and laudable reasons. Through her utilization of the ego defense of Rationalization, she evaded recognition of the otherwise intolerable aspects of her attitudes and behavior. She had accordingly preserved the dependency and neurotic gratifications which stemmed from what was in essence a very destructive relationship.

The neurotic "gains" of the mother however, were achieved and preserved at the cost of sacrificing any chance for a more soundly based constructive and satisfying relationship. Further self-defeat lay in this being at the cost of her daughter's maturity, and the deprivation of any real love between them. The complex was supported, but at great cost to both people involved. Illustrated are both the *Ego-Maintaining Rationalization* and the *Complex-Supportive Rationalization*.

Rationalization is an unconscious endeavor to provide the ego with plausible, acceptable, and rational reasons for actions and motives. In this way, appeasement of the conscience or superego and society is sought. Rationalization is often employed to maintain or enhance one's self-esteem.

Rationalization can operate to hold criticism "in check," in anticipation that something will work out well, or until after something pending has transpired. A medical student detected this in the reaction of his classmates to their summer service assignments.

The junior class regularly divided these positions among its members. Prior to its being placed in operation, the plan adopted received unanimous approval. However, after the positions had been apportioned, those who received the less desirable assignments noted flaws and objections. Criticism before apportioning was rationalized by some in hopes of receiving a favorable assignment (which would hold criticism in abeyance), while others might keep earlier criticism silent and rationalized afterwards because they made out so well. Rationalized "sour-grapes" attitudes were also expressed by several toward the more coveted positions, after these had been lost.

2. *Goal Devaluation*

A. EASING DISAPPOINTMENT, LOSS, AND FRUSTRATION.—When a person fails to obtain a desired goal, it is an understandably common tendency to try and make that goal seem less worthwhile and attractive. In that way, one seeks to ease the sense of disappointment or frustration, and to avoid feelings that might be too hard to bear. The sharp knife of loss is dulled.

Devaluing the unobtainable, as illustrated in the following instances, is fairly frequent. It is a variant of the succeeding Sour-Grapes type of Rationalization. (See also pp. 201 and 457.)

Case 133

Devaluing the Unobtainable

A young premedical student failed to secure the admission into medical school which he greatly desired. He was, however, later able to gain entrance into dental school as a substitute. This was for him a major defeat in life, which he had difficulty in accepting. As part of his endeavors to adjust to his new situation, he gradually developed a most critical attitude toward medicine. This included criticisms about

individual physicians and the entire medical profession, which a short
time past he had sought so hard to join.

As part of his devaluing endeavors, after a year or so he regarded
the physician's life as uninviting and strenuous. As he remarked one
day, "I wouldn't be a doctor for anything.... They are on call 24 hours
a day, and have no life of their own.... Even if they make any kind
of living, they will never find time to benefit much from it with the
schedules they have to keep.... It's a terrible way to live!...." He rationalized away his hurt, disappointment, and loss by devaluing what
had proven unobtainable.

B. SOUR-GRAPES RATIONALIZATION.—The operation of the dynamism
is referred to as "sour grapes" when it is employed as above to devalue an
unobtainable goal. The classic example of Rationalization springs from
Aesop's fable of *The Fox and the Grapes*.

This type of Rationalization is widely recognized, and hearing the expression "sour grapes" is not uncommon. People have long been aware of
such human attempts to devalue something that one really wishes to have,
when it has proven to be unobtainable.

Case 134

Sour Grapes

A fox was particularly fond of grapes. One day when he was
very hungry he spied some beautiful, luscious grapes hanging high on
a vine. He wanted some, but found they were above his reach. He
jumped and jumped and jumped, but was unable to get any. Finally
he gave up in despair.

As he walked away from the vineyard he said, "They were probably
sour grapes anyway. Anyone can have them for all I care. Who wants
sour grapes? Certainly not I!"

His reaction was an effort to salve his disappointment over the loss;
the classic instance of the *Sour-Grapes Rationalization*.

3. Motive-Rationalization

Self-deception and justification are major functions and consequences
of the mechanism of Rationalization. These are so much a part of the
intent of the dynamism that they are present to some degree in every instance. Frequently the ego defense is related to justifying aspects of motivation, and we accordingly refer to this type of its operation as *Motive-
Rationalization*. (See also *Ineffective Rationalization*, p. 397.)

The next case offers an example of a relatively superficial instance of
Rationalization, in which the function of self-deception was important in
relation to the motivation of a young doctor. There are many examples of
Motive-Rationalization to be encountered. Many of these will have points
of general similarity to the following instance.

Case 135

Motive-Rationalization

A young physician was working in the psychiatric service as part of
his residency training. In the course of doing admission studies, he was

assigned the case of an attractive young woman. During the ensuing week, while working up her history, he commented several times to his colleagues about how interesting he found this young woman's problems to be.

He decided that he wanted to work with her in intensive therapy during his period of training. Shortly thereafter he formulated plans to continue the therapy following his transfer to the next department.

The resident's colleagues did not share his evaluation of interest. In fact, they felt she would be a trying and difficult therapeutic problem. However, the resident's enthusiasm won him the approval of the staff to begin therapy.

After a number of therapy sessions with this young lady, it became increasingly evident to his supervisor that the case was extremely complex, and the prognosis guarded. Further, during his supervisory hours, it was soon apparent that the resident's interest was more personal than psychiatric. This was discussed tactfully, the Rationalizations were partly recognized and the resident found that his interest decreased.

He had been unaware (or certainly not fully aware) of his more basic and emotional motivations. These had been covered over by rather thin Rationalizations; an instance of *Motive-Rationalization*.

The following is an example of a commonly encountered type of Rationalization in which its devaluation function is employed to promote comfort and satisfaction; to lessen frustration and dissatisfaction. For some this process which is called *Material Devaluation* is a necessary one. Many similar instances of this defensively-aimed operation are far less obvious.

Case 136

Devaluation of the Material

The life employment of a 66-year-old man was working on a railroad section gang. His income was quite limited. While he found satisfactions in his work, there were many material things quite beyond his reach. He had devalued the advantages of many of these long since.

Should a friend extoll the virtues of a Cadillac for instance, his response would be along the line that he would certainly never own one. They were not worth the cost, too large to handle easily and burned too much gas.

He wouldn't want to own a house in the more desirable section of town. There had been two floods (one 86 and one 40 years earlier); his part of town was higher. He did not want a deep-freeze and he disapproved of TV. The list included many items and reasons.

Not only did this function of Rationalization help him justify what he maintained, but it also aided him in softening any disappointments about what he couldn't have. He did not recognize, as did his friends, some of the inconsistencies with which his reasoning was peppered.

The laborer above had developed a fair number of Rationalizations to lessen the attraction of the unobtainable. The process of Material Devaluation is intended to provide a measure of solace in easing frustration and deprivation. The strength and breadth of the process as in the foregoing can afford at times a rough level of the "real," i.e., basic and underlying, desires for what is outwardly devalued.

The following instance is an interesting illustration of self-deception and justification contributed to by stubborn Rationalizations during therapy. An inaccurate self-picture was maintained, with considerable self-defeat resulting as an inadvertent consequence. It also illustrates the Alcoholic Rationalization as mentioned later.

Case 137

Rationalization in Self-Deception

A 28-year-old professional woman in therapy occasionally used alcohol immoderately, a few drinks having considerable effect. In these instances, her behavior was hasty, ill-considered, and indiscreet. Included would be a loose tongue, lessened inhibitions, and later regrets. There were several episodes of sexual promiscuity. Subsequently she regularly suffered from severe headaches. It was clear that the episodes were indeed headaches to her—both figuratively and literally.

This attractive young woman had a powerful and rigid conscience and her conduct occasioned her most stringent self-disapproval. This she managed to deny over the course of many months of therapeutic study, however, partly through maintaining an entrenched Rationalization that she was "allergic" to certain brands of bourbon. As long as she could remain convinced of this, then the episodes were not due to the quantity of alcohol, nor her failure to exercise restraint or judgment in ways best designed to ensure self-approval. The Rationalization sought to deflect, and to defend against, the heavy weight of her condemnation.

This type of operation of the dynamism is not infrequently employed and continues a dangerous kind of self-deception. Through it this patient was able to preserve a destructive pattern of behavior which provided certain gratifications but was quite self-defeating, with the potential for still more hurt.

In the following example, the self-justification and deception is of a greater extent and seriousness. Herein, it was of such a level and extent as to be considered almost delusional. A combination of Denial and Rationalization were operative (p. 56 ff.).

Case 138

Rationalization and Denial

A middle-aged man was a particularly unpopular hairdresser at a fashionable salon. He had a certain following, however, and despite his overbearing manner, insufferable vanity, and contemptuous attitudes toward co-workers and clients alike, was able to continue with a measure of success for some years. Gradually, however, these more troublesome personality traits became further accentuated. As this transpired, his clients decreased.

Soon this process had become a vicious circle, with each development seeming to speed the other. It was not many months before he became unwanted and a liability. One day he received the inevitable advice that he might be well advised to look elsewhere for a position.

He remained completely blind to any possible contributions to this train of events. He talked in glowing terms about how: (1) everyone admired and loved him, (2) the artistry of his work was unequaled, (3) he must make a move to better himself while still young, and (4) his co-workers were extremely sorry to see him go (on the contrary, only through the knowledge of his early departure were they able to remain civil).

His self-confidence was empty and his claims and views of himself hollow and transparent to all save himself. Everyone knew he had been fired and felt it was long past due.

Justification has interesting ramifications. People not only employ Rationalizations in this service personally, but also for family members, friends, and figures in literature. Not many think of Robin Hood as bad. How many regard him as a thief?

Case 139

Rationalizations for Robin Hood

Robin Hood was the leader of a band of robbers. Their victims were the rich, who were generally represented as being in various ways less than admirable. This in itself might have been an insufficient justification, but, to the relief of the reader perhaps, Robin Hood reputedly turned all his loot over to the poor, which for many not only absolved him of blame but helped make him an admirable character.

The success of the Robin Hood legends is in part based on the knowledge that readers will employ Rationalization in evaluating his activities. Possibly one cannot condone stealing, but giving away stolen goods to needy folk makes it more acceptable. Factors of Identification and Idealization play a role in the popularity of the tales, as do the inclusion of heroic deeds, escapades, and other features.

Certain face-saving operations are likely to receive contributions from Rationalization which is sometimes conscious and at other times less so. The following is an example of a rather frequently encountered type of occupational and scholastic face-saving.

Case 140

Rationalization for School Failure

A 19-year-old university sophomore was doing poorly in his scholastic work. This he could not admit. As the spring term grew to a close, he still was unable to recognize the gravity of his situation, or to study with the greater effort so urgently needed.

One month prior to the end of the semester he dropped out of his class and enlisted in the Navy.

To friends he explained this move as due to anticipating the draft, so as to have his choice of service. He devalued the advantages of an education or a degree. In the process, his precarious position at the University was forgotten. He rationalized his reasons for leaving in an endeavor to try and salve his feelings over failing.

In the foregoing instances, Rationalization results in the justification of conduct, beliefs, failures, or attitudes through assigning reasons which are other than those actually motivating the person. The reasons given are more or less plausible and are more personally and socially acceptable.

Rationalization fills a significant function in its promotion of justification and self-deception. It is important to recognize the implicit but unwitting self-defeat which is present in so much of this. The examples cited illustrate these features to an extent and in more flagrant instances. Much, of course, of what transpires in the emotional vicissitudes of people is far more subtle in nature.

4. *Protection Against Anxiety*

Protection against the generation, presence, or effects of anxiety is a basically intended function of Rationalization. This function plays a more or less apparent role in each of our case examples.

When one's ideas, feelings, or drives come into opposition with personal or social standards the resulting conflict gives rise to anxiety. Through the evolvement of Rationalization, opposing systems of ideas, needs, and associated feelings can come into contact but through an intermediary which so influences the incompatibilities, that these become more or less concealed. The individual, consciously or unconsciously, seeks for and finds specious reasons that enable him to regard certain specific actions of his own, or of others, as justified by the circumstances. Opposing ideas thus can enter the mind, but only after their logical significance has been distorted through Rationalization. The conflict which would have existed between them otherwise is obviated.

Rationalization is a defense against anxiety. It keeps the individual from awareness of those motives and wishes which otherwise are at variance with his standards, ideals, or expectations. The constant potential for danger and for self-defeat lies in its masking reality, and in its keeping various facts from oneself even though these may be important for objectivity and for adjustment. The hazard of providing oneself with a false picture of reality is substantial.

Rationalization is dependent on language and communication. It tends to modify one's realistic self-evaluation. One must justify one's behavior to oneself or to others. The quantity and quality of Rationalization can indicate the level of dependence on others' opinion for one's self-esteem.

It is not always apparent or adequately presented that conscious efforts are constantly called into play to combat anxiety, to prevent it, or to minimize its effects. Conscious rationalizations seeking to lessen responsibility or blame comprise a major part of these attempts.

The following instance illustrates an effort to shrug off responsibility through the employment of quite transparent rationalizations. It is doubtful if this man really persuaded anyone, including himself. At the most he may have succeeded in talking himself into feeling a little better about his time and energy-wasting error.

Case 141

Conscious Rationalization to Evade Responsibility

A 34-year-old biologist was engaged in research work with assays of biologic material. The immediate object was to improve a certain culture media. In instructing his technicians, he made a particular point of the nutritional requirements for a particular organism and stressed that the exact amount of each element must be present in the ideal media. He suggested varying the proportion of these components to determine which combination provided the most rapid rate of growth. He recited from memory the percentages as required.

A week was spent preparing the media; the work based on the figures quoted. The bacteria was inoculated into the media, and the plates
were carefully incubated. Series were set up in a regular time sequence.

At intervals during the three subsequent weeks, the technicians
noted that there was no growth in any of the preparations. They were
dismayed. The biologist was also disturbed at the loss of work and time.
On checking the growth component figures which he had earlier recited
so glibly, he found that one of them was misquoted to the extent of
toxic levels.

In discussing this later he first denied giving the specific figures.
Next he offered a number of rationalizations for his error. Still later he
said, "Well I'm sure if it hadn't been me who made the mistake, it
would have probably been someone else.... We can't all be perfect all
the time...." With these and similar comments he sought to spare himself criticism, to rationalize his failure, and to lessen responsibility.

Let us proceed to consider several additional special major types of
Rationalization.

D. ELEEMOSYNARY RATIONALIZATION

1. On Behalf Of. . . .

There are a number of major types of Rationalization that warrant
comment. First let us consider a general kind of philosophy of certain
persons according to which, for example, in the name of sweet and gentle
charity—anything goes. This of course does not have to be confined to
charity or to a charitable organization. It can operate with any group, organization, church, or cause which a person regards as sufficiently worthwhile, important, deserving, or to which he assigns an overriding significance.

Doing something thus in the name of, in view of, or for his cause,
then for many people allows a greater and wider latitude of action. More
is permissible and he can view things a bit (or a great deal) differently
from usual. The evolution of a type of Rationalization becomes possible
through which relaxation, or even suspension, of one's more usual standards takes place. This process is a prominent one in our culture.

Because of its nature, its mode of operation, its relative distinctness,
and its cultural significance, we have sought to invite further attention to it
through assignment of the name of *Eleemosynary Rationalization*. The term
emphasizes its frequent relation to charitable and other worthwhile causes.
This process can be a conscious operation, an unconscious one, or a
combination of both.

2. Modification of Usual Codes

There are several factors which are important in facilitating Eleemosynary Rationalization. The first involves the possession or assignment to the
cause or group of a position of special importance, righteousness, or worthwhileness by the person concerned.

A second element relates to the seeming lack of personal, selfish advantage to be derived. The activity and sought-after gains are conceived as being for something outside of oneself. A picture of selflessness is promoted. For many this makes the employment of a modified or different set of ethical standards for one's conduct more permissible in these situations. The following is a brief illustration.

Case 142

Eleemosynary Rationalization

A church group was negotiating for the purchase of a new parsonage. The chairman of the committee, comprised of leading businessmen, was a real estate man of substantial reputation and excellent standing. With his approval, the committee deliberately violated at least two major ethical real estate principles, in a way he would never have tolerated in his firm. First, the salesman who originally interested the group in the property and conducted the early phase of negotiations was a time ignored. Secondly, a man from another firm was induced to take over. Since it was for the church, he was persuaded to forgo a commission.

The first salesman was wronged. Calling in the second firm wronged the first firm. This was a breach of realty ethics. In addition, an exclusive sales contract between the owner and firm number one was violated. All of this was neatly rationalized by the committee on the basis of saving their church the sales commission.

Those wronged of course might have sought recourse in law, but the loss of good will in instituting procedings against a church group ruled this out, even had they been so inclined.

The second firm's initial reluctance to enter into the transaction was overcome by similar Rationalizations to those already made by the committee, as to the need, worthwhileness, public service aspects, and lack of personal gain, together with their fear of turning down the church group.

Eleemosynary Rationalization permitted for the people concerned a considerable elasticity in their usual personal codes and standards in this instance. Considerations of conscience were replaced by feelings of virtue, service, and accomplishment.[1] The committee was commended by the congregation.

The above example happens to concern a church group. This intriguing type of Rationalization, however, can be found operating in relation to many types of service in behalf of many organizations and causes.

Eleemosynary Rationalization may be evolved in regard to activities undertaken for the school, the firm, society, profession, fraternity, organization, or group. A relaxation of one's usual code of ethics is rationalized on the basis of for whom it is done.

3. Absence of Gain Illusory

As mentioned, an important criterion in delineating Eleemosynary Rationalization is the supposed absence of personal gain. This is, of course, a fiction and quite illusory. It can be true strictly from a monetary standpoint. As a member of a group which gains something however, one also

---

[1] As an ironic footnote to this instance, it was learned independently that the owner actually had been prepared to accept a purchase contract via the first salesman for several thousand dollars less than that finally negotiated. This was equivalent to nearly twice the sales commission "saved."

gains in various ways, even though the conscious thought is directed toward the group and does not concern oneself.

Far more important, is the recognition one may receive in turn from the benefited group, which often constitutes the real personal gain. Gains in terms of enhanced prestige, reputation, achievement, acceptance, recognition, position, or honor, can provide more important, driving or complex, but often subtle motivations for many people than mere monetary gain. These can also remain more hidden, and more difficult of assessment.

Finally, the opportunity to act arbitrarily, ruthlessly, sexually, authoritatively, competitively, or hostilely in the guise of serving a worthy cause can afford the opportunity for a hidden avenue of expression for these kinds of otherwise disapproved or disowned intrapsychic drives and their secret gratification.

4. Historical Perspective

Lest the claim be advanced that Eleemosynary Rationalization is a symptom of our particular culture, it might be worthwhile to observe its operation in historical perspective. This kind of basis for stretching, suspending, or relaxing one's conscience is not new.

"In the name of God. . . ." and "In the name of the King. . . ." have a timeless ring. Under such noble umbrellas of sanction, how many injurious, destructive, or foul acts have been committed? Dark and evil actions have been adjudged to be good or noble All kinds of misdeeds have thus come to be viewed as patriotic or holy.

At first glance, the foregoing may seem far removed from overexalted views held of science, scientific achievement, or a given business enterprise in some quarters today, in which, for instance one may hold that, "no sacrifice is too great," or "let's not have too many scruples—they will only delay progress." Perhaps the distinction is not so great.

Social and personal standards are also vulnerable at times to variants of another hoary doctrine of Rationalization, according to which "the end justifies the means." Ethical and moral principles can go by the board.

The Renaissance offers many "Christian" examples of *Eleemosynary Rationalization*. These include some of the otherwise reprehensible activities of Crusaders, the trials and tortures of the Inquisition, and the exorcising of "witches." Included are bases for many actions designed to enforce the rigid and restrictive religious controls and harsh demands for conformity, exercised in various countries through the centuries by various religious sects and groups, particularly against religious and other minority groups. Religious zealots often demand conformity, are seldom noted for tolerance and find ample justification for restrictive or persecutory practices.

In more recent decades we have observed the Party or State emerge to secure overriding prominence in Nazi Germany, in Communist Russia, and elsewhere. In their service, "staged" trials, extorted "confessions," the psychologic conditioning horrors of Prisoner Processing (brainwashing) and mass murder have not only been condoned, but viewed laudably by many, and subsequently developed to a high state of efficiency.

These represent samplings of the many ways throughout the course of history in which Eleemosynary Rationalization has been employed. It is an interesting concept in which fortunately there are fewer of the more striking illustrations as noted above, evident in more recent years.

E.   SOCIAL OR COLLECTIVE RATIONALIZATION

1. Social Phenomenon

There is another interesting type of Rationalization which involves the large scale and shared development of Rationalizations for motives and behavior. Here we refer to those which are collectively employed by a national or geographical group, a class of people, a political party, or a large organization. Instances of this interesting class are referred to as *Collective* or *Social Rationalization.*

Through Collective Rationalization a group of people share common activities, motives, or behavior, which they collectively seek to justify. What is individually eschewed can thus become more or far more acceptable, or even laudable when pursued and rationalized collectively, with one's group, club, or nation.

2. Supporting Extermination

Certain relationships to Eleemosynary Rationalization are present in some instances. The *Concept of Collective* or *Social Rationalization* also has widespread applications in both past and present. We must at least briefly observe a marked example from the recent tragic era of the vicissitudes of the Jewish people.

Case 143

Social Rationalization

The operation of Collective Rationalization is apparent in certain types of political behavior prior to and during World War II. A marked occasion applied to the years when Nazi policy dictated the systematic slaughter of millions of Jews. The people concerned needed Collective Rationalization to sanction the genocide, as well as individually to allow participation, approval, the maintenance of nonawareness, or the inhibition of their disapproval and opposition.

In support of such deeds, numerous rumors and propaganda efforts were current from time to time. Stories about the alleged vicious and traitorous designs of the Jews were widely circulated and swept through Germany.

Although there was little or no factual basis for them, these rumors were believed by large segments of the population. A fair amount of this was deliberately propagated and disseminated, but this was by no means true for all. The underlying needs helped to promote the spontaneous generation of stories and prejudicial attitudes which contributed to this major instance of Collective Rationalization.

The foregoing type of Rationalization was widespread. It was *Collective* or *Social Rationalization,* that is, a kind of Rationalization involving a class of people, a political party, a geographic area, or part of a national group.

3. Car Purchase; Sexual Rationalization

At times the label of Social Rationalization seems appropriate for the widespread, semicultural pattern in which numbers of the American public support and justify their frequent replacement of automobiles. There is a widespread tendency through Rationalization to make the purchase of a new car seem the economical, practical, or necessary thing to do. One thus endeavors to make the acquisition less a luxury, indulgence, "keeping up with the Joneses," or that of competitively having a newer car than brother Tom.

Another rather widespread type which we refer to as *Sexual Rationalization* was prominent during World War II. Through this operation of the ego defense, the widespread relaxation of morals and personal scruples took place about sex. Servicemen and their girl friends thus evolved various personal and even patriotic Rationalizations to allow, explain, and excuse the relaxation of their more usual moral scruples about sex and sexual relations. (See also *Case 104,* p. 200.)

A fair variety of individual Sexual Rationalizations may be encountered in intensive therapeutic study. The needs of people to justify and explain various personally and socially conflictual sexual activities and behavior is widespread. (See also *Case 102,* p. 198.)

F.   FAMILIAL RATIONALIZATION

1. Equitable Regard

Another special type of Rationalization deserves mention at this time. It is widely prevalent, probably necessary in many instances, and contributes to emotional equanimity. Through it, parents help to preserve their beliefs, which are personally important in varying degree as to their equality of regard and treatment of their children. In view of its family setting and function, it is called *Familial Rationalization.*

Parents often have strong needs to provide fair and equal treatment to each child. This includes material things as well as regard and affection. Of these, the former are easier to make equal, although inequities in this area can require the evolution of various Familial Rationalizations.

2. Equality an Ideal

Insofar as love, regard, and affection for children are concerned, the achievement of complete equality is more an ideal than actually possible.

For a fair number of parents, however, the illusion must be carefully preserved that absolute equality is maintained.

Various large and small inequities in parental regard are likely to exist however. These are emotionally charged. As a consequence, Familial Rationalizations are employed to preserve the belief that full equality is present. These are widely variable in nature and can extend from the most subtle to the gross and evident.

G. IN SYMPTOMS AND EMOTIONAL ILLNESS

1. Ubiquitous Role

The operation of this major ego defense can be observed in most of those persons with emotional illness who have the good fortune to enter intensive psychotherapy. A significant function in its relation to emotional illness lies in its contribution to the secondary defenses, an important concept which we shall shortly mention further. In view of its pervasive and ubiquitous role in the entire field of emotional illness, these functions need to be stressed and a point or so added.

Rationalization can be of importance for the obsessive patient, together with a number of other ego defenses including Isolation, Projection, Repression, Symbolization, and Undoing. The emotionally sick patient seeks to explain himself in acceptable terms. Through the dynamism of Rationalization he substitutes more tolerable motives, thoughts, and sentiments for intolerable ones, or modifies his views of the latter.

2. The Supporting, or Secondary Delusion

Rationalizations are vital to the maintenance of delusionary beliefs. In delusions, the patient ignores and discards those facts that are incompatible with his delusion, or rationalizes them in such a way that their significance is effectually downgraded. In other words, incongruities are denied or rationalized.

Rationalization is often responsible for what we term the *Supporting* or *Secondary Delusion*. This operation leads to the further elaboration of such erroneous beliefs. They are evolved by the psyche to bridge over the incongruities between the primary delusion and actual facts of experience. The Supporting Delusion comprises a further powerful secondary defense of the original or primary delusion. In severe cases, this defensively-intended process gives rise to the development of complicated delusional systems, as further defenses are required when existing ones prove insufficient.

The Secondary or Supporting Delusion upholds and defends the first or primary delusion. This constitutes the erection of defenses to defend defenses, and brings us to our next important conception.

3. Concept of Secondary Defense; Symptom-Defensive Rationalization

The symptoms of emotional illness are defensively-intended and directed. As such, they are *primary defenses*. Often they are unable to stand alone. They require support and defense in turn.

These endeavors are called *secondary defenses*. In other words, *the symptoms, defenses in themselves, are in turn defended.* This is the important and vital concept, which has been earlier described, of the secondary defense. In the operation of this process, a major type of Rationalization often makes a significant contribution. Actually, one of the major rationales in the Rationalizations encountered in conjunction with emotional illness is observed to lie in the support and defense of symptoms.

These major endeavors of the dynamism comprise a significant group indeed, which are accordingly termed the *Symptom-Defensive* type of *Rationalization*. They contribute substantially to the resistances which must be dealt with in psychotherapy.

4. The Alcoholic Rationalization

In instances of alcoholism one is likely to encounter the operation of Rationalization. Rationalizations are often advanced as reasons for drinking, or in devaluing its destructive and self-defeating consequences. Essentially these are in support of the drinking as a symptom-crutch. They are thus to be included with our group of *Symptom-Defensive Rationalizations,* comprising a subtype which we call *Alcoholic Rationalization.* Another instance concerning the employment of confabulation in Korsakoff's syndrome was cited in *Case 7, p. 24.*

The alcoholically-habituated person may rationalize his drinking on the basis of needing to cool off when the weather is hot; when it is cold he drinks for warmth; when elated to celebrate; when depressed, to drown his sorrows. He may become an expert in rationalizing his alcoholism. See also earlier *Case 137.*

Case 144

Rationalization in Alcoholic Habituation

A psychiatric resident reported this example concerning his landlord. The latter, a retired businessman, was given to excessive drinking. One evening, after heavier than usual indulgence, he became ill. He sent for his family physician, who told him in urgent terms that he absolutely must give up the use of alcohol. He finally agreed, seemingly without reservations.

The next morning the young psychiatrist met him at breakfast. It was immediately apparent that he had had a change of heart. He had already had his first morning highball.

In response to a query, the landlord asserted that his doctor was wrong in requiring the sudden relinquishment of alcohol. The doctors for years had told his father to give up alcohol, but this advice "had never bothered him." However, as soon as he gave it up, he died.

The landlord described in detail how his system was used to alcohol. Deprivation would definitely injure him. At this juncture in the presentation of his rather shallow *Symptom-Defensive Rationalizations*, he was ready to begin drinking his breakfast dessert.

This kind of *Alcoholic Rationalization* is a superficial justification and defense. One may thus succeed to an extent in kidding oneself. He rarely convinces others. Variations are not uncommonly met with in medical practice.

H. DYNAMICS

1. Nonconformity with Ego Ideal

In the process of growth and maturation, the human psyche develops an ideal concept of what it should be, This is taken over largely from parents, other significant persons, and society and it helps to make up the superego. However, the ego is constantly under pressure for the outward expression of basic and hidden inner, or so-called instinctual impulses. Although these have been repressed, the continuing energy of the repressed drives is sometimes too powerful to be thwarted by the process of Repression alone, and one or more of the impulses may threaten to emerge.

The result not infrequently is the outcropping of some form of behavior or feeling that may not be acceptable to the ego's concept of itself in varying degree, since it is not in conformity with the ego ideal or superego. This brings on conflict and anxiety, which in turn gives rise to the automatic calling into employment of the various ego defenses, and ultimately the elaboration of character defenses and symptom formation. Let us, however, return to the ego.

2. More Creditable Alternatives. Characterologic Rationalization

The ego is now in the position of having behaved or reacted unacceptably, that is, in a fashion that cannot be condoned. It, therefore, consciously or unconsciously, looks for more acceptable and more creditable motives to account for its behavior and for the associated emotional and underlying feelings. These alternate motives which perhaps are made to be acceptable to the unconscious portion of the ego and to the superego become conscious, and become attached to the action by the ego. This particular form of unconscious self-deception is Motive-Rationalization as noted earlier.

Through Rationalization, the underlying true impulses and drives are replaced in consciousness by alternates, pseudological explanations, and by more acceptable conscious reasons to account for the behavior or feelings in question. Rationalization provides more tolerable and creditable alternates.

Rationalization is one of the most universally employed defensive mechanisms in everyday life. This is hardly surprising since it is a favorite method of coping with unresolved conflicts. Rationalizations are likely to be invested with strong emotion because they cover up otherwise distressing facts. Although comforting, we have observed how they can lead to self-deception, self-defeat, and support delusions. When possible, people avoid having their pride hurt, and rarely enjoy seeing their naked selves. Everyone seeks to save face.

As a consequence, people tend to keep their guard up, to be on the defensive, to avoid being forced to make ego-deflating admissions. Rationalization can afford an easier, more acceptable route which is "chosen" in preference.

The following instance illustrates how Rationalization can influence attitudes and behavior over a period of time. This might be regarded as an illustration of *Characterologic Rationalization*.

Case 145

Long-Term Effects of Rationalization

An instructor in college chemistry entered psychotherapy. History disclosed that he had been a premedical student at one time. After years of difficult work, he applied to medical school in 1936. Admission was very difficult to secure. He was one of those refused, on the basis that his grades did not meet the medical school's standards. He persuaded himself that his grades were not better because he really didn't care for medicine. Otherwise he would have spent more time studying, and would have received better grades. Therefore, he reasoned, "I really didn't want medicine anyway. . . ." He had gradually added similar Rationalizations to those of other students, devaluing his unobtained goal.

He continued his education, and went on to secure a doctorate in chemistry. Later he was appointed to a teaching position at a college where many of his pupils were premed. Here, his course was extremely feared by premedical students through the years. During one period he failed 40 percent of the class in introductory chemistry. When his record for failing students came up for discussion, he explained that he flunked so many because medicine is an extremely difficult field and only those who have exceptional ability should be in a position to apply for admission to medical school.

Following study of this and related attitudes over a period of time, he found many significant connections with personal experiences reaching back into his college days. He had been taking out some of his long-buried hostility and resentment on his students. (See also *Scapegoat Reaction.*) This was kept from awareness through Rationalization.

Rationalization endeavors to provide plausible and acceptable, i.e., seemingly rational reasons for actions and motives. When successful the superego or conscience, is apparently satisfied. This is a main endeavor of this intrapsychic mechanism. Rationalization at times is a selective support to the mechanism of Denial. The ego attempts to maintain or build up one's self-esteem through Rationalization. In *Case 81* (p. 152), we observed Identification supported by Rationalization (pp. 245–6).

Rationalization can serve as the mechanism for advancing more socially accepted reasons for one's conduct, as noted. The bases of these Rationalizations stem from quite personal motives, such as mastery, competitive striving, social approval, and sex, which are then disowned and unrecognized. Rationalization also helps "explain" evasions of responsibility. Through this dynamism, the person may turn his anxiety into a more rational kind of fear. There is at times a relation to guilt. The ego invites motives which are consciously acceptable, to hide the underlying ones which are not acceptable. In this manner, Rationalization can seek to absolve feelings of guilt and responsibility.

We have observed that Rationalization is evolved as a route to try and secure reconciliation between one's standards and behavior. Rationalization can serve as an attempted defense against the exposure to oneself or others of violent, unethical, and socially-disapproved motives. Similarly, Rationalization can provide plausible explanations to account for motives springing from completely unconscious sources. Rationalization is an unconscious justification.

3. Relation to Other Ego Defenses

As is frequently the case with ego defenses, Rationalization is rarely observed alone. Upon occasion it is to be found operating in conjunction with, and as an accessory to nearly every other dynamism. We have observed how the ego endeavors through Rationalization to explain away the unpleasant or unacceptable. Disapproved motives are denied in this fashion, and apparently irrational acts are justified. Rationalization is often closely related to Denial, and at times it is very difficult to differentiate between these two major ego defenses. *Case 137* illustrates this relation. Conscious denial can be similar to Rationalization (p. 62). At times Rationalization may also be regarded as a selective support to the mechanism of Denial, as noted in *Case 23* (p. 64). (See also p. 459.)

Rationalization is also related to Compensation (p. 34 ff.) of which it can comprise a type. Confabulation constitutes a Denial, is compensatory and can also be regarded as a form of Rationalization. See *Case 7* (p. 24).

There must be a process of self-justification operating almost continuously. If the ego did not actually triumph, was not sustained and boosted, it has to do so at least in retrospect. One accordingly finds extenuating circumstances for one's own lapses, failures, weaknesses, failings, or unacceptable behavior.

Brierley holds that Rationalization is an important "adjutant or auxiliary to Repressions," in that it makes the Repression of consciously intolerable motives easier through unconsciously supplying an acceptable motive in place of one which would ordinarily appear irrational or unacceptable. Through Rationalization, it is made to appear reasonable to the person concerned, and hence acceptable. Intellectualization (p. 474) is akin to Rationalization.

Rationalization also bears some relation to the ego defense of Idealization (p. 123 ff.). Rationalization and Idealization of the so-called instinctual impulses often occur together. Emotional and instinctual attitudes are acceptable on condition that they can be justified as reasonable. Finding acceptable reasons for his behavior one can thus avoid becoming aware of actually being driven by instinctual impulses.

Idealization in turn can perhaps serve as one type of Rationalization. The realization that a requirement of the ego ideal is going to be achieved enhances self-esteem. As a consequence the individual can remain blind to recognizing that through the Idealization there can be secured a measure of outward expression of basic drives that ordinarily would have to remain repressed.

I. SUMMARY

1. Making the Unacceptable Acceptable

Rationalization is an ego defense through which one seeks to make the unacceptable acceptable. Plausible explanations are provided for that which is constantly repugnant. Through the use of this dynamism, one unconsciously endeavors to justify otherwise intolerable aspects of oneself. Conflict resolution and intrapsychic mediation are significant goals. These are sought, usually through trying to make disapproved impulses, motives, or emotional feelings, more acceptable. Through Rationalization, one "kids himself" in various ways, or tries to talk himself into or out of, something. More reasonable explanations are thus sought or provided for oneself and others.

Rationalization has many functions. These are various and widespread; conscious, unconscious, and mixed. They vary from the man who disguised the reasons he wished a new car, by making it appear a necessity through Rationalization, to the Rationalization of behavior by the hypnotized subject of his suggested posthypnotic behavior (*Posthypnotic Rationalization*), or to the person exhibiting the *King David Reaction,* who thereby explains his otherwise untoward emotional feelings.

Various kinds of failure, shortcomings, or poor performance can be rationalized, some of which can result in serious consequences for the person concerned. Several illustrations were offered. The *Recognition-Deferment Rationalization* trades the potentially severe self-defeat involved in avoiding prompt recognition, for the short-term and often illusory gain of being spared some painful recognition for the present.

2. Major Functions

This mechanism provides an added block to conscious recognition of things about oneself or others which would prove painful. One's self-picture can be protected (*Ego-Maintaining Rationalization*), and the course of interpersonal relationships can be greatly affected or influenced. Devaluation of an unobtained or unobtainable goal (*Sour-Grapes Rationalization*) is another major function of this ego defense. This has been so frequently employed and so widely recognized as to lead to the expression "sour grapes" being carried over from the classic instance in Aesop's fable into common usage.

A third major function includes unconscious justification and self-deception. This appears to some extent in every instance. Rationalization can occur in reference to motives (*Motive-Rationalization*), behavior (*Behavioral Rationalization*), a distorted self-picture, one's evaluation of or by others, fictional or historical characters, poor performance, sexual activity (*Sexual Rationalization*), personal failures, and many other situations.

A fourth major function is its intended protection against anxiety, which is basic to its operation and is present in each instance of Rationalization. Finally, as a mediator of conflicting psychic forces, it seeks to reconcile personal or social standards with inner needs.

3. Special Types

Six special types of Rationalization merited our consideration. *Complex-Supportive Rationalization* aids in supporting and maintaining an important emotional complex or relationship which is conflictual and often self-defeating. In *Material Rationalization,* one devalues material possessions which are beyond his reach. *Eleemosynary Rationalization* refers to the relaxation or suspension of one's usual ethical standards, being thus justified on the basis of the worthwhileness of a group, organization, or cause, and in view of the supposed lack of personal selfish gain to be so derived. Modification of one's codes of behavior or ethics thereby becomes permissible. The illusion in this type of Rationalization was also discussed briefly in its historical perspective.

Collective or *Social Rationalization* is the widespread justification by a national group, a class of people, a party, and so on, for the shared Rationalization of behavior, motives, or guilt. The large-scale, that is, the social or collective, development of Rationalization may allow or forgive something which otherwise would not be permissible individually. What is termed *Sexual Rationalization* can have many applications and facets. Its widespread employment during a period of national crisis, as in World War II was noted.

Familial Rationalizations are employed to maintain one's picture of the ideal of equality being present in one's parental affection and regard for each child in a given family.

Symptom-Defensive Rationalizations are those which contribute significantly to the maintenance and support of symptoms and character defenses.

4. Final Points

Rationalization is pervasive in living. It is even more so in instances of emotional symptoms and illness, in which it can play an important role. Symptoms are primary defenses. Once established, their maintenance and defense in turn can become a vital matter. In other words, *the symptoms, a defense in themselves, are in turn defended.* This thesis has been advanced earlier. It is the important *Concept of Secondary Defense.*

Building secondary defenses in emotional illness is a major endeavor of Rationalization (the *Symptom-Defensive Rationalization*). Concepts of the *Primary Delusion* and the *Supporting* or *Secondary Delusion* were offered. *Alcoholic Rationalization* is a not uncommon subtype of this dynamism.

The dynamics were discussed as we proceeded. A final section emphasized and added a few points. The positions of the ego and superego in relation to Rationalization were noted. This dynamism can play an important role in long-term characterologic evolution. When this function is apparent, as a sixth major type, it is termed *Characterologic Rationalizations.* A few of the many relationships of this major ego defense to other dynamisms were noted. It rarely operates except in conjunction with another or more additional mechanisms.

J. CROSS-REFERENCES TO *THE NEUROSES* *

Rationalization
In Nature of Anxiety (Chapter 1)
  as a defense by ego, in dealing with anxiety; p. 24.
  employed, to explain cause of discomfort; p. 15.
In Illusory Gains (Chapter 2)
  as conscious endeavor, in conscious secondary gain; p. 61.
  employed, in neurotic gain of *King David Reaction;* p. 76.
In Character Reactions (Chapter 5)
  as a *personality type;* p. 233.
  of compulsive overeating; p. 298.
  of emotional feelings, in *Obsessive Personality;* p. 255.
  of rigidity, in sexual activities of *Obsessive Personality;* p. 297.
  use of, in posthypnotic subject; p. 240.
In Obsessive-Compulsive Reactions (Chapter 6)
  encouraged, in development of obsessive defenses; pp. 323, 374.
  in *First Line of Defense* of *Obsessive Personality;* p. 343.
  of behavior, in *Impulsive Reactions;* p. 356.
  of preoccupation with detail (*Preoccupation-Defense Concept*); p. 334.
  of repressed data, in *King David Reaction;* p. 345.
  of sexual limitations, by *Obsessive Personality;* p. 329.
  of thievery, in *Obsessive Personality;* p. 335.
In Fatigue Reactions (Chapter 7); of incomplete endeavors, in Fatigue as; p. 403.
In Fear and Its Avoidance (Chapter 9); of *Relationship-Distance* defense; p. 524.
In Phobic Reactions (Chapter 10)
  of neurotic symptoms, in phobic reaction (Case 113); p. 555.
  of phobic object, in *Phobic Dilemma;* p. 562.
In Soterial Reactions (Chapter 11); of food hoarding, as a *Security Operation* (Case 127); p. 621.
In Dissociative Reactions (Chapter 13)
  of behavior, in post-hypnotic subject; p. 820.
  of conscious fear and worries, expressed in dreams; p. 746.

---

* From Laughlin, H. P. *The Neuroses.* London, Butterworth & Co., Ltd., 1967.

In Neuroses-Following-Trauma (Chapter 14)
  as a psychologic defense against danger; p. 874.
  of resistances, to psychotherapeutic insight; p. 887.

K. REVIEW QUESTIONS

Sample self-check questions on Chapter 17 and Rationalization for the student, psychiatric resident, and board candidate.

1. Distinguish *Rationalization* as an ego defense from justification. Discuss its role in internal compromise and reconciliation.
2. How does posthypnotic suggestion support the existence of the unconscious? Rationalization?
3. What is meant by *Complex-Supportive Rationalization?*
4. Describe and give an illustration of *Eleemosynary Rationalization.*
5. *Minor Rationalizations* include the
    (A) Posthypnotic, (B) Recognition-Deferment, (C) Ego-Maintaining, (D) Motive-Rationalization, (E) Sour-Grapes, (F) Material, (G) Alcoholic, (H) Sexual, and (I) Behavioral types. Select four for description, including examples from your clinical experience.
6. Collect instances of *Collective* or *Social Rationalization* from personal observation.
7. Discuss briefly how *Familial Rationalization* can influence family relationships.
8. What is the significance of *Symptom-Defensive Rationalization* in: (1) neuroses?; (2) perpetuating psychopathology?; (3) psychotherapy?; (4) *Secondary Defense Concept?*
9. Outline what is meant by *Characterologic Rationalization.*
10. What are the roles that Rationalization can play in the following:
    A. *Concept of Emotional Exploitation.*
    B. Devaluing the unobtainable.
    C. Self-deception.
    D. Goal devaluation.
    E. *Engulfment Concept.*
    F. Historical and literary figures.
    G. Protection against anxiety.
    H. Personal standard modification.
    I. King David Reaction.
    J. Personal acquisitions.
    K. The *Supporting* (Secondary) *Delusion.*
    L. Operation of other dynamisms.

CHAPTER 18

REACTION FORMATION

. . . Outward Reaction Against Disowned Drives

A. NATURE OF REACTION FORMATION

    1. Definition. 2. Characterologic Development a Reaction Against Disowned Drives. 3. Added Facets of Interest: a. A Literary Instance; b. Progression to Unconscious; c. Social and Behavioral RF's.

B. TYPES AND ILLUSTRATIONS

    1. Characterologic Reaction Formation. 2. Social Benefits. 3. Effects on Self-Estimation. Attitude-Symptoms.

C. PARENTAL STANDARDS REVERSED OR REENFORCED

    1. Contra-Parent RF. 2. Political Reversal. 3. Standards-Reenforcement. Parental Reaction Formation.

D. DYNAMICS OF REACTION FORMATION

    1. Defense Against Awareness or Action; To Avert Anxiety. 2. Intrapsychic Reversal. 3. Personality Modified. 4. Consciously Disowned.

E. REACTION FORMATION AND OTHER EGO DEFENSES

    1. Inversion. 2. Compensation. 3. Rechannelization. 4. Repression and Denial.

F. CHARACTER TRAITS AND NEUROTIC SYMPTOMS

    1. Symptomatic Reaction Formations. 2. Military Reaction Formations.

G. SUMMARY

    1. Leaning Over Backwards. 2. Outward Reversals.

H. REFERENCES (FROM *The Neuroses*)

I. REVIEW QUESTIONS

A. NATURE OF REACTION FORMATION

1. Definition

Reaction Formation is *an ego defense or mental mechanism operating outside of and beyond conscious awareness through which major outward attitudes, complexes, motives, and needs develop, which are the opposites of consciously disowned ones. These can embrace large areas of the personality. A conscious reaction is accordingly evolved, reversing the disowned inner drive, against which it thereby defends.*

Through the operation of the dynamism of Reaction Formation, at times abbreviated as *RF,* personally and socially more tolerable and acceptable drives and goals are developed which are the antithesis of the inner hidden ones. These had been earlier relegated to the unconscious through their Repression. Attitudinal and characterologic reactions frequently evolve through operation of this dynamism.

A *reaction of the opposite* accordingly takes place, through which outward attitudes of overconcern or oversolicitude, for example, may develop to aid in the concealment and control of inner feelings which are the reverse of these. Sexual drives, for instance, may be replaced through the operation of Reaction Formation by opposite attitudes of prudishness or excessive morality. Major drives of an aggressive and hostile nature may be reacted against, as may their opposites. These frequently are *characterologic evolvements* of considerable significance.

The awareness and potential expression of disowned and repressed emotions, drives, and complexes is guarded against through the development of reversed outward attitudes and traits. This is the defensively-intended Reaction Formation against them.

2. Characterologic Development a Reaction Against Disowned Drives

Reaction Formation is an auxiliary to Repression, in relation to which it is often to be regarded as a further progression or *secondary elaboration* (see earlier references). Its aims and intent are defensive. The outer characterologic development reverses the hidden inner drive and further hides, guards, and inhibits it. Reaction Formation protects against dreaded awareness or action in response to disowned inner drives.

The operation of this dynamism as we have already noted can lead to substantial characterologic change, and can contribute significantly to character and personality trait development. When this transpires, for purposes of emphasis and convenience we refer to this major type and consequence as *Characterologic Reaction Formation.*

Divergent views exist as to the nature of Reaction Formation. RF may be viewed by some as merely the behavioral denial of unconscious conflict. Others would regard RF as operating whenever a repressed impulse is replaced by another of opposite or antagonistic character. The ego-defensive operation through which this is brought about and the end result as well, are considered Reaction Formations.

This dynamism results in the automatic prevention of certain painful or dangerous thoughts from entering consciousness through the development of opposing attitudes and types of behavior. These opposite attitudes as noted, serve as further significant barriers in keeping the painful or dangerous thoughts out of awareness.

We might also define Reaction Formation as the development of a pattern of attitudes and reactions which contradict the inhibited one, in order to provide the maximum amount of cover and control. Reaction Formation is also a noun, naming the resulting attitudinal and character-ologic formations. They comprise secondary opposing attitudes, which develop through psychic endeavors to deny or to repress certain impulses, or to defend the person against dangers stemming from his instinctual drives.

RF attitudes are likely to be cramped and rigid ones, as might be expected in view of their function in hindering the expression of contrary impulses. These contrary impulses however, sometimes nevertheless break through into outward expression in various concealed and devious ways. The original opposite (repressed) attitude or drive still exists in the unconscious as can be sometimes determined through the analytic process in therapy. A Reaction Formation may well come to make use of and reenforce existing drives, the aims of which are opposite to the aims of the original drive.

3. Added Facets of Interest

A. A LITERARY INSTANCE.—Examples of this mechanism are not too difficult to find. One may suspect their existence in acquaintances in social situations, or find them in literature and history.

The character of Uriah Heap provides a classic literary instance. He was a cringing, subservient, and obsequious creature of Dickens' crea-tion, who underneath and in reality was mean, aggressive, destructive, and hostile. Through the operation of Reaction Formation, he had, to an extent and at least, outwardly become the apotheosis of, and the symbol for subservience and obsequiousness. Finding instances of historical or literary recognition of RF operation from the past would provide added interest-ing support for the *Concept of Historical Validation* as outlined in the succeeding chapter (p. 301).

B. PROGRESSION TO UNCONSCIOUS.—The evolvement of Reaction Formations is not difficult to understand. When an impulse or feeling is unwanted, one seeks to suppress it. He may guard against it to the extent that he goes in the opposite direction. There is an analogy to the person who is afraid of falling from a building or cliff, and who leans over back-wards or retreats, away from the edge of the threatening height.

The extension of this type of consciously defensive counter or reversed reaction, into its becoming an unwitting and unconscious process consti-tutes the ego defense of Reaction Formation.

C. SOCIAL AND BEHAVIORAL RFS.—There are illustrations of Reaction Formation to be found in social experience, some of them superficial. The reader may have encountered the person who is noisy, loud, and bumptious at a party. His friends defend him, pointing out that in reality he is a very shy and insecure person. Such of course may be correct and the operation of Social RF contributory or responsible.

The individual availing himself of this type of behavioral defense avoids having to consciously admit to himself or others that he is inwardly timid, unsure, and fearful. When sufficiently marked and extensive, this is a psychic protective device which can involve the operation of Reaction Formation. Named for their field of operation this class includes *Behavioral RFs* and *Social RFs* and brings us by progression to the wider more significant characterologic functions of the dynamism.

B. TYPES AND ILLUSTRATIONS

1. Characterologic Reaction Formation

As anticipated, Reaction Formation enters into broad areas of character formation and personality development. The consequences of this inevitably influence one's social adjustment and the quality of one's interpersonal relationships. In the following case, the defensively-evolved Emotional Allergy is illustrated, as is the Characterologic Reaction Formation.

Case 146

Reaction Formations in Personality Development

(1) *Self-Assertiveness Lacking.* A 34-year-old research worker sought treatment because her interpersonal relationships were unsatisfactory and unsatisfying. During the past several years she had become gradually more aware and distressed about this.

During the course of therapy, it became increasingly apparent that she was unable even to look out properly for her own best interests. Any aggressive tendencies were so deeply buried that she lacked a normal and healthful level of self-assertiveness. In accord with our *Concept of Categories of Aggression* (see *The Neuroses*, p. 321 ff.) she had little or none of the essential type known as *Constructive Aggression*.

(2) *Emotional Allergy.* There had been an inordinate amount of tension in her early home life, largely generated by her mother's excessive demands upon all family members. Her mother had been a minor tyrant, requiring subservience from all. Her father's intermittent efforts to placate were a sorry measure of how ineffectual he was. These would secure remission of a temporary nature only. Several of her siblings on occasion would rebel or fight back. Not so this young woman.

She had in attempted defense developed an *emotional allergy* to the frequent conflict and turmoil in the home. She couldn't stand the demands and tyranny. She found arguments abhorrent and overreacted to any form of interpersonal tension, whether or not she was personally involved. This progressed to the point of considerable ensuing self-defeat.

(3) *Reaction Against Hostility and Aggressiveness.* From an early age she had begun defending against anything like this in herself. Assigning the primary responsibility for the dissension in the home to her mother, she struggled against Identification (Chapter 9) with her (although almost inevitably she had unwittingly taken over and possessed a number of her mother's attributes, in several important areas). She felt that she "must avoid being like that at all costs." Her own hostility and resentment were too threatening to be allowed any outward expression. Accordingly they eventually became deeply buried.

These early struggles involved conscious efforts at suppression, plus the more important unconscious Repression, eventually of anything even remotely argumentative, hostile, or in opposition. This was successful to the point that as an adult her character formation allowed no room for assertiveness.

This major development comprised a Reaction Formation against competitive and aggressive strivings, early repressed and unconscious, since they were too dangerous and threatening to her to allow them to be subjectively experienced. The consequences permeated her life. Lacking even a spark, she had doubtless impressed many potential friends as being dull and uninteresting.

(4) *Added Defenses.* This patient's mother had suffered from a tremendous need to be involved in conflict. This had contributed in a major way to the demands, arguments, and resulting tension and turmoil in the home. The daughter had also of course developed other defenses in addition to her emotional allergy to conflict and tension.

She had cultivated a faculty for "shutting things out," through a great ability to concentrate on reading and study. Then she couldn't hear (mother's calling her, for instance), see, or have very much awareness of the troubling things going on about her. In addition, she had identified with her father, as the "good parent" and the one she regarded as being "right" in the family struggles and contention.

In the above case, the Reaction Formation had influenced this young woman's entire life, as reflected in her personality development and many of her attitudes. It illustrates the broad scope of this ego defense often present as one of its distinguishing features, and one which sometimes differentiates it from the dynamism of Inversion (Chapter 13). The latter is usually characterized by a more narrow and specific scope.

It is clear from the foregoing instance that Reaction Formation can play a major role in the life of a given individual. It also illustrates the *Characterologic Reaction Formation* and the *Concept of Emotional Allergy.* Instances of Compensatory Characterologic Development which are akin were summarized in *Cases 2, 3,* and *4,* pp. 20–22.

2. Social Benefits

The operation of this dynamism and its consequences can enter into the unwitting determination of avocations and vocations. In the next case this is illustrated. Part of the results secondarily serve a highly useful social purpose somewhat akin to certain consequences of Rechannelization (Chapter 19), in addition to subserving vital intrapsychic defensive needs.

Case 147

Reaction Formation of Socially Beneficial Attitudes

A 28-year-old clothing manufacturer entered therapy complaining of inability to be forceful and assertive in his business. A facet of his personality about which he prided himself was his generosity, especially to handicapped people. The employees of his company numbered among them over 80 percent handicapped persons. He had received favorable mention in the newspapers on a number of occasions in connection with his socially commendable work with the handicapped. His first girl friend had been a victim of polio, with considerable residual paralysis. Their planned marriage had been broken off because of her parents' implacable objections on religious grounds.

Family history revealed that his father had long had a severe physical defect, marked by a bad limp. During the course of prolonged intensive therapy, it became clear that he had actually long harbored deep, unconscious resentments and hatred toward his father. This had played a major role in his early psychologic development. His strong affectionate and sympathetic feelings for handicapped people ultimately proved to be in large part a Reaction Formation against the consciously intolerable and repressed hostility toward his handicapped father.

In this case, Reaction Formation resulted in the control of otherwise intolerable negative feelings and aided in their successful Repression. Their outwardly reversed expression became socially approved. This characterologic development is not unlike that found in Rechannelization (Chapter 19). There are also similarities in this particular employment of a major unconscious psychologic endeavor to examples in which the process of Inversion (Chapter 13) is operative. The effects of this major defensive operation had thoroughly permeated this man's life.

3. Effects on Self-Estimation. Attitude-Symptoms

Reaction Formation can play an important role in how one views himself. This in turn can exert major influences on how he is likely to be viewed by others.

In the following instance, a young lady in therapy had suffered from a very low level of self-esteem, and had presented a typically subservient attitude to others. This ego defense had contributed to the characterologic development of what are called *attitude-symptoms,* in distinction from other types of emotional symptoms as manifested physically, psychologically, or physiologically.

Case 148

Reaction Formation in the Development of Attitude-Symptoms of Subservience and Low Self-Esteem

(1) *Scapegoat Reaction.* A 24-year-old girl was the youngest of three sisters. Their mother was austere, distant, critical, and demanding. As a consequence, much of their self-expression was aired when the mother was not around. Often this took the form of the older ones teasing, provoking, and making fun of their younger sister. In this way, they would vent some of their hostility toward mother by "taking it out," so to speak, on a less formidable personage.

The brunt of this antagonism undoubtedly fell upon this youngest girl who became the scapegoat of her sisters. This created and served to intensify her own inner hostility, anxiety, and conflict. Her efforts to fight back in childish ways were quite ineffective. They were only likely to produce still more ill treatment in return, and she had no vent for her own inner feelings.

She was inevitably the last to wear hand-me-downs and the last to receive new clothes. She was also the last to acquire any privileges, freedom, or independence from the parents. Finally, she was the last to pass through the school which both of her sisters had attended and where they were often held up before her as unwelcome and resented examples.

(2) *A Reaction of the Opposite.* She had inevitably developed the strongest of aggressive and hostile feelings toward her mother and siblings. These people had prevented the satisfaction of her basic needs for expression and self-reliance, and for her recognition as an independent individual. Her puritanic superego however had helped make these feelings intolerable to her. In order to deal with the resulting conflicts, through Repression she disowned her hostile attitudes, and then still

further replaced them with opposite ones through a "reaction of the opposite."

Whereas when she was much younger she had at times tried to fight back, or to be "firsty," now she went out of her way to give in cheerfully to others' wishes. A major *attitude-symptom* of subservience evolved. She seemed to want to be last in everything, and denounced herself as inferior.

This reversal of a whole broad segment of her personality permeated her life and extended to small details. When going through a doorway, she would insist on holding the door open for everyone else, whether male or female, acquaintance or stranger. Sometimes she would stand by in such a situation for quite a time, until everyone had passed through or until someone else more determined insisted that she proceed.

(3) *Hidden Evidences of Hostility Breaking Through.* Reaction Formation usually affects a whole complex of attitudes and motives, and is generally not as efficient as the operation of the less complex or narrower ego defenses. This patient's repressed feelings continued to struggle for conscious acknowledgment. Constantly, in subtle ways, they were able to break through the sometimes ragged line of defense against them. In certain other far less obvious ways she had become a good deal less gentle and careful.

As examples, in handling inanimate objects and in doing things around the house, she repeatedly broke or damaged small items. Outwardly she was unconcerned about this destructiveness. She was herself in turn taking out a bit of her unconscious hostility more safely on these inanimate objects. This was a second instance of the Scapegoat Reaction in operation.

Her seeming carelessness and clumsiness had deeper roots in unconscious motivations. In essence these had become sufficiently marked as trends to also comprise behavioral or attitude-symptoms. Their explanation was not as simple as might have been suggested by superficial impressions.

C. PARENTAL STANDARDS REVERSED OR REENFORCED

1. Contra-Parent RF

One particularly interesting major type of Reaction Formation is that which develops against parents, or more particularly against part of the parental standards. Through it the adoption of reversed views and attitudes (to the parental ones) occurs. Although not generally recognized, this phenomenon in greater or lesser significance is not an infrequent occurrence. It is one which is called *Contra-Parent RF* (or Parental Standards RF). The resulting attitudes are similarly Contra-Parent RFs.

In this type of psychologic operation, the ego defense has been unwittingly utilized for somewhat different purposes than previously outlined. Contra-Parent RFs evolve as (part of) a rebellious process against parents or a particular set of parental attitudes or goals which have been rejected. As part of this type of process, reversed views or attitudes evolve and prevail. In this form of Reaction Formation the person concerned may develop outward goals which are distinctly less socially desirable; on the other hand, they may be more so.

The rebelliously motivated attitudinal development through the "reaction of the opposite" can result in the nearly complete rejection and reversal of a given set of parental attitudes. The child may thus have most strongly disapproved of certain aspects of the familial setting, and have unconsciously developed reversed traits. The son of an alcoholic father may become a teetotaler, or a rabid and crusading prohibitionist. There are many instances in which the preacher's son or daughter proverbially "throws over the traces" of the moralistic views and religious atmosphere of the home. In these instances and many others of *Contra-Parent RF*s the child no longer heeds or follows the precepts by which he was raised. He turns away completely from his parents in certain major areas of their views, attitudes, and behavior.

2. Political Reversal

The following is an interesting instance in which a son evolved and strongly espoused opposite political views from those of his father.

Case 149

The Son of a Politically Liberal Father Becomes Ultraconservative

A Representative who had served several terms in Congress had made his political reputation on the basis of liberal views and attitudes, and because of progressive stands which he took with regard to current issues. The family life necessarily had centered around the father's political career. Around the age of 12, the oldest son began to show an interest in political affairs. However, from the beginning, his interests had been on the conservative and reactionary side.

His views, ideas, and behavior developed into ones which were along strikingly ultraconservative lines. This was in direct contrast to the tenets of his father's political philosophy. Instances are also, and perhaps more often, to be observed in which the parental views and the child's contra-reactions to them are the other way around.

By the time he was 14, this lad on his own initiative, made contacts with several Congressional leaders from the party opposed to that of his father. At election times he "campaigned" as actively as was possible for a youth, not for men in his father's party, but for those who were his father's political opposites.

This boy's "reaction of the opposite" found its expression in the field of politics, and he took his stand on the opposing side from that of his father. This became a fixed pattern in later life. In other respects, the son was cooperative, obedient, and fitted well into the family. However, there were many both obvious and subtle influences on family members and relationships. He had completely reversed his father's political philosophy in this instance of *Contra-Parent RF*.

In Franklin D. Roosevelt's family, son John took an active part in the activities of the Republican Party in New York State. His father, mother, and two brothers were nationally prominent leaders in the Democratic Party. In some measure this Political Reversal may have represented a similar kind of "reaction of the opposite."

3. Standards-Reenforcement. Parental Reaction Formation

We have observed how Reaction Formation can contribute to the evolution of attitudes. Hereby they evolve in opposition to feared unconscious impulses, which they are intended to help control. On the other hand the operation of Reaction Formation can also serve to reenforce parental standards, as in the following brief instance.

Case 150

Reenforcement of Sexual Taboos

A 31-year-old patient was characterized by prudishness and by his strong and open disapproval of anything sexual in nature. On slight provocation he would declaim against sweater girls in magazines, in opposition to suggestive billboards, sexy movies, off-color stories, or lax morals. He was quite critical of typically female attire. He could not tolerate his wife's wearing bathing suits, shorts, or any but the most conservative of clothes.

This man basically had strong sexual drives. However, he had even stronger needs to disown them at least to a considerable extent. Accordingly, he outwardly maintained his relative disinterest in sex and was highly critical and contemptuous of others who admitted theirs. Any attempt in early sessions to pursue leads or engage in open discussion of anything even tangentially related to sex was fruitless and made him anxious.

He had been raised in a rigid household marked by strong Victorian standards. There were early family pressures to conform. His Reaction Formations served to aid in the control of his feared sexual drives and to help him to better fit into the family. The reenforcement of parental standards was a further consequence, illustrating the *Standards-Reenforcement* function and type of RF.

Reaction Formations are also evident in another significant sphere of the parent-child relationship. Herein there is overprotectiveness and exaggerated parental overconcern. These can progress to the extent of becoming attitude-symptoms. This class of operation of the dynamism is *Parental Reaction Formation*.

Parental RFs represent a defensive outward attitudinal reaction in the parent against subconsciously feared and opposite inner urges. Parental oversolicitude can develop in this manner as a defense against buried reverse trends.

D. DYNAMICS OF REACTION FORMATION

1. Defense Against Awareness or Action; To Avert Anxiety

Through the ego defense of Reaction Formation, dangerous desires and impulses are prevented from entering consciousness, and any chance of their being carried into action becomes more remote. Repression is reenforced. Through its operation, types of behavior and attitudes develop which are opposite from the ones which are maintained in the unconscious. It is as though the person says in effect: "See, I really don't want what is objectionable. Far from it. As you can plainly see, I want the reverse!"

Two of man's basic, so-called instinctual impulses ultimately are preservative-hostile and sexual in nature. With reactive patterns of excessive kindness, fairness, morality, and idealism, humans seek to protect themselves against the dangers resulting if they were to follow their inner impulses of anger, sex, or rage. The goal is protective and defensive. One seeks to avert anxiety. In this way, through the use of the dynamism of Reaction Formation, their self-evaluation is maintained and enforced.

2. Intrapsychic Reversal

Reaction Formation protects the ego against the return to consciousness of repressed impulses from within the psyche. In repressing an intolerable instinctual drive, together with the reenforcement of Repression through the secondary elaboration of Reaction Formation, the ego utilizes the psyche's capacity for what we call *instinct reversal.*

The process of instinct-reversal when operative through RF, is fully automatic and unconscious. In the successful Reaction Formation the conscious self cares nor knows naught of the impulse or its intrapsychic reversal. The only awareness is of the external reversed reaction; the opposite subjective feelings. The operation of the ego defense of Reaction Formation represents vicissitudes of repressed drives of a fair degree of complexity.

3. Personality Modified

As noted, Reaction Formations represent both the consequence and the bolstering of an established Repression. Dependent of course, upon the degree of "success" of the Reaction Formation the Repression can become more established and secure, avoiding the need for continuing and oft-repeated reenforcement. Reaction Formations often avoid such repetitive needs, through effecting a once-and-for-all definitive change in the character structure.

The person who has evolved staunch RFs does not have to urgently mobilize new ego defenses when a so-called instinctual danger threatens. He has revised his personality structure and attitudes as if this threat were constantly present, so that he is prepared whenever the danger occurs. As an example of the successful Characterologic RF we can note the presence of certain obsessive attitude-symptoms. Thus through his excessive orderliness and cleanliness evolved as RFs against deeper and more instinctual interests in dirt and disorder, the obsessively oriented person may have resolved otherwise serious intrapsychic conflicts.

4. Consciously Disowned

In summary, Reaction Formation results in the outward reversal of basic internal drives and needs. These become expressed in their outward conscious form as defensively-evolved attitudes, character traits, or as large segments of the total character structure. Reaction Formations operate in an attempt to keep repressed such inclinations as are consciously disowned.

We see, then, that Reaction Formation is often operative in conjunction with and in close alliance to other ego defenses of which the principal one is Repression. Let us consider several of these relationships and some points of distinction.

E. REACTION FORMATION AND OTHER EGO DEFENSES

1. Inversion

In comparison with Reaction Formation, Inversion (Chapter 13) usually has a more limited application to a specific idea or feeling. It does not reflect as much of the long-term major characterologic developmental process usually thought of in conjunction with Reaction Formation. This latter is described as a "reaction of the opposite," while Inversion is a more direct, isolated and complete "turning around" or reversal, of a specific discrete original impulse, wish, and so on. Inversion is often 100 percent effective in its narrower area (pp. 194 and 203–4).

Reaction Formation involves a larger area of the psyche than Inversion. Operating in such a broad area there is a greater likelihood for unevenness of effectiveness. Remnants of the repressed opposite drive can remain unchanged or be only partially changed, and elements of the repressed material can secure a measure of direct or concealed outward expression.

In the "reaction of the opposite" there are generally distinct, consequential, and reversed changes in an entire area of conscious feeling and behavior, although this distinction affords some elasticity. An area of feared hostile impulses can be further defended against and denied through the reversal of the entire emotional complex. The replacing subjective feeling and behavior can reflect great solicitude or tenderness; the hostility would have been repressed and the latter further reenforced. Added differential features between the two dynamisms were noted in the discussion of Inversion (p. 193 ff.).

2. Compensation

Reaction Formation and Compensation frequently are closely allied and differ only in scope. Accordingly, we might regard Reaction Formation as an intrapsychic, characterologic type of *over*compensation in which, for example, compensatory behavior has become exaggerated to the extent that inner hostility and aggression outwardly become oversolicitude and overtenderness. The complete albeit usually more narrow, limited, and specific reversals effected through the dynamism of Inversion sometimes are to be viewed similarly. In these overdevelopments, via whatever psychic route, the person concerned further denies his original wish and strengthens its Repression.

The following case illustrates a kind of characterologic overcompensation that is closely allied to Reaction Formation. A clear distinction here is difficult and perhaps really somewhat academic. In this instance the subjective deficiencies were compensated for through the development of traits which were largely in the opposite direction. In other words, the Compensation unconsciously resulted in the gradual evolution of personality traits and behavior which were, outwardly, the opposite of those existing internally. As noted, this type of Compensation also serves as a secondary elaboration in the further Denial of the hidden and rejected attributes.

Case 151

Overcompensation for Timidity

A 42-year-old lawyer, in the early course of analytic treatment, related with pride and at some length stories of his repeated physical aggressiveness. This was a pattern of behavior which extended into adult life. Upon slight provocation at times, he physically assaulted men of greater stature. This had continued into the recent past.

As analytic study progressed, it became increasingly clear that in reality, and on a more hidden level, he was a timid and fearful person. He had successfully repressed these attributes and had unconsciously developed outward attitudes of a reverse nature.

This was accompanied by considerable pride and increased self-esteem. He had overcompensated for his underlying timorousness and fearfulness, which he had consciously rejected as unacceptable. This development can also be viewed as a Characterologic Reaction Formation.

3. Rechannelization

Reaction Formation can at times, represent a "half-way house" between symptom formation and Rechannelization or Sublimation (Chapter 19). When this situation prevails, the RF is not fully developed or successful. The consequence is one of considerable expense in terms of psychic energy, because the Repression has to be continuously maintained, as does the reenforcing RF. *Case 147* illustrates a related, socially beneficial Reaction Formation.

We must not think that Reaction Formations of wide scope, as is true also with Rechannelization and symptom formation, are simple activities; they always involve intrapsychic operations of a high degree of complexity. Fenichel held that Rechannelization is related to Reaction Formation in the same way that the successful elaboration of the superego is related to an immutable Repression of the Oedipus complex. See Chapter 19, p. 296 ff.

4. Repression and Denial

Reaction Formation can function as a major aid to Repression and Denial. We have observed several illustrations. At times the operation of this dynamism may be witnessed attempting to defend against, and as a further reenforcement in the Denial of (unconscious) homosexual lean-ings. It may unwittingly contribute to certain attitudes, an understanding of which can help to account for the vigorousness and zeal employed by some in the discovery and prosecution of homosexually oriented men. This is illustrated in the following instance.

Case 152

**Reaction Formation in the Detection and Arrest
of Homosexually Oriented Persons**

A certain law enforcement officer in a large city gained a measure of notoriety for his activity and zeal while serving on the vice squad. His forte was the arrest of homosexually inclined individuals. He took great personal satisfaction in tracking them down. In his hands, legal prosecution came considerably closer to persecution. The amount of dedication in the performance of his duties was unusual. It was not infrequently remarked upon by his associates, one or two of whom had correctly, but fortunately silently, suspected some of the hidden bases for its generation.

His way of apprehending the hapless homosexually oriented male was to have himself "picked up" in a public park or lavatory. On observation he was himself effete, mincing in attitude, with slightly effeminate mannerisms. It was not entirely by accident that he was good "bait," and that homosexual persons selected him as an object for their advances, when in effect thus tacitly invited to do so. His methods if not actually representing entrapment, often came close to it.

Seemingly as an aid to the Repression of his own strongly rejected and consciously disowned homosexual drives, this officer had become a rabid foe of homosexuality. His "success" in his official duties was a result of these attitudes and resulting zeal. They had evolved earlier as a "reaction to the opposite," in the service of added control of dangerous and feared unconscious forces.

It may be that those most eager to participate in so-called "Vice Crusades" are sometimes unwittingly employing and exhibiting the results of a kind of Reaction Formation. This has defensively evolved against their own similar but consciously disowned drives in order to help hide from themselves and others their powerful interests and desires for sexual expression.

F.   CHARACTER TRAITS AND NEUROTIC SYMPTOMS

1. Symptomatic Reaction Formations

Reaction Formations can have overall effects upon the character structure or upon more limited segments. This should be apparent by now, but may stand some further emphasis. We have observed how overcompliance, subservience, and obsequiousness are examples of character traits that can develop as Characterologic Reaction Formations. What is thereby accomplished is the further containment of large, otherwise buried, and unacceptable areas in the unconscious.

Similarly, other groups of defensive character traits may evolve which are carried through life. If effective, following their establishment they will show little further progression. However, if they prove inadequate or if the individual concerned is subjected to sufficient added emotional stresses, the defensively-intended traits may develop further, or be replaced or supplemented by more overt neurotic symptoms.

At times single character traits, as in the classical example of the housewife who is obsessively clean, may be looked upon as Reaction Formations. Whenever this dynamism produces or substantially contributes to symptom evolvement, these are instances of *Symptomatic-Reaction Formation*.

The following case is a further brief illustration of character development as a consequence of Reaction Formations.

Case 153

Characterologic Development a Consequence of Reaction Formation

A 54-year-old patient was characterized by a meek and nonaggressive personality. Most of his time outside of business hours was spent in doing church work. He was considered to be one of the "pillars of the church," serving on practically all of its various councils and committees. Although he did a great amount of work, he could not oppose policies which he believed to be wrong. He was self-effacing, mild-mannered, and meek. This characterologic overdevelopment, while protective and psychologically vital to him on the one hand, exacted a severe toll in limitation and self-defeat on the other.

Let us briefly consider this man's family background. Continually ridiculed by a hypercritical father who ruled the household on an "old country" standard, one might have perhaps expected that the son would become hostile and rebellious. Why then should he become a meek and retiring person, greatly interested in "doing good" through the church? Through a "reaction of the opposite," his intense feelings of hostility had early become ones of an opposite, reversed character. Through this means he denied their existence to himself and to the outside world and reenforced their further control and Repression.

There was an interesting sidelight. We know that Reaction Formation is seldom 100 percent effective, as is more likely found with Inversion. One clue as to some of the unconscious feelings present became apparent through recognizing and studying another side interest. When not actually engaged in the work of the church, this chap's favorite diversion was in watching TV and movies concerned with violence. This kind of entertainment attracts many people, of course, but not identically as with this man.

He didn't react to these shows as exciting or horrifying, but rather as relaxing. The more violent the scenes and action of the characters, the more relaxing the programs. Occasionally he would be described as having fallen asleep with a serene expression, while on the TV, guns roared and victims fell. While aiding in the determination of major characterologic patterns, the Reaction Formation was nevertheless not so effective as to completely stifle the expression of his inward unconscious interests in aggression and violence. Certain satisfactions lay in part in these vicarious experiences, and was unconsciously achieved.

2. Military Reaction Formations

To those with military experience, an interesting illustration of a combined type of overcompensation and Reaction Formation may be familiar. What is referred to here is the overly correct serviceman, who makes a ceremonial point of saluting smartly, and in other ways, slightly —or even more than slightly—overdoing his showing of "respect" to his officers.

The man concerned is quite unaware that this exaggerated military correctness is a way of reenforcing control over his more concealed and unconscious resentment of a particular officer, of the military, or perhaps of authority in general. It may of course also represent the overt expression of partly or clearly conscious hostility with a subtle tone of mockery in it. In any event, this kind of behavior may nettle or annoy his officers to some extent, but if it is not too exaggerated, how is it possible to reproach him?

Such behavior sometimes might be transposed verbally from the man's unconscious as follows: "Actually I hate your guts. I certainly don't respect you in the least, but I have to conceal this, not only from you and the others, but even more so from myself. That is why outwardly I show every manifestation of respect, although I really only go through the motions. If I obviously respect you to such an extent, yon can't possibly, nor can I myself, be aware of how hostile I really feel underneath."

G. SUMMARY

1. Leaning Over Backward

Reaction Formation is an important ego defense which is alternately referred to as a "reaction of the opposite," or in abbreviated form as *RF*. Through its operation as an unconscious process, attitudes, complexes, and behavior evolve, which are the reverse of consciously disowned (repressed) urges. Effortful conscious endeavors are made in a similar direction. *Characterologic Evolvements* through RF can be of considerable significance. Reaction Formation serves to reenforce Repression and is a further step beyond Denial. The concept of *Attitude-Symptom* was stressed.

Reaction Formation can enter into symptom formation as cause or contributor (*Symptomatic Reaction Formations*), is an important factor in a number of types of neurotic reactions, and can be a potent contributing force in character development (*Characterologic Reaction Formation*) and in modifying personality. It is an operation of intrapsychic reversal, generally for broad areas, and is seldom 100 percent effective. The literary character of Uriah Heap is illustrative. *Social* and *Behavioral RFs* were noted. The conception of *emotional allergy* was offered.

Reaction Formation is an intrapsychic process of "leaning over backward" through the reversal of disowned instinctual drives. Personality development is influenced, socially beneficial attitudes may develop, and the level of one's self-estimation may be determined in part through its operation. Reaction Formation may take place against parental attitudes and standards (*Contra-Parent RF*), or, on the other hand, serve to aid in their acceptance and maintenance through the *Standards-Reenforcement* function. *Political Reversals* on this basis were illustrated. *Parental*

Reaction Formations reverse and guard against the outer expression of personally disowned attitudes toward and about a child.

2. *Outward Reversals*

This major dynamism results in the development of outward reversal of basic internal drives and needs, particularly those which are ultimately aggressive-hostile and sexual in nature. Attention was invited to the psyche's capacity for *instinct reversal.* Comparisons, distinctions, and relationships were observed between this dynamism and those of Inversion, Compensation, Rechannelization, Repression, and Denial. The potentially significant relationship to Overcompensation was discussed and illustrated.

A number of comments were offered about the dynamics of Reaction Formation. Essentially it is an intended defense against awareness, action, and anxiety. The intriguing subject of *Military Reaction Formations* received comment. RF as with other dynamisms, can serve a *secondary elaboration* function.

H.   CROSS-REFERENCES TO *THE NEUROSES* *

Reaction Formation
In Nature of Anxiety (Chapter 1); to parental standards, as a source of anxiety (*reaction-of-the-opposite*); p. 35.
In Character Reactions (Chapter 5)
    as a character defense
        in *Conversion Personality* (Table 12); p. 260.
        in obsessive traits (Freud); p. 235.
        in *Obsessive Personality;* pp. 245–6.
    against anal-eroticism, in *Defiance-Submission Conflict* of *Obsessive Personality;* p. 293.
    to counter hostility
        in *Depressed Personality;* p. 271.
        in military correctness; p. 280.
        supermoralism as, in *Obsessive Personality;* p. 260.
In Obsessive-Compulsive Reactions (Chapter 6)
    as a defense against awareness, in *Obsessive Personality;* p. 361.
    in *First Line of Psychic Defense* of *Obsessive Personality;* p. 343.
In Hygeiaphrontic Reactions (Chapter 8); overprotection as, against hostility for child, by parent; p. 479.
In Phobic Reactions (Chapter 10); against hostility, into idealized image of mother; p. 578.

I.   REVIEW QUESTIONS

Sample self-check questions on Chapter 18 and Reaction Formation for the student, psychiatric resident, and board candidate.

    1. What is *Reaction Formation* or RF? What internal needs enter into its evolvement?
    2. To what do the following terms refer?

---

* From Laughlin, H. P. *The Neuroses*. London, Butterworth & Co., Ltd., 1967.

    A. *Social Reaction Formation.*
    B. *Constructive aggression.*
    C. *Emotional Allergy Concept.*
    D. *Attitude-Symptoms.*
    E. RF in *Political Reversals.*
    F. *Standards-Reenforcement* function of RF.
    G. *Instinct reversal* capacity.
    H. *Characterologic evolvement.*
    I. Psychic process of "leaning over backward."
    J. *Behavioral RF.*

3. How does Reaction Formation influence character formation? What is *Characterologic Reaction Formation?*
4. What is the potential role of RF in relation to parental standards? Explain the *Contra-Parent RF.*
5. What is the defensive intent of *Parental Reaction Formation?*
6. List points in distinguishing RF from Inversion.
7. Note the relations of RF to the dynamisms of Compensation, Denial, Repression, and Rechannelization. What is the *secondary elaboration* function?
8. What is *Symptomatic Reaction Formation?* How can it contribute to character formation? To psychopathology?
9. Outline the concept of *Military RFs.*
10. Discuss the dynamics of Reaction Formation. What is the fate of the disowned drives?

CHAPTER 19

RECHANNELIZATION

*... Instinctual Diversion or Sublimation: Unconscious
Drives Rechanneled into Constructive Channels*

A. The Nature of Rechannelization

1. Energies Rechanneled into Acceptable Endeavors: a. A Constructive Dynamism; b. Personally and Socially Valuable. 2. Origins of Term Sublimation. Rechannelization Preferred. 3. Definition: a. Repressed Drive Expressed; b. Sexual and Aggression Rechannelization.

B. Types of Rechannelization

1. Personal-Tragedy Rechannelization (PTR): a. Great Undertakings Initiated; b. Concept of Historical Validation; c. Szu-Ma Chien the Historian. 2. Characterologic Rechannelization: a. Major Role in Personality and Character Development; b. Identification and Rechannelization. 3. Vocational Rechannelization: a. Major Professional and Vocational Commitments; b. Rechannelization Gradual; c. Sexual Energy Diverted; d. Contributing to Career Commitment; e. Rechanneling Thwarted Parental Drives. 4. Avocational Rechannelization: a. Partial and Multiple Sublimations; b. Gardening as Avocational Sublimation. 5. In Emotional Illness: a. Ineffective, Incomplete, Contributory, and Preventive Rechannelization; b. Therapeutic and Improvement-Rechannelization. Prognostic-Sublimations. 6. Sublimation-en-Therapy.

C. Dynamics

1. By Analogy: a. Psychic Energy; b. Niagara Falls Analogy; c. Concurrent Evolvement of Superego and Sublimation. 2. An Ideal Solution. 3. Defensive Reactions to Psychiatric Concepts. 4. Acceptable New Channel.

D. Summary

1. Rechannelization. 2. Types of Rechannelization. 3. Psychodynamics.

E. References (from *The Neuroses*)

F. Review Questions

A. THE NATURE OF RECHANNELIZATION

1. Energies Rechanneled into Acceptable Endeavors

A. CONSTRUCTIVE DYNAMISM.—Among all the ego-defensive mechanisms, Sublimation or perhaps preferably *Rechannelization* is the most advanced and highly developed. In terms of social benefit, aesthetics, and cultural achievement it is the most important. Rechannelization is usually to be regarded as the most developed of what has been termed the *Higher Order* or *Less Primitive Group* of dynamisms. Through its operation, the energy of personally and socially intolerable impulses and drives is often successfully redirected into acceptable channels. Their direction and aim thus become deflected and redirected toward more approved substitute goals.

Rechannelization, Sublimation, and Instinctual Diversion are employed herein as alternate terms for this constructive mechanism. Through its operation, instinctual forces are more or less permanently harnessed. Rechannelization contributes to character and personality development. It plays a major role in the amelioration and resolution of emotional conflict, in the prevention of anxiety, and in the maintenance of emotional health. This dynamism supplies a disguised but useful external outlet for otherwise blocked or intolerable inner drives. Internal energies are rechanneled into consciously acceptable and laudable endeavors.

B. PERSONALLY AND SOCIALLY VALUABLE.—Through their Rechannelization, inner drives which press for recognition that would prove unacceptable, and for action that would be destructive, secure disguised outward expression and constructive utilization through their unconscious diversion into approved and useful pathways. In other words, Sublimation results in the deflection of one's intrapsychic energy (from personally and socially unacceptable drives) into higher, nonaggressive and nonsexual activities. These are individually creative and useful. They are often of social and cultural value as well. See *Case 147*, pp. 23–4.

Many social and professional activities of the most praiseworthy nature represent successful Rechannelizations. The operation of this major ego defense can lead to the highest creative endeavors in art, medicine, law, teaching, architecture, business, research, politics, exploration, government, scientific achievement, philosophy, and many other diverse fields of human activity. Indeed, one would not be far wrong to assume the operation of Rechannelization or Sublimation to some extent on an empirical basis, in most instances of dedication, application, devotion to an endeavor in life, marked achievement, or success.

2. Origins of Term Sublimation. Rechannelization Preferred

To make sublime is to elevate, to dignify, or to ennoble. A sublime person is one who is prominent for nobility of character or attainment. Something sublime is exalted, lofty, free from dross and impurities, or eminent. Sublimation means to elevate, purify, raise on high, make sublime, and refine.

In chemistry, the process of sublimation affords a certain analogy to its employment in a psychologic sense. Herein it is a process of refinement and purification, in which a substance is vaporized by heat and recondensed, securing its separation from less vaporable impurities.

Roots for the term and concept of Sublimation are traceable to a Latin word of which the infinitive form is *sublimare,* meaning "to raise on high." In English Sublimation is derived from the past participle form *sublimatus,* "having been raised on high."

The background and origins of the name for this ego defense are of interest in understanding: (1) the concept of Sublimation; (2) the nature of the important intraphysic endeavor which this term describes and; (3) something of the views of those who originally adopted this term for application in the behavioral sciences.

For something to be elevated indicates that it has been low. Purification follows prior impurity and dross. The process of dignification or ennobling connotes the lack of these; baseness, or perhaps pettiness. Raising on high or elevating conveys the existence of such needs and a preceding lowness of stature or character.

The so-called instincts and unconscious drives are neither good nor bad per se. They exist. It is true that they are often intolerable to the ego or self, but this does not necessarily mean they are base, wrong or bad. Moral judgments are best not made. They can lead to bias and impede or interfere with objective study and scientific research into these vital areas.

It has always been most difficult, if not impossible, to divorce value judgments and moral overtones from the consideration of instinctual aggressive, and sexual drives. That which is nonconstructive, socially unacceptable, culturally harmful, or self-defeating, often enough becomes "wrong," "evil," or "bad" in people's eyes. The original selection of this particular term suggests the presence of moral judgments about instinctual drives which become sublimated.

From this standpoint, the adoption of an alternate term for this important intrapsychic process might offer advantages. We have accordingly suggested and preferred using the term of *Rechannelization* or perhaps that of *Instinctual Diversion.* A more neutral term would more likely lack an implication of a moral judgment, a view which we would encourage. Accordingly as noted, we have used these terms interchangeably.

3. Definition

A. REPRESSED DRIVE EXPRESSED.—In Rechannelization, the otherwise intolerable instinctual drive secures a disguised but welcome and constructive external expression. In its new guise it secures utilization in a personally and socially more acceptable avenue. There are certain similarities in our views of Rechannelization and its operation, to those of Conversion (Chapter 3). Sublimation was originally used as a dynamic term in discussing the vicissitudes of the sexual instincts. Sexual energy was regarded as being sublimated (rechanneled) into constructive avenues of aesthetic and creative endeavor.

The early analysts considered Sublimation the most healthful method employed by the psyche in dealing with repressed sexual drives. The term "sexual" in this usage had a broader connotation than ordinarily assigned, usually including anything pleasurable or sensual. In our current conceptions of repressed drives there is ample justification for broadening our conceptions of Sublimation or Rechannelization so as to apply them equally to all unconscious urges.

Through their rechanneling, inner libidinal energy becomes outwardly expressed as nonlibidinal. Similarly the energy of aggression, hostility, and related drives becomes expressed in outwardly nonaggressive terms. A blocked ambition or goal and the consequent affect can lead to the operation of what is sometimes a more superficial type of Rechannelization. Let us then offer a definition for our alternate terms.

Rechannelization, Sublimation, or Instinctual Diversion are the terms for *a major ego defense or mental mechanism operating outside of and beyond conscious awareness, through which instinctual drives which are consciously intolerable, or are blocked and unobtainable, are diverted so as to secure their disguised external expression and utilization in channels of greater personal and social acceptability. In successful Rechannelization the direction and aim of the repressed drives has been permanently deflected into new pathways of creative endeavor.* Through Rechannelization, intrapsychic energy becomes thus usefully redeveloped into socially more accepted extrapsychic expression. The consequence is personal gain, often with additional aspects of social and cultural gain.

The activities and behavior that result from the operation of Rechannelization are often highly useful and constructive. The more we study this interesting dynamism the more likely it seems that Instinctual Diversion is a universal phenomenon. Thus, it is probable that every successful individual has rechanneled a portion of the energy from his instinctual drives into useful kinds of endeavor. Since the consequences of Sublimation are so often personally and socially constructive, it is understandable that psychiatrists generally regard it as a healthful process.

A constructive rechanneling and outward expression is thus secured for energy which would otherwise be denied a culturally acceptable outlet. In regard to its significant role, a colleague once declared that "love and Sublimation make the world go 'round." The *Constructive Rechannelization* refers to a broad group which includes all the personally and socially beneficial operations and consequences of the dynamisms. (*Case 188,* p. 405.)

B. SEXUAL AND AGGRESSION RECHANNELIZATION.—Through operation of the dynamism of Rechannelization an individual's antisocial impulses are made socially acceptable. Instinctual Diversion can lead to covertly securing gratifications of sexual drives through nonsexual activities. Resolution of the frustrations of basic urges can be affected through the substitution of socially more acceptable goals. The dynamism of Rechannelization serves as a process through which infantile sexual and pleasurable aims are exchanged for those which are no longer sexual and which are on a socially acceptable level. The so-called "instinctual" drives otherwise producing shame and guilt are repressed, and their energy thus utilized in the pursuit of more suitable objects.

Rechannelization represents one basic intrapsychic route for resolving emotional conflicts, through which the individual concerned "finds" alternate socially acceptable ways for securing gratification for otherwise unacceptable unconscious desires and wishes. While the new routes may not offer as direct or as complete a measure of satisfaction, they ease his conscience and aid in his satisfaction with himself. Importantly they are usually alternate routes of which society in general approves.

Rechannelizations may be also considered as *psychic compromises,* which society finds of value. In the present social and cultural order a great deal of one's sexual drives must be thwarted. If this thwarting or frustration is followed by the turning of the psychosexual energy into unproductive and self-defeating channels, the individual can develop symptoms of emotional illness. A neurosis can evolve. Instead, if this energy and drive has been automatically deflected into constructive and productive channels, the process and the consequences are *Sexual Sublimations* or *Rechannelizations.* These comments apply equally, of course, to unacceptable and otherwise buried aggressive drives, which lead to *Aggression Rechannelization.* For illustrations see *Mental Mechanisms,* pp. 76–118.

B.   TYPES OF RECHANNELIZATION

1. *Personal-Tragedy Rechannelization (PTR)*

A. GREAT UNDERTAKINGS INITIATED.—Historically, the understanding of man's motives has been a matter of great difficulty, even under the favorable circumstances of the cooperation of the person concerned. Analysis or intensive psychotherapy, in which the patient's conscious efforts are wholeheartedly enlisted to work with the therapist in seeking self-understanding affords the ideal situation. Nonetheless, the defensive mechanisms influencing behavior still are often most elusive and recondite. If in this most favorable climate one finds the unraveling of motivation and defenses difficult, it is not surprising that instances of deep self-revelation through the centuries are not too common.

Throughout the course of history, one finds men who have been outstandingly motivated in pursuing some given line of endeavor. Their goals have been pursued with a notable singleness of purpose and accompanied by a tremendous investment of energy. Undoubtedly the process of Rechannelization has entered into many such noteworthy careers, but mostly the operation and contributions of this important ego defense in these instances has been only subject to surmise.

One relationship is worthy of note in the initiation and sequence of certain of great human undertakings. In a number of instances there has been a clear relationship to great personal tragedy: loss, misfortune, deprivation, persecution, torture, and mutilation. At times the consequent endeavor represents a Compensation (Chapter 2). Other ego defenses may also be called into play singly or in combination. The frustration, anger, and psychic pain which results, is of such an intolerable level that it cannot, must not, indeed dare not secure recognition or any direct outward expression.

Undoubtedly, much has to be repressed in conjunction with personal tragedy, but is too energy laden to remain completely buried and dormant. One constructive pathway lies in some of the internal and otherwise blocked fury and rage being diverted, altered, and changed in direction so as to secure expression in sublimated form. When successful, the operation is the *Personal-Tragedy Rechannelization,* or as we prefer to abbreviate it sometimes, the PTR. The term for the result of the harnessed and rechanneled drive is the same. It is initiated or stimulated by great personal misfortune.

B. CONCEPT OF HISTORICAL VALIDATION.—Rarely one can find evidence of an appreciation of some of the foregoing and the operation of the PTR on the part of some observant and perceptive scholar from the past. This is in accord with the intriguing *Concept of Historical Validation* (see also p. 226 and p. 240). In the study of human behavior and motivation, according to this conception one can hypothecate that a given "new" pattern, term, or concept most likely has already been noted by some wise scholar from the past. The terms and language may be different, but the idea will prove to be essentially similar.

Sufficiently thorough research can uncover such an antecedent frequently enough to help validate the discovery historically. Rarely one might deliberately employ the *Concept of Historical Validation* as a criteria in the assessment of an "original" concept. This was in fact done for example, in the case of the *King David Reaction* (Chapter 16).

C. SZU-MA CHIEN THE HISTORIAN.—The Historical Validation Concept is illustrated in the following instance of a PTR dating back over two thousand years, in which the Chinese historian Szu-Ma Chien, following castration, undertook the monumental task of compiling a history of ancient China. He provided us with thoughtful comments in analyzing his motivation. Drawing on his own experience he forcefully and insightfully pointed out how great loss or suffering can be followed by the pouring of energies into new and constructive channels. His account also illustrates the interesting *Scapegoat Reaction* noted earlier (Chapter 5).

In this instance, as in others which Chien cites, great personal tragedies led to the production of famous classics. We also observe through this illustration how significant Rechannelizations also evolve in adulthood. Sexual and aggressive drives with no acceptable outlet can thus be diverted and rechanneled into a major constructive endeavor.

His account represents our present earliest documented instance of a major Personal-Tragedy Rechannelization. Chien of course did not employ present day terms, which are of recent adoption. However, his evident perception, empiric recognition, and description are of such clarity that modern clinical terminology is hardly missed.

Case 154

Personal-Tragedy Rechannelization (PTR)

(1) *Scapegoat Reaction.* Szu-Ma Chien was an outstanding historian of ancient China, born in the 2nd Century B.C. Some years prior to his undertaking this great endeavor, China had come under attack by the Mongolians. The Chinese Emperor of the time was greatly worried and sent an army under General Lee against them. As nomads without towns or settlements, however, the Mongol raiders were an elusive enemy. Although General Lee acquired a reputation for competence and destroyed thousands of Mongols, he had great difficulties, lost his route across the Gobi Desert, and eventually was forced to surrender.

The Emperor, upon learning of this disaster, became enraged, and punished the hapless general by imprisoning his family. A friend of Lee, Szu-Ma Chien protested and sought to defend him. His arguments not only did not help his friend, but made the all-powerful ruler furious with him. He became a further scapegoat. As a consequence the Emperor ordered that Szu-Ma Chien be castrated.

(2) *Monumental Undertaking Results.* Szu-Ma Chien suffered deeply. He was deeply angered, depressed, and humiliated. This personal tragedy, however, eventuated in his becoming a great historian. As a consequence he came to devote his remaining years to writing *Shih-Chi,* a history of China from the year 2,700 B.C., and one which proved to be a peerless contribution to Chinese archives and literature. It was a monumental undertaking. It illustrates the PTR as a major type of *Constructive Rechannelization.*

In the introduction to *Shih-Chi,* the author provides a perceptive account of the motives underlying this tremendous achievement. "…. After I suffered the punishment for General Lee I asked myself repeatedly, 'Is it my fault? Now, my body has been incapacitated. What can I do?"

(3) *Constructive Rechannelization.* "Through my grief I thought of King Wen who wrote the *Book of Change* when he was imprisoned by his foe; I thought of Confucius who began to write his *Annals* when he was almost starved to death. I thought of Chu Ynen, the great poet of Kingdom Tsu, who completed his masterpiece *Freedom from Sorrow* when he was exiled from his country by the King; I thought of Tso Chiu who edited the *Anecdotes* when he lost his sight; finally I thought of Sun Wu who accomplished the *Philosophy of War* after his feet were amputated.

"The immortal writings through the generations were done by those who had suffered … profound sorrows … in the struggle of saving their shattered souls…. This is … the true motivation (through) which I … devoted myself to … history…."

2. *Characterologic Rechannelization*

A. MAJOR ROLE IN PERSONALITY DEVELOPMENT.—Rechannelization plays a major role in the molding of personality and in the development of character traits. Thus, for example, such abilities and traits as studiousness, research ability, intellectual curiosity, and literary interests may be determined through Sublimation.

In certain traits, as we have observed, other ego defenses such as Idealization (Chapter 8) and Reaction Formation (Chapter 18) can also play an important role. Resulting character formation can illustrate the operation of several dynamisms and compromises. Traits from the constellation comprising the Obsessive Personality (see *Table 17, p.* 247, *The Neuroses*) can have their origins in Reaction Formation and Rechannelization.

Obsessive traits include the major ones of meticulousness, preciseness, acquisitiveness, exactness, and parsimoniousness. The related character defenses or traits of orderliness, frugality, and obstinacy originate as partially sublimated, or rechanneled, carryovers from the vicissitudes of the era of bowel training in infancy.

B. IDENTIFICATION AND RECHANNELIZATION.—Sublimation is related to Identification (Chapter 9), a relationship that is more readily pointed out in the type of Rechannelization leading to attitude development, certain vocational drives, and character trait formations. In many of what are accordingly termed *Characterologic Rechannelizations,* the redirected aim and goal of the drive (and formation) is influenced through Identification. These effects may be gradual and subtle. They are no less important and vital. When early Identifications are limited, the capacity for Instinctual Diversion is also likely to be restricted.

Certain influential people in early childhood (or certain facets or segments of them) often come to serve as unwitting models. Needs and "efforts" to identify provide ample inducement in given instances to help to determine the direction of the rechanneled drive. When the Rechannelization is successful, the instinctual drive does not remain repressed, is not erased, nor is the amount of energy therein necessarily reduced. It is the direction and goal that are modified and substituted. Altering the object of the drive makes it acceptable, tolerable, and useful from both personal and social standpoints. This modification permits the drive's discharge and satisfaction.

Because the direction (and/or object) of the drive has been deflected and redirected, the original drive apparently vanishes. In the successful Sublimation, it is just as adequately and effectively discharged through its new outlet. This is a healthful result, in distinction from the damming-up of blocked and undischarged kinds of id drives, which lead to neurotic manifestations.

3. Vocational Rechannelization

A. MAJOR PROFESSIONAL AND VOCATIONAL COMMITMENTS.—Reference has been made to the widespread contributions of Rechannelization to many vocational and professional activities. Instinctual Diversions may be responsible or contributory, to varying extents. They may be so major as to account for an entire lifetime activity, which can achieve any degree of success. On the other hand, they can be minor, unapparent, and, as a consequence, of less moment to either individual or society.

We refer to these major operations of the ego defense as *Vocational* and *Avocational Rechannelizations* (or Sublimations). Both types are important personally; they are also significant in the social scheme of things.

B. RECHANNELIZATION GRADUAL.—The Rechannelization of aggressive and sexual drives generally is a very gradual affair. Their harnessing and redirection is seldom sudden, dramatic or apparent, and therefore is unlikely to be readily observed by the average person.

Instinctual Diversions can also evolve quite slowly, taking a decade or more. While this process can begin at any time, it often begins to evolve during the so-called Latent Phase of personality development (see *Table 9*, pp. 328–9).

C. SEXUAL ENERGY DIVERTED.—Sublimation was originally studied exclusively in relation to the sexual "instincts" or drives, and their resulting changes and redirection. Herein we are purposely inviting further attention and emphasis to the operation of this important dynamism in relation to other basic needs and drives, thwarted ambitions, and blocked goals. In so doing, however, we do not want to lose sight of the important role of Rechannelization in the vicissitudes of the sexual drives.

At times the Rechannelization of sexual energy takes place to an excessive extent beyond what is objectively optimal. This is illustrated in the following example of Vocational Rechannelization. This person mobilized a tremendous amount of energy indeed, which he constructively utilized in many areas of activity.

This, however, was at the cost of a normal sexual adjustment. So much of his sexual drives was sublimated that he became partially impotent. This is also an instance therefore of what is termed *Sexual Rechannelization,* as well as one of *Excessive Sublimation* or *Rechannelization.* In addition this instance affords us an opportunity to present and stress the significant *Principle of Libidinal-Investment in Therapy.*

Case 155

Excessive Rechannelization of Sexual Drives

(1) *Substantial Achievements.*   A 48-year-old business executive sought psychotherapy because of marital problems. The most striking single feature early noted was his tremendous energy. This he had employed with very considerable success in a number of areas.

In his professional work he had achieved national recognition. He was the youngest member of his firm's board of directors and had headed up several civic and professional organizations, all of which comprised a major *Vocational Rechannelization*. There were added consequences of the Instinctual Diversion of his tremendous energies.

Although he was intensely occupied business-wise, he had built his own summer home. People asked with amazement, "Where does he get such energy?" or "How can that man get so much done?"

A business associate had once commented, "He handles the equivalent of three full-time jobs!" Interestingly, the associate was unaware of several more concurrent activities.

(2) *Relative Impotence a Consequence.* Outstandingly productive and potent in so many areas of his life, he was almost completely impotent in the sexual sphere. An interesting feature of this symptom-handicap was his seeming near lack of awareness of its existence and his indifference to the loss and its effects, despite the problem having contributed substantially to his marital difficulties. This can be noted in relation to *la belle indifférence* in Conversion (Chapter 3) and *Paranoid Indifference* (Chapter 15). It comprised a powerful *secondary defense* and a resistance in therapy. The executive was a person of superior adequacy, in all areas save the sexual.

The supporting psychologic structure of his adjustment had led to interesting side effects characterwise, in his attitudes and judgments of others. He expected everyone to be a "doer." Once quite tolerant, laziness had become a cardinal sin. His children had to be busy. He had gradually become more demanding of them.

(3) *Excessive Rechannelization.* It became increasingly clear during the course of therapeutic study that the energy of sexual drives had been sublimated into work and professional activities. (*Sexual Sublimation*). The underlying needs had been intrapsychic and powerful and had progressed beyond any optimal redirection of excessive psychic energy to the extent of *Excessive Rechannelization*. As a consequence his sexual adequacy was sacrificed.

One can perhaps view this process in another way. Sexual outlets of course do not have to be thwarted by external factors. They can be most effectively blocked by intrapsychic needs and forces.

(4) *Principle of Libidinal-Investment in Psychotherapy.* The key to success in this man's therapy lay in securing the investment of a sufficient segment of his profuse and basically libidinal energy in the work of treatment. When this was accomplished the project of self-study began to make steady and satisfactory progress.

This illustrates an important "must"; a requirement in therapy, in accord with what we refer to for convenience and greater emphasis as the *Principle of Libidinal-Investment in Psychotherapy.*

This man's wife had come to bitterly resent his work. This is hardly surprising. An astute person, she had some intuitive understanding of her husband's psyche and conflicts. On one occasion, for example, she wrote: "... Our sex life has become almost nil. The energy he pours into his work comes from this, and that's why I've so bitterly resented it ..." His major professional achievements, substantial income, recognition, and what these obtained for the family in material benefits and position were inadequate compensation for her.

In considering the Vocational Rechannelization of sexual drives we must not neglect the interesting symbolism sometimes to be encountered in the choice of occupation. Two interesting instances come to mind. One concerns an artistically inclined and dedicated stone mason. He took great delight and pride in matching stones as to size and color, and shape, and even more particularly in filling holes, interstices and gaps with stones of perfect fit, using a minimum of mortar. There appeared to be symbolic elements present from both anal and sexual areas. A second case relates to a professional explorer and mountain climber whose increasing eagerness to achieve the summit while climbing reflected a significant measure of sexual symbolism. His growing tension and strivings in the climb were a burden to his less motivated companions. In another example, exhibitionism was rechannelized into acting. Various such instances can provide interesting possible types of sexual symbolism for speculative interpretation.

Certain instances of Vocational Sublimation indicate the inimical consequences which can follow when: (1) the mechanism is incompletely operative, (2) it affords inadequate protection in the face of psychic trauma, or (3) it breaks down under new stresses. Emotional problems multiply. Emotional symptom defenses of various kinds can be initiated.

D. CONTRIBUTING TO CAREER COMMITMENT.—Sexual drives can develop and be influenced in various ways so as to become homosexual in aim. These can be repressed, and the repressed drives rechannelized or sublimated in turn. This led in the following instance of Instinctual Diversion to a successful career in interior decorating. The energy of the repressed homosexuality was constructively harnessed and utilized in a personally and socially approved manner.

Repression was maintained and personal and social conflicts avoided. Some secret gratification was secured through the occupation as well as the opportunity it afforded for being among women, which for this person had a symbolic meaning of belonging, that is, of being one of them.

Case 156

Rechannelization: Homosexual Drives Diverted

A 48-year-old businessman was referred by an internist because of functional gastrointestinal symptoms and entered therapy. He had pursued a highly successful career as an interior decorator. To say that his work was important to him is an understatement. It had become his basis for living, his *raison d'être*. Into it he had poured all his interest and energy, some of which under other circumstances might have gone into other avenues.

History disclosed an absence of sexual activity or interests in this direction. Following considerable study it became clear that his orientation was latently homosexual. In other words, his sexual inclinations were homosexual, without this being known to him or reflected in his behavior however, since it had been so throughly repressed from consciousness long ago. Most of the drive had been successfully diverted into occupational channels.

He derived great satisfaction from his successes, his prestige in the field, and from his close relationships with his largely female clientele. The decorator was never happier than when he was with a group of female colleagues. Here he would carry on animated discussions at great length. Assuming a leadership position, he was not only in effect one of the group, but a particular, or preeminent one. There was secret homosexual envy of the female position and this secured a measure of disguised gratification.

In this instance, this area of defensive patterns was not fully explored. Reasons for this decision included the reasonably stable adjustment achieved, his lack of interest in change, and the long-standing and established nature of his defenses. The goals of therapy were limited accordingly.

The Instinctual Diversion had been successful enough for practical purposes to have secured a compromise resolution for conflictual repressed drives. Consciously intolerable and subject to potential social censure, the energy of his sexual drives had thus managed to secure alternate acceptable and constructive utilization.

The foregoing kind of Vocational Sublimation is generally subject to psychiatric study and treatment, particularly in instances where the psychic operation has been only partially successful. Further, the unconscious meanings, gratification, and symbolism of the vocation can vary greatly. Needless to say, the entrance of men into what are ordinarily regarded as women's fields, or women into men's fields does not give rise to an *a priori* interpretation of latent homosexuality. Instances come to mind, however, of similar Vocational Rechannelizations in a highly successful male cook, a male hairdresser, and a woman's magazine editor.

E. RECHANNELING THWARTED PARENTAL DRIVES.—Satisfactions of a maternal nature are denied to many women. Spinsterhood, the loss of spouse by death, separation or divorce, and barrenness for various reasons are not uncommon bases for the frustration of maternal wishes for children. The resulting thwarted drives can secure new sublimated outlets through a number of highly useful vocations. Not uncommon avenues for Vocational Rechannelization include teaching, nursing, foster mothering, leadership in youth activities (YMCA, Scouts, religious groups), counseling, and social work. Other vocations also are not far afield from motherhood.

The original and the substituted goals in Sublimation do not have to be clearly related. Women in such a position may also enter religious orders or take up a diverse variety of occupations and professions. The choice of vocation in Rechannelization is highly individual and is limited only by the individual capacity for symbolism, associations, and unconscious needs. There are fairly few real limits.

The "choice" of an avenue for Sublimation is not determined solely by chance. In many instances, the connections may be difficult to uncover. In many others, one has not the opportunity. The most successful Rechannelizations leave no traces in conscious awareness. Special techniques of study are required, such as are available via free association, dream analysis, and psychotherapeutic study. Further, since successful Rechannelizations provide a resolution for otherwise intolerable drives, these are likely to lead to greater emotional equanimity, not to therapy.

The psychiatrist thus has a greater opportunity by and large to study those instances and types of Rechannelization which are less successful, incomplete, or which for some reason falter. These are the ones more likely encountered in therapy since they fail to achieve their purpose; fail to avert conflict, anxiety, and neurosis.

In the following example, surgery ended the possibility of motherhood. This was a great blow to this woman. It was successfully weathered by the pouring of her energies into law, a field she had earlier abandoned

after an initial year of training, in order to be married. In her case, the
prior interest afforded a readily available outlet into which she could unconsciously divert the energy of her blocked drives. Some motivation had
already been present for the earlier interest in law, in addition to which
her husband was also an attorney. The internal process of Rechannelization
was initiated with inner struggle, but once begun and with such a convenient channel available, it rapidly gained momentum and significance.

Case 157

Maternal Instincts Rechanneled

A 34-year-old lawyer had displayed a great amount of energy and
initiative in achieving success. After earlier completion of one year
in law school she had left her graduate studies in favor of marriage,
to resume her legal schooling some years later. During the later renewed
work toward her law degree (which she accomplished in night school)
she also held a position of considerable responsibility during the day.
Following completion of her studies with honors, she had been entirely
devoted to the practice of law, in which she achieved a fair degree of
success.

Sometime prior to reentry into law school she developed carcinoma
of the cervix and had a hysterectomy performed. She had been married
for 5 years prior to the operation. It had been the fervent wish of both
husband and wife to have a large family. Despite efforts and medical
assistance there were no children. The operation dealt the final blow
to their hopes. It saved her life, but ended further pursuit of the long-
standing goal.

For a number of reasons they would not consider adoption. Her
emotional health was threatened. Fortunately, however, her blocked
strivings were successfully rechanneled into intense work in graduate
school, and later in her legal career.

4. Avocational Rechannelization

A. PARTIAL AND MULTIPLE SUBLIMATIONS.—We have noted that
Sublimations do not necessarily lead to vocations, although most great endeavors of man receive contributions from this intrapsychic operation.
Much of our drive and energy ultimately stems from so-called instinctual
sources. These can be quite powerful, and when all or most of such force
follows a single channel it is not surprising that it can lead to major cultural and social gains.

Major instances of Rechannelization are far more striking and invite
attention far more readily than do minor ones. Partial Rechannelizations
are somewhat different, in that through their success in a limited way, the
intended defensive purpose is not subserved or is only partially and incompletely so. As a consequence, such instances are more likely to secure
notice socially or therapeutically.

Let us propose an analogy in which one's total instinctual energy is
likened to a powerful stream of water. All of it may follow a single channel and with great force. However, some of it may follow side passages of
varying size. These can in turn exert effects with little or no particular
relation to the remaining main stream. Such effects may or may not be

important. However in accord with our analogy, Instinctual Diversions may be partial and are accordingly termed *Partial Rechannelizations.*

Rechannelizations of drives also are not necessarily limited to a single avenue, and these sometimes may be called *Multiple Rechannelizations* or Sublimations.

In our study of Major Rechannelization we can ourselves direct a segment of our attention toward the many minor Sublimations which can evolve in the utilization of instinctual energy. Hobbies and many various kinds of "side" pursuits and interests ultimately secure their motivation through Sublimation. For convenience and in the interests of the scientific shorthand we employ in the field, we call these particular minor rechannelings of instinctual energy *Avocational Sublimations* or Rechannelizations. They are large in number and far more common than one might ordinarily think.

B. GARDENING AS AVOCATIONAL SUBLIMATION.—Avocational Rechannelizations, however, are not necessarily limited to minor ones. We know that for some people a supposed avocation approaches a vocation in terms of the level of one's commitment of interest, energy, and time.

This evolvement is more likely true when the Rechannelization serves important intrapsychic needs, as illustrated in the following case. While this woman suffered from emotional problems, it was apparent that Instinctual Diversion had been successful in one major area and had stood her in good stead. The development of what was a major Avocational Sublimation may have prevented a more severe illness or a psychotic break.

Case 158

Avocation of Gardening a Major Sublimation

(1) *Avocational Rechannelization: Bright Spot in a Clouded Vista.* A 39-year-old housewife entered intensive psychotherapy because of chronic anxiety. This had become a considerable handicap. Somatic symptoms due mainly to muscular and visceral tension had gradually increased.

This lady had one significant activity which brought her satisfaction and pleasure; namely, her absorbing hobby of gardening. It was a real salvation for her. She hated housework, socializing was disturbing and stirred up anxiety. Most leisure-time activities, such as reading, sports, or TV were boring.

(2) *Extremely Obsessive Parent.* Gardening however had come to hold a special place for her, particularly the planting, transplanting, weeding, and earth handling aspects. She was never happier nor felt better than after she emerged from a long day of working in her garden; hands and face grimy, clothes soiled and soaked with perspiration. She would begin such a day with "an eager look and a sparkle in her eye" (according to family) and end it with "great feelings of accomplishment and satisfaction" (her words).

Her mother was a terribly rigid and obsessive person, insisting on the strictest cleanliness for the entire household. After the birth of the patient, her mother had become even more strict along these lines, if such a thing were possible.

As an infant and into early childhood, the importance of being clean was drilled into her over and over again. To the mother's dismay it had been difficult to keep the child clean—perhaps harder than most children. During these early years she had seemed to enjoy playing in dirt. At times it appeared that she was deliberately defying and engaging in a power struggle so as to vex her mother with this behavior. This conflictual situation had a great deal of dynamic significance for both persons.

(3) *Forced Repression and Rechannelization.* The mother's efforts were crowned with "success." As the child grew older, her love of dirt completely disappeared. By the time she was seven, she was already an overly orderly, clean child. This gradually became an ingrained part of her character, and she remained obsessively clean (although not so much as her mother) during her adult life, except in relation to her gardening.

Her forcibly suppressed and repressed interests in dirt and dirtiness had become gradually rechanneled and reexpressed in not too obscure terms through her gardening. This was a useful occupation and the one exception which mother had, at least tacitly, approved. This Rechannelization had been very useful for this patient.

5. In Emotional Illness

A. INEFFECTIVE, INCOMPLETE, CONTRIBUTORY, AND PREVENTIVE RE-CHANNELIZATION.—Discussion thus far has emphasized the successful Rechannelizations or Sublimations, those which contribute to emotional health. Some note has been made of those which are partial, insufficient, or falter and come under surveillance in therapy. We have learned that Instinctual Diversion can resolve the pressure of basic inner drives in one area while leaving another untouched. This leads us to the discussion of the Sublimations which are encountered in, or which can take place during emotional sickness.

Partial, Ineffective, and Incomplete Rechannelizations can contribute to the onset of an emotional illness. One can observe at times how the greater effectiveness of the operation of this dynamism could have had or has had a preventive effect, the *Preventive Rechannelization.* The poor Sublimations can, and are more likely to be, the ones encountered in the course of an illness; can contribute to the symptomatology.

B. THERAPEUTIC AND IMPROVEMENT-RECHANNELIZATION, PROGNOS-TIC-SUBLIMATION.—Rechannelization can occur during the course of emotional and mental illnesses. The operation of Instinctual Diversion is possible during various stages of neurosis and psychosis. There are a number of varieties. In some of these, the energy and aim of destructive drives clearly becomes rechanneled into constructive activities.

More pronounced instances are to be observed among hospitalized psychotic patients. In one such variety of Rechannelization, the new interests and endeavors are correctly welcomed by staff and personnel, as indicative of improvement, although not necessarily recognized by name. What we accordingly term *Improvement-Sublimations* or *Prognostic-Rechannelizations,* have encouraging prognostic significance.

These instances can be most often observed to take place in the improvement and recovery phases of an emotional illness. They are most prominent perhaps when operative in the more assertive and destructive patients. The following is an instance illustrating the operation of the Prognostic-Rechannelization.

Case 159

Improvement-Sublimation in Psychosis

(1) *Acute Destructive Episode Precipitates Hospitalization.* A 32-year-old patient had suffered the recent onset of an acute psychotic illness. He had been an accountant and also had considerable mechanical ability. Hospitalization was precipitated by an acute episode in which he was building a boat in his sister's garage, when visitors of hers arrived. For obscure reasons, the interruption had been most upsetting.

His reaction was violent. He grabbed a crowbar and started tearing up his sister's house. The police intervened and he was shortly admitted to the state hospital.

(2) *Wrecking Energy Rechanneled.* On the admission ward, in any way he could manage, he continued his wrecking operations. At various times he succeeded in breaking up pool tables, a pingpong table, water fountains, bathroom equipment, and the exercising equipment in psysical therapy. He was placed on tranquillizers and attempts were made to interest him in therapy. Slowly these efforts were successful, and he began to participate in ward meetings. His destructive behavior ceased.

Instead his energy began to be rechanneled into more constructive avenues. This was a process of Improvement-Sublimation which gained momentum. He began making things for the ward. He prepared molds and made dozens of ceramic items.

(3) *Improvement-Rechannelization also Prognostic; Remission Achieved.* His constructive work continued. He fashioned metal ash trays to supply the entire hospital. After a time he began working in the hospital shops, where he designed and produced complicated toys for underprivileged children, including a remarkable animated dog. He did much of the mechanical work on a hospital exhibit being readied for a medical convention and shortened the legs of scores of beds so as to meet specifications for open ward use.

He was transferred to an open ward where he remained active, but his work continued to be channeled into useful ends. No more destructive tendencies were exhibited. Ultimately with the working out of some other problems, he was discharged from the hospital with the psychotic phase of his illness in remission, to continue psychotherapy on a private outpatient basis.

6. Sublimation-en-Therapy

Sublimation is a Higher Order ego defense. It is frequently thought of in connection, and more likely to be found in, the more mature. Therapy is an educational process of considerable depth and one which promotes emotional maturation. It is not surprising therefore, if upon occasion one encounters evidence of Sublimations evolving during the course of long-term intensive psychotherapy. This is *Sublimation-en-Therapy* and its operation is related to the foregoing type. It should be stressed, however, that the more successful and durable Instinctual Diversions generally are likely to be too gradual and subtle of onset and presence for ordinary observation.

Sublimation of part of the following patient's sexual drive took place over the course of more than 3 years of treatment. This example is also illustrative of *Improvement Rechannelization.*

Case 160

The Improvement Sublimation: Maturation During Psychotherapy

A 36-year-old engineer entered therapy because of professional and social problems. The former were due to loss of interest, as distinguished from a lack of ability. The latter included several problems, among which were those as a consequence of avid girl-chasing, in which he paid little attention to social custom or the fine sensitivities of others' feelings.

As therapy progressed, he gradually developed personality traits on the more mature side. Over several years his sexual drives moderated and came within socially acceptable bounds.

What happened to his energy, previously allowed such free expression? This had very gradually and imperceptibly become (unconsciously) thoroughly harnessed, to secure a rechanneled expression in greatly increased professional interests and work. Both personally and socially the advantages were substantial. Both problems in essence were resolved together.

His work increased greatly in caliber and enhanced his professional reputation. His firm came to depend upon him for the more difficult assignments. This was a far cry from his status at the beginning of his therapeutic work. In 5 years he became a partner.

C. DYNAMICS

1. By Analogy

A. PSYCHIC ENERGY.—We have found it useful in understanding the dynamics of Sublimation or Rechannelization to employ several analogies. One, to channeling a powerful stream, has been mentioned. A second is the related analogy to Niagara Falls, to follow.

We must bear in mind that each unacceptable drive or impulse that undergoes Repression requires a certain amount of psychic energy to maintain it in its repressed state. This is in accord with the KEP. (*Kinetic-Energy Principle*) in the maintenance of Repression, see later Chapter 21. Each repressed impulse theoretically detracts from the total amount of such energy that is available to the individual in the ordinary pursuits of living. In this situation, Instinctual Diversion has a vital role to play. This operation results in the conservation and more healthful utilization of psychic energy.

As outlined in our discussion thus far, Rechannelization may be viewed as the diverting of purely instinctual energy and purpose toward aims which society looks upon with greater favor, and which are therefore also more acceptable to the ego or self. In this way, the energy associated with primitive and unacceptable (id) drives becomes transferred and redirected into socially more useful goals.

B. NIAGARA FALLS ANALOGY.—A million tons of water each 2 minutes plummets with devastating force over the combined American (167 feet high and 1,400 feet wide) and Canadian (158 feet high and 2,950 feet wide) sides of Niagara Falls. The tremendous energy of this vast amount of falling water can be compared to the energy of the unacceptable unconscious impulse. Such a force is irresistible. The water also inevitably constantly exerts wearing and erosive effects which might be likened in turn to the potentially destructive effects of unconscious impulses when they are bottled up and denied expression, or when they are not sufficiently controlled or constructively directed.

Near Buffalo, engineers constructed great diversionary channels which directed huge streams of water from the Niagara River (constructively) into operating hydroelectric turbines. A portion of the energy and the dynamic force of the falling water was thus usefully redirected and converted into generating electricity, to supply light and power to a wide area.

The rechanneling of the water from the falls through the hydroelectric plants was an effective diversion of part of the otherwise eroding force into constructive channels. Some of the destructive potential was averted.

This is similar to the diversion of the instinctual energy of otherwise destructive impulses into socially constructive endeavors, which takes place in Rechannelization or Sublimation. In the psychic process, a far larger proportion of the energy potential may be diverted and rechanneled into new, constructive, and useful pathways of endeavor.

Through Rechannelization when it is successful, emotional conflict is averted or resolved. Instinctual drives secure acceptable utilization. Emotional health and maturity is promoted. It is not without good reason that we refer to Rechannelization as a healthful ego defense. Properly also, we describe it as the most highly developed and most advanced of the *Higher Order* group of dynamisms. In the following discussion, we shall review and underline a few of our comments thus far, and perhaps add one or two.

C. CONCURRENT EVOLVEMENT OF SUPEREGO AND SUBLIMATION.—By definition, the mechanism and process of Sublimation usually leads to the evolvement of aims and activities that are acceptable to both self and society. Since the substituted aims (secured through Sublimation) must of necessity have the acceptance of society, effective Rechannelization cannot be fully accomplished until the individual has reached a sufficiently mature stage of development. He must have reached a point where he can begin to recognize what is and what is not acceptable to the world.

The process of Sublimation often reaches a high peak of activity during the so-called *Latent Period,* that is, the ages from 5 or 6 to 10 years. See *Table 9* in the following chapter. Foundations for later elaboration of the defense of Sublimation are also frequently laid down during this era. Further, it is during this period that the superego elaborates more completely.

Thus the development of the superego (roughly the conscience) and the evolvement of precedents for patterns of psychic defense can take place more or less together. We have also observed that Sublimations are initiated or receive their real impetus at almost any juncture in living.

In our society, rage and sex must be held in check. In other words, instinctual tensions must be discharged in modified, diverted, disguised, periodic, deferred, and in various substitute or indirect ways. These must be ways which are acceptable socially, unless more or less serious social conflict is to be engendered.

2. An Ideal Solution

Not everyone has the same psychic capacity for the evolution of Rechannelization. This internal ability is one which is highly variable. However, the psychologic capacity of the child to develop successful Rechannelizations may be one index of his ability to achieve emotional maturity.

The early analysts first advanced the theory of Sublimation and emphasized the important part it plays in individual adjustment. They viewed Sublimation as the most healthful means of coping with repressed infantile sexual material. The infant experiences drives and impulses for which he can find no suitable, safe, or acceptable expression. These impulses are repressed. In the continuing efforts of the organism at adaptation, as it is more and more exposed to environmental experiences and pressures, some of these repressed impulses lose their original libidinal or aggressive connotation.

In the resulting desexualized state, or minus their aggression, they become more readily attached to another drive which is convenient by virtue of association, hidden meaning, or symbolism. The substituted drive or new channel allows a form of outward expression that is more socially acceptable, and hence more acceptable to the individual. We have seen the results of this process in prior case studies; also see *Mental Mechanisms,* pp. 76–117 (and *Mental Mechanisms, Cases 19* through *38*).

In general, we have come to view successful Rechannelization as the best solution for the outward expression of the energy of unconscious, that is, repressed, instinctual drives. The energy provides the dynamic force, but in the process it has become more controlled and rechanneled.

3. Defensive Reactions to Psychiatric Concepts

When the concept of Sublimation (Rechannelization) was introduced around the turn of the country, society was still in the rigid and strait-laced Victorian Era. There was an emphasis on the suppression and repression of all things sexual, and often sensual as well. Matters pertaining to sexual or eliminative function were strictly taboo. Any really open discussion was practically unthinkable. It was as though in the effort to achieve a higher cultural plane, people must ever more thoroughly divorce themselves from their more basic "instinctual" drives.

In such an atmosphere it was hardly surprising that relationships of character formation to oral, anal, and genital function in infancy and early childhood were often defensively and vigorously discarded. To many, these findings seemed farfetched and absurd. To some, depending on their earlier conditioning, they were revolting. The finding of roots of neuroses and emotional illness in the vicissitudes of the instincts and in resulting emotional conflict, was for some decades widely rejected.

This is far less true today. However, the conception of an infantile interest in smearing being rechanneled into vocations of painting or art work, urethral erotism into firefighting, or destructive infantile aggressiveness into slaughtering and meat handling, is still offensive to many people. Perhaps even the possibility of such relationships is threatening to some, in that they touch too close to personal Repressions, areas which seem more safely avoided.

A more widespread defensive reaction to be expected today on the part of the general public is that of scepticism. Many physicians do not find dedication to pathology, surgery, or obstetrics as possibly representing successful Rechannelizations particularly palatable. They are content however to maintain a sceptical attitude, usually without pursuing the matter further, although more study might prove interesting and informative—both generally and personally.

4. Acceptable New Channel

Much of the foregoing in text and example has been not only descriptive, but has also helped to bring out many important elements of the dynamics of Sublimation or Rechannelization, how and why it develops, and the psychologic consequences of its operation. Rechannelization is an automatic and unconscious process. It is defensive and constructive. Unconscious emotional drives thus become more useful, and more acceptable to both the individual and society. Rechannelization (as an interchangeable term for this dynamism) is an advanced member of the Higher Order group of dynamisms. (See p. 290.)

Through Sublimation, discharge of the energy becomes possible in more acceptable form. Thus we see that in healthy emotional adjustment and in sound personality development, this dynamism plays a useful and important role. Instinctual Diversion is an ideal solution for the management and constructive utilization of the instincts and their psychic force.

D. SUMMARY

1. Rechannelization

Sublimation is a major ego defense through which the energy of instinctual drives and intolerable repressed material secures disguised outward expression and constructive utilization. It is a constructive dynamism, with personal and social values. Unconscious drives are diverted into more constructive channels of endeavor. A new outlet becomes substituted with resulting psychologic advantage. *Psychic compromises* are evolved. Types of Sublimations or Rechannelizations include the *Major* or *Minor, Complete, Multiple, Successful, Characterologic, Partial,* and *Incomplete.*

Rechannelization makes a major contribution to mental and emotional health. Through this dynamism there is a diversion of drives into personally and socially approved channels of endeavor. *Rechannelization* and *Instinctual Diversion* were suggested as alternate and interchangeable terms which can offer us certain advantages.

Sublimation is likely universal in that, to varying extents, everyone rechannels part of his basic drives into personally aesthetic and socially acceptable avenues. Society gains, and cultural advantages may accrue. More noteworthy Rechannelizations have led to outstanding careers in practically every field of human activity.

2. Types of Rechannelization

The introduction of this concept met with considerable resistance in the Victorian Era. However, Sublimation has had some implicit recognition for a long time. It can follow great misfortune in the *Personal-Tragedy Rechannelization* or PTR, of Szu-Ma Chien, as illustrated in *Case 154,* in the examples mentioned therein, and in other outstanding instances throughout history. Great undertakings have been initiated or fostered as a consequence. In this connection, the interesting *Concept of Historical Validation* was mentioned again (Chapter 16). Sublimation can play an important role in the formation of a number of character traits and in personality development (*Characterologic Rechannelization*). The *Scapegoat Reaction* received mention, as did the *Kinetic-Energy Principle* or KEP. in maintaining Repression.

Vocational Rechannelizations are of great importance individually and socially and contribute to career commitment. Several instances were illustrated. Laudable contributions not infrequently result. Success in many occupational and professional pursuits owes its achievement to the operation of this vital intrapsychic defensive process. Rechannelization can lead to a vocation, reestablish a prior one, or result in accelerated activity in one already existing.

Sexual Rechannelization (or Sublimation) refers to this process in relation to the more constructive redirection of sexual drives, as does *Aggression Rechannelization* in relation to aggressive and hostile drives. *Excessive Sublimation* describes the type in which the degree of Rechannelization is so great as to unduly sap the strength of the normal sexual or aggressive drives.

Avocational Sublimations constitute another important group. Some of these are difficult to distinguish from vocational rechannelings in their great commitment. Many, however, are of the nature of hobbies, part-time interests, and sidelines. Often they serve a very useful and even vital purpose in individual psychology. The Rechannelization of homosexual and thwarted maternal drives was illustrated.

Important Rechannelizations (Sublimations) can occur during the course of a neurosis or psychosis, more striking ones occasionally being evident in the recovery phase of a disturbed psychotic patient, as illustrated. The *Principle of Libidinal-Investment in Psychotherapy* was formulated (*Case 155*) to stress the necessity for such a commitment, in securing a reasonable measure of therapeutic success.

Types of Sublimation or Rechannelization which are more likely to contribute to emotional illness include the *Ineffective, Partial, Multiple, Contributory, Excessive,* and *Incomplete.* The *Preventive Rechannelization* can be encountered. The *Improvement* or *Prognostic* type occurs during therapy and is likely to parallel the degree of or forecast recovery. During treatment, *Sublimation-en-Therapy* may transpire as a moderately long-term characterologic development. *Improvement Rechannelization* was illustrated in *Case 160.*

3. Psychodynamics

Sublimation is healthful. It is the one ego defense in which all divisions of the psyche, the id, ego, and superego, operate in concert. In the most successful instances one can only surmise its existence, since it leads to contentment, equanimity, happiness, and emotional health and seldom to the psychiatrist's office. The psychiatrist is the person who is more likely to encounter the Sublimations or Rechannelizations which are partial, incomplete, or which tend to break down. The *Niagara Falls Analogy* was offered, and defensive reactions to psychiatric concepts received comment.

In sublimation or Rechannelization (which is the ideal process for the resolution of the conflicts stemming from otherwise potentially or actively destructive inner drives), a channel for outward expression is gradually provided which is acceptable to oneself and to society. At a high level of activity from 5 or 6 to 10 years of age, when the superego is being concurrently established, Sublimation can evolve at any juncture in one's subsequent life.

Sublimation is similar in definition to Conversion. It is close to Reaction Formation in operation but differs in scope, direction, and end results. Substitution is a requisite to its operation in that substitutive aims and goals are adopted. Rechannelization is the most developed and advanced of the ego defenses. It plays an important role in the securing and maintenance of emotional and mental health, in personality development and in the progress of healthful maturation.

In conclusion it is clear that Rechannelization is to be considered as one of the more significant in the senior ego defenses. For those sufficiently interested in this major process of Instinctual Diversion, some additional data will be found in the chapter entitled Sublimation in *Mental Mechanisms,** pp. 76–118. Included therein also are a dozen more case illustrations.

---

* From Laughlin, H. P. *Mental Mechanisms.* London, Butterworth & Co., Ltd., 1963.

E.   CROSS-REFERENCES TO *THE NEUROSES* *

Rechannelization (Sublimation)
In Nature of Anxiety (Chapter 1)
   as a reaction to anxiety; p. 24.
   in acculturation of child (*First Tenet of Parental Role*); p. 23.
In Character Reactions (Chapter 5)
   contribution of R., in character trait development; p. 288.
     of *Obsessive Personality;* pp. 235, 245.
       Abraham's theories; p. 292.
     lack of, in *Conversion Personality defenses* (Table 19); p. 260.

F.   REVIEW QUESTIONS

Sample self-check questions on Chapter 19 and Rechannelization for the student, psychiatric resident, and board candidate.

1. Briefly describe the operation of this major ego defense. Cite two examples from your clinical experience.
2. Which is your preference among the alternative terms of *Rechannelization, Sublimation,* and *Instinctual Diversion?* Why? Each offers certain advantages. What are they?
3. Outline briefly the *Personal-Tragedy Rechannelization* or PTR.
4. What does the *Historical Validation Concept* stress?
5. How can *Characterologic Rechannelization* play a major role in personality development?
6. Cite consequences of: (1) the *Excessive Sublimation* or *Rechannelization;* (2) the *Vocational* and *Avocational* types.
7. What is meant by *Partial* and *Multiple Rechannelization?*
8. Name the types of Rechannelization which are factors in emotional illness. How can they so contribute?
9. Select six of the following concepts for definition and example.
    A. *Psychic compromise.*
    B. *Constructive Rechannelization.*
    C. *Sexual Rechannelization.*
    D. *Libidinal-Investment Principle in therapy.*
    E. *Prognostic-Rechannelization.*
    F. *Kinetic-Energy Principle* or KEP.
    G. *Latency Period in relation to Sublimation.*
    H. *Sublimation-en-Therapy.*
    I. *Complete Rechannelization* or *Instinctual Diversion.*
    J. *Aggression Sublimation.*
10. Why is Rechannelization or Sublimation sometimes described as an ideal solution?

---

* From Laughlin, H. P. *The Neuroses.* London, Butterworth & Co., Ltd., 1967.

CHAPTER 20

REGRESSION

*... Ego-Retreat: Psychologic Withdrawal Toward
a More Protected and Dependent Position*

A. THE NATURE OF REGRESSION

1. Directional-Tenet of Regression. 2. Definition. 3. Psychologic Retreat. 4, Major and Minor Regressions. 5. Motives and Mode of Action: a. Proportional Ego-Response Law; b. Ultimate-Dependency-Goal Concept; c. Attitudinal and Behavioral Regression. 6. Partial, Total, and Mixed Regression.

B. CHILDHOOD REGRESSIONS

1. Tidal-Progression of Maturity Concept. 2. Reaction to New Sibling: a. Understanding Aids Dissolution; b. Increasing-Complexity Principle. 3. Disciplinary-Regression. 4. The Regressive-Indicator. "Pushing" a Child. 5. Conflict-Indicators Reactivated.

C. THE MAJOR STAGES OF PSYCHOSEXUAL DEVELOPMENT

D. DYNAMICS

1. Reversion Under Stress; a. Illness-Regression; b. Sexual Regression. 2. To Era of Earlier Gratification: a. Dependency Needs Multiply; b. Psychologic Recapitulation Route (PRR) Concept. 3. Retreat for Ego Defense. 4. Advance at Cost of Regression-Retreat. 5. Complete or Total Regression.

E. FIXATION

1. Any Level. 2. Law of Maturity. 3. Types of Fixation.

F. REGRESSION IN EMOTIONAL ILLNESS

1. The Regression-Gauge. Pathologic Regressions: a. In Every Illness; b. Evidence of Illness. 2. In Neuroses: a. Dependency-Seeking Principle; b. Phobic Regression; c. Hygeiaphrontis, Phobia, Delusion, and Depression; d. Conversion Regression; e. Hypnotic Regression; f. Depressive Reactions; g. Fatigue States; h. Hygeiaphrontis. Vicious Circle of Self-Defeat Concept in Neuroses; i. Obsessive-Compulsive Reaction; j. Neuroses-Following-Trauma. 3. Massive Regression: a. Psychotic Reaction a Regression; b. Progressive Development in Schizophrenia; c. Infantile Patterns Readopted; d. Assessment Valuable.

G. REGRESSION AND THERAPY

1. Concept of Tidal-Progression. 2. Dependency Gratification:
a. Overdependency Feared; b. Trend Toward Emotional
Health Concept. 3. Regression Treatment: a. Early Unmet
Needs Filled; b. Bowen's Approach; c. Maximal Support; d.
In Alcoholism; e. Maturity Fostered.

H. SUMMARY

1. Ego-Retreat. 2. The Making-up-for Principle. 3. Normal
Regression. 4. Pattern Established: a. Many Bases; b. Emotional Recapitulations; c. Fixation. 5. Dependency Needs Significant.

I. REFERENCES (FROM *The Neuroses*)

J. REVIEW QUESTIONS

A.   THE NATURE OF REGRESSION

1. Directional-Tenet of Regression

Regression is a major form of personality defense. It represents a
psychologic retreat. In Regression there is an emotional reversion in varying degree to an earlier and less mature level of adjustment and development. Patterns of reaction appropriate to this level may be adopted, or the
prior ones reactivated. This is a retreat toward a dependent position which
is such a prominent and regular feature of the unconscious regressive endeavors that we refer to it as the *Directional-Tenet of Regression*. Regression always (and by definition) takes place in this direction.

Regressive manifestations can relate to any area or aspect of living,
particularly including those appearing in: (1) emotional reactions; (2)
behavior; (3) patterns of thinking; and (4) general level of adjustment.
Interesting regressive phenomena occur in response to otherwise overwhelming emotional conflict and stress. Regressions evolve in consequence
to the ego unconsciously seeking a more tolerable situation.

2. Definition

Through the automatic and consciously effortless process of Regression, the ego retreats toward a safer and more defensible position, toward
the only ones it knows—those already experienced, a more satisfactory era
from the past. Such a retreat reflects an inability to cope with life as it is
experienced, some significant aspect of living, or the current situation.

By definition, Regression is *a major psychologic endeavor, operating
outside of conscious awareness, through which an individual retreats to an
earlier and subjectively more satisfactory level of adjustment. Through
Regression there is a psychic-emotional withdrawal toward a more pro-*

tected and dependent position. Regression is the principle and most direct form of *ego-retreat.*

Regressive phenomena may vary from *Partial* and *Minor* ones, to *Major Regressions* of considerable significance. What we term *Massive Regression* takes place in certain psychotic reactions. Regression and regressive manifestations may be symbolic, actual, or a combination, and may involve any aspect of living. This senior dynamism belongs with the more primitive, less advanced group of ego defenses. It is a Lower Order type of intrapsychic defensive process.

3. Psychologic Retreat

Regression differs somewhat from other ego defenses. It is convenient to speak of the operation of many dynamisms as unconscious endeavors of the ego. In some distinction, Regression involves a retreat by the ego, partially or in toto.

In other mechanisms the ego rearranges things, unconsciously effects different ways of seeing them, and makes various kinds of intrapsychic adjustments. These are internal, within itself. In Regression, the ego itself seeks to return to an earlier and safer, more satisfying level. A *Making-up-for Principle* may also be involved, see later (p. 352). In line with the foregoing comments, we view the process of Regression as a distinct phenomenon.

4. Major and Minor Regressions

The capacity and tendency to regress are individual and vary widely. The need also, of course, is quite variable. While the ease and frequency of employing Regression varies—and while only a limited number of people evolve repressive patterns of responses to stresses in childhood, which are retained by some into adulthood—a basic capacity to regress exists in most people. In this sense Regression sometimes serves as a last-ditch defense, to fall back on when other, established emotional-psychic defenses fail. Then, at least theoretically, anyone subjected to sufficient stress will regress. Regressive manifestations are likely to evolve with many during the vicissitudes of living.

We have found it useful personally and clinically to classify Regressions as *Minor Regressions* and *Major Regressions*. Minor Regressions frequently reflect a patterned type of response. They are often interesting phenomena, as distinguished from being of great significance as far as psychopathology is concerned. They are usually partial, simple, temporary, and not a prominent feature of illness.

Major Regressions include the massive behavioral reversions associated with psychotic reactions, which can progress to the infantile level. By definition they are of considerable significance, occupying a position of prominence in a given individual, his emotional adjustment and illness.

Major Regressions can include aspects of behavior which are more or less characteristic of the oral phase of personality development.

The Major Regressions are automatic, unconscious, and occur in response to an overwhelmingly stressful situation. They represent a desperate, last-ditch, and defensively motivated strategic withdrawal by the ego. They can comprise a significant feature in almost any type of emotional illness.

5. Motives and Mode of Action

A. PROPORTIONAL EGO-RESPONSE LAW.—Regression takes place in response to overwhelming unconscious needs for safely and security. A haven, refuge, and more secure position is sought. Regression represents a desperate psychic endeavor to restore a measure of emotional equilibrium. Through it the harassed and weakened ego seeks to stablilize itself on an earlier, simpler level. The aim and intent is to preserve emotional synthesis, which the ego "fears" would otherwise disintegrate, flying apart in total disorganization.

To a considerable extent in the operation of this defense, the more overwhelming the assault, the farther the ego retreats. This is in accord with what we term for emphasis the *Law of Proportionual Ego-Response* in Regression. The validity of this law is illustrated clinically in many instances of regressive retreat in emotional illness in which this defensively-intended route has been unwittingly adopted and pursued.

B. ULTIMATE-DEPENDENCY-GOAL CONCEPT.—In Regression a safer base of operations is sought. In this sequence, the ego longs for and finally must have, surcease from tension, danger, anxiety, stress, and responsibility—for relief from assault. As the ego unconsciously seeks a more protected and less exposed position, the psychologic retreat is toward a position of dependence.

Theoretically, the ultimate goal of Regression would be to retrieve the complete dependency position sacrificed in the process of birth. This is the *Concept of the Ultimate-Dependency-Goal* in Regression. Less technically, Regression might be viewed approximately as seeking acceptance, love, and security.

C. ATTITUDINAL AND BEHAVIORAL REGRESSION.—We have earlier defined Regression as "the psychic process of returning in a more or less symbolic fashion to an earlier and subjectively more satisfactory (but actually more infantile and immature) level of adjustment." This definition remains applicable. Thus, through Regression there is the readoption of infantile modes of gratification. Regression is always to an earlier level as noted, the particular level depending on the individual patient's background and needs. It is an attempted retreat from stress toward what is unconsciously viewed as a more dependent, protected, simpler, and less responsible position. This is in accord with our Directional-Tenet of Regression.

The following case is illustrative. In this clinical example Regression was a major feature in a psychotic reaction precipitated by the death of a woman's father. Both *Attitudinal* and *Behavioral* Regressions were in evidence.

Case 161

Regression in Attitude and Behavior

(1) *Leads to Hospitalization.* A 32-year-old woman was hospitalized following the onset of a severe emotional illness. This had been precipitated by the death of her father some months previously, for whom she had long been housekeeper and nearly sole companion.

A sister described how the patient had changed from a "well-adjusted person" into one who became "more and more childlike." She had frequent crying spells," became increasingly talkative, constantly complained about things not being done for her, and demanded increasing attention. The Regression led to her being admitted to a hospital, urgently requiring psychiatric care.

(2) *Attitudinal and Behavioral Regression.* During interviews she spoke in high-pitched, childish, pathetic, and whining tones, with the intermittent tearful and pathetic interjection of, "My daddy is dead. My daddy is dead!" This she moaned sadly, over and over. Although partly able to care for herself, this was more on an 8-year-old level than that of an adult. She piteously denied hostility, "... Everyone is so nice to me. ... I just love everyone. ..." Instead of feeling concern over her major problems in living, she became upset instead over something to do with her daily care, weeping, for example, over not having more milk. This was an instance of a *Major Regression* in an illness of psychotic level.

For many, many months she was helpless and dependent. She constantly invited advice, help, and solicitude from fellow patients, staff personnel, visitors; from anyone who would listen. She referred to the way her mother used to carry her around in her arms, demonstrating by motions how she was "so carefully carried." Her emotional reactions reflected a Regression to at least the level of middle childhood. Manifestations of both *Attitudinal* and *Behavioral* Regression were prominent.

(3) *Long-Term Improvement.* This patient's response to the overwhelming stress of her father's death was an unwitting Regression to a more protected and dependent past level of adjustment. This is in accord with the *Directional-Tenet of Regression.* The degree and the completeness of the regressive features were in direct proportion to the severity of the emotional reaction, illustrating the *Law of Proportional Ego-Response in Regression.*

Hospitalization was required for 2 years, with continuing intensive psychotherapy on a private basis. She recovered from the acute psychotic phase of her illness. Her adjustment and level of maturity gradually improved substantially.

6. Partial, Total, and Mixed Regression

The retreat in Regression is away from the current stresses, conflicts, and responsibilities, which have proven too complex and are not possible of solution on an adult level. Regression is a way of saying in effect: "I can't continue," or "I can't keep up the pace."

Accordingly, the person involved retreats psychologically, that is, regresses toward a prior level of integration and adjustment. Regression may be *Partial,* affecting one area of the personality and adjustment, or *Total,* affecting the individual in toto. Regression may take place to any preceding level of personality development, or in what we occasionally encounter as the *Mixed Regression,* to aspects of several prior levels. In the latter event, regressive manifestations from different levels are present together.

B.   CHILDHOOD REGRESSIONS

1. Tidal-Progression of Maturity Concept

Regression may be a normal or a pathologic phenomenon. As observers of childhood development, we recognize that progress toward his eventual maturation by the child is more by "fits and starts" or "ups and downs," than through an unremitting, forward progression. There is nothing necessarily pathologic about this movement. Alternately forward and backward, the process of maturity normally makes progress, with more movement in the "forward" than in the "backward" direction. This is the expected course of events. This phenomenon is the *Tidal-Progression of Maturity* or development (p. 346).

In healthful personality development, of course, the overall direction will be along the line of steady progression. The setbacks are of a minor nature and temporary. These are better accepted and understood in their more proper long-range perspective, in accord with the Tidal-Progression Concept. When these are apparent they comprise what we call *Normal Regression.* Viewed in this light, parents are less likely to be disturbed by their presence, and will be more effective in coping with any resulting problems.

It is useful to continue our study of clinical instances of Regression with those of childhood. These comprise an important subgroup, which we name *Childhood Regressions.* They are frequently of a simple enough nature. Often comprising slight exaggerations and in line with the Tidal-Progression Concept, Minor Regressions are frequently encountered. They do not have to be pathologically significant. This is a matter for individual evaluation in each instance. Regressions are at times abetted, marked by, or secured in part through Fantasy (pp. 113), also see *Case 65* (p. 118–9).

2. Reaction to New Sibling

A. UNDERSTANDING AIDS DISSOLUTION.—Mild instances of Behavioral Regression are frequently manifested as a consequence of the conflicts engendered by relationships with a sibling. Feelings of competition and envy are often involved. Variations of this situation provide common bases for Minor Regression. An example of these Childhood Regressions includes the toilet-trained child who begins to wet or soil, for instance following the stress of the advent of a new brother or sister. A child who has learned to drink from a cup may temporarily prefer bottle feeding, in reaction to conflicts so generated.

Fortunately many Childhood Regressions tend to be self-limited. Parental understanding and judicious management assists in their gradual dissolution.

B. INCREASING-COMPLEXITY PRINCIPLE.—Many variations of this type of reaction can be seen. Childhood Regressions also of course take place in older children. In general, the older or actually *the more mature the person, the more complex and subtle regressive manifestations are likely to be in response to conflict and stress.* This defines the principle through which we recognize that increasing complexity in emotional manifestations is proportional to the level of maturity achieved.

What we accordingly refer to as the *Principle of Increasing-Complexity* in emotional manifestations has many applications in their therapeutic understanding and resolution. The alert observer-therapist can find continuing application of this principle in his professional work.

The following illustrates a common instance of Childhood Regression.

Case 162

Regressive Manifestations Follow a New Baby

A 9-year-old youngest child had occupied the center of the family stage for years. Relatives referred to her as the baby of the family. Her parents preferred calling her, "Baby," neglecting her real name. She was pampered and "made over" by three older brothers and two sisters. Except for the inevitably retarding influences from this setting, she was mature for her age, and enjoyed acting "grown-up."

It was an unfortunate day when a new baby arrived. Linda's behavior unconsciously came to reflect many regressive features, in response to envy and the threat of being displaced from her favored position. She began sucking her thumb. The tone of her voice assumed a childlike higher pitched quality. She cried easily and constantly demanded attention. In many respects her behavior became closer for a time to that of a 2- or 4-year-old.

Gradually her new role in the family became clarified and was without major loss in status. Aided by judicious parental management, the initial insecurity wore off. Within several months the Minor Regression faded and she returned to her more usual level of adjustment.

3. Disciplinary-Regression

Regressive behavior may be observed in response to physical injury, pain, sickness, and psychologic hurt. While these are more readily observed in childhood, as we shall learn they also occur with adults.

One interesting temporary Childhood Regression is sometimes observed to take place following punishment. Herein comfort and solace are sought, as well as reassurance from several standpoints. Referred to as *Disciplinary-Regression,* it is also to be encountered elsewhere, as with certain prison inmates.

The following case illustrates a brief regressive reaction to a spanking.

Case 163

Disciplinary-Regression

The mother of a 6-year-old boy became angry when he poured a box of soap flakes over the floor. This followed a series of unrelated, extra-familial difficulties. Her response was consequently aggravated. As punishment she meted out a severe spanking.

The little boy was hurt, emotionally as well as physically. A little later he was observed curled up in a chair, arms and legs in flexion in a fetal-like position. His thumb was in his mouth, something he had not done for 2 years. He had located his old favorite blanket (his soteria, an object-source of security: Chapter 11, pp. 607–639 in *The Neuroses*) and had it close to him for comfort.

A Childhood Regression took place when this little boy found the situation painful because of emotional stress. He was seeking to go back to a period where things were more satisfactory.

His position, resumption of thumb-sucking, and resurrecting his soteria, as his "portable security," were regressive manifestations. This instance also illustrates the *Disciplinary-Regression* and the *Minor* (temporary and nonpathologic) *Regression*. After a time, when comfort had been secured, the regressive manifestations were discarded as no longer necessary.

4. The Regressive-Indicator. "Pushing" a Child

The wise parent and teacher learn that development in its various aspects should not be pushed too hard. The child has to proceed at his individual pace. He can be encouraged and assisted to the extent which he desires and can use. Reactions which can follow too much pressure or too great demands should be avoided. When recognition of the foregoing is lacking or these principles are not followed, various unfortunate events can take place.

The overeager parent may more than defeat his aims. Untoward emotional sequelae can develop. These include regressive tendencies, which contribute to maturation delay, or to ground being lost instead of gained. Regressive features manifested in attitudes or behavior can serve the astute observer as a useful *Regressive-Indicator*. The RI helps invite attention to the fact that too much is expected of a child, or that he is under undue pressure. This was true in the following instance.

Case 164

Regressive Behavior Signals Difficulty

A 9-year-old boy was in the sixth grade of public school. For his age, he was large in size and above average in intelligence. He had been advanced two grades ahead of his contemporaries. Often he was pushed to his limits of capability in class. More was expected of him because of his size and because he actually was smart.

During recess, after a period of mental exertion and strain in class, he played in the sand pile with toy bears and soldiers together with the second grade boys. His classmates were playing baseball and football. When playing in the sandpile he felt relaxed and secure. His reaction during recess periods was not merely a relieved, "Now I can be my age." This was carried further, his play was on a regressed level.

An observant teacher fortunately noted this regressive manifestation as a signal of trouble; a *Regressive-Indicator*. As a consequence it became possible to effect some environmental readjustments and more serious trouble was averted.

Parents had best not push children too hard in their education, socialization, or maturation. The results may be self-defeating. The onset of regressive manifestations can serve as a red flag of warning.

Recognition of these principles and the wish to emphasize the conception led to formulating the concept of the Regressive-Indicator, one which could prove helpful for parents, teachers, and therapists. Awareness of the presence of a Regressive-Indicator can lead to a constructive change of pace or revised approach with a given child.

5. Conflict-Indicators Reactivated

The many symptoms which occur in relation to anxiety and tension can have regressive aspects. In early childhood, what we have earlier termed *Conflict-Indicators*, including as examples nail-biting, nightmares, sleepwalking, and bed-wetting, are not infrequently encountered. Often these gradually subside with no specific treatment. People speak of children "outgrowing" or "growing out of" such things—as though increased age accomplished this in and of itself. It is not age, but rather greater security and maturity which are responsible.

The presence of a Conflict-Indicator may be encountered particularly or recur, in response to the stress of situational and interpersonal change. A first camp experience, visit away from home, going away to school or others of the more Specific Emotional Hazards of Childhood or Adulthood (SEHC and SEHA; *The Neuroses* pp. 33–4, 38, and 119) are examples. Regressive factors can play a role in the initiation and reactivation of CIs as also in the unwitting selection of emotional symptoms.

The following instance illustrates symptom-recurrence (actually *Conflict-Indicators*) from an earlier era, in response to the joint pressures of being away at college and semester examinations.

Case 165

Recurrence of Conflict-Indicators

A freshman college student was away from home for the first time and found adjustment difficult. Nevertheless, he managed fairly well and made a few friends, by whom he was well regarded. This continued until semester examinations when pressures increased. He had somewhat of a struggle, but weathered the period.

It was during this additionally stressful time that he developed urinary frequency, occasional enuresis, suffered nightmares, and bit his nails. This was a recurrence of Conflict-Indicators not present since early childhood.

Their return was in direct response to the stress and tension of the examination period, superimposed on a somewhat less than excellent adjustment to college, and being away from home. There were contributory regressive factors. He fought down a desire to give up school and to return home. During subsequent examination periods throughout college the same difficulties returned, fortunately in diminishing degree.

These and similar manifestations help comprise a class of emotional phenomena which have been termed Conflict-Indicators, as noted. (See *The Neuroses,* pp. 406, 671, 756, and 797.) Under later stress such manifestations can recur.

The recurrence of Conflict-Indicators is quite evident with some persons in response to the emotional stresses of military service in wartime. During World War II CI manifestations were frequently observed as recurrences under the stresses of induction and basic training, as well as later in response to the psychologic pressures of wartime operations.

C.   THE MAJOR STAGES OF PSYCHOSEXUAL DEVELOPMENT

One cannot always draw clear lines of distinction between Childhood and *Adult Regressions.* In general, regressive reactions and manifestations in adulthood tend to be more significant. With sufficient observation and study, Regression or regressive tendencies are to be found in every case of emotional illness. Major Regressions in adulthood are of course largely confined to the more grave cases.

We have referred to the concept of *Tidal-Progression of Maturation* and its expected unevenness as a normal progression. The development of maturity progresses gradually. Scientists in the behavioral and social fields have evolved and use certain terms in discussing personality development. Psychiatrists and psychologists refer to the maturation process as *Psychosexual Development.*

Stages of this progression have come to be further identified and labeled for purposes of convenience, classification, communication, and reference. They are approximate as to years. Currently there is a certain amount of variation and overlapping as to meanings and usage.

The following *Table 9* outlines the major periods of human personality development as we view them. Although psychosexual development is divided into levels or stages, it should be emphasized that this is a continuing, evolving and dynamic process; not one which is in any way static. We have prepared and included this data as a convenient reference source for those who might so wish. It is offered with the hope that it will help the reader clarify, delineate, and compare the various sometimes overlapping labels more commonly employed in discussing personality development of infants and children.

Table 9

Eight Major Stages of Man: His Development and Adulthood

This tabulation is offered to aid the interested student by providing a source for ready reference. Alternate terms employed by various authorities are included.

The chronologic ages as assigned are not absolute and can vary within moderate limits, without necessarily indicating abnormal or retarded personality development. The various periods or stages overlap, as does the terminology used in the field.

Regression can occur psychologically, emotionally, and/or behaviorally toward any earlier level of adjustment. This may be complete, partial, or mixed. It may include elements of several earlier stages (*Mixed Regression*). Although *Total Regression* can transpire, most often it is *Partial*. To an extent Regression can be symbolically achieved.

A. **Intrauterine.**

B. **The Infantile Period.** Also is referred to by some as the *Narcissistic* or *Autoerotic Period*. The Infantile Period extends from birth onwards for approximately the first 3 years.
   1. *Oral Stage*. Extends from birth to 12 or as long as 24 months, and occasionally longer. During this stage the infant is primarily *mouth-oriented*.
      a. *Oral Erotic Phase*. This term and phase refer to the positive, sensual, more pleasurable, and "loving" aspects of the *Oral Stage*.
      b. *Oral Sadistic Phase*. This term and phase refer to the negative, hostile, aggressive, and "retaliatory" aspects of the *Oral Stage*.
   2. *Anal Stage*. Extends from the ninth to the twelfth month, or for as long as 36 months. Awareness of anal function begins and gains prominence personality-wise. Needs for control and mastery of bowel and eliminative function plus the accompanying interpersonal relationships and their vicissitudes, can have significant primordial influences upon personality and character trait development, and upon emotional adjustment.
      a. *Anal Erotic Phase*. Refers to the more pleasurable aspects of the *Anal Stage*.
      b. *Anal Sadistic Phase*. Refers to the more aggressive, hostile, withholding, and manipulative aspects of the *Anal Stage*.

C. **The Oedipal Period.** Also referred to by some as the *Genital Stage, Phallic Stage,* or *Early Childhood*. Extends approximately from the third to the sixth or seventh year. During this period the elaboration of the superego (that is, the conscience) has begun. This receives a great stimulus as the Oedipal situation is resolved.

D. **The Latent Period** or **Middle Childhood.** This period extends from the sixth to the tenth or eleventh year. Actually "latent" is somewhat of a misnomer, insofar as emotional maturity is concerned. The process of psychosexual development is a continuing one and is not latent for any substantial period. Thus apparent latency is likely to be misleading.

E. **The Period of Puberty.** This period extends from the tenth to the thirteenth or fourteenth year.

F. **Adolescence.** The period of "teens." From 13 through 17, to the nineteenth year.

G. **Adulthood.** The stage of relative maturity; the *Heterosexual Stage*. From 17 or 19 years, to senescence.

H. **Senescence.** The onset is individual and quite variable. It begins from age 65 to 85 years or later.

D. DYNAMICS

1. Reversion Under Stress

A. ILLNESS-REGRESSION.—The evolution of regressive manifestations indicates the inability of the individual to continue functioning at the level of maturity which has been achieved. Also indicated is the inability to continue in the present situation as it exists for the person concerned. The presence of certain manifestations usually associated with early years, including the Conflict-Indicators of thumb-sucking, nail-biting, bed-wetting, temper tantrums, and masturbation, can have regressive meanings as we have learned. The symbolism and unconscious significance of these manifestations, whether they are new, continuing, or recurrent, are important, but are often difficult to ascertain.

The reversion to, or recurrence of the emotional manifestations of childhood whether psychic or physical, can occur under various conditions of stress. (*See Case 165.*) The stress can progress to where it becomes too great for the individual to maintain an adult-type adjustment.

The foregoing occurs sometimes in response to the stresses of major physical illness or surgery. This is *Illness-Regression*. Emotional maladjustment or illness may preexist, but does not have to have been major or apparent. Regressive manifestations include the development of hygeiaphrontic preoccupation (overconcern-with-health), but the implications and significance of these phenomena are not necessarily identical.

The following instance illustrates Behavioral Regression. Since it evolved in response to the stress of serious illness, it also comprises Illness-Regression.

Case 166

Illness-Regression

A 67-year-old woman was admitted to the ward of a large city hospital with intestinal carcinoma. She was told the serious nature of the illness. This was a great shock. After trying briefly to deny its existence, she managed to acknowledge it but continued to experience great difficulty in adjustment.

This frightened and desperate woman posed a problem to hospital personnel. She made continuous demands on the staff for bodily comforts. After lying briefly in one position, she would cry out loudly and repeatedly for the nurse, wanting her position changed. She was quite able to move about herself.

Invariably she wanted to be fed. Could she have an apple, or some special item of food? She sought constant attention in a child-like, dependent fashion and complained constantly. Her's was a major instance of *Illness-Regression* following the stress of onset of physical illness, hospitalization, and the shock of recognition of its grave import.

The patient regressed in part to an infantile level. At times her *Behavioral Regression* was reminiscent of the helpless infant, crying to gain attention and care. Following what fortunately proved to be successful surgery and recovery, there was slight improvement behaviorally. Ten months later, assisted by supportive psychotherapy, she had improved considerably. With the severe psychic shock of discovering serious illness, she had become temporarily unable to continue adjusting on an adult level.

B. SEXUAL REGRESSION.—We have outlined several types of Regression. To these we should add that of Sexual Regression. Herein there is a reversion from more typically adult expressions of sexuality to antecedent infantile ones. Sexual manifestations of Regression are varied, sometimes significant, and always of interest.

How is the effectiveness of Regression determined? How is it viewed? Regression may be considered as a vitally needed defense or as a major feature of illness. In the first instance it can represent a necessary gain to the hard-pressed ego.

Regression illustrates the capacity of the psyche under stress to find gratifications and satisfactions at a simpler level when ones of a higher level are not available, or because they would engender too much tension or strain. Regression has also been regarded as one form of *psychologic flight,* through which the person avoids situations in which forbidden impulses and resulting anxiety could be aroused.

Regression describes the surrender by the personality of some level or part of the level of integration, adjustment, and maturity already achieved, as a consequence of intolerable emotional stress. It may be readily manifest to the observer, yet is likely unconscious on the part of the regressing person. We learned that Regression is related to Conversion and its manifestations (pp. 50–51).

With Regression, segments or aspects of the person's behavior and reactions revert to antecedent and more primitive patterns. Regression reflects the psychologic seeking of a more comfortable milieu. In terms of the individual's past experience, Regression is a retreat to the position in development which is "remembered" (unconsciously of course) as providing him the most gratification.

2. To Era of Earlier Gratification

A. DEPENDENCY NEEDS MULTIPLY.—As an attempted means of conflict resolution, we have learned how some individuals, in response to sufficient conflict and stress, unconsciously resort to psychologic, emotional, or behavioral reversion. This is in part or (in certain Major Regressions) whole, to an earlier and less mature level of adjustment than had been subsequently attained. The retreat is toward a prior, more satisfying level, where there were fewer demands and less responsibility.

This psychologic retreat may be symbolic only, or it may be manifested in any one or several of a number of symbolic activities. The retreat is always toward an era in which external emotional sources of supply resulted in gratifications being more readily obtained, or more satisfactory. Dependency needs multiply under stress. In sufficient strength, they demand gratification. Regression contributes to seeking a dependency position. Added minor motivations include those embodied in the *Dependency-Seeking* (p. 338) and *Making-up-for* (p. 352) *Principles.*

B. PSYCHOLOGIC RECAPITULATION ROUTE (PRR) CONCEPT.—Any earlier era may fit the ego's view and needs in Regression. At times there is psychic reversion to a childhood period which was significant because of illness. This can represent an important era of gratification because of the extra care, attention, and love received at such times. Parental worry and concern over health also come to be valued by the child, especially when acceptance or love are lacking.

To the unconscious of course, the physical pain or the symptoms associated with an illness can be less important than its emotional significance. The latter can lead to the recreation of manifestations of an illness on an emotional basis, through Regression. Originally organic in origin, the recapitulation of such symptoms in later years is on a psychologic basis.

To emphasize this pathway for symptom elaboration and psychic influence on their form, character, and locale, this is termed the *Psychologic Recapitulation Route* (or PRR) and *Concept* in the evolvement of symptomatology. See also *Case 171,* pp. 340–1.

In the unconscious endeavor to return to this earlier significant era, various elements associated with the illness, or the time of the illness, can be regressively recapitulated. Herein also, symptom pain can inadvertently fit in with self-punishing, masochistic needs.

In the following case illustrating the PRR, a young woman developed severe fatigue and backaches in an unconscious emotional readoption of the earlier physical symptoms of a serious and prolonged childhood illness. *Case 171,* to follow shortly, has similar PRR features. This type of recurring symptomatology likely represents both the: (1) direct, partial Regression to the earlier level, and (2) an outward expression of the (unconscious) regressive wishes.

Case 167

Regressive Recapitulation of Symptoms of Childhood Illness. The PRR.

A 34-year-old housewife was in psychiatric treatment because of a number of psychologic and physical manifestations. The prominent feature among the latter was distressing back pain in the kidney region. She also suffered from fatigue of such a level as to be at times nearly incapacitating. There were no physical bases for these.

The patient had resisted vigorously the idea of a relationship to emotional factors, as a part of her Secondary Defense (of the symptoms). After she became reconciled to this possibility, we learned that they came on, or were increased, with emotional stress. Eventually, the story of a 14-month childhood bout with kidney infection was elicited. Many of the details, including the pain and the debility, had been "forgotten."

Significantly, during this period she had received the ultimate in care. Her every need was met, her wishes anticipated. She had been pampered in a way reflecting her mother's great concern, although not in a way best designed for her own future interests, from the psychologic viewpoint.

Partially, she unconsciously sought retreat to this more sheltered, protected, and dependent era of her life. At the same time another part of her unconsciously feared and dreaded this desire, fighting to keep it repressed and thus more under control. Its strength and the possibility of its "taking over" were terrible threats. Thus, it was too hazardous. The earlier era was "too good"—i.e., too tempting and thereby too dangerous. The intrapsychic way of trying to cope with this danger was through the Repression of memories and associated feelings.

With stress, there was a greater wish and need for Regression. At these times the repressing forces wore thin, and the repressed wishes threatened to break out into consciousness. Trouble resulted. The symptoms evolved as a partial expression and also represented a Compromise Formation (see p. 454). They comprised a Regression, in addition to being a disguised outward expression of the unconscious regressive wishes. The regressive manifestations, recapitulated through the PRR gradually faded out, with minor recurrences, during the course of therapy.

3. Retreat for Ego Defense

Regression is a return to earlier modes of thought, action, or behavior which takes place in response to urgent inner needs. As an ego defense, its operation is unconscious, as stressed repeatedly. When the individual is unable to cope with his life situation through the employment of familiar and established responses, he reverts to earlier ways of response. As we learned earlier (p. 166) Incorporation is one such primordial pathway to which the hard-pressed ego can revert. Frustration can also contribute to ego defensive Regression. Its main function is that of psychic defense.

In the endeavors of the psyche to cope with otherwise unmanageable stress and to maintain ego integrity, the ego, making use of Regression, retreats to less mature responses. Regression comprises a retreat, undertaken by the ego in its defense.

4. Advance at Cost of Regression-Retreat

Regression may sometimes be viewed as an example of failing compensation, or as an evidence of an *emotional decompensation,* a concept earlier formulated. The partial failure to maintain one's integration in the face of the untoward consequences of one's strivings and conflicts may thus in part be relieved through "permitting" the psyche to slip back into earlier, easier, more comfortable, and less responsible ways.

Sometimes an advance in one area of personality development or maturity is achieved at the cost of Regression in another. A person achieving considerable success in a profession (his ability to do this is usually an evidence of maturity) may have foregone various social obligations, civic duties, or other responsibilities indicative of maturity. This principle was illustrated in an instance of Childhood Regression, *Case 164.*

Regression arises through the inability of the ego to cope with otherwise intolerable problems of reality. Thus, having achieved a more mature state of adjustment, the hard-pressed psyche faced with such stress relinquishes involuntarily some of its advances, and returns to a more immature and infantile level.

We have noted that Regression may be partial, when the psyche so requires. Further inability to resolve conflicts and stress may lead to more complete Regression. This brings us to the following topic.

5. Complete or Total Regression

We have observed the uniqueness of Regression as a defensive process. Its difference from other mental mechanisms is one of a kind and extent. We have viewed it as an ego operation, in which the ego plays an active role in the retreat which takes place, as well as occupying a passive position. It is a response of the ego to stress (overwhelming stress in the case of Major Regression), as well as something which happens to it.

It can be a partial response, especially in Minor and what we term *Temporary Regressions.* It is also sometimes a *Complete* or *Total Regression,* a gross process in which the entire ego organization regresses. The latter theoretically can progress to the extent or level of a pre-ego state of personality development.

Fenichel observed also that the role played by the ego in Regression is different from the part it plays in other defense mechanisms. Most dynamisms are set in motion by the ego. Regression happens to the ego. At times Regression is precipitated by unconscious needs and strivings which have been blocked from more direct satisfaction. A precondition for the evolvement of Regression as a defensive mechanism is an individual weakness of the ego organization.

When the individual concerned is sufficiently blocked and thwarted, he may turn again to the mechanisms and conditions of adjustment that were existant in some given and more successful phase of his earlier development. There is a resulting retreat in part to this earlier phase as subjectively recalled and evaluated by the psyche. For the purpose of Regression, essentially only a favorable era of childhood is significant and so recalled and in effect reactivated.

E. FIXATION

1. Any Level

There is a close relationship between Fixation and Regression. We would define Fixation as *a more or less complete arrest, or cessation of personality development at some given level.* Fixation may be temporary, semipermanent, or continue unchanged. The same bases which lead to Regression can also determine a fixation of maturation.

Fixations take place at any level or stage of psychosexual development and maturation. They are far more likely to be partial than complete. Their duration is quite variable as noted, all the way from the very transient to those which are apparently permanent.

2. *Law of Maturity*

Fixation, although closely allied to Regression, also differs significantly from it, in that Fixation describes *an arrest or cessation of personality development;* while Regression conveys the meaning of a return to a former phase. Both Fixation and Regression take place as defenses in response to emotional stress. The normal pattern of personality development is in the overall direction of growth, progression, and increasing maturation. See earlier *Tidal-Progression Concept.*

Fixation and Regression represent interruptions of the normal pattern. The *Law of Maturation* states that other things being equal, *the state of maturity steadily advances, so as to move progressively forward over any reasonable given period of time.*

Fixation can have its interesting illustrations at any phase or stage of psychosexual development. Not infrequently, Fixations take place in the teen-age and preadult stages. The concept of a fixation-arrest is generally thought of in conjunction with some particular phase of maturation which is likely to be an uneven process, as we have learned.

3. *Types of Fixation*

Fixation may be *Temporary, Semipermanent,* or *Permanent.* In certain additional instances it is as though the personality encounters an area of more stubborn emotional opposition in its progress, which is only gradually passed through over the course of years.

The following example illustrates several important points. This man developed an emotional Fixation at what was approximately a college sophomore level, lasting over the course of 5 years. There had been little progression. This was a Semipermanent type of *Maturation-Fixation.* During the course of considerable intensive therapy, he was gradually able to gain a clearer picture of himself, with resulting substantial improvement.

Case 168

Maturation-Fixation

(1) *Undergraduate Athletic and Social Success.* A young college student was quite popular, and usually commanded the social center of attention with ease. He had received publicity as one of the nation's top athletes and was showered with honors in two sports.

Attendance at Princeton represented the achievement of a cherished dream. He was raised in an industrial area near Chicago and, by dint of hard work in school and on the athletic field, won a scholarship.

(2) *A Pattern Evolves.* During 4 college years, little fazed him, although academic interests and successes left something to be desired. Following graduation, he secured a position with a leading brokerage firm in New York.

For the first few months, no one saw him back at school; then with increasing frequency he turned up for weekends. As the months passed, he began spending some week days at school. With succeeding visits he enjoyed drinking more heavily. His time was spent with old friends from the football team and club. With these groups he would "perk up" and become the "life of the party." Soon, however, everyone else would have to get back to his duties. He would sulk about for a day or so, and finally head back to New York.

This behavior established a pattern which persisted for several years. There were many factors contributing to his Fixation. His position in the firm was at the bottom of the pile. His co-workers were hard working young men, anxious to get ahead. It became apparent that he was judged on the basis of his value to the company. In order to have the stature of previous years, he must lift himself to the top of the heap by proving himself in the new arena of business. This was easier said than done.

Emotionally, he was not capable of developing fast enough to meet the demands of his abruptly changed situation. The maturing influences of college had been largely lost to him for a number of reasons. The achievements that enabled him to be such a success in college no longer counted substantially in the business world. The disappointments and frustration were considerable.

(3) *Fixation at Point of Success.* His response was a Fixation to that period of life where he had his happiest, most successful, and satisfying days. Its effect, of course, tended to be self-defeating, since the more he relied on his attempt to hang on to this past, the less chance for business success. This illustrated the Vicious Circle of Self-Defeat Concept, often to be observed in conjunction with emotional difficulties.

With further study it turned out that each of the longer "sprees" at college were preceded by some work failure. His emotional maturation had not developed past that of a college sophomore and was not capable of serving him adequately in graduate life. Fixation as a mode of defense sought to make his failures more tolerable and to help allay the resulting anxiety. His adjustment improved substantially during the course of a difficult and prolonged analysis.

The following instance has considerable similarity. Although details are lacking in regard to the dynamics of the Fixation, the presence of the phenomenon is reasonably clear. Some of the consequences of this instance of partially fixated maturation through the years are evident and others can be surmised.

This unfortunate man had no interest in psychotherapy, and would have presented a difficult therapeutic problem, had it proved possible to secure interest. This was an instance of the more permanent type of partially arrested development.

Case 169

Fixation at College Level

Beginning with their freshman year as college students, several classmates attending the social functions, football games, dances, and fraternity parties, made an observation in common. At most of these affairs, one person was generally more boisterous than the rest. His behavior was less controlled and he tended to be more intoxicated and rowdy than others. He created the impression of being a conspicuous nuisance. The remarkable thing about this was that he happened to be a grey-haired, middle-aged individual. On appearance alone, he would have been taken for a responsible and sedate business man.

On one occasion, one of the students having the opportunity, asked him how he could come to these functions. He replied, "Son, my wife thinks I am crazy, but I'll always be a college man at heart!" As the conversation continued, it was soon apparent that he had been a college hero, campus social light, and football star.

This man had never been able to cope with an adult society, which would accept or reject him on the basis of more adult merits. He had become in part fixated at the college level of his development, at a stage in which he had been happy and secure.

There is considerable variety in the degree of Regression. Thus Regression by no means necessarily proceeds to the infantile stage. Regarding the actions of human beings as though they were actors on a stage, Menninger remarked that "there are certain other felicitous phases (from prior experience) which the actors are prone to recall, and there is an everpresent propensity to lapse into the older and easier situations instead of proceeding with newer and harder ones. The actors, finding the real words and acts of their parts difficult, substitute false lines."

". . . .Actors whose parts were played long since, and who should have left the stage, may force their way back, so that the play, instead of proceeding with the third act, let us say, reverts to a clumsy anachronistic reproduction of Act I." Clinging to infantilism through Fixation or regressing to infantile modes of expression and behavior can proceed to alarming extremes, giving way ultimately to emotional illnesses of various types.

F.   REGRESSION IN EMOTIONAL ILLNESS

1. The Regression-Gauge. Pathologic Regressions

A. IN EVERY ILLNESS.—Regression is present in some measure at least in every emotional illness. This varies from subtle regressive changes in behavior, emotional reactions, or attitudes, to the kinds of Major Regression which can be encountered in the severe psychotic reactions.

We have observed that the level of Regression and how thoroughly it is operative are individually widely variable. On the other hand, the relationship between the extent of Regression and the severity of the illness in which it is present may well be one of direct proportion. This however, is not invariable. Likewise, the level and extent of Regression is not necessarily a good index as to the prognosis of a given illness.

One may observe acute psychotic episodes which are relatively short-lived, in which regressive behavior has been marked. On the other hand, the relative presence and extent of this psychologic retreat can occasionally serve as what we term a *Regression-Gauge;* (1) in indicating the depth of certain psychoses or neuroses.

This Gauge may also see service in measuring: (2) the impact and the effects of stress; a person's vulnerability in a given stressful situation; (3) the progress of therapy and the prognosis, particularly in the psychoses; and (4) the general effectiveness of other intrapsychic defense mechanisms. (See also p. 345 for number 5.)

B. EVIDENCE OF ILLNESS.—Regressions represent a return to an earlier simpler, safer, or more satisfying era. They may be a symptom or a signal of pathology. Only when they become exaggerated, excessive, or self-defeating can they be regarded as evidence of illness. These criteria however delineate what we refer to accordingly as *Pathologic Regressions*.

Although in many neurotic reactions, Regression is not apparent, regressive tendencies, or their close cousin Fixation, can be regarded as everpresent to some extent in emotional illnesses. It is so widespread a feature that space must allow us a few comments and illustrations.

2. In Neuroses

A. DEPENDENCY-SEEKING PRINCIPLE.—Regression is a major ego defense. It is a psychologic retreat. In the large group of neurotic reactions we have found it convenient and useful clinically to regard Regression as a dependency-seeking process. This is in accord with what is named the *Dependency-Seeking Principle* in the inner motivation to regress. Through it the harassed ego seeks a less exposed and more dependent position. Dependency needs are gratified. It is related to our earlier Concept of the Ultimate-Dependency-Goal (pp. 332 and 352).

According to the Dependency-Seeking Principle (DSP) *earlier unsatisfied or rekindled dependency needs from the earliest years or new ones, seek gratification.* These are likely to have been repressed, to lie apparently dormant, until the stimulus of new threat or tension comes along. Careful observation is likely to reveal regressive trends in every type and instance of neurotic reaction.

B. PHOBIC REGRESSION.—Accordingly we expect to find regressive manifestations in the neuroses. Among these, it is not too startling to find that a specific Phobic Reaction may be regressive, or may indicate regressive wishes. In the following interesting instance the symptom represented elements in the conflict over repressed dependent needs and over secret regressive longings. The DSP was operative. In condensed fashion, vomiting symbolized for this patient the longed-for state of being dependent, and in defense against this, in reversed fashion, it became the object of a phobia.

This phobic manifestation served partially to deny the unconscious wishes, and to aid in their Repression. One learns upon studying the dynamics of phobias that *the object of dread and fear (or what it symbolically represents) is at the same time secretly (unconsciously) sought after and longed for.* (See Chapters 9 and 10 *The Phobic Reactions,* pp. *515–607,* in *The Neuroses.*) This is the so-called *Phobic Dilemma.* This double attitude toward the phobic object also prevailed in the following instance.

Case 170

The Role of Regression in a Phobic Reaction

(1) *Phobia Defends Against Dependency Strivings.* A 31-year-old housewife had four children in rapid succession. Coping with their care and management became increasingly difficult. The development of serious marital conflicts in addition proved too much. The onset of an emotional illness followed, in which a phobia of vomiting was a prominent feature.

During the course of intensive and prolonged psychotherapeutic study, this eventually proved to be an expression in condensed, symbolic, and reversed form of desperately strong but consciously disowned needs for dependency. It was the only expression permitted outwardly of her regressive trends. These were rekindled and exaggerated in response to emotional stress.

(2) *Contributions by Anxious Parent.* She had been overprotected and sheltered throughout childhood and later, by an anxious mother, herself insecure and unable to love her child. The overconcern had served as a substitute for acceptance and love, but accordingly had been still more sought after and more valued by the child.

The mother said admonishingly, over and over again, such things as, "Don't do too much or you'll be ill . . ." "Don't eat that; it might make you sick . . ." "Be careful of swinging, so you don't get sick . . ."

When the child became ill, mother was terribly frightened. An upset stomach or the child's "throwing up" during a childhood illness was anathema, and would stimulate all manner of anxious concerns.

(3) *Reversal of Secret Wish to Be Ill.* Her position of great dependence was consciously abhorrent to the child, although also the subject of tremendous inner conflict. When pressures became too great in later life, a return to this earlier era was secretly longed for. The Dependency-Seeking Principle was operative.

Her outward dread of vomiting, on a deeper level represented in reversed fashion her secret wish to be sick; i.e., to secure the dependent position and anxious concern which would gain this for her. Coming closer in therapy to recognition of the meaning of her symptom, one day she exclaimed with great feeling, "I really want to be sick, so mother will take over . . . will take care of me! . . . ."

C. HYGEIAPHRONTIS, PHOBIA, DELUSION, AND DEPRESSION.—The foregoing type of symptom, with its regressive implications, is likely to be found only in more marked cases. Another similar but more serious instance is recalled from clinical experience. Herein phobic formation had progressed into hygeiaphrontic delusion, illustrating the interrelations which can exist between phobia, hygeiaphrontis (hypochondriasis), depression, and delusion evolvement.

The dread and fear of syphilitic infection and resulting paresis had become a horrible and intolerable "established fact" to a 47-year-old machinist. Repeated negative clinical and laboratory studies failed to be reassuring. He was on the verge of suicide for several months. His phobic-hygeiaphrontic state sought to serve a number of unconscious purposes, including the regressive seeking of a dependent position, in accord with the DSP and similar to the above instance. To an extent this was achieved, as he became helpless, unable to work, and required great care for a 9-month period.

Suffering from an illness of psychotic depth, this patient was treated extra-murally. He made an excellent recovery with 18 months of intensive psychotherapy. This was a fortunate and gratifying outcome. He has remained well since.

In the neurotic reactions and in the character neuroses we find, as noted, that Regression is usually far less evident although it occurs. It is also far less marked than in this instance, or as it can be in the psychoses more generally. Let us consider briefly several additional types of neurotic regression.

D. CONVERSION REGRESSION.—There is a strong potential for Regression in the Conversion Personality. When character traits of this particular personality constellation are present, regressive trends can be expected, especially if emotional illness should impend. In general, persons of this personality grouping are less mature, with ego defenses of a less advanced order. With personality development less organized, perhaps more loosely organized, Regression sometimes seems to take place more readily.

In the Conversion Reactions (hysteria), this process of ego defense is almost to be expected. The gross Somatic Conversions are usually regressive, and the determination of the form these will take is contributed to by unconscious dependency wishes. The trait of suggestibility is important. The PRR can help determine symptom type, form, and locale.

In the following instance of Conversion Reaction, regressive factors entered into the unwitting selection and psychic elaboration of headaches, fatigue, and oversleeping as major presenting symptoms. These represented the conversion of unconscious conflict into physical symptoms and illustrate Conversion Regression. In condensed and symbolic fashion, life was a tremendous headache to this woman, as was her marriage, the responsibilities of her family, and her adult role.

The illness and the symptoms thereby also represented unconscious regressive wishes for a return (the PRR in symptom elaboration) to the dependent position of her childhood at around age 11, plus the conflict over this. The DSP was very much in evidence. There are interesting similarities to the preceding *Case 167*.

Case 171

Regression and Conflicts over Dependency

(1) *Interest in Therapy Enlisted.* A 34-year-old housewife entered treatment following a suicidal attempt. She had suffered from excruciating conversion headaches for 18 months, for which she had undergone exhaustive but negative medical studies and treatment. Other major symptoms included severe *Emotional Fatigue*,[1] fatiguability, and oversleeping.

Initially, this patient had little interest in therapy, as a staunch resistance and secondary defense of her symptoms. Fortunately it proved

---

[1] Presumptively present when there is a level of subjective fatigue present which is out of proportion to the amount of physical and mental effort expended. See also Chapter 7, *The Fatigue Reactions* in *The Neuroses*, pp. 379–441.

gradually possible to enlist her active interest and participation. Psychiatric treatment extended over several years, during which understanding of the symptoms was gradually gained and their resolution secured.

(2) *Dependent Status Regained.* In childhood at age 10 to 11 she suffered a long debilitating illness marked by fever, overwhelming lassitude, repeated severe headaches, and the receipt of great care and solicitude from many, especially including that from a devoted aunt who hardly left her side. Much of this had been "forgotten" by the child.

". . . . It seems so strange that I remember so little of that!" This was at first glance surprising, in view of an otherwise very excellent memory. ". . . . As much as I loved Aunt Helen, I didn't even remember that she was there!" ". . . . I didn't recall at all having headaches or the tiredness until Mother talked about them with me . . . now it begins to come back. . . ."

Although she finally came to remember the illness and many details, the haziest features in her recall had to do with the dependency gratifications received, and the symptom features which were unwittingly recapitulated in her adult sickness. In effect, *these were too good to remember!* Along with her dependent needs, these memories had been repressed. Their recall might stimulate an already too dangerous craving.

Through Regression the longed-for state was to an extent, however self-defeating, unconsciously regained through illness. The present symptoms had followed the Psychologic Recapitulation Route in their evolvement, as earlier outlined. (See pp. 332–3.)

(3) *Aunt Helen's Engrossing Project.* To help understand the nature of the conflict, one must appreciate the impact of the early serious illness on the child, and appreciate the tremendous amount of attention and care received by her. ". . . . It was not just Aunt Helen. . . . Everything I wanted during those months was done. . . . From everything Mother has told me, I must have been terrifically spoiled. . . . Many gifts came to me—sometimes as many as 8 to 10 a day! . . . some even from strangers. A great deal was done for me by people we scarcely even knew . . . and Aunt Helen constantly hovering over me, to do anything she could. . . ."

She had become a special project for her teachers and classmates, and the family doctor "never missed a day." As one measure of her aunt's devotion, the latter broke a long-standing mutual compact with a girlhood friend—to come and stand by whoever became ill—in order to remain with the child. During her niece's illness, the friend became ill and died. Despite terrific conflicts over her obligation, the aunt did not budge from the child's bedside. She had become Aunt Helen's special and all engrossing project in life.

(4) *Symptoms Influenced by Regressive Needs.* As the earlier illness subsided, one medical consultant reportedly said, "There is nothing wrong with her now except too much mother, father, and Aunt Helen. . . . Let her live a normal life!"

Regression to the earlier dependent phase represented a retreat to a less exposed and safer haven. Secretly longed for, these needs became too strong for continued containment under the stress of increased family responsibilities and conflicts. Her illness ensued, with its nature and symptoms determined in part by her unconscious regressive needs along the PRR and her deep conflicts over dependency.

E. HYPNOTIC REGRESSION.—Under hypnosis, with a "good" subject, various levels of Regression can be induced. This interesting phenomenon has been discussed elsewhere (see p. 821, *The Neuroses*). Interesting experiments can be conducted through this medium, although all necessary care and safeguards must be taken for the welfare of the subject.

Hypnosis is not a toy. A serious potential for adverse effects exists at the hands of the beginner or the less perceptive and understanding operator.

F. DEPRESSIVE REACTIONS.— Regressive trends can be found in most cases of neurosis, although as noted they may not be nearly so marked nor as potentially understandable in illnesses of this level. Unconscious secondary gains (epigain) are present in the depressive illnesses. There may be some degree of Regression present, extending back to early oral levels in the more severe cases, with an implied appeal for the dependence that is customary in infancy.

In these severest of Emotional Depressions, it is as if the individual were pleading: "Look at me; I'm absolutely helpless. I have to be taken care of and looked after." Thus, in the Regression which occurs, the patient unconsciously seeks attention, sympathy, love, solace, affection and protection.

G. FATIGUE STATES.—In the Fatigue States and Neurasthenia, the patient unwittingly becomes placed in a less responsible position, in a more passive one. Insofar as this is sought after unconsciously, emotional fatigue and the Fatigue States are manifestations of Regression. This was illustrated also in *Case 171*.

The unconscious attempt is made via the symptoms to return to the dependent and protected position of early childhood. From this point of view, the Fatigue State especially can represent in toto a regressive kind of retreat.

H. HYGEIAPHRONTIS. VICIOUS CIRCLE OF SELF-DEFEAT CONCEPT IN NEUROSES.—Overconcern-with-Health or preferably Hygeiaphrontis (hypochondriasis), may also represent, at least in part, an unconscious regressive retreat toward a more dependent position. This can result in a type of character formation which might be called the Hygeiaphrontic Personality as outlined elsewhere, in which there is exhibited preoccupation with self and function, regressive trends, and perhaps also some social seclusiveness. This type of Character Reaction or the corresponding neurosis can be regarded as a psychologic retreat—into somatic and physiologic self-absorption. When this occurs, it is of varying degree.

The resulting withdrawal of interests from external objects is unconscious and regressive. However, the casual observer may interpret it merely as egotism and self-centeredness. Thus, the Hygeiaphrontic Personality may, in self-defeating fashion, secure the very reverse of the love and affection that he craves. There can result a tragically vicious circle of increased need for love with more narcissism, followed by more rejection, which stimulates more need, and so on. This outlines the *Concept of the Vicious Circle of Self-Defeat in the Neuroses* referred to earlier.

The regressive trends which occur in sick people become a familiar part of hospital experience. *Case 166* was an example. Their proper recognition, understanding, and management can make the difference between an average nurse or intern and an outstanding one. A correlation between level of Regression and severity of illness is not necessary. The following exaggerated instance is one which is not infrequently encountered, albeit usually in far more subtle forms in most medical experience.

Case 172

Somatic Preoccupation (Hygeiaphrontis)

A young male patient on a medical ward had been hospitalized for a relatively minor intercurrent infection. His was a better than average level of intelligence. His diction denoted superior education. Despite these presumed assets, which have little or no bearing on the relative presence or nature of emotional conflicts or upon the level of emotional maturity, he was for a time the most difficult patient on the ward. This was not a reflection of the physical severity of his illness.

He sought attention and being cared for so desperately as to make himself *persona non grata,* and to ensure the defeat of such dependency needs. He complained incessantly about every facet of his hospital existence, no matter how trivial. Given the opportunity, he would describe in microscopic detail innumerable subjective complaints. His constant dwelling on aches and pains led the ward personnel to recognize how much he relished the attention his behavior sought to elicit. His attitudes differed greatly from those of his pre-illness make-up. While quite out of keeping with his more usual self, they did not seem incongruous to him.

"Attention-seeking" was too superficial and casual a label to apply to this young man. On a deeper level he was seeking to satisfy desperately urgent dependency needs. While he made a nuisance of himself, his behavior was symptomatic, and an indicator of powerful regressive trends. It was the outward manifestation of an unconscious retreat toward an earlier and subjectively more satisfying and secure milieu. Following his recovery his earlier adjustment level gradually reasserted itself. This was a Temporary Regression.

I. OBSESSIVE-COMPULSIVE REACTION.— Regressive trends are likely to be more deeply buried in the Obsessive-Compulsive group of neuroses. When this type of defense breaks down as inadequate, under overwhelming conflictual stress, and a psychotic reaction ensues, a Major Regression may occur.

Fenichel commented on the role of Regression in this type of neurosis. The compulsive neurotic patient, ". . . experiences a conflict between his phallic oedipal wishes and his castration fear, substitutes anal-sadistic wishes (remnants of childhood) for his oedipal demands. . . ." In this manner Regression is a means of defense. In other words, unresolved oedipal conflicts are "exchanged" for antecedent ones.

J. NEUROSES-FOLLOWING-TRAUMA.—Neurotic illnesses following upon trauma are more or less clearly regressive in character. Often there is an appeal, although it may be wholly unconscious, for dependency. The ego, having had a desperate blow in its attempt to cope with the environment, retreats to an antecedent state that is more comfortable, that relieves it from tension and strain.

It always must be borne in mind of course that such Regression is involuntary, that it is entirely beyond conscious awareness. It is a special type of ego defense, a process in which the ego stages a strategic withdrawal and retreat.

3. Massive Regression

A. PSYCHOTIC REACTION A REGRESSION.—The most marked examples of *Complete* or *Massive Regression* are to be observed in cases of psychotic illness. Psychoses are regressive processes. Here the total behavior can come to approximate any preceding level, including the very early infantile. In hallucinations the person regresses to primitive forms of perception (p. 69). Psychoses are often Major Regressions, in which the ego as a whole retreats. Beyond the psychotic *breaking point* behavior frequently regresses.

Conduct which would not be considered abnormal or inappropriate in children may be regarded as quite inappropriate, or as an evidence of illness, in the adult. A psychotic reaction can represent a massive psychologic retreat, withdrawal, flight, or a way of hiding from the current situation, and from life itself. A psychotic reaction can also in itself constitute a Regression. (See also p. 170.)

B. PROGRESSIVE DEVELOPMENT IN SCHIZOPHRENIA.—During the onset of a psychosis, the evolution of the illness is sometimes reflected in the progressive adoption of regressive behavior. This is illustrated in the following instance, in which Massive Regression took place in a severe schizophrenic type of psychotic reaction.

Case 173

Major Regression in Schizophrenia

(1) *Adjustment Crumbles.* A 25-year-old woman had been having increasing difficulty carrying out her responsibilities as a wife and mother of two small children. There were all kinds of major emotional conflicts. Finally, things reached a point where she could no longer continue. Emotional symptoms began. Her adjustment began to crumble.

As these manifestations progressed, she spent an increasing amount of time sleeping. She neglected her household chores and found herself unable to discuss problems with her husband. Following an argument, she would cry for hours and behave childishly in various ways.

(2) *Regression Deepens.* This situation became progressively worse over the succeeding months. Her contact with reality became more and more tenuous. She became unable to care for her home. Her time was spent playing with dolls, "playing house," eating candy and lollipops in preference to food. She came to consider her children in semidelusional fashion as "playmates." At other times, she was withdrawn and uncommunicative.

On occasion, when her husband tried to locate her, she would hide under a table or behind a chair. At other times she would play childlike games. She grimaced and laughed inappropriately. This reaction comprised a *Massive Regression.*

(3) *Prolonged Hospitalization with Limited Treatment Resources.* This patient was very sick emotionally and was hospitalized, with the diagnosis of Schizophrenia, hebephrenic type.

As the psychotic reaction became established, she had steadily regressed in many respects, so that a considerable proportion of her behavior approximated that of the 3- to 4-year-old level. After several years, sadly she had shown little response to the very limited therapeutic resources available at the state mental hospital. The Massive Regression continued with little change while observation was possible.

C. INFANTILE PATTERNS READOPTED.—The above case provides us with an excellent example of the *Massive* or *Complete Regression*. It also fits into the categories of the *Psychotic Regression* and the *Major Regression*. One observes how it can lead to an actual and literal return to infantile modes of behavior and living. Psychotic patients may become feeding problems. They can become incontinent in bowel and bladder function.

Clothes may be discarded. Relationships with others can approach those of the level of early childhood or infancy. Destructive, explosive, and assaultive behavior, including occasional instances of murder, can take place, as the restrictive bonds of inhibition and learned social convention are lost in the psychotic process.

D. ASSESSMENT VALUABLE.—Sometimes drawing lines of distinction between a neurotic and a psychotic reaction may be aided by an assessment of the Regression. This is another important application (number five) of our Regression-Gauge. (See p. 337.) Thus, in psychotic depressions the Regression is ordinarily more apparent, more complete, and more drastic than in neurotic depressions. (See also *Table 10*, p. 147 in *The Neuroses*.)

The level of Regression does not necessarily remain unchanged in the psychotic patient. It can seem adamant to change. On the other hand, regressive manifestations can advance or recede as to number and level, dependent upon a number of factors. Their recession is generally a favorable sign and can indicate progress in therapy, in accord with the Regression-Gauge Concept.

In the following instance, a psychologic retreat to a lower level took place temporarily as the regressive response to the vacation of a staff member.

Case 174

A Psychotic Regression Increases

A 26-year-old chronically ill schizophrenic patient had been hospitalized for nearly 10 years. During this time she was withdrawn and seclusive. She talked infrequently, preferring to be alone, and showing fright and even panic when approached. Generally, she was easy to manage, the only difficulty being occasional marked regressive traits including incontinence and infantile behavior. She was typical of the tragic long-standing "back-ward" case of schizophrenic psychosis.

Two years earlier a young resident psychiatrist had begun to take an active interest in her. He began visiting her daily, seeking to interest her in activities. Gradually and very slowly, the patient became more alert and interested. Regressive manifestations receded and became less frequent. She began going to OT and worked on simple projects. To those who knew her, the changes were substantial.

Although the patient had never openly indicated any attachment for or feeling toward the therapist, these became quite apparent when the latter took a 2-week vacation. In spite of trying to prepare the patient she began regressing immediately. Under the stress of separation from the only person she had had any relationship with in years, the patient again became incontinent, played with feces, and withdrew from social contacts. She would not eat unless spoon fed, and paid no attention to personal needs. She needed, in fact, as much caring for as an infant, to which level she had again regressed. Assessment of the Behavioral Regression as a Regression-Gauge provided a good indication of the status of her illness.

Two months after the return of the physician, she had once more regained her earlier achieved level of adjustment. Progress continued slowly thereafter.

G. REGRESSION AND THERAPY

1. Concept of Tidal-Progression

In analogous fashion to the *Tidal-Progression of Personality Development* and *Maturation* (p. 324), the progress of therapeutic understanding and emotional adjustment is likewise uneven. This too can have its ups and downs, and these are to be expected in a significant *Concept of Tidal-Progression in Therapeutic Progress*.

Thus Regression not surprisingly, is occasionally to be encountered during the course of treatment. Sometimes it takes interesting or bizarre forms. Often these are Minor Regressions and are of brief duration.

In the following instance, a regressive feature developed during the course of intensive psychotherapy. Herein it appeared to be evidence of the reluctance to move ahead. Serving as a resistance to further insight and progress in treatment, the manifestations comprise a *Resistance Regression*. It accordingly aided in the Secondary Defense of the symptoms and supported the *status quo* of the character structure and the neurosis (i.e., the *neurotic status quo* as earlier noted).

Case 175

A Regressive Episode in Therapy

(1) *Crucial Juncture Creates Stress.* A 36-year-old single patient from a learned profession was in his third year of successful analysis. He had reached a point where certain major issues had become clarified for him, pointing clearly to the need for some important changes in his attitudes. He struggled indecisively for some time on the brink of a move toward increased maturity. This was a crucial juncture, with considerable resulting stress.

One day he hesitantly reported some difficulty with bowel control. At seemingly unaccountable moments his anal sphincter would relax involuntarily. A small amount of fecal material would be extruded. This caused him considerable discomfort and embarrassment over a period of 3 or 4 weeks. Rather significantly, this occurred on several occasions during the course of therapy sessions.

(2) *Highlights Reluctance to Progress.* This was a regressive phenomenon, reflecting his reluctance to move ahead. As he became able to analyze it, he was saying in effect, "You see, I can't take this step that I think I should. It's too much to expect. . . . See how really helpless and infantile I still am . . . I need to be taken care of more, instead of assuming more responsibility myself!" This regressive feature highlighted his feelings of helplessness and reluctance to progress further. It symbolized his otherwise hidden regressive needs and served as a Resistance Regression.

"Further, through my Regression I will to this extent return to the better, earlier level, where so many things were not expected of me . . .

when I didn't have to be grown up, when people looked out for me. . . .
Through my childish difficulty, I demonstrate my helplessness to change
my ways. . . . You and I can't possibly expect me to really 'grow
up'! . . ."

2. Dependency Gratification

A. OVERDEPENDENCY FEARED.—It has been recognized that Regression can play a role in the recovery of certain patients from serious emotional disorders. For a number of individuals, a degree of dependency gratification by the therapist can be very useful, with the necessary proviso, of course, that the therapist is thoroughly aware of what transpires in the treatment situation.

There is widespread uneasiness in professional circles over the possible development of overdependency. Many fear that allowing a temporary source of external emotional supplies to become important is quite hazardous. This is largely based on the fear that this might set up an inimical pattern that the patient would be unable or unwilling to relinquish. At times the fear is a reflection of strong unconscious dependency needs of the therapist, and his uncertainty, conflicts, and fears about this personal area.

B. TREND TOWARD EMOTIONAL HEALTH CONCEPT.—In accord with a favorite conception of the author, there is however, a certain basic and counteracting overall *Trend Toward Emotional Health* operative for people generally. With any encouragement, this will aid in the individual progress toward independence and maturity. However, some therapists, as a consequence of their concern over fostering undue dependency lean far over backwards so as not to provide external support.

To establish just the proper balance between need and supply (as may be possible to provide), and to develop the sensitive and discriminating kind of judgment to be of optimal value in this respect, is of course one of many difficult requirements for the therapist. There are no hard and fast rules, no convenient road markers. One essential is that the therapist himself be reasonably mature and emotionally stable. This is in addition to thorough training and experience.

When these assets are present, there is little danger to be feared from overdependency. In most instances, with some degree of accuracy, he can decide upon the optimum course to pursue for his patient's best interests. One therapeutic modality would maintain a rigid withholding of dependency gratification, a second might allow a certain rationed allowance, and a third avoid any so vigorously as to present a cold and hard front to the patient.

3. Regression Treatment

A. EARLY UNMET NEEDS FILLED.—As a logical progression from the preceding comments, we can hypothecate another approach in therapy which would lean over the other way from the midline. Herein dependency needs would be purposely gratified insofar as feasible and possible, and Regression would be allowed or even encouraged. This approach sometimes finds application in various degrees or modifications in the treatment of the neuroses.

In the therapy of the psychoses, the employment of a more active dependency gratification and the encouragement of Regression is at times possible and is more frequently employed. Its rationale is based upon the theory that the foundations for the most severe types of psychotic reactions are laid down in the first years of life. In what we call *Regression Treatment,* the emotional needs of the patient which were not met during the early crucial years are made up for, insofar as possible. This is through the combined efforts of the therapist, the hospital, and the therapeutic milieu. The so-called therapeutic community can contribute substantially. In Regression Treatment, marked Regression is permitted and accepted, or actively encouraged, as in the following case:

Case 176

Regression Treatment in a Psychotic Reaction

An 18-year-old-girl was admitted to a mental hospital with typical symptoms of an acute Schizophrenic Reaction. She was untidy, mute, heard voices, gestured and grimaced, would not dress herself, and sometimes required forced feeding. In many respects her level of adjustment had regressed to the 18-month age level. She was chosen for a trial at *Regression Treatment,* as an instance of a difficult therapeutic problem with little progress otherwise.

Nurse, therapist, and attendants were selected on the basis of their expressed interest in an experimental program, and their capacity to fill a parental-like (primarily a mothering) role. Instead of encouraging behavior more appropriate to her age, every assistance and help which she could accept was made freely available. To feed or dress her was welcomed by staff members. Care was not given grudgingly, or in any way disapprovingly. What was asked was provided in a cheerful and (insofar as possible) affectionate manner. Actually what were to an extent at first their deliberate and conscious efforts to be fond, were fortunately followed by the gradual development of genuine fondness by the staff members concerned. They came to more adequately and genuinely appreciate the psychologically hard-pressed position of this patient, and her lack of responsibility for her illness and its manifestations.

During 3 months of intensive therapy, complete dependency gratification, and the tacit encouragement of Regression, the patient took the initial steps in renouncing some of these, after an early period of accepting them completely. Improvement increased in speed. With the inevitable reverses, another 5 months found her greatly improved and about ready for discharge home. Continued intensive psychotherapy on a private basis along more conventional lines continued subsequently, with further substantial improvement in her emotional adjustment.

B. BOWEN'S APPROACH.—Bowen introduced and applied an interesting and more positively regressive kind of treatment approach. Related to the foregoing, his method goes much further. In it the patient's Regression is considerably more actively encouraged. He has enjoyed substantial success in several noteworthy instances, including one or more in which the person concerned was chronically and nearly hopelessly habituated to alcohol. His regime is based upon the further refinement of certain interesting theoretical considerations about Regression.

Accordingly, certain patients maintain a minimal level of social adjustment only through the expenditure of great psychic energy. Even minor stresses can force them to employ psychotic defenses in order to preserve a semblance of emotional equilibrium. One psychologic treatment design employed wittingly or not by many in the therapy of the psychoses would "engraft" the ego of the therapist on the weakened ego of the patient. A more common and alternative treatment design would strengthen the weakened ego with a supportive relationship, while the ego reassembles preexisting or new defenses and strength. The first treatment design takes over and forces help, while the second makes help available.

This brings us to still another, and third treatment design which may be used occasionally by experienced therapists in those hospital settings which are able to permit a maximum of time and attention to one patient. This removes the patient from as much external expectation and responsibility as possible. At the same time it provides as much support as the patient can utilize. This milieu and treatment approach which not merely allows but actively encourages Regression has been named *Regressive Therapy.*

C. MAXIMAL SUPPORT.—Ideally, the overall therapeutic environment in Bowen's Regressive Therapy should meet the needs of the developmental level to which the patient can "allow" himself to regress, during the course of his treatment. It should be maintained as long as the patient has the need for and can permit the Regression.

As noted, some psychiatrists believe the patient consciously wants the Regression (and that the physician ought, in more usual circumstances, to stand against it). Some hospitalized psychotic patients in a severely regressed state may present a picture conveying this impression. This has not been the invariable experience. The reverse can be observed in those situations where minimal expectation and maximum support have been possible. This was also illustrated in the preceding case.

Patients are more likely, on a deeper level, to be anxious about Regression. If the environment which permits the Regression becomes insecure through increasing expectations or removing support, the patient can quickly utilize any ego defense at his disposal to escape the Regression, even though the defense mechanisms are psychotic ones. If it is possible to maintain a Regression in Regressive Therapy long enough, the patients seem to grow out of the Regression in a solid, orderly fashion, with the development of more adequate defenses than previously available. Subsequent Regressions, if they take place, or are encouraged in such patients, have been less severe and shorter in duration.

The environmental milieu which is created in Regressive Therapy provides freedom from responsibility and maximum support. It will permit Regression to proceed, should the basic ego structure be significantly impaired. The degree of Regression depends on the degree of ego dysfunction and the ability of the environment to attain and maintain the conditions which permit Regression. In other words, the average neurotic patient ordinarily would not and could not regress to any significant degree. The ego does not permit Regression if there is a readily available defensive mechanism to prevent it, and if there are sufficient psychic resources so that it is not required.

D. IN ALCOHOLISM.—The situation is different in the severe psychotic reactions. Here the ego is usually sufficiently disorganized so that Regression can take place to a varying extent. In Regressive Therapy this trend is not only discouraged, or merely permitted; it is encouraged.

This type of treatment design has been used by Bowen with different patients. Each type presents a challenge and a different management problem. Regressive Therapy has found application in instances where alcoholism is the major problem. The following is a summary of the procedure with an alcoholic patient.

Case 177

Regressive Therapy in Alcoholism

(1) *Regressive Approach Selected.* A 35-year-old man had been seriously habituated to alcohol since college. He had at least one episode of delirium tremens. Business and family relationships were greatly impaired. He completed 3 years of classical analytic treatment, during which time there had been periods of sanitarium care. Little basic improvement resulted. One month after terminating analysis, he was in another severe drinking episode accompanied by his usual regressive behavior.

He refused further analysis, but had no ideas as to what he would like to do. A plan was devised to permit him to remain in the Regression. This was chosen in preference to seeking merely to "dry him out" once more, and to attempt to force him, probably again prematurely, to attempt resumption of a functioning level on a more or less adult level.

(2) *Problems in Management.* The regressive procedure was initiated by starting him on insulin subshock treatment as a vehicle to make acceptable the constant nursing attention he demanded when regressed. Paraldehyde was given on demand, rather than forcing him to give it up. The Regression deepened, and anxiety about being alone became so great that it was allayed only by supplying special nurses who cared for his every need around the clock.

There were repeated serious problems, requiring careful judgment in maintaining and furthering this particular treatment design. On one such occasion, he developed paraldehyde hallucinosis, and asked indirectly for the therapist to take away the drug. He was left to make his own decision about whether to continue or cut it down. He reduced the paraldehyde.

(3) *Gradual Emergence; Achievement of a New Level.* His deep Regression continued for four and a half months, during which time he became most painfully aware of his intense wish to stay in this "cared for" state for life. He tried many ways indirectly to force the therapist to act so as to terminate the program. He was given to understand that it would be provided until he could give it up himself. From this junc-

ture, he brought the program to a close, emerging from the regressed state in planned steps for which he did the planning, and for which he took the responsibility.

He became an outpatient and continued for 6 months the intense psychotherapy relationship developed during the Regression. He emerged on a new level with a much higher order of psychic functioning and social responsibility. In the subsequent two and a half years he was left with the responsibility of "weaning himself" from the psychotherapy relationship. This he did through increasingly infrequent contacts. There were Minor Regressions and episodes of depression. Occasionally he tried to "really hang one on," but found he could no longer drink to this degree, and stopped himself.

E. MATURITY FOSTERED.—Regressive Therapy is Bowen's term for *the therapeutically encouraged and induced surrender by the personality of some level or part of the level of integration, adjustment, and maturity already achieved.* With the Regression, segments or aspects of the person's behavior and reactions revert back to earlier, more primitive patterns of living. The patient's needs are gratified and he is completely cared for. When the Regression is "grown out of," over a period of time, the ensuing level of adjustment will be better and more stable than before the illness. A measure of more solid emotional maturity will have been achieved.

This is a highly specialized treatment approach. Its successful utilization requires highly skilled and experienced personnel, and the most ideal surroundings and is better not attempted otherwise.

Regression is the unconscious psychologic seeking after a more comfortable level. "Measured" by the individual in terms of his past experience, the result is a retreat toward the position in his earlier development which he "remembers" as providing the most satisfaction.

H. SUMMARY

1. Ego-Retreat

Regression is a major ego defense through which the ego stages a psychologic kind of retreat. Through it, one's thinking, conduct, emotional reactions, any aspect of living, or the total person may revert in part or in whole to some earlier stage of adjustment and development. This is invariably toward a more protected and dependent position, in accord with the *Directional-Tenet of Regression.* It differs from other defense mechanisms in that the ego itself withdraws; this is something that happens to the ego. Regression is a significant form of *psychologic retreat.*

We have classified Regressions as *Major* or *Minor,* depending upon their level, extent, inclusiveness, significance, and pathologic import. *Massive* or *Psychotic* Regressions are sometimes encountered in severe psychotic manifestations.

Regression frequently includes a greater or lesser amount of psychic withdrawal. Although often present together, Regression and Withdrawal (Chapter 27) should not be confused. Occasional instances of Regression can be encountered (see *Case 226,* p. 490) in which withdrawal is not a feature, and which thus help to distinguish these defensively-intended endeavors.

As a means of attempted resolution of conflict, the individual response to additional stress of sufficient strength sometimes results in psychologic, emotional, or behavior reversion, in whole (*Total Regression*) or in part (*Partial Regression*) to an earlier, less mature level of adjustment than had previously been attained. The *Law of Proportional Ego-Response* describes the level of Regression as being in direct proportion to the individual level of stress, when this route of psychic retreat is evolved.

2. The Making-up-for Principle

The retreat is toward some prior, more satisfying level, where there were fewer demands and less responsibility. The retreat may be symbolic only, or it may be manifested in a number of symbolic activities. It is toward an era in which gratifications (that is, external emotional sources of supply) were more readily obtained and/or were more satisfactory. According to the *Ultimate-Dependency-Goal* in Regression, the theoretical end point of the process would be the neonatal, complete position of dependency.

Regression is frequently manifested in attitudes and behavior. When sufficiently prominent clinically these warrant the descriptive designations of *Attitudinal Regression* and *Behavioral Regression*. When aspects of several different levels are reverted to at the same time the operation comprises the *Mixed Regression*.

The retreat may also be viewed as being toward the era in which dependency supplies first failed, as though to relive, to pass through this once more—and better so, this time. This is in accord with what we have termed the *Making-up-for Principle* in the motivation for Regression.

3. Normal Regression

Regression is a defensive seeking of a safer position by the hard-pressed ego, the return to a more secure era from one's past. It is a way of saying, in effect, "I can't continue," "I can't keep up the pace," or "I can't stand my life and its stresses."

The process of development normally follows what we termed the *Tidal-Progression of Maturity,* an uneven process marked by ups and downs. Some of the temporary "downs" when apparent may be regarded as *Normal Regressions*. These are particularly to be observed in children. The concept of *Childhood Regression* was outlined, briefly discussed, and several instances noted. Understanding and patience contribute to their dissolution.

The important (*Principle of Increasing-Complexity*) in emotional manifestations (p. 325) was stated and further observations of its many applications was urged. An interesting type of *Disciplinary-Regression* can follow punishment of various kinds of incarceration.

4. Pattern Established

A. MANY BASES.—The early employment of Regression as a defense may initiate a pattern which can continue into adulthood. Some common situations, such as the arrival of a new sibling, are at times followed by regressive behavior which is often temporary. Regression can follow pain, punishment, illness, or emotional stress of many kinds.

Regressive behavior can serve as an important and useful signal of present or impending emotional difficulty, or more serious difficulty. This principle is basic to an important concept of the *Regressive-Indicator*. Recognition of these by parents, teachers, therapists, and by others can be quite useful. *Conflict-Indicators* were mentioned (p. 327), with the observation that they can recur as a regressive manifestation under sufficient stress.

B. EMOTIONAL RECAPITULATIONS.—Regression can enter into the return of old manifestations or symptoms of emotional stress and conflict from earlier years. These represent both recurrences and what are termed *Emotional Recapitulations*. These may have been originally emotional, or physical in which the physical established a model for later developments on an emotional basis. An Emotional Recapitulation in response to the stress of major illness or surgery is an aspect of and is termed *Illness-Regression*.

Regressions take place unconsciously to an era of earlier gratification, as it has seemed to the person concerned. There are many interesting features such as the unwitting later recapitulation of symptoms from a childhood illness. As dependency needs multiply under stress, the PRR or *Psychologic Recapitulation Route* can help to determine the form, character, and locale of emotional symptoms.

The eight major stages of man, including his phases of personality development and adulthood were tabulated for ready reference and to aid in clarifying some of the overlapping terminology. (*Table 9*, p. 328–9.) The *Secondary Defense Concept, Emotional Decompensation,* and *Temporary Regression* received mention. *Pathologic Regressions* are those observed in conjunction with emotional pathology.

C. FIXATION.—Fixation refers to the cessation or arrest of development. They may be *Temporary, Semipermanent,* or *Permanent.* The dynamic bases for Fixation are analogous to those for Regression. Fixation may occur at any level of psychosexual development. Both Fixation and Regression are important concepts in emotional and mental illness. The *Law of Maturity* stated that ordinarily the level of maturity tends to move progressively albeit intermittently forward.

Regressive features can be expected in every case of emotional illness, although they may be of considerable or of little significance, and their presence may be most difficult to prove. The *Regression-Gauge* can be an occasional useful measurement in at least five aspects of emotional illness. *Maturation-Fixation* was illustrated in *Cases 168* and *169*.

5. Dependency Needs Significant

Regression and unsatisfied dependency needs from infancy and early childhood are closely related. This is in accord with the *Dependency-Seeking Principle* in the inner motivation to regress. Regression does not proceed as far in neurotic reactions and, although universally present, is less significant, less apparent, and far less marked than in the psychoses. Nonetheless, regressive features, conflicts over Regression, regressive influences in symptom selection, and conflicts over dependency take place in the various types of neurotic reactions, several of which were discussed in this connection.

Conversion Regression and the Psychologic Recapitulation Route (PRR) for symptom evolvement were illustrated. The *Vicious Circle of Self-Defeat Concept* in the neuroses was illustrated.

Massive or *Complete Regressions* and the most marked illustrations of this process are to be found in the psychotic reactions. These were illustrated. Attention was invited to conflicts over dependency needs. The *Resistance Regression* was illustrated (*Case 175*).

Therapeutic progress is an uneven progression, in which Regression may occur. This statement summarizes our important *Concept of Tidal-Progression in Therapeutic Progress*. Some of these are small ones and temporary, as illustrated. The *Concept of a Basic Trend Toward Emotional Health* received mention. Dependency gratification in therapy was discussed, as was the interesting *Concept of Regression-Treatment* and *Bowen's Regressive Therapy*.

I.   CROSS-REFERENCES TO *THE NEUROSES* *

Regression
In Nature of Anxiety (Chapter 1); as an ego defense against conflict; p. 24.
In Illusory Gains (Chapter 2)
    in "Gains" of Emotional Illness (Table 6); pp. 77–8.
    in relation to *epigain* (Table 4); p. 65.
    regressive retreat, into emotional illness; p. 71.
      in *endogain* of schizophrenia (Case 11); p. 74.
In Anxiety Reactions (Chapter 3); a factor, in destructive (pathologic) anxiety; p. 119.
In Depressive Reactions (Chapter 4)
    degree of, in Neurotic *vs.* Psychotic Depression (Table 10); p. 147.
    in dynamics of Depression, regressive reactivation of primary shock (Bibring); p. 162.

---

* From Laughlin, H. P. *The Neuroses*. London, Butterworth & Co., Ltd., 1967.

to earlier antecedent position; p. 183.
to oral level, in Depressive *epigain;* pp. 181, 184.
In Character Reactions (Chapter 5)
  as a maturity-fixation in Obsessive person; p. 293.
  potential for, in character defenses of *Conversion Personality* (Table 19); p. 260.
  unsuccessful, in Hygeiaphrontic Vicious Circle; pp. 283–4.
In Obsessive-Compulsive Reactions (Chapter 6)
  overlying Conversion, in analysis difficulties of Obsessive persons (Fenichel); p. 365.
  to withholding, in anal function (an expression of anger); p. 353.
In Fatigue Reactions (Chapter 7)
  to dependent position (a *regressive retreat*); p. 410.
    Case 84; p. 411.
  principle feature in Neurasthenia (Table 23); p. 428.
  to infantile level, in *Emotional Fatigue* (Case 82); p. 405.
In Hygeiaphrontic Reactions (Chapter 8)
  fixation, in relation to Regression, in *Hygeiaphrontic* overconcern; pp. 467, 476.
  in comparison of *Hygeiaphrontis* with Depression; p. 449.
  into narcissistic somatic preoccupation, in *endogain* of *Hygeiaphrontis;* pp. 481, 484, 508, 510.
  in traumatic occupational neuroses; p. 496.
  regressive retreat, dynamically represented by *Hygeiaphrontis;* pp. 447, 489.
    as an *Interest-Absorption Defense* (Case 90); pp. 454–5.
      progressive; p. 462.
    in *Episodic Hygeiaphrontis;* p. 483.
    in *Hygeiaphrontic epigain* and *endogain* (Table 26); p. 511.
    in *Hygeiaphrontic Reactions;* p. 482.
    Case 100; p. 485.
    into Fantasy, in onset of psychosis (Case 96); p. 472.
    in *Secondary Defense Concept* (Case 101); p. 487.
      as a resistance to therapy; p. 505.
    upon failure to attain goals (Case 94); p. 466.
In Conversion Reactions (Chapter 12)
  an important mechanism, in Conversion Reactions; p. 691.
  a *regressive retreat,* in Sensory Conversion; p. 688.
  in symptom formation of Conversion Reaction; p. 693.
  to dependency, in conversion pain; p. 668.
  unconscious wish for, in identification with *emotional prototype* (Case 145); p. 694.
In Dissociative Reactions (Chapter 13)
  induced, through hypnosis; pp. 821–2.
    reported by Rosen; p. 824.
  in *regressive retreat,* somnambulism as; p. 796.
  sought as an escape
    in psychodynamics of Fugue; p. 799.
    in *Retrograde Fugue* (Table 42); p. 796.
In Neuroses-Following-Trauma (Chapter 14)
  a characteristic, in *Traumatic Neuroses;* p. 875.
  featured, in *endogain* and *epigain* of *Traumatic Neuroses,* as *Hygeiaphrontis* (Case 182); p. 873.
    to a dependent position (Case 177); p. 861.
  in Compensation Neuroses, dependency needs met; pp. 884–5, 895.
    in *Therapeutic Impasse;* p. 888.

In Military Reactions (Chapter 15); induced, in *Prisoner-Processing* of Cardinal Mindszenty (Case 191); p. 942.

J.   REVIEW QUESTIONS

Sample self-check questions on Chapter 20 and Regression for the student, psychiatric resident, and board candidate.

1. Comment on the nature of *Regression*. How does it represent a psychologic ego retreat? What is the *Directional-Tenet of Regression? Law of Proportional Ego-Response? Concept of Ultimate-Dependency-Goal* in Regression?

2. Distinguish *Major* from *Minor Regressions*. What is meant by *Partial, Temporary, Pathologic, Total* and *Mixed Regression?* The *Phobic Dilemma?* The *Making-up-for Principle?*

3. How does the *Concept of Tidal-Progression of Maturity* influence the clinical assessment of Regression? Psychotherapy?

4. Give instances from your clinical observation in illustration of seven of the following:

    A. *Attitudinal* or *Behavioral Regression.*

    B. *Normal Regression.*

    C. *Increasing-Complexity Principle.*

    D. *Childhood Regression.*

    E. Anal Sadistic Phase.

    F. *Emotional Decompensation.*

    G. *Regression-Gauge* in emotional illness.

    H. *Dependency-Seeking Principle* (DSP).

    I. *Vicious Circle* of *Self-Defeat* in neuroses.

    J. *Massive Regression.*

5. What are the implications of the *Regressive-Indicator* or RI in child development? *Disciplinary-Regression* for parents or teachers? *Conflict-Indicators* in relation to Regression?

6. Outline the stages of psychosexual development.

7. What should physicians in other specialties know about Illness-Regression? Distinguish Fixation from Regression.

8. Discuss the role of dependency needs in Regression.

9. How do regressive needs contribute to the unwitting utilization of the *Psychologic Recapitulation Route* or PRR in the evolvement of emotional manifestations?

10. A. Comment on the value of concepts about Regression to therapy.

    B. What is the *Tidal-Progression Concept* in psychotherapy? *Resistance Regression? Trend Toward Emotional Health Concept? Regression-Treatment?* Regression as a *secondary defense?*

CHAPTER 21

REPRESSION

. . . Assignment to the Unconscious

A. AUTOMATIC AND CONSCIOUSLY EFFORTLESS PROCESS

1. Major Role in Emotional Illness and Health: a. Assignment to Unconscious; b. Key Concept in Behavioral Sciences. 2. Definition; Association-Repression; KEP: a. Involuntary Relegation; b. Basic Process. Early Activity; c. KEP: Kinetic-Energy Principle. 3. Suppression Distinguished.

B. HISTORICAL NOTES

1. Herbart, Schopenhauer, and Charcot. 2. Bernheim, Janet, Breuer, and Freud: a. Bernheim; b. Janet; c. Breuer and Freud.

C. PRIMARY AND SECONDARY REPRESSIONS

1. Primary or Primal Repression: a. Primordial Defense; b. Untoward Events Significant. 2. Secondary Repression: a. Awareness Precedes; b. More Accessible Form; c. Major and Auxiliary-Repressions. Repression-by-Association. 3. Minor Repressions.

D. USEFUL CONCEPTIONS

1. Law of Universal Affect: a. Affect Bound to Object; b. Definition. Implications in Memory. 2. Emotional-Object Amalgam (EOA). 3. Memory and EOA. 4. Electronics Analogy.

E. REPRESSION, MEMORY, AND RECALL

1. Every Aspect of Living. 2. Nietzsche and Darwin. 3. Convenient Memory. Psychologic Blindness. 4. Loss Through Affect Association.

F. DYNAMICS

1. Anxiety or Threat of Anxiety. 2. Importance in Health and Illness. 3. Beginnings of Repression: a. Repression Within Unconscious; b. Censorship Pattern Established. 4. Effects Upon Character Formation and Behavior.

G. REPRESSION AND EMOTIONAL ILLNESS

1. Goals in Therapy. 2. Failure Leads to Psychopathology. Principle of Overextension: a. When Derepression Threatens; b. Reenforcements Mobilized. 3. Repression and Neuroses.

4. Derepression and the Acute-Anxiety-Attack or AAA. 5. Derepression in Therapy: a. Judicious Pace Best; b. Therapeutic Aims; c. Free Association.

H. SUMMARY

1. Automatic Forgetting. 2. Types of Repression. 3. Added Conceptions.

I. REFERENCES (FROM *The Neuroses*)

J. REVIEW QUESTIONS

A. AUTOMATIC AND CONSCIOUSLY EFFORTLESS PROCESS

1. Major Role in Emotional Illness and Health

A. ASSIGNMENT TO UNCONSCIOUS.—Repression or its threatened failure is the precursor of all the ego defenses and plays a significant role in all of the neuroses, character neuroses, and functional psychoses. It is accordingly appropriate that we accord it a prime position in our survey of the emotional dynamisms.

Through its ego-sustaining and protective effects, Repression plays a vital role in maintaining emotional health. We have described the ego defenses as the foundation—the building blocks—of modern dynamic psychiatry. This is in accord with an earlier concept of the dynamisms comprising the *First Line of Psychic Defense.* Understanding their functions and operation is a requisite to comprehending human behavior. Continuing the analogy, Repression may be regarded as psychiatry's cornerstone.

Repression is the term for an automatic and consciously effortless kind of memory loss. In these terms, it appears misleadingly simple as an emotional-psychic process. Through the operation of Repression, ideas, impulses, and emotional feelings which are consciously repugnant and thereby intolerable to the individual for various reasons, are assigned to a deeper layer of the psyche, which we call the unconscious. Thereby, the unconscious becomes the repository for much that is painful in fantasy, ideation, or experience; for that which proves to be consciously intolerable. Repression is the process of assignment to the unconscious.

B. KEY CONCEPT IN BEHAVIORAL SCIENCES.—What is repressed does not remain dormant or necessarily quiescent. Although thus submerged and ordinarily inaccessible to voluntary conscious recall, the repressed material remains active, emotionally charged, and potent.

Accordingly, that which has been repressed can contribute to emotional difficulties: (1) if new emotional pressures or threats place too great a burden on the repressing process; (2) if internal pressures for expression of repressed material become too great for its continued containment; (3)

if the repressing forces become sufficiently weakened; or (4) through various combinations of the foregoing. The concept of Repression is a key one in the behavioral sciences.

2. Definition; Association-Repression; KEP

A. INVOLUNTARY RELEGATION.—We can define Repression as *the automatic, effortless, and involuntary assignment or relegation of consciously repugnant or intolerable ideas, impulses, and feelings to the unconscious.* Following this defensively and protectively intended process, *such material is not ordinarily subject to voluntary conscious recall.* Repressed material includes data which never really entered consciousness, in addition to that which, having once been in conscious awareness, has subsequently been assigned or relegated to the unconscious through its Repression. *Anxiety and the threat of anxiety is the active force which brings about Repression.*

Considered as an ego defense or dynamism, Repression is the one which is most widely used. It is a universally employed process of psychologic defense. It is at times closely related to Denial (p. 80), with which it may overlap. It can be regarded as dissociative (p. 96) in its effects. Repression involves forgetting and memory loss, but more than this, the memory loss is a "directed" and purposeful kind. It is unconsciously directed, however, by psychic expediency, and its purpose is ego defense. Conflictual, disturbing, and painful wishes, thoughts, and urges are thereby banished from consciousness.

Repression is operative in the service of attempted conflict resolution, seeking surcease for an embattled and harassed ego. As noted, the motive force for Repression ultimately comes from anxiety, or the threat of anxiety. Similarly, these same needs, to allay, or to circumvent anxiety and its effects, help to ensure continued Repression. The experiencing of anxiety is usually the subjective signal when derepression threatens. At this juncture, other ego defenses may be called into operation as emotional reenforcements. Should these prove inadequate as defenses, emotional symptoms may be evolved, an emotional illness can be initiated, or an existing one aggravated.

B. BASIC PROCESS. EARLY ACTIVITY.—This important process is particularly active during early years. However, Repression continues to operate throughout life. Repression is a primitive and first-line dynamism through which the ego defensively endeavors to lessen, resolve, and prevent emotional conflict, and consequent anxiety. Repression is a basic process, since it is a prerequisite to the elaboration of the other ego defenses.

Many ego defenses are called into operation as reenforcements of Repression. As to classification, this dynamism belongs with the less advanced or Lower Order Group of dynamisms, of which it is the foremost and the most widely employed.

From our introductory comments, one can see how very important the concept of Repression has become in medicine, psychiatry, and the behavioral sciences. It is one of the cardinal tenets of modern psychiatry. Through the operation of Repression unacceptable thoughts are expelled from consciousness. It is the fundamental defensive mechanism of the ego. In addition to its vital   ! basic role in emotional illness and health, an understanding of Repression is crucial in appreciating the many factors influencing memory and recall.

In addition to the present data, some supplemental material together with 10 illustrations are available to those sufficiently interested in Chapter 2 entitled Repression, in *Mental Mechanisms,** pp. 27–76.

C. KEP:KINETIC-ENERGY PRINCIPLE.—Although the process of Repression can allay the conscious experiencing of conflict, it can contribute to the continuation of unconscious conflict through maintenance of data in a repressed or poorly repressed status. This interferes with its resolution. What is repressed and remains repressed however poorly, continues inaccessible to therapeutic scrutiny and the healthful potential for conflict resolution.

It is a tangential but basic tenet in our conception of Repression that each drive or impulse that undergoes Repression requires a certain amount of psychic energy to maintain it in its repressed state. This is what we name for convenience and emphasis the *Kinetic-Energy Principle* in Repression. It is an important concept in its own right. The more poor or incomplete the Repression or the stronger the striving, the more energy is required (p. 312).

Repressed strivings may attempt to escape by various means, especially by undergoing various modifications through the operation of other ego defenses. Such strivings may also, of course, secure varying measures of outward expression in disguised, modified, and symbolic forms.

Another interesting and significant feature of Repressions concerns our observation that in many instances they are overdetermined. By this we refer to the process tending to carry along more data into the unconscious than is required.

Stated in other words, the otherwise painful data which "requires" Repression tends to take along with it additional and more neutral, associated material into the seeming limbo of the unconscious. The operation of the dynamism leading to this additional repressed data is the intriguing type which we term *Association-Repression*. The operation and its influence is frequently to be noted by the perceptive clinician. The material so carried along comprises *Association-Repressions*. This process is alternatively labeled *Auxiliary Repression* [1] or *Repression-by-Association*.

---

* From Laughlin, H. P. *Mental Mechanisms.* London, Butterworth & Co., Ltd., 1963.

[1] A concept overlapping with a later one concerning the overextension of Repression, which is more applicable to emotional illness; the *Principle of Overextension* in Repression.

3. Suppression Distinguished

The terms Repression and Suppression are frequently confused in lay usage. In the interests of clarity, it is worthwhile to point out the distinction. Suppression is *the process in which one makes deliberate and conscious efforts to forget, control, and restrain; one thus actively seeks to subjugate unacceptable thoughts or desires, with the individual concerned being clearly aware of the attempt.*

Through Suppression, one directs his attention away from undesirable thoughts, objects, or feelings; actively seeks to forget them. It is a consciously directed effort to banish from awareness; a conscious effort to forget. Through Suppression one seeks to subdue and to quell. In the correct use of this term then, there is an implied conscious effort to keep down and to restrain; to try to forget. Suppression is conscious, deliberate, and effortful. (*Case 146*, pp. 282–3.)

Repression, on the other hand, is the automatic relegation from consciousness of the unacceptable thought or wish. In distinction, it is an unconscious and involuntary process. There may be no conscious effort; no awareness of the wish or striving, nor of its unacceptability. When something has been successfully banished from consciousness, it has been repressed; we correctly employ Suppression to describe the conscious effort in this direction.

B. HISTORICAL NOTES

1. Herbart, Schopenhauer, and Charcot

The German word *verdrangung,* or repression, appears to have been earliest employed in a sense close to our present usage by the psychologist Herbart in 1824. The idea was implied by Schopenhauer in 1844, and doubtless also by others, before or since. The fruits of further research in uncovering additional evidence of early recognition will be of interest. One might anticipate that the findings would further bear out our Concept of Historical Validation (see earlier, *Chapter 19*).

Professor Jean M. Charcot (1825–1893), a genius of his time and a pioneer French psychotherapist, undertook significant work with hypnosis in the decades following 1870, clinically demonstrating several levels of consciousness and its dissociation. He experimentally reproduced symptoms identical to certain of the marked Somatic Conversions (hysteria) of that day. His work and demonstrations were indeed momentous. Among their contributions they made evident the existence of unconscious (repressed) data and its influences.

Among many others of that day, Sigmund Freud (1856–1939) attended several of Charcot's demonstrations, and was notably impressed, commenting how with "... this incomparably fine piece of ... research

... the psychical mechanism of ... (a conversion) phenomenon was for the first time disclosed. ..." *The Neuroses,* p. 648.

2. *Bernheim, Janet, Breuer, and Freud*

A. BERNHEIM.—In the 1880's and 1890's, Hippolyte-Marie Bernheim (1840–1919), professor of clinical medicine at Nancy, France, undertook important experiments in the use of hypnosis. He was probably the first to apply the term neurosis to hysteria and other reactions now labeled as neuroses. Bernheim apparently quite well recognized that certain acts could be devoid of conscious intent or origin.

Freud was clearly familiar with his work, writing (in 1895): "I had myself seen Bernheim producing evidence that the memories of events during somnambulism (a hypnotic state) are only apparently forgotten in the waking state and can be revived. ..."

B. JANET.—In the final decades of the 19th century, events were progressing rapidly toward recognition, acceptance, and establishment of the psychologic bases of many illnesses. Pierre Janet (1859–1947), a distinguished pupil of Charcot, introduced the important concept of dissociation.

His resulting theories as to the splitting of the stream of consciousness, also helped further demonstrate the existence of a powerful body of unconscious data.

C. BREUER AND FREUD.—*Das unbewusste* (the unconscious) a term used earlier (Hartman in 1869, and others) was originally introduced to psychiatric usage by Breuer in 1895. This term was adopted, developed, and more firmly established as a concept through the extensive writings of Freud.

Joseph Breuer (1841–1925) first recognized that patients could be induced to relive painful but "forgotten" (that is repressed) emotional situations from past experience. He found that the recall of psychologically painful experiences could lead to the more or less permanent surrender of Conversion (hysterical) symptoms.

This was a momentous discovery in regard to the psychogenesis of neurotic symptoms. It further proved the existence of the unconscious, the operation of repression, and confirmed Charcot's research. His findings and clinical results encouraged further study, and attracted Freud's attention, interest, and participation. A collaborative relationship developed and continued for some years, was highly productive, and had a profound influence on both men.

In experiments with posthypnotic suggestion, Bernheim discovered that subjects were embarrassed when attempting to explain their behavior in the posthypnotic state. The embarrassment vanished as the subject was induced to recall the facts which had been lost to recall.

Breuer and Freud studied these phenomena further and concluded that there was an important dynamic process operative. This process resulted in the active relegation of emotionally painful material from consciousness into the unconscious. Accordingly, they employed the term Repression (its first specific use in its current dynamic sense), beginning in 1893, to express this meaning.

Today we regard Repression as a major ego defense, bringing about (when successful) the dismissal of intolerable emotional data from consciousness. Through it, the ego excludes from awareness areas of id drives, conflictual material, and subjectively or socially intolerable thoughts, events, and emotions. Through the operation of Repression, the subjective experiencing of an emotion, for example anger in an otherwise personally appropriate situation, may not occur—or love, or passion, or envy, or resentment, and so on.

C. PRIMARY AND SECONDARY REPRESSIONS

1. Primary or Primal Repression

A. PRIMORDIAL DEFENSE.—From our discussion thus far, it might be apparent that we can delineate two major kinds of Repressions. One of these is comprised of very early psychic material which is largely "instinctual," or the subject of infantile fantasies (Chapter 7). Most of this never actually entered consciousness. We have found it convenient and useful to refer to this type of Repression as *Primary* or *Primal*. This is in distinction from the Repressions of later conscious data which are *Secondary*, occurring as they do frequently in response to superego and social pressures.

Primary (or primal) Repressions include material from fantasies, instinctual drives, certain very early experiences in the life of the individual, and primordial emotional conflicts. Aspects of the so-called instinctual drives involved are predominantly and ultimately aggressive or sexual in nature, as are their consequences, derivatives, and resulting conflicts. Their Repression is a primordial defense. Nonawareness aids in control, spares conscious conflict, removes the threat of disapproval, punishment, or retaliation, and averts anxiety.

B. UNTOWARD EVENTS SIGNIFICANT.—A knowledge of the potential for and existence of the process of Primary Repression has practical importance in a number of disciplines. Undoubtedly instances of Primary Repression play a major role in infancy and, as such, can have an important effect upon subsequent emotional and personality development. It is a grave mistake to blithely assume that the infant has no unconscious, that it contains little or nothing, or plays no significant role. It is likewise very much in error to believe routinely that painful or untoward events will have no effect at all upon him, that "It doesn't matter,"... "he is too little" ... "he won't remember it anyway."

Some of us believe that Primary Repressions can be the more important and vital ones for certain individuals. This is in accord with the view that the ultimate antecedent roots of the major psychoses are most likely laid down in the first 2 years of life.

Rank was impressed with the impact of parturition. This sequence of events constituted for him the "birth trauma," a potentially significant area of Primary Repression. Others have discounted the emotional significance of the birth experience for the neonate for various reasons. (See *"Theory of Antecedent Conflicts"* in *The Neuroses*, p. 492.)

2. *Secondary Repression*

A. AWARENESS PRECEDES.—Within the category of Secondary Repressions we include any and all repressed material including feelings, experiences, and impulses, which at one time have been clearly conscious. We find it appropriate to call them Secondary Repressions since: (1) they usually occur later (that is afterwards or secondarily) in life than the primary ones, and (2) they take place following (i.e., secondary to) their originally having been in conscious awareness.

It is this latter major type of Repression which was early recognized by Breuer and Freud. Secondary Repression was basic to the analytic theories which they developed. Freud considered these the important ones, an evaluation which was almost unanimously held, at least until sometime after 1930.

B. MORE ACCESSIBLE FORM.—Certainly the Secondary Repression is more accessible, tangible, encountered, familiar, and likely to be worked with in the treatment situation. Secondary Repressions more immediately underlie the common symptoms of emotional illness, such as anxiety, conversion, obsessions, phobia, and depression.

The neurotic reactions represented by these symptoms comprise the bulk of clinical work of modern students of psychodynamics. Secondary Repression takes place in response to individual (intrapsychic) needs. The *raison d'être* in its operation also receives important contributions from interpersonal and social pressures. Many memory lapses and losses illustrate Secondary Repression.

Both types (Primary and Secondary) of Repression, however, are of vast importance to us in our formulation and understanding of conceptions concerning: (1) personality development, (2) the adaptive efforts of the organism, and (3) therapeutic endeavors.

C. MAJOR AND AUXILIARY-REPRESSIONS. REPRESSION-BY-ASSOCIATION. —The following instance illustrates the early and complete Repression of a painful experience. We cannot say at just what time after the event this discard from consciousness took place, whether the memory loss was gradual, or instantaneous and massive. From other sources the Repression appeared to have been complete by 8 years of age, or 3 years after the event. It could conceivably have transpired at nearly any given point following the terrible tragedy.

Powerful motives in this instance of Repression were present in the intense level of emotional feelings experienced. This is a striking and dramatic example of the complete Repression of a significant event. It is an illustration of what we call the *Major Repression.*

What is termed, for purposes of distinction and emphasis, the *Auxiliary-Repression* also is illustrated. Auxiliary-Repression includes the discard of related but less personally significant and vital data through a process of *Repression-by-Association.* Some measure of this carrying along of seemingly more neutral material is to be expected almost routinely in the operation of Major Repression.

Case 178

A Drowning Repressed

A 5-year-old girl visiting with her family at a seashore resort, was assigned to look out for her little sister, aged two. Their mother left them at a play area while grocery shopping. Shortly thereafter, perhaps bored or annoyed with this assignment, the older child began playing with two girls of her own age, ignoring her sister.

The 2-year-old wandered across the road and down a lane where a bulkhead bordered the bay. Here she may have played a bit; been fascinated by the water. Somehow she fell in and drowned.

This was a terrible tragedy. The family tried to forget. The surviving sister, Helen suffered terribly from feelings of responsibility and guilt.

After a time she no longer spoke of the event nor gave any indication of its recollection, an endeavor aided by family members also eager to forget. They had not referred to the sister as far as Helen could recall, although confirming the events upon inquiry much later. This was a Major Repression.

Helen was led to the recall of the long-repressed tragedy many years afterwards through her analysis, in which dream material provided leading clues. Through operation of the process of Repression-by-Association, data which was associated with the painful primary material for repression but which was more emotionally neutral was carried along into the unconscious. Also uncovered in therapy, this illustrated the Auxiliary-Repression.

The event albeit repressed, had been of significance in her psychic development. Its derepression and analysis proved beneficial.

3. Minor Repressions

Repressions cover a wide range. Those of the magnitude of the foregoing Major Repression are rare. Far more common are the reflections of what might be termed *Minor Repressions,* to be observed in the myriad of memory lapses in everyday living. These may be of little moment. Occasionally they can be quite significant.

Memory blocks can betray inner feelings which one wishes hidden; at other times they may be an inconvenience or a nuisance. For the introspective student they can be intriguing and fascinating.

In acknowledgment of the wide clinical variations of the process of

Repression, we have suggested labeling them on suitable occasions as major or minor. Thus as noted earlier, there are Major Repressions and there are Minor Repressions. Such designations are suitable depending on their scope, and upon the relative importance of the repressed material. When a distinction is made, it should be on the basis of clinical evaluation and professional judgment.

In the following instance, failure to recall parental anniversary dates was an annoying and troubling difficulty which persistently defeated efforts to conquer it. Inability to resolve the problem was a measure of the strength and tenacity of the repressing forces. This example is one of Secondary Repression which also probably better illustrates the Minor type of Repression, although for the person concerned this particular difficulty at times certainly seemed a major one.

Case 179

Repression of Anniversary Dates; Minor Repression

A 33-year-old man in therapy frequently gave verbal testimony to his affection for his parents. There was no doubt that much of this was quite genuine. It might have been a bit surprising therefore to learn of his considerable problem in remembering their birthdays, anniversaries, and other special dates. Superficially, this might have seemed more remarkable since his family attached greater meaning to such occasions than do others. At the same time, however, this point was also a give-away as to the significance of his problem.

Realizing that his parents were hurt by his failures and omissions in this area, this chap went to great lengths to avoid these lapses. He carefully circled the appropriate dates on his calender. He bought and addressed greeting cards, having them ready to send, only to find after the important date passed that he would have forgotten to mail the message. Try as he would, he seemed unable to observe these important dates.

He stoutly maintained for a long time that his only feelings toward his parents were positive ones. His struggle over their anniversaries, however, was one indication of the presence of more mixed emotions. The Repression of dates important to them was a way of allowing some otherwise concealed, partial expression of the hostile segments of his feelings, and aided in their continued Repression.

The study of this problem, plus several similar ones of some moment, made his stated position of unmixed affection increasingly untenable. When he became able to realistically face the hostile elements in his attitudes, and to cope with them constructively, the problem over the recall of anniversaries melted away.

D.   USEFUL CONCEPTIONS

1. Law of Universal Affect

A. AFFECT BOUND TO OBJECT.—In seeking an understanding of Repression it becomes clear that an association and binding of emotion, or affect, has taken place to the thought concerned. It is this associated emotional feeling that helps provide the motive force, the reason for the Repression. Repression does not occur by chance. It is defensively intended.

A memory, thought, or urge thus becomes assigned to the unconscious because the attached affect is unpleasant; repugnant; consciously intolerable. It may be threatening, painful, or frightening, and thereby anxiety-provoking. Its banishment is intended to spare one the associated feelings. Thus, there is an affective (emotional) basis for every instance of Repression, every memory lapse, every time something is forgotten. One may not know what it is, but it is always present.

It is often easier to be aware of emotional feelings which are unpleasant. They bother us, are troublesome. Clinically, with sufficiently detailed scrutiny we learn, however, that everything, no matter how small or large, has a quantum of associated affect, emotion, or as it is sometimes referred to, *emotional charge.* The attached affect may be minimal and insignificant, as it often is, or it may be important and meaningful. It may be pleasant and positive, unpleasant and negative, or a mixture of the two.

The foregoing helps outline the basis for the conception of a *Law of Universal Affect,* as formulated earlier (*The Neuroses* pp. 279, 586–9, also p. 85) and found to be a convenience in communication and teaching. This labels a significant principle concerning the universal attachment of affect to everything; to each item of thought, person, idea, word, dream, fantasy, subject, and so on—in short, to every object.

The attachment by the individual of a quantum of affect to each object is routine and so much to be anticipated that it is regarded as a law of the psyche, and has been so named. This conception is a vital one in our understanding of Repression, resistance, and memory, as well as the factors which influence the flow and reporting of associations in psychotherapy.

B. DEFINITION. IMPLICATIONS IN MEMORY.—The Law of Universal Affect is defined as *the basic psychologic premise that every idea, thought, or object, no matter how minor, seemingly trivial, or apparently neutral, has a distinct quantum of affect attached.* The amount of affect or emotional charge may be so small as to be infinitesimal, but it is nonetheless present. It can have an important effect upon the retention or discard from memory of an idea or word, as well as on its relative ease of recall. The emotional feeling so possessed by an object (that is, associated with it) may be positive, negative, or mixed. It is automatically assigned in kind and extent by the person concerned.

The kind or quality of associated affect of course is quite important. The amount is also important, although we tend to overvalue this aspect and assign relatively less significance to the quality. The operation of the Law of Universal Affect leads us to an interesting related conception.

2. Emotional-Object Amalgam (EOA)

Recognition of the attachment of a certain quantum of affect, or emotional feeling, to each and every object, led to formulating the Law of Universal Affect. It is sometimes convenient, perhaps inescapable, that the two—the object, plus its inevitable emotional charge—come to be regarded together as a unit.

Considering the combination of the two together can serve a useful purpose. Attention may come to be more specifically directed to the affective component. Accordingly we use the descriptive term *Emotional-Object Amalgam, or EOA.* The adoption of this label has had an added advantage in emphasizing the existence of the bond, pointing out the firm nature of the union, and noting the presence of both components.

An Emotional-Object Amalgam may be defined as *the compound, union, or amalgam which is formed by the close association and attachment of an emotional charge to its object.* According to this concept, an object and its attached affect are considered together, as a unit. The EOA represents a relatively stable union, which ordinarily tends to continue, and is not readily disrupted. The affect or emotional significance has become firmly attached to a person, object, event, name, event, circumstance, or situation.

The kind and quality of emotional charge attached to any given object can be highly variable individually. This is contributed to by the presence and level of hidden symbolic significance. We can find important applications for the EOA concept in the study of psychodynamics, as, for example, in the evolvement of phobias. As earlier described, we observe the detachment of an overload of anxiety (at the time of a critical attack) with its displacement (Chapter 5) externally to a new object.

The "selection" of a phobic object is determined by various factors. Once established, the object, plus its newly bound emotional significance, constitutes an important type of Emotional-Object Amalgam. The phobic EOA is a neurotic object-source of fear and dread.

The *Soteria* comprises an important analogous (but converse) type of EOA. The Soterial Reactions are discussed in Chapter 11 (pp. 607–639) of *The Neuroses.*

3. Memory and EOA

Memory tends to be more highly selective than is usually recognized. In accord with the foregoing concepts, the possibly minute amounts of affect which are associated with each item are important. They have an important bearing upon what is retained, and what is readily recalled. With training a person can learn to recognize pleasant versus unpleasant connotations however minor, that places, names, terms, and ideas hold for him. This is an intriguing as well as a worthwhile endeavor. Its potential is great for unraveling the bases for memory lapses.

More often than we are aware, the "control" of memory is subject to the seeming whims and vagaries of the affect side of the Emotional-Object Amalgam. The functions of memory, memory loss, and recall operate automatically and unconsciously. The trained observer often can perceive an instance of these only after it has taken place, if then. At this later time it may be possible to follow associations and seek bases for the lapse.

Newcomers in psychiatry generally find little difficulty in understanding the Law of Universal Affect or the concept of the Emotional-Object Amalgam. They seem reasonable. At this point, however, some questions may be raised: How can such small amounts of affect have such a potent effect? If these amounts are often so minute that we tend to be unaware of them, how could they prove so influential? We have found one useful explanation in an analogy to electronics, as follows.

4. Electronics Analogy

In electronics one necessarily learns to think in terms of microvolts. These are extremely minute amounts of electrical energy. They cannot, of course, be seen or felt. Indeed, they are not detectable by ordinary means. Their measurement requires special equipment. Despite their minute strength, however, they have a crucial role in certain electronic circuits.

Minor changes in electrical potential, actually in terms of a few microvolts can sometimes change or reverse an entire complex circuit. The tiniest variations can result in the difference between the success of a function as planned, or the circuit being blocked or reversed. This is a physical phenomenon which is usually readily accepted. Still, the involved functioning of electronic circuits is a simple matter compared to the complexity of our human emotional-psychologic-mental apparatus.

When it can be demonstrated how tremendous functional differences can follow changing the direction of a few microvolts, it seems hardly surprising that the energy of the emotional charge of Emotional-Object Amalgams can result in blocking, repression, difficulty in memory, recall, and alteration of function and response. This is the *Electronics Analogy*, designed to help in understanding the concept of the EOA and its pervasive influences on mental content.

E. REPRESSION, MEMORY, AND RECALL

1. Every Aspect of Living

During our discussion, it should be increasingly apparent that emotional factors consistently and profoundly influence Repression, memory, and recall. This is so basic to human life that it can hardly be overstressed.

The faculty of memory is most vital. It enters into every aspect— large and small, daily as well as long-term—of living. There are a great many minor but potentially troubling memory lapses and blocks which can be observed in day-to-day life.

Lapses of memory are sometimes serious, often problematic, at times trivial or embarrassing, and occasionally amusing. In the following instance, the blocking of a name became quite personal. In this interesting and unusual instance the person forgot his own name, and attempts an analysis of contributing factors.

Case 180

Forgetting One's Own Name

"I was a member of a social fraternity during my college days. I had pledged despite the strong objections of my parents.... They believed fraternities to be a waste of time, a source of bad associations and habits, and a colossal waste of money. My attitudes toward the fraternity were overshadowed by their opinion of the club as unsavory, and I felt some very definite uncertainties about the 'rightness' of my belonging ... I had not overriden their judgments without great conflicts and feelings of disloyalty, rebellion, 'badness,' and guilt ...

"An important annual activity of the organization was to conduct a 'rush week' to get new members. This was a time when school work was abandoned. All our efforts were turned to meeting as many of the prospective rushees as possible, and trying to favorably influence the more select candidates to join our ranks.... Each day until late at night, was spent meeting the new boys seeking to convince them of the assets of fraternity life: excellent relationships, good study habits of our group, and the economy that our house offered. Since I had mixed feelings about these, I was not always the best salesman....

"One day, toward the end of the week, I joined a small group of candidates and automatically started to introduce myself. Can you imagine the peculiar sensation I experienced when I found I could not remember my own name ... I started the conversation with, 'How do you do? I am....' I absolutely could not think of my own name. It was very embarrassing, to say the least ... I tried to pass off my distress and confusion by offering some lame excuses, such as how tired I was, and so on.... It was pretty weak! ...

"I believe my parents' attitudes, with their great influence from early years, were far more important than I had consciously realized. I knew very well that what I was doing was against my parents' wishes. The activities of rush week with the adjournment of scholastic work, bore out some of their pronouncements....

"There was also my own deep conviction that what I was doing was wrong; therefore I was 'wrong.' The outward manifestation of this evaluation of myself was exhibited by forgetting my name ... I was so wrong that for the moment I was no longer even entitled to a name, or at least to my own—the one my parents had given me...."

2. Nietzsche and Darwin

As noted earlier, awareness of forces influencing Repression has been long evident to observant scholars. Philosophers and scientists have made similar observations concerning memory and the facility of recall. Two interesting examples are readily available, one from Nietzsche and a second from Darwin. Nietzsche in *Jenseits von Gut und Bose* wrote: "I have done that, says my memory. I cannot have done that, says my pride, and remains inexorable. Finally—memory yields." This statement indicates Nietzsche's grasp of an important principle at times applicable in memory and its Repression.

Charles Darwin further demonstrates this kind of insight, as reported in the book *The Life of Charles Darwin,* by his son, Francis. The elder Darwin says, "I had during many years followed the Golden Rule, namely, that whenever a published fact, a new observation or thought came across me, which was opposed to my general results, to make a memorandum of it without fail and at once; for I had found by experience that such (contrary and thus unwelcome) facts and thoughts were far more apt to escape from memory than favorable ones."

The scientist who strives for scientific objectivity had best be guided by this premise. Persons engaged in research are likely (and hopefully so) to learn early the influences which "wishful thinking" can have upon their observations, interpretations, and recollections.

3. Convenient Memory. Psychologic Blindness

This brings us to another important aspect of memory and forgetting. This is the widespread phenomenon which has been termed *convenient memory.* Characteristic is that one tends to better recall that which is personally more advantageous, conveniently "forgetting" what is not. Many unwitting influences can play a role in its operation.

The convenient memory can be conscious or not. At times the "convenience" of the loss is such as to suggest its being feigned. As a defense it has social uses, of course. Consciously or not, and to a greater or lesser extent, one prefers and perhaps actively seeks to view himself, and to have others view him, in the best possible—the most favorable—light. This endeavor can lead to various conscious and unconscious machinations. These may vary from the slightest shading of the interpreting of events, to himself and to others, to deliberate and major deceptions. The influence of "wishful thinking" can be strong indeed.

Recollections may be lost completely, altered, or reversed. These needs are so human and understandable that at least milder operations in their service are seldom regarded harshly, and in their social context are likely to be viewed charitably.

4. Loss Through Affect Association

The loss from ready conscious recall of a thought, a name, or a term almost invariably occurs because it carries some unpleasant connotation. In other words, the affect associated with the lost item is disagreeable and enters into the loss. The trained and reflective person can often explain memory losses through identifying the affect associated, if he approaches the problem properly and without preconception or bias. A relaxed neutral attitude fosters free association, which is the recommended approach.

Finding a basis or reason for the loss is in accord with the *Principle of Scientific Determinism,* according to which every occurrence or phenomenon has an explanation. This important principle applies in psychologic areas, as it does in the physical sciences. The basis may or may not be found and if found, this may prove easy or difficult. However, one should not be satisfied with an explanation in which the basis is attributed to mere chance.

Most people have had the annoying or embarrassing experience of being unable to recall the name of a person who is actually well known. This can even occur with a person with whom there is daily contact. Despite how hard one tries, the name will not present itself, even though it's possible to summon up a mental picture of the person. Similar instances may become less frequent as one gains ability in securing awareness of underlying reasons for memory lapses. Finding them can represent a challenge, and the bases when uncovered can be most interesting.

F.   DYNAMICS

1. Anxiety or Threat of Anxiety

Let us pause at this juncture to make an additional comment or so about the dynamics of Repression; as to how the ego defense of Repression operates. Through the intrapsychic process which we term Repression, painful, disturbing, and conflictual thoughts or experiences are pushed into the unconscious. Consciously of course this process is an effortless one; there is no awareness of the "push."

We have stressed that the impetus in accomplishing Repression ultimately comes from anxiety, or from the threat of anxiety. It is this intense psychic kind of pain which provides the basic motive and force for Repression.

2. Importance in Health and Illness

We have noted the universality of the process of Repression. It has been stated that Repression plays a vital role in emotional health, precedes the evolution of the various ego defenses, and contributes to the initiation of all manner of symptoms of emotional illness. A categorical statement about hazards or injury resulting from the operation of Repression therefore is rather difficult, since *it would appear that we can regard Repression as indispensable to both mental health and mental illness.*

Its protective function is certainly vital in many instances. Its operation can provide an essential respite to a hard-pressed ego, allowing time for recuperation, mobilization of inner resources, and preparation for new onslaughts from one's external or internal environments. An organically oriented psychiatrist who poorly valued psychotherapy and understood it less, used to say in an effort to belittle, that Repression cured far more patients than did psychotherapy.

His statement was technically correct, although it would be more accurately stated as relieved, or afforded a measure of conflict resolution, rather than as "cured." However, in view of the universality and pervasiveness alone of the ego defense of Repression in the absence of more compelling points of argument, his efforts to belittle the effectiveness of psychotherapy on this basis were ineffective, at least for the initiated.

3. Beginnings of Repression

A. RETAINED WITHIN UNCONSCIOUS.—Primary Repression is most often a part of the general reaction of the undeveloped early ego in response to threatening sexual and aggressive impulses, retaliation for having them, and so on. In this type of Repression the impulses are perceived and held within the framework of the unconscious, never escaping into awareness. Because they are not permitted conscious perception by no means indicates they no longer exist.

Sometimes repressed data are reflected in the content of the fantasies of infants and small children. The clinician observes effects and influences from repressed material. The repressed continues to be present and potent, although hidden, and represents a constant forceful potential unless rechanneled or otherwise harnessed or psychologically neutralized in some manner.

We have indicated the requirement for continued psychic energy to maintain Repressions, in accord with the KEP. One cannot say how much is required by a given individual, nor necessarily why Massive Repressions are more successfully made or maintained by some than by others. One's capacity to repress is affected by his psychic-emotional makeup and by his environment, especially including the interpersonal. This is likely established early in life.

B. CENSORSHIP PATTERN ESTABLISHED.—Primary Repressions and the patterns so established help to determine the capacity for later Repression under appropriately stressful initiating circumstances, as well as what can happen later in various psychologic areas. This applies to the super-ego taking over certain roles earlier exercised by parents. In this manner, a pattern of self-censorship is established which can last for life.

Primary Repression also enters into the establishment of primordial patterns of coping with both aggression and sex. These patterns in modified form also carry over into adulthood. Finally, there are important implications in connection with each as regards the vicissitudes of one's interpersonal relationships and one's abilities in dealing with people—closely or more at arm's length.

4. Effects Upon Character Formation and Behavior

Mention must be made of the important effects which Repression exerts upon character trait formation, and also upon behavior. We are aware of many important influences of the ego defense in this area and the many interrelationships which exist between its operation and the developing psyche. A volume could be written.

It would be unfortunate and hazardous to think of Repression merely as a negative force, a loss, or simply an absence of something. The results in personality development at times may serve to significantly accentuate outwardly reversed qualities, or invite attention to different ones. The personality as observed by others cannot directly display nor express that which is repressed.

G. REPRESSION AND EMOTIONAL ILLNESS

2. Goals in Therapy

It is in the area of emotional illness that professionals in the health field find some of the most important and significant applications of our concepts of Repression and its principles of operation. In every case of emotional illness—neuroses, character neuroses, and functional psychoses —in the study of their psychic foundations, one will inevitably find repressed material.

The recovery of repressed material from the unconscious, its recognition, acceptance, and the patient's learning to cope with and healthfully and constructively integrate derepressed data, are fundamental goals of dynamic psychotherapy and analysis.

2. Failure Leads to Psychopathology. Principle of Overextension

A. WHEN DEREPRESSION THREATENS.—Repressions are universal. They can be variously essential, helpful, useful, or at least not harmful. They can also be handicapping and self-defeating. Repression can be excessive. Repression is part of the endogain of neuroses and dynamisms, as in Conversion (Chapter 3).

When too much is demanded of the repressing forces, when too large a chunk of emotionally charged material is presented for this psychic burial process, or when the repressive forces falter and repressed material threatens to emerge into consciousness, the emotional difficulties, often in the form of symptomatology and psychopathology, ensue.

New and more pathologic defenses may be evolved. Various symptoms of emotional illness can develop. Psychopathology develops when the threat is too great, or when what we refer to as derepression threatens.

As noted, energy is required, in line with the *Kinetic-Energy Principle in Maintaining Repression,* to keep unacceptable impulses and other unconscious material in a repressed state. If the need for the required energy becomes too great, Repression alone may prove insufficient to keep the material submerged. When this happens, other methods of coping with the hidden drives, emotional conflicts, and resulting tensions are called into play. These include various additional ego defenses or dynamisms. Denial is often related to Repression, as noted in earlier references (Chapter 4), or may be an adjunct.

B. REENFORCEMENTS MOBILIZED.—Thus, other intrapsychic defensive processes such as Identification (Chapter 9), Introjection (Chapter 12), Rechannelization (Sublimation) (Chapter 19), Rationalization (Chapter 17), Fantasy (Chapter 7), and others, may be called upon unconsciously as defensively-intended reenforcements. Should these supplementary defenses fail in turn, they may become pathologically exaggerated, and/or the hidden impulses may make their appearance externally in disguised and symbolic form as symptoms of emotional and mental illness. Character defensive traits may be regarded in a comparable light to the more specific ego defenses, as to their intended purposes, effects, and possible symbiotic relations with emotional dynamisms and symptoms. See Chapter 5, *The Character Reactions,* in *The Neuroses,* pp. 227–307.

In instances of psychopathology, Repression is always exaggerated, its failure (derepression) has always threatened. As a defense it is overdone. Protectively intended, it over inhibits; extends farther than is psychically necessary. This is the *Principle of Overextension in Repression* and the repressing process. According to this principle *in emotional illness when banishing the intolerable through Repression, more material is carried along than is psychologically required.*

Thus some of the repressed data would prove consciously tolerable, were awareness permissible. This is borne out in psychotherapy, in which derepression is deliberately fostered. This is an overlapping principle with that of Auxiliary-Repression, particularly emphasizing the overinhibitory function of Repression in relation to clinical psychopathology.

3. Repression and Neuroses

In our work with the neuroses, we have found that Repression plays an important role in the psychodynamics of each case. Various neurotic symptoms can develop following Repression when it constitutes an inadequate or unsuccessful defense. (See *Case 102,* pp. 197–8.)

Unsuccessful repressive defenses leading to symptomatology include: (1) excessive or massive Repressions; (2) insufficient, partial, or inadequate Repressions; and (3) exaggeration of supporting or supplemental ego defenses to a self-defeating, psychologically uneconomic, and pathologic level. Repression leads far more readily to neurotic symptomatology when it fails to adequately perform its allotted task. Its role in Somatic Conversion (hysteria) was noted, and in Conversion generally (Chapter 3). Its role in various neurotic reactions has received further attention in *The Neuroses.*

4. Derepression and the Acute-Anxiety-Attack or AAA

Repressions are mostly silent. It is when derepression threatens, when a breakthrough into conscious awareness impends, that difficulty arises. Crisis can impend. A most acute and severe manifestation is the Acute-

Anxiety-Attack, or AAA. This is among the most disturbing and painful conditions to which man is heir. The following instance is illustrative.

Case 181

Repression Falters; the Acute-Anxiety-Attack

(1) *A Typical AAA.* A 31-year-old machinist was driving home from work one evening when he suffered an Acute-Anxiety-Attack or AAA and was brought to the hospital emergency room.

He was feeling tense, but otherwise well upon leaving work. Initially he experienced numbness and tingling in his legs. This was premonitory and rapidly followed by wild fright and a sense of impending doom. He could identify no initial emotional feeling, nor recall any precipitating or disturbing thoughts.

(2) *Clinical Features.* "Something terrible was about to happen, but I didn't know what it was ... I couldn't stand it. I was completely panic stricken ..." His heart beat wildly and breathing was labored. He was sure he was about to die. He managed to pull his car over to the curb, and a policeman helped him with a cab.

Upon arrival at the hospital, he was visibly shaken. He looked the picture of panic, which he described and was blanched, trembling, and dyspneic. His pulse and respiratory rates were increased, and blood pressure elevated. These kinds of readily observable changes afford ample proof to the greatest sceptic as to the acute and major functional changes which can accompany anxiety. They hardly serve as a measure, however, of the level of subjective emotional stress and tension generated.

(3) *Identification Facilitates Recapitulation.* History from several sources confirmed increasing nervousness and uneasiness for about 2 years, since his father's death. He began working then for a boss whose volatile temperament and characteristics were similar to his father's. The two never got along well, and the patient constantly thought of quitting. However, he continued to work for his boss because he "didn't want to let him down." On the day of his AAA, they had their first open argument, and he threatened to leave.

Briefly, his problems hinged upon repressed hostility toward his father and the conflicts this created. His father's death might have produced more immediate problems, if the relationship with his new boss had not served as a timely replacement. Identification of boss occurred with father, with the former becoming a substitute, allowing continuation of an established pattern of emotional reaction and relationship.

The threat of an open break with the boss was symbolically one with the father. This mobilized, recreated, and rekindled long-standing conflicts and added a new external danger. The conflicts had been unconscious. As fuel was added and they flared anew, derepression threatened and the Acute-Anxiety-Attack ensued. This man did well in therapy. He has not had an AAA for some years.

5. Derepression in Therapy

A. JUDICIOUS PACE BEST.—The therapist must keep in mind the possible consequences of derepression during treatment. Making the unconscious conscious is useful in therapy, so that derepression becomes an essential part of the therapeutic process. Sometimes this is painless or relieving. Sometimes it is painful. However, this must be handled judiciously and with due regard for the patient's relative ability at any given time to tolerate anxiety and to integrate new insights. One should encourage the patient to proceed at his own best and psychologically optimal pace. Urgency or "pushing" in the therapeutic situation can defeat its intent.

When one studies the symptoms of the neuroses, he learns increasingly that symptom evolvement is a likely consequence of partial and incomplete ("unsuccessful") Repression. Symptoms are often symbolic and disguised outward representations of various elements of unconscious conflicts, of which at least one aspect has been repressed.

There are usually several important unconscious purposes served in symptom formation. For example, the symptom may permit a partial disguised (and perhaps symbolic) external expression of an otherwise disowned wish. Elements of self-punishment in secret or more apparent form are likely to accompany secret gratification when secured.

At times, factors within the treatment situation constitute a threat. These are not always easy to fathom. Sometimes they are not reported. Sometimes they cannot be; they are unconscious. At other times, existing conflicts may be activated, or new ones created. Recognition of the existence of repressed material and its influence aids in the handling of these problems. Repression also can follow such conflicts.

B. THERAPEUTIC AIMS.—Forty years ago, the recovery of repressed data was the major aim of most psychoanalytic endeavors. The more current view includes wider vistas, as therapeutic aims in analysis and psychotherapy broaden. This is a constructive development which is reflected in the following *Table 10*.

Table 10

Modern Aims of Therapy

This outline of current treatment aims is offered to emphasize broader vistas. These succeed older more narrow aims of Repression dissolution per se, as prevalent some decades ago.

In treatment today, major psychotherapeutic goals generally include:
A. Constructive readjustments, adaptation, and reorientation to life generally.
B. Resolution of emotional conflicts.
C. Improved capacities and effectiveness in developing and maintaining satisfactory interpersonal relationships.
D. Emotional growth and maturity.
   As regards Repression more specifically:
E. Making the unconscious conscious; that is, the recovery of repressed material, including the recall of early memories.
   1. Derepression is undoubtedly a requirement for, as well as a consequence of successful therapy in varying measure, plus
   2. Facilitating its progress.
F. Recognition, study, elucidation, modification, reconciliation, and integration of repressed affects.
G. Insight promotion; the securing of a more accurate self-picture.

C. FREE ASSOCIATION.—In analytic therapy, techniques of free association are employed to encourage the recovery of repressed data. These are valuable. Such recovery is not easy, however, nor readily secured. The patient cannot report what he does not know. Sometimes, however, associations bring out suggestive or leading data. Slips of the tongue are occasionally significant.

While space does not permit thorough discussion, the significant role of dreams and their study should be stressed. Work with dreams can assist in ferreting out hidden conflicts, lost memories for early events, repressed motives and feelings.

As an experienced participant-observer, the therapist can often suspect and be alert for what lies still hidden from his patient-colleague. In addition to disguised and symbolic representations of repressed data in dream content, the physician may observe evidences of otherwise concealed and repressed drives as reflected in apparently inconsistent or irrational reactions and behavior.

For purposes of convenience in this exposition we have tried to isolate Repression as an ego defense. However, any real isolation is impossible. Every clinician recognizes its role in the operation of all the dynamisms. He utilizes this therapeutically and practically. Other defenses operate in conjunction with Repression; are called into play as reenforcements, and help to integrate the external manifestations of otherwise repressed impulses with other elements of the personality and society.

H. SUMMARY

1. Automatic Forgetting

Repression is an automatic forgetting. It is a major process employed by the ego to assign repugnant ideas and impulses to a seeming but misleading "oblivion" in the unconscious, from whence they are not subject to ready recall. Their presumed dormancy here is a relative matter, since they remain energy-laden and potent. Repression is an automatic, consciously effortless process of assignment to the unconscious of painful data, which plays a major role in emotional illness and health. It is a key concept in the behavioral sciences.

In distinction, suppression is the conscious effort to forget, control, and restrain, in contrast to the automatic relegation of Repression. In Repression, one is not aware that the process has taken place. A conception of the ego defenses views them as the *First Line of Psychic Defense.* Repression is particularly active in the early years.

The *Concept of Historical Validation* points out the likelihood of prior knowledge or recognition of a valid psychologic principle by earlier scholars (Chapter 19). Thus a "new" conception in the behavioral sciences can likely be found to have had some measure of prior recognition. Such research may be used to validate a concept or theory.

Repression-by-Association or *Auxiliary-Repression* was outlined. The resulting repressed data are *Association-Repressions,* an overlapping concept with the Principle of Overextension in Repression. The *Kinetic-Energy Principle,* or KEP was formulated to stress the requirement for continuing psychic energy to maintain material in the repressed state.

The work of Charcot, Bernheim, Janet among others, paved the way for early contributions by Josef Breuer and Sigmund Freud concerning the unconscious and Repression. Freud's continuing study and extensive writing played a leading role in the development of dynamic theory for the next several decades. He recognized that the basis of Repression lay in anxiety and that it was one of a number of important ego defenses.

2. *Types of Repression*

Primary or *Primal Repressions* include repressed data from infancy and later, most of which never really entered consciousness. Included are "instinctual" material and infantile fantasies. Important influences from Primary Repressions bear upon personality development, emotional health, and the establishment of significant emotional patterns for subsequent life.

Secondary Repressions follow later in time than the infantile primary ones. They take place secondarily to their having once been in conscious awareness. They are more frequently encountered in treatment and in living and are more accessible to observations. Both Primary and Second-ary Repressions are of great importance.

An entire complex or an actual experience may be repressed when psychic stress or trauma is sufficiently great. This is more common in earlier years. An instance of a *Major Repression* was cited in which memory of death by drowning of a child was repressed by her older sister, who had been assigned responsibility for looking after her. *Minor Repressions* occur of dates, names, words, phrases, meetings, various aspects of oneself or one's feelings, and a wide variety of items.

Repressions were accordingly also categorized as *Major* and *Minor.* There are *Partial, Auxiliary,* and *Total* Repressions. *Massive Repressions* are occasionally encountered in severe psychotic reactions.

2. *Added Conceptions*

Several conceptions were offered or reformulated, having proved useful personally and in teaching. The *Law of Universal Affect* emphasizes the basic premise that every thought, idea, word, or object possesses a quantum of associated affect; an *emotional charge.* This is true no matter how apparently neutral or minor the object may seem. The *Emotional-Object Amalgam* or EOA, is a convenient label for the unit comprised of an object plus its attached affect. This concept and term emphasizes: (1) the presence of the emotional component; (2) the existence of the bond; and (3) the firm nature of the compound.

In stressing the potential importance and influence of very small amounts of attached affect, the *Electronics Analogy* was formulated, comparing the significant effects of minute affective components in various EOAs, to the similar major influences produced by a change in electric potential of a few microvolts. The latter exert influence in certain complex (but far less so than with human emotions) electronic circuits. A *Chemical Analogy* might also be offered, drawing a comparison between often minute emotional charges in the EOA and the tiny plus or minus charges of the ions of a solution and the considerable influence these can exert in determining the direction of a given chemical reaction.

Concepts of the EOA have significant applications in memory. Minute amounts of positive or negative affect have great influences on the relative ease and facility of memory and recall, as well as Repression. Lapses of memory can be serious, major, and often problematic. Minor ones are sometimes embarrassing, often troubling, and occasionally amusing. Such lapses are all of interest and take place with great frequency. Memory is a vital faculty in human existence which warrants further research.

Wishful thinking can play a role in memory and in Repression and is a potential pitfall for the unwary scientist. Nietzsche and Darwin noted this. The term *convenient memory,* refers to conscious or unconscious forgetting where this is an advantage or convenience. The Principle of Scientific Determinism received mention. *Psychologic blindness* is the defensively-intended maintenance of nonawareness about some aspect of oneself, not infrequently concerning factors which are condemned in others. It can be self-defeating. Through Repression an inaccurate self-picture can be perpetuated. Recall often proves more difficult or impossible when there is unpleasant associated affect.

Repression follows anxiety or the threat of anxiety, which is its major motive force. It is a protectively-intended operation which can afford necessary respite for a hard-pressed ego. We may regard Repressions as both necessary and vital, and at the same time expect to find them in association with the operation of every ego defense and at the basis of every emotional illness. Thus Repression would be indispensable to both emotional health and illness.

Important applications of the principles of Repression are to be found in connection with the neuroses, character neuroses, psychoses, and their treatment. According to the *Principle of Overextension* in Repression, this defensively-motivated dynamism results in more data being carried over into the unconscious than might be psychically necessary. This is the over inhibiting function of Repression in conjunction with emotional illness.

Symptom development is a likely consequence of partial and incomplete Repression and threatened derepression. Several clinical examples were presented in which Repression was an outstanding feature. Its threatened failure was stressed in relation to the AAA (*Case 181*). Applications to therapy were considered. Derepression was discussed, together with a deemphasis of its earlier preeminent role in analytic therapy. *Table 10* listed the modern aims of insight therapy.

I. CROSS-REFERENCES TO *THE NEUROSES* *

Repression
In Nature of Anxiety (Chapter 1)
    defined; p. 17.
    dreams as a facilitation to R., a *Contribution to Emotional Health;* p. 39.
    in *frustration sequence* (anxiety⟶Repression⟶emotional symptoms); p. 32.
    of anxiety
        in phobic formation; p. 16.
        in psychogenesis of emotional manifestations; p. 20.
        motive force for R.; p. 51.
    of conflict
        as attempted resolution; pp. 21–2.
        equated with "fight" or "flight"; p. 24.
    of hostility
        core of every neurosis (Alexander); p. 28.
        in *ejaculatio praecox;* p. 9.
In Illusory Gains (Chapter 2)
    of conflict, in "gains" of emotional illness (Table 6); pp. 77–8.
    of dependency needs
        in *epigain* of emotional illness; p. 68.
        in paranoid individual; p. 75.
    of disowned aspects of self, in negative *King David Reactions;* p. 76.
    of hostility, in *Somatic Conversion* Reaction (Case 11); p. 72.
    of intolerable impulses,
        a defensive undertaking; p. 58.
        in disguised emotional symptoms; p. 59.
        in *endogain* of obsessive endeavors; p. 74.
        in primary gain, *endogain* (Table 5); p. 69.
In Anxiety Reactions (Chapter 2)
    dissolution of R. threatens, in Anxiety Reactions; p. 120.
    maintained, through defensive denial; p. 91.
    of hostility, in *anxiety-equivalent;* p. 102.
    of intolerable impulses, pathway to emotional illnesses (Table 7); p. 87.
    recall of R., important in intensive psychotherapy; p. 125.
    reenforced by ego
        in resistance to insight; p. 126.
        in *Secondary Defense Concept;* p. 97.
        in *Symptoms-Longevity Principle;* p. 127.
In Depressive Reactions (Chapter 4)
    of grief, encouraged (Case 31); p. 166.
    of hostility
        depression as last desperate attempt toward; p. 159.
        in *Concept of Diffuse-Retardation;* p. 157.
        in ego support, by therapist; p. 211.
        in masochism and sadism of Depressive Reactions; p. 177.
        in negative side of ambivalence; pp. 188–9.
            Case 35; p. 180.

---

* From Laughlin, H. P. *The Neuroses.* London, Butterworth & Co., Ltd., 1967.

in psychodynamics of depression (Table 14); pp. 178–9; also p. 219.
of sexual drives, less stringent today; p. 212.
vs. depression (Case 34); p. 176.
In Character Reactions (Chapter 5)
in formation of character traits; pp. 245–6.
massive, primary R., in traits of *Conversion Personality* (Table 19); p. 260.
of disowned data, results in diminished sexual activity of *Obsessive Personality;* pp. 295–6.
of hostility
in clinical depression (Case 59); p. 276.
in *Conversion Personality* (Case 52); p. 265.
in *Depressed Personality;* p. 271.
in evolvement of Conversion character traits; p. 262.
in overdevelopment of character traits (Case 50); p. 251.
of rage, in development of *Conversion Personality;* pp. 269–70.
successful, in obsessive traits (Freud); p. 235.
unsuccessful
in threat of derepression, in level of depression; p. 275.
overdevelopment of character traits, attempt to combat; p. 302.
In Obsessive-Compulsive Reactions (Chapter 6)
as a mechanism,
in psychodynamics of depression and obsession; p. 349.
in psychodynamics of *hygeiaphrontis* and obsession; p. 352.
in psychodynamics of Obsessive-Compulsive Neuroses; pp. 315, 373.
according to Freud; p. 314.
in *First Line of Defense* of obsessive person; p. 343.
in onset of obsessive symptoms (when derepression threatens); p. 337.
in relation to treatment
derepression necessary; p. 360.
in *Triple Defense* of obsessive person; p. 370.
of hostility
in *Antecedent Conflict* (*Defiance-Submission Concept*); pp. 339, 341.
in genesis of obsessive doubting (Case 71); p. 347.
in genesis of obsessive thoughts (Case 70); p. 344.
in genesis of obsessive traits; p. 322.
in obsessive patterns of defense (Case 65); p. 325.
successful, in obsessive defenses (*Inverse Anxiety-Symptom Ratio*); p. 323.
of sexual impulses, in *Compulsive-Security Ritual* (CSR) (Case 74); p. 354.
reenforcement of R.
in *King David Reaction;* p. 345.
in kleptomania (*Secondary Defense Concept*), (Case 75); p. 358.
through obsessive manifestations; pp. 319, 374.
sought, through compulsions and obsessions; p. 311.
In Fatigue Reactions (Chapter 7)
in etiology of Neurasthenia; p. 425.
of actual goals, in dynamics of boredom; p. 415.
of hostility
in danger of derepression (Case 84); p. 412.
reenforced by fatigue (in *Dependency-Dilemma of Infancy*); pp. 411, 437.
of prohibited impulses
maintained
in *endogain* of fatigue; pp. 408–9.
in fatigue and depression (Table 21); p. 407.

unsuccessful
 in *Fatigue Indicator,* in threatened derepression in therapy; p. 434.
 inverted into depression; p. 405.
 in *Teakettle Analogy;* pp. 406–7.
In Hygeiaphrontic Reactions (Chapter 8)
 body language, expression of R., in Somatic Conversion; p. 467.
 hygeiaphrontic symptoms, a defense against derepression; p. 482.
  in *Symptom-Barrage;* p. 505.
 massive R., in primitive emotional reactions; p. 497.
 of anxiety, in bases of *hygeiaphrontic* symptoms; p. 444.
 of dependency needs
  Case 97; pp. 474–5.
  in *epigain* of hygeiaphrontis; p. 494.
 of disowned impulses
  in *Attention-Absorption Defense* (Case 101); p. 488.
  in *endogain* of *hygeiaphrontis;* p. 481.
   Table 26; p. 511.
 of hostility
  in *Concept of Defensive-Layering* (Case 93); p. 465.
  into somatic concerns (Case 100); p. 486.
  inverted into *hygeiaphrontis* (Case 102); p. 500.
 of infantile fantasies (*Theory of Antecedent Conflicts*); p. 491.
 of sexual impulses, in psychodynamics of *hygeiaphrontis* (Freud); p. 449.
In Fear and Its Avoidance (Chapter 9)
 in threat of derepression as anxiety source; pp. 516–17.
 of hostility, derepression threatens (Case 110); p. 539.
 of instinctual drives, enforced by society; p. 520.
In Phobic Reactions (Chapter 10)
 defense of R.
  by diversion; p. 549.
  in *endogain* of phobia; pp. 547–8.
  in Freud's theories; pp. 550, 552.
 of dependency needs, in *phobic ambivalence;* pp. 578, 602.
 of hostility
  displaced, to phobia of flowers (Case 119); p. 572.
  in *Oral Dependency Conflict* (Case 125); p. 598.
  in phobic evolvement (Case 117); p. 567.
  in *Psychic Indigestion Concept* (Case 120); p. 573.
 of intolerable impulses
  in *Situational Phobia* (*Critical Attack of Anxiety*); p. 582.
  in symptom formation in neuroses; pp. 563, 593.
 of sexual impulses, in *Critical Displacement Phobia;* p. 580.
In Soterial Reactions (Chapter 11)
 in comparison of phobia and *soteria* (Table 30); p. 628.
 in principal mechanisms of *Soterial Reaction;* p. 627.
 of bases for *soteria,* in *Security Operations* (S.O.), (Case 127); p. 621.
 of dependency needs, in *soterial endogain;* p. 626.
In Conversion Reactions (Chapter 12)
 of disowned impulses
  body language, an expression of; p. 643.
  in Conversion convulsions; p. 685.
  in Conversion *endogain* (Table 36); p. 691; also p. 700.
  in determination of symptoms (Table 37); pp. 697–8.

in diagnosis of *Physiologic Conversion* (Table 31); p. 655.
in dynamics of symptom formation; pp. 662, 690, 716.
    Breuer's Dissociation in; p. 648.
in function of symptoms (Fenichel); p. 671.
in psychodynamics of *Somatic* and *Physiologic Conversions;* p. 642.
in sequence of reactions of Conversion Hysteria; pp. 550–1.
massive, in *Conversion Epidemics;* p. 703.
through *Secondary Restrictions;* p. 688.
of homosexual strivings, in aphonia; p. 680.
of hostility
    in Conversion pain (Case 137); p. 668.
        according to Fenichel; p. 703.
    in *Interpersonal Perpetuation Concept;* p. 665.
of oral sexual strivings, in *globus hystericus* (Case 146); dysphagia; (*emotional-equivalents*); p. 696.
In Dissociative Reactions (Chapter 13)
Amnesia as
    massive extension of; pp. 784–5.
    Table 41; pp. 777–8.
a source, in depersonalization (Table 40); pp. 764–5.
defined, in relation to memory loss; *p.* 776.
facilitated
    by approach of Alcoholics Anonymous (A.A.); p. 783.
    in induced dissociation and automatic writing; p. 810.
of conflict, in *Overall-Language Concept* in Dissociative Reactions; p. 742.
of dependency needs, initiates fugue in *Total Reaction to Crisis* (T.R.C.), (Case 171); p. 798.
of disowned data
    expressed in dreams; pp. 745, 776.
    in *Dream's Contribution to Emotional Health;* p. 749.
    in dissociated physiologic expression (Case 152); p. 735.
of painful event, in *Janet's Dissociation;* p. 734.
recall of
    in hypnosis; p. 821.
    through free association in therapy (Freud); p. 823.
In Neuroses-Following-Trauma (Chapter 14)
a factor, in *Total Reaction to Crisis* (TRC); p. 858.
in *raison d'être* of Neuroses Following Trauma; p. 873.
of awareness, a protective endeavor (in resistances to therapy); pp. 886–7.
of fear, in *Critical-Displacement Phobia* of snow (Case 176); pp. 855–6.
of infantile hostility, in obsessive *hygeiaphrontis* (Case 182); p. 873.
of unconscious wish to suffer, in Traumatic Neuroses; p. 869.
In Military Reactions (Chapter 15)
of guilt, in *Unit-Guilt Reaction*
    Case 186; p. 923.
    Case 188; pp. 927–8.
    Case 189; p. 932.
of hostility, in traumatic interpersonal situation (*Antecedent Conflict Theory*) (Case 187); p. 925.

J.   REVIEW QUESTIONS

Sample self-check questions on Chapter 21 and Repression for the student, psychiatric resident, and board candidate.

1. Why do many psychiatrists ascribe a major role to the function of *Repression* in both emotional illness and emotional health?
2. Outline the respective scope of *Primary Repressions* and *Secondary Repressions*. Why attempt a distinction?
3. Explain the *Law of Universal Affect*. Give an example of its application in relation to: (1) memory; (2) psychotherapy; and (3) the phobia or soteria.
4. Discuss briefly the implications of the *Emotional-Object Amalgam* or EOA in living.
5. Illustrate the clinical concepts of the *convenient memory* and *psychologic blindness*. How do they influence: (1) interpersonal relationships?; (2) psychotherapy?
6. Define:
   A. Suppression.
   B. *Kinetic-Energy Principle* (KEP).
   C. *Auxiliary-Repression*.
   D. *Repression-by-Association*.
   E. *Electronics Analogy*.
   F. First Line of Psychic Defense.
   G. *Minor Repression*.
   H. Affect association.
   I. *A Chemical Analogy*.
   J. Relation of anxiety to Repression.
7. Comment on the role of Repression, its threatened failure, and de-repression in the onset of psychopathology, the AAA (Acute-Anxiety-Attack), and free association.
8. Outline the *Principle of Overextension* in Repression. What are its implications in symptomatology and therapy?
9. What are the presentday aims of psychotherapy?
10. Discuss the relationship of memory to Repression. Why is Repression especially active in early years?

CHAPTER 22

RESTITUTION

. . . Unconscious Amends and Reparation

A. NATURE OF RESTITUTION

    1. Reparative Intent: a. Inner Guilt Feelings Motivate; b. Useful Clinical Concept. 2. Definition: a. Making-up-for Process; b. Distinguishing from Similar Dynamisms. 3. Conscious Restitution: a. Many Instances Effortful; b. Enforced Restitution and Restitutive Reenforcements; c. Restitutive Acts in Relationships; d. Operation Conscious and Unconscious.

B. TYPES OF RESTITUTION

    1. Interpersonal Restitution. Restitutive-Behavior; a. Responsibility and Amends Assessment Subjective; b. Minor Restitution; c. Prominent Effects of Guilt and Restitutive Endeavors; d. Principle of Never-Enough. 2. Public Restitution: a. Voluntary Restitution; b. Criminal Restitution. Enforced Restitution. 3. Social Restitution: a. Society Benefits; b. Pious Restitution; c. Restitution-via-Charity. 4. Restitution-by-Proxy. 5. Restitution in Dreams; 6. Business Restitution; Restitution-in-Abeyance. 7. Legacy Restitution.

C. SUMMARY

    1. Superego Pressure. 2. Interpersonal and Public Restitution. 3. Social Restitution. 4. Restitution-by-Proxy and Other Types.

D. REFERENCES (FROM *The Neuroses*)

E. REVIEW QUESTIONS

A. NATURE OF RESTITUTION

1. Reparative Intent

A. INNER GUILT FEELINGS MOTIVATE.—Restitution is a major ego defense. It is an unconscious intrapsychic operation evolved primarily in response to guilt feelings. Through Restitution the ego seeks to make amends for injury; to effect reparation for hurt, suffering or wrongdoing.

Restitution involves the unwitting performance of actions designed to make good losses or damage believed to have been inflicted. This generally but not always, has been at the hands of the person concerned or a group of which he is a part. The intent is reparative. The reparation seeks to indemnify the injured person, group, firm, public, society, or nation. To the extent this is deemed sufficient, feelings of guilt and responsibility are assuaged.

Restitution is one of several related ego defenses which are similarly evolved in unconscious endeavors to ease guilt. Through their operation, the ego seeks to mollify the psychic pain of a disapproving conscience, or superego. The dynamisms of Undoing (Chapter 25), Atonement-Penance (Chapter 26) and others also operate toward this goal. Restitution belongs with the *Higher Order* ego defenses. (See p. 430.)

B. USEFUL CLINICAL CONCEPT.—As one of the more advanced dynamisms, Restitution is less primitive and its evolution is more often associated with correspondingly advanced stages of personality development. Accordingly, its being called into play requires the demands of a well-developed conscience; one which can exert sufficient pressure upon the ego to so respond.

We originally described and named Restitution as the mechanism operating outside of conscious awareness whose object is the satisfaction of conscious or unconscious guilt feelings. We have found the delineation and employment of this concept useful clinically, in communication and teaching. It has been proffered to clinicians more widely as a possible convenience, as have the dynamisms of Inversion (Chapter 13), Absolution, Deferment, Devaluation (Chapter 26), and others.

2. Definition

A. MAKING-UP-FOR PROCESS.—Restitution may be defined as *an ego defense or mental mechanism operating outside of and beyond conscious awareness, through which the ego seeks to make amends and reparation to a person or group for losses which have been inflicted, or for injuries and damages for which responsibility is assumed, generally by the perpetrator, and as these are subjectively assessed.*

The assessment, often an unconscious one, may be realistic, partly so, or not at all. Objectivity is by no means a requirement for the bases of internal needs requiring the evolution of a given dynamism.

The unconscious does not require objectivity, rationality or consistency in its operations and they are often absent. The same applies to the emotions as experienced, having as they do elements and contributions from the unconscious.

Restitution is a defensive intrapsychic process of the ego which is automatically called into play by superego pressure, largely on the basis of unconscious feelings of guilt and responsibility. Through its operation, the individual unwittingly seeks to make-up-for his prior bad conduct; for damage consequent to his "instinctual" impulses, wishes, or fantasies, actions in response to them, or possibly for merely having had them. Restitution is a making-up-for process.

B. DISTINGUISHING FROM SIMILAR DYNAMISMS.—There are similarities as noted, between the operations of Restitution and Atonement-Penance. In the latter ego defense, however, methods of making-up-for unconscious guilt cover a wider range. In distinction, Restitution is a more specific and direct attempted repayment to the wronged party. Atonement-Penance may be unconsciously pursued through more diverse channels, usually including the self-infliction of pain, frustration, illness, defeat, injury, loss, or failure (pp. 450–453).

In Restitution, actual reparation is attempted, through the direct compensation and reimbursement of the injured party. This is in a rather narrow and definite sense, although of course also outside of awareness. Finally, in Restitution the connotation of punishment is not implicit to the process, as it is when the defense of Atonement-Penance is employed.

Undoing is a more primitive, magical Lower Order process. Through this ego defense as discussed later, something which is done is in effect undone. It is then as though the "something" had not been done in the first place. Undoing is closely related to Repression. It is less specific, developed, or selective, but likely to be more massive in its operation. Restitution operates in a more narrow sense and is less frequently observed. While guilt similarly can be important in initiating the dynamism of Undoing, as a motive force it is not as exclusive a basis as it tends to be in Restitution (p. 426 ff.).

Restitution involves some restorative act, activity, or behavior. At times it can be regarded as one way of Undoing or an aspect of Atonement. Restitution can also provide a means of Compensation (Chapter 2). In some instances of Rechannelization (Chapter 19) there can be restitutive elements, and an occasional restitutive process can approach Rechannelization in the amount of resulting constructive activity and social gain.

3. Conscious Restitution

A. MANY INSTANCES EFFORTFUL.—Conscious acts of restitution are not uncommon. One does something (or perhaps thinks or feels something) and on later reflection decides that this was destructive, injurious, or unfair. He seeks to make up for it. The following instances are illustrative.

Several friends were sitting together on the beach. They deliberately and repeatedly made one of the group who was knitting, lose track in counting 118 stitches for the sweater she was starting. Observing that this had "gotten under her skin," one of the ring leaders in the teasing, unobtrusively took over and made the count for her.

A businessman came to regard an earlier negotiated agreement as unfair for the other party and spontaneously and gratuitously modified the terms. In similar instances, the person might "make it up" to the other party in various ways. A woman mailed payment to a store to cover an unpaid for item. Most apologies when sincere, are attempts at Restitution. Others which are not, often seek to convey such an impression (p. 429).

An exacting conscience requiring scrupulous honesty can require disproportionate efforts by an individual to make restitution, as for a penny too much change. Abraham Lincoln hiked miles to return a cent. We are aware of course that the honesty of some people shows glaring inconsistencies. There may be great concern and one may lean over backwards, being painfully honest about small items, at the same time nonchalantly accepting dishonest gains from great ones. (See also p. 440.)

B. ENFORCED RESTITUTION AND RESTITUTIVE REENFORCEMENTS.— The principle of making restitution for wrongdoing is widely accepted in society. It is implicit to the philosophy of criminal law. When a prison sentence has been completed we speak of the prisoner as having "paid his debt to society." The debt is incurred through the commission of a criminal act, for which he makes what we term *Enforced Restitution* by serving out his sentence.

The Enforced Restitution exacted by law, may not satisfy the individual's subjective or unconscious sense of guilt. In some instances however additional restitutive acts may be demanded by inner needs as we have illustrated elsewhere. (*Mental Mechanisms* [Blue Book] *Case 91*). Such restitutive reenforcements may be performed without any conscious awareness of their connection and inner motivation. The concepts of Enforced Restitution and *restitutive reenforcements* have additional clinical applications in psychiatry.

C. RESTITUTIVE ACTS IN RELATIONSHIPS.—A worker may have "goofed off" on the job, feel guilty, derelict of his responsibilities, and as a consequence, double his efforts for a time to make up for the lapse. A supervisor grants extra time, or a concession to an employee because of feeling he has demanded too much.

A mother buys a child ice cream or takes him to a movie because of feeling guilty about an undue punishment. A lover treats his girl with special consideration and tenderness following an untrue accusation, unfair judgment, or shabby treatment. Such efforts are often not designed so much to win favor, as to ease one's own self-critical feelings.

D. OPERATION CONSCIOUS AND UNCONSCIOUS.—Restitutive acts are legion in human relationships and all manner of instances might be recounted. The important points however, are: (1) that they occur with some frequency; (2) that the distinction between the aims and goals of their conscious and their unconscious operation is not necessarily marked; and finally (3) the transition from one to the other is not very difficult, nor too uncommon. The margin between them at times is indistinct.

Thus, Restitution takes place outside of conscious awareness, an operation in which the intended restitutive act, behavior, or attitude as undertaken has lost its conscious connection with its inner motivation and goal, the latter remaining unconscious. In other words, the restitutive act may be carried out consciously enough. Its basis is hidden in whole or in part. Explanations if made, often are Rationalizations. These may be required so as to have an acceptable or plausible motive. Such an endeavor would thereby aid in maintaining the Repression of the guilt feelings.

B.   TYPES OF RESTITUTION

1. Interpersonal Restitution. Restitutive-Behavior

A. RESPONSIBILITY AND AMENDS ASSESSMENT SUBJECTIVE.—Unwittingly making amends and rendering repayment for wrongs as subjectively assessed, which are inflicted upon those close to oneself constitute a major group of Restitutions. This group comprises instances of what we term *Interpersonal Restitution.*

An act or behavior may be impulsive, unthinking, or injurious and lead to guilt and remorse. This sequence can progress, producing inner needs for Restitution. Restitutive acts between people result. The process is that of Interpersonal Restitution.

B. MINOR RESTITUTION.—Interpersonal Restitution, or other types do not have to be major and significant. Indeed, instances of Restitution are far more frequently minor ones. The rarer, striking instances, however, are likely to attract more attention. These usually are drawn on for case examples in order to more forcibly illustrate the point at hand. While this is unfortunate because of its undue emphasis, it is necessary and serves a useful purpose.

In keeping with our concepts of ego defenses, the person concerned is consciously unaware that he has made (or sought to make) Restitution. Awareness is generally only gained through special circumstances or analytic and psychotherapeutic techniques.

C. PROMINENT EFFECTS OF GUILT AND RESTITUTIVE ENDEAVORS.—In the example to follow, guilt and attempted Restitution played a major role in a young woman's life. The consequence was the development of a pattern of what is termed *Restitutive-Behavior.* This had been true to an extent in earlier years, as in the present era. Guilt played a significant role in her symptoms of anxiety and its effects, as it can in character development. It led to the decision to seek therapy.

She paid an unduly stiff price for her limited satisfactions in the form of guilt feelings over partly fancied neglect of her children and impositions on her mother. The continuing battle between her overly strict conscience and ego, with the consequent evolvement of Restitutive-Behavior, exerted a constant influence upon her actions and behavior. Her level of guilt feelings as subjectively experienced, was quite inappropriate when assessed objectively.

Case 182

Neurotically Exaggerated Guilt Feelings Motivate Restitutive-Behavior

(1) *Widow Seeks to Reconstitute Her Life.* A young woman was left a widow with two small children. She was partially provided for by insurance and could have made ends meet. However, she found a job as a private secretary—a position she enjoyed. Her children were cared for by her mother. She had made valiant efforts in seeking to refurbish her life.

A casual observer might have thought her fortunate to secure satisfactions through her work, but we soon learned that she felt quite guilty over this. She also suffered from guilt feelings over her mother taking over daytime care of the children, something in fact that the mother, a widow herself, actually enjoyed very much—as did the children. Resulting conflicts produced tension, nervousness, and led to gastrointestinal malfunction.

She entered therapy because of anxiety symptoms which were further exaggerated as a consequence of attentions by her employer. Courting her, he proposed marriage.

(2) *Restitutive-Behavior in Evidence.* During the course of therapy, the presence of strong unconscious guilt feelings toward mother and children were increasingly in evidence through a process of Restitutive-Behavior. This was undertaken outside of awareness of the need or intent, which remained unconscious.

Although her mother did not demand, need, ask, expect, or even particularly want it, the daughter insisted on paying an unrealistic sum for lodging and board. Her behavior towards her reflected exaggerated concern and solicitude. She showered the children with gifts and attention, to the point of overindulgence.

(3) *Healthful Modifications Follow Elucidation.* Through her behavior she unwittingly sought to pacify a neurotically severe superego. The latter filled her with guilt feelings over supposed neglect of her children during the day, and "impositions" on mother.

Clarification and elucidation of these factors in therapy led to more realistic appraisals, attitudinal and behavioral modifications, and considerably greater comfort. Her attitudes and behavior over a period of time had illustrated both the *Restitutive-Behavior Concept* and that of *Interpersonal Restitution.*

D. PRINCIPLE OF NEVER-ENOUGH.—The above instance illustrated another interesting and fairly oft-observed facet of Restitution; the trend toward its continued and increasing strength of operation. This is what we call the *Never-Enough Principle* or *Spiral.* The NEP helps explain the ineffective Restitution and why it tends to ever widen its scope. In certain instances which are at times noteworthy, this principle is illustrated as the restitutive activity proves to be insufficient.

This can comprise a tragically self-defeating kind of circular spiral reaction, as the restitutive endeavors prove to be "never enough." The behavior, desires, thoughts, and feelings which lead to the need for the psyche to evolve a Never-Enough Spiral, whether these be neurotically evaluated or not, do not abate. To the contrary they are more likely perhaps to gradually increase (p. 471).

The restitutive efforts in turn also increase, but since the underlying conflicts are not resolved, they are never sufficient to accomplish their purpose, that is, to indemnify to the extent necessary to fully allay or nullify the unconscious guilt feelings. The circular, spiral type of self-defeating operation as outlined by the NEP is the consequence.

So it had been with the young widow. Guilt-ridden for years, she had elaborated an unending pattern in which guilt feelings were steadily generated, to be followed as regularly by an increase in restitutive efforts. It was only possible for her to surrender this pattern after the unconscious was made conscious. Recognition and acceptance were followed by more objective views, a sounder self-evaluation, conflict resolution, and more constructive ways of coping with sources of guilt.

The Never-Enough Principle enters into the elaboration of patterns of exaggeration of various dynamisms and neuroses. When established, such patterns are not readily elucidated or surrendered. Therapeutic resolution was prolonged and difficult with the widow, but far less so than is sometimes true.

Interpersonal Restitution can be sought or occur in any relationship. It may be observed in parent-child relations, in the same direction as the foregoing case, or reversed. It is encountered between siblings and in other blood relationships. Interpersonal Restitution can operate in friendships, teacher-student relations, employer-employee, military, and business relationships, as well as others. Examples of these were included in our earlier work, *Mental Mechanisms* (pp. 223–252).

2. Public Restitution

A. VOLUNTARY RESTITUTION.—The major type of Restitution we term *Public Restitution* includes two particular subtypes: (1) that which is demanded and required *by* the public from an individual through due process of law, and (2) that which is voluntarily made *to* the public by the individual. These subdivisions are named *Enforced Restitution,* as noted earlier, and *Voluntary Restitution.*

Every year, municipal, state, and federal agencies receive unexpected remittances from people seeking to make up for past deficiencies. Prominent among these is the U.S. Internal Revenue Service. However, many bureaus and departments receive them. So also do banks and business firms. *Case 185* illustrates one basis as to how such a remittal may be made and notes the phenomenon of *Token Restitution.* Occasionally, one of these unsolicited receipts is sufficiently interesting or unusual to be picked up by the press.

More often such Voluntary Restitutions are not noteworthy enough as the foregoing, to be reported however, receiving routine treatment and no public notice. Most of these instances of course are deliberate and planned. The bases underlying the action however are not always fully in awareness. The persons concerned may identify themselves or prefer to remain anonymous. The sums involved are often petty, but occasionally there are sizable amounts. Overall the total sums however, are appreciable.

Not all Public Restitutions are so clearly planned. Not all are monetary, since restitutive endeavors find many and devious pathways. The U.S. Treasury maintains special accounts for unidentified, "lost," and unclaimed funds. These moneys arrive by various routes. It is probably safe to assume that a certain proportion of such "lost accounts," "accidents," or failures to be more specific about the identity or purpose of a payment, are unconsciously motivated in part at least by more or less unwitting restitutive needs.

Presumed carelessness is by no means a matter of mere chance alone. The intensive study of specific instances of accidents and mischance demonstrates repeatedly that such "chance," like other behavioral phenomena, tends to follow the Law of Scientific Determinism. Reasons and underlying bases may be obscure and difficult or impossible to uncover, but they exist.

B. CRIMINAL RESTITUTION. ENFORCED RESTITUTION.—Reference was made to the concept of Enforced Restitution to the public, considered complete when a prison term has been served out. The debt has supposedly been paid for that offense and the slate wiped clean in what is called *Criminal Restitution*. This may be correct technically as far as the law is concerned. It may not be correct to a victim, nor to the transgressor or his unconscious.

A troubled conscience can lead to continuing efforts to make Restitution; restitutive reenforcements. These can be both conscious and unconscious. In many instances of Restitution, conscious acts are more direct and apparent. These can still have contributing subconscious motivations which are not apparent.

Changes in attitudes, behavior, and character motivated by minor restitutive needs, are more subtle, far less apparent, but hardly less significant. They are more likely also to be more indirect, often being expressed toward others and the public generally. Further, society and the public may come to be the unseeking beneficiary of characterologic modifications. Public Restitution then can sometimes merge into the following interesting major category of Social Restitution.

3. Social Restitution

A. SOCIETY BENEFITS.—*Social Restitution* has been so named because society, or some segment of it, benefits from the indirect, less specific, and generalized endeavors at reparation which evolve. Recipients of resulting benefits have some relation or association with the injured parties, little relationship, or none. In any event, society in general is a beneficiary.

Repression of guilt feelings is a goal of unwitting efforts at Restitution. Success of this endeavor is dependent in turn upon the success of restitutive efforts in meeting the inner needs for them, as well as the pressures exerted by the superego. Social Restitution at times approaches the dynamism of Rechannelization or Sublimation in its operation, scope, and consequences.

Social Restitution manifests its activity in less dramatic fashion. Included are the contribution of kindly services, charitable works, and contributions to worthwhile and beneficial organizations, civic groups, religious bodies, and social agencies. Social Restitution unwittingly helps to account for many activities that are socially useful and worthwhile.

B. PIOUS RESTITUTION.—The following instance illustrates the influence of Restitution in contributions of work and money to a church. These activities on behalf of his church by a prominent builder and congregation leader helped for a time to keep in check certain guilt feelings over his more selfish gains from the affiliation, and similar factors in originally securing membership.

Case 183

Social Restitution; Church Contributions to Assuage Guilt

(1) *Guilty Feelings Come to Light.* A 58-year-old man had become a successful builder in a medium-sized city. He was a leading member of the largest church, to which for years he made increasing donations. He had originated a movement to build a new church, worked toward its realization, and sizably contributed to the building fund.

The builder became ill, seriously so. During the course of the illness the sick man told the minister about his deep feelings of guilt. When he joined the church it was in part for business reasons.

He had been well aware of the business contacts he might make. The financial value of his church affiliation was prominent among the reasons for his seeking membership. He felt very guilty about this.

(2) *Minister Recognizes Neurotic Features.* He had some very limited awareness that his increasing contributions of time, money, and interest might have some relation to guilt. However, any full awareness of his endeavors representing an effort to make up for his having personally and selfishly used his affiliation was lacking. He was unaware of the restitutive aspects helping to motivate his church work.

His concern was with his guilt, which was first consciously recognized. He could not appreciate his many useful contributions. These had lost their ability insofar as keeping his guilt feelings repressed, partly under the added stress of illness, plus serious family problems.

Fortunately, the minister had an excellent understanding of the situation and recognized neurotic factors in the level of his parishioner's feelings. The alleged hypocrisy in joining the church was also overrated. He arranged for referral for possible therapy.

(3) *Social Restitution Active.* During a series of intensive psychotherapeutic interviews, among other insights, the builder gained a clearer view of the restitutive factors in his church activities. Undertaken in behalf of a religious institution, they also comprised a subtype of *Pious Restitution.* Concurrently with his insight however, he came also to recognize their social usefulness and to properly credit himself.

His endeavors did not cease, although he discontinued them for a time, while he was getting his bearings. When resumed, they were on a more genuine and sounder basis, and have continued. The church in which he was a leader continued to exercise a powerful and constructive influence and made many useful contributions to the community.

His inner guilt feelings and resulting efforts at Restitution had aided substantially in making these social benefits possible. This was an example of Social Restitution.

C. RESTITUTION-VIA-CHARITY.—When one is aware of its possible operation and perhaps looks for it, consequences of the ego defense of Restitution come under observation clinically a fair number of times; not infrequently in the work of character analysis. In Restitution, the goal is to assuage guilt by doing something about it. Charity and charitable works afford a convenient and frequent route as we have illustrated in *Mental Mechanisms*. This is *Restitution-Via-Charity*.

In the following instance a lady continued a veritable barrage of gifts. Her largesse in what proved to be a significant reparative endeavor, was sufficiently distributed to nearly approach being considered as an instance of Social Restitution!

Case 184

Restitution Through Gifts

A socially prominent middle-aged woman entered treatment following a suicidal attempt. What amounted to a social trademark was her largesse as a giver of gifts.

House guests—and she had many—received an "arrival gift," and on departing a "departure gift." Anniversaries, birthdays, and special occasions were marked by gifts. Christmas meant hundreds of gifts with 10 weeks of intensive preparation.

During treatment, the early and more superficial layer of interpretation was that the concentration on gift giving was a "social promotion" type of activity. The subsequent meaning was a pathetic buying of attention, friendship, and regard, by a woman quite insecure, despite many advantages. The uncovering of successive layers of significance was in accord with the *Concept of Defensive-Layering* (see p. 465 in *The Neuroses*).

Eventually, a third and deeper layer of concurrent significance emerged, revealing her endeavor to be one of unconsciously sought Restitution. This was mainly in two areas: *first*, as an apologetic and restitutive making up to her acquaintances and friends for the relatively greater material advantages she enjoyed. *Secondly*, this was a general kind of reparation and Restitution for the kind of person she considered herself to be; the reflection of an unrealistically low level of self-esteem.

The analysis of this complex led to her attitudes and drive about gifts losing their compulsive and driven character. Her interpersonal relationships improved substantially.

4. Restitution-by-Proxy

An interesting aspect to the clinical study of guilt feelings is that they do not necessarily have to follow, nor do restitutive endeavors only seek to make up for one's own acts. For various reasons, and to various degrees, one may come to feel guilty or responsible for the misdeeds of a son, a child about a parent, one sibling about another, or a man about his spouse.

This provides the background for the intriguing type of restitutive activity appropriately named *Restitution-by-Proxy* as earlier illustrated in the "blue book" of *Mental Mechanisms*. Through this process one makes Restitution for the actions (or failure to act) of another person, about which he feels in some measure responsible.

Illustrations are to be observed during the course of psychiatric treatment. Its operation may be surmised at times in social situations. Thorough validation of instances however, is often difficult, even when study is feasible.

5. Restitution in Dreams; The Dream-of-Regret

Restitutive and reparative acts are not confined to conscious efforts nor to outward activity in response to unconscious demands. Restitution can provide a meaningful theme for daydreams, fantasy, and nocturnal dreams. Dream content can reflect otherwise unconscious guilt feelings and needs for making Restitution. These can be analogous to the operation of Undoing (Chapter 25), as expressed in dreams.

When the opportunity no longer exists for direct reparation to the person concerned, its only possible expression may be through a fantasy or dream. This situation we call the *Dream-of-Regret*. This dream expresses feelings like those of the lines:

> "Of all sad words of tongue or pen,
> The saddest of these, 'It might have been'." [1]

Occasional illustrations of this type of dream are encountered clinically.

The internal needs for Restitution can contribute to the manifest or latent theme of dreams. Manifest dream content may or may not reveal restitutive needs, the unraveling of which can require considerable study and analysis.

6. Business Restitution; Restitution-in-Abeyance

In thinking of people making Restitution, one's ordinary tendency may be to think in terms of money. In the foregoing discussion we have accordingly stressed that this ego defense encompasses a far wider range of restitutive activities. Various avenues for Restitution are prominent in business relationships. These provide instances of what may be termed *Business Restitution*. Taking various forms, they may be conscious, unconscious, or both. Many instances are available clinically to the observant therapist.

When funds or goods have been embezzled or misappropriated the evolution of Restitution as an intended ego defense may follow. Whether conscious or not, restitutive operations can take odd and varied forms. Minor dishonesties are rationalized in various ways. Many remain undiscovered as do many endeavors at Restitution.

In the following instance, we observe the conflict between accepting a dishonest gain, versus its restoration. This led to an interesting compromise; a type of suspended reaction in which both the gain and its Restitution were held in abeyance. This is an example of what we refer to as *Restitution-in-Abeyance*. It also illustrates the uneasy emotional compromise

---

[1] John Greenleaf Whittier, "Maud Muller," 1854.

occasionally encountered clinically in psychiatry, which we term the *Suspended Reaction*. (See *Compromise* Formation, p. 454.)

Case 185

Restitution-in-Abeyance

(1) *Rationalization Ineffective.* A 54-year-old vice president of a large merchandising firm was in intensive psychotherapy because of certain character traits which had resulted in professional limitations and social handicap.

Some years earlier, in the course of an ambitious and energetic career, he had been a store manager for a national chain. While in this position, he intermittently embezzled money from the firm. While each amount was small, the total was appreciable. This he sought to justify on the basis that he was not adequately paid. The attempted Rationalization was ineffective.

(2) *The Suspended Reaction.* Having moved on to another firm, after several years he worked for the chain again temporarily during a 3-week vacation. In lieu of collecting pay, he asked the firm to leave the money "on credit against future purchases." After this was arranged, he felt more comfortable, although he would still have denied blame or guilt. Note, however, that he did not surrender claim to the money, when it would have been easily possible to place it in with company funds.

Both realization of his improper gain, and its Restitution were held in abeyance in a kind of uneasy compromise of his conflicting feelings. Neither accepting payment nor surrendering his claim to it, comprised an illustration of what is termed clinically the *Suspended Reaction.*

(3) *Token Restitution.* Some period of time elapsed, after which he made substantial purchases from the firm. Instead of calling upon the existing credit, he paid the bill in full. As long as the money remained in their hands, he had made a *Token Restitution* for the funds earlier misappropriated. However, the money also remained available to him since it was held to his credit and at his call.

Through the resulting conflict and struggle with his conscience, he paid dearly for the earlier lapses. This served as an Atonement-Penance (Chapter 26).

With the elucidation of the conflict through therapy, he decided to make the Token Restitution more real. How could he do so without disclosure, in that he was unwilling for his defection to be known? He met this dilemma by using the deposited funds to pay for merchandise, and anonymously mailed a cashier's check to the firm.

7. Legacy Restitution

Restitution is not uncommonly sought through the provisions of a will. Attorneys and executors sometimes are aware of this type of sought-after *Restitution-by-Will*. There are many varied and interesting examples to be garnered of what may be alternatively termed the *Legacy Restitution*.

People can suffer guilt feelings about the vehicle of their success, or its effects. This may enter into the establishment of trust funds and foundations. This possibility is perhaps illustrated by the Nobel Peace Awards.

Case 186

Restitution-by-Will; The Nobel Awards

Alfred Nobel discovered dynamite and several important derivatives. Successful in the development and exploitation of his products as a businessman, he accumulated a great fortune. Biographical data strongly implies the presence of certain personality problems and emotional conflicts. He was a lonely, unhappy man, plagued with hesitancy, self-doubt, and probably guilt over the destructive employment of his explosives.

Nobel's super explosives were vastly superior to those hitherto available. While they found many peaceful uses, they made possible a new level of military performance—more destructive and lethal wars. Through their availability, more soldiers died and more destruction resulted. Within himself, Nobel must have suffered acutely from the havoc resulting from the martial employment of his explosives.

In his later life, he became interested in movements for peace. Upon his death in 1896, a major portion of his fortune was set aside to establish annual awards, of which perhaps the most famous are the Nobel Peace Prizes. By devoting funds derived from the manufacture and sale of war facilitating explosives to the promotion of peace, a measure of Legacy Restitution may have been "intended" for their destructive consequences.

C.   SUMMARY

1. Superego Pressure

Among the major ego defenses employed in response to superego (and social) pressure arising from guilt is that of Restitution. Through its evolvement one unwittingly seeks to make up for, to make reparation, for injury or loss which has been inflicted. Evaluation of such harm or hurt is subjective and may or may not be realistic. It has been defined as a making-up-for process. We have found it suitable and a matter of convenience in teaching and communication to name this important intrapsychic process *Restitution.*

Restitution is one of the more advanced dynamisms. Its intent is defensive and reparative; making amends in response to guilt feelings. It has similarities to Undoing and to Atonement-Penance, from which distinctions were also made. Conscious, effortful restitution is common and differences from the unconscious operation of the ego defense are not necessarily substantial. The principle of Restitution for wrongdoing, for damages inflicted, for hurt, and for criminal acts is widely prevalent and well recognized.

2. Interpersonal and Public Restitution

Interpersonal Restitution includes that which is made for wrongs as subjectively assessed, suffered at one's hands by those in close interpersonal situations. Many of these comprise *Minor Restitutions,* which are not necessarily significant clinically or personally. They particularly include intrafamilial instances, and may influence behavior in very minor, to major ways. Some of these consequences illustrate a *Concept of Restitutive-Behavior.* Guilt and restitutive endeavors can have prominent characterologic and symptomatic influences.

Public Restitution includes that which is demanded by the public, by due process of law, plus that which is voluntarily made. Public Restitution is less stringent today and the Talion Law has been largely abandoned. Subdivisions of this type are *Enforced Restitution* and *Voluntary Restitution*. That made by the serious offender legally, is *Criminal Restitution*. What are called *restitutive reenforcements* occur as added restitutive endeavors when Enforced Restitution as required by law for example, does not satisfy unconscious guilt.

3. Social Restitution

In Social Restitution society in general benefits from the restitutive endeavors. Herein, the resulting major changes can approach those in quality resulting from the operation of the mechanism of Rechannelization (Chapter 19). Occupations may be chosen and one's life work influenced. In the *Pious Restitution,* a religious institution becomes the beneficiary.

The *Never-Enough Principle* and *Concept* or NEP is widely operative in psychic defenses. In Restitution this term refers to pitfalls in some restitutive processes, so that both guilty needs and restitutive efforts continue to slowly increase in a circular fashion; the *Never-Enough Spiral.* Restitution is made but it is "never enough."

Social Restitutions at times are illustrated through contributions to church and to charity. *Restitution-via-Charity* and that sought through giving gifts, received brief reference. The important *Concept of Defensive-Layering* was mentioned.

4. Restitution-by-Proxy and Other Types

Restitution-by-Proxy may occur in which one person makes Restitution for another's deeds or omissions. The needs to effect Restitution are reflected in certain dreams. One illustration is found in the *Dream-of-Regret.* Instances of Restitution are fairly frequent in business affairs (*Business Restitution*), in which they may take many forms besides the monetary.

The interesting uneasy compromise type of *Restitution-in-Abeyance* was illustrated. This provides a significant illustration of the *Suspended Reaction Concept* in psychiatry. The *Ineffective Rationalization* was also illustrated in *Case 185.* Inevitably, as in this instance, its lack of effectiveness leads to the evolution of other defenses.

Restitution also takes place through bequests in *Restitution-by-Will,* alternatively referred to as *Legacy Restitution.* In the *Token Restitution,* reparation is not always made and is only symbolic or token in nature.

D.   CROSS-REFERENCES TO *THE NEUROSES**

Restitution
   an ego defense against anxiety; p. 25.
   making-up-for reparation, in obsessive manifestations; p. 327.

---

* From Laughlin, H. P. *The Neuroses.* London, Butterworth & Co., Ltd., 1967.

E. REVIEW QUESTIONS

Sample self-check questions on Chapter 22 and Restitution for the student, psychiatric resident, and board candidate.

1. What provides the motive force for the unwitting evolution of *Restitution* as an ego defense?
2. We speak of possible *restitutive reenforcements* being evolved when *Enforced Restitution* is insufficient. Explain.
3. Describe and illustrate *Interpersonal Restitution*.
4. How does the *Never-Enough Principle* or NEP find application in restitutive endeavors? The *Concept of Defensive-Layering?*
5. Provide instances from social or clinical experience of the major types of *Public Restitution*.
6. A. Define and illustrate *Social Restitution*.
   B. Define and illustrate the subtype of *Pious Restitution*.
7. Explain how the following can find application in clinical practice:
   A. *Minor Restitution*.
   B. *Restitutive-Behavior*.
   C. *Token Restitution*.
   D. *Restitution-via-Charity*.
   E. *Business Restitution*.
   F. *Restitution-by-Proxy*.
   G. *Suspended Reaction Concept*.
   H. Superego pressure.
   I. *Criminal Restitution*.
   J. Conscious and unconscious guilt.
8. How does the *Dream-of-Regret* function in relation to restitutive needs?
9. What is *Legacy Restitution? Restitution-by-Will?*
10. Compare and contrast the operation of Restitution with that of the related *Guilt-group* of dynamisms; Atonement-Penance, Undoing, and Compensation.

CHAPTER 23

SUBSTITUTION

... Psychologic Alternative Provided

A. NEW OBJECT ASSIGNED
   1. In Many Areas. 2. Definition. The Symbiotic-Substitution.
   3. Relations with Other Dynamisms.

B. NATURE OF SUBSTITUTION
   1. Conflict Resolution: a. Essential in Phobic Defense; b.
   Characterologic Implications. 2. In Obsessive Reactions: a.
   Counterirritant-Substitution; b. Other Types.

C. SUBSTITUTION IN THERAPY

D. SUMMARY

E. REFERENCES (FROM *The Neuroses*)

F. REVIEW QUESTIONS

A. NEW OBJECT ASSIGNED

1. In Many Areas

As a psychic operation, Substitution is the process of replacing an act, object, thought, attitude, or satisfaction with another. In Substitution, a psychologic alternative is provided. One object displaces another. It may be similar, related in kind, or of a different order. Substitution can be conscious or operate unconsciously.

As an unconscious process, Substitution is one of the major ego defenses. Herein it operates outside of awareness, and through its use a consciously intolerable goal, emotion, or object, for example is displaced by one which is more acceptable or approved. A new object is assigned to stand in place of one which is psychologically repugnant or intolerable. Substitution is one of the more advanced, Higher Order dynamisms.

The aims of Substitution include allaying anxiety and resolution of emotional conflict. In general, the substituted object is something that is psychologically more innocuous, acceptable, desirable, and admissible to conscious awareness by the person concerned.

There are many types of Substitutions which take place, and can be observed clinically in many areas. Awareness of their operation varies widely. Sexual aberrations represent a form of Substitution. An activity involving physical exertion as with an active sport, can provide a substitute outlet for aggressive impulses (Activity Substituion). Fantasies attempt to provide unrealistic and substitutive satisfactions. Various Substitutions for bisexual gratification are found through such activities as courting, love stories, exercise, masturbation, dancing, and avocations. There are many examples and variations.

Substitution is also encountered in increasingly complex fashion with major consequences in behavior, personality adjustment, and character development. For example, an author employed his writing about people and about personally forbidden situations in interpersonal relationships as an acceptable substitute for unacceptable participation. The devotee of erotica may similarly substitute reading and fantasy for action.

In what is described as the *Self-Aggrandising* Substitution, a man dwelt upon self-assumed areas of prowess in athletics and courting, thus replacing occupational ones in which his achievements were mediocre. This type of operation of the ego defense can bear a close kinship to Compensation. We shall offer further illustrations of the operation of Substitution following its definition. It is prominent in the Phobic and Obsessive Compulsive Reactions.

2. Definition. The Symbiotic-Substitution

As a conscious process, Substitution results in the displacement of one object, goal, or satisfaction, by another one. In our present psychiatric context, we would define Substitution as *the ego defense or mental mechanism operating outside of and beyond conscious awareness through which an unacceptable or unobtainable goal, emotion, drive, attitude, impulse, interest, or need, which is consciously intolerable and repugnant, is replaced by a more acceptable one.* The ego is provided with a psychologic alternative.

In other words, Substitution refers to the unconscious process of replacing one object with another. New and more innocuous or obtainable acts, objects, thoughts, attitudes, and satisfactions may be so substituted for the original ones.

Sometimes the dynamism of Substitution functions alone. At other times it is operative together with other mental mechanisms, with which it is intimately related. In certain of these conjoint processes—for example with Displacement in the Phobic Reactions—its intrapsychic operation is termed a *Symbiotic-Substitution*.

3. Relations with Other Dynamisms

Displacement and Substitution are often observed functioning together (p. 87). In *Case 50* (p. 90), they were illustrated operating in conjunction. The Symbiotic-Substitution is particularly prominent in the phobic type of defense. Herein we observe how a significant emotional charge can be displaced from one object to another.

In similar fashion, hatred can be diverted from a person where it would lead to emotional conflict or danger, to someone else where this seems safer, less conflictual, and perhaps to some extent justified. At other times it is not a person but an act, which is consciously objectionable and intolerable and becomes the object for the operation of Substitution. A murderous impulse may be replaced through the Substitution of a minor aggression, or be displaced toward another person, substituted as a safer object. (See pp. 87 and 238.)

In another type termed *Activity Substitution,* as noted, hostility and aggression may be expressed or at least to some extent released, through the Substitution of some more impersonal type of activity, such as wood-chopping, bowling, or a punching bag. Earlier, in *Case 29* (p. 67), we observed Substitution reenforcing Denial.

The dynamics of Substitution and Replacement (Chapter 27) are almost identical. Replacement is a minor ego defense through which the object of emotional feelings is replaced by another which is similar. The operation of Substitution and its relationships with other ego defenses can be ascertained with some frequency in individual psychotherapy. Substitutions are sometimes noted and discussed in group therapy.

The following instance illustrates the operation of this ego defense in pronounced form, as a new and more tolerable set of interests and activities were adopted in substitutive fashion. The scope of this operation and its consequences are reminiscent of the dynamism of Rechannelization (Chapter 19). (See references pp. 129 and 317.)

Case 187

Substitution for Disturbing Interests

(1) *Remodeling Projects Provide Satisfaction.* A 35-year-old married woman in therapy had successively undertaken the remodeling of three homes. As soon as one home was completed it was sold and the family would move to another, which was tackled in turn.

Each remodeling was a major undertaking. She threw her energies into this endeavor. As a consequence, plus imaginative ability, the finished results were excellent. She gained a certain reputation and had offers to continue her absorbing occupation on a professional basis. She "... enjoyed all of this immensely.... You've no idea how much satisfaction I secure from this work ... I was really only content and satisfied at these times...."

During the course of her intense interest and activity, a number of emotional conflicts were active and smoldering. The relationship with her husband, a successful engineer and inventor, had never been satisfactory. Their marriage was on the rocks. There were serious difficulties with both parents. Finally, being a mother to three small children was intolerable.

(2) *An Important Defensive Operation.* Under these circumstances Substitution of the absorbing interests in remodeling was hardly surprising. The home and family conflicts seemed insoluble. Problems

were "... so painful and seemed so insurmountable that I didn't even want to consider them.... Couldn't think of them at all ... I know now that it was a substitution of new interests and problems for ones which had become too painful. (Attention-Focus Substitution). I couldn't stand to think about those things.... This was a way of avoiding a situation that I simply couldn't tolerate any more."

Her successful Substitution seemingly preserved a measure of equanimity. In its absence her emotional situation would have deteriorated more drastically. This had been an important defensive operation. Its elucidation aided her therapy.

B.   NATURE OF SUBSTITUTION

1. Conflict Resolution

A. ESSENTIAL IN PHOBIC DEFENSE.—Substitution ultimately operates as a defense against anxiety. As a clinical example, when disowned rage threatens to come into conscious awareness during a treatment session, an obsessively repetitive train of thinking may ensue as a defensively-motivated Substitution. Thus, also in Obsessive neuroses, the repetitive thought or obsessive rumination displaces a more disturbing unconscious one; serves as a substitute. The Substitution defends against the anxiety which the disturbing thought would produce. See Chapter 6, *The Obsessive-Compulsive Reactions* in *The Neuroses* (pp. 307–379).

As noted, Substitution operates conjointly with other ego defenses. Together with Displacement in the evolvement of the phobic defense, an external object is substituted for the internal one, which is thereby more readily maintained in its repressed state in the unconscious. Displacement (Chapter 5) is the name for a major ego defense and is employed in describing the dynamics of the phobias, where the actual internal but unwitting object of fear and dread is displaced by a substitute external one.

In phobia formation, Substitution and Displacement are essential dynamisms. Together they operate so as to bring about the Substitution of an external and consciously recognized object of fear and dread for the disowned one.

In an illustration of six major points in the dynamics of a phobia in A Phobia of Travel, *Case 121* (p. 576), *The Neuroses: First,* Repression had taken place, and the patient no longer was aware of the negative side of his early ambivalent feelings or dependency needs. *Secondly,* the anxiety had been displaced externally onto travel, which had become the phobic object. *Third,* the external phobic object was a Substitution for the original, disowned internal area of concern. *Fourth,* externalization had occurred, with disowned emotional feelings bound to the new target for fear and dread through the dynamisms of Displacement and Substitution (pp. 462–4).

In this case, the *fifth,* travel became the disguised outward symbolic representation and object for otherwise disowned and disturbing ideas and needs. Finally and *sixth,* this entire complex intrapsychic operation was in the service of controlling, checking, and denying anxiety.

As with other ego defenses, Substitution ultimately operates in the endeavor of conflict resolution, seeking to allay and to prevent resulting anxiety. The six aspects cited may be found in the underlying psychodynamics of many Phobic Reactions.

B. CHARACTEROLOGIC IMPLICATIONS.—The conflict resolution bases of characterologic developments are not often readily discernable, but are nonetheless most important. In *Case 187*, we noted some of the major events which can transpire.

The following description from a man's early life in the Middle East presents an interesting instance of substituted aims and activity. These contributed to what possibly comprised in level a Rechannelization. Due to the circumstances, only surmises are possible as to psychodynamics.

Case 188

Substitution Contributes to Rechannelization

(1) *An Aggressive Little Girl.* "Thirty years ago there was a little girl about my own age in my country. We used to play together with many other boys and girls. This girl developed a great pleasure in sticking other kids with pins, thorns, or any penetrating object she could find. She greatly enjoyed seeing somebody jump in fright.... Her favorite trick was to steal up behind someone who was not watching, and stab them with whatever she had in her quick little hand.... A long, strong thorn was usually the weapon, and their back seat her favorite target. The second most favored place was the back of the neck....

"Sometimes she would get a hit from her more sensitive victims, but that only made her worse. She would retaliate with a more penetrating stab.... Her parents thought it was cute at first, but later when she sometimes exercised her darts on their bottoms, the cuteness faded, and stronger measures were taken. She was not allowed to play with us, in addition to other forms of punishment.... This treatment gradually worked, and spared us considerable suffering....

(2) *After 14 Years; Channeled into Substitute.* "At ten I left the village and did not see her for a long time. Fourteen years later, in the summer of 1956, I went back to visit my family, and she was among the old friends I met. She was now married and had four children. When I saw her again she had a needle in her hand. However, now she held it so delicately, and instead of using it on someone's seat, she was producing the finest embroidery I had ever seen. No one in the village could match her exquisite work.

"As a little girl she had considerable aggressiveness which she expressed rather openly. Thorns she could easily obtain and children were ever-present. Restraint was not overstrong.

"Later, however, her aggressiveness was forcibly suppressed. It gradually came to be expressed in a way suitable to her and through media which her environment could supply, namely, needle, thread, and cloth.... This was a successful rechanneling of new and commendable aims for an aggressive drive that was unacceptable...."

The Substitution as described in the foregoing instance, undoubtably contributed to a Constructive Rechannelization of early aggressive-sadistic drives (p. 299).

2. In Obsessive Reactions

A. COUNTERIRRITANT-SUBSTITUTION.—In Obsessive-Compulsive Reactions, we occasionally observe clinically the unconscious ideational Substitution of something less disturbing. Several of these are illustrated in the appropriate chapter in *The Neuroses* (pp. 307–379).

Anxiety makes it impossible for the obsessively-oriented individual to control the recurrent disturbing thoughts in obsessions, despite his desire and efforts. The intrusion of an unwelcome obsessive thought, as we learn, seeks to prevent anxiety by serving as a substitute for a subjectively less welcome thought or impulse.

The obsessive person commonly evolves a number of mechanisms for intended ego defense. His unconscious employment of Displacement and Substitution is common; Displacement of affect to a new object, and the Substitution of the new object for the repressed one.

The following instance illustrates the more or less deliberate Substitution of new concerns for existing obsessive ones. This is an example of what we term the *Counterirritant-Substitution* in which a new source of concern or irritation becomes preferable, since it detracts from the existing one. A segment of attention is thus redirected toward the CS, and absorbed by it. The magnetic attraction of the obsession is lessened accordingly.

Case 189

Substitution of New Concerns for Obsessive Ruminations

(1) *Obsessive Preoccupation with Homosexuality.* A 23-year-old graduate student narrowly missed a psychotic episode when his obsessive system of personality defenses broke down. Fortunately, he was able to get into therapy and this crisis was averted.

He continued to have periods of stress during treatment. Manifestations at these times were obsessive ones. They involved the recurrent intrusion of disturbing thoughts about homosexuality.

These were most distressing. He devoted a great deal of effort to their attempted control and suppression. His attempts were limited in success, as is usually the case with obsessive intrusions. He suffered a great deal.

(2) *Smoking Abandoned, Producing New Concerns.* This young man had been a heavy smoker for years. He derived great satisfaction from cigarettes and was dependent upon them. One day he decided to give up smoking. He realized this would cause him considerable strain and trouble. However, he sought this deliberately.

He had decided that the anticipated concern, stress and struggle over giving up smoking would provide a more tolerable substitute for his obsessive ruminations about homosexuality, which were very much a cause of distress. For a time the deliberately created Counterirritant-Substitution was to an extent effective.

The Counterirritant-Substitution may also be employed in various guises by persons suffering from emotional depression, anxiety, tension, certain painful conversion symptoms, and in occasional instances of Hygeiaphrontic Reactions. Employment of the CS may be the result of a conscious effort or comprise an unconscious endeavor.

The obsessively burdened person on occasion may welcome the CS discomfort of a severe cold. As a substitute, the latter somewhat forcefully occupies, absorbs, and diverts attention. The following is a less conscious example of this type of Substitution.

Case 190

The Counterirritant Substitution

A young man suffered from terribly empty, desolate, and lonely feelings. Many of these had been repressed. He had no friends, and his family was distant. Each new disappointment in the interpersonal sphere threatened to force renewed recognition of his inner desolation. This would be followed by compulsive masturbation, although he was unaware of the connection. While this practice afforded some measure of comfort and solace, it was also associated with considerable emotional conflict.

Masturbation was consciously repugnant and he suffered from guilt. These feelings, albeit painful in and of themselves, were a more tolerable substitute for the inner ones which threatened derepression. This was an instance of the unwitting operation of the Counterirritant-Substitution.

B. OTHER TYPES.—Additional interesting types of Substitution are to be in the obsessive pattern of defense and in other neurotic defensive patterns of reaction as well. Through the *Antidotal-Substitution* one makes up for a hurt, loss, or injury. Certain Soterial Reactions can include elements of this process. In Depressive Reactions, the depressive feeling may be combatted through inadvertently securing "another hurt which will hurt more," as another variant of the Counterirritant type of Substitution.

Through what for convenience we refer to as the *Attention-Focus Substitution,* one may obsessively bury himself in work or an avocation. This can represent unconsciously a more acceptable focus for attention and interest, serving as a substitute for that of a more painful life situation or interpersonal difficulties. It is a function of the dynamism which can be significant. Certain distinctions from Replacement may be noted, p. 487.

Substitution of course can be more symbolic. In the following instance "house tidying" as an achievement which was possible to manage, had been the Substitution for "life tidying," which seemed impossible to achieve. Also illustrated is the Attention-Focus Substitution.

Case 191

Substitution of House Tidying

(1) *Perfection Housekeeper.* A housewife for years devoted herself to housekeeping. She had become the perfectionist housewife *par excellence.* Everything was immaculate.

Her overdeveloped ability to keep things in order, however, was in marked contrast to an inability to keep her life in order. There were no satisfactory friendships. Her marriage had collapsed, and relationships with children were distant and strained. As her life situation deteriorated, interests in order increased. She could not tidy up her life. Her house she could tidy.

The Substitution had been an obsessive salvation, desperately needed. Among its defensively-motivated functions was that of the Attention-Focus Substitution.

(2) *Obsessive Components Lessen.* Through prolonged therapy this lady was able to gain major beneficial insights. She became increasingly the master of her fate and able to make constructive adjustments. As these were effected the obsessive components in the house-tidying lessened their grip. She came to recognize and understand the Substitution, its symbolism and effects.

In her words, "I had to keep my house terribly neat and clean.... It no longer seems necessary. It no longer helps me feel more orderly.... I can see now how it was an effort to get order and system in some area of my life. Now I have some....

(3) *Dynamism Served Vital Defensive Needs.* "The cleaning and housekeeping are only good for their own sake any longer.... It's just the room I'm organizing, not my head!...Oh, I still keep things neat and clean, but not so desperately. It doesn't serve the same needs...I can keep my life tidy; the house is not a substitute any more...."

The house which she could keep tidy had been a tragic substitute for her life which was disorganized and chaotic, and which she could not keep tidy.

The Substitution evolved in support of a vitally needed obsessive orientation. Energies could be poured into the substituted endeavor with tangible results. Attention and interest were defensively refocused into a more tolerable area, as an instance of the Attention-Focus Substitution.

C.   SUBSTITUTION IN THERAPY

Our final two instances concern Substitution as its operation may become evident in the therapeutic situation. In these examples the attenuated, concealed, and thereby safer expression of anger became permissible. In each the therapist was the actual target for hostile feelings, but these had been deflected through Substitution, to become directed toward related but tangential, less hazardous targets.

Case 192

Substitution Allows Resentment Expression

(1) *Lateness and Small Talk Resented.* A 41-year-old broker was in intensive therapy. He was handicapped by certain character traits, including diffidence, lack of directness, and reticence. One day the therapist was late. On beginning the session, he briefly chatted informally, stopping shortly as it became apparent that the patient's participation had fallen off.

After a period of silence, punctuated by sporadic remarks of little consequence, the patient talked about inconveniences in therapy. He complained about the schedule and difficulties in meeting. He talked of the expense and requisite sacrifices. His position in the therapeutic relationship must indicate masochism.

He said, "I am masochistic to continue (therapy) without putting in a lot more time in raising questions! I ought to consider a lot of things about the lack of advantages and merit. A person would have to be a masochist to enjoy this situation!" He continued for some time in a general vein about his self-sacrificing efforts in keeping treatment going.

(2) *Underlying Anger More Personally Directed.* Some sessions later it came out how angry he had been with the doctor. He very much resented the lateness. The friendly chit-chat had added further "insult

to injury" as a "waste of my time . . . talking about trivialities . . . using something (time) that was properly mine. . . ."

The Substitution of subject matter so as to provide a related but tangential target, took place unconsciously as an important defensive operation. As such it allowed an indirect and thereby safer route for the expression of resentment. In this way his anger became transposed. He pursued a self-righteous theme of "See how much I do for the therapy and to make it possible." A significant implication was the unspoken reproach, "Why don't you work at it also?"

(3) *Gain to the patient.* The patient was of course unaware of the Substitution. This was worked out later. The unwittingly sought gain was that the affect secured expression in part, the Substitution allowing this in attenuated form and toward a tangential target.

This was safer in that further generation of hostility, or retaliation, was far less likely. Further, what he expressed was couched in such a way that it might conceivably generate sympathy for his difficult situation, rather than feared counter responses should his anger become evident.

Case 193

Substitution of Family Doctor for Therapist as Resentment Target

(1) *Traumatic Background; Early Needs Not Gratified.* A 31-year-old woman suffered from a Schizophrenic Reaction. Hospitalization was not essential, however, and she was treated successfully as an out-patient. Therapy sessions were three times weekly for several years. During most of this time she was plagued with overwhelming dependency needs. This was the inevitable consequence of deep emotional needs which had never been gratified.

Her mother suffered a psychotic decompensation when the patient was two. Subsequently the little girl was moved from one foster home to another. This resulted from a traumatic series of events and the development of constructive and permanent emotional attachments was impossible.

(2) *Ambivalent Feelings Develop.* Dependency and regressive features in the illness were manifested in the original symptoms, including overwhelming fatigue, inability to make decisions, emotional instability, fear of being alone, and the desired escape into sleep.

As the mother of a young child, and because her husband was the dependent victim of alcoholic habituation, no one in her environment could give her any of the care she herself cried for. As a result, she was hostile toward everyone. She could not allow this any outward expression, or conscious awareness.

In therapy attempts were made to gratify some of this dependent longing through support, fostering interests, and a planned program of activity. Inevitably, however, the therapist had been unable to be the "good mother" for whom the patient longed. As her positive feelings toward him grew stronger, her underlying hostile ones also increased. Her attitude toward him became strongly ambivalent.

(3) *Clues Suggest Substitution.* In one therapeutic session she began recounting difficulties she had with her family doctor. Her little girl had become ill. When she called the physician he was hesitant about coming. ". . . .He has been like that before. He just doesn't seem interested. Surely it is not too much to expect that the doctor will be available when he is really needed. . . . He acted that way with me earlier . . . I went to him for help and he irritably said he didn't know what was the matter with me, and did nothing. . . ."

As she continued, the hostile feelings became more intense. Fury flashed in her eyes. The strength of her anger was out of proportion to the incident described. As an added clue, in a slip of the tongue she said "you" instead of "he" when referring to the family physician. By the end of the session she was relieved and felt less tense. These clues together with other background data suggested the operation of the Substitution.

(4) *Substitution Provides a Safer Object.* From what she said it appeared that the real object of her anger was the therapist, whom she felt was not sufficiently interested or doing much. This was confirmed. To express or feel this was too anxiety-provoking, as it meant to her the end of the relationship. Instead, she unconsciously employed the dynamism of Substitution. She consciously experienced anger toward the family physician instead of her therapist. As a more removed and safer target she was able to express it. (See Index references to the *Scapegoat Reaction.*)

The family physician unwittingly became the substitute object for rancor and resentment. As a more acceptable substitute for her conscious emotional feelings, these had been unconsciously displaced and their partial discharge achieved through the resulting disguised expression. As frequently occurs, the ego defenses of Displacement and Substitution were operating together in a symbiotic kind of relationship, illustrating the *Symbiotic-Substitution.* Elucidation of the operation of the dynamism in this instance aided therapy and opened the way for recognizing similar instances of Substitution as well as the operation of other ego defenses.

D. SUMMARY

Through operation of the Higher Order ego defense of *Substitution* a psychologic alternative is provided, for example in the form of a new object or target. Thoughts, attitudes, and satisfactions can also be substituted. The aim is conflict resolution and averting anxiety. Substitution operates in many areas.

In the *Self-Aggrandizing Substitution,* an area of actual or unreal achievement or prowess takes the place of unsuccessful ones in one's contemplation. In conjoint operation with another dynamism as frequently occurs with Displacement, the process is one of *Symbiotic-Substitution.* These two defenses regularly operate together in the Phobic Reactions. In the *Activity Substitution,* hostility may be released through a substituted activity such as a sport. Interests, as in *Case 187* can find a substituted area for their direction.

Substitution can have significant implications in individual characterologic evolution. It can contribute to Rechannelization. The *Counter-irritant-Substitution* can sometimes be observed in Obsessive Reactions, in which attention and concern become directed to a substitute area, away from obsessive ruminations. This can be a deliberate or unwitting process.

A hurt, loss, or injury may be made up for through an *Antidotal-Substitution.* One may bury himself in an avocation or vocation via the *Attention-Focus Substitution.* The operation of various types of Substitution can be observed in therapy, as illustrated in *Cases 192* and *193.*

E. CROSS-REFERENCES TO *THE NEUROSES* *

Substitution
In Nature of Anxiety (Chapter 1); psychogenic symptoms as, for subjective anxiety; p. 5.
In Depressive Reactions (Chapter 4); of objects, encouraged by therapist; p. 211.

---

* From Laughlin, H. P. *The Neuroses.* London, Butterworth & Co., Ltd., 1967.

In Obsessive-Compulsive Reactions (Chapter 6)
  in *First Line of Psychic Defense* of obsessive person; pp. 343, 374.
  of repetitive thought, a defense against anxiety (*Preoccupation Defense*); pp. 311, 344.
    in obsessive doubting (Case 71); p. 348.
    of early incident (Case 70); p. 345.
    underlying bases for S.; p. 367.
In Hygeiaphrontic Reactions (Chapter 8)
  of physical symptoms
    in *Bodily Expression* of emotional conflicts; p. 481.
    in *Flight-to-the-Physical Concept;* p. 463.
    in unconscious translation of emotional conflicts; p. 484.
    for (parental) love and acceptance; p. 479.
      in *epigain* of *hygeiaphrontis;* p. 485.
In Fear and Its Avoidance (Chapter 9); of external object, for internal fear, in phobic evolvement; p. 518.
In Phobic Reactions (Chapter 10)
  of external object
    as a mechanism in phobic evolvement; p. 602.
    for another external danger, in castration complex; p. 552.
    for inner conflict in *Emotional-Object-Amalgam* (EOA); p. 571.
    in *anxiety-induced cathexis;* p. 585.
    in *Critical-Displacement Phobia;* p. 580.
    in *Gradually Evolving Phobia;* p. 578.
In Conversion Reactions (Chapter 12)
  of symptom
    as a distorted form of sexual action; p. 685.
    to secure disguised gratification (*Flight-to-the-Physical*); p. 663.
In Dissociative Reactions (Chapter 13)
  of figure for self, in dream symbols; pp. 751–2.
  of symptoms hazardous, under hypnosis; p. 824.

F.   REVIEW QUESTIONS

Sample self-check questions on Chapter 23 and Substitution for the student, psyciatric resident, and board candidate.

1. What are the defensively-intended aims of Substitution?
2. Cite five common clinical instances of the operation of this ego defense.
3. What type of Substitution bears a kinship to Compensation?
4. With what dynamism is *Symbiotic-Substitution* most prominently associated?
5. How does the *Activity Substitution* function?
6. Why is the *Counterirritant-Substitution* or CS more frequently encountered in conjunction with obsessive defenses?
7. Define the *Attention-Focus Substitution*. Give an example from your clinical experience.
8. How can Substitution operate as a defense in relation to powerful inner hostility and resentment?
9. What is meant by *Antidotal-Substitution?*
10. Cite ways in which Substitution can influence psychotherapy.

CHAPTER 24

SYMBOLIZATION

... Unconsciously Established External Representation

A. STANDING IN PLACE OF

    1. Emotional Significance Assigned or Acquired. 2. General and Individual Symbols. 3. Background Notes. 4. Definition. The Condensation Symbol.

B. UTILIZATION PERVASIVE

    1. Required in Communication. 2. In Adjustment and Neuroses. 3. In Dreams; Dream-Symbols: a. Relation to Object Represented; b. Multiple Symbolization; c. Guidepost Dreams and Therapy; d. Law of Increasing Complexity of Dreams. 4. In Emotional Illness: a. Tenet of Variable-Interpretation; b. Symptom-Symbol Concept; c. Association to Similars or Opposites; d. Emotional-Object Amalgam.

C. SUMMARY

    1. Concealed Outward Expression Achieved. 2. Possibilities Limitless.

D. REFERENCES (FROM *The Neuroses*)

E. REVIEW QUESTIONS

A. STANDING IN PLACE OF

1. Emotional Significance Assigned or Acquired

The symbol is a general or individual, often abstract, representation for some particular idea, complex, or object. The utilization of symbols may be conscious and deliberate, partly conscious, or unconscious. With the latter, one is consciously aware of the symbol but not of what it represents, or that it represents something. In other words the symbol stands in the place of or represents something different, but this different object or complex is outside of conscious awareness.

Affect or emotional feelings become attached to the new object-symbol. It accordingly becomes an EOA—emotional-object amalgam. (See also p. 379–80.) The symbol acquires meaning and emotional significance. This can directly reflect the level of meaning and significance of what the symbol stands for.

The object-symbol may have started out as a more or less neutral item. Its "selection" can be through chance, association, or some special individual significance. Wittingly or not the symbol comes to stand in the place of, or to represent something else. Because of the attachment of emotional significance, it frequently comes to have a considerable and sometimes seemingly undue level of importance.

The American flag has symbolic connotations for most citizens. As everyone knows it is simply comprised of colored textiles. When these are combined together however in the prescribed fashion—bars of red and white, a smaller field of blue, with white stars—the resulting flag conveys considerable meaning and significance. Emotional feelings often are generated. This is true for most national flags, particularly when they are displayed in a parade, carried in battle, or children pledge allegiance.

2. General and Individual Symbols

What we term the *General Symbol* to help distinguish this major type includes all symbols which convey similar meanings and significance generally, that is to a large group, if not to most people. Through its more or less common recognition, the General Symbol widely recalls or represents something. As instances of General Symbols, white stands for or symbolizes purity, the elephant and lion strength, and the cross, Christianity.

Certain General Symbols can convey multiple meanings, the particular meaning being dependent on the situation. The color red for example, can symbolize danger, courage, stop (cars), fire, blood, or business loss (debits; red ink).

There are many areas for employment of the General Symbol. They are especially observed in religious rites, patriotic and military situations, fraternal groups, and professional organizations.

What are referred to in distinction, as *Individual Symbols* do not require wide use or acceptance. They are of sufficient significance for the individual concerned, evolved in response to his own inner motivation and needs, and serve a psychic function of greater or lesser moment. This is their *raison d'être*.

The meaning and significance of the Individual Symbol is most individual and specific. Their presence not only may be not apparent to others, but most important, they often are not apparent to the person concerned. See pp. 305–6, and p. 440.

Symbolism is the practice or art of using symbols. Through symbolism one invests otherwise less significant objects with symbolic meaning. The invisible or abstract becomes expressed or represented by means of a concrete visible object or representation. In art the halo around the heads of saints or members of the Holy Family is an identifying symbol, one with which most people become familiar. In psychiatry we learn that ideas or visual representations can stand for others. A symptom can symbolically stand for or express elements of hidden emotional conflicts. Symbolism finds employment in many fields of interest and endeavor.

3. Background Notes

The use of symbols has been widespread in every culture, past and present. Symbols have been used in some way or other as representations in almost every kind of human activity. This has been especially true in religious rites. In primitive societies, symbols are used as charms or totems in religion, witchcraft, voodoo, tribal ceremonies, and magic.

The employment of symbols is widespread and by no means restricted to primitive peoples, nor the less sophisticated groups in our present milieu. Nonetheless, Symbolism is ordinarily to be regarded properly as being a *Lower Order Dynamism.*

The use of symbols has origins in the dim regions before the beginnings of recorded history. Symbols are used today to convey secret meanings. They are an aid to communication. As noted with the General Symbol, they serve important functions in religious, patriotic, professional, and fraternal organizations.

We have learned elsewhere how certain symbolic objects in the *Soterial Reactions* can come to have a neurotic association of special significance in the direction of protection and security. In converse fashion to evolvement of the phobia, the soterial object is unwittingly set up as an emotional object-source of comfort and safety. See *The Soterial Reactions,* in *The Neuroses* (pp. 607–639).

4. Definition. The Condensation Symbol

Symbolization is a widely evolved ego-defensive process operating outside of and beyond conscious awareness through which an external object, becomes the disguised outward representation for another internal and hidden object, idea, person, or complex. Standing for a number of objects, it may serve as what we term the Condensation Symbol. In dreams and symptomatology esepecially, the *Condensation Symbol* can play a prominent role.

The *symbol* is originally a more or less neutral item which is set up to stand for or to represent something often to some extent associated. Through the operation of Symbolization, emotional significance is attached. As a result, the symbol can come to have what apparently is an undue level of emotional meaning.

Any item or object when evolved to represent another is a symbol. As in dreams a symbol is often a considerable abbreviation, standing for a number of things and illustrating the Condensation Symbol. In addition to its outward and conscious aspect, the symbol also has inner, unconscious connections and associations for the individual or the group.

There are many common examples of symbols. In day-to-day living, such items as money, words, pictures, parables, allegories, fairy tales, dreams, and emotional symptoms have symbolic meanings.

B. UTILIZATION PERVASIVE

1. Required in Communication

The utilization of both General and Individual symbols is widespread indeed. Symbolic meanings come to be accepted so matter-of-factly that in the first variety one must often stop and consider, to be able to recognize that a General Symbol exists.

As noted, Individual Symbols frequently are not so recognized. The capacity for Symbolization is an important human resource. It can be constructive and useful, or a manifestation of and attempted defense in emotional illness.

Repressed material in both normal and sick people often secures symbolic expression. Behavior can be symbolic. Many emotional symptoms are symbolic representations of one or more aspects of the individual's unconscious conflicts. Mannerisms and items of dress can have symbolic meanings. The applications of symbolism are individually and culturally so wide that this brief chapter summary of certain related aspects must suffice in view of space limitations. A volume could prove inadequate to cover the subject.

Written and spoken languages are based on the use of symbols— words, signs, or sounds. In communication between individuals and groups, these symbols convey meanings. It would be impossible to conceive of communication between people without the use of symbols. The print which we read consists of black marks of various shapes on paper. It is because of their symbolic meanings that our present words convey meaning.

2. In Adjustment and Neuroses

As we progress in studying Symbolization to include the complexities in adjustments and relationships, illustrations become more complex but hardly less pervasive. Symbolization is admirably illustrated in the Soterial Reactions. The soterial object is a symbol to which added significance has become ascribed. It thereby becomes an emotional-psychic source of comfort, security, and protection to the person concerned. The reversed significance is encountered in the Phobic Reactions.

The goal of home ownership had come to symbolize recreating an earlier ideal era for a certain driven and unhappy man. This period in his middle childhood years, during which his parents succeeded in buying their own farm, had been the only happy period in his life.

In a reaction somewhat akin to the soteria, a middle-aged married woman treasured an old blanket. This had long occupied the foot of their bed. Originally a gift from an earlier fiance who lost his life, it had come to symbolize the earlier relationship, what it meant, and its tragically unfulfilled promise. Its presence made the present marriage more acceptable. It was valued accordingly.

The importance of symbols in symptomatology and in the neuroses generally, has been illustrated throughout an earlier study of the patterns of neurotic reaction in *The Neuroses.* We speak of the symbolic meaning of a symptom, for example, in cases of Conversion Reaction. The literature of dynamic psychiatry is replete with case histories in which symbolism plays a role.

Through the operation of Symbolization, patients come to utilize a conscious idea or mental image as a symbol, for the unwitting purpose of concealing from themselves a more objectionable unconscious need or urge. Symbols aid in the ego's needs for concealment and distortion, and help to maintain Repression. Symbolization of psychopathologic import is commonly observed and can be striking in regressive states, psychoses, childhood, and dreams.

3. In Dreams; Dream-Symbols

A. RELATION TO OBJECT REPRESENTED.—Symbolism is a regular part of the normal and universal language of dreams. Situations, persons, or objects may be disguised and represented by different object-symbols or person-symbols. Symbolism is one of three basic factors in dream interpretation, the others being condensation and convergence, as confirmed through the study of many, many dreams and associations to them. What we refer to as the *Dream-Symbol* superficially at least need bear little resemblance to the object or person for which it stands.

Symbolization in dreams is a Repression-facilitating process, aiding in the disguise and distortion of unconscious wishes, desires, impulses, and ideas. Their expression in dream content is achieved in symbolic and therefore concealed fashion. Thus, the symbol in any given dream sequence may be similar, completely different, or perhaps the exact reverse of the object, idea, wish, or impulse, for which it stands. There are associative connections, of course, between the hidden idea and its outward representation; its symbol. However these are hidden in the personal life of the individual. All of this is inaccessible to ordinary awareness.

It is at times possible to unravel the meaning of dreams and Dream-Symbols through the technique of free association. The unconscious selection of the symbol does not depend on intellect or logic. Symbolization fundamentally is an emotional process.

In dreams there is a tendency for certain dream symbolism to be similar from person to person, and dream to dream. We must carefully bear in mind however that there is no universal language of symbols in dreams. The meaning of a given Dream-Symbol is not unequivocal. Even for the same dreamer, a symbol may have different meanings. For six dreamers a similar figure or object-symbol can prove to have six different interpretations. This is in accord with the *Tenet of Variable-Interpretation* when applied to dreams. It will be outlined shortly (p. 419).

B. MULTIPLE SYMBOLIZATION.—Perhaps the most readily available source of the Individual Symbol is in the dream. In many dreams abstract thoughts and concepts require representation in concrete form; they must be symbolized. This also aids in the disguise of the true meaning of the dream. The latent content tends to remain latent.

The following dream with its foreshortened interpretation illustrates the employment of what we term *Multiple Symbolization*. In clinical experience dreams not uncommonly illustrate similar varieties of MS.

Case 194

Dream-Symbols

(1) *Manifest Content.* "I was in Germany during the war. There was fighting. The Germans were going to attack and I felt doomed. . . .

"Then the scene shifted. I found a bolt of expensive woolen material and thought of taking it home with me. A General came by and told me that it was half cotton and wouldn't be any good. He was of course right and I felt ridiculous for making the mistake. . . ."

This man's voluminous associations summarized below revealed the following Dream-Symbols. Study of these helped uncover the latent content.

(2) *Associations Reveal Dream-Symbols and Bring Out Latent Content.* 1. *War;* fighting; attacking. All represented the dreamer's violent anger, which he intensely feared. His fears included being attacked directly, as well as in retaliation for his own aggression.

2. *Germans;* The national background of the dreamer's banker and principal backer in business was Germanic. They had recently strongly criticized him. Outwardly he had accepted this meekly, but was really quite angry.

Their joint attack could indeed prove overwhelming and perhaps "doom" him, at least in a business sense.

3. The dreamer, a manufacturer of boy's clothing, had an intense desire to do better than his father, who was in the same business. He had suffered repeated failures, however, which would culminate in his father telling him he was worthless.

The second dream scene symbolized this entire complex. The expensive cloth represented his desires to excel; the General, his father; the adulterated cloth, his father's criticism of him.

The foregoing dream included a number of symbols, illustrating Multiple Symbolization. Its analysis was beneficial in the man's therapy (see also *Case 210,* pp. 652–3).

C. GUIDEPOST DREAMS AND THERAPY.—In the following instance multiple symbols are again present. As with what we label *Guidepost Dreams,* their special value in the therapy situation is illustrated. Usually the dream is so termed to stress its position of directional significance.

A young woman had been in therapy a short time. She had little conscious awareness of the direction and strength of her feelings about the analysis. These were already well established. Some of her attitudes and feelings became apparent, however, through a series of three short dreams which occurred the night before an early therapeutic session. These dreams and their interpretations follow.

Attitudes Toward Therapy Symbolized

1. "I was on the beach dressed in a very sheer, filmy gown. I was standing up, but it seemed I was lying down too ... I felt embarrassment and shame...."

2. "I walked into an old room. Someone was sitting at a desk reading an open book which was the story of my life."

3. "I badly needed a pair of glasses. A kindly man with big, horn-rimmed glasses said he would help me secure a similar pair."

There were, of course, many symbolic elements in each of these brief dream sequences. Most interesting was the Symbolization of the psychotherapy and the patient's attitudes toward it.

1. A very sheer, filmy gown.... This is garb through which she can be seen. Lying down was her position in therapy sessions.

2. The book containing the story of her life.... In the therapeutic situation she seeks to make her life, through a deliberate process of therapeutic study and analysis become an "open book." It is of course made available to the therapist to "read."

3. The man with the horn-rimmed glasses.... This figure stands for the therapist, who will help her secure similar glasses, that is, find the way to see more clearly. The need for glasses also symbolized the recognition of her need for treatment. The kindly man (the physician) already possessed glasses, symbolizing his ability to see more clearly.

To the above young lady, therapy meant in part someone looking through her—into her personal, intimate life. Many hidden things would become apparent, some of which caused her embarrassment and shame. This Guidepost Dream was useful in the therapy, helping to point out especially to the therapist, the way treatment was headed.

D. LAW OF INCREASING COMPLEXITY OF DREAMS.—Dreams which occur early in the course of therapy are likely to be revealing about the patient's attitudes, as in the foregoing instance. This helps explain adoption of the term, Guidepost Dream. This is more likely to be true where the person is unsophisticated about the latent meaning of dreams, when he has not yet learned to unravel their messages or their symbolism.

As the therapist comes to realize with experience, the internal censor develops greater resources and later can more effectively conceal and obscure the message of a dream. *An increasing facility for the unwitting concealment, and disguise of latent dream content is likely to progress in direct proportion to the dreamer's increasing competence in unraveling their meaning.*

This is the underlying principle in the *Law of Increasing Complexity* of Dreams. It has been so termed for the purpose of stressing this major concept concerning dreams and their interpretation. In other words, recognition of the concept and law indicates our understanding that the latent meaning of a dream tends to become more concealed and hidden, in direct proportion to the increase in the level of sophistication achieved by the dreamer about dreams and their interpretation.

The following additional interesting example again stresses the added significance of the Guidepost Dream in therapy. It helps convey in symbolic terms the dreamer's initial attitudes about therapy.

Case 196

The Guidepost Dream

(1) *The Dream Reported.* A 40-year-old professional man regarding himself along in years had the following first dream. It was reported during session number three.

"I was taking a brand new friend on an inspection tour of an older house. There were many rooms. It seemed strange, and yet very familiar, as though I had lived in it.

"It was in a bad state of disrepair, and dirty, too, which for some reason I had to keep my friend from seeing. The walls were all cracked. I kept running ahead, frantically putting on a new clean coat of wallpaper as we went on, so he wouldn't see the dirt and the cracks. I had to present it in a good light!"

(2) *Analysis of the Symbolism.* In his Guidepost Dream the "inspection tour" symbolized the analysis. The "older house" is himself, with "many rooms." The "bad state of disrepair" indicates his need for treatment. The "cracked walls" helped to symbolize this as well. "Cracked" is a common slang term for serious emotional difficulties. Dirtiness stood for and described how he viewed certain aspects of his life.

"I had to keep my brand new friend (the analyst) from seeing" indicates his fear of letting the therapist see, or know how badly off things are. This, plus the "frantically putting on a clean coat of wallpaper," symbolized his need for, and his secret intent to conceal things in the course of treatment, so the therapist "wouldn't see." Poor man, it was like having to "clean the house before the maid comes"; one doesn't dare let the maid see the dirt!

(3) *Premature Interpretation.* Prematurely, partial interpretation of this dream was undertaken. At an early juncture in therapy this was a technical error and disadvantageous. Two of the untoward consequences were: (1) a cessation of dreams for several months, which upon resumption were far more complex and involved, and, (2) a more guarded and defensive approach to therapy. As a Guidepost Dream, it proved an excellent directional indicator.

Needless to say, despite this patient's conscious protestations to the contrary, his frantically urgent "wallpapering" endeavors as noted in the dream, rather aptly characterized much of the resistance encountered in therapy over the course of 4 years. For this man, the beneficial results of therapy however, were beyond measure.

4. *In Emotional Illness*

A. TENET OF VARIABLE-INTERPRETATION.—In emotional illness, symbolism is especially to be encountered in the psychotic individual whose activities, mannerisms, dress, possessions, and behavior may symbolically express all kinds of otherwise hidden, that is, repressed, unconscious material. An understanding of the symbolic "language" of the psychotic person is difficult to gain.

Since there is a lack of uniformity in the interpretation of symbolism encountered in serious emotional disorders (and in others), the same object-symbol can have three interpretations for three persons. This comprises an important *Tenet of Variable-Interpretation* in psychiatry. In accord with this important tenet, the interpretation and meaning of *a given symbol, dream, symptom, or other psychic manifestations, can vary widely from person to person.* (See also p. 417.) This tenet has been formulated to help stress the individuality, especially in the interpretation of dream symbols, in distinction to the past tendency by some to too often accord them common meanings.

In the symbolism accompanying and a part of emotional illness, there is a displacement of emotional charge from the original object, which remains hidden, to the external symbol. It is characteristic of the symbol that it has been endowed with more meaning and significance to the individual, or to the group concerned, than might be casually suspected.

B. SYMPTOM-SYMBOL CONCEPT.—Emotional symptoms can in themselves be symbols. A newly married young woman had an obsessive, domineering, and rigid husband. Figuratively, he soon proved to be "more than she could swallow." This reaction to him had progressed to the literal, as she came to develop a painful functional disorder of swallowing. The swallowing symptom was directly symbolic—representative of her difficulty in living.

Severe functional backaches in analogous fashion can represent the symbolic expression of feelings that burdens of living, a relationship, problem, or situation are greater than one can bear. Like the old man of the sea, life with spouse, parent, or child, is thus secretly regarded and expressed symbolically, as a more or less intolerable burden.

Symbolism is frequently encountered in the Conversion Reactions, as noted. It enters into symptom choice, since for the individual some special hidden significance enters into both his choice of symptom, and its location. The operation of Conversion (Chapter 3) allows for the symbolic expression of an impulse which is consciously disowned, because it is disapproved and unacceptable to the superego, to society, or to both.

Many emotional symptoms are largely symbolic or are symbolically-determined. When such is the case, for purposes of identification and distinction we refer to these as *Symptom-Symbols.*

Symbolization is a primitive emotional-psychic process. Through it, an unconscious urge or impulse receives some measure of gratification in a consciously disguised form and Repression is maintained.

C. ASSOCIATION TO SIMILARS OR OPPOSITES.—Symbolization as an ego defense operates on bases of association and similarity, or in some cases, differences and opposites. One object comes to stand for, or to represent some other object, through some particular and often quite obscure and hidden quality or aspect which they have in common for the individual concerned.

The association is often so slight or tangential that, except through special techniques of study, it is overlooked by the conscious mind. Through Symbolization emotional values are transferred from the original object to another; its symbol which stands in its place.

D. EMOTIONAL-OBJECT AMALGAM.—In summation, Symbolization is a widely and unwittingly employed psychic process which operates outside of and beyond conscious awareness, through which an object, usually external, becomes the disguised outward representation for another internal and hidden object, complex, or a number of objects. Symbolization is a more primitive or *Lower Order* type of ego defense.

The ego selects some more or less neutral item as a symbol and uses it unconsciously to stand for something else. This other item, through its connection with the hidden one, comes to have more meaning and emotional significance attached to it than it would have in and of itself.

The symbol thus comprises what is referred to as an EOA or *emotional-object amalgam*. The symbol has an emotional significance far beyond what might objectively be expected.

C. SUMMARY

1. Concealed Outward Expression Achieved

Symbols serve to distort and to conceal. In clinical psychiatry they are unconsciously established external representations to which emotional significance is assigned. They stand in place of something which remains in the unconscious.

The process of Symbolization is often a vital psychologic function. Through the distortion and concealment achieved, the evolution of symbols helps the ego to maintain Repression, which, as we have learned (Chapter 21), is so necessary for the avoidance of anxiety. This is particularly applicable in the latent content of dreams. *Dream-Symbols* are universally employed.

Symbolization is a defensively-intended process utilized in health and in illness. Its psychologic prominence rests particularly upon its wide use in childhood years (*Childhood Symbolization*), in dreams (*Dream-Symbols*), in regressive states, and in the psychoses. The *Condensation Symbol* represents a number of objects at the same time and accordingly can be prominent in dreams and emotional symptomatology. When the process of Symbolization is prominent in symptom formation and especially when the symbol is a symptom, the consequence is termed a *Symptom-Symbol*.

Symbols are requisite for communication. They are important in adjustment and neuroses and their utilization is pervasive.

In emotional health and illness, repressed material threatens to break through into awareness, to find a direct or more or less symbolic outward expression. In emotional illness, the symbolic object may come to have a neurotic association of special significance. This may be as regards protection and security, as in the soteria, about which more has been said in *The Neuroses*.

When symbolism is encountered in emotional illness, we find a displacement of emotional attachment from some original object (which remains hidden and outside of conscious awareness). Characteristic of the symbol is its endowment with emotional significance.

Formulation of a *Law of Increasing Complexity in Dreams* stressed the tendency for increasing complexity, obscuration, and disguise of the dream's latent content, in direct proportion to the dreamer's increasing sophistication concerning dreams and their interpretation. *Multiple Symbolization* is fairly common in clinical experience and is encountered in the study and interpretation of dreams and other emotional manifestations.

2. Possibilities Limitless

In psychotic individuals, symbolism is observed in various bizarre activities, interests, mannerisms, and behavior, all of which may be looked upon as the symbolic and outward expression of all types of otherwise hidden, that is, repressed thoughts, ideas, wishes, impulses, and otherwise intolerable data.

Experience has shown that there is no uniformity in the symbolism of emotional disorders, or their interpretation. The same is true for dreams. This is in accord with the *Tenet of Variable-Interpretation* in psychiatry.

The name of *Guidepost Dream* is assigned to the first significant dream following the initiation of therapy, to help emphasize its special position of importance as a directional indicator for the therapist. Two examples were cited. The hazards of premature interpretation of dreams were noted in *Case 196*.

There are practically no limits as to the possibilities for the evolving and employment of Symbolization both for the individual—*Individual Symbols*—and culturally—*General Symbols*. Behavior may be symbolic; symptoms can be a symbolic guise for internal, forgotten, unacceptable, condemned ideas, thoughts, wishes, or impulses.

Symbolization operates in conjunction with other dynamisms. In Rechannelization, for example, repressed drives return in symbolic guise, in such a way as to become more acceptable to the superego or conscience, as well as to society, and in conformity with the requirements of external reality. The symbol comprises an important type of *emotional-object amalgam* or EOA.

D. CROSS-REFERENCES TO *THE NEUROSES* *

Symbolization

In Depressive Reactions (Chapter 4)

of hostile/aggressive forces

in masochism of accident-proneness; p. 198.

in inverted sadism of Depressive Reactions, electroshock therapy serves as punishment; pp. 217–18.

in suicide

acting out, expression of; p. 193.

in *Symbolic Authority Concept;* pp. 195–6.

inverted sadism of; pp. 205, 220.

of lost love object (concomitant destruction of)

due to death; p. 188.

in *Depression of Success;* pp. 185–6.

in *Antecedent Conflict* of Oral Phase (Case 39); p. 187.

in suicide (*Lost Object Reunion*); p. 206.

of return to the womb, in "death wish" of suicide; p. 208.

In Character Reactions (Chapter 5)

as a mechanism in *Conversion Personality* (Table 19); p. 260.

of anal-erotism in obsessive characteristics (Abraham); pp. 292–3.

of moral purity, in obsessive bodily cleanliness (Case 52); p. 290.

In Obsessive-Compulsive Reactions (Chapter 6)

a reenforcement of Repression

in *Compulsive Security Rituals* (CSR); pp. 351–2.

in onset of obsessive symptoms; p. 337.

in *First Line of Defense* of obsessive person; pp. 343, 374.

of conflict between id and superego

in obsessive concern over eliminative function; pp. 353–4.

in religiosity (Case 73); p. 353.

of hostile/aggressive impulses

inverted (Case 70); p. 344.

in overcautious driving (Case 64); p. 318.

toward siblings, recapitulated in children (Case 65); p. 356.

of unconscious forces

in acting out of *Impulsive Reactions;* p. 352.

related to obsessions; p. 345.

In Hygeiaphrontic Reactions (Chapter 8)

of internalized (good and bad) breasts, in overconcern with cancer (Case 101); p. 488.

of unconscious conflicts, in *Bodily Expression;* p. 481.

In Fear and Its Avoidance (Chapter 9)

as the reverse of phobia, *soteria* as; p. 527.

in *Psychic Pain;* p. 533.

In Phobic Reactions (Chapter 10)

of hostile/aggressive impulses

into phobia of cats (Case 120) p. 573.

into phobia of theaters (Case 117); p. 567.

of latent stimulus, by manifest stimulus (phobic object); p. 548.

of loss of dependent position

in dynamics of phobia; pp. 575–6.

into phobia of travel (Case 121); p. 577.

of threat of retaliation, into phobia of horses (Case 111); p. 551.

---

* From Laughlin, H. P. *The Neuroses.* London, Butterworth & Co., Ltd., 1967.

of unconscious impulses
   displaced to external object, in phobias; p. 556.
   in *Critical Attack of Anxiety;* p. 602.
   in *phobic ambivalence;* p. 570.
   in *Phobic EOA* (Emotional-Object-Amalgam); p. 585.
   in *phobic endogain*
      in phobia of flowers (Case 119); p. 572.
   in symptom formation; pp. 563, 578.
   in selection of phobic object (Table 28); p. 583.
In Soterial Reactions (Chapter 11)
   in comparison of phobia to *soteria* (Table 30); p. 628.
   of oral object of dependency
      food as, in overeating; p. 631.
   in psychodynamics of *soteria evolvement;* pp. 612, 636.
   in *Security Operations* (SO); p. 620.
   in selection of soterial object; pp. 626–7.
In Conversion Reactions (Chapter 12)
   in *First Line of Defense* of Conversion Reactions; pp. 691–2.
   in symptom choice and *Peg Concept* (Table 37); p. 697.
   of hostile impulses
      in paralysis of arm (Case 136); p. 666.
      in *Red Ink Cure* (Case 148); p. 709.
   of repressed and repressing forces
      in bases of Sensory Conversion; p. 687.
      in Conversion *endogain;* pp. 700, 716.
      in Conversion Hysteria; p. 651.
      in *physical-translations* of figures of speech; p. 660.
   symptoms as S.
      as defense against acting out; p. 671.
      in Conversion aphonia; p. 677.
      in Conversion tics and convulsions; pp. 685–6.
      in *endogain* of Conversion symptoms; p. 671. Table 36; p. 690.
      expression of unconscious conflicts
         in *body language* of *Somatic Conversion;* pp. 641, 643–4, 662, 690.
         in *physiologic language* of *Physiologic Conversion;* pp. 642, 644.
         in psychologic expression of *Psychologic Conversion;* p. 643.
      in Conversion *epigain;* p. 693.
      in diagnoses of *Somatic* and *Physiologic Conversions;* pp. 689–90.
      in dysphagia (*literal-symbolic expression*), in *Psychic Distaste Concept;* p. 696.
      in interpretation and *Rule of Individual Symbolism;* p. 699.
      in dreams; p. 708.
      in substitutive gratification; p. 663.
      in *Symptom-Barrage* in therapy (Case 135); p. 664; also p. 665.
In Dissociative Reactions (Chapter 13)
   of escape, in *Symbolic Escape* of depersonalization; p. 767.
   of literal and figurative flight in *Concept of Psychologic-Flight Avoidance* in Dissociative Reactions; p. 724.
   of unconscious forces
      expressed in dreams; pp. 745–6.
      disguised through Displacement; p. 748.
      in *Dream's Contribution to Emotional Health;* p. 749.
      in manifest (distorted) content overlying latent content; p. 747.
      in research of dream symbols; p. 821.

in *Rule of Individual-Symbolism;* p. 753.
through splitting-off of parts of self; p. 752.
through symbolic substitutes; p. 751.
expressed through somnambulism; p. 755.
in inducing confessions, narcosis welcomed as *Symbolic Authority;* p. 819.
in *over-all language* of Dissociative Reaction; p. 742.
in seeking or acting out of fugue; pp. 798, 801–2.
related to episodes of traumatic amnesia; p. 781.
In Neuroses-Following-Trauma (Chapter 14)
a factor in individual vulnerability to Traumatic Neuroses; pp. 867, 893.
in *Antecedent Conflicts Theory;* p. 888.
in *Concept of Psychologic Soil;* p. 868.
individual, in *Total Reaction to Crisis* (TRC); pp. 859–60.
in *Final Straw Concept* (Case 177); p. 861.
of dependency needs, *Compensation Neuroses* as (Table 44); p. 877.
in *Symptoms as an Implied Preference;* p. 885.
of emotional conflict, expressed in psychologic and physiologic symptoms; p. 851.
in *epigain* and *endogain of Traumatic Neuroses;* pp. 873–5.
in *raison d'être* of Neuroses-Following-Trauma; p. 873.
In Military Reactions (Chapter 15)
of escape, in depersonalization as a *Prognostic Signal Flag* (PSF); p. 922.
of mastery, in *Desensitizing Purpose of the* (repetitive) *Dream;* p. 917.
of unconscious conflicts
in final (precipitating) traumatic event; p. 911.
in post-combat *Unit-Guilt Reaction* (Case 189); p. 932.
in traumatic relationship to earlier antecedent (Case 187); p. 925.
symptoms as S.
expressed as tremors in *Concept of Defensive Over-reaction;* p. 918.
in individual's *Total Reaction to Trauma* (TRT); p. 926.
in *Rule of Individual Symbolism;* p. 914.

E.   REVIEW QUESTIONS

Sample self-check questions on Chapter 24 and Symbolization for the student, psychiatric resident, and board candidate.

1. Comment briefly on the significance of symbols in modern culture. Define *Symbolization* as an ego defense.
2. Differentiate the *General* and the *Individual Symbol.*
3. What is the *Tenet of Variable-Interpretation* and its application to *Dream-Symbols?*
4. What is the value of the *Guidepost Dream* in therapy?
5. Briefly discuss the role of symbolism in dreams. What principle underlies the *Law of Increasing Complexity of Dreams?*
6. How does the *Tenet of Variable-Interpretation* relate to Symbolization in emotional manifestations? Can you illustrate from your clinical experience?
7. List the hazards in premature interpretation in therapy.
8. What are *symptom-symbols?* Cite examples observed.
9. The symbol comprises an important type of *emotional-object amalgam* or EOA. Explain.
10. Distinguish between latent and manifest content in dreams; in emotional symptomatology. What is the *Condensation Symbol? Multiple Symbolization?*

CHAPTER 25

UNDOING

. . . Psychic Erasure

A. THE NATURE OF UNDOING

1. Adoption in Psychiatric Terminology. 2. Definition.

B. TYPES OF UNDOING

  1. Confession: a. The Confession-Discrepancy; b. The Judas or Ineffectual Confession; c. Confession-Undoing Cycle. 2. Crime and Punishment. 3. Alcohol: The Hangover Paradox. 4. Expiative Undoing. 5. The Undoing Spiral.

C. MOTIVATED BY GUILT

  1. Childhood Undoing. 2. The Behavioral Undoing Cycle. 3. With Every Type of Guilt: a. Wide Bases; b. The Undoing Phrase.

D. UNDOING WHILE ASLEEP

  1. The Undoing Dream. 2. Dream-of-Erasure. 3. Sleepwalking and Sleeptalking.

E. IN OBSESSIVE-COMPULSIVE NEUROSES

  1.Repetitive Symptoms. Tidal Undoing. 2. Obsessive Order and Rituals. 3. Undoing in Therapy—a Secondary Defense.

F. SOCIAL UNDOING

G. NOTES ON DYNAMICS, AND ADDITIONAL ASPECTS

  1. Symbolic Undoing: a. In Prayer; b. Compulsive Rituals (CR). 2. Compulsive Handwashing. 3. Relationship-Undoing.

H. SUMMARY

I. REFERENCES (FROM *The Neuroses*)

J. REVIEW QUESTIONS

A. THE NATURE OF UNDOING

1. Adoption in Psychiatric Terminology

To undo is to render null and void. When something is undone, it is as though whatever was done had not been done. Through Undoing, what has been done is undone. The original condition existing before the act, thought, or deed is restored. While Undoing has added meanings, the foregoing ones are those which have come to be employed in psychiatry. Through the evolution and employment of Undoing as an ego defense, in similar fashion one may undo, or seek to undo psychologically that which the ego finds repugnant and intolerable.

Adoption of the concept and term of Undoing is quite recent. Closely associated with the Obsessive-Compulsive Reactions, recognition of its operation depended upon recognizing them and gaining an understanding of their dynamics. In 1838, Esquirol first described the condition of obsessive doubting, later named by Falret *la maladie du doute.* Morel introduced the term obsession in 1861, and some years later, in 1878, Westphal further described and defined the condition. By 1910, obsessive neuroses were rather well delineated clinically.

As a psychic defense, Undoing is especially to be observed operating in the psychodynamics of the obsessions. In fact this dynamism is one which functions fairly regularly in the Obsessive-Compulsive group of neuroses. Nonetheless it was not until after the turn of the century that much work of value was undertaken as to their psychodynamics, in which Abraham was the pioneer. Progress continued at a slow pace.

Only in 1926 in the appendix to Freud's *Inhibition, Symptoms and Anxiety,* did " 'undoing' what has been done" receive mention, together with Regression and Isolation, as defensive techniques employed in the obsessional neuroses. In 1936, Freud described conscious (effortful) undoing as "the resolve to treat an occurrence as *non arrive."* Undoing as an ego defense operates unconsciously toward the same end and more. Magically it negates not merely the effects of a disowned urge, drive, act, or experience but the event itself. When successful Undoing comprises what we term *psychic erasure.*

2. Definition

Undoing is a major mental mechanism through which the person concerned unconsciously endeavors to resolve conflict and to allay or avoid consequent anxiety. This is sought through the erasure, that is the Undoing, of what he has thought, felt, or done, as this is evaluated subjectively to be intolerable.

What is done is undone. The Undoing operation may be effected in symbolic or magical ways. Through Undoing one seemingly abolishes and annuls the disapproved or overly painful thought, act, omission, or deed. Frequently motivated by guilt, relief may be sought from the burden of an otherwise critical conscience; of self-disapproval.

Undoing is one of the more primitive and magical dynamisms. It is usually to be regarded as one of the Lower Order group of mechanisms. Through this intrapsychic defensive process, one endeavors to erase and undo a prior act, thought, or impulse. We are ready to attempt a formal definition.

Accordingly, Undoing is *an intrapsychic ego defense or mental mechanism operating outside of and beyond conscious awareness in the endeavor to actually or symbolically undo something which has been done, including a thought, wish, impulse, or act, the commission, omission, or experiencing of which has proven consciously intolerable. Undoing is a process of psychologic erasure.* Undoing is usually a more basic and primal kind of defense, often similar in level to the dynamisms of Denial and Incorporation. It can, however, also involve more complex psychologic functioning of a higher level. Through Undoing the ego seeks to erase, to reestablish a prior status quo, to completely undo.

In understanding the basis and operation of this dynamism, a simple analogy can be drawn from everyday experience in which a person does something, and finds himself sorry. Emotional feelings in such instances vary in intensity from slight to intolerable. There are regrets. These can influence the person's behavior and reactions. There are many possibilities. He may try to make up for it in restitution. He may rationalize. He may behave as if it had not happened, as if it didn't exist, or as if everything were exactly as before. With the latter he may be trying to deny, erase, annul, or undo.

The child gains familiarity with the approaches to handling his regrets in interpersonal situations at an early stage. We once observed a little girl deliberately hit her younger brother with a toy. At once she ran over to hug and kiss him. She wanted to console, make up for, and thus undo the injury and hurt she had caused. Her behavior was motivated by feelings of responsibility, guilt, and regret.

The more deliberate and conscious types of Undoing through attempted reparation or other routes also take place in an analogous fashion on an unconscious level. While the same name may be applied to each, Undoing leads to more disguised or symbolic outward expressions in the unconscious process.

B. TYPES OF UNDOING

1. Confession

A. THE CONFESSION-DISCREPANCY.—Some individuals employ various kinds of confession as a way of Undoing. In this way, they consciously or symbolically seek to wipe the slate clean. Confession comprises a major type of Undoing and one which is frequently employed. Colleagues frequently cite confession as first among the more frequent routes of Undoing. For some people, confessing can be a useful and successful way of abolishing an act, thought, wish, or impulse which the ego finds unacceptable. Their confession can be deliberate and superficial and vary in sincerity.

Confessions and the need to confess can prove to be out of proportion to the supposed injury, sin, or evil when subjected to objective assessment. When the element of subjectivity is sufficiently marked to lead to such a lack of proportion, we term this the *Confession-Discrepancy*. The CD can be very important.

Thus the need to confess can accordingly be neurotic in origin and unrealistic. In appropriate instances the astute, perceptive, and understanding hearer will likely surmise: (1) the presence of neurotic needs; (2) the existence of further (unconscious) motivation for confessing than the supposed wrong; and (3) the presence of a Confession-Discrepancy with its indications for further inquiry when appropriate and feasible.

B. THE JUDAS OR INEFFECTUAL CONFESSION.—Confession and attempts at repentance do not always succeed in Undoing the wrong for the injured party. This is also true in so far as the person who has done the injury is concerned. When the latter is applicable, this endeavor comprises what is termed for purposes of delineation and emphasis the *Ineffectual Confession.*

As a prominent biblical example, Judas had a change of heart and sought to return the 30 pieces of silver received for betraying Christ. However his confession of the betrayal and attempted restitution of the blood money did not undo the act nor relieve his feelings of guilt and remorse.[1] The Pharisees responded to his confession of wrongdoing with "What is that to us? See thou to that." Judas' reaction was to seek self-destruction—the ultimate in attempted retribution and atonement.

What we alternatively call the *Judas Confession,* after its prominent and antecedent formulator, is an ineffectual type of Undoing-Confession. It is ineffectual because the hearer is indifferent and unaffected, or it doesn't accomplish its intent in so far as the confessor is concerned.

C. CONFESSION-UNDOING CYCLE.—Confession may be misused. By this we mean that confession sometimes is made by someone merely so as to be able to begin over again. This he proceeds to do, presumably more secure in the implicit knowledge that he can once more confess, and then repeat the cycle. This pattern of repeated Undoing can involve confession to a friend, parent, priest, or spouse. Needless to say, religious authorities hardly look with favor on the misuse of confession in this manner. This circular operation comprises the *Confession-Undoing Cycle.*

To many the thought or the wish alone is viewed as being close to or identical with the act. To them, a personally intolerable thought or wish would accordingly be regarded as conveying almost equal responsibility and guilt as would that of the corresponding act. Because of this, Undoing

---

[1] The Pharisees would not take the money. Blood money was not acceptable for the treasury. Judas flung it at their feet and departed. His guilt was not eased. While attempting to hang himself, Judas met his end by falling over a precipice. The money was used to buy burial ground for strangers.

in its various forms often becomes even more important as an extra- or intra-psychic defensive endeavor.

2. Crime and Punishment

A similar kind of *Punishment-Undoing Cycle* is sometimes observed operating in the sequence of crime and punishment for the criminal. Certain criminals at the time of their crime behave as if arranging for their apprehension. Their discovery is unwittingly made certain.

As an example, not too long ago, at the scene of a break-in in Washington, D.C., the burglar "accidentally" left behind one of his business cards with his picture on it. He had dropped it while at the scene of the crime, where it would be almost certainly and promptly picked up. It was. The burglar was quickly apprehended and taken into custody.

For the criminal, making restitution is a way of Undoing. Restitution may be made individually or towards society more generally. These endeavors may be conscious or unconscious. The process may be indistinguishable from Atonement-Penance (Chapter 26). The following instance of criminal reparation in the service of Undoing is of interest.

Case 197

Volunteers for Medical Research

Some time ago a medical news program was nationally televised. The subject was concerned with research attempts to transplant cancer cells into healthy volunteers.

This important series of medical experiments took place at a large penal institution. While potentially useful to people generally, the individual risk could have been great. Many of the persons concerned when interviewed expressed quite candidly their reasons for volunteering for the frightening research. Among their reasons, one could observe some conformity.

All of them had committed crimes. To a man they expressed albeit in varying terms and to a varying extent, the wish to make retribution and to undo the wrong. Seemingly, through their restitutive good works guilt would be assuaged, the crime and its effects (to an extent) undone.

Certain repetitive symptoms whose function appear to have a basis in intended Undoing are sometimes encountered in *criminals-in-fact*. These are also to be observed in what for purposes of distinction we term *criminals-by-wish,* or fantasy. Each can evolve the operation of the dynamism in *Criminal-Undoing*. In many instances, the dynamics have to be based upon surmise and presumption.

As a recent instance a prominent racketeer comes to mind who was repeatedly linked to crimes of violence. This man spent an average of 90 minutes daily scrubbing himself in the shower. In addition, he had a hand-washing compulsion, which required at least 10 to 20 daily washings. Speculative analysis would suggest the presence of guilt and possibly an intended Undoing operation in the psychodynamics of his ritualistic scrubbing.

3. Alcohol: The Hangover Paradox

For some persons, the suffering from a hangover following alcoholic overindulgence serves to help wipe the slate clean. In this type of Undoing, the discomfort and pain is unconsciously employed to erase or undo the self-disapproval and whatever "wrong" has resulted. It is as though the more suffering, the better one may regard himself for what happened the night before. In this sequence, seemingly paradoxically, the more one suffers physically, the better he will feel emotionally. This is what we call the *Hangover Paradox*. While not common, occasionally it is encountered as part of his routine pattern of reaction for the alcoholically habituated person.

For some, the drinking bout and its consequences (from behavior and possible misconduct) are abolished and atoned for through the morning-after malaise. An overindulgent drinker can use his remorse and hangover symptoms to an extent, to wipe out the last such event, sometimes in order to permit the next. One can readily see how this need might psychologically serve to help bring on or increase the symptoms of a hangover.

4. Expiative Undoing

Operation of the ego defense of Undoing can be clearly observed in certain obsessive-compulsive symptoms that are made up of two opposed actions in sequence, the second being the reverse of the first. Inversion (Chapter 13) can contribute to this process (see also p. 204). Acts, behavior, or symptoms that represent expiations belong with this category. The psychodynamic intent of what we accordingly call *Expiative Undoing* is the annulment of prior acts. The second reversed act is more or less unwittingly and automatically so directed. Expiative symptoms often indicate the ego's subscription to the possibility and magic of Undoing.

Expiative Undoing can enter into everyday living and social relationships. It can become more complex and lead to more than the simple doing-undoing sequence. Let us take the clinically not uncommon example of the young man who becomes obsessed with the belief that he has made an unfriendly comment. After a time he is forced to return to try and undo this. This is the simple doing-undoing sequence of Expiative Undoing thus far, which brings us to our next topic.

5. The Undoing Spiral

As implied, the foregoing sequence can progress. In his Undoing endeavor our young man only succeeds in inadvertently making a new hostile laden comment which is at least as offensive as the first. His uneasiness grows. His hostility has been further revealed. His obsessive ruminations increase as do his needs for attempts at reparation and Expiative Undoing. The more hostility he has the greater can be his needs to convince people of its absence.

If the young man tries again, what will happen? Through the attempt alone to undo, he perhaps further betrays his concern and negative feelings. Might he not make things still worse? Such a more involved and repetitive pattern is of course marked, but one can see that all manner of variations of this theme can occur. People can unwittingly follow similar patterns with repeated phone calls.

This type of repetitive doing and Undoing on occasion sets up a vicious circle. It can establish what we term the *Undoing Spiral*. Having the potential for substantial self-defeat, the Undoing Spiral is most frequently evolved in systems of obsessive defenses. In the symptomatology and life of an occasional person it can play a most significant role.

C.   MOTIVATED BY GUILT

1. Childhood Undoing

Guilt is the most frequent motivation and stimulus for the operation of Undoing, in childhood as well as with adults. Guilt feelings are both conscious and unconscious. There are many possible variations, and this subject has interesting ramifications with all age groups. At times Undoing follows quite spontaneously as an addendum to a hostile comment. This was illustrated in *Case 87* (p. 167). Undoing can be a simple, almost childlike dynamism. When motivated by emotions of guilt and remorse, these feelings are for something done, or merely thought about. In instances observed in childhood, the basic feelings may be fairly nebulous, and guilt too definite a label to apply.

2. The Behavioral Undoing Cycle

Upon occasion the clinician will observe a given pattern of behavior which is highly suggestive of an Undoing kind of operation. Such an endeavor may operate in awareness, or partially so. Sometimes it is accessible to consciousness only with the greatest of difficulty, if at all.

Instances of the above may be encountered in therapy, as illustrated in the following example. Herein what is termed the *Behavioral Undoing Cycle* was in unwitting operation. Awareness was gradually gained, although with considerable difficulty. When its elucidation had been achieved, this pattern of behavior was surrendered. It no longer made sense, or perhaps after its analysis it made too much sense. Its retention was no longer psychologically economic and became unnecessary.

Case 198

Undoing Through Indulgence and Sex

(1) *Unrealistic Level of Guilt Significant.* A young real estate salesman was in treatment because of handicapping personality traits

and sexual conflicts. Symptomatic of the latter, an interesting pattern of attending burlesque shows was noted which afforded him substitutive gratifications. He paid heavily for these through feelings of guilt. His attendance was compulsive.

During the show he experienced erotic stimulation, accompanied by feelings of superiority to the women, who undressed before him. Because of accompanying emotions of shame and guilt, he attended the shows secretly when on business trips. Although he had never been "caught," he constantly feared detection. He returned home miserable, his level of guilty feelings out of proportion, as assessed objectively. What might have represented an innocuous activity was revealed by the level of feelings to have a great deal of personal significance.

(2) *A Behavioral Undoing Cycle.* For a few days following each such occasion he was unusually kind to his wife. He indulged her in various ways. He helped with the children and housework. After a time, and especially if he could successfully have sexual intercourse (impotence was a significant problem), his guilt lifted and he felt himself again. The cycle was over, to begin on the next trip.

Through his burst of kindness to his wife and having sexual relations, he had undone the self-assessed guilty act of attending the burlesque show, and what this meant to him—including his hostility to women generally and his wife in particular. Having erased all this, he was free to repeat the cycle. Underlying motivations as well as the regular existence of the sequence, including the periods of indulgence, was initially outside of awareness. Awareness led to understanding. His therapy made substantial progress and relationships improved.

The above brief excerpt may convey to the reader the presence of additional interesting dynamics operative in this young man's psyche. The Behavioral Undoing Cycle was surrendered with its thorough elucidation.

3. With Every Type of Guilt

A. WIDE BASES.—One might review all the possible consequences of human behavior which occasion guilt. Guilt feelings have wide bases indeed. We would suspect that with each, sooner or later one would come across instances in which the ego defense of Undoing had been evolved. Undoing is associated with every type of guilt.

People tend to suffer guilt more frequently in relation to aggressive and sexual drives. Guilt is also often present concerning life and death. Many people disapprove of abortion. This may be based upon moral, ethical, religious, or legal grounds. Guilt feelings are commonly associated. As ever with guilt feelings, these may be realistic or neurotic in level. The following instance illustrates the endeavor to cope with them through the operation of Undoing.

Case 199

Undoing Follows Abortion

(1) *Conscience Violated.* A young husband and wife had to work hard to set up housekeeping and support themselves. They were having a struggle. They planned not to have a child for 2 years. An earlier arrival would be disastrous to their uncertain finances. However, within a short time the wife became pregnant. Her emotional response was as to a major catastrophe.

Although strongly disapproving, in her despair her conscience was violated. She secretly had an abortion performed, an act regarded as a major sin. She suffered deep guilt feelings. These continued and if anything, increased. She energetically sought to undo the wrong, her endeavors in this direction being both conscious and unconscious.

(2) *Undoing Compulsion.* She began talking incessantly about her desire for a child. For months this was the main topic of conversation, at least as far as she was concerned. Daily she covetously admired the window displays of the Stork Shop. She became occupied knitting and sewing infants clothes.

This troubled young woman had a compulsion to undo what she had done. Becoming pregnant again was a way. She could hardly wait until this became feasible. Her increasingly strong feelings of desire for a child, and becoming pregnant, together with expressing them prominently were part of her endeavor to assuage her feelings of guilt, erase her sin, and undo the abortion.

Patterns of behavior are not infrequently associated with Undoing. Something of this has been illustrated. Repetitive acts as with the following pattern can also be performed on the basis of unconscious needs for Undoing.

B. THE UNDOING PHRASE.—Another category of repetitive activity which represents an intriguing form of Undoing is the oft-repeated phrase. It may be expressed frequently and automatically, with the person concerned little aware of its use, frequency, or intent. When so used, it is called the *Undoing Phrase*.

The repeated use of the Undoing Phrase may be of such prominence as to help characterize the person. It comes to serve as a personal trademark. This interesting form of Undoing is illustrated in the following example.

Case 200

The Undoing Phrase

A 34-year-old salesman had a habit of speech which was more apparent to his friends than to himself. Frequently he would add, "Maybe I'm wrong" to his statements. This appeared as an automatic kind of afterthought. It had a slightly apologetic tone. In view of its prominence, it had come to serve as a personal trademark. After attention was invited to his vocal mannerism in the course of therapy, he began to observe its frequency and analyze its bases.

The analysis underscored two major purposes, one of Undoing and a second of seeking reassurance. "Maybe I'm wrong" would regularly follow any comment of his about someone which was critical in the slightest. The sequence was that of: (1) attack, (2) remorse, and (3) Undoing.

He felt badly (comprised of elements of guilt, anxiety, apology, fear of retaliation, and remorse) over the criticism. The "maybe I'm wrong" sought backing, agreement, and reassurance. It was an attempt to "tone it down a bit," an apology, and a way of "blunting the attack." This was a form of Undoing undertaken repeatedly and automatically. Understanding the intended function of the Undoing Phrase led to dissipation of the needs and process.

Following the elucidation of the characteristic phrase in the foregoing instance, it became more rare. During the subsequent months of a successful analysis, it vanished.

D. UNDOING WHILE ASLEEP

1. The Undoing Dream

The wish-fulfilling role of dreams is well established. At times this function reflects underlying needs for the erasure or annulment of a guilt-laden act, or taking events back to before it happened. Similarly, dreams can be a vehicle for the expression of remorse and atonement.

The following illustrates a repetitive type of dream in which the regretted act was undone. It is an instance of what we refer to as the *Undoing Dream*.

Case 201

Omission Undone in an Undoing Dream

An 8-year-old boy put his cat in an unused chicken house. The family was due to leave the next day on an extended vacation trip, and in the excitement he neglected to release the pet, or arrange for its care. His omission led to a sad result.

Upon their return, the cat was dead, a victim of starvation. The boy felt intensely guilty. Shortly afterwards he had a vivid dream of returning home once again from the trip. In the dream he found the cat still living and active. In his dream he erased the death and the consequences of his failure. The omission was undone. His feelings in the dream were ones of relief and happiness.

This was an instance of the Undoing Dream. It became a repeated one. It occurred again with slight variations on an average of three times yearly for more than 30 years. Its repetition conveyed the continuing presence of unconscious regret and self-condemnation. The dream served an Undoing function. When this became clarified through its analysis after many years, it ceased to recur. The underlying need was no longer present.

2. Dream-of-Erasure

Many dreams have similar elements. In attempting to recreate events so as to wipe out a disturbing event or memory, this goal is consistent with what we know of its wish-fulfilling functions. This transpired in the preceding instance. It becomes increasingly clear in the following two dreams which illustrate a particular variant of the Undoing Dream.

This specific type of dream is encountered only occasionally, but nevertheless is of sufficient moment and frequency to warrant its designation as the *Dream-of-Erasure*.

Case 202

The Dream-of-Erasure; a Conviction Reversed

A 52-year-old businessman was having a difficult struggle getting reestablished after serving a year in prison. This followed his conviction on several counts of criminal negligence in the management of others' funds. The trial and conviction were the most bitterly painful events in his life.

One day he related a particularly vivid dream. In the dream all the events of his trial were recapitulated exactly—up to the point of the verdict. In the dream, however, the jury foreman announced that they had found for acquittal.

One can imagine the pleasant feelings associated with this dream. One can understand how he hoped for its return. In one blow his conviction and all its resulting painful consequences were undone.

Case 203

The Dream-of-Erasure; A Sequence in Living Undone

A 37-year-old housewife went to a cocktail party, leaving her visiting mother to manage the children and put them to bed. Upon return everything was fine. An hour later, however, tragedy struck when her mother suffered a fatal heart attack.

The daughter reproached herself bitterly and unrealistically about her responsibility. She believed things might have been different if her mother had not looked after the children.

She had an interesting Dream-of-Erasure after a month, in which the evening's events were in part undone. In the dream she returned from the party in time to get supper for the children and put them to bed herself. Her mother was a background figure, smiling benignly. She had erased the tragedy in her dream. As a dreamer she had undone the bases for her self-reproach.

3. Sleepwalking and Sleeptalking

Communications while asleep occasionally take another and intriguing form. Some people talk while sleeping. Because of their awareness of this possibility, plus the prospect of one's inadvertently making self-revelations, or confessions, certain people are quite uneasy over talking in their sleep. For similar reasons people often fear anesthesia or intoxication. They may be consciously unaware of the basis for their apprehensions.

Instances of sleepwalking and sleeptalking can symbolically or more directly illustrate a type of Undoing. Confessions are encountered thus. One may recall from Shakespeare, Lady Macbeth's confessional while asleep as witnessed by her attendant and a summoned doctor. Although she concludes with the oft-quoted "What is done cannot be undone," one may wonder about her dream work reflecting a measure of defensively-intended Undoing.

E.   IN OBSESSIVE-COMPULSIVE NEUROSES

1. Repetitive Symptoms. Tidal Undoing

Sometimes the mechanism of Undoing fails, that is, the defense is invaded by the warded-off impulses. This helps us understand several phenomena in the Compulsion Neuroses. Among them is the repetitive compulsive act, in which an increase in the number of repetitions becomes necessary. This transpires because no repetition gives sufficient reassurance that the act is done without its instinctual intention.

This may be observed, for instance, in certain forms of counting compulsion, in which the person must perform a given number of repetitions.

These are necessary in order to free himself from the necessity of still further repetitions. If they are not performed exactly and precisely, that is, in the prescribed manner, he must begin them over again. The alternative is anxiety and tension.

Case 204

Repetitive Telephoning

A 38-year-old obsessional patient in analysis frequently made phone calls in series of three.

Eventually as the dynamics of these came under scrutiny, we learned that they followed a typical sequence. Call number one was marked by his being on the nasty and offensive side, in his view. The second call sought to deny and to undo the first through offering apologies. Call three in turn undid the Undoing.

In the final call in the series he revoked the apologies and under-scored the original hostility. At times, of course, the intent and affect involved were not at all striking except to him and might only become apparent through careful analysis of a given sequence.

The reader can readily surmise from the above how with added anxiety, conflicts, or stress, or with the threatened failure of the Undoing operation, additional calls or series of calls might be required. This is a back and forth process which may appropriately be termed *Tidal Undoing.*

2. Obsessive Order and Rituals

While space will not permit consideration of the widespread role of Undoing in the Obsessive-Compulsive group of neurotic reactions, this subject merits attention. As in the foregoing case, the operation of this ego defense can closely approach that of Denial, may act in concert with it as an example of the *emotional symbiosis,* or represent a further progression.

There is no doubt that Undoing is a significant if unwitting aim in many obsessional rituals and in the frequent obsessive need for order. As with other symptoms in this major type of neurosis, their careful study and analysis will often reveal the operation of this dynamism.

3. Undoing in Therapy—a Secondary Defense

Undoing can play a role in treatment. It is of practical importance to note the employment of Undoing as a resistance phenomenon, especially in the analysis and psychotherapy of the obsessive patient. In a typical instance of this operation, an interpretation will be offered the patient, who seemingly quite readily accepts it. However, especially to the dismay of the young therapist, the next session (or three) will be spent rejecting, arguing, and disproving what was proffered—in effect Undoing the earlier acceptance. This is *Resistance-Undoing.*

Resistance-Undoing comprises a significant mode of resistance. It provides added interesting illustrations of the important *Concept of Sec-*

ondary Defense, according to which the psychologic symptom—a defense in itself—is in turn (i.e., *secondarily*) defended.

The psychotherapist can help minimize the effects of Resistance-Undoing through avoiding premature interpretations, especially to his obsessive patients, preparing the groundwork carefully, and proffering an idea or insight not too far in advance of when the person would arrive there himself.

F.   SOCIAL UNDOING

As noted, the operation of Undoing is common to persons evolving obsessional defenses. These are widespread. Accordingly its operation can be anticipated in a wide variety of situations. A frequent type is that which we identify as *Social Undoing,* in which either an offense or a compliment is to an extent undone almost simultaneously with the doing.

Examples of Social Undoing are frequently thought of in a rather offhand fashion as awkwardness, a slip of the tongue, or perhaps as an absence of "social graces" or "good breeding." Social Undoing may be so slight or subtle as to pass unnoticed, sometimes because the listener automatically and selectively excludes it from his awareness and recognition.

The following are instances. These are hardly subtle, still there was a degree of automaticity in each. Several were clearly inadvertent.

Case 205

Social Undoing

"That is such a becoming dress; I like it every time you wear it."

"Your hat is very attractive; it's just like the one that Elsie (the speaker's maid) has."

A woman remarked upon a certain dress being suitable for an older person, whereupon a second woman present, agreeing, remarked, "Yes, indeed, the owner is about forty-five." Suddenly realizing the first woman was older than this herself, quickly added, "and she thinks the dress is too old for her."

"Your girls are so cute; it's too bad they have your straight hair."

"What a terrible play! I didn't like the way your boy passed the ball, but he is an excellent passer most of the time."

"I don't go for your kind of music and I don't see how anyone could like it; however, I am sure there are many people who do."

"Your new little car looks awful nice, but you wouldn't catch me in one."

"Congratulations on your promotion. I guess you know they asked four other men to take that job before you took it."

"Your house is so fine and spacious; it's unfortunate that it's too much for you to keep straightened up."

"He is an excellent host. Too bad he monopolizes the conversation."

"My wife has so many odd friends that we have to get Christmas presents for, although I like most of the people and shopping is fun."

G. NOTES ON DYNAMICS, AND ADDITIONAL ASPECTS

1. Symbolic Undoing

A. IN PRAYER.—In understanding the intrapsychic operation of Undoing, it is sometimes helpful to observe instances of its conscious operation. The progression of this operation and its relegation to the unconscious through Repression can be helpful in clarifying our views of Undoing as an intrapsychic defensive process.

The following instance was of interest. It illustrates this chap's childhood struggles to cope with a troubling situation.

Case 206

Undoing Blasphemous Thoughts

"While I was a youngster, it was my obligation to spend several hours each Saturday morning at the synagogue praying. This was something I had to do, but I would have much preferred to go outside and play football or baseball. During warm or pleasant weather, I would be very unhappy. It was boring. My discontent and unhappiness would be increased by the sounds of other children playing.

"Frequently I was rebellious. In anger I would sit and grumble to myself. Blasphemous thoughts passed through my mind—especially thoughts of hating and denouncing God, because He was responsible for my having to come to the synagogue every week. Immediately after these thoughts I would feel extremely guilty. I would try to undo these intolerable ideas by praising God and saying to myself that I loved Him. I would thank Him for his goodness and mercy.

"I had to repeat these opposite thoughts several times, otherwise I would become distraught. I was not comfortable until I completed these praises. Only when I told Him many times of my love and devotion would I feel I had undone the wrong of my complaining and bitter thoughts. . . ."

Fenichel cited a case which is a progression from the foregoing and comprised an obsessive-compulsive symptom. A young man followed a compulsively repetitive pattern of praying, in which the prayer was immediately followed by slapping his mouth. On a conscious level, his obsessive praying was for his mother's health and reflected love and concern. The praying, however, was also unconsciously and symbolically intended to ward off and keep repressed certain death wishes which he simultaneously harbored, but which could not be admitted to awareness.

His unique symptom recapitulated conflicting feelings toward mother. The compulsive slapping of his mouth following the prayers was a symbolic means of putting back, that is, Undoing the prayer. The prayer, originally a compulsive warding-off and Undoing type of symptom, was in turn undone. It represented an interesting form of *Tidal Undoing* as cited above.

B. COMPULSIVE RITUALS (CR).—There are a number of fairly common and not too significant compulsive rituals which comprise a defensively-intended symbolic Undoing. A child who errs in stepping on a crack in the pavement, because he has been sedulously avoiding this, may undertake various involved acts or further rituals in order to magically undo whatever presumed evil or danger the crack-stepping evokes.

We may observe children or adults surreptitiously crossing their fingers upon telling a fib. The finger-crossing is intended to undo (the wickedness of) the untruth. When the Devil is mentioned, some people similarly ward off, that is, undo in advance, the evil of Satan by crossing themselves.

People attempt to undo various kinds of disapproved actions through making culturally acceptable gifts, services, or sacrifices. Indeed, throughout human history sacrifices have been a widespread means of trying to make up for or seek Restitution for misdeeds, and in this way undo whatever transgressions may have been committed. This approach has operated with families, groups, tribes, races, and nations (p. 389).

Guilt has been a widespread and pervasive manifestation in individual and group experience since the race evolved. In view of the discomfort evoked through this characteristically human emotion, it is not surprising that all kinds of emotional conflicts develop, and many dynamisms are called into operation.

2. Compulsive Handwashing

In the neuroses, *Symbolic Undoing* is illustrated by a number of emotional manifestations. Among these, a striking symptom is the one of compulsive handwashing. This terribly disturbing and at times disabling symptom generally includes attempts on the part of the individual concerned at expiation and Undoing in response to unconscious guilt. If this were successful, if it could really erase and wash away the source of guilt, this compulsion would well serve its unconsciously intended purpose. Guilt would no longer threaten. Tragically, however, this is often not enough. The deep despair of these persons, which can lead to their seeking therapy, can arise from the implicit recognition that the Undoing operation can never be sufficient.

This was understood by Shakespeare in Macbeth, in which the hapless Macbeth was encouraged by his wife to commit murder. He recognized the futility of trying to wash away the blood stains (representing guilt) from his hands, when he cried:

> "Will all great Neptune's ocean wash this blood
> Clean from my hand? No, this my hand will rather
> The multitudinous seas incarnadine,
> Making the green one red."

Macbeth refers figuratively of course, to the futility of cleansing his conscience of guilt feelings. The deed could not be undone.

The symbolism of compulsive washing usually is found to have a dynamic basis in the unconsciously attempted Undoing of sin, evil, or badness, as these come to be subjectively assessed by the person's superego. Undoing is part of the attempted endeavor of placating the conscience or superego. See also discussion of symbolism, pp. 412–425 and Index references.

3. Relationship-Undoing

Undoing can have significant effects upon interpersonal relationships. These are often subtle, likely to be difficult of verification, and often can only be surmised at best. Subtle Undoing is frequently unwitting.

We tend to utilize the more marked instances encountered in psychotherapeutic experience for illustrations of the manner in which Undoing influences a pattern of relationship. When so delineated whether subtle or apparent, we refer to these instances as *Relationship-Undoing*. The following case is an example of such resulting influences of Relationship-Undoing in a marriage.

Case 207

Sexual Relations Undo

A young woman reported to the therapist her lack of interest in sexual relations. Her husband's overtures failed to elicit much response. Indeed, this was his major complaint about the marriage.

As the pattern of sexual activity in the marriage unfolded, it became clear that there were still other instances in which, in some contrast, the wife was not only interested in sex but was the aggressor. The lack of consistency invited scrutiny.

The contrasting occasions on study proved to follow spats with her husband. She would end these with a verbal tirade, forcefully enumerating over and over all his faults and shortcomings, as assessed by her. The husband, a mild, quiet, unassuming fellow, would usually suffer in silence through the verbal barrage. After the episode she was remorseful about the tirade and its effects, much of this on a less than conscious level.

Shortly after this sequence of events, her sexual interests were aroused and she initiated love making. It eventually became apparent to her during the course of therapy that her overtures and sexual interests represented a way of Undoing the tirade. It was an unconscious endeavor to erase and make reparation for the hurt and injury, about which she felt responsible and guilty.

With this pattern of behavior she said in effect, "I have hurt you. I will undo this hurt by providing love and sexual satisfaction which you usually don't get. I will be more the kind of wife you want. I will make up for my deficiencies in our relationship as a way of Undoing my tirade and the hurt it has occasioned." In view of the prominent effects upon the interpersonal situation this was an example of *Relationship-Undoing*.

Through therapy the above patient gained an understanding of various psychologic factors handicapping her sexual adjustment. As a consequence, she was able to achieve a more satisfactory relationship. As this was effected, her needs for the defensively-motivated tirades abated, and the sequelae of guilt and Undoing was no longer appropriate.

The following incident illustrates the ways in which the operation of Relationship-Undoing can function in child-parent relations. Following a

Fantasy (Chapter 7) it also illustrates the fantasy-generated need for and process of *Fantasy-Undoing*.

Case 208

Fantasy-Undoing

A colleague found his small son hunting for something in the street. The lad was reluctant to discuss the incident, but his father gradually was able to secure an interesting explanation.

The child was looking for tacks and nails. He hadn't found any. He had earlier had a fantasy of throwing nails into the streets to puncture his Dad's tires. His searching made him "feel better."

The prime dynamism operative in this instance was Undoing. Through it he undoes the Fantasy; i.e., *Fantasy-Undoing*. Through additionally safeguarding against other nails, he carries this further, as a form of Restitution.

H.   SUMMARY

To undo is to render null and void, to restore the preexisting conditions. Undoing is a process of *psychic erasure*. Although an obsessional reaction, in which the mechanism of Undoing is prominent, was described prior to 1850, the recognition and early attempts at delineation, and definition of this dynamism waited 100 years.

Undoing is a major ego defense through which an act, thought, omission, desire, or impulse is erased. Its defensive intent is to spare one the consciously intolerable disapproval of a critical conscience. It is an intrapsychic process in which one unwittingly endeavors to abolish, annul, and *undo* a prior deed or wish. The underlying needs are based upon subjective evaluation. There are many types of Undoing.

Confession can be used as a way of Undoing. The *Confession-Discrepancy* or CD describes the situation when there is a significant gap between the wrongdoing as objectively assessed, and the subjective need to confess. Sometimes Undoing is employed to wipe the slate clean at least partially, so that one may feel freer to resume or repeat an act. When this can be identified as a pattern it constitutes the *Confession-Undoing* Cycle. An analogous pattern of crime and punishment with the criminal comprises the *Punishment-Undoing Cycle*. An undoing act frequently follows a consciously intolerable or sinful thought or impulse. Both *criminals-in-fact* (as distinguished from) and *criminals-by-wish* can evolve the Undoing process.

Undoing may be found in connection with any type of human behavior which evokes guilt feelings. Some of these were illustrated. There are interesting applications in criminal experience (*Criminal-Undoing*), and in alcoholism, with the *Hangover Paradox* a possible consequence. The *Judas Confession*, alternatively an *Ineffectual Confession*, is one which fails to procure the intended goal. Guilt and remorse are not ameliorated.

Inversion (Chapter 13) may occur in which a second reversed act symbolically undoes the first in *Expiative Undoing*. The *Undoing Spiral* may be encountered as a significant progression. The most frequent motivation for Undoing is guilt. Instances are found in childhood (*Childhood Undoing*), as illustrated in several case examples. These may be minor or major and they may continue, to exert a major influence in the person's life. A major behavioral pattern can develop which reflects the operation of Undoing. These are sometimes encountered in therapy. *Case 198* illustrated what is accordingly termed the *Behavioral Undoing Cycle*. Its overall consequences are more likely to be destructive, in distinction from those of Rechannelization (Chapter 19). In therapy one observes Undoing most frequently in relation to otherwise intolerable aggressive and sexual drives.

Repetitions, obsessions, a..d compulsions often reflect operation of the dynamism of Undoing. The repetitive act may illustrate what is termed *Tidal Undoing*. Limited and partial success, or failure, in the ego defense's operation leads to more repetitions, when these are marked by the symbolic intent of Restitution and Undoing. The *Undoing Phrase* was illustrated (*Case 200*).

Undoing can occur, often symbolically, while asleep. *Case 201* illustrated Undoing in a long-standing repetitive dream (The *Undoing Dream*). The *Dream-of-Erasure* as a specific variant of the foregoing was cited and illustrated (*Case 202*). Understanding conscious efforts at Undoing can help us better understand the progression of this process into the automatic, unwitting, and unconscious.

The major role of Undoing in obsessive symptoms was discussed. Undoing can contribute to a Secondary Defense type of resistance in therapy. Instances of *Social Undoing* and *Symbolic Undoing* were offered. *One phase of compulsive rituals* (CR) in everyday life (such as sidewalk-crack avoidance or stepping) can have an Undoing intent. Tidal Undoing as mentioned above refers to a back and forth process—a sequence in which repetitions are required; to do, to undo, and to undo the undoing. Certain compulsive rituals may be illustrative.

Undoing is encountered in the neuroses, particularly in the Obsessive-Compulsive group, as exemplified in compulsive handwashing. It is illustrated in literature, as in *Macbeth*. It can have many important defensively-motivated consequences and effects, including those upon the development of attitudes (*Attitudinal Undoing*), character structure, in fantasy (*Fantasy-Undoing*), interpersonal relationships (*Relationship-Undoing, sexual relations (*Sexual Undoing*), and many areas of living. Entering into an *emotional symbiosis*, it can operate in conjunction with a number of other ego defenses. Undoing occurs in therapy as *Resistance-Undoing*, in which it can comprise a significant illustration of the *Secondary Defense Concept*.

I. CROSS-REFERENCES TO *THE NEUROSES* *

Undoing
in *First Line of Defense* of obsessive persons; pp. 343, 374.

---

* From Laughlin, H. P. *The Neuroses*. London, Butterworth & Co., Ltd., 1967.

in *epigain* and *endogain* of Neuroses-Following-Trauma; p. 875.
not a factor, in Case 190, of *Prisoner Processing;* p. 939.

J. REVIEW QUESTIONS

Sample self-check questions on Chapter 25 and Undoing for the student, psychiatric resident, and board candidate.

1. Give a definition for the ego defense of *Undoing.*
2. What is meant by the *Confession-Discrepancy* or *CD?* How can Undoing contribute?
3. Describe the *Judas* or *Ineffectual Confession,* the *Dream-of-Erasure.*
4. Why might religious authorities view the *Confession-Undoing* and *Punishment-Undoing Cycles* with disfavor?
5. Cite examples from personal or clinical observation for the following:
   A. *Criminal-Undoing.*
   E. *Childhood Undoing.*
   F. *Behavioral Undoing Cycle.*
   B. *Criminals-by-wish.*
   C. *Hangover Paradox.*
   D. *Expiative Undoing.*
   G. *Undoing Phrase.*
   H. *Undoing Dream.*
   I. *Social Undoing.*
   J. *Compulsive Ritual or CR.*
6. Explain the operation of the *Undoing Spiral.*
7. Discuss the role of Undoing in repetitive symptoms. What is the function of *Tidal Undoing?*
8. Does the category of *Resistance-Undoing* support the *Concept of Secondary Defense?* Explain.
9. What is: (1) *Relationship-Undoing?;* (2) *Fantasy-Undoing?;* (3) Symbolic Undoing?; (4) the role of Undoing in compulsive handwashing?; (5) *psychic erasure?*
10. Why might Undoing best be grouped with the *Lower Order* group of dynamisms?

PART 3
SELECTED "LESSER" DYNAMISMS

CHAPTER 26

MINOR EGO DEFENSES

A. ABSOLUTION . . . PSYCHIC REMISSION

    1. Release From Responsibility and Guilt. 2. Definition. 3. In Psychotic Reactions. 4. Demands of Conscience. 5. Many Avenues. 6. Relation to Guilt-Group of Dynamisms.

B. ATONEMENT-PENANCE . . . AMENDS AND REPARATION FOR WRONG

    1. Guilt Basic to Group. 2. Sorrow, Repentance, and Punishment. 3. Examples and Influences. 4. In Psychologic Alopecia.

C. COMPARTMENTALIZATION . . . PROCESS OF EMOTIONAL SEGREGATION

D. COMPROMISE FORMATION . . . UNCONSCIOUS MEDIATION AND ARBITRATION

E. CONDENSATION . . . TELESCOPING INTO A SINGLE REPRESENTATION

    1. Symbol Represents Several Objects. 2. In Dreams and Other Manifestations.

F. CONVERGENCE . . . MULTIPLE FACTORS COME TOGETHER

G. DEFERMENT . . . EMOTIONAL POSTPONEMENT

    1. In Recognition, Experiencing, and Expression. 2. Continued Functioning in Emergency.

H. DEVALUATION . . . REDUCED SIGNIFICANCE

I. DISTORTION . . . UNCONSCIOUS CHANGE AND DISGUISE

    1. Affects, Aims, and Drives. 2. The Aggrandizing Distortion.

J. DIVERSION . . . DEFLECTION OF ATTENTION AND INTEREST

K. EXTENSION . . . EMOTIONAL SCOPE INCREASED

    1. Definition. 2. Major Types: a. Phobic-Extension; b. Symptom-Extension; c. Tribal and Cultural Extensions; d. Characterologic Extension. Concept of Character Trait Balance; e. Dependency-Extension.

L. EXTERNALIZATION . . . OUTWARD REDIRECTION

    1. Definition. 2. Psychodynamics.

M. Fainting . . . Unconscious Perceptive Surrender

    1. Definition. 2. Unconscious Response to Psychic Conflict.

N. References (from *The Neuroses*)

O. Review Questions

A. ABSOLUTION . . . PSYCHIC REMISSION

1. Release From Responsibility and Guilt

Absolution is a minor ego-defensive process which operates uncon-sciously. Through Absolution the ego endeavors to secure release from otherwise intolerable consequences, painful emotional feelings, and penal-ties. There are often moral connotations, including the remission of sins, as these are subjectively assessed by the person concerned, or by church authorities and religious doctrine.

Unconsciously sought, Absolution can masochistically result in self-derogation, self-punishment, and emotional depression. In its ultimate progression it can make contributions or lead to occasional instances of suicide. Conscious and unconscious feelings of guilt and remorse bring this dynamism into operation. It cannot operate until the elaboration of the superego has taken place. This helps to establish our view of Absolution as belonging with the more advanced, Higher Order dynamisms.

2. Definition

Absolution is derived from the Latin *absolutio,* to absolve. Absolu-tion is the release from obligation, debt, or responsibility, or from the consequences of guilt. Through Absolution one is set free from guilt, sin, or penalty. Absolution is the forgiveness of an offense; in civil law repre-sented by an acquittal; in religion by the remission of sins.

In our psychiatric adoption these meanings are directly carried over. Absolution may of course be sought deliberately and consciously. It can also become a complex intrapsychic endeavor, in which case its operation is on the same plane of consciousness as other ego defenses.

We define Absolution as *an ego defense or mental mechanism operat-ing unconsciously through which one seeks and/or secures a measure of freedom from guilt or penalty, remission of sins, or forgiveness for an offense. Release from responsibility, consequences or obligations are the defensively-intended aims and goals of the dynamism.*

3. In Psychotic Reactions

In certain psychotic reactions one may observe striking instances of the intrapsychic endeavor of Absolution. At times the desperate, unconscious seeking of forgiveness can influence the psychologic generation and content of hallucinations. This is illustrated in the auditory sphere in the following case.

Case 209

Hallucinations in Absolution

(1) *Punitive Superego.* A 19-year-old girl developed insoluble emotional conflicts because of greatly overdeveloped moral and ethical standards. In efforts to conform to them, she attempted unsuccessfully to suppress sexual interests. She condemned herself bitterly for several minor incidents of a sensual nature.

Her level of guilt was unrealistic and neurotic. An archaic superego exacted harsh and masochistic punishment. As her problem-coping defenses proved ineffectual, life was intolerable, and the onset of a Schizophrenic Reaction ensued.

(2) *Hallucinatory Comfort.* An early prominent feature in her illness was hearing God's voice. She heard Him say, "Martha, you are a good girl," . . . "Your sins are forgiven," and a few times, "Heaven awaits you, child." To her the voices were not imagined. They afforded a measure of Absolution.

This young lady derived transient comfort from these absolutional hallucinatory experiences, deeply convinced as she was of her worthlessness and terrible guilt. This was a desperate, unconscious endeavor at securing Absolution. We eventually learned that she had projected certain "forgotten" comforting comments long earlier made by a spiritual advisor. These helped to provide the content of the hallucinations.

This patient secured Absolution in part through creating the forgiving voice of God. To her the experience was real, although in fact comprising a serious symptom of a major psychotic reaction.

4. Demands of Conscience

A punitive superego enters into the bases for evolving the guilt-group of dynamisms, in which Absolution is included. It is important to bear in mind that the function of the superego (roughly the conscience) is primarily emotional, as distinguished from intellectual or rational. Attitudes, demands, and censure by the conscience are not necessarily consistent with what might be adjudged appropriate or realistic by an objective observer.

It is important to keep this in mind in assessing the level of unconscious guilt of a given individual. *The automatic and unconscious evaluation of the presence and significance of one's wrongdoing is a subjective matter which is highly variable for every individual.* The existence of needs to be punished, or to atone is likewise variable. Mangammal, Queen Regent of Madura, India (1689–1706), gave more than six million dollars to charity to atone for using her left (instead of right) hand in placing a betel nut in her mouth.

A person's wrongdoing may be realistically evaluated, neurotically judged, or some of both. However, it is the subjective appraisal and judgment by the person concerned which is the important feature from the standpoint of adjustment and emotional health. These characteristics of the conscience can help us better to understand the operation of the ego defenses in general, and the guilt-related group of dynamisms in particular.

5. Many Avenues

Persons take many routes trying to absolve themselves from blame and responsibility. These avenues are both conscious and unconscious. Their intent may or may not be recognized.

A middle-aged attorney's marriage was breaking up. He followed what we call the *third party route* in his endeavors to secure what amounted to a "Certificate of Absolution." His understanding of motivation was limited. He induced a friend to contact his wife so as to firmly establish the impossibility of a rapprochement.

Communicated by letter, her response absolved him of responsibility for further efforts, and in part for his contributions to the marital collapse.

6. Relation to Guilt-Group of Dynamisms

Absolution is closely related to other members of the guilt-group of ego defenses. The aim is often the same; the endeavor similar.

The guilt-group also includes the dynamisms of Atonement-Penance, Restitution, Retribution, Undoing, and sometimes Denial and other ego defenses. Instances of each of these can be observed to operate on occasion in the service of Absolution.

B. ATONEMENT-PENANCE . . . AMENDS AND REPARATION FOR WRONG

1. Guilt Basic to Group

Unconscious guilt contributes to the evolvement of many of the ego defenses. Prominent among these is the interesting guilt-group of dynamisms. As noted above, it includes Absolution, the present one of Atonement-Penance, together with those of Restitution, Retribution, Undoing, and at times Denial. See p. 388; *Case 185,* p. 397; and pp. 429, 430.

Guilt-group members can often be distinguished and identified clinically. They possess in common the unconscious aim of alleviating guilt. As a consequence, their function and operation is often overlapping. Their separate delineation clinically can be difficult at best, and on occasion is either not feasible or must needs be contrived.

Most members of the guilt-group are being considered together with what we name the *Minor Ego Defenses.* This is to distinguish them from what we sometimes refer to as the 22 *senior dynamisms* or *group,* because the latter are generally more prominent.

Terming them minor or lesser may or may not be appropriate, depending upon how one regards them, and the situation in which a given dynamism is operative. They are also so termed at times by virtue of being less specific or more difficult to delineate. Certainly when any one of them plays a major role in an individual's psychology, it is not a minor mechanism, at least as far as he is concerned. See earlier references in the chapter on Restitution, Chapter 22. This is true for any member of the minor group of ego defenses or *junior dynamisms*. See Index references to Reparation.

2. Sorrow, Repentance, and Punishment

Through operation of the dynamism of Atonement the ego arranges amends for wrongdoing or injury. Reparation and satisfaction are rendered. The concept of unwitting expiation for sins and transgressions overlaps. (See Expiation Undoing, Chapter 25.) Our co-consideration of Penance indicates its close relationship and frequent association with Atonement.

Penance generally refers more definitely to what is regarded as sinful. It's operation implies regret or sorrow. In Penance punishment is undergone as part of the penitence for sin. According to certain church doctrine, Penance may be made through confession with sorrow, in which case it is followed by forgiveness. The ego defense of Atonement-Penance indicates the presence of regret, sorrow, and repentance.

Unconscious endeavors which are partially or wholly motivated by inner needs for atonement and Penance encompass a wide variety. Unwitting, masochistic, and tragic contributions may be made through Atonement-Penance to self-defeat, emotional symptoms and illness, accidents, and failures. Many less than conscious contribtutions are made to the ways in which an individual unwittingly contributes to his own loss, self-defeat, poor relationships, and personal misery.

3. Examples and Influences

Atonement carries into legal concepts and punishment. The wrong-doer has atoned for wrongs throughout history. In 1406, a court in Cordova sentenced a wife-killer to build an Arch of Atonement; a gate and tower which stand today. A young man deliberately destroyed prized hobby gear in atonement for masturbation. An individual learned through analysis that his compulsive-driven and often filled-with-misery preoccupation with newspapers (a like preoccupation to that of his father) had in it elements of Atonement-Penance for having rejected his father and his traits most thoroughly—taking over unwittingly and retaining an aspect about his father about which perhaps he was openly most critical.

These dynamisms can influence one's outlook, in line with the gloomy and pessimistic prediction that "for every smile, a tear must fall." Accordingly, an individual reported in therapy that "I cannot allow myself to be happy, because I'll have to atone for it . . ." It was as though to be happy was somehow wrong, or bad; enjoying life more than he was entitled to, and that this must be made up or atoned for. See *Hangover Paradox,* alcoholic bouts, p. 431.

4. In Psychologic Alopecia

The following instance illustrates a number of aspects of Atonement-Penance in a marked instance of psychic-emotional alopecia. The study of a dream proved significant.

Case 210

Hair Loss in Atonement-Penance

(1) *Psychotherapy Initiated.* A 36-year-old divorced bank teller was referred for evaluation and possible psychotherapy because of progressive loss of hair. History disclosed that upon two earlier occasions a similar loss progressed to total baldness. Medical and dermatologic studies eliminated organic factors, and uncovered suggestive emotional features in certain of the patient's self-depreciatory attitudes.

The results of the preliminary studies were borne out, and a series of psychotherapeutic interviews, recommended and begun. As therapy began, it was soon learned that this man harbored a great amount of guilt and self-condemnation. Some of this related to aggressive feelings, but the majority was tied to sexual matters.

(2) *Intense Sexual Guilt.* Several traumatic childhood experiences helped lay foundations for certain attitudes about himself. Once a small playmate told his mother about incidents of mutual masturbation. These reflected childish curiosity and interest of the two boys. On learning of this the patient's mother became upset.

"She came and took me home and whipped me. She found a piece of lath some place and just beat me and beat me. Finally the lath went to pieces and she stopped. Maybe she was too tired by that time. . . . I was afraid she was going to kill me. . . ."

"I could never make advances toward women. My mother beat me whenever she believed I had any sexual interests. . . . I was always afraid of her. . . . I've always doubted if she was really my mother, in view of how cruel she was. . . . There was never any affection. But anything about sex would really set her off! I felt nothing was so bad or wrong as sexual feelings. . . .

"I always felt I had done something terribly wrong in childhood. . . . Never felt good or worthy afterwards. . . . It changed my whole outlook on life. It was after that beating that I first had asthma. It just came on one night. . . ."

(3) *A Recurrent Disturbing Dream.* After some time in treatment, this man had a disturbing dream recur which he had experienced on several previous occasions. The manifest content of his dream follows.

"A snake is going to get me. He comes for me but I can't move. I am terrified and I wake up frightened and yelling. Something is going to get me. It keeps coming back. The snake is crawling at me. I try to get away and fall. Everyone; all the world. I try to crawl away and escape but it's like dragging. . . . He's going to get me."

His associations to the dream dealt with his terribly guilty feelings, belief in his unworthiness, sinfulness, and fear of and need for punishment. There were frequent references to the devil, as represented by the snake, and why he was pursued. Significant associations led to his loss of hair and its symbolic meaning as atonement and penance for his sins, and as such, a prominent sign, so that everyone, "all the world, will know."

(4) *Dream Element Associations.* The following are extracts from the profuse associations to dream elements. Note the presence of condensation, convergence, overdeterminism, and other principles of dream association, symbolism, and interpretation.

[Snakes?] "Snakes are bad. Everything evil is in snakes. The devil. Going to get after me; like the snake in the dream. Always afraid of the devil. . . . Seem always afraid that something's going to get me. The devil gets sinners. I think I must be the worst. He's certainly going to get me. . . ."

"Snakes and me are strange. . . . I have no fear of them. When I was real little I handled them and played with them as a child. I scared my sister with them. I handled coral snakes—those real dangerous snakes we have down in Florida, and I handled large ones too. I thought they were very pretty. . . . This was before that worst beating. . . ."

[Comes for me?] "The devil. . . . I haven't much fear of dying, but in the dream I'm afraid. . . . I don't regret anything except those two times (sexual incidents) in childhood. I was so bad. . . ."

[Crawling?] "I'm crawling on my stomach to try and get away from the snake. I associate the snake with that awful business in childhood, as if my past would catch up with me and mean my death. Or worse, everyone, all the world, would know! Then I would be socially outcast; couldn't go on living. I guess that's about the same thing. . . . What worse punishment is there?"

[Fear?] "When things go adverse, the fear mounts and grows until things seem insurmountable. Sometimes then I think of suicide. . . ."

[Everyone knows? All the world knows?] "If my hair comes out again; that is what I fear. . . . When that happens I'm a pitiful spectacle. . . . The whole world, everyone knows. . . . The Lord punishes me by making my hair fall out."

"It's like some of those evil people from medieval Europe. . . . Some of those terrible sinners would become penitent. Then their heads would be shaven and they are forced to walk on the street. This is a sign so everyone will know. . . . All the world knows! . . ."

(5) *Progression of Alopecia Reversed.* This dream and its associations came at an important juncture in therapy. It served to clarify, underline, and reenforce prior data from therapeutic study. Through it the patient sharply gained awareness of the important psychic endeavor of unconscious Atonement-Penance represented by the alopecia.

This provided a striking and unique example of self-punishment and retribution. The rate of hair loss decreased shortly after therapy began, about two-thirds of it having been lost by then. After completing the dream work, the loss stopped and the hair slowly began to grow back. His therapy continued successfully. A year later he again had a full head of hair. After 9 years there was no recurrence.

Instances are not common in which one's hair is the vulnerable site for the impact of severe emotional stress. The foregoing is the most marked example of its kind in our experience. Still, less prominent instances occasionally occur. When they do, they can challenge one's credulity in addition to the clinicians's ingenuity, in working out the dynamic and physiologic bases.

A student reported a family instance in which a car's driver suffered an area of alopecia 4 inches in diameter within 12 hours of striking and badly injuring a child. In a related phenomenon, rarely a person's hair turns white overnight following a severe emotional shock or strain.

C. COMPARTMENTALIZATION ... PROCESS OF EMOTIONAL SEGREGATION

Related to the defense of Isolation (p. 476) is the psychic operation of Compartmentalization. We define Compartmentalization as *an unconscious emotional process through which the ego segregates segments of experience, mental activity, or opposing and conflictual elements of psychic conflict, to-gether with their associated emotions and cognition into separate compo-nents or compartments.*

Successful Compartmentalization may allow sharper focus on the problem at hand through sparing one the simultaneous impingement of an additional one, or several others which may well be conflictual, inconsistent, or in opposition. Compartmentalization can be effective even though these potential competitors are otherwise pressing and/or of some moment. It is a defensively-intended psychic-emotional process of segregation of a given element or component.

The operation of Compartmentalization assists in avoiding the simul-taneous consideration of conflicting areas. Through their segregation a compartmentalized coexistence is possible. What would otherwise comprise a sharp emotional inconsistency becomes tolerable.

For example, a man regarded his mother as the person closest to him, and simultaneously was also intensely hostile to her. The latter was strong enough that he avoided any discussion of her or related areas. Seemingly grossly inconsistent and the source for great emotional conflict, his attitudes were compartmentalized. This he had managed with such success that he was unaware of conflict. *Relationship Compartmentalization* can aid in the maintenance of two or more relationships which are other-wise conflicting or incompatible.

Prejudicial attitudes as well as inconsistencies can be better main-tained through their emotional segregation. What we term *Incomplete Compartmentalization* can contribute to psychopathology. This is the faulty operation of the dynamism and can lead to symptoms of confusion, impaired ideation, and interference with verbal facility.

D. COMPROMISE FORMATION ... UNCONSCIOUS MEDIATION AND ARBITRATION

In Compromise Formation *the ego serves as a mediator in the en-deavor to settle differences. Conflicting drives, aims, needs, goals, or standards may be thus compromised unconsciously. A compromise is evolved and formed. In the successful operation of this mediating process, emotional conflicts are averted, resolved, or compromised.*

The consequence is establishment of an *Emotional Compromise,* an alternative term for the *Compromise Formation;* both terms naming the process and what it eventuates. Its effects are likely to be reflected, al-though in disguised form, in what is consciously and externally apparent.

Although elaborated protectively, not all Compromise Formations prove to be healthful ones by any means. This is readily illustrated, in that many symptoms in the emotional illnesses represent defensively-intended but ineffectual Compromise Formations, or have such aspects. These may be considered variously as *Partial, Neurotic,* or *Unsuccessful* Compromise Formations. See *Case 15* (p. 40), and *Case 167* (pp. 332–3).

In effecting compromises, the ego serves as the mediator. Arbitration and mediation is sought principally between the id and the superego, or between the id and external demands for social conformity. Formation of the Emotional Compromise results. (See also pp. 252 and 396–7.)

E.   CONDENSATION ... TELESCOPING INTO A SINGLE REPRESENTATION

1. Symbol Represents Several Objects

Condensation is an interesting intrapsychic process which is particularly important in dreams and in symbolism. Through its operation several concepts, ideas, or needs are condensed in their figurative representation so that a single symbol, object, or figure serves to stand for them.

The process of Condensation almost routinely takes place in the psychic overdetermination of emotional symptoms. It also represents a particular form of the dynamism of Distortion, through which unconscious material is represented in condensed, disguised, and usually symbolic form. Through the telescoping operation of Condensation one object, figure, or symbol can represent several.

In dreams, a number of latent elements may be fused thus into a single manifest symbol, object, or representation. Condensation is the dynamic process through which an unwitting fusion of events, emotions, mental pictures, or emotional elements transpires. This allows the presenting and external symbols or figures to represent multiple items. As noted in our discussion of Symbolization (Chapter 25), their emotional charge or affect is transferred. Recognizing its telescoping effects is basic to an understanding of this dynamism (p. 416 ff.).

2. In Dreams and Other Manifestations

Most dreams have symbolic elements and employ Condensation. A dream figure frequently represents the Condensation of several persons. A popular 20-year-old girl was attracted to a number of young men, among whom she could make no choice. She liked aspects of each. One session she reported "the oddest dream." A young man arrived for a date. However, he wore the clothes of a second. He was driving the car of a third and in the latter's reckless manner. She had, in her dream, unconsciously condensed significant elements of three persons into a single dream figure. The dream confirmed and underlined her indecision and mixed attractions. See also *Case 210*, p. 452.

We observe the operation of this dynamism in the production of many emotional manifestations. In dream symbolism it often acts in close concert with the two other members of the important dynamic triad of Convergence, Overdetermination, and Condensation.

F.   CONVERGENCE ... MULTIPLE FACTORS COME TOGETHER

The important principle of Convergence is basic to the study of associations. In their production we learn that multiple associations and repetition increasingly point or converge toward a common goal, meaning, or interpretation. Convergence operates psychologically to produce a single result from the contributions and coming together of multiple factors.

Different stimuli can converge to produce a single end result. Convergence contributed to the bases for a Scapegoat Reaction in *Case 48* (p. 88). In emotional phenomena there is generally a confluence of unconscious determinants toward the production of one manifestation. In other words, a number of psychologic forces incline together so as to converge. In the unconscious, a symbolization thus can represent and result from the Convergence of various needs or determinants.

Through the operation of Convergence as an ego defense, a single expression stems from the coming together (the converging) of a number of psychic factors. These have been more or less associated. In psychotherapy, what we term *Association Convergence* is an important concept. As they are produced in the treatment process, associations tend to become stronger, closer, clearer, and converge. Unconscious meanings become more apparent as the process of Association Convergence progresses.

G.   DEFERMENT ... EMOTIONAL POSTPONEMENT

1. In Recognition, Experiencing, and Expression

As an ego defense, Deferment unconsciously secures an emotional postponement. Its operation is particularly noteworthy in relation to the awareness, recognition, and experiencing of emotional feelings. The advantage sought is defensive. Time is gained. By putting something off, it may become more tolerable. One can better brace oneself, take care of more urgent emergency needs, or be better able to cope later with what has been delayed.

A frequent defensive consequence of the automatic employment of Deferment ensures more efficient performance in emergencies. This function of the dynamism is at times related to Dissociation (Chapter 6), which can operate in its service.

2. Continued Functioning in Emergency

The woman in the following instance was a pillar of strength through several family emergencies. These included a heart attack, a cerebral accident, and two deaths. Deferment of the impact on each occasion contributed to her ability to function and continued efficiency. She reported:

Case 211

Deferment of Emotional Impact

"In an emergency or accident I've always had this quality. My emotions get put off as long as there's a need to do something. They get postponed. . . . Instead of feeling something right at the time, it gets stopped cold for a while. . . . It's quite automatic with me.

"I have no tears. . . . I don't get emotional at all, at least until later; sometimes much later. Then I feel it all, but in the meantime I can function very effectively. . . . Later it's okay to feel, I guess. . . . I no longer need to be efficient."

In *Case 47* (p. 87), we observed that a capacity for Deferment was requisite to Personal-Feeling Displacement. Blocking or Repression of an idea or striving can represent Deferment (p. 88). Also see *Case 57* (p. 104, and references, pp. 256–7.

H.   DEVALUATION . . . REDUCED SIGNIFICANCE

Devaluation is a minor dynamism or mental mechanism through which the ego lessens or decreases the meaning of an event, strength of a wish or drive, pain of hurt or disappointment, impact of aggression and hostility, and so on. Through Devaluation the level of emotional significance is reduced, psychologically and unconsciously.

Devaluation is motivated by the need for self-protection. The endeavor is to guard and maintain the ego. Conscious efforts at Devaluation are not uncommon, and their progression into an unconscious operation is not difficult to understand.

A person may laugh and make fun (and often more pointedly so) of what is threatening and frightening. The threat of injury or death is far more tolerable when it can be a subject for jokes, amusing anecdotes, or scoffing. Many means of Devaluation exist. Devaluation can be a way station toward certain types of Denial, as was illustrated in *Illness Denial, Case 36* (p. 73; also *Case 133,* p. 259; pp. 260–1; and *Case 145,* pp. 273, 275).

When an ambulance went to pick up a sick person, the man laughed and joked with the driver. He kidded about the precautions taken, and scoffed at "all the fuss." He laughingly denied anything was really wrong, and talked of "much ado about nothing." There actually was a great deal wrong, and on a less superficial level he was fully aware of it. In this instance the driver, a perceptive person recognized the defensive intent.

Jokes, stories, and cartoons about psychiatry and psychiatrists reflect elements of this process. Thereby the unfamiliar, unknown, and to some threatening, is to an extent devalued. A review of sources of humor published in the decades after the turn of the century indicated the operation of an analogous process in relation to medicine and physicians.

I.   DISTORTION ... UNCONSCIOUS CHANGE AND DISGUISE

1. Affects, Aims, and Drives

Distortion is a minor ego defense or mental mechanism operating outside of conscious awareness, through which change, misrepresentation, or alteration is secured in an affect, aim, drive, or object. Distortion reenforces Repression and nonawareness. Awareness of unconscious material and its nature is thus thwarted. Concealment and disguise are aided; outward expression is further restrained and disguised.

Distortion in the direction, nature, and object of drives can occur. There may be a Distortion of either the object, affect, or both, in the *emotional-object amalgam,* or EOA. Emotional feelings as these are experienced or expressed, can be distorted. Distortion can be intended to preserve a cherished picture, to others or to oneself, similarly to that in Idealization (Chapter 8). The father whose son has done quite poorly may exaggerate and overvalue the latter's achievements through this process.

2. The Aggrandizing Distortion

Distortion may be evolved in the service of seeking self-enhancement. This can be an unwitting operation, promoted deliberately, or both. It is what we term the *Aggrandizing Distortion*. In some instances, as in the following, this endeavor may be pursued avidly and repeated sufficiently, so as to gradually gain a measure of conviction.

Case 212

The Aggrandizing Distortion

A middle-aged businessman had done little of importance. He had been a mediocre student, and just one of the boys in his fraternity. On occasion he played in intramural sports, never doing particularly well. His friends were of the minus personality category, among whom he perhaps gained by comparison.

When he left college he obtained a respectable but minor banking job on the basis of his college degree. His fellow workers were impressed with his educational background. As time progressed, he began to embroider his past. He told how he barely missed getting a Phi Beta Kappa key. He described being president of his fraternity and starring on the college football team. He gradually became a local figure of mild importance, based in part upon a considerable exaggeration and distortion of his past accomplishments.

The above are fragments of an elaborate tapestry which was fabricated. Through the distortions of his past experiences, this chap came to picture himself more as he had long wished. The process of self-enhancement may have been undertaken deliberately in the beginning. It represented a major instance of the *Aggrandizing Distortion*, that to a considerable extent he had come to believe.

A Distortion can be evolved when one is motivated by sufficient needs. A grossly overweight man who was hospitalized failed miserably in following a dietary regimen. He snacked, nibbled, secured candy bars surreptitiously, and in many small ways defeated the efforts of staff personnel to help him with the problem. In a defensively-motivated process of Distortion, he came to blame these people bitterly for the failure to lose weight.

During World War II it was not uncommon to encounter angry servicemen complaining bitterly about the military establishment and its performance. In some of these instances, the outbursts of resentment represented a defensively distorted expression of inner feelings of failure, inadequacy, and self-censure concerning personal performance.

An original protectively-intended aim can become distorted. An intern had trouble doing venipunctures for his women patients. Analysis revealed overprotective attitudes originally induced toward his sisters in early years, with a major impetus to this having followed his inadvertent injury of one with an icepick. Through Extension and Distortion, the inhibition resulting from overprotectiveness limited his effectiveness in an unrelated medical procedure, and one needed in the treatment of his patients.

Distortion in one's views of his goals or motives aids in placing them in a more acceptable light. A businessman's overly zealous drive for money or power can thus come to be viewed as being for the welfare of his family, firm, associates, or so he can contribute more substantially to charity.

A housewife on a stringent diet regularly consumed her children's leftovers. Her distorted reasons which were to avoid waste, aided in the concealment of less approved needs for food, and resulting solace and comfort. Distortions are sometimes akin to Rationalization, which they can support (p. 274) in illustration of the *emotional symbiosis* concept. As in the foregoing instance, they can be close to the surface. (See also pp. 199, 226, and 421.)

J. DIVERSION ... DEFLECTION OF ATTENTION AND INTEREST

The employment of Diversion, as with most defensive endeavors, can vary from the conscious and deliberate to the automatic and unconscious. In instances of the latter, we consider it appropriate to classify Diversion as a minor dynamism or mental mechanism. In some instances, Replacement (Chapter 27), Substitution (Chapter 23), and other ego defenses operate in the service of Diversion, function with a diversionary intent, or their operations have a defensively-diversionary effect.

A 32-year-old married mother was under great tension, suffering from intense emotional conflicts and feelings of desperation. Her only respite lay in the forceful Diversion from these feelings occasioned by caring for a child. These Diversions were conscious, and in part consciously directed. She was less aware of underlying conflicts and needs.

An instance of a 38-year-old businessman was in some contrast. For him the Diversion of attention and interest into more minor areas of concern was arranged unconsciously. Thus concern over accumulating leaves, washing his car, or a disordered desk drawer served as effective Diversions from deeper and more major concerns. The latter included overdue interest on a loan, completing a bid for a contract, and his wife's mention of separation. For this businessman, the Diversion was an automatic, unwitting, and internally directed process. Consciously what should have rated as major concerns were regarded surprisingly lightly, if at all; the diversionary ones instead seemed major in the quality and amount of attention and worry devoted to them. An alternate term and concept for a major type of Diversion is the *Attention Absorption* defense, especially prominent in Obsessive Reactions (The Neuroses, pp. 311–313 and 487–489).

K.   EXTENSION ... EMOTIONAL SCOPE INCREASED

1. Definition

Through Extension, the scope of an emotional complex is unconsciously increased. Its boundaries are enlarged so as to include additional areas. The added areas are ones which are related by contiguity, continuity, or association. Extension is an intrapsychic process whose defensive intent is to bolster defenses which already have evolved.

Extension can be considered as a minor ego defense. As such it would be defined as *a mental mechanism or ego defense operating outside of and beyond conscious awareness, through which the scope or boundaries of existing defenses or those of an emotional complex or reaction are enlarged (that is, extended) to include areas which are adjacent or contiguous; physically or by emotional association.*

Extension exerts influences and effects in many emotional phenomena. It is related to Generalization (Chapter 27), from which a distinction may be difficult to make. Space allows us the mention of several major types of operation of Extension.

2. Major Types

A. PHOBIC-EXTENSION.—The phobic type of defense illustrates the operation of Extension. With the onset of a phobia, sometimes there is later an Extension of the internal threat and danger, resulting in the concomitant Extension of (conscious) phobic fear and dread so that new phobic objects are established. These can come from the locale of an Acute Anxiety Attack (AAA). As an example of a phobia evolved in the context of an AAA, the color red became a new phobic object. The girl concerned wore a red dress and jacket while suffering an AAA. For another person buses were added when an AAA came on while riding in a bus.

In various ways, established phobic defenses can be extended. Dynamically, this occurs when sufficient Displacement has not taken place and the generation of an unstable surplus of anxiety continues. Elements of new locales, as AAAs recur, become further objects for phobic avoidance. This process is labeled *Phobic-Extension*. Likewise, objects related through association can become phobic objects, when this defensively-intended pattern extends. We have observed illustrations of these principles in the appropriate chapters of *The Neuroses.*(See pp. 515–607.)

In Phobic-Extension, one may view the process as seeking to aid one in escaping all the situations in which one would suffer anxiety. In their psychic avoidance, the boundaries for phobic dread are extended.

B. SYMPTOM-EXTENSION.—In the situation where an emotional symptom fails to satisfy its defensive aim, Extension can follow. This is often a significant development, one which we term *Symptom-Extension*. It refers to the tendency for symptom defenses in the emotional illnesses to increase their boundaries, scope, numbers, and influence. Emotional pathology tends to extend with the incomplete symptom defense. This is an important concept in psychopathology.

This major type of Extension finds illustration in conjunction with most neurotic symptoms. Particularly included are instances of Symptom-Extension encountered in relation to obsessive manifestations, compulsive rituals, hygeiaphrontic concerns, conversion symptoms, soterial dependence, and character reactions (*Character Defense Extensions*). The phobic defenses as noted above are included.

Actually nearly any kind of neurotic or psychotic manifestation can be followed by Symptom-Extension. Likewise the activity, scope, and influence of a given dynamism, complex, or emotional reaction may be extended in response to continuing powerful internal needs. When sufficiently marked, these may be respectively labeled *Dynamism-Extension, Complex-Extension,* and *Reaction-Extension*.

C. TRIBAL AND CULTURAL EXTENSIONS.—Tribal and Cultural Extensions comprise major group-types of the process. Through them, for example, superstitions grow and legends are enhanced. Supernatural or religious beliefs may be fostered.

The scope of such Extensions may be familial, tribal, or national. The names assigned reflect their group nature and wide scope of influence.

D. CHARACTEROLOGIC EXTENSION. CONCEPT OF CHARACTER TRAIT BALANCE.—As noted, one can anticipate with some frequency a certain amount of Extension of character and personality traits. With these defenses this is usually a progressive phenomenon which we refer to as *Characterologic Extension*. As a process it may be incredibly slow and gradual, or on rare occasions fairly rapid. Through it a defensively-evolved trait increases its scope and significance in the personality of the person concerned.

In instances of progression arrest, what is called a *Character Trait Balance* is achieved. This is alternatively referred to as a relative *characterologic status quo* (analogous to the *neurotic status quo* concept) which prevails when a given trait subserves its intended defensive function.

Further Characterologic Extension is not a requisite emotionally. Both Trait Extension and Balance are useful conceptions in character analysis.

Extension of defensive needs can influence character development in more involved ways. Let us briefly cite two instances.

Case 213

Characterologic Extension

A middle-aged woman had a reputation for selflessness and a host of friends for whom she was constantly doing things. She was not contented or happy however. Analysis ultimately traced some of the origins of her engrossing pattern of doing for others.

These needs had developed unwittingly as an Extension of an antecedent pattern of relationship with a sister. Through doing for her, she denied otherwise intolerable hostility and competitiveness. These needs however continued and grew, as life became more complex and relationships multiplied. Extension of the pattern gradually led to the inclusion of many other persons.

Case 214

Characterologic Extension; a Student's Problems

A college junior long had difficulty in participating in class discussions. This varied in degree from reluctance to impossibility. Although many social situations were reacted to with similar difficulties, the scholastic handicap alone was major.

Analysis led to the conclusion that the dynamism of Extension had been active. During early years he was a constant target of censure, criticism, and ridicule from three older brothers. He came to fear their reactions to his ideas. Offering a comment came to be dreaded, to the extent that he often defensively retreated into silence.

His father was dead, and such protective efforts as his mother made were ineffectual. If anything, they served as an impetus. It is not surprising that the reaction to his brothers, through its unwitting and protectively-motivated Extension, gradually came to include many people and groups. Tragically, to an extent he had unwittingly come to live in a world of cruel brothers.

E. DEPENDENCY-EXTENSION.—In conclusion, mention must be made of this important type of Extension. Dependency needs, their objects, and means of gratification can undergo progressive Extension. Such an evolvement when identified is appropriately termed Dependency-Extension. This type of Extension frequently contributes to Regression (Chapter 20).

L.   EXTERNALIZATION ... OUTWARD REDIRECTION

1. Definition

Externalization is used in a psychiatric context in referring to the outward redirection of emotional drives, problems, conflicts, and emotions. The fear and dread of the phobia, for instance, is an externalized fear, having been displaced from its original, hidden, internal object.

For those who would use Externalization to describe an intrapsychic defensive process, we can define it as *a minor ego defense or mental mechanism operating outside of and beyond conscious awareness through which the emotion from an internal emotional conflict, or one of its elements, comes to be outwardly directed.*

Problems, repressed data, and emotional complexes can also be externalized. Consciously unrecognized drives may thus secure an outward direction. For the small child, Externalization can be an early and continuing type of defense against anxiety.

2. Psychodynamics

The following instance concerned a little boy.

Case 215

Refusal to Enter Family Car

The father of a 5-year-old was troubled when his son refused to enter their new car. The little boy could give no reason. Access to the bases for his reaction was gained later through therapy.

This reaction resulted as the fairly simple externalized and acted out manifestation of deeper fears of accidents, dangers of traffic and streets. These fears had resulted from protectively-intended and induced parental overinhibitions.

The outward externalized manifestation of his fears was the more specific and difficult-to-understand refusal to enter the new car. In the Externalization of this complex, the conscious connections to underlying less specific fears had been lost.

In the development of phobic reactions, Displacement and Externalization take place regularly. The above instance is essentially a phobic process, although diffuse and not well developed. It is not too untypical of some of the less complex phobic processes of childhood. Most phobias such as claustrophobia and acrophobia, examples of developed and identifiable ones, illustrate Externalization. (See footnote, p. 221 and references, pp. 223 and 404.)

Externalization is also illustrated in hygeiaphrontic (hypochondriacal) concerns and Conversion Reactions, among others. Herein elements of otherwise unconscious conflict are externally manifested through symptoms, in which awareness of a link to the underlying bases has been lost. Seemingly vital Repression is thereby facilitated.

The following abbreviated example is cited to illustrate aspects of both Externalization and Extension. They were present in an instance of phobic hygeiaphrontis with strong masochistic components.

Case 216

Phobic Hygeiaphrontis; Extension and Externalization

A young married U.S. soldier in Viet Nam had a brief leave in Japan. A sexual experience produced intolerable emotional conflict because of strict, personal ethicomoral codes, and precipitated a serious emotional illness. The personal repercussions were tragic and the Army lost a highly effective soldier.

Initially he expressed concerns over contracting gonorrhea. These had been seemingly laid to rest following medical studies ·vith negative findings and reassurance. However, the reassurance was short-lived. His original concerns returned and in full force.

They quickly extended to include added fears and dread, including as objects in turn, syphilis and genital cancer. Their rapid progression in scope and magnitude represented further Externalization of the raging fires of the underlying conflicts. The point was soon reached beyond which reassurance and logic were of no avail.

The nature of this man's fear and dread was more hygeiaphrontic than phobic, although it partook of elements of both. Consciously he could not face his deep self-condemnation. His concerns became externalized to gain a related but partly disguised expression, but in a guise which unwittingly led to anguish and suffering in the masochistic consequences. He eventually recovered, however carrying residual personality effects. His effectiveness from the service viewpoint was ended.

M. FAINTING ... UNCONSCIOUS PERCEPTIVE SURRENDER

1. Definition

Fainting is an automatic, primitive type of defensive reaction through which one shuts off perception. The temporary cessation of painful psychic stimuli is secured. Emotional feelings cannot be experienced.

We can regard Fainting as a minor mental mechanism in view of its protective intent and bases, and since it bears a relationship to certain other defensive reactions, such as selective memory loss, inattention, hearing, and vision. All of these have related goals in shutting out perception, or in the loss of earlier perceptions. Fainting might be more accurately viewed as a dissociative blocking of perception, when the latter becomes too painful to tolerate.

Fainting is *the sudden and complete loss of consciousness. Its origin is psychologic. Fainting occurs in the absence of sufficiently strong physical trauma, injury, or disease.* Fainting is a major type of *Fragmental Dissociation,* together with the amnesias, depersonalization, dreams, and somnambulism. These reactions have been considered in some detail, in turn, and elsewhere (*The Neuroses,* pp. 770 ff.). As a minor dynamism, the mention of several situations in which Fainting has been operative may be appropriate.

2. Unconscious Response to Psychic Conflict

An emotional eleventh grade girl with serious scholastic problems, fainted when a history teacher announced an unexpected test toward the end of the school term. She escaped the situation; and the test.

A mother fainted when her cherished son told of his impending departure for military service. A young lady fainted in response to conflicts generated by seeing a movie on sex hygiene.

On two occasions fainting attacks of a mother-in-law deferred a planned second honeymoon. A young woman whose husband had been overseas a year, fainted when told she was pregnant. Repeated fainting attacks of a young student-nurse in the delivery room resulted in a change of career.

Circumstances which initiate Fainting sometimes fail to do so when repeated. Thus a woman who fainted when her husband was wheeled off to the operating room did not repeat this on a subsequent occasion several months later. This was despite the fact that the second operation was for cancer. The successful outcome of the first operation apparently lessened the psychic threat of the more serious second instance to a tolerable level.

In occasional instances, the initiating circumstance for Fainting is one of relief, as when the fears of an anticipated loss or tragedy suddenly prove groundless. Fainting is encountered at times in relation to the Conversion Personality, and there are relationships to Conversion (p. 43).

Episodes of Fainting may have further significance. At times, the unconscious adoption of this type of defense is considered as prodromal or a step in the progression toward a later amnesia or fugue. The psychodynamic bases of an episode of Fainting is likely to be intriguing to the student, and of significance for the person concerned.

N. CROSS-REFERENCES TO *THE NEUROSES* *

Minor Ego Defenses
Absolution
   ultimate in A., in dynamics of suicide; p. 207.
Atonement-Penance
   a factor, in *Defiance-Submission Conflict* of Obsessive-Compulsive Reactions; pp. 321, 341.
   in comparison of self-punishing features of Dissociative vs. Conversion Reactions; p. 786.
   in expiation elements in dynamics of suicide; pp. 205, 207.
   in need for atoning punishment in *Hygeiaphrontic Reactions;* p. 482.
   in psychic pressures, in Inducing Confessions (Table 39); p. 818.
   sought, in self-punitive aspects of Conversion symptoms; p. 863.
Compartmentalization
   as aid to freedom from emotional stress, in *la belle indifférence* of the Conversion Reaction; p. 672.
   defined as a main function, in the process of Dissociation (Case 156); p. 741; also p. 927.
      of self, in Conversion Reactions; p. 682.
Compromise Formation
   as an attempted defense
      against anxiety (Table 1); p. 20.
      in mechanisms of Conversion Reactions; p. 642.
   as a resolution of emotional conflict, in somnambulism; p. 755.
   in Conversion symptoms
      cramps, tics and mannerisms as examples of; p. 671.
      in *Somatic Conversion,* in relation to incidence of, in World War II; p. 912.
   minor, in dynamics of Anxiety Neuroses; p. 117.
   supermoralism as CF, in *Obsessive Personality;* p. 255.
Condensation
   in distortion and disguise of Conversion symptoms; p. 716.
   of concepts, fused into single symbolic representation of Conversion Reaction; p. 691.

_____

* From Laughlin, H. P. *The Neuroses.* London, Butterworth & Co., Ltd., 1967.

of consciously unacceptable impulses
>   important, in the study and interpretation of dreams; p. 747.
>   in dream representations; p. 745.
>   in dynamics of the dream; p. 750; (Hadley); p. 751.
of fear
>   and self-doubt, into direct fear of social relationships; p. 542.
>   in manifest content of phobic object; p. 548.
through Convergence, of unconscious needs in Overdetermination of Conversion symptoms; p. 702.

Convergence
a major tenet, in the principle of Free Association
>   in dreams; p. 747.
>   expressed in single dream symbol; p. 751.
in the production of *hygeiaphrontic* symptoms; p. 489.
of major components, in the motivations for suicide; p. 208.
of underlying forces, in any given symptom of *Somatic Conversion;* p. 702.

Deferment
of acuity of trauma, in *Individual-Appropriateness-of-Response Principle;* p. 926.
of affect, in *Emotional-Impact-Deferment* (E.I.D.); p. 731.
>   in death of parent (Case 150); p. 732.
of physical symptoms, in effects of trauma
>   in *EID;* p. 864.
>   in *time lags;* p. 863.
>   in *Total Reaction to Crisis* (TRC); p. 865.

Devaluation
of suicidal attempt, by family members; p. 205.

Distortion
in *First Line of Psychic Defense* of Conversion Reaction; p. 691.
of antecedent relationship, in transference situation of obsessive patients; p. 365.
of good object, into food as *soteria,* in overeating; p. 631.
of reality in schizophrenia, compared to depersonalization; p. 763.
of repressed data, expressed in dreams; p. 746.
>   in dynamics of the dream; p. 750.
>   in manifest content of the dream; p. 747.
of traumatic event, in dreams (to gain mastery) in *Desensitizing Purpose of;* p. 857.

Diversion
of attention, from feared./desired interpersonal relationships (Case 104); p. 523.
of conscious awareness, away from underlying bases of phobia; p. 549.
of disowned traits, in *endogain* of *King David Reaction;* p. 76.
of emotional feelings, encouraged by parents, in *Principle of Inhibition* of obsessive persons; p. 323.

Extension
in Anxiety Reactions (Chapter 3); in *Principle of Extension,* in *Acute Anxiety Attacks* (AAA); pp. 96, 131.
in Depressive Reactions (Chapter 4)
>   of emotional restriction, in depressive *epigain;* p. 182.
>   of grief, in *Grief States;* p. 167.
>   of the *Implicit Command* of rejection, in motivations for suicide; p. 208.
in Character Reactions (Chapter 5); of desire for maturity, in *Obsessive Facade;* p. 248.
in Obsessive-Compulsive Reactions (Chapter 6); of *Compulsive Rituals* (CR), into ceremonial rites; p. 351.

in Fatigue Reactions (Chapter 7)
   of depression, served by *Emotional Fatigue* (Table 21); p. 407.
   of parental insecurities into *Fatigue Reaction* (Case 82); p. 405.
in Hygeiaphrontic Reactions (Chapter 8)
   of early intrauterine comfort, in earliest interpersonal relationships; p. 493.
   of the literal into the figurative, in *Psychic Distaste Concept;* p. 473.
in Phobic Reactions (Chapter 10)
   of phobia to flowers, to certain chemical odors (Case 119); p. 571.
   of phobic dread, to related, associated or adjacent areas; p. 578.
in Soterial Reactions (Chapter 11)
   of maternal comfort, to external object (*soteria*); p. 608.
   of value of home, into a *Soterial Refuge;* p. 630.
in Conversion Reactions (Chapter 12); symptoms disguised through E., in mechanisms of Conversion Reaction; pp. 692, 716.
in Dissociative Reactions (Chapter 13)
   of defensive pattern of avoidance, in amnesia (Case 167); p. 780.
   of functions of the dream, through somnambulism; p. 754.
   of Repression, amnesia as; p. 784.
in Neuroses-Following-Trauma (Chapter 14); of early vicissitudes, in precipitating stress (*Theory of Antecedent Conflicts*); p. 866.
in Military Reactions (Chapter 15); to country, of early parental relationships in war neuroses; p. 920.
Externalization
in dynamics of phobia
   in external *peg concept;* p. 529.
   in phobic *endogain;* p. 548.
   in phobia of cats (Case 120); p. 573.
   in phobic pattern of psychologic flight; p. 541.
   of internal fear; p. 16.
   utilized with Displacement; p. 524.
of dependency needs
   cathected through Displacement to new object; p. 578.
   in phobia of travel (Case 121); p. 576.
of source of security, to *soteria;* p. 610.
Fainting
as an *antecedent prototype* to fugue; p. 797.
as a form of Dissociation; p. 723.
   in *Fragmental* type of *Dissociation;* p. 770.
      definition and incidence of F.; p. 771.
      in *Psychic Reduplication* and *Ostrich Concepts;* pp. 772–3.
as gross perceptual surrender, in Conversion fainting; p. 687.
   as *Janet's* type of *Dissociation;* p. 734.
   in Conversion epidemics (*Emotional Contagion Concept*), in military situations; p. 915.
in response to traumatic event, as a defensive reaction; p. 852.

O.   REVIEW QUESTIONS

Sample self-check questions on Chapter 26 and the *Minor* or *Junior Ego Defenses,* for the student, psychiatric resident, and board candidate.

   1. Which major and minor dynamisms would you place with the *Guilt-Group* of ego defenses? Can you define and cite an illustration of each from clinical experience?

2. What are the "pros" and "cons" for categorizing a score or more of ego defenses as *minor, lesser,* or *junior?*

3. What are the defensively intended motivations underlying the evolvement of *Absolution, Atonement-Penance, Deferment, Extension,* and *Fainting?*

4. "A process of emotional segregation" and "unconscious mediation and arbitration" describe the operation of which dynamisms? Describe their operation.

5. Explain the following terms and concepts:
   A. *Incomplete Compartmentalization.*
   B. *Emotional Compromise.*
   C. *Condensation.*
   D. *Association Convergence.*
   E. *Emotional Postponment.*
   F. *Aggrandizing Distortion.*
   G. *Emotional Symbiosis Concept.*
   H. *Diversion.*
   I. *Characterologic Status Quo Concept.*
   J. *Fragmental Dissociation.*   .

6. What is the function of *Devaluation?*

7. Discuss the role of *Extension* in emotional illness. What is: (1) *Symptom-Extension;* (2) *Characterologic Extension;* (3) *Dynamism-Extension;* (4) *Phobic-Extension;* and (5) *Dependency-Extension?*

8. Outline the intended operation and scope of *Externalization.*

9. Comment on the concept of *Fainting* as a psychic defense. How does Fainting relate to emotional conflict?

10. What features are shared in common by the minor ego defenses?

CHAPTER 27

MINOR EGO DEFENSES II

A. FIRE DRILL . . . PREPARATION FOR CONTINGENCIES

B. GENERALIZATION . . . EMOTIONAL DIFFUSION

    1. Definition. 2. Pervasiveness Promoted. 3. Emotional Diffusion. 4. Attitudinal-Generalization. 5. Combatting Estrangement. 6. Contributions to Prejudice.

C. INTELLECTUALIZATION . . . PLACING ON AN INTELLECTUAL PLANE

    1. Characterologic Intellectualization. 2. Resistance-Intellectualization. 3. Intellectualized Retreat.

D. ISOLATION . . . AFFECT DIVORCEMENT

    1. Definition. 2. Clinical Instances.

E. OVERDETERMINISM . . . EMOTIONAL MANIFESTATIONS ENSURED

F. PERSONAL INVULNERABILITY . . . VIEWING ONESELF AS INDESTRUCTIBLE

    1. Effectiveness Enhanced. 2. Converse of Hygeiaphrontis: a. Aanalogy to Phobia and Soteria. b. Opposites Defensive.

G. REPLACEMENT . . . AN OBJECT, EMOTION, OR PERSON REPLACED

    1. Like Replaces Like. 2. Symptom-Replacement. 3. Relationship-Replacement. 4. Obsessive Replacements.

H. RETRIBUTION . . . PSYCHIC REQUITAL

I. RETROSPECTIVE DEVALUATION . . . EMOTIONAL SIGNIFICANCE DOWNGRADED

    1. Painful Made Tolerable. 2. In Many Varieties of Experience. 3. Operation Progressively Complex.

J. REVERSAL . . . EMOTIONAL TURNABOUT

    1. Characterologic Reversal. 2. Sexual Reversal. 3. Added Clinical Types.

K. SPLITTING . . . SEPARATION INTO COMPONENTS

L. UNWITTING IGNORANCE . . . DEFENSIVE RESTRICTION OF FACULTIES

M. WITHDRAWAL . . . EMOTIONAL-PSYCHIC RETREAT
    1. Defensively-Motivated Distance. 2. Associated with Regression.

N. EGO DEFENSES

O. REFERENCES (FROM *The Neuroses*)

P. REVIEW QUESTIONS

A. FIRE DRILL . . . PREPARATION FOR CONTINGENCIES

Many interesting defensive patterns are to be observed in clinical psychiatry. While not often sufficiently prominent to warrant being so labeled because of the prime position it has secured in a person's adjustment, nonetheless what we term *Fire Drill* is encountered.

In illustration of this defensively-evolved reaction pattern, an occasional person frequently, urgently, and automatically mobilizes his emotional resources as though to combat a psychic fire. He is prepared, overly so. He holds psychic-emotional fire drills over and over again. Such a fire may rarely if ever eventuate, but he is constantly prepared and ready, should there be one.

Fire Drill can be defined as *a minor ego defense or mental mechanism through which the individual concerned urgently mobilizes his emotional resources in preparing for an anticipated crisis or emergency.* The unconscious motivation is to anticipate and prepare for unwelcome contingencies. In this pattern of reaction, which seeks to avert unpleasant surprise, there are often similarities to another important ego defense, that of *Pessimism.*[1]

The following instance illustrates the defensive response pattern of Fire Drill.

Case 217

Fire Drill

A businessman was to meet with officials from the Navy Department. His long-standing pattern of response to upcoming situations was to conduct repeated Fire Drills in anticipation. This instance was typical although marked.

In the painful Fire Drills held on this occasion, anticipation and preparation for the meeting was rehearsed over and over again, during which his emotional response approached panic. This was an automatic kind of reaction which was more or less typical. As with earlier examples of the pattern, there were a number of major defensively-intended unconscious aims, among which the following were prominent:

---

[1] Pessimism can comprise an important type of what we term an *Attitudinal Symptom.*
Instances of the psychologic functioning of Pessimism in turn can be regarded as comprising the functions of a dynamism, and examples of its ego defensive operations can not be infrequently observed in the clinical and social setting.

The increased concerns were intended as a self-whip and spur to stimulate greater preparation. If sufficiently prepared, he would be able to meet any contingency; weather any crisis. Any difficulty could be handled. To this end, every question must be answerable; therefore every figure and statistic must be at his fingertips. This goal was attainable more in theory than in practice. His preparatory endeavors accordingly became increasingly frantic, the result being to defeat their intent.

Further, through anticipating (however painfully) the worst, he cannot be disappointed or hurt. Having braced himself for every conceivable problem, presumably he is fully prepared. Unpleasant surprise would be avoided. He could not be caught flat-footed. The success of the meeting, and the protection of his feelings would be assured if the anticipatory Fire Drills adequately served their intended purposes.

Through Fire Drill, one may repeatedly anticipate or seek to prepare for many given dreaded events. An interesting tie-in with the dynamism of Identification can transpire. Herein the psychologic Fire Drills are conducted by figuratively placing oneself in the shoes of another person who is suffering through a given painful, problematic, or catastrophic situation. Some people do this repeatedly in relation to potential financial problems, others with sickness and death, and so on. For instance, a woman repeatedly conducted such emotional "drills" concerning her own child and situation, after a friend's child developed a grave illness.

The self-defeat in Fire Drill can be prominent. Once adopted, this pattern can become pervasive. In accord with our *Never-Enough Principle* (also *Never-Enough Spiral,* see p. 391), one may never be able to conduct enough such drills.

As one person long habituated to this defensively-intended pattern observed sadly, "I keep going through so many alarms and crises that are unnecessary. . . . I shouldn't have to do it and seldom do they really get me ready for contingencies like I'd like. I'm always ready to fight a fire . . . (and) one almost never develops. This is good, but it's such a waste of energy. . . . I can't seem to stop it. . . ."

B.   GENERALIZATION ... EMOTIONAL DIFFUSION

1. Definition

Generalization is a minor dynamism which is closely akin to Extension, and from which a clear distinction may be difficult or impossible. Through it, an important emotional diffusion is secured which the ego intends to help protect and conserve emotional feeling, as the defensive alternative to its particularization.

Biases and prejudices may spread through their Generalization. Intolerance can be further generated. Attitudes toward individuals may become generalized so as to apply to groups. Attitudes toward authority are a frequent subject for Generalization.

By definition, Generalization is *a minor ego defense or mental mechanism through which emotional feelings and attitudes which are experienced toward a particular object or person come to be applied more generally.* Through the process of Generalization an emotional feeling may become less pronounced through its defensive diffusion. The same amount of affect when it is distributed among a number of people may seem more tolerable; less threatening. Generalization, however, can also lead to the generation of stronger affect, as more target-objects for emotional feelings are included.

2. Pervasiveness Promoted

A young researcher became angry with his project director. His resentment and anger rapidly became generalized so as to include most of his associates. He said, "Soon I was angry with everyone. . . ." He partly withdrew into silence, tending to become more distant from people in general.

A second young man was having a difficult courtship. When he thought of his more successful rival, he would experience overwhelming feelings of helplessness, powerlessness, and frustration. These feelings threatened to generalize so as to include most aspects of living. Generalization can result in attitudes increasing in scope. Their pervasiveness is promoted.

Following an involved hassle with a co-worker, a young woman found herself treating everyone particularly nicely. There were elements of Compensation (Chapter 2) in this, to make up for the disturbance and contributions of her role in it. Another underlying and deeper layer of significance was uncovered as is often to be expected, in line with the Concept of Defensive Layering. Herein, the Generalization of her anger had taken place and others were included. This transpired for various reasons; including their presence as mere bystanders; their failure to more actively support her.

The "being nice" aided in the Denial (Chapter 4) and concealment of the underlying generalized hostile feelings, which had come to include other people.

3. Emotional Diffusion

The instance to follow illustrates the defensively-motivated diffusion of emotional feelings through the process of Generalization. This emotional phenomenon is referred to as *Emotional Diffusion*. It is an interesting process which is occasionally to be observed in clinical practice.

Case 218

Emotional Diffusion

A 32-year-old newspaperman had been dominated throughout early life by an insecure mother and a rigid controlling grandmother. As an adult anything which suggested direction or domination by a woman made his "blood boil." As an example, he once developed great resentment and anxiety upon reading a magazine article on the theme of the alleged undue influence and control of American men by their women-folk.

This man worked out an understanding of the intended gain of what proved to be an unwitting employment of the dynamism of Generalization. Through its operation his feelings would be spread out so as to apply in a more diluted fashion toward womankind in general. Otherwise too threatening and seemingly intolerable because of their nature, power, and originally specific direction toward two prime but hazardous targets, they were defensively diffused. The operation was one of *Emotional Diffusion*.

Following an episode of typically strong affective response in this area, he exclaimed, "Here again is where I feel safer through Generalization!" He thus automatically avoided particularization; the threat and danger of experiencing stronger, possibly uncontrollable feelings toward the closer members of his family.

His emotions were diffused in this way toward a wider, more general target which included many people. Defensively-intended, it prevented him from coming to grips with his affect which was actually directed toward far more specific targets. Substitution was involved here also, of course, but a particular type. Together with Generalization, the operation secured a measure of the sought-after and protectively-intended Emotional Diffusion. Its price was in the lack of knowledge, inadvertent influences on his life, and the self-defeat engendered. Following its therapeutic elucidation the pattern of response was surrendered.

4. Attitudinal-Generalization

Generalization is observed to operate at times in relation to attitudes toward authority, in what we call the Anti-Authority Generalization. This reaction can become so major as to be attitudinal, and exercise a significant influence on one's character structure.

In the following instance, the not uncommon reaction of rebellion against authority became generalized. This type of reaction can operate so as to promote an individual's devotion to communism or other political ideologies and systems. There are a number of types of Attitudinal-Generalization to be observed.

Case 219

Anti-Authority Generalization

A young college graduate long resented authority. This had its origins in his parental relationships, from which it gradually spread to become general. Any rule, regulation, or authority evoked an automatic kind of perverse response. Unwittingly and routinely he would directly or more subtly block or render these impotent. This psychic pattern represented an Anti-Authority Generalization, a major type of the Attitudinal-Generalization, as evolved by an occasional individual.

Through his work in therapy he came to increasingly recognize ways in which his unconscious came to push him around. As he analyzed it, "I've generalized this attitude toward authority.... Policemen are social symbols for authority and I hate them! I know this isn't rational, but as far as I'm concerned, any cop has six strikes against him to start....

"Authority sets up a kind of a fight; a contest. If it's maintained, you are beaten; if it is broken or defeated, you win!"

Until he became able through therapy to recognize the irrational elements in his reactions, this man had a pronounced and generalized intolerance of authority, rules, or any kind of restraint.

In some contrast to possible benefits of diffusion through Generalization as illustrated, this reaction kept him in a constant state of undeclared war with society. It had become an automatic and unwitting conflict in which he had little say.

5. Combatting Estrangement

Generalization is frequently employed in a way which tends to mitigate feelings of estrangement or difference. Some people regularly generalize from their own experience or feelings with this motivation playing a significant role in the operation. They apply their *Personal Yardstick* indiscriminately (see p. 226). Generalization of their attitudes can become so widespread that everyone is viewed as possessing similar views.

Frank Harris once noted an incident in which a friend made a Personal Yardstick Generalization, based on personal experience. The friend claimed in his sister's presence to her embarrassment, that boys rather regularly learn about sex with their sisters.

6. Contributions to Prejudice

Extension and Generalization almost invariably contribute to the development of racial, religious, and social prejudices. A shopkeeper, for instance, had several experiences in which townsmen of Slavic extraction refused to pay bills. He developed bitter, resentful, antagonistic, and prejudicial attitudes toward anyone of Slavic origin.

An individual can come to make Generalizations about a person or persons which are designed to support an existing preconception. A farmer decided that a neighbor was responsible for a missing prize heifer. Until proven wrong, he found to his own satisfaction all manner of generalized supporting evidence.

For the student, dislike or bias toward an instructor, his methods, or material is often enough generalized to include the subject, or vice versa. The way a child comes to interpret and to relate to an early significant adult frequently comes to serve as a model for later relationships. His reactions can become generalized subsequently toward persons of the same sex.

A young woman for example, thus came to fear and hate men and was angered by them. Tragically, she was never able to get close enough emotionally to a man to enjoy a satisfying relationship.

C. INTELLECTUALIZATION ... PLACING ON AN INTELLECTUAL PLANE

1. Characterologic Intellectualization

In medical circles and popularly as well, Intellectualization is often used to refer to a more conscious process than the ego defense. However, Intellectualization can well operate outside of conscious awareness.

For those who would accord it recognition as a mental mechanism, its meaning is akin to that of Rationalization. In this context, its operation of course must be unwitting. The individual thus endeavors defensively to divorce the disturbing emotional significance from conflicts or complexes, through an intellectualized approach and operation. It is a process through which the emotional is placed and dealt with on an intellectual plane.

Intellectualization is a frequent defensive operation in a number of areas. It can serve as a welcome retreat for some when faced with emotionally disturbing situations or conflicts. In these, the process can be direct and superficial, or involved, concealed, and indirect.

Along the lines of the former, a certain young lady would thus react in an intellectualized fashion, whenever her sensual feelings threatened to become aroused. In such a situation she would conversationally undertake discussion of Freud's views, Kinsey's or Masters and Johnson's findings, historical research, or sociology theory.

Illustrating the more involved type of operation we occasionally observe an individual with an overall intellectualized orientation and approach to life. Affective experience comes to be generally restricted in what we refer to as *Characterologic Intellectualization.* This kind of orientation is evolved in the long-range defense against painful awareness of emotional conflicts, frustrations, and tragedies.

Intellectualization is a commonly observed character defense of the Obsessive Personality. It is frequently encountered among the defenses of the person who suffers from an Obsessive-Compulsive Reaction.

2. Resistance-Intellectualization

Both as a conscious process and as an unconscious endeavor, Intellectualization frequently plays a role in Secondary Defense and resistance in psychotherapy. This is *Resistance-Intellectualization.* Its role can be a major one. Psychiatric treatment is not an intellectual exercise, it is an emotional process. Without aspects of the latter, its potential for substantial benefits is vitiated. Still, we can understand how much easier it is for the person in therapy to keep his discussion at times and the process on a more comfortable and less personal, intellectual plane!

Indeed a certain measure of such respite is probably essential for each person so engaged. In view of its prominence and in emphasis, we term this the *Principle of Intellectualization-Respite.* There are frequent applications in intensive psychotherapy and analysis.

As a dynamism, the endeavor of Intellectualization seeks to provide and maintain psychic insulation from disturbing and painful emotional feelings. Through this mechanism, the ego endeavors to place emotionally laden matters on a more comfortable intellectual plane. As such the process is reminiscent of Rechannelization (Chapter 19). Intellectualization is also related to the dynamisms of Substitution (Chapter 23), Compensation (Chapter 2), and Rationalization (Chapter 17) among others, and seeks to reenforce Repression (Chapter 21).

3. Intellectualized Retreat

Some persons literally retire into intellectual pursuits. This is intended as a defensive avoidance of emotional conflict and a retreat from the difficulties and pain incident to interpersonal relationships. Accordingly this state of affairs is termed the *Intellectualized Retreat*. Further, an intellectual goal may be more feasible of achievement than one with a basis which is more definitely aggressive or sexual. It can provide one basis for withdrawal, p. 489.

The *Intellectualized Retreat* is defensively evolved in conjunction with certain specific SEHA (specific emotional hazards of adulthood) or otherwise intolerably frustrating life situations.

As examples, the IR can represent a withdrawal from an unsuccessful marriage, and follow the loss of a close companion or a failure to achieve a cherished goal. In these situations, this process can evolve as a defense against the onset of an emotional depression. Intellectualization is a less primitive, Higher Order dynamism.

D.   ISOLATION . . . AFFECT DIVORCEMENT

1. Definition

In the field of psychiatry the concept and term of Isolation refer to the divorce of affect from an object or idea. As a possible consequence, this may serve to allow its conscious consideration more comfortably and feasibly. In other words, the idea or impulse is isolated from its emotional context. The affect component of the EOA (emotional-object-amalgam, see Chapter 21) is detached. The bond between object and its emotional charge is broken. Concepts of Isolation have been occasionally utilized by authorities heretofore, usually in discussing the dynamics of the Obsessive-Compulsive Reactions.

For our present purposes, Isolation can be defined as *a minor ego defense or mental mechanism operating outside of and beyond conscious awareness through which an idea or object is divorced and isolated from its emotional connotation. The emotional side of the emotional-object amalgam or EOA has been detached.* Isolation is a psychic process of affect divorcement.

Isolation is the intrapsychic defense sometimes evolved when the emotional charge has been too painful or too great. Divorcing its charge leaves the object emotionally isolated, or neutral. In various instances, the clinician can observe the divorce of affect from ideation and content. Through the dynamism of Isolation the ego secures the separation of otherwise intolerably painful affect from a given event, striving need, idea, or event.

In accord with another concept of Isolation as a defense, in personal adjustment it serves a distance-promoting function. This provides a route which leads toward aloofness and personal isolation. Loneliness often follows as a consequence. Isolation is allied to the defense of Compartmentalization (p. 453).

Isolation is closely related to Dissociation, can operate in its service, and a distinction may be difficult. It may occasionally serve as a variant of Dissociation. In similar but reversed fashion, cases of fugue or multiple personality may be viewed as securing the Isolation (from the balance) of a series of painful conflicts or a section of the personality. Various major segments and their painful associated emotions are thus isolated from awareness.

2. Clinical Instances

To a clerk stealing was unacceptable. Emotional conflict and inconsistency were seemingly squashed however through Isolation of the affect from petty acts of pilfering supplies. Among others, firemen often successfully isolate fear and apprehension from their hazardous duties. A kind of emotional detachment is thereby secured which is akin to Dissociation.

The psychotherapist can hear the recital of past traumatic events from which affect has been isolated. Reported quite matter-of-factly, we recall an illustrative instance each of incest, beating, and rape. It was clear in each case that before the Isolation took place, great emotional significance had been attached.

Death wishes from the past or present toward parents, children, or spouse, may be so reported in detached fashion in therapy. The physicians' professional detachment with patients, in contacts with infectious diseases, and death, often reflect the operation of Isolation. See also *Case 103,* p. 199.

At times the forces of Repression can relax their defensive restriction because of a protective kind of Isolation. On occasion murderous impulses, for example, can safely gain awareness when the process has functioned with sufficient effectiveness. Through the operation of Isolation, they have become sufficiently stripped of emotional significance. Chances of otherwise feared overt action has become negligible.

E. OVERDETERMINISM . . . EMOTIONAL MANIFESTATIONS ENSURED

The operation of Overdeterminism is similar to that of Convergence (see p. 456). Through Overdeterminism *the bases of psychic and emotional phenomena are not merely determined as expected in accord with the doctrine of scientific determinism, but further, they are overdetermined.* Since this process takes place outside of conscious awareness and contributes to defensively-motivated emotional manifestations it probably merits consideration together with the ego defenses.

Through the operation of Overdeterminism, the occurrence of a given emotional manifestation, reaction, symptom, or dream-symbol is ensured. Earlier references more specifically in relation to dreams, were included in *The Neuroses* (see p. 744 ff.). In *Case 48* (p. 88), Overdetermination likely contributed to evolving a pattern illustrating the *Scapegoat Reaction.* The process of Condensation (p. 455) contributes almost routinely.

Overdeterminism plays an important role in every symptom and indeed in every emotional manifestation. It accounts for the multiple associations, bases, and representations which are found to underlie symptoms and symbols, as we explore these in psychotherapy and analysis. Thus, there is almost no symptom of the neuroses or psychogenic psychoses in which successful analysis does not ultimately reveal a number of important contributory facets. Through these the particular manifestation is overdetermined, and individually so.

F.   PERSONAL INVULNERABILITY ... VIEWING ONESELF AS INDESTRUCTABLE

1. Effectiveness Enhanced

Viewing oneself as indestructable or invulnerable is a commonly evolved defense and one which is often effective. Termed *Personal Invulnerability,* or abbreviated as PI, through its operation one can face danger and hazard with considerably more equanimity. It has not heretofore been sufficiently delineated as a specific defense mechanism, which it can be indeed. *Through this endeavor, one more or less and often implicitly, comes to believe in his own indestructability. A detachment is secured which makes functioning possible or contributes to more effective function.* As an ego defense it is often related to Isolation and Dissociation.

Personal Invulnerability is likely to appear with more prominence in times of stress and hazard, in wartime operations, in dangerous occupations, and in any situation involving personal danger. This particular defense has received earlier comment in the chapter entitled *Military Reactions and Prisoner Processing* in *The Neuroses* (pp. 891 ff.). At this time we shall enlarge on our conception of Personal Invulnerability. The PI operation can constitute a major pattern of psychologic defense.

2. Converse of Hygeiaphrontis

A. ANALOGY TO PHOBIA AND SOTERIA.—On careful consideration, we learn perhaps with some surprise that the broad range defense of Personal Invulnerability might be regarded as the converse of Hygeiaphrontis or Overconcern-with-Health. If correct, this would tend toward assigning it a considerably more prominent position among the psychic defenses.

It should not be surprising that such recognition has not been accorded heretofore. In seeking to understand this view of the PI defense, an analogy may be drawn to the respective positions of the phobia and soteria to each other. As with the Phobic Reaction, the Hygeiaphrontic Reaction leads to trouble, pain, difficulty, complaints, seeking for help and medical attention.

Similarly, as with the soteria, when the defense of Personal Invulnerability is effective, it ordinarily produces feelings of comfort, protection, solace, and security. Although elements in both the Soteria and PI can engender substantial self-defeat, each is far less likely, if at all, to produce pain, or to become the subject for complaint, seeking help or medical attention.

B. OPPOSITES DEFENSIVE.—What we classify and term Pessimistic Hygeiaphrontis constitutes a major psychic defense. In this endeavor, one comes to constantly anticipate, fear, dread, or conjure up various frightening possibilities as to physical illness and threats to health and well-being. When the worst is anticipated, whatever eventuates can hardly be more painful or difficult, and is likely to be less so. Further, unpleasant surprises and painful shocks are guarded against and forestalled. Pessimistic Hygeiaphrontis thus can individually comprise a significant intended-defense.

It is of interest that the converse reaction of PI is likewise an intended defense. Adoption of attitudes about death, injury, ill health, and illness for example, that "It can't happen to me" forestall fear, worry, and concern over health matters, as well as painful apprehension over possible danger, hazard, and physical threats.

Although quite opposite, each of the foregoing comprises a major psychic defensive endeavor. Each also has the built in potential for self-defeat. These potentials usually are more readily discernible in instances of Hygeiaphrontis, than they are in the operation of the converse defense of Personal Invulnerability.

G.   REPLACEMENT ... AN OBJECT, EMOTION, OR PERSON REPLACED

1. Like Replaces Like

Replacement is *an ego defense or mental mechanism operating outside of and beyond conscious awareness through which the real underlying (i.e., unconscious) object or feeling is replaced on the conscious level by another similar or related one. An emotion, attitude, object, symptom, or relationship can also be replaced by another.* This intrapsychic mechanism of defense at times is almost identical with Substitution, from which an important distinction can sometimes be made, in that like tends to replace like in Replacement, while in Substitution this is not a requisite, or is considerably less apparent.

Replacement is also related to Displacement (Chapter 5) and their usage overlaps. Thus on occasion it also may be used correctly in describing the dynamics of the phobias, where the actual internal but hidden object of fear and dread is replaced by a related external one. In Compensation (Chapter 2) one may replace a deficient skill or a presumed lack, with another similar but developed one.

The concept of psychic-emotional Replacement finds a fair diversity of applications. It particularly applies to relationships. It can enter into the Scapegoat Reaction or Spiral (See Chapters 5 and 23 on Displacement and Substitution). A boy found a Replacement target for his hostility in the form of a smaller, more manageable lad, since the real object, a large bully, was too threatening.

A shipping crate filled with excelsior replaced a radio amateur's prized equipment as the target for destructive rage, following oft-repeated failures and frustration with the complex apparatus. In *Case 3* (p. 21) we observed the characterologic replacement of timidity by aggressiveness in an instance of overcompensation. Replacement can also occur with Conversion (Chapter 3, p. 29). See also references pp. 129; 402 ff., and *Case 115*, pp. 230–1.

2. Symptom-Replacement

In the following instance the disappearance of one symptom was followed by its Replacement. The Replacement symptom was evidently required by and subserved similar unconscious needs to the earlier one. When identified this type of development is called *Symptom-Replacement.*

Likewise, a symptom banished through suggestion may be promptly replaced by another. The replacement symptom can prove to be more self-defeating and malignant. This has been observed in instances of attempted symptom removal under hypnosis.

Case 220

Symptom-Replacement

A 43-year-old lawyer was in the third year of a moderately successful analysis. Upon occasion he had worked out the basis for minor psychophysiologic ills. Modification of the symptoms usually followed.

At this juncture in therapy, to his irritation he developed an annoying and persistent dry cough. It interfered with work and sleep. For a number of cogent reasons he was convinced that the cough was of psychologic origin. Despite considerable time and effort invested over a 2-week period, however, he was unable to analyze contributing psychologic factors. He was unable to secure relief from this troublesome symptom. He became increasingly frustrated.

One night, in a fit of exasperation over his inability to lick this problem, he decided that since his cough was psychologic it was silly for it to continue. He simply would not stand for it to do so further. He willed it to vanish! With this ironclad resolve, he stopped coughing, promptly went to sleep, and slept soundly for 11 hours (the first time in several weeks). The following morning he woke up free of the cough. He was elated.

Unfortunately his elation was short-lived. Before the day was half gone he suffered a severe backache. It was painful enough to restrict his activities to at least the same extent as the cough, which it replaced. This was an instance of *Symptom-Replacement*. Some significant emotional data was subsequently uncovered and released. Although seemingly not directly related to the back pain, the latter as is sometimes to be observed, was relieved.

Symptom-Replacement as in the foregoing instance does not have to be in kind, but undoubtedly the new manifestation endeavors to serve the same unconscious needs.

Another person was subject to psychophysiologic bouts of gastric distress. This manifestation on occasion would be replaced by a need to scratch or dig at his scalp. With the onset of the latter Replacement, the earlier distress regularly vanished.

One activity can automatically replace another. In *Case 20* (p. 59), speaking was replaced as an avenue for libidinal investment. Overindulgence in eating can replace that with alcohol, and vice versa. Smoking may similarly be interchangeable with candy and sweets, the like satisfactions being in the main psychologic. A contractor rapidly gained 20 pounds on giving up smoking. A hobby, interest, or gratification can replace another.

3. Relationship-Replacement

As noted, Replacement is important in relationships. A wife can serve as an unconsciously arranged Replacement for mother, a husband for father.

What is termed *Relationship-Replacement* may be sought and adopted unwittingly for a lost parent, child, spouse, or pet. The reaction involving "rebound" from a lost love has elements of Replacement. The following examples are illustrative.

Case 221

A Relationship-Replacement

A 33-year-old housewife entered therapy for several valid reasons. One of these concerned problems arising from a close relationship with an older woman. This alliance had continued on an intense basis for two and a half years. The older friend was an art teacher to whom the patient went for lessons, and the relationship grew. Its intensity had been such as to arouse doubts, questions, criticism, and antagonism from friends and family.

Her husband denounced the "over-influence" of the friend. She was cited for neglect of her family by the mother-in-law, who wondered if she was being unfaithful. Two friends implied that the relationship was homosexual. The patient herself could not for a considerable time understand its importance. Over a period of time in therapy this gradually became clear.

This relationship eventually proved to have been an attempted *Relationship-Replacement* for a more vital but unsatisfactory one. Her mother had an unusual and successful career as an architect. In the early years of the patient's life, there was little of her attention, interest, and time available. She lacked much of the mothering for which she longed. This lack and longing had been successfully repressed. Its later expression took place in the attachment to the teacher. This was an unwitting endeavor, in which she sought Replacement for the earlier lack.

Certain corollaries were of interest in this case. These included interesting parallels with her mother. For example, her mother also had an overpowering interest (as had the teacher). This was her profession; while the patient's was a relationship. Architecture and art, however are similar. Further, the patient's children were in a similar position to her own earlier one. The great need underlying the attachment is illustrated by the teacher's relative lack of ability, gross physical appearance, and repugnant (except to the patient) personality traits.

A distinction from Substitution has been noted in that Replacement tends to be in kind, or the needs are similar. One glass is employed to replace another glass; a similar figure comes to replace a parental figure in one's automatic reactions and responses, and so on. To continue the analogy, in Substitution this takes a different turn. Thus a pitcher or a can is employed as a *substitute* for a glass; an unlike figure comes to substitute for a parent in one's automatic reaction and response, or a dream-symbol can substitute for an object which is quite different.

Case 222

A Series of Relationships Replaced the Paternal

A 32-year-old business woman gradually worked out in therapy some of the important but hitherto hidden bases for a series of destructive relationships with men. We learned that these sought to replace, and in ways more favorable to her, the earlier paternal one.

As a little girl she wanted to reverse the relationship as it existed with her domineering, authoritative, and dictatorial father. She secretly wanted to control her father—to "lead him around by the nose," as she was. This had been impossible; very much so. This, however, had not detracted from its desirability, nor from her wish. There was a greater possibility that she might achieve this reversed role in each one of the series of later Relationship-Replacements. To an extent she had.

Other unfulfilled needs could be unwittingly pursued: competitiveness, revenge, hostility, and sexuality. These had not been possible with father, or if so, they might now be pursued with more success. Still the pattern was self-defeating. First, the more "successful" it was, the poorer and more miserable the relationship, the faster it would deteriorate, and the sooner it would be terminated. Second, partly since the real object (father) was not involved the *Never-Enough Principle* became operative, so that the degree of "success" achieved was never enough, the underlying needs were never really satisfied, and repetitions were required, so long as this pattern could remain in obscurity. There had become established an instance of the *Vicious Circle of Self-Defeat,* not infrequently encountered in the relationships of the neurotic person.

The defensive gains as sought were those of securing a position of relative indifference; to not care; to control rather than be controlled; to be less vulnerable to hurt and rejection. Achieving a measure of this, as she had always wanted with her father, was more feasible with the unwittingly sought Replacements. It was, however, a tragically hopeless pattern, which required thorough elucidation for its surrender.

Anger may secure a Replacement object when sufficiently blocked. Pat didn't get along with Jack. His mother violently opposed quarrels and fights. The relationship held to a wary neutrality. Pat, however, suddenly developed an intense dislike for Jack's dog, as a related *Object-Replacement* for his master.

It was noted that we might regard the phobia as requiring an external

Replacement object for the attachment of fear, threat, and anxiety. This is also possible in the soteria. It is true with a number of other types of emotional reactions, including the obsessively recurrent thought.

4. Obsessive Replacements

For a young person, analysis revealed that frequent and painful obsessive intrusions about homosexuality replaced still less tolerable hostility. Awareness of the dangerous hostility was further blocked.

The following instance provides another, more complex illustration of *Obsessive Replacement*.

Case 223

Replacement in an Obsessive Reaction

A young school teacher developed obsessive concerns over details of grammar. These might concern a punctuation mark, part of speech, or word meaning. Her degree and depth of preoccupation with these were considerable and served as a partial measure of the significance of the underlying concerns which they sought to replace. Analysis gradually succeeded in working these out. In this instance, the similarity and relatedness of the Replacements lay in deeper layers of the dynamics but was nonetheless present.

In brief, the manifest content of the ruminations included *Obsessive Replacements* for her: (1) feared and thereby dangerous sexual thoughts, which might lead to (forbidden) intercourse or masturbation; (2) social defeats, including a lack of acceptance generally, and a recent rejection by a social-professional group; and (3) overall loneliness and unhappiness.

Little time or energy was thereby available for these three major areas of concern. This was invested instead in the obsessive Symptom-Replacements, in fighting their intrusion and attempting their control. As awareness of the nature of these needs increased, they in turn decreased.

H.   RETRIBUTION ... PSYCHIC REQUITAL

As a minor ego defense or mental mechanism, Retribution refers to *the unconscious granting or inflicting of one's deserts as his requital for good or for evil, more especially for the latter. Objects for such requital are assessed according to their merit, as this is subjectively evaluated.* Not only are other persons included for such assessment and Retribution, but the individual is himself. Retribution belongs to the Guilt-Group of Dynamisms and as such is related to the ego defenses of Atonement-Penance, Absolution, Undoing, and the other members of the group. It is one of the more developed, Higher Order dynamisms.

In Retribution, the individual concerned unwittingly takes over the function of providing awards and punishments for others or himself, as a Divine Providence might do. In effect, he becomes the jury, judge, and the one who carries out the judgment, meting this out according to the merits of the case as subjectively assessed by his own superego. Needless to say, one is more likely to note instances of self-punishment or punishment of others through Retribution, than the granting of awards or favors. However each can be observed by the perceptive clinician. (See *Criminal Reparation* in *Case 197,* p. 430.)

Retribution plays a role in most if not all instances of suicide. Its contribution can vary widely in extent and significance in each case, but is likely to be an unwitting factor of some moment. It can influence the self-punishing and masochistic aspects of a given emotional reaction or symptom-element.

Retribution and its effects or needs for it, can influence one's choice of occupation. It can affect one's success in play or work, for a day or a period of time. It can add to or detract from one's enjoyment of an occasion or achievement.

Retribution can exert subtle but significant influences in many areas of living, in which its role is likely quite unsuspected by those so influenced, or their associates.

I. RETROSPECTIVE DEVALUATION ... EMOTIONAL SIGNIFICANCE DOWNGRADED

1. Painful Made Tolerable

Retrospective Devaluation or in its alternative abbreviation RD, is an important defensive operation which can be a variant of Rationalization (Chapter 17). Through RD, *one unconsciously endeavors to downgrade the emotional significance of an event in retrospect.* The level and seriousness of painful emotions is lessened. Their impact is blunted. Retrospective Devaluation has important functions of an ego-protective and sustaining nature and is frequently employed. It is a Higher Order type of unconscious, defensively-intended operation.

Through their Retrospective Devaluation, losses, hurts, disappointments, frustrations, and failures become less significant and thereby more tolerable. An emotional feeling is downgraded in quality, meaning, pain, and personal significance. This is a kind of unconscious RD which, when operative for an earlier unobtained or unobtainable goal, is similar to the *Sour Grapes* variety of *Rationalization* (see earlier). Also see reference, p. 197.

2. In Many Varieties of Experience

Retrospective Devaluation is an ego defense in many varieties of human experience. Space allows brief mention of typical instances in which such endeavors appear. Among these, the operation of RD is frequently found in conjunction with broken relationships; unsuccessful competitions, jilting, and extramarital affairs. The variety is limited only by the possible range of human experience. Painful loss or experience is devalued in its retrospective consideration, making the wounded heart easier to heal.

The import and seriousness of quarrels may be devalued. In one such instance, prior to their RD these had precipitated a suicidal attempt.

Suicidal attempts per se are frequently downgraded in the individual's subsequent assessment of their import. Sometimes the degree of downgrading is in direct proportion to their earlier level of seriousness.

The emotional significance of a divorce and its surrounding events was emotionally downgraded by one of the parties. A serious auto accident in which several people were injured was retrospectively devalued by the driver responsible, in a self-protective endeavor. The one time semiserious plans for the murder of an associate were later so devalued by the person concerned.

3. Operation Progressively Complex

Retrospective Devaluation can operate in relation with any experience or emotion. This process, together with its consequences, is not always simple. As an ego defense, RD can operate in progressively more complex ways. The complaining spouse in a divorce who suffered greatly from loneliness and regrets, met her ex-husband 5 years later. By this time she had substantially devalued the significance of an earlier affair of his, which precipitated the legal action. This was in part a reflection of regrets and secret longing for the earlier happy days of the marriage.

A young man achieved considerable success through his excellent performance as a cheer leader. He took pride and satisfaction in his achievements. Through certain psychologic avenues he gained an increased awareness of the motivation for these achievements, which lay in Compensation (Chapter 2) for the lack of success in a more direct and active type of sports participation. He came to devalue in retrospect the cheer-leading expertise achieved. This was an unfortunate consequence, since the compensatory elements in its motivation did not make his achievements any less worthwhile.

A desperately unhappy patient once reported his plans to kill a repairman, who he believed was cheating and taking advantage of him. There was no doubt as to the urgency of his feelings and intent. Five years later, in referring back to this, he mentioned it merely as "the idle thoughts I had once about shooting Mr. Andrews." In a major RD operation he had greatly downgraded the seriousness of the incident. Its import had become minimal. That which had been so terribly disturbing and threatening to him a few years earlier no longer resulted in a ripple in his stream of life.

Finally we should note a relationship to Depersonalization (Chapter 6), in which this type of defense is employed in the service of, or in conjunction with Retrospective Devaluation. Herein, upon later recall, the distressing emotion or complex is treated as being unreal, and "not really like me."

As an instance of the foregoing, a young man was troubled by homosexual ruminations and repeated obsessive feminine Identifications, or those which he so regarded. Two round objects, for example, in fantasy, became two breasts under his shirt. Quite distressing to him each time, there were many such thoughts. Following resolution of the conflicts of this particular era, their later recall was of interest in illustrating some of the defenses which had become operative. His ruminations in retrospect now seemed unreal; "not a part of me . . . ," "not my thoughts at all." A measure of unwitting Depersonalization had been achieved, contributing to the Retrospective Devaluation of the earlier troubling and conflictual material.

Retrospective Devaluation is not far removed from a similar unconscious endeavor, that of *Retrospective Falsification*. Both processes, as related dynamisms also might be regarded as variants of Distortion (Chapter 26).

J.   REVERSAL . . . EMOTIONAL TURNABOUT

1. Characterologic Reversal

Reversal is a more general term than Inversion, from which, however, a clear distinction can be difficult. *Denoting the unconscious alteration to the opposite, Reversal can refer to position, direction, order, sequence, relation, and bearing.* Thus as dynamisms, both Inversion (Chapter 13) and Reaction Formation (Chapter 18) might be regarded as forms of Reversal, and indeed they each accomplish Reversals, albeit in a more specialized sense.

The following instance illustrates the *Characterologic Reversal*. A powerful influence was exerted through the rejection and Reversal of a distinct parental pattern.

Case 224

Characterologic Reversal: A Daughter Reverses Mother's Pattern of Handling Finances

During the course of therapy a 39-year-old married mother of four children brought out an appalling lack of information about family finances. She knew nothing about income, expenses, budget, or obligations. It was surprising that she could maintain such a state of ignorance, when she had managed her household for years. It had not occurred to her that this was worthy of interest. Her lack of interest about money matters seemed perfectly normal. It had come to be accepted by her husband, after repeated earlier efforts to interest her were futile.

As one might suspect, this woman's attitudes about fiscal affairs had important roots in the past. In distinct contrast, her mother knew everything about family finances. Her mother was responsible for running the family business as well. She successfully handled the income and outgo for both. The patient's Reversal of her mother's attitudes was an unwitting consequence of her disapproval and rejection of all this, and partly a reflection of resentment and hostility.

The mother's attachment to the business was experienced as a competitive distraction from interest in the home, children, and domestic affairs. As a consequence this had secretly become the object of the greatest resentment and criticism. The unconscious Reversal followed. Her mother's particular area of fiscal competence and interest had become the reverse of this for the daughter in a major Characterologic Reversal. Its analysis was followed by the generation of moderate interests in financial matters.

In such an instance as the above, there are likely to be other ramifications. The mother, for example, long planned for the daughter to take over the business and it was later offered free—lock, stock, and barrel. She in turn had no interest in the offer, which was accordingly refused. The business, once very successful gradually deteriorated and became worthless.

2. Sexual Reversal

Various types of Reversals occur in attitudes toward sex. When appropriate these are termed *Sexual Reversals*. The following instance is illustrative.

Case 225

Sexual Reversal: Pleasurable into Aversion

A 32-year-old married woman discussing problems in sexual adjustment mentioned an absence of breast sensation. We learned that this went farther. Caressing or fondling her breasts was repugnant. An unpleasant response to this form of sexual play had been present for years and currently was of such strength as to warrant reference as an aversion. This was more marked in relation to marital relations.

Her attitude was more striking when found to represent a Reversal of attitudes dating back to teen years. Earlier, breast stroking was stimulating and represented the most appealing part of sex play. This was a major Reversal of attitude and reaction. In its analysis three factors were prominent.

First was an experience in her later teens while visiting friends at a mountain resort. She met a young man on a blind date to whom she was greatly attracted. There was a heavy petting session in which she became very passionate after her breasts were caressed. An attempt at intercourse followed which was sufficiently successful to result in the loss of virginity. A terrible event in her view, it was accompanied by shame and self-condemnation.

Breast sensation became associated with this painful episode. The Reversal was in part self-deprivation punishment for allowing herself to be carried away and for the abortive pleasure derived. At the same time it served a defensive purpose as an added measure of self-restraint, control, and inhibition.

Overlapping with the above are the second and third factors. Pre-existing self-consciousness, doubt, and feelings of inadequacy over the size and shape of her breasts became reactivated and stronger. Finally, the Sexual Reversal was more in keeping with strongly developed and rigid moral-religious values. She thoroughly accepted the biblical injunctions as to sinfulness of pleasures of the flesh; believing it wrong to have interest, or take pleasure in such activities.

An artist was studied one time who had come to reverse his interests in portraying women as nude and sensual objects, into picturing wholesome outdoor or girl-next-door types. This had been his unwitting defensive response to personal and family pressures.

3. Added Clinical Types

Secret hostility and jealousy are sometimes concealed and their Repression ensured through their outward expression in Reversal. A college student harboring a great deal of hostile envy and jealousy toward his brother became a vigorous protagonist and campaigner when the latter ran for election as student council president.

A coed's secret attraction for a fellow student remained thoroughly masked for several years, largely through its Reversal into a contentious, critical, and argumentative attitude towards him. The endeavor was to protect herself from the dreaded possibility of rejection.

In a more generalized but similarly protective operation, a professional woman's overall attitudes toward people of coldness and distance, represented a Reversal. Thereby an unconscious defense was established against social intimacy and the vulnerable position of close relationships. Reversal associated with Denial was noted in *Cases 23* (p. 64) and *25* (p. 65).

Reversal can be a factor in homosexuality. Feelings of inadequacy may be present. Discomfort or antipathy toward women can develop via this route. A Reversal of earlier attraction into dislike and repulsion toward women can help incline the person concerned toward his own sex as a safer, more available, acceptable, and comfortable area of social contact. Also see references in relation to *Mood Inversion,* p. 201, 203, 205, *Case 126,* p. 247, 285–6, and *Case 170,* p. 339.

K. SPLITTING ... SEPARATION INTO COMPONENTS

Splitting refers to *a minor ego defense or mental mechanism through which the (emotional-object amalgam), or components of emotional complexes or states, are split off for purposes of their more ready defensive management, denial, isolation, or in order to achieve more protection.*

Splitting of mixed and undifferentiated affects experienced toward an object begins with the infant. These gradually come to be more safely separated through this process into several components, as for example, into negative and positive aspects, or love and hate.

Through Splitting, the isolation of otherwise conflicting drives and actions is secured. This serves to lessen or avoid their conflictual impingement. See *Case 62* (p. 115), for an instance of *Splitting-through-Fantasy,* which contributed to sexual gratification.

The ego utilizes Splitting in maintaining a less conflictual integration, preserving its view of itself as "good" and acceptable, in contrast to the "bad" object which is then maintained as external. This dynamism can aid in distinguishing internal from external reality.

Splitting is related to Denial (Chapter 4), in that it may set the stage for the latter ego defense so to speak, through providing a split-off segment of affect, which then can be more readily denied. Splitting allows a clearer view of an affect, appears to lessen subconscious overlapping and confusion, and leads to its more ready disposition and management. For overlapping concepts with Dissociation, see Chapter 6. Also *Case 53* (p. 100).

The concept of Splitting, as a dynamism, has not enjoyed wide adoption. Its utilization and value in the field has been accordingly limited.

L.   UNWITTING IGNORANCE ... DEFENSIVE RESTRICTION OF FACULTIES

The poor development, application, and employment of one's mental faculties is not ordinarily viewed as defensive, nor as a dynamism. Still, poor memory, slowness of understanding and thinking, and the failure to dispel one's ignorance can reflect the consequences of important defensive needs. Promoted and maintained unwittingly, these limitations can play a most major role in the performance and in the potential of an individual.

Appreciation of this concept which we term *Unwitting Ignorance,* alternatively abbreviated UI, is most valuable in understanding the psychologic contributions and emotional bases for instances of mental limitation and retardation. Its importance in the speed and ease of learning and education can hardly be overstressed. In order to help underline the significance of this premise, we might regard Unwitting Ignorance as a dynamism. UI is a conception of the underdevelopment of mental faculties and restriction of their optimal utilization as comprising an important defensively-intended unconscious endeavor of the ego. See also discussion pp. 214–217.

It is not difficult to perceive possible advantages in maintaining ignorance. As examples of UI, it is as though the person says in effect, "If I don't know, I can't be held responsible, nor can others so hold me. . . ." ". . . I can't expect this performance, knowledge, or achievement of myself —nor can anyone else expect it of me. . . ." A lack of know-how in an occupation, in tackling a given procedure, or for completing a chore may spare one being expected or asked to do it. The reader can doubtless find many examples of the utilization of UI as an intended defense.

Maintaining ignorance is related to *psychologic blocking* and to *selective inattention* (Chapter 21). It offers similarities to instances of defensive forgetting and fainting. It is reminiscent of the *Ostrich Concept* (Chapter 4), especially insofar as its built-in capacity for self-defeat is concerned.

M.   WITHDRAWAL ... EMOTIONAL-PSYCHIC RETREAT

1. Defensively-Motivated Distance

Withdrawal is *an unconsciously and protectively motivated retreat, especially from aspects of external reality. Through it, one withdraws to a greater or lesser extent from contacts, relationships, social situations, and painful conflicts.* Withdrawal is *an emotional-psychic retreat from life and living.* It generally implies retreat toward a more dependent position.

A prominent feature of Withdrawal is lessened communicativeness. Responsiveness is likely diminished, as is spontaneity. The lay description of "withdrawing (or retreating) into one's shell" often aptly expresses some of the intent and meaning of what we classify as a *Behavioral Mechanism*. Withdrawal is alternatively regarded as a defensively-motivated reaction, an emotional manifestation of illness, and as what is termed an *Attitudinal Symptom.*

What we refer to as *Psychologic Insulation,* as unwittingly sought or secured through other dynamisms such as Intellectualization, is also sought through the operation of Withdrawal. Withdrawal is a protectively intended endeavor. Similar in some of its defensively-intended aspects to the Ostrich Concept as described earlier, the self-defeat implicit in its over-development is also analogous.

Introversion is a major manifestation of Withdrawal. Herein, to a varying extent, interest tends to be protectively withdrawn from the external world. Withdrawal can become a prominent manifestation in the major emotional illnesses, as typically so in cases of Schizophrenia. Withdrawal as a vital psychologic retreat in the psychoses, can be viewed as one of nature's means of protection and defense. This is in accord with the earlier (p. 101) *Concept of Dissociated Psychotic-Survival.*

2. Associated with Regression

Withdrawal is not to be confused with Regression (Chapter 20), with which it is frequently if not regularly associated to some degree. Both are related to dependency needs. As noted earlier (p. 320 ff.), they should be distinguished.

An occasional instance is encountered in which Regression is prominent, and Withdrawal minimal. The following example is illustrative. Herein Regression was prominent in a Schizophrenic Reaction. Withdrawal was minimal, in an emotional reaction of *Regression-Sans-Withdrawal.* (See also reference, pp. 351–2.)

Case 226

Schizophrenic Regression-Sans-Withdrawal

A 24-year-old male patient had been hospitalized for 7 years with a chronic Schizophrenic Reaction. On admission, prominent features included Regression, Withdrawal, and noncommunicativeness. After 5 years the Withdrawal gradually receded and he became freely communicative.

Appearing 18 years of age, his regressive level of behavior approximated the 8- to 10-year level. This was characterized by childlike thinking, uncertainty, approval seeking, and dependency. He considered himself a little boy, and believed others did also. (Example Sentence Completion: My family thinks of me . . . "as a very nice little boy.")

He was "little boyish" in mannerisms, talking, voice, and laughter. Otherwise, he was well oriented and his affect usually appropriate. His mother was reluctantly admitted to be his ideal. He was definitely not withdrawn.

In the foregoing case the Regression was maintained, in the absence of Withdrawal. The latter manifestation had receded. Actually this young man had become quite communicative, often spontaneously so, outgoing, more extrovertive than introverted, but all of these on an 8- to 10-year-old level. He had achieved a *psychotic status quo* type of adjustment on a regressed level. This instance helps us distinguish the major defense of Regression from the frequently associated, emotionally symbiotic, protectively-intended manifestation of Withdrawal.

Withdrawal is a frequently less recognized, and less marked type of automatic defensive operation, but one which is present in many emotional reactions and can be observed in conjunction with many conditions of emotional stress. To some degree, it is likely to accompany every type of emotional illness, and indeed, approaches the universal in its operation at some point in one's individual psychology. Dependency needs are prominent in its underlying bases. See references p. 110, *Case 174,* p. 345, and 351.

N.   EGO DEFENSES

The discussion of the preceding chapters has been concerned with various unconscious endeavors; the major or senior and minor or junior ego defensive mechanisms, through which conflict resolution and freedom from anxiety are sought. The mental mechanisms have been stressed as individually important psychic-emotional processes evolved by the ego.

We recognize that it is often not possible to draw sharp lines of delineation between the various dynamisms. Their functions frequently overlap. Regardless of this, it is certainly clear that the ego defenses as named, outlined and described herein provide us with a useful series of concepts for the study of the psychodynamics of emotions and behavior.

As we conclude our formal study of the mental mechanisms, we may regard them basically as endeavors of the ego to resolve emotional conflict. They can serve a useful purpose and contribute to working out a harmonious emotional adjustment. Ego defenses need not disturb the personality or its stability. We have also observed, on the other hand, how they can progress pathologically, leading to self-defeat and interference with living.

Dynamisms are most widely operative, although in varying degree. Their influence can be minor, or extend so as to color and influence one's total character structure and life adjustment.

O.   CROSS-REFERENCES TO *THE NEUROSES* *

Minor Ego Defenses II
Fire Drill
   related to
        the *Be Prepared Defense,* of *Hygeiaphrontis;* p. 487.
        the *Pessimism Defense,* of obsessive persons; p. 252.
Generalization
   of a phobia, to include related areas in phobic *endogain;* p. 578.
        in phobia of people (Case 114); p. 557.
   of fear of parents, to social relationships as a whole; p. 33.

* From Laughlin, H. P. *The Neuroses.* London, Butterworth & Co., Ltd., 1967.

Intellectualization
    encouraged by parents, in developing the *Principle of Inhibition* (of emotions) in
        the obsessive person; p. 323.
    in Fenichel's difficulties in analysis of Obsessive Reactions; p. 365.
        in *Secondary Defense Concept;* p. 366.
    to be avoided, in the therapy of *hygeiaphrontic* persons; p. 508.
Isolation
    as an insulating effect, in *Distance-Promotion Defense* of *hygeiaphrontic* person;
        pp. 506–7.
    in distance promoting defenses, in sexual relationship of *Obsessive Personality;*
        p. 297.
    in Fenichel's difficulties in analysis of Obsessive Reactions; p. 365.
    in *First Line of Defense* of obsessive persons; pp. 343, 374.
    marked use of, by *Hygeiaphrontic Personality;* p. 283.
    of inner affect, in *Obsessive Facade* (Case 69); p. 339.
Overdeterminism
    as a factor, in the character defenses of *Conversion Personality* (Table 18); p. 260.
    in *First Line of Defense* of Conversion Reactions; p. 691.
    in selection of phobic object (Case 119); p. 572.
    in the study and interpretation of dreams and dream-symbols; pp. 747, 751.
    more evident, in the *Gradually Evolving Phobia;* p. 575.
    of phobias, makes therapeutic resolution difficult; p. 596.
    of symptoms in Conversion Reactions (Doctrine of Scientific Determinism); pp.
        701–2.
    principle of, illustrated in multiple determinants of *Hygeiaphrontis;* p. 486.
    reenforces the motivations for suicide; p. 208.
    through the Convergence of forces to produce symptom, in *Hygeiaphrontic Re-
        actions;* p. 489.
Personal Invulnerability
    Concept of, in susceptibility to stress; p. 919.
    omnipotent responsibility, converse of; pp. 922–3; (Case 186).
Replacement
    in *Nature of Anxiety* (Chapter 1)
        as indirect expression of anxiety; p. 5.
        of external authority, internally by conscience (superego); p. 35.
    in *Illusory Gains* (Chapter 2); of early deprivations, in *epigain* of Somatic Con-
        version (Case 11); p. 71.
    in *Depressive Reaction* (Chapter 4); of important parental figure, in *Depression
        of Success;* p. 187.
    in *Obsessive-Compulsive Reactions* (Chapter 6)
        as reenforcement to Repression, in onset of obsessive symptoms; p. 337.
        for self-defeating attitudes, in *Team-Work Tenet in Psychotherapy;* p. 363.
        in *First Line of Defense* of obsessive persons; p. 343.
        of unconscious impulse, by obsessive idea; pp. 317; (Brill) p. 346.
        of warm positive feelings, by hostile ones (Case 65); p. 325.
    in *Hygeiaphrontic Reactions* (Chapter 8)
        of *hygeiaphrontic* concerns, by psychologic ones (*Concept of Defensive Layer-
            ing*); (Case 93); p. 465.
        of lost dependency object, by overconcern with health (Case 102); p. 500.
        of real love and acceptance, by attention-demanding somatic preoccupation
            (Case 100); p. 486.
        of unconscious emotional feeling, by external *hygeiaphrontic* concerns; p. 484.
    in *Conversion Reactions* (Chapter 12); of character defenses under additional stress,
        by physical symptoms in *Conversion Personality;* p. 716.

in *Dissociative Reactions* (Chapter 13); of anxiety, by depersonalization (*anxiety-equivalent*); p. 759.

Retribution
  in *Nature of Anxiety* (Chapter 1); for disowned hostile feelings (Case 5); p. 15.
  in *Illusory Gains* (Chapter 2); for distorted expression of unconscious conflicts, in psychogenic symptoms; p. 59.
  in *Depressive Reactions* (Chapter 4); expressed by the act of suicide; p. 207.
  in *Obsessive-Compulsive Reactions* (Chapter 6); for acting out of hostility, in overcautious driving (Case 64); p. 318.
  in *Hygeiaphrontic Reactions* (Chapter 8)
    a factor, in the *endogain* of *hygeiaphrontic* and *Concept of Visceral Masochism* (Table 26); p. 511.
    for unconscious impulses, in *hygeiaphrontic* suffering; p. 482.
  in *Phobic Reactions* (Chapter 10)
    for unconscious guilt, in phobic *endogain;* p. 563.
    for unconscious hostility, in phobia of cats (Case 120); p. 573.
  in *Conversion Reactions* (Chapter 12)
    for symbolic expression of unconscious impulses
      in masochism of *Somatic Conversion;* p. 642.
      in *epigain* and *endogain* of *Somatic Conversion;* p. 690.
    for symbolic gratification of disowned impulse, in dynamics of Conversion symptoms; pp. 671, 716.
      in aphonia; pp. 680, 688.
      in Conversion *endogain* (Table 36); p. 691; also p. 700.
      in gait-disturbance; p. 684.
      in *rage-equivalent;* p. 683.
      in Sensory Conversion (Fenichel); p. 688.
  in *Dissociative Reactions* (Chapter 13)
    a factor, in injury resulting from somnambulism; p. 757.
    for guilty fear, in behavior of victims of fugue; p. 799.
    represented in amnesia and fugue, by "arranging apprehension"; p. 786.
  in *Neuroses-Following-Trauma* (Chapter 14)
    in subjective evaluation of trauma (*raison d'être* of Traumatic Neurosis); p. 873.
    need for R., insufficiently served by minor trauma, in Neuroses-Following-Trauma; pp. 769, 771.
  in *Military Reactions* (Chapter 15)
    sought, for hostile feelings, in *Unit-Guilt Reaction* (Case 188); p. 928.
    sought, in (masochistic) acting out behavior of serviceman; pp. 917–18.
Retrospective Devaluation
  employed to secure comfort, as a defense against danger; p. 875.
Reversal
  of appearance, in *Obsessive Facade;* pp. 240, 326, 332.
    Table 17; p. 348.
  of desire to escape, into phobia of concern for wife's emotional health (*phobic ambivalance*); (Case 118); p. 570.
  of omnipotent feelings, into omnipotent responsibility in *Unit-Guilt Reaction* (Case 186); p. 923.
  of secret wish, into phobic dread (*Phobic Dilemma*); p. 562.
  of unconscious feelings, into obsessive doubting; p. 347.
    of husband's love (Case 71); pp. 347–8.
  of unconscious material, in dream symbolism; p. 751.
  of unconscious thought, into meaningless obsession; p. 346.

Splitting
  away of emotional segment through Displacement, in the phobia; p. 556.
  degree of S., varies in Dissociation; p. 741.
  depersonalization, a consequence of S.; pp. 759, 765.
  dramatic, in the Dissociation of personality in Conversion Reactions; p. 682.
  in definition of Dissociation and its dynamics; pp. 726, 740.
  massive, in *Alternating Dissociation;* p. 732.
        in Split Personality; pp. 806–9.
  of area of consciousness, in *Janet's Dissociation;* p. 734.
  of consciousness, in dynamics of the fugue; pp. 766, 794.
  of mental activity, in dream functions; pp. 744, 754.
        in Dissociation within dream; p. 752.
  of painful affect, in *Affect Dissociation* (Table 38); p. 729.
        in *Emotional-Impact-Deferment* (EID.); (Case 150); p. 732.
        in protective purpose of Dissociation; p. 731.
  of reality, in *Bleuler's Dissociation* (schizophrenia); p. 736.
        in psychoses; p. 740.
  of recollections, in definition of amnesia; p. 733.
Unwitting Ignorance
  amnesia as; pp. 773–791.
  related to, *selective inattention* of Sensory Conversion; p. 688.
  reminiscent of, the *Ostrich Concept;* pp. 772–3.
Withdrawal
  a factor, in the *Hygeiaphrontic Vicious Circle* of the *Hygeiaphrontic Personality;*
        p. 284.
  as social isolation, in the *Antiseptic Personality;* p. 285.
  covered by agitation, in *Anxious Depression;* p. 191.
  in definition of Neurotic Depression; pp. 154–5.
  in symptomatology of Depressive Reaction (*Implicit Command of rejection*);
        p. 175.
  into dependent position, in Neuroses-Following-Trauma; pp. 885, 888.
  of interests
        in both *Hygeiaphrontic* and Depressive Reactions; p. 499.
        in *Reactive Depression* (Case 38); p. 185.
        into somatic preoccupation in *Hygeiaphrontic Reactions;* pp. 506–7.
  sought, in loss of dependent position in *Depression of Success* (Case 39); p. 187.

P. REVIEW QUESTIONS

Sample self-check questions on Chapter 27 and Part II of the *Minor*
or *Lesser Ego Defenses* for the student, psychiatric resident, and board
candidate.

  1. A. Discuss the potential for self-defeat implicit in the evolvement
        of a defensive pattern of *Fire Drill.*
     B. How can Fire Drill relate to: (1) the *Never-Enough Principle*
        and (2) the *defense of pessimism?* In what ways might tthe op-
        eration of pessimism meet the criteria for being regarded as an
        ego defense?
  2. A. The ego defense of *Generalization* is described as *emotional
        diffusion.* Explain the defensively-attempted gain.
     B. The *Anti-Authority Generalization* is a major type of *Attitu-
        dinal-Generalization.* Can you outline another type?

C. What is the potential for self-defeat inherent in the *Personal Yardstick Generalization?*

D. How can Generalization promote: (1) pervasiveness and (2) prejudice?

3. A. Define *Intellectualization.*

B. What are the effects of *Characterologic Intellectualization?*

C. The role of *Resistance-Intellectualization* can be substantial in therapy. Can you cite an instance from experience?

D. Give several bases for people evolving an *Intellectualized Retreat* or IR.

E. What is the rationale supporting the *Principle of Intellectualiza-tion-Respite* in therapy?

4. A. Define and find examples of *Isolation.* What is meant by *affect divorcement?* How does this tie in with the *Emotional-Object Amalgam* (EOA) *Concept?* Can you recall or find clinical in-stances?

B. How can *Overdeterminism* ensure the elaboration of emotional manifestations? Can you distinguish its operation from that of *Convergence?*

5. A. The *Personal Invulnerability Defense* or PI is intended by the ego to aid and preserve effectiveness in the face of danger. Explain its operation in this endeavor. Under what circum-stances is this defensive process more prominent and more fre-quently to be observed?

B. What is *Pessimistic Hygeiaphrontis?*

C. Contrast the defensively-evolved reactions of the phobia and *Hygeiaphrontis* (Overconcern-with-Health) with those of the *Soteria* and *PI.*

6. A. Define *Replacement.* Can you distinguish it from *Substitution?* How can it relate to: (1) phobias; (2) *Compensation;* (3) the *Scapegoat Reaction;* and (4) hostility?

B. Can you find illustrations of: (1) *Symptom-Replacement?* (2) *Relationship-Replacement?;* (3) *Object Replacement?* and (4) *Obsessive Replacements?*

C. Reference was made to the *Never-Enough Principle* and the *Vicious Circle of Self-Defeat.* How can illustrations of these evolve in relation to the operation of Replacement? In relation to two other dynamisms of your choice?

7. A. What is the ego defense described by the alternative term of *Psychic Requital?* How does it operate? What functions are assumed by the ego? How can it play a contributory role in the psychodynamics of suicide?

B. Explain the defensive motivations for *Retrospective Devaluation* or RD. Cite situations of conflict, stress, frustration, or loss which can lead to its protectively-intended evolvement.

C. What rationale could you advance in according *Retrospective Falsification* admission to the status of a dynamism.

D. Define and outline the emotional-psychic operation of *Splitting.* How can it relate to Denial, affect, and one's self-estimation? Can you recall the reference to *Splitting-through-Fantasy?*

8. A. Cite areas for operation of the "emotional turnabout" termed *Reversal.*

B. Can you find an instance of *Characterologic Reversal?* or *Sexual Reversal?*

9. A. The unwitting defensively-motivated restriction of one's intellectual faculties and resources comprises a widespread psychic operation termed *Unwitting Ignorance*. Can you find examples of its operation in several areas?

    B. Have you ideas as to why it has been heretofore accorded such slight recognition and appreciation?

    C. How can UI be related to *psychologic blocking, selective inattention*, and recall?

10. A. 1. Define *Withdrawal*. How does it classify as a *Behavioral Mechanism?* an *Attitudinal Symptom?* What is the latter?

    2. Can you give a clinical instance of *Psychologic Insulation?* What other dynamisms can contribute and what is the inherent self-defeat?

    3. Do you recall the *Concept of Dissociated Psychotic Survival?*

    4. Discuss the relation between *Regression* and *Withdrawal*.

    5. How would you employ the concept of the *psychotic status quo?*

    B. 1. If sharp lines of delineation are impossible, why do we study the ego defenses in more or less individual fashion?

    2. What determines which dynamisms are evolved by the ego?

PART 4
APPENDICES

GENERAL REFERENCES

1. Abraham, K. Three papers. *In* Jones, E., ed. Selected Papers in Psychoanalysis. London, Hogarth Press, 1949.
2. Adler, A. Organ Inferiority. Washington, Nervous and Mental Diseases, 1917.
3. ———— The Practice and Theory of Individual Psychology. New York, Harcourt, Brace & Co., 1924.
4. Alexander, F. Fundamentals of Psychoanalysis. New York, W. W. Norton & Co., Inc., 1948.
5. ———— and Ross, H., eds. Dynamic Psychiatry. Chicago, University of Chicago Press, 1952.
6. Allport, G. W. Personality, A Psychological Interpretation. New York, Henry Holt & Co., 1938.
7. Bernheim, H. Suggestive Therapeutics. New York, London Book Co., 1947.
8. Bowen, M. Personal communication. Chevy Chase, Maryland, 1954.
9. Breuer, J., and Freud, S. Studien uber Hysterie. Leipsig, Autick, 1895.
10. ———— Studies in Hysteria. New York, Basic Books, Inc., Publishers, 1957.
11. Brown, J. F. The Psychodynamics of Abnormal Behavior. New York, McGraw-Hill Book Company, 1940.
12. Brierley, M. Personal communication. Keswick, Cumberland, England, 1954.
13. ———— Trends in Psychoanalysis. London, Anglobooks, 1951.
14. Bychowski, G. General Aspects and Implications of Introjection. Psychoanal. Quart., 25:530.
15. Chodoff, Paul. Adjustment to Disability, J. Chronic Dis., 9:6, 1959.
16. Coleman, J. C. Abnormal Psychology and Modern Life. Chicago, Scott, Foresman & Company, 1950.
17. Dengrove, E. Behavior therapy 1 Psychoanal. Forum, 53:2, 1966.
18. Eliot, C. W. Harvard Classics V. 5:47, New York, Collier Press, 1910, pp. 721–816.
19. English, O. S., and Pearson, G. H. J. Common Neuroses of Children and Adults. New York, W. W. Norton & Co., Inc., 1937.
20. ———— The Emotional Problems of Living. New York, W. W. Norton & Co., Inc., 1945.
21. ———— and Finch, S. Introduction to Psychiatry. W. W. Norton & Co., Inc., 1954.
22. Fairbairn, W. R. D. Psychoanalytic Studies of the Personality. London, Tavistock Publications, 1952.
23. Fenichel, O. The Psychoanalytic Theory of Neurosis. New York, W. W. Norton & Co., Inc., 1945.
24. Freud, Anna. The Ego and the Mechanisms of Defense. New York, International Universities Press, Inc., 1946.
25. Freud, S. Collected Papers, London, Hogarth Press, 1950. Vol. I, first six papers.

26. —— The Interpretation of Dreams, 3rd ed. New York, The Macmillan Co., 1933.
27. —— and Miss Lucy R. *In* Breuer, J. and Freud, S. eds. Studies in Hysteria. New York, Basic Books, Inc., Publishers, 1957.
28. Gibson, Robert W., Cohen, M. B., and Cohen, R. A. The Dynamics of the Manic Depressive Personality, Amer. J. Psychiat., CXV. 12, 1959, p. 1102.
29. Glover, E. Pathological Character Formation. *In* Lorand, S., ed. Psychoanalysis Today. New York, International Universities Press, Inc., 1944.
30. Hart, B. The Psychology of Insanity. New York, The Macmillan Co., 1931.
31. Hartmann, E. von. Philosophie dis Unbewussten. Berlin, 1869.
32. Healy, W., Bronner, A. F., and Bowers, A. M. The Structure and Meaning of Psychoanalysis. New York, Alfred A. Knopf, Inc., 1936.
33. Heimann, Paula. Developments in Psycho-Analysis. London, Hogarth Press, 1952, p. 147.
34. Herbart, J. E. Psychologie als Wissenschatt. Konigsberg, 1924.
35. Hinsie, L. E., and Shatzky, J. Psychiatric Dictionary, 2nd ed. New York, Oxford University Press, Inc., 1953.
36. Holy Bible. 2 Sam.:11, 12, *passim*. Matt. 27:3–10. Acts 1:18.
37. Horney, Karen. The Neurotic Personality of Our Time, New York, W. W. Norton & Co., Inc., 1937, p. 38.
38. Hunt, Joseph McV. Personality and the Behavioral Disorders. New York, Donald, 1944.
39. Isaacs, Susan: The Nature and Function of Phantasy in Development. *In* Psycho-Analysis, p. 90.
40. James, W. The Principles of Psychology. New York, Henry Holt & Co., 1940, Vol. 1.
41. Janet, P. Le Sentiment de Depersonalization. Paris, 1908.
42. Jones, E. Papers on Psychoanalysis, 5th ed. Baltimore, The Williams & Wilkins Co., 1948.
43. Kardiner, A. *In* Lorand, S., ed. Psychoanalysis Today. New York, International Universities Press, Inc., 1944, p. 190.
44. Klein, M. Psychoanalysis of Children. London, Hogarth Press, 1949.
45. —— The Psychoanalysis of Children. London, Hogarth Press, 1954, pp. 201–205.
46. —— Contributions to Psychoanalysis. London, Hogarth Press, 1950.
47. —— The Early Development of Conscience. *In* Lorand, ed. Psychoanalysis Today. New York, International Universities Press, Inc., 1944.
48. —— Developments in Psychoanalysis. London, Hogarth Press, 1952.
49. Kuhn, Clifford C. Personal communication. 8/15/64.
50. Landis, C., and Bolles, M. M. Textbook of Abnormal Behavior. New York, The Macmillan Co., 1946.
51. Landis, C. and Bolles, M. M. Textbook of Abnormal Psychology. N.Y., The Macmillan Co., 1950.
52. Laughlin, H. P. Author's Bibliography; See following Part B, 1948–1970.
53. Le Gault, O., Denial of Operation, and Certain Other Post-lobotomy Symptoms, Psychiatry, XVII:2, 1954.
54. Lewin, Bertram D. The Psychoanalysis of Elation. New York, W. W. Norton & Co., Inc., 1950.

55. Maslow, A. H., and Mittelmann, B. Principles of Abnormal Psychology. New York, Harper & Row, Publishers, 1951.
56. Masserman, J. H. Principles of Dynamic Psychiatry. Philadelphia, W. B. Saunders Co., 1946.
57. Menninger, K. A. The Human Mind. Garden City, N.Y., Garden City Pub. Co., 1930.
58. ――― Love Against Hate. New York, Harcourt, Brace & Co., 1942.
59. ――― The Mind in the Making. New York, Alfred A. Knopf, Inc., 1930.
60. Noyes, A. P. Modern Clinical Psychiatry, 4th ed. Philadelphia, W. B. Saunders Co., 1953.
61. O'Kelly, L. I., and Muckler, F. A. Introduction to Psychopathology, 2nd ed. Englewood Cliffs, N.J., Prentice-Hall, Inc., 1955.
62. Orgel, S. Z. Psychiatry Today and Tomorrow. New York, International Universities Press, Inc., 1946.
63. Sadler, W. S. Practice of Psychiatry. St. Louis, The C. V. Mosby Co., 1953.
64. Schopenhauer, A. Die Welt als Wilk und Vorstellung, 2nd ed. Leipzig, 1844.
65. Searles, H. F. Data Concerning Certain Manifestations of Incorporation. Psychiatry, 14:397, 1951.
66. Shaffer, Laurance F., The Psychology of Adjustment, An Objective Approach to Mental Hygiene. Boston, Houghton Mifflin Company, 1956.
67. Shakespeare, W. Macbeth: Act II, Sc. 2; Act III, Sc. 2; Act V, Sc 1.
68. Slotkin, J. S. Personality Development. New York, Harper & Row Publishers, 1952.
69. Spock, B. The Pocket Book of Baby and Child Care. New York, Pocket Books, Simon & Schuster, Inc., 1946.
70. Strecker, E. A., Eoaugh, F. G., and Ewalt, J. R. Practical Clinical Psychiatry, 7th ed. 1951.
71. Symonds, P. M. The Dynamics of Human Adjustment. New York, Appleton-Century-Crofts, 1946.
72. Thorpe, L. P., and Katz, B. The Psychology of Abnormal Behavior, 1959.
73. Weinstein, E. A., and Kahn, R. Denial of Illness, Springfield, Ill., Charles C Thomas, Publisher, 1955.
74. Wells, F. L. Social Maladjustments: Adaptive Regression. *In* Murchison, Carl., ed. A Handbook of Social Psychology. Worcester, Mass., Clark University Press, 1935.
72. Young, K. Personality and Problems of Adjustment, 2nd ed. New York, Appleton-Century-Crofts, 1952.

BIBLIOGRAPHY OF AUTHOR

I. BOOKS:

1. 1948–1958. *Directory of Psychiatrists and Clinical Psychiatric Facilities in the Washington Area.* (Founder and) *Ed.* through *5 ed.*: (*1st*, 1948; *2nd*, 6/1949, pp. 46; *3rd*, 5/1951, pp. 54; *4th*, 1953–1954, pp. 70; *5th*, 1957, pp. 88, and *Suppl.* 5/58, pp. 8). Washington, D.C., The Washington Psychiatric Society.

2. 1949–1954. (with M. deG. Ruffin) *An Outline of Dynamic Psychiatry* (4 revs). Washington, D.C., The George Washington Univ. Medical School, pp. 257. (4th rev., 1954).

3. 1952–1967. *A Psychiatric Glossary, 7 eds.* (*1st*, 1952–1953, pp. 19; *2nd*, 11/1953, mimeo, pp. 25, Washington, D.C., Amer. Psychiat. Assn.; *3rd*, 1953–1954, in item #2 above, pp. 219–232; *4th*, 8/1954, *in* Simon, *et al. Univ. of Calif. Syllabus ZM*, pp. 81–107; *5th*, 1955–1956, pp. 96, Washington, D.C., Amer. Psychiat. Assn.; *6th*, in item #5 below, pp. 693–745; *7th*, in item #10 below, pp. 950–1029.)

4. 1955. *The Psychoneuroses* (Lectures). Washington, D.C., The George Washington Univ. Medical School, pp. 116.

5. 1956. *The Neuroses in Clinical Practice.* Philadelphia, and London, W.B. Saunders Co., pp. 802.

6. 1962. *Ed. Psychiatry: Vol. 6* (Part XIII, pp. 320). *In* Cantor, *Ed. Traumatic Medicine and Surgery for the Attorney, Washington, London and Toronto, Butterworths; Neuroses Following Trauma: Vol. 6*, pp. 76–126.

7. 1963. *Mental Mechanisms* (Blue Book). London, England and Washington, D.C., Butterworths, pp. 262.

8. 1967. *Le Nervosi nella Pratica Clinica.* (Trans. by Mario Farne.) G. Barbera Universitaria, Florence, Italy, C.E. Giunti, pp. 880.

9. 1967. *The Emotional Reactions to Trauma.* London, England, Butterworths, *Supplement* to *Traumatic Medicine and Surgery for the Attorney*, pp. 86.

10. 1967. *The Neuroses.* Washington, D.C., Butterworths, pp. 1076. New York, Appleton-Century-Crofts, pp. 1076.

11. 1978. *Ed. The A.C.Pn. Archives* (*4th ed.*). Frederick, The American College of Psychoanalysts, pp. 58.

12. 1970 and 1979. *The Ego and Its Defenses.* New York, Appleton-Century-Crofts (1970–77) and Jason Aronson, Inc. (1979–84), pp. 560.

13. 1979. *Ed. The A.C.Psych. Archives* (*4th ed.*). Frederick, The American College of Psychiatrists, pp. 128.

14. 1983 (est.) A *Contemporary Dictionary of Psychiatric Terms and Concepts.* In preparation. Est. pp. 960.

II. PAPERS:

15. & 16. 1949. (with Commission Members) *Occupational Insecurity Among Employees of the U.S. Government.* Personnel Administration (*Part I*, 3/1949, pp. 4–8; *Part II*, 5/1949, pp. 18–22).

17. 1949. *Constitution; The Washington Psychiatric Society.* Washington, D.C., W.P.S., pp. 10.

18. 1951. - and Hall, M., *Manual of Psychiatry for Executives; An Experiment in the Use of Group Analysis to Improve Relationships in an Organization.* Amer. J. Psychiat. 107:493–497.

19. 1952. *Constitution Drafts. Amer. Acad. Psychoanal.* Washington, D.C., pp. 12.

20. 1952. Series of Papers. *The U.S. Psychological Strategy Board.* Various titles. Mimeo., Washington, D.C., *Nos. I* through *VI.*

21. 1953. *Suicide; Impulse and Remorse.* Quart. Rev. Psychiat. Neuro., 8:19–26.

22. 1953. *Anxiety, Its Nature and Origins*: An Introductory Essay to a Series on the Psychoneuroses. Med. Ann. D.C., 22:401–412.

23. 1953. *Research in Sleep Deprivation and Exhaustion:* An Invitation to Further Observation and Study. Int. Rec. Med., 166–305–310.

24. 1953. *The Anxiety Reactions: The Acute Anxiety Attack or Panic, Anxiety and Tension States* and *Anxiety Neuroses. A.* Med. Ann. D.C., 22:463–473 (No. 9, September), *B.* Digested in G.W. Univ. Med. Ctr. Courier (1954), and *C.* Acta Neuro-Psychiatrica (1960); Istanbul, Kader Basimevi.

25. 1953. *A Psychiatric Contribution to the Development of Executives—* The Development of a Psychoanalytically Oriented Approach to Training in Human Relations. Bethesda, Md., National Institutes of Health, pp. 30.

26. 1953. *The Dissociative Reactions. Dissociation, Double Personality, Depersonalization, Amnesia, Fugue States, Somnambulism* and *Hypnosis.* Med. Ann. D.C., 22:541–552.

27. 1953. *The Conversion Reactions.* Med. Ann. D.C., 22:581–594.

28. 1953. *Depression. Some Dynamic and Clinical Features of Depressive Character Defenses, Psychoneurotic Depression, and Suicide.* Med. Ann, D.C., 22:653–672.

29. 1954. *The Psychiatric Aspects of Fatigue: Emotional Fatigue, Fatigue States and Neurasthenia.* Med. Ann. D.C., 23:22–37.

30. 1954. *King David's Anger. I.* Psychoanal. Quart., 23:87–96 (No. 1, January). *II.* J. Pastoral Care, 8:147–153 (No. 3, Fall). *III.* Digest Psychiat. Neurol., 22:207. *IV.* (1972) *Konig David's Zorn* in *Psychoanalytische Interpretation Biblischer Texte.* Yorick Spiegel Regensburg, pp. 224–32.

31. 1954. *An Approach to Executive Development. Five Years Experience with Analytically Oriented Groups of Executives.* Dis. Nerv. Syst.,

15:12–22.

32. &33. 1954. *Overconcern-with-Health. Somatic and Physiologic Preoccupation; Hypochondriasis.* Med. Ann. D.C., *Part I,* 23:96–105 (No. 2, Feb.) and *Part II,* 23:147–152 (No. 3, March).

34. 1954. *The Obsessive Personality: The Clinical and Dynamic Features of the Obsessive Character Defenses.* Med. Ann. D.C., 23:202–214.

35. 1954. *Psychosomatic Medicine.* D.C.T.B. Assn. Bull., No. 40., p. 4.

36. & 37. 1954. *The Obsessive-Compulsive Neuroses.* Med. Ann. D.C., *Part I,* 23:264–272. (No. 5, May) and *Part II,* 23:322–331 (No. 6, June).

38. 1954. *Executive Seminars in Human Relations In The United States Government.* A Group Approach to Management Improvement. Int. J. Group Psychother., 4:165–171.

39. &40. 1954. *Fear and Phobias.* Med. Ann. D.C., *Part I,* 23:379–391; and *Part II,* 23:439–448.

41. 1954. (with M. deG. Ruffin) *A Biographical Review of the History of Psychiatry. In* Simon *et al. Univ. of Calif. Syllabus ZM.* Berkeley and Los Angeles, Univ. Calif. Press, Mimeo., pp. 107–114.

42. &43. 1954. *The Neuroses Following Trauma.* Med. Ann. D.C., *Part I,* 23:492–502; and *Part II,* 23:567–580.

44. 1957. *Contributor: Medical Dictionary, Dorland. 23rd ed.* Philadelphia, and London. W.B. Saunders Co.

45. 1957. *Depression and the Suicidal Attempt. State of Mind* (Ciba) 1:No. 6 (June–July).

46. 1958. *The Role of Sleep in Emotional Health. I. State of Mind* (Ciba) 2: No. 4 (April). *II. Child-Family Digest,* 17, 24–27 (No. 4, July–August). *III. Courier of the G.W. Univ. Med. Ctr.,* pp. 20–24 (December, 1958). *IV.* Med. Bull. Mont. Co. Med. Soc., III:4, pp. 12 (April, 1959).

47. 1958. *Counseling and Psychotherapy by Non-Medical Personnel* (Editorial) Med Ann. D.C., 27:7 (1958; July), pp. 357–9. II. Med. Bull. Mont. Co. Med. Soc. II:4–5 (No. 8, August, 1958).

48. 1958. *On Problems and Needs in Mental Health Education* (Statement). Nat'l. Assembly on M.H.Ed., Ithaca, Cornell Univ., pp. 2.

49. 1958. *Psychiatry in Asia and the Middle East.* Amer. J. Psychiat., 115–193–202.

50. 1958. *A Historical Note on the Amer. Acad. of Psychoanal.* (Appendix) Private. Chevy Chase. (Rev. 1967). pp. 56.

51. 1959. *The Mental Mechanisms.* Med. Bull. Mont. Co. Med. Soc., III:12 (No. 9, Stptember).

52. 1959. The Mental Mechanisms. *Compensation.* Med. Bull. Mont. Co. Med. Soc., III:12–26 (No. 10, October).

53. 1959. The Mental Mechanisms. *Inversion.* Med. Bull. Mont. Co. Med. Soc., III:17–34 (No. 11, November).

54. 1959. The Mental Mechanisms. *Undoing.* Med. Bull. Mont. Co. Med. Soc., III:21–39 (No. 12, December).

55. 1959. *India, Land of Medical Challenge.* Med. Bull. Mont. Co. Med.

Soc., 3:17–20 (No. 2, February).

56. 1959. *An Outline of Basic Psychiatry for Board Examiners.* 3rd Revision. Private. Chevy Chase. Mimeo. pp. 31.

57. 1960. The Mental Mechanisms. *Sublimation.* Med. Bull. Mont. Co. Med. Soc., 4:15–39 (No. 1, January).

58. 1960. *European Psychiatry: England, Denmark, Italy, Greece, Spain, and Turkey.* Amer. J. Psychiat., 116:769–776.

59. 1960. (Rev.); Kubie, "*Neurotic Distortion of the Creative Process.*" Ment. Hyg., 44:2, p. 301.

60. 1960. *Denial: A Primitive Dynamism of Disavowal and Disclaiming.* Med. Bull. Mont. Co. Med. Soc., IV:3; pp. 19–24.

61. 1960. *Denial in Alcoholism, Depression and Psychic Pain,* Ed. Bull. Mont. Co. Med. Soc., IV:4; pp. 20–24.

62. 1960. *Denial in One's Self Picture,* and *A Cultural Dilemma.* Med. Bull. Mont. Co. Med. Soc., IV:5; pp. 19–23.

63. 1960. *The Operation of Denial in Pysical Illness,* and *The Denial of Death.* Med. Bull. Mont. Co. Med. Soc., IV:6; pp. 23–28.

64. 1960. *Denial* (conclusion of series) Med. Bull. Mont. Co. Med. Soc., IV:9; pp. 18–24.

65. 1961. (Rev.); Loftus, "*Meaning and Methods of Diagnosis in Psychiatry,*" Cur. Med. Dig., 28:1; pp. 30 (Jan.).

66. 1961–62. *Constitution. The Eastern Psychoanalytic Assn.* For references and history see 1970 *EPA Archives, 3rd ed.* The Eastern Psychoanalytic Association, Washington, D.C., pp. 58.

67. 1962 (Rev.); Spotnitz, H. "*The Couch and the Circle:* A Study of Group Psychotherapy." Mental Hygiene, 46:1, January, 1962, p. 140.

68. 1962. Co-editor. *Handbook.* Washington, D.C. The Washington Med. Surg. Soc., pp. 28.

69. 1962. *The Depressions;-Clinical Understanding and Management.* (for the N.P.E.F.) New York, T. Bates & Co. Manual.

70. 1961. (Rev.); Rigney and Smith, "*The Real Bohemia,*" Cur. Med. Dig., pp. 38.

71. 1961. *Neurosis, Conditioning, and the Rule of Impression Priority.* J. Med. S.N.J. 58:454–61.

72. 1961. *The Current Status of Psychiatry in the United Kingdom.* Amer. J. Psychiat. 118:308–310.

73. 1961. (Rev.); Barton *et al.* "*Impressions of European Psychiatry,*" Nervous and Mental Dis., 133:6.

74. 1962. *Neuroses and Trauma. In* Belli, *Ed. Trial and Tort Trends:* Belli Seminar. New York, Bobbs Merrill.

75. 1962. *Neuroses Follwing Trauma. In* Cantor, *Ed. Traumatic Medicine and Surgery for the Attorney.* Washington, D.C., Butterworths.

76. 1962–63. *Constitution. The Amer. Coll. Psychiatrists.* Included with Historical Notes: In 1969, *Handbook, 2nd ed.* The American College of Psychiatrists. Silver Spring, Md., and Chicago, Ill., pp. 56.

77. 1963. (Rev.); Jacobs, "*Western Psychotherapy and Hindu Sadhena*," Amer. J. Psychiat., 119:7; pp. 698.
78. 1963. *The Med Re Fund: A Retirement Program for Maryland Physicians.* Maryland State Med. J., 12:340–5.
79. 1963. Co-editor, *Handbook. Med. Arts Soc. of Greater Wash.* (*2nd ed.*); pp. 28, Washington, D.C.
80. 1964. (Rev.); Sher, *Ed.* "*Theories of the Mind*," Mental Hygiene, pp. 330.
81. 1964. Historical Sketch; "*The Washington Med. and Surg. Soc.*," Med. Ann. of D.C., 33:633 (December).
82. 1966. *The Age of Anxiety.* Panhellenic Union for Mental Hygiene, Parnossos Aud., Athens, Greece, pp. 10.
83. 1966. *Conversion Reactions. Ann. Report: Dept. of Psychiatry,* Athens Univ. Sch. Med., Athens, Greece, pp. 12–17.
84. 1967. Ed., "*Handbook*," *3rd. ed. The Medical Arts Society* of Greater Washington, pp. 28.
85. 1967. *Unraveling The Phobic Defense. I.* Amer. J. Psychiat., 123:1081–87. Excerpts: *II.* Dig. Psychiat. Neur., 35:100(3–67); *III.* Psychiat. Dig., April, 1968.
86. 1968. *Contributor; Dorland's Pocket Medical Dictionary. 21st ed.* Philadelphia, W.B. Saunders Co.
87. 1968. *Membership Trends in the American College of Psychiatrists.* (Sixth Ann. Mtg., Boston, 5.11.68) Regents Minutes; A.C.P.N.L.; A.C. Psych. Archives. Chevy Chase. The American College of Psychiatrists.
88. 1968–69. *Constitution* (final revision). *The American College of Psychoanalysts.* Washington, D.C., Am. Col. Psa., pp. 8.
89. 1969. *The E.R. Defense. Eleemosynary Rationalization. N.L. #3,* February, 1969, New York, American Society of Psychoanalytic Physicians, pp. 2.
90. 1969. (Rev.) Lewis, N.D.C., and Strahl, M.D., *Eds. The Complete Psychiatrist.* Psychiat. Dig., April, 1969, pp. 61.
91. 1969. *The Royal Medico-Psychological Association of Great Britain* and *Psychiatry in the United Kingdom*—A Report to the Board of Trustees of the American Psychiatric Assoc. (photographs). October 25, 1969, pp. 16. Also *British Officialdom: Psychiatric News* (A.P.A., Washington, D.C.), February, 1970, p. 30.
92. 1970. *An Analysis of the Registrants of The American College of Psychiatrists Graduate Education Program* (Third Annual Seminar, Atlanta, February, 1970). Summary, A.C.P. 2.14.70; *Board of Regents Minutes* and *The A.C.P. Archives.*
93. 1970. *The Surburban Maryland Chapter of Psychiatrists or S.M.C.P.: The Founding of a Psychiatric Organization.* Bethesda, Maryland. XV:4, pp. 47–51 (photographs), April.
94. 1970. *Psychiatry in the United Kingdom.* Amer. J. Psychiat. 126:12 (June); pp. 1790–94.
95. 1970. *The Academy Movement: Historical Notes on the Origins and*

Founding of The American Academy of Psychoanalysis, Bethesda, Md., (October), pp. 54 (appendices).

96. 1971. (Rev.) Assn. for Research in Nervous & Mental Disorders, *"Perception and Its Disorders."* Hamburg, D.A., Pribam, K.H. & Stunkard, J.J., *Eds.,* Psychiatry Digest. 32:9, September, 1971, pp. 64–5.

97. 1971. *Membership Ceiling: Pros and Cons.* (Ninth Annual Meeting, Washington, D.C., 5.1.71). A.C. Psych. Minutes and N.L. Bethesda. The American College of Psychiatrists.

98. 1971. (Rev.) Ralph W. Heine, Psychiatry Digest. *"Psychotherapy,"* 32:10, October, 1971. pp. 65–6.

99. 1971. *The Royal College of Psychiatrists: A Salute.* Amer. J. of Psychiatry, 128:761–3, 1971 (December).

100. 1972. The Psychoneuroses. *In "In Current Therapy (1972)."* Conn, Howard F., *Ed.* Philadelphia, W.B. Saunders, 1972. pp. 804–10.

101. 1972. *On the Art of Psychotherapy: Useful Conceptions for the Clinician.* In Commemorative Vol. to John M. Dorsey. Krystal, Henry, *Ed.*

102. 1972. *Konig David's Zorn. Psychoanalytische Interpretaticonen Biblischer Texte.* Yorick Spiegel, Chr. Kaiser, Munchen, pp. 224–32.

103. 1972. *The A.C.Pn. Newsletter, Vol. III* No. 2, June 1972, *Editor.* The American College of Psychoanalysts, Washington, D.C.

104. 1972. *The Emotional-Traumatic Reactions. In* Gray's *Attorney's Textbook of Medicine,* Chapter 104, L. Caswell, *Ed.* New York, Matthew Bender.

105. 1973. *The A.C.Pn. Newsletter, Vol. IV* No. 1, March 1973, *Editor.* The American College of Psychoanalysts, Washington, D.C.

106. 1973. (Rev.) Maurice Levine, *"Psychiatry and Ethics,"* Amer. J. of Psychia., 130:10 (October, 1973), pp. 1164.

107. 1974. *The A.C.Pn. Newsletter, Vol. V* No. 1, Mid-Year Issue, January, 1974. The American College of Psychoanalysts, Washington, D.C.

108. 1974. *The A.C.Pn. Newsletter, Vol. V* No. 2, February Issue, 1974. The American College of Psychoanalysts, Washington, D.C.

109. 1974. *The A.C.Pn. Newsletter, Vol. V* No. 3, Annual Meeting Issue, April, 1974. The American College of Psychoanalysts, Washington, D.C.

110. 1975. *The Psychoneuroses.* In *The Encyclopaedia Brittanica, 15th Ed.* Vol. 15, pp. 166–173, Chicago.

111. 1975. *The A.C.Pn. Newsletter, Vol. VI* Nos. 1, 2 9 3 (January, March, June, 1975) The American College of Psychoanalysts, Washington, D.C.

112. 1975. *Five Major Challenges in Medicine and Psychiatry* (s. Spafford Ackerly Distinguished Professor Lecture, 4.18.75). University of Louisville, Louisville, Kentucky. pp. 22.

113. 1975. *The A.C.Pn. Archives. 1st Ed.,* American College of Psychoana-

lysts; April, Washington, D.C.

115. 1976. *Critique and Analysis, with Six Related Concepts* (Hon. discussant for *The 36th Annual Meeting of The South, Psych. Assn. Program;* Oct. 4–7, 1975) Ch. XIII, pp. 185–211. Endo Labs, Garden City, New York.

116. 1976. *Ed., The A.C.Pn. Archives, 2nd ed.* The American College of Psychoanalysts, Bethesda, Maryland. pp. 44.

117. 1977. (with C.C. Kuhn) *Hysterical Neuroses.* In Conn, H.F., *Ed., Current Diagnosis, 5th ed.,* Philadelphia & London, W.B. Saunders.

118. 1977. *Neuroses: An Overview. Int'l. Encyclopedia of Psy., Psych., Psa. and Neur.,* Wolman, B., *Ed.;* New York, Van Nostrand, Reinhold Co. *Vol. VIII,* pp. 58–64.

119. 1977. *The A.C.Pn. Newsletter. Vol. VIII, Ed.* Winter (January), Annual Meeting (March) and Summer (June) Issues. Frederick, Maryland.

120. 1977. *Ed., The A.C.Pn. Archives, 3rd ed.* The American College of Psychoanalysts, Frederick, Maryland. pp. 50.

121. 1978. *Ed., The A.C.Pn. Newsletter, Vol. XI* Nos. 1, 2 & 3 (January, March, June, 1978) The American College of Psychoanalysts, Wash., D.C.

TABLES

1. The Ego Defenses or Mental Mechanisms   7

2. Major Types of Behavioral-Conversion   38

3. Dissociative Reactions; Comparative Data   98–101

4. Features of the Unhealthful Fantasy   113

5. Idealization: the Internal Psychologic Intended-Functions of a
   Major Dynamism   125

6. Bases for Application of the Personal Yardstick   153–154

7. Introjection: Major Distinguishing Features of the Ego Defense   182

8. The Ego Defenses. Aims, Functions and Consequences   214

9. The Eight Major Stages of Man: His Development and
   Adulthood   328

10. Modern Aims of Therapy   377

CASES

1. Behavioral Compensation for Small Stature 19
2. Compensatory Character Development by a Military Officer ... 20
3. Aggressive Overcompensation for Timidity 21
4. Compensation for Disapproved Behavior 21
5. Don Juanism: Compensatory Success as a Lover 22
6. Compensation in Powerful Motors; Avocational Compensation ... 22
7. The Compensatory Use of Confabulation 24
8. Demosthenes Compensated for a Speech Impediment 24
9. Theodore Roosevelt's Successful Compensation 25
10. Paraplegia; a Major Somatic Conversion in Childhood 34
11. Headaches During Therapy 35
12. Primary and Secondary Gain 36
13. Pseudoconvulsions 39
14. An Acute Behavioral Conversion 40
15. An Acute Pseudoepileptic Behavioral Conversion;
    Followed by a Major Somatic Conversion Reaction 40
16. Behavioral Conversion in Overall Activity 41
17. Sensory Loss and Partial Paralysis 45
18. Identification and Conversion; Symptom Compathy 46
19. Somatic (Motor) Conversion Follows the Threat of Injury
    and Wife's Illness 48
20. Denial-for-Confidence 59
21. The Antitherapeutic Denial 62
22. Denial of Painful Past Events 63
23. Denial of Sterility and Desire for Children 64
24. Denial in One's Self-Picture 64
25. Denial in the Image of Another 65
26. The Denial of Impropriety 65
27. Denial-in-Aging 66
28. The Denial of Problems, Including Overdrinking, as an
    Insoluble Block to Therapy 67
29. Denial and Substitution in Chronic Alcoholism 67
30. Denial in Alcoholism of Husband and Son 68
31. Denial of Pregnancy 70
32. A Psychotic Episode with Denial of Painful Reality 70
33. Denial of Loss 71
34. Denial in the Death of a Parent 71
35. Sexual Denial 72
36. Denial of Cancer 73
37. Illness Denial in Terminal Illness 74
38. Illness Denial and Its Mortal Prognosis 75
39. An Illusion-of-Continued-Living 76
40. Denial-of-Death 77
41. Denial-of-Death and Neglect of Cancer 78
42. Denial in the Death of a Child 78
43. Denial-of-Death in the Grief-Stricken 78

510

44. Denial of the Destructive Consequences of Extramarital
    Sexual Experience ... 79
45. Denial Supports Idealization ... 80
46. Jealousy is Denied ... 81
47. Personal-Feeling Displacement and Deferment ... 87
48. The Scapegoat Reaction ... 88
49. Sexual-Object Displacement ... 89
50. Substitution and Displacement ... 90
51. The Displaced Complex ... 90
52. The Convenient Target ... 91
53. Dissociation of Feelings in Therapy ... 100
54. Dissociation of Responsibility ... 100
55. Dissociation of Affect in a Schizophrenic Patient ... 102
56. Dissociation: "Someone Else's Children" ... 103
57. Dissociation: Depersonalization as a Defense Against
    Impact of Painful News ... 104
58. Depersonalization Dissociates Affect ... 104
59. Authorship and Cabdriving ... 105
60. Fantasy in Adolescence ... 111
61. Fantasy-Pattern in Dependency and Hostility ... 114
62. Fantasy Allows Sexual Gratification ... 115
63. The Fantasy Lesson-Function ... 116
64. Fantasy Useful in Psychotherapy ... 118
65. Fantasy, a Resistance in Psychotherapy ... 118
66. Retreat into Fantasy ... 119
67. A Literary Idealization; Hamlet's Father ... 124
68. The Impossible Standard ... 126
69. Reluctant Surrender of an Idealized Image ... 127
70. Marital Idealization ... 129
71. Substitute-Idealization ... 129
72. Group Compathy; Emotional Feelings of Sadness Shared ... 140
73. Predecessor Identification; Social Purpose Subserved ... 141
74. Mannerism Identification ... 142
75. Identification in Personality Development ... 143
76. Basking in Reflected Glory, in Dreams ... 144
77. Identification with a Movie Star ... 146
78. Criminal Identification and the Spurious Confession ... 147
79. Identifying with the Wrongdoer ... 147
80. Military-Unit Identification Begins Before the Fact ... 150
81. Substitute Gratification Through Vicarious Identification ... 152
82. A Standard is Held Up ... 155
83. Parental Identification Succeeded by Interpersonal Identification ... 155
84. Symptom Identification in Hygeiaphrontis
    (Overconcern-with-Health) ... 156
85. Identification in Psychotic Reactions ... 157
86. Underdog Identification ... 157
87. Sibling Rivalry and Incorporation ... 167
88. Incorporation Expressed by a 4-Year-Old ... 167
89. Parental Incorporation, Mother's Patterns of Reaction ... 169
90. Marital Engulfment ... 171
91. Views About Money Internalized ... 175
92. Postural Attitudes Taken Over ... 176
93. Internalization of Prejudicial Attitudes ... 178

94. Internalization   178
95. Introjection in Onset of Depressive Reaction   184
96. Introjection and Abdominal Pain   185
97. Psychotic Introjection   186
98. Adolescent Fears of Kissing   187
99. Idealization, Identification, and Partial Introjection   188
100. Attraction-Inversion into Homosexuality   196
101. The White-Washing Operation; Retrospective Denial and
     Memory-Inversion   197
102. Standards-Inversion in Sexual Behavior   197
103. Inversion of Therapist's Role; A Distortion in Therapy   199
104. The Ego-Enhancing Inversion   200
105. A Major Mood-Inversion   202
106. Projection of Affect: "I dislike them" Becomes
     "They dislike me"   222
107. Psychologic Blindness to Child's Behavior   224
108. Profanity: External versus Personal   225
109. Debt Payment   225
110. The Mirror-Defense   227
111. Projection of Responsibility   227
112. Self-Critical Feelings Projected; PVC Evolved   228
113. Intended Defense Against Recognizing Resentment;
     Gives It Away   229
114. A Minor Projection   230
115. Diffuse Paranoid Projection   230
116. Negative Projection   231
117. Projected Anger   232
118. Shakespeare Uses the Nathan Device   240
119. King David's Anger in Hamlet's Reaction   240
120. The Negative King David Reaction: Unrecognized
     Resemblance Stimulates Identification and Projection,
     with Production of "Royal Anger"   241
121. King David's Anger   242
122. King David's Anger in a Combat Hero   242
123. The Negative King David Reaction: A Physician feels
     Disgust toward Certain "Strangers"   243
124. Violence Fostered   244
125. A Positive King David Reaction   246
126. Positive King David Reaction Self-Defeating   247
127. Inversion of Exhibitionism Sets Stage   247
128. Protection of Neurotic Gains Through Rationalization
     and Denial   252
129. Rationalization Justifies Behavior of Posthypnotic Suggestion   253
130. Rationalization for Failure in Weight Reduction   255
131. Loss of Affection Rationalized   257
132. Ego-Maintaining and Complex-Supportive Rationalization   258
133. Devaluing the Unobtainable   259
134. Sour Grapes   260
135. Motive-Rationalization   260
136. Devaluation of the Material   261
137. Rationalization in Self-Deception   262
138. Rationalization and Denial   262
139. Rationalizations for Robin Hood   263

140. Rationalization for School Failure 263
141. Conscious Rationalization to Evade Responsibility 264
142. Eleemosynary Rationalization 266
143. Social Rationalization 268
144. Rationalization in Alcoholic Habituation 271
145. Long-Term Effects of Rationalization 273
146. Reaction Formations in Personality Development 282
147. Reaction Formation of Socially Beneficial Attitudes 283
148. Reaction Formation in the Development of Attitude-Symptoms of Subservience and Low Self-Esteem 284
149. The Son of a Politically Liberal Father Becomes Ultraconservative 286
150. Reenforcement of Sexual Taboos 287
151. Overcompensation for Timidity 290
152. Reaction Formation in the Detection and Arrest of Homosexually Oriented Persons 291
153. Characterologic Development a Consequence of Reaction Formation 292
154. Personal-Tragedy Rechannelization (PTR) 302
155. Excessive Rechannelization of Sexual Drives 304
156. Rechannelization: Homosexual Drives Diverted 306
157. Maternal Instincts Rechanneled 308
158. Avocation of Gardening a Major Sublimation 309
159. Improvement-Sublimation in Psychosis 311
160. The Improvement Sublimation; Maturation During Psychotherapy 312
161. Regression in Attitude and Behavior 323
162. Regressive Manifestations Follow a New Baby 325
163. Disciplinary-Regression 326
164. Regressive Behavior Signals Difficulty 326
165. Recurrence of Conflict-Indicators 327
166. Illness-Regression 330
167. Regressive Recapitulation of Symptoms of Childhood Illness. The PRR 332
168. Maturation-Fixation 335
169. Fixation at College Level 336
170. The Role of Regression in a Phobic Reaction 339
171. Regression and Conflicts over Dependency 340
172. Somatic Preoccupation (Hygeiaphrontis) 343
173. Major Regression in Schizophrenia 344
174. A Psychotic Regression Increases 345
175. A Regressive Episode in Therapy 346
176. Regression Treatment in a Psychotic Reaction 348
177. Regressive Therapy in Alcoholism 350
178. A Drowning Repressed 365
179. Repression of Anniversary Dates; Minor Repression 366
180. Forgetting One's Own Name 370
181. Repression Falters; the Acute-Anxiety-Attack 376
182. Neurotically Exaggerated Guilt Feelings Motivate Restitutive-Behavior 391
183. Social Restitution; Church Contributions to Assuage Guilt 394
184. Restitution Through Gifts 395
185. Restitution-in-Abeyance 397
186. Restitution-by-Will; The Nobel Awards 397

187. Substitution for Disturbing Interests   403
188. Substitution Contributes to Rechannelization   405
189. Substitution of New Concerns for Obsessive Ruminations   406
190. The Counterirritant Substitution   407
191. Substitution of House Tidying   407
192. Substitution Allows Resentment Expression   408
193. Substitution of Family Doctor for Therapist as Resentment
       Target   409
194. Dream-Symbols   417
195. Attitudes Toward Therapy Symbolized   418
196. The Guidepost Dream   419
197. Volunteers for Medical Research   430
198. Undoing Through Indulgence and Sex   432
199. Undoing Follows Abortion   433
200. The Undoing Phrase   434
201. Omission Undone in an Undoing Dream   435
202. The Dream-of-Erasure; a Conviction Reversed   435
203. The Dream-of-Erasure; a Sequence in Living Undone   436
204. Repetitive Telephoning   437
205. Social Undoing   438
206. Undoing Blasphemous Thoughts   439
207. Sexual Relations Undo   441
208. Fantasy-Undoing   442
209. Hallucinations in Absolution   449
210. Hair Loss in Atonement-Penance   452
211. Deferment of Emotional Impact   457
212. The Aggrandizing Distortion   458
213. Characterologic Extension   462
214. Characterologic Extension; a Student's Problems   462
215. Refusal to Enter Family Car   463
216. Phobic Hygeiaphrontis; Extension and Externalization   463
217. Fire Drill   470
218. Emotional Diffusion   472
219. Anti-Authority Generalization   473
220. Symptom-Replacement   480
221. A Relationship-Replacement   481
222. A Series of Relationships Replaced the Paternal   482
223. Replacement in an Obsessive Reaction   483
224. Characterologic Reversal: A Daughter Reverses Mother's
       Pattern of Handling Finances   486
225. Sexual Reversal: Pleasurable into Aversion   487
226. Schizophrenic Regression-Sans-Withdrawal   490

INDEX

The more substantive conceptions and reformulations of the author are in *italics* to help facilitate their identification.

AAA. See *Acute Anxiety Attack.*
Abeyance, Restitution-in-, 397, 399
Abortion, 433
Absolution, 448–50
  Certificate of, 450
  definition, 448
  Guilt Group Dynamisms and, 449
  Higher Order Dynamism, 448
  psychic remission as alternative and descriptive terms, 448
  psychotic reactions and, 448
    hallucinations providing *Absolution,* 449
Absorbing interests, 114, 403
  Fantasy and, 114
  Substitution for emotional conflicts, 403
Absorbing knowledge, *Incorporative Learning* as, 172
Acceptance, 134, 143, 146, 151
  Group Identification and, 151
  love-object Identification and, 134
  mother longed for, 143
Accidents, *Atonement-Penance* and, 451
Acquaintances, *Personal Yardstick* (PY) and, 153
Acquittal, 448
Acting, *Rechannelization* of exhibitionism and, 306
Acting Out, 38
  Major Types of Behavioral Conversion, neurotic and psychotic, 38
Activity, 41–42
  Behavioral Conversion into, 25
  Dissociation of, 96
  pursuit of concurrent as, 106
  Substitution, expression of aggression and, 402–3
Actor Identification, 136, 158
Acute Anxiety Attack (AAA), 375, 376, 380, 460
  derepression and, 375
  Extension of phobic fear, 460
  Repression falters, 376, 380
Acute Conversion Behavior, 37 ff.
Addiction, drug
  Denial operative in, 62
  promotion of fantasies, 119

Adjustment, 415, 441
  contributions by ego defenses, 9, 211
  to life, dynamisms and, 213
  Mixed Regression levels and, 320, 324, 329, 352
  sexual, 72
  superior, in elation, 202
Adler, Alfred, Compensation and, 25
Admiration, *Characterologic Identification* and, 142
Admired people, Identification with, 149
Adolescence, 111, 329
  Fantasy-Life, 111
  Major Stages of Man, 329
Advertising, *Primary and Secondary Appeal* in, 149, 159
Affair
  best friend's wife and, 200
  desire for father and, 118
  Rationalization and, 252
Affect, 94 ff., 136 ff., 476 ff.
  appropriate, absence of, in psychosis, 103
  Association, 371
  detachment of, 94
  Dissociation, 94–96
    alternate term for, 97, 476
    Depersonalization and, 104
    schizophrenia and, 102
    therapy, 100
  Distortion and, 458
  divorcement, *Isolation* defense and, 476 ff.
  Emotional-Object Amalgam (EOA) and, 412
  equivalent, 47 ff.
    heartache as, 47
    la grippe as, 47
    translation of figurative into literal, 47
    type of symptom, 48
  Inversion, 201
  isolation, 47
  Projection and, 221, 222
  repugnant, assigned to unconscious, 367
  splitting, 97
  universal attachment, 367
  Universal Law, 97, 366, 367, 397

Affection. See also *Love.*
  Rationalization of loss of, 257
Affective Identification, 136 ff.
Aging, Denial-in-, 66
Aggrandizing Distortion, self-enhancement through, 458
Aggrandizing, Self-, in Substitution, 402, 410
Aggrandizement, emotional, 123
Aggression, 417. See also *Hostility.*
  Activity Substitution and, 403
  Constructive, lacking, 282
  Criminal Identification and, 147
  diverted in external expression, 299, 316
  Fantasy and, 116
  Reaction Formation and oversolicitude, 289
  Rechannelization and, 298–99, 316
  suppression of, 283
Aggressive drives, 280, 402–3, 410
  Activity Substitution as outlet, 402–3, 410
  Reaction Formation against, 280
Aggressive/hostile, 329
Aggressiveness
  overcompensation for timidity, 290
  suppressed through Substitution, 405
Aggressive urges, 110, 125, 186
  disowned through Idealization, 125
  Fantasy as partial discharge of, 110
  Introjection defending against, 186
Aggressor Identification, 159
Aims, 303, 317, 403, 405
  direction, in *Rechannelization,* 303
  diversion, 317, 403
  substituted, 405
Air Force, *Military-Unit Identification* and, 150
Alcoholic Rationalization, 24, 67, 262, 271
  Confabulation as, 24
  Denial of problem, 67
  examples of, 262, 271
Alcoholism, 24, 65 ff., 262, 271, 348 ff.
  Bowen's treatment, 348 ff.
  Denial of, 65 ff.
  fantasies promoted, 119
  personality development and, 143
  Rationalization and, 262, 271
  Regressive Therapy, 350
  Secondary Defense of, 68
Alibi, counterfeit, 147
Allergy, Emotional, 282–83, 293
Alliance, Emotional, Identification as, 133, 135, 158
Allies, group affiliation and, 151
Alopecia, psychologic, *Atonement-Penance* and, 452
Alternating Dissociation, 95
Alternating Personality, 95, 98
  Dissociative Reactions and, 98

Alternative, psychologic, Substitution and, 401
Amalgam, Emotional-Object (EOA). See *Emotional-Object Amalgam.*
Ambition, blocked, *Rechannelization* and, 299
Ambivalence, 90, 169, 404, 409
  feelings of, 404, 409
    Repression of, in phobia dynamics, 404
    toward therapist, Substitution for, 409
  negative, repressed, 90
Amends, 386, 451
  Atonement-Penance and, 451
  unconscious, *Restitution* as, 386
Amnesia, 50, 95, 98, 464
  conflict expressed in, 50
  Dissociative Reaction and, 95, 98
  Fainting prodromal to, 464
Amorphous Dissociation, diffuse anxiety and, 95, 105
Analogy
  Chemical, *Emotional-Object Amalgam* and, *Electronics,* in Repression, 369, 379
  Iceberg, Fantasy and, 109
  Niagara Falls, psychic energy in, 312, 317
Anal Stage, 329
Analysis, 90, 377, 434. See also *Psychoanalysis; Treatment.*
  Defensive-Layering Concept (DLC), 395
  dissociative mechanism, 100
  dreams and
    beneficial, 417–19
    Condensation in, 455
    symbolized as inspection tour, 419
    Undoing, repetitive, 435
  finances, Reversal of attitudes and, 486
  headaches and, 35
  Interpersonal Identification and, 154
  obsessive patient, *Resistance-Undoing* and, 437
  Principle of Intellectualization-Respite in, 475
  of self, by Margaret Brierley, 77
  Sexual Reversal and, 487
  successful
    overdetermined emotional manifestations and, 478
    Replacement and, 483
  values, 224
Analytic study of *Displaced Complex,* 90
Analytic therapy, free association in, 377
Anesthesia, 44, 45, 46, 436
  Conversion and, 45–46
  feared, self-revelation and, 436
  of legs, *Sensory Conversion* and, 45
  "stocking" and "glove" varieties, 44

Anger, 87–88, 116, 184, 409. See also *Hostility.*
  checked, *Fantasy Lesson-Function* and, 116
  displaced, *convenient target* and, 87, 91
  King David Reaction and, 238, 239, 241 ff.
  pattern of, 88
  Projection of, 232
  Royal, 238 ff., 248
Anniversary dates, failure to recall, as *Minor Repression,* 366
Antecedent (Primordial) *Introjects,* 189
Antecedents of Projection, 223
Anthropologists, primitive incorporative rites and, 164, 172
Anti-Authority Generalization, college graduate and, 473
Anticipation, *Fire Drills* and, 470
Antidotal Substitution, 407, 410
Antisocial, 38, 299, 304–5, 316
  behavior, *Conversion* and, 38
  impulses, *Sexual Rechannelization* and, 299, 304–5, 316
Antitherapeutic Denial, 61–62
  mother representing, 62
Anxiety, 104, 148, 211, 222–23
  Acute, Attack, 375, 376, 380, 460
  avoidance
    Conversion and, 44, 51
    Counterirritant Substitution and, 406
    repetitions and, 437
    Undoing and, 427
  concurrent with symptoms, in *Incomplete Symptom Defense,* 44
  controlled, through phobia, 404
  Depersonalization and, 104
  diffuse, Dissociation and, 95
  Emotional Contagion Concept and, 140, 159
  freedom from, 210, 491
  Hysteria, 50
  Incomplete Symptom Defense Concept and, 44
  Projection as defense, 223
  Rationalization as defense, 256, 264
  Regression as surcease, 322
  Repression impetus from, 359, 372
  self-punishment aided by, 148
  Substitution as defense, 404
Apathy as *Secondary Defense,* 196
Aphrodisiacs, 165
Appeal, Primary and Secondary in Advertising, 149, 159
Appraisal, self-, 227, 236, 237, 241
Appropriate affect, absent in psychosis, 103
Approval, *Identification* goal, 146
Arbitration, unconscious, alternate and descriptive term for Compromise Formation, 454

Artistic style, Identification and, 143
Assessment of people, *Personal Yardstick* and, 153
Assimilation, psychic, alternative and descriptive term for ego defense of Incorporation, 163
Association, Affect, 371
Association Convergence, 456
Association, 371, 452, 460
  analytic therapy and, 377
  Convergence and, 456
  converse of Dissociation, 95
  to dream elements, 452
  Dream-Symbols revealed, 417
  Repression and, 356, 358, 360, 364–65, 378
Asthma following beating, 452
Athletic prowess, *Secondary Appeal in Advertising* and, 149
Atonement, 450 ff.
  dreams as expression of, 435
  -Penance, 387, 388, 430, 450 ff., 484
    alopecia and, 452
    embezzlement and, 397
    examples of, 451
    Guilt Group of Dynamisms, and, 450
    Minor Ego Defense, 450
    punishment in dynamics, 451
    Restitution relationship to, 388
    Undoing similar to, 430
Attack, Conversion, 43
Attention
  -Absorption defense, Diversion as alternate term for, 460
  deflection of, Diversion as, 459
  -Focus Substitution, 404, 407, 459–60
    employment of, 407
    new interests for painful problems, 404
  Hypothesis, 9, 14
  inattention vs., *Unwitting Ignorance* (UIC) and, 489
  new focus for, 156
Attitude(s), 284–85, 288, 470, 480
  anticipated, 226
  Generalization and, 472
  Internalization of, 178
  -Inversion, 201
  parental, assimilated, 170
  prejudicial, Compartmentalization and, 454
  Regressive-Indicator based on, 326, 353
  Reversal of, 64
  self-deprecatory, of depressed patient, 183
  sex inversion and, 197, 204
  -Symptoms, 284–85, 288, 293, 470, 490
    low self-esteem as, 284
    obsessive, as successful *Characterologic Reaction Formation,* 288

Attitude(s) (con't.)
  Pessimism as, 470
  Reaction Formation and, 284, 288
  subservience as, 285
  Withdrawal as, 490
  taken in, 174
  toward therapy symbolized, 418
Attitudinal-Generalization, 473
Attitudinal Regression, 322–23, 330, 352
  in psychotic reaction, 323
Attitudinal-Undoing, 443
Attorney, 140, 246, 397, 450
  awareness of *Legacy Restitution,* 397
  death of, *Group Compathy* and, 140
  latent hemosexuality of, 246
  third party route for Absolution, 450
Attonement Penance, 450
Attraction-Inversion, 196–97, 204
  homosexuality and, 196
Attractions, inexplicable, *King David Reaction* and, 236
Attributes, 142
  Characterologic Identification and, 134
  emulated better when person idealized, 130
  parental, unwittingly taken over, 149
  Projection and, 221, 227
Author, *Side-by-Side Dissociation* with, 105
  biblio. of present, 502 ff.
Authority, 179, 473
Automatic
  forgetting, 357 ff.
  writing, in Dissociative Reactions, 98
Automobiles, *Social Rationalizations* and, 269
Autonomic Conversion and language, 31–32, 51
Auxiliary-Repression, 360, 364, 365, 375, 378–79
  drowning and, 365
Aversion, *Sexual Reversal* and, 487
Avocational Compensation Concept, 20, 31–32, 39
Avocational Rechannelization, 308–10, 316
Avocations, Compensation and, 22
Avoidance, 220
  of anxiety, 44, 51, 211, 406, 427, 437
  defensively intended, 211
  of the intolerable, through Denial, 79
  of sexual interest, 73
Awareness blocked through *Recognition-Deferment Rationalization,* 256–58, 275

Bad influences for children, people as, 148

Backache, *Symptom-Replacement* and, 480
Balance, 461–62
  Concept of Character Trait, 461
Balanced Neurotic Position (BNP), 461–62
Baldness, *Atonement-Penance* and, 452
Banishment of intolerable affects, Repression and, 367
Basic need, *Primary Appeal* and, 149
Basic Trend Toward Emotional Health (BTEH)
  Concept of, 34, 347
  Hypothesis of, 226
Basking in Reflected-Glory, Concept of, 144, 158
Bathsheba, 236
Bed visits, Denial of impropriety and, 66
Behavior, 18–19, 26, 32, 37
  Antisocial, *Conversion* and, 38
  assaultive, *Massive Regression* and, 345
  Criminal, *Conversion* and, 38
  justified, group, 256, 268–69, 276
  patterns, 41
  reconciled, 252, 274, 276
  Regressive-Indicator based on, 326, 356
  Restitutive, 390, 391, 398
Behavioral
  Compensation, 18–19, 26
    small stature and, 19
  Conversion, 32, 37 ff., 51
    Childhood, 40
    explained, 32
    la belle indifférence of, 40
    major types, 38
    overall activity and, 41
    pseudoepilepsy as, 40
    trauma preceding, 39–40
  language, 33, 42, 50
    Conversion of conflict as, 42
    Dissociative Reaction as, 50
  Mechanism, Withdrawal as, 489
  Rationalization, 256, 261 ff.
  Reaction Formation, 281, 293
    Social Reaction Formation and, 281
  Regression, 323, 324, 330, 346
    assessment of, as *Regression-Gauge,* 346
    carcinoma and, 330
    childhood, 324
    in psychotic reaction, 323
    science, Repression key concept in, 358
  Undoing Cycle, 432
Belonging, 150, 151
  Group Identification and, 151
  Military-Unit Identification and, 150
Bernheim, Hippolyte, 362
Bias, moral judgments and, 298

Biologist, responsibility evaded through *Conscious Rationalization,* 264
"Birth trauma," Otto Rank and, 364
Bisexual gratification, substitution for, 402
Blake, William, *raison d'être* of Identification, 133
Blanket as soterial object, 326
Bleuler's Dissociation (Schizophrenic Dissociation), 102–3, 106
Blindness, psychologic, 380
Blind-spots, psychologic, 223–24, 233
Blocking
  awareness of the unacceptable, 256–58, 275
  Deferment requisite to, 457
  Denial and/or *Deferment* and, 69, 96
  dissociative, of perception, Fainting as, 464
  Emotional-Object Amalgam and, 369
  of goal, 201
  of idea, 69
  Unwitting Ignorance and, 489
BNP (*Balanced Neurotic Position*), 461–62
Body language, 33, 52
Bowel training, *Rechannelization* and, 303
Bowen's treatment in alcoholism, 348 ff.
Brainwashing, *Eleemosynary Rationalization* and, 268
Breaking point, 344
Breast, 91, 189
  replaced by thumb, 91
  represents both good and bad objects, 189
Breuer, Joseph, 30, 362
  "forgotten" experiences relived and, 362
  Freud and, Conversion concept, 30
Brierley, Margaret, analysis of self and, 77
BTEH (*Basic Trend Toward Emotional Health*), 34, 226, 347, 354
Building blocks of psychodynamics, 5–6
Business Restitution, 396, 399
Businessman, 63, 458
  Aggrandizing Distortion, 458
  Denial of painful past, 63

Cab driver, *Side-by-Side Dissociation* and, 105
Cancer, 74, 81, 164–65
  Behavioral Regression and, 330
  Denial of, 73, 78
  in *Multiple Denial,* 77–78
Cannibalism, *Literal Incorporation* and, 164–65

Capacities, Denial of limitations of, 81
Catastrophes, *Public Denial* of, 61
Cause, devotion to, *Eleemosynary Rationalization* and, 265
CD (*Confession Discrepancy*), 428, 442
Celebrity-Seeker, 144, 158
  in *Basking in Reflected-Glory Concept,* 144, 158
  in dreams, 144
Censor, internal, 177. See also *Conscience; Superego.*
Central Identification, 136, 140, 158
  compathy and, 140
  role in many aspects of living, 136
CF (*Compromise Formation*), 41, 333, 454–55
Chance, Law of Scientific Determinism and, 393
Changes
  primary, functional or physiologic, 52
  secondary, structural or physical, 52
  tertiary, functional and structural, 10, 52
Changing Trends Concept, 215
Channels, constructive, 300, 301
  Personal Tragedy Rechannelization and, 300
  Rechannelization and, 301
Character, 20, 141
  Defense Extensions, 461
  formation, 279, 293, 373
    Repression and, 373
  trait, 200, 461
    Balance, 461
  development, Inversion and, 200
Characterologic
  change, trait adoption and, 141
  Compensation, Denial and, 20, 27
  development as consequence of Reaction Formation, 280, 292
  Extension, 461–62
    scholastic handicaps and, 462
  formations, named for Reaction Formation, 281
  Hypertrophy, Concept and *Principle of,* 18, 26
  Idealization, Identification and, 130, 131
  Identification, 134, 142, 158
    attributes acquired through, 134
    course of life and, 142
    trait adoption and, 142
  Intellectualization, Rationalization akin to, 474–75
  Internalization, 174–75, 179
    of parents' views on money, 175
  Inversion, 198, 205
  Rationalization, 254, 272, 273
    definition, 272

Characterologic (con't.)
  long-buried hostility and, 273
  major, 254
  Reaction Formation, 146, 280, 282,
      283–84, 288, 290, 293
    as overcompensation for timidity,
        290
    personality development and, 280
    successful, in obsessive *attitude-
        symptoms*, 288
  Rechannelization, 302, 316
    personality development and, 302
  Reversal, mother's pattern in handling
      finances, 486
  status quo, 199, 272, 346, 461–62
    Concept of Character Trait Balance
        equating, 461–62
    defenses supported through Ration-
        alization, 272
    Resistance-Regression and, 346
    Secondary Defense and, 199
Charcot, Jean M., 51, 361
  Conversion experiments, 51
  Repression experiments, hypnosis and,
      361
Charity, 265, 395
  Eleemosynary Rationalization and, 265
  Restitution-Via-, through gifts, 395
Chemist, *King David's Anger* and, 242
Childhood
  Conversion, 33–34, 40
    paraplegia as, 34
    subsiding spontaneously, 34
  Denial, play and fantasy and, 76, 80
  Fantasy
    Denial and, 76
    universal in, 111–12
  Identification, 159
  illness, *Regressive Recapitulation of,*
      332
  Internalization in, 175
  paraplegia, *Somatic Conversion* and,
      34
  phobia, 463
  Regression, 324, 352
    new baby and, 325
  Specific Emotional Hazards of, 71, 327
  Undoing, 432, 443
    guilt and, 432, 443
Childlike level of *Fantasy-Regression,*
    119
Children, 264 ff.
  Bad Identifications and, 148
  Contra-Parent Reaction Formation,
      286
  as *convenient target,* in *Scapegoat Re-
      action,* 88
  Denial
    in death of, 78
    of failures of, 81

Children (con't.)
  Familial Rationalization in parents'
      treatment of, 256, 269–70, 276
  Fantasy Undoing by, 442–43
  incorporated parental attitudes, 169
  orally expressed incorporative attitudes,
      167–68
  regressive behavior, 326
  vicarious experience by parents, 151
Choice of symptoms in *Hygeiaphrontis,*
    156, 190
Church, 266, 394, 399
  contributions in *Pious Restitution,* 394,
      399
  ethical principles violated, in *Eleemos-
      ynary Rationalization,* 266
CI. See *Conflict Indicator.*
Cinema, *Personal-Feeling Displacement*
    while attending, 87
Circle, Vicious. See also *Cycle; Spiral;
    Vicious Circle.*
  Pathogenic, Concept of, 10, 14
  Projective (PVC), 221, 223, 233
  of *Self-Defeat,* 41, 336, 342, 482
Cleanliness as *attitude-symptom,* 288
Clumsiness, unconsciously motivated, 285
Cold, *Counterirritant Substitution* and,
    407
Collective Rationalization, 256, 268
Combat, 36–37, 51, 242–43
  Conversion, 36–37, 51
  hero, 242–43
    King David's Anger and, 242
    overcompensation for guilt, 242–43
Comfort, 325, 415
  Childhood Regression and, 325
  soterial object and, 415
Communication
  Compathic, 138–40, 158
  conversion headache as, 35
  General and *Individual Symbols* req-
      uisite to, 415
  lessened through Withdrawal, 489
  media, *Mass Identification* in, 145
  nonverbal, *symptom language* as, 36
Compartmentalization, 453–54
  definition, 453
  Incomplete, 454
  Relationship, 454
Compathic, 136 ff., 158
  Communication, 138–40, 158
  Identification, 136 ff., 158
Compathy, 46, 47, 136 ff., 158
  as *Affective Identification,* 136, 140
  alternate term for *Emotional Identifi-
      cation,* 137
  definition, 47, 138–40
  Group, 139–40, 158
  Individual, 139, 158
  sexual experience and, 139

Compathy (con't.)
Symptom, 46–47, 139, 158. See also *Symptom-Identification; Recapitulation, emotional; Psychologic Recapitulation Route* (PRR); *Illness Regression.*
vicarious experiencing through, 140
Compensation, 13, 17 ff., 294, 388
Avocational, 22, 26
powerful motors and, 22
awareness of process followed by *Retrospective Devaluation*, 485
Behavioral, 18–19
Characterologic, 20, 27
military officer, 20–21
confabulation in Korsakoff's syndrome, 24
Deficit (*Deficits of Illness*), 23, 26
definition, 17–18
Dream, 23
disapproved behavior, by storekeeper, 21
Group, 19, 26
Individual Psychology and, Adler's principle tenet and, 25
King David Reaction (KDR) and, 242
National, 19, 26, 128, 131
Personal, 18, 26
physical deficiencies and, 18
Power, 20, 22–23, 26
Public-Figure Enhancement as, 26
Rationalization and, 274
Reaction Formation and, 20, 289
Sexual, 21, 27
for stature, 18
Substitution akin to, 402
Vocational, 22, 27
Competition, 118, 222, 324, 482
mother and daughter, 118
Regression in childhood and, 324
Relationship-Replacement and, 482
underlying, 222
Complete
Rechannelization, 307–9, 316
Regression, 344–45, 354
Complex, 90, 256, 258, 276, 289, 460, 461
Displaced, 90
emotional, Extension and, 460
-Extension, 461
reversed, 289
-Supportive Rationalization, 256, 258, 276
Complexity
of *Dreams, Law of Increasing*, 418, 422
in *Emotional Manifestations*, 325
Compromise
emotional, 454
-Formation, 41, 333, 454–55

Compromise (con't.)
hemiparesis and, 41
Neurotic, 454
Partial, 454
Regression and, evolution of symptoms as, 333
unconscious mediation as alternative and descriptive term, 454
gain and *Restitution*, 369
Internal, 251 ff.
psychic, *Rechannelization* as, 300, 315
Rationalization and, 252
Compulsion, 154, 430, 434, 436–37, 440
handwashing as *Symbolic Undoing*, 30, 440
Neuroses, repetitive symptoms in, 436–37
telephoning and, 437
repetition, 154
Compulsive
rituals, as *Symbolic Undoing*, 430, 439, 440, 443
sexual behavior, 89
Compulsory activity in Fantasy, 114
Concept. See also *Law; Principle; Tenet;* and individual key words and italicized entries.
Advanced Defenses, 12
Association Conversion, 456
Association Repression, 356, 358, 360, 364–65
Attention Absorption Defense, 460
Attention Hypothesis, 9
Attitude-Symptom, 284, 285, 293, 470, 490
Balanced Neurotic Position, 461–62
Basic Trend Toward Emotional Health, 34, 226, 347, 354
Basking in Reflected-Glory, 144, 158
Central Identification, 140
Changing Trends, 215
Characterologic Hypertrophy, 18, 26
Character Trait Balance, 461
Compathic Communication, 138–40, 158
Compathy, 46–47, 136 ff., 158
Confession Discrepancy, 428, 442
Conflict Indicator, 38, 170, 325, 327, 330, 353
Conversion, 30
Conversion-Escape, 48, 52
Somatic Conversion and, 48
Cultural Vogue, 215
Defensive-Layering, 391, 395, 399, 472
Generalization and, 472
Restitution-Via-Charity and, 395
Dissociated Psychotic Survival, 101, 490
in psychotic reactions, 101
Withdrawal and, 490

Concept (con't.)
  Dream of Erasure, 426–27, 435–36, 442–43
  Electronics Analogy, 369, 379
  Elucidation, Therapeutic, 223, 233
  Emotional Allergy, 282, 283, 293
  Emotional Alliance, 133, 135, 158
  Emotional Contagion, 140, 159
  Emotional Engulfment, 170–72, 253, 258
  Emotional Exploitation, 171, 258
  Emotional Health, Basic Trend Toward, 34, 226, 347, 354
  Emotional Recapitulation, 353
  Emotional Sensitization, 453
  Emotional Symbiosis, 89, 125, 204, 437, 459
  Endogain, 31, 49, 52, 125
  Energy, Principle of Kinetic, 360, 379
  Engulfment, 170–72, 253, 258
  Epigain, 45, 49, 52
  Equivalents, Affect-, 47, 52
  Euphemistically-Intended Disguises in suicide, 69
  Excessive Rechannelization, 304, 316
  Fantasy-Lesson Function, 166
  Functional-Structural Progression, 10, 52
    primary, secondary and *tertiary* changes in, 52
  Group Compathy, 139, 158
  Guidepost Dream, 417–19, 422
  Hand-in-Glove, in Relationships, 171
  Historical Validation, 226, 240, 248, 281, 301, 316, 361
    King David Reaction recognition by Shakespeare, 240
    literary recognition of Projection, 226
    Personal-Tragedy Rechannelization and, 301–2
    Repression and, 361
  Hygeiaphrontic Personality, 342
  Impression-Priority Rule, 129, 145, 152, 159, 178, 237
  Incomplete Symptom Defense, 44
  Intellectualized Retreat, 476
  Janet, 96, 106
  Level of Defenses, 12 ff.
  Mirror-Defense, 220, 221, 226–27, 234
    Projection as, 226–27
  Multiple Denial, 77
  Ostrich, 60, 81, 489, 490
    in Denial, 60, 81
    reminiscent of *Unwitting Ignorance,* 489
    Withdrawal and, 490
  Overextension in Repression, 360, 375, 380

Concept (con't.)
  Paranoid Indifference, 103, 230, 231, 234, 305
  Pathogenic Vicious Circle (PVC), 10, 14
  Peg, Rationalization and, 254
  Personal Invulnerability, 60, 63, 478–79
  Personal Yardstick, 146, 152–53, 159, 223, 226, 233, 246, 474
    Generalization of attitudes and, 474
    Identification and, 146
    new relationships; and, 153
    Projection and, 223, 233
    as universal measuring device, 226
  Physiologic Conversion, 31–32, 51
  Primary Appeal in Advertising, 149, 159
  Primitive Dynamisms, 12 ff.
  Projective Vicious Circle, 221, 223, 233
  Psychologic Recapitulation Route (PRR), 332, 340–41, 353
  Regression-Gauge, 337, 345–46, 354
  Repression-by-Association, 359, 360, 364, 378
  Restitutive-Behavior, 398
  Secondary Appeal in Advertising (SAAC), 149, 159
  Secondary Defense, 14, 52, 67–68, 197, 199, 205, 213, 218, 276, 304–05, 332, 346, 353
    Conversion and, resistance to analysis and, 36, 49
    emotional dynamisms and, 211
    primary defense and, 11
    Rationalization and, 277
    Symptom-Defensive Rationalization and, 271
  Secondary Delusion, 270, 277
  Secondary Repression, 364, 379
  Self-Defense, 97, 104, 106
  Self-Esteem Maintenance in Therapy, 33, 52
  Side-by-Side Dissociation, 96
  Somatic Conversion, 31, 34, 36, 42 ff., 340, 361
  Soteria, 125, 128, 326, 368, 415, 478–79, 483
  Suspended Reaction, 397, 399
  Symptom Identification, 156
  Symptom-Symbol, 420
  Tenet of Variable Interpretation, 417, 420, 422
  Tidal-Progression, 324, 329, 335, 346, 352, 382, 480
    of Maturity, 324, 329, 335, 352, 382, 480
    of Therapeutic Progress, 346, 353, 356

Concept (con't.)
  Ultimate-Dependency-Goal, 322, 352
  Unwitting Ignorance (UIC), 489
  Vicious Circle of Self-Defeat, 41, 336,
    342, 482
    in *Behavioral Conversion*, 41
    in *Maturation-Fixation*, 336
    in Neuroses, 342
Conception, Fantasy of, as oral process,
  187
Concern, substitute for acceptance and
  love, 339
Condemnation, 228, 239
  of another, in negative *King David Re-
    action* (KDR), 239
  of self, Projection leading to *substi-
    tute target*, 228
Condensation, 416, 455
  dreams and, 416, 455
  Symbolization and, 455
Condensation Symbol, 414, 421
Conditioning, earlier relationships and,
  152
Confabulation, 24, 274
  defined, 24
  as Denial, related to Rationalization,
    274
  Korsakoff's syndrome and, 24
Confession, 146–47, 159, 267, 428, 436,
  442
  Discrepancy, 428, 442
  Eleemosynary Rationalization and, 267
  Judas, 429, 442, 444
  Multiple, in murder and violent crimes,
    146–47, 159
  sleepwalking and sleeptalking and, 436
  Spurious, notoriety sought through,
    146–47
  Undoing Cycle, 429, 442–43
Confidence, Denial-For-, 59–60, 81
  speaking ability and, 59
Confidence, shyness and, 202
Conflict(s)
  allayed, 104
  avoidance of, 119, 210
  elucidation of, through therapy, 397
  emotional, 4, 30, 90, 209, 440, 463,
    491
    awareness prevented through, 90
    guilt feelings and, 440
    sexual experience and, 463
  expressed functionally via *Physiologic
    Conversion*, 50
  id, ego, and superego, 91
  Indicator Concept (CI), 38, 170, 325,
    327, 330, 353
    development contributed to, by
      SEHC, 327
  Incorporative trends and, 170

Conflict(s) (con't.)
  mild Regressions in childhood and,
    325, 327, 330
  recurrence of, 327
  internal, Externalization of, in pho-
    bia, 221
  intrapsychic, 4 ff.
  Oedipal, 124
  parental, 118
  resolution, 71, 210, 405, 427
    Denial and, 71
    Substitution as endeavor at, 405
    Undoing and, 427
  sexual, 88
  transmutation of, conversion and, 30
Conflicting drives, Compromise Formation and, 454
Confusion, faulty Compartmentalization
  and, 454
Conscience, 31, 168, 443–44. See also
  Superego.
  Characterologic Inversion and, 198
  demands of, *Absolution* and, 449
  development of, 168
  as internal censor, 177
  placated through *Undoing*, 441
  Rationalization appeasing, 259
Conscious
  Compensation, 24, 25
    Demosthenes exemplifying, 24
    Theodore Roosevelt exemplifying,
      25
  Denial, efforts at, 80
  Identification, imitation as, 135
  Rationalization, responsibility evasion
    and, 264
  Restitution, 388, 398 ff.
Conservative views, *Contra-Parent Re-
  action Formation* and, 286
Constrictive life, 46
Constructive
  Aggression, 282
  Fantasy, 109, 112–13
    in adult imagination, 112
    in planning, 109
  Rechannelization, 299, 302, 405
    Substitution and, 405
Contagion, Emotional, 140, 145
  mobs and riots as, 140
  psychologic epidemic, 145
  of sadness, 140
Content, latent and manifest, 112, 117
Contingencies, *Fire Drill* as preparation
  for, 470–71
Contra-Parent Reaction Formation, po-
  litical attitudes and, 285–86,
    293
Contributory Rechannelization, 310, 317
Convenient memory, 57, 81–82, 375
  psychologic blindness as, 371, 380

Convenient Target, 87, 91–92
  for angry feelings, 91
  of *Displaced Complex*, 91
  as object for Displacement of feelings,
    87
Convergence, 88, 416, 452, 456, 476, 477
  adjunct to Displacement, 88
  Association, 456
  dreams and, 416, 452
  as minor ego defense, 456
  Overdeterminism and, 477
  Scapegoat Reaction and, 456
  symbolization resulting from, 416, 456,
    476
Converse of phobia, *soteria* as, 125
Conversion, 11, 29 ff.
  Acting-out in, 37–38
  anxiety and, 44, 51
  Attack, 43
  Autonomic, 32, 51
  Behavioral, 32, 37, 38, 40, 41, 51
    acute, 40
    as *Behavioral Language*, 33, 37, 51
    in child, 40
    major types, 38
    as overall activity in teacher, 41
  Childhood, 33, 40, 51
  Combat, 36–37, 51
  concept of, 30
  definition of, 32
  Delinquency, 38
  derepression in, 32
  diathesis, 39
  Displacement and, 50, 90
  Dissociation and, 50
  endogain, 49, 52
  epigain, 48, 52
  Escape, Somatic Conversion and, 48,
    52
  as *Great Imitator*, 44
  Headache, 35
  intelligence in, 45
  Language, 32–33, 45, 51–52
  manifestations, figurative into literal,
    30, 47
  Minimal, 38
  Motor, 43, 45, 48–49, 51
  pain and, emotional into physical, 48
  paralysis, 41, 48
  -Personality, 45, 69, 170, 345, 465
    Denial and, 69
    Incorporation and, 69, 170
    Regression in, 340
    traits revealed in, 45
  Physiologic, 31, 32, 51
    definition of, 32
    Progression of, 51
  -Reaction, 31, 41, 48, 103, 340, 416,
    420, 463

Conversion (con't.)
  endogain, 31
  la belle indifferènce in, 41, 103
  *Self-Esteem Maintenance Principle
    in Therapy* and, 33
  Surgery-in-Abeyance Rule in, 48
  Symbolism in *Symptom of Choice*, 420
  Transparency Theory and, 36, 52
  Regression, 340–41, 534
  relationships
    Denial, 51
    Identification, 50
    Regression, 50–51
  Repression in, 31, 44
  resistance in psychotherapy, 49
  Sensory, 44, 45
    paralysis as, 45
  Sexual, 30, 43
  Social Behavior, 37–38
  Somatic, 31, 34, 36, 42 ff.
    Conversion-Escape and, 48
    epigain in, 49
    expression of conflict in, 50
    gross motor and sensory changes,
      42 ff.
    hypnosis and, 361
    la belle indifferènce in, 45, 69
    paralysis and, 41, 45
    regressive features in, 340
  Symptoms
    affect equivalent, 47, 52
    Conviction erased, in *Dream of
      Evasive*, 435
    Compathy, 46
    Denial and, 69
    elaboration, dynamic sequence of
      events in, 51
    Fainting, 43
    First Line of Psychic Defense ap-
      plies, 49
    formation, 30
    gain of endogain and epigain, 49
    Identification, 46, 435–36. See also
      *Psychologic Recapitulation
      Route* (PRR).
    surrendered when recalled, 362
  -in-Therapy, 35–36, 51
  transmutation of emotional conflict, 30
Convulsions, 39, 40, 67
  alcoholic, Denial of, 67
  in *Behavioral Conversion*, 40
  pseudoconvulsions, 39
Coordination, Motor Conversion and, 43
Cough, *Symptom-Replacement* and, 480
Counterirritant Substitution, 406, 407,
    410
  masturbation as, 407
  neurotic reactions and, 407
  Obsessive-Compulsive Reaction and,
    406

Courtship, Fantasy in, 115
CR (*Compulsive Ritual*), 430, 439–40, 443
Creative endeavor, *Rechannelization* and, 297
Crime
  punishment and, 442
  violent, *Multiple Confessions* and, 146
Criminal
  Acting-Out Concept, 38
  Behavior, 38
  Dream-of-Erasure, 435
  -in-Fact, 430, 442
  Identification, 146–47, 159
    Multiple Confessions, 147
    Spurious Confessions, 146
  Punishment-Undoing Cycle, 430
  Restitution, 393, 398–99
  Undoing, 430, 442
  -by-Wish, 430, 442
Crises, unnecessary, in *Fire Drill*, 471
Criticism
  of colleagues through Projection, 227
  of self, projected, 228
CS (*Counterirritant Substitution*), 406–7, 410
Cultural Evolvement of the *General Symbol*, 422
Cultural Extension, 461
Cultural Vogue Concept (CVC), 215
Cycle. See also Spiral; Vicious Circle.
  Behavioral Undoing, 432, 443
  Confession-Undoing, 429, 442
  Punishment-Undoing, 430, 442
Cyclic swings of mood, 201

Danger dismissal via Denial, 60
Darwin, Charles, memory Repression and, 370–71
Das unbewusste, 362
Daydreams, 76, 109, 111, 114
  Fantasy and, 76, 109
  inadequacy and, 111
  of romance, 114
Death
  Denial-of-, 60, 71, 75, 76, 78
    Aging, 66
  of father, *Major Regression* and, 323
  frustration rechanneled and, 307
  Impossible Standard and, 126
  Introjection and, 187
  King David Reaction and, 238
  wishes
    affect detached from, 477
    repressed, 439
Debt, slow repayment of, 225
Deception, self, 68, 251, 262
Decompensation, Emotional, 333, 353
Decompensation, psychotic, 409

Dedication, *Rechannelization* and, 297
Defeat of self, 9, 12, 21, 41, 101, 125 ff., 222, 228, 335–36, 342, 451, 471, 482
Defects, self-evaluation and, 18 ff.
Defenses, 3 ff., 10, 97, 209 ff., 374, 491. See also *Dynamisms.*
  Advanced, 12
  against action, 39
  Attention Absorption, alternating concept and term with *Diversion*, 460
  Depersonalization, 104
  depression threatening, 374
  exaggerated, 10
  Fainting as, 464
  First Line of Psychic, 49, 358
  functions, 213–14
  Higher Order, 12–14
  inadequacies, symptom formation and, 10
  Incomplete Symptom, 22, 44
  Layering, 391, 395, 399, 472
  Lower Order, 12–14
  Mirror-, alternate and descriptive term for Projection, 220, 221, 227
  primary, 6–8, 10–11, 49, 211, 277
  Primitive, 16
  Secondary *D.*, *Concept* of, 10–11, 14, 36, 52, 67–68, 71, 197, 199, 213, 218, 271, 304–5, 332, 346, 353, 437, 443
    Conversion and, 49
    explanation of, 11
    Rationalization and, 277
    resistance in therapy and, 36, 199
    Undoing and, 437, 443
    Sophistication level and, 215, 419
    synthesis and integration and, 96
    tabulated, 7
Defensive Layering Concept (DLC), 391, 395, 399, 472
  Generalization and, 472
  Restitution-Via-Charity and, 395
Defensive reactions to psychiatric concepts, 314
Deferment, 88, 96, 257, 456–57
  blocking or Repression and, 96
  Displacement and, 88
  Dissociation and, 456
  emotional impact and, 457
  emotional postponement and, 456
  Recognition-, Rationalization, 257
Deficiencies made up through compensation, 17 ff.
Deficit Compensation, 23, 26, 372
  illness and, 17 ff., 392
Deficits
  Denial of, 75
  of Illness, 23, 26

Déjà vu, 98
Delineation, *Inversion* from Reaction
    Formation and, 203
Delinquency, Conversion, 38
Delusion
  Denial and, 57, 69, 70, 78
  formation
    Denial-of-Death, 77
    Illness Denial, 73
  grandiose, 232
  Identification and, 157, 159, 160
  Incorporation and, 170
  Introjection and, 186
  Persecution and, 231
  primary, 270, 277
  Projection in, 222
  psychotic, 186
  Rationalization and, 270
  Regression and, 339
  Secondary, 270, 277
Demosthenes, 24
Denial, 20, 39, 56 ff., 129, 204, 274, 450
  -in-Aging, 66
  aiming at conflict resolution, 71, 79
  of alcoholism, 66–68
  Antitherapeutic, 61–62, 68, 81
  avoidance of conflict and, 79
  blocking or Regression and, 69, 96
  childhood, 76
  -for-Confidence, 59, 81
  of conflict through Conversion, 69
  conscious, 80
  Conversion and, 51, 69
  -of-Death, 60, 71, 75
    of child, 78
    in "Grandfather's Clock," 77
    humor and, 80
    in "Little Boy Blue," 77
  definition of, 58
  delusions and hallucinations and, 57,
    69, 78
  Devaluation and, 73
  in diathesis of
    Depressive Personality, 71
    manic-depressive psychosis, 57
    paranoid conditions, 69
    persecutory beliefs, 69
  drug addiction and, 62
  Euphemistically-Intended Disguises, 69
  extramarital sexual experience and, 79
  of failures of children, 81
  Fantasy and, 57, 76, 80, 111
  Grief-Stricken, 78, 82
  guilt and, 69
  as handicap, 75
  idealized picture of another and, 66
  Idealization and, 80, 129
  Illness, 73–74, 82, 457
    cancer and, 73

Denial (con't.)
  Devaluation and, 457
  terminal, 74
  Illusion-of-Continued Living, 76–77,
    78, 82
  of impropriety, 65, 84
  Introjection and, 68
  Inversion and, 65, 196
  of jealousy, 81
  King David Reaction (KDR) and,
    237, 244
  of limitations of capacities, 81
  of loss, 71
  as *Lower Order ego defense*, 57, 58,
    70
  Mass, 82
  memory loss and, 71
  Multiple, death and, 77–78, 82
  National, 60–61, 82
  Omission, 79–80, 82
  Ostrich Concept and, 60–61, 81
  other dynamisms and, 80
  pain and, 62, 63, 64
  Personal Invulnerability and, 60, 63
  pleasure principle and, 75
  of pregnancy, 70
  primitive negation, as alternate and
    descriptive term, 57
  Primordial, Projection and, 68, 223
  Psychologic Disavowal and, 56
  psychotic episode, 70
  Public, 69, 82
  Rationalization and, 262
  Reaction Formation and, 280, 289–90
  repressed impulses and, 38
  Repression and, 60, 359, 374
  responsibility and, 81
  Retrospective, 197
  as second defense, 82
  in SEHC, 71
  self-deception and, 68
  self-esteem and, 66
  in self-picture, 64
  Sexual, 72–73
    conflict resolution and, 71
    by student, 72
  somnambulism and, 69
  Splitting and, 488
  Standards-Inversion and, 198
  of sterility, 64
  Substitution reinforced by, 403
  Symptom D., 73
  of threats of danger, 60
  Undoing and, 437
Dependence, Regression toward, 322
Dependency
  conflict, regression following, 340 ff.
  -Extension, 462
  Fantasy-Pattern in, 114
  -Goal, Ultimate-(UDG), 322, 352

Dependency (con't.)
  gratification, in Regression, 347
    encouraged, 348
  manifested, in Schizophrenic Reaction, 490
  needs, 338–39
    awareness of, Fantasy aids in blocking, 114
    Group Identification and, 151
    multiplication of, Regression and, 331
    purposely gratified in therapy, 348
    Repression of, phobia and, 404
    satisfaction of, in *Hygeiaphrontis,* 343
    Schizophrenic Reaction and, 409
    of therapist, reflection of, 347
  -Seeking Principle, 331, 338 ff., 354
    sleep desire and, 409
    strivings, phobia and, 339
    supplies, retreat toward era when provision failed and, 352
Dependent position, 45–46, 47, 320–21, 339, 490
  epigain equates, 45
  phobia of vomiting and, 339
  Regression and, 320
  Symptom-Compathy and, 46
  unconscious wish for, 47
  Withdrawal toward, 320
Depersonalization, 95, 98, 103, 464, 485–86
  defense, 104
  Dissociation and, 95, 98, 103, 104
  feelings of unreality in, 103
  Retrospective Devaluation and, 485
  Self-Defense Concept and, 104
Depreciation of self, 183
Depression, 171, 182, 184, 201, 202, 406
  cocoon of, 202
  Counterirritant Substitution employed in, 406
  cyclic, *Parental Engulfment* and, 171
  elation through *Inversion,* 201
  Introjection and, 182
  recriminations transposed in, 184
Depressive-introject, 183–84, 190
Depressive Personality, 71, 200
  Denial by, 71
  Inversion of hostility and, 200
Depressive Reactions, 183–84, 202, 215, 342, 407
  Counterirritant Substitution and, 407
  depressive-introject, 183–84
  incidence, among intellectually favored, 215
  Introjection and, 183–84
  Inversion of, 202
  regressive trends in, 342
  Repression of anger in, 184

Deprivation, 261, 301
  frustration of, eased, 261
  Rechannelization and, 301
Derepression, 218, 374 ff., 580
  in Conversion, 32
  danger of, in Depressive Reaction, 184
  fostered, 375
  important aspect of psychotherapy, 212
  judicious handling essential, 376
  prevention of, 9
  signaled by anxiety, 359
  therapeutic, 212, 377
  threatened
    Counterirritant Substitution and, 407
    ego, 228
    evolvement of *Ego Defenses* and, 211
    symptoms, 374
Destructiveness, *Scapegoat Reaction* and, 285
Detachment
  Isolation and, 477
  Personal Invulnerability and, 478
Determinants, unconscious, in Convergence, 456
Determination, Principle of Scientific, 371
Devaluation, 256, 275
  educational advantages, 263–64
  function of, in Rationalization, 261
  Goal, 273
    Rationalization and, 261
    unobtainable devalued, 259
  Material, 261
  progression toward Denial, 73
  Retrospective, 197, 484–86
  self-protection and, 457
Devalued educational advantages, 263
Development
  Character Trait, 200
  in childhood, 324
  personality, 135, 143, 328
  Psychosexual, 328–29
Device, Nathan, 236, 240, 248
Dexedrine, physicians' Denial of addiction to, 62
Diathesis, Conversion, 39
Diet, Distortion and, 458, 459
Diffuse Projection, 230, 234
Diffusion, emotional, alternate term for Generalization and, 471, 472
Digestion, *figurative,* Incorporation and, 163 ff.
Dilemma, Socio-Sexual, 72–73, 82, 115
Directional-Tenet of Regression, 320, 323, 351
  in attitude and behavior, 323
  regressive endeavors and, 320

Direct Proportion of Symptom-Prominence to (its) Secondary Defense, Principle of, 11, 14

Directly Proportional Ego-Response in Regression, Law of, 322, 352

Disavowal, Psychologic, alternate term for Denial, 56

Disciplinary-Regression, 325–26, 353

Discrepancy, Confession-, Undoing and, 428, 442

Disease, intractable, Denial and, 74

Disguise
  Euphemistically-Intended, 69
  unconscious, Distortion as, 458

Disillusionment, Shattered Ideal and, 127

Displaced Anger, 87–88

Displaced Complex, 87, 91
  toward more convenient target, 90. See also Scapegoat Reaction.

Displacement, 86 ff., 404, 422, 463, 479–80
  of affect in Counterirritant Substitution, 406
  Conversion and, 90
  definition of, 86
  Displaced Complex, 90
  of emotional charge in symbolism, 420
  Intrapsychic Transference, alternate term for, 86
  as Lower Order defense, 86
  of object through Substitution, 402
  Personal-Feeling, 87, 92, 457
    Deferment and, 87
  Phobic, endogain of, 86
  Primal, thumbsucking (ACI) as, 91–92
  Replacement and, 479
  Repression and, 86
  Scapegoat Reaction, 87–88, 92–93, 182, 238, 248, 301, 480
    children as, 88
    wife as, 91
  Sexual-Object, 88–89, 92
  Substitution and, emotional symbiosis and, 89–90

Dissension, mother and, 282

Dissimulation, social, Attitudinal Inversion as, 194

Dissociated Psychotic-Survival, 101, 106, 490

Dissociation, 50, 94 ff., 477, 478
  Affect, 94, 95, 99, 100, 102, 104, 106
    Depersonalization and, 104
    ideation and, 106
    Law of Universal Affect and, 97
    schizophrenic patient and, 102
    in therapy, 100
  alternate term for ego defense of Affect Dissociation, 97
  Amorphous, 95, 105

Dissociation (con't.)
  BBC (after Braid, Bernheim, and Charcot), 98
  Bleuler's, 102, 103
  as converse of association, 95
  Comparative Data and, 98–100
  Conversion and, 50
  Deferment and, 456
  definition of, 94
  Dissociative Reactions and, 94
  of emotional significance from object, 94
  Fragmental, Fainting as, 43, 464
  Induced, 98
  Isolation and, 477
  Janet's, 96, 106
  Mental Function, 104–6, 108
  painful news and, 104
  Personality, 95–97, 106
    Janet Concept alternate term for, 96
    portion of ego split off in, 97
  as psychologic flight, 95
  psychosis, 101, 102, 106
  psychotic, Concept of Dissociated Psychotic-Survival in, 101
  of Responsibility, 100
  Schizophrenic, alternate term for Bleuler's Dissociation, 102
  Self-Defense Concept in Dynamism Elaboration in, 97, 104, 106
  Side-by-Side, 96, 98, 105, 106
    concept of, 96
    in Dissociative Reactions, 98
  splitting-off-process in, 97
  unreal feelings in, 95

Dissociative
  blocking of perception, Fainting as, 464
  depersonalization, 104
  psychologic flight and, 105
  Reactions, 50, 94 ff.
    as Behavioral Language, 50
    Comparative Data, 98, 100
    Dissociation and, 94
    expression of conflict in, 50
    Pharmacologic, 100
    Traumatic Encephalopathy as, 100
    types of, 95
  Repression as, 359
  Splitting, 95, 99, 102, 105, 115, 408

Distance in Withdrawal, 489

Distortion, 455, 458–59
  Aggrandizing, self-enhancement through, 458
  Emotional-Object Amalgam and, 458
  Extension and, 459
  Idealization similar to, 458
  Interpersonal identification and, 154
  Personal Yardstick and, 226

Distortion (con't.)
Rationalization and, 459
reality, 232
Repression reenforced, 458
Resistance Inversion and, 199
Retrospective Devaluation as variant, 486
Symbolization and, 421
Diversion, 296 ff., 317, 403, 459–60
aims and goals, through Rechannelization, 317, 403
Attention *Absorption Defense,* 459–60
Instinctual, 298, 305, 316
alternative and descriptive term for Rechannelization or Sublimation, 296 ff.
major vocational *Rechannelization* as result, 305
sexual energy, 304
Divine Providence, *Retribution* and, 483
Divorce, 70, 307, 485
Denial of, 70
frustrates maternal drives, 307
Retrospective Devaluation and, 485
Divorcement, Affect, alternative and descriptive term for *Isolation,* 476
DLC (*Defensive Layering Concept*), 391, 395, 399, 472
Doctor. See also Physician.
as *substitute target,* 409
Don Juanism, 21–22, 26
alternative term for *Sexual Compensation,* 21
compensatory success as lover, 22
Double Personality, 95
DPS (*Dissociated Psychotic-Survival Concept*), 101, 106, 490
Dream(s), 98, 109, 158, 416 ff.
analysis, unconscious *Rechannelization* and, 307
atonement need and, 451
of *Basking in Reflected-Glory,* 144
Compensatory, 23
Condensation in, 414, 455
Dissociative Reactions and, 98
-of-Erasure, 435–36, 443
criminal conviction reversed through, 435
living sequence undone in, 436
Fantasy and, 116
Guidepost, 417–18, 422
attitudes toward therapy indicated, 418
special value in treatment, 417
Increasing Complexity of, Law of, 418–19, 422
interpretation, three basic factors in, 416
manifest content, 417

Dream(s) (con't.)
recurrent, of snake, 452
-of-Regret, 396
Restitution in, 396
sophistication level and, 419
Symbols, 416–17, 421
associations reveal, 417
object represented and, 416–17
Undoing, wish fulfillment in, 435, 443, 448
Variable-Interpretation, Tenet of, 417, 420, 422
world, 111
Drill, Fire, 470–71
Drives, 201, 205
aggressive, 183, 298, 304
altered through *Distortion,* 458
instinctual, *Rechannelization* and, 298, 308
neurotic success and, 216
repressed, symbolic form of, 422
sexual, 245, 299, 312
Excessive Rechannelization of, 304, 316
Reaction Formation against, 280
value judgments and, 298
vicissitudes of, 304
Drowning, repressed memory of, 365
Drug addiction, Denial in, 62
DSP. See *Dependency-Seeking Principle.*
Duchess of Malfi, 225
Dynamics, 4, 183, 402. See also *Psychodynamics;* individual ego defenses.
phobias, 404, 479–80
of Rationalization, 272
of *Rechannelization,* 312
in suicide, 184
Dynamism(s) (alternatively termed ego defense and mental mechanism), 5 ff., 209 ff.
consequences of employment, 214
Defense, Incomplete, 22
definition of, 6
as ego synthetic, 185, 209 ff.
elaboration, *Self-Defense Concept* in, 97, 106
exaggeration of, 221
-Extension, 461
Guilt Group of, 386–87, 449–50, 483
Absolution, 450
Atonement-Penance, 450
Restitution, 387
Retribution, 483
Undoing, 450
Higher Order, 12–14
hypertrophy, 183
intended functions, 212
Lower Order, 12–13
Major and *Minor,* 7, 217, 450–51

Dynamism(s) (con't.)
  Prime or Primary, 7
  primitive, 12
  Secondary, 7, 11

ED (*Ego Defenses*), 4 ff.
ED (*Emotional Decompensation*), 333, 353
Editor, Displacement of anger in, 88
Education devalued, 263–64
Educational process, psychotherapy as, 212
Ego, 3 ff., 91, 97 ff., 209 ff., 386, 398, 447 ff., 491 ff.
  acceptable motives, Rationalization and, 259
  aided through Fantasy, 109
  defense, Denial as, 58
  defense of, Dissociation and, 97
  Defenses, 3 ff., 134–35, 209 ff., 333, 350, 447 ff. See also dynamisms and mental mechanisms.
    Aims, Functions and Consequences, 214
    Concept of Secondary Defense, 211, 218
    effects of hypertrophy, 96, 211
    further conceptions concerning, 209
    Higher Order, 12–14
    Lower Order, 12–13
    Major (alternatively *prime, primary* or *senior*), 6–7
    major influences in adjustment, 211
    Minor (alternatively *secondary* or *junior*), 6–7, 447 ff.
    modify and allow safer expression of repressed strivings, 360
    Primary, 6
    psychic pain and anxiety, 210
    psychopathologic sequence, 211, 218
    Repression and, 358
    Secondary, 6
    type of evolvement, intelligence and, 215
    understanding of, 212, 219
  development, Internalization and, 176
  disruptive, 96, 106, 183
  early childhood, 76
  employs
    Devaluation, 457
    Splitting, integration and, 488
  -*enhancement,* Identification and, 134
  -*Enhancing Inversion,* 200–01, 254
  functions, memory and perception as, 76
  -*ideal,* 125, 272, 275
    nonconformity, anxiety and, 272
    unobtainable, 125

Ego (con't.)
  integrity, 96, 106, 183, 213, 333, 488
    contributed to by balance, 96
    maintained through bolstering intra-psychic mechanisms, 213; Repression, 33
  -*Maintaining Rationalization,* 254, 257
  mediates superego demands, 31, 256
  motives for actions, 259
  portion splits off in Dissociation, 97 ff.
  pressure on, repressed drives and, 272
  psychologically undoes intolerable, 429
  reparation sought by, 386
  -*Response in Regression, Law of Directly Proportional,* 477, 528
  -*Retreat,* 319, 343, 351
    Neuroses-Following-Trauma and, 343
    proportional to stress, 322, 352
    Regression equates, 319, 351
  seeks to resolve conflicts, 210
  serves as mediator, 256, 454
    in Compromise Formation, 454
    between superego and id, 256
  splitting of Dissociation and, 94 ff.
  Fenichel's theory, 76
  as *substitute target,* 182
  symbols aiding, 416
  -*synthesis,* 96, 106, 134, 183, 214, 333
    defensively-intended aim, 214
    Identification and, 96
    Introjection as, 183
    loved object, 134
    proper balance and, 96, 183
  threatened, potential derepression and, 228
  universality, 4 ff.
  withdrawal, in Regression, 322
EID (*Euphemistically-Intended Disguises*), 69
Elaboration, Self-Defense Concept in Dynamism, 97, 106
  superego and, 313, 328–29, 448
Equanimity, therapy and, 60
Elation, 60, 201–2
  Denial and, 60
  derepression and, 201–2
Electronics Analogy in Repression, 369, 379–80
Eleemosynary Rationalization, 256, 265 ff., 276
  absence of gain illusory, 266
  definition of, 265
  historical perspective in, 267
  Prisoner Processing and, 268
Elucidation. See also *Therapy.*
  conflict, 397
  Identification destructive, 153
  KDR helpful, 242
  Projection, 223

Elucidation (con't.)
  sexual patterns, 115
  symptoms unable to survive, 30
  Therapeutic, 223, 233
Embezzlement, *Restitution* in, 397
Emergencies, Deferment and, 456
Emotional
  Aggrandizement, alternative and de-
    scriptive term for Idealization,
    123
  Allergy, conflict and, 282, 283, 293
  Alliance, alternative and descriptive
    term for Identification, 133, 135
  Amalgam Concept, 367–68
  block, alternate term for psychologic
    blind-spot, 224
  charge, 367, 379
  complex reversed, 289
  Compromise, alternative and descrip-
    tive term for Compromise For-
    mation, 454, 468
    conflict, 9, 30, 37, 477
    avoidance of psychic pain, 4
    conversion of, 37
    Displacement and, 90
    guilt and, 440
    resolution, 9, 210, 491
      Fantasy and, 110, 113
    within psyche, 31
    Somatic Conversion and, 50
    universality, 4
  contagion, mobs and riots as, 140, 159
  crippling, *Parental Incorporation* and,
    169
  Decompensation, Regression and, 333,
    353
  Depression, Introjection and, 183
  detachment, *Isolation* and, 477
  diffusion, Generalization as, 471, 472–
    73
  Dynamisms, 209 ff. See also alternative
    terms of ego defenses and men-
    tal mechanisms.
  Engulfment, Incorporation and, 171
  equanimity, 9
  equilibrium, Regression and, 322
  Exploitation Concept, 171, 258
  extrusion, Projection and, 222
  Fatigue, 114, 340
    Regression and dependency conflict
      and, 114
    State, Fantasy Pattern in, 340
  health, 214
    Concept (*and Hypothesis*) *of Basic
      Trend Toward,* 34, 226, 347,
      354
    definition of, 217
    major role of
      Identification, 135
      Rechannelization, 317

Emotional (con't.)
  Regression, 321
  Repression, 358, 372, 374, 378
  repressed material in symbolic ex-
    pression, 422
  Identification, alternate term for *com-
    pathy,* 137, 138, 158
  illness, 137, 419–20
    bases of, rejected instincts and, 315
    contributed to by *Bad Identification,*
      148
    prejudice and, 216
    primary defenses in, 271
    Regression in, 337
    Repression and, 358, 372, 374, 378
    symbolic expression, 422
    term, preferred to "mental illness,"
      215
  impact, 102, 457
    avoidance of, through *Affect* Disso-
      ciation, 102
    Deferment of, 457
  *Manifestations, Principle of Increasing
    Complexity* in, 325, 352–53
  maturity, 324, 328, 351–53
    Denial and, 57
    Personal Yardstick and, 226
    preferable in marriage, 72
  -*Object Amalgam* (EOA), 192, 367–
    68, 379
    Chemical Analogy and, 380
    Distortion and, 458
    Isolation and, 476
    Symbolization and, 412, 421, 422
  overestimation, Idealization as, 123 ff.
  pain, Conversion of, 48
  phenomena, overdetermined, 477
  Postponement, 456–57
  priority of earlier impressions, 145,
    152, 154, 159, 237
  problems, intelligence and, 214
  -*psychic retreat,* alternative and de-
    scriptive term for Withdrawal,
    489
  reactions. See also individual entries,
    e.g., *Anxiety; Conversion Re-
    action; Depression.*
  recapitulations, Regressions as, 353.
    See also *Illness-Regression; Psy-
    chologic Recapitulation Route*
    (PRR); *Symptom-Identification.*
  reversal, 193, 203, 205
  Segregation, 453
  Sensitization Principle, 453
  significance, 94, 413, 422
    attachment to symbol, *EOA* and,
      413, 422
    Dissociation of, 94
  supplies, external, 125, 132, 331, 347
    gratification and, 331

Emotional (con't.)
  idealized object and, 125
  temporarily provided, 347
  symbiosis, between dynamisms, 64–65,
      90, 92, 180, 262, 410, 443
  cooperative interaction in *KDR,* 238
  Displacement and Substitution, 9,
      89, 90, 402, 404–5
  Idealization and Identification, 8, 125
  Inversion and Undoing, 204, 402,
      442
  Rationalization and *Distortion,* 459
  relationship as, 46
  Undoing and Denial, 437
  symptoms, as symbols, 420
  synthesis, Regression and, 322
  turnabout, alternate and descriptive
      term for Reversal, 486
Emotions, bases of illness, 216
Empathy, 136–38, 158
  definition of, 137
  essential attribute for successful psy-
      chotherapist, 138
  Projective Identification and, 136–38
Emulation encouraged by parents, 155
Endogain, 31, 49, 52, 125
  primary gain of:
      Conversion and, 31, 49, 52
      Idealization and, 125
Enemies, *literal incorporation* of, 164
Energy, excessively rechanneled, 304
Energy, Principle of Kinetic, 360, 379
  sexual, diverted, 299
Enforced Restitution, 389, 392–93, 399
  exacted by law, 389
  Public, 392, 399
Engineer, 231, 312
  Improvement Sublimation and, 312
  Negative Projection and, 231
Engulfment, 170–71, 195, 258
  Concept of, in interpersonal relation-
      ships, 170, 195, 258. See also
      Vicarious.
      Complex-Supportive Rationalization
          and, 258
      Incorporation and, 170
      Inversion and, 195
  Emotional, Incorporation and, 171
  Marital, 170–71
  Parental, 170
Enhancement, 26, 114, 115, 120, 134,
      458
  ego-, Identification and, 134
  Gratification, Sexual Fantasy-System
      and, 114, 115
  Public-Figure, Compensation and, 26
  Self, Aggrandizing *Distortion* and,
      458
Envy
  disowned, Rationalization and, 254

Envy (con't.)
  Displaced Complex and, 91
  homosexual, of female position, 306
  Mannerism Identification and, 142
  mild Regressions of childhood and,
      324
EOA. See *Emotional-Object Amalgam.*
Equanimity, 9, 60, 213, 307, 317, 404
  achieved through therapy, 60
  constructive contributions, 9
  parental, 169
  psychologic homeostasis as, 213
  Substitution and, 404
  vital role of *ego defenses* in, 9
Epidemic, psychologic, 140, 145. See
      also *Emotional Contagion.*
Epigain, 45, 49, 52
  definition of, 49
  of Somatic Conversion, 45, 49, 52
Equivalents, Affect-, 47, 52
ER (*Eleemosynary Rationalization*), 256,
      265 ff., 276
Erasure, 426, 427, 435, 436, 442, 443
  Dream-of-
      conviction reversed through, 435
      living sequence undone in, 436, 443
  Psychic, alternative term for Undoing
      and, 426 ff.
Erotic phase, 329
Escape, Conversion-, Somatic Conversion
      as, 48
Esteem-self, 33, 66, 214, 237, 243, 259,
      264, 273, 284
  Self-Maintenance Principle in Therapy,
      33
Estrangement, Generalization and, 474.
      See also *Depersonalization.*
Ethics, relaxation of, 266
Euphemistically-Intended Disguises, 69
Ewe Lamb Parable, 236–37, 248
Exaggeration of dynamisms, 221
Example held forth by parents, 155
Excessive Rechannelization of sexual
      drives, 304–5, 316
Executive, Fantasy of, 119
Executors, *Legacy Restitution* and, 397
Exhibitionism, 247, 306
  Positive King David Reaction and, 247
  Rechannelization and, 306
Experience
  sexual, 79, 139, 463
  vicarious, through *compathy,* 140
Expiative Undoing, 204, 431, 442
  definition of, 431
  emotional symbiosis between *Inversion*
      and Undoing leads to, 258
  Inversion occurring in, 442
Exploitation, Concept of Emotional, of
      child by parent, 258

Extension, 459, 460–61, 463, 471, 474
   Character Defense, 461
   Characterologic, 461–62
      Character Trait Balance and, 461
      scholastic handicap and, 462
   Complex, 461
   Cultural, superstitions and, 461
   definition of, 460
   Dependency, 462
   Distortion and, 459
   Dynamism-, 461
   Generalization and, 460, 471
   Phobic, 460
      hygeiaphrontis, 463
   Reaction, 461
   Regression in *Dependency,* 462
   Symptom, 461
   Tribal, 461
Extermination, *Social Rationalization*
   and, 268
External Emotional Supplies, 125, 132,
   331, 347
Externalization, 221, 462–64, 472
   Concept of Defensive Layering (DLC),
      472
   of fear by five-year-old, 463
   of internal conflict in phobia, 221
   in *phobic hygeiaphrontis,* 463
   psychodynamics, 463
Extramarital sexual experience, Denial
   of censorship of, 79

Facade, outer, 175, 247
Face-saving
   avoided during therapy, 45
   Ego Enhancing Inversion and, 200
   Rationalization and, 200, 263
Fact, Criminals-in-, 430, 442
Faculties, intellectual, *Unwitting Igno-*
   rance and, 489
Failure of defenses, 211
Fainting, 43, 95, 98, 464–65, 467–68
   Comparative Data, 98
   Conversion Personality and, 43
   defensive shutting off of perception, 464
   definition of, 464
   Dissociation and, 43, 98, 464
Fairbairn, 164, 176
Falling in love, Idealization and, 126
Falret, Jean-Pierre, 427
False pregnancy, 70
Falsification, Retrospective, 486
Familial Rationalization, equal treatment
   of children, 256, 269–70
Fantastic Person, 125–26, 130, 221, 233
   Idealization and, 125
   Projection and, 221, 233
Fantasy, 56, 58, 109 ff., 375, 379, 402
   adolescent, 111

Fantasy (con't.)
   aggression and, 116
   bases of, 109 ff.
   childhood, 57, 111, 112, 120, 442, 443
   Constructive, 109, 112–13, 120
   definition of, 110
   Denial-in-, 57, 76, 111
      in adulthood, 76
      in childhood, 57
      Melanie Klein's treatment of, 111
   Denial of reality, 57, 80
   Dissociative Splitting and, 116, 488
   dreams and, 116
   drugs and, 119
   Iceberg Analogy, 109, 117
   of infant, expectations of, 223
   infantile, Incorporation and, 164
   intercourse, 118
   latent content, 112, 117, 120
   Lesson-Function, 116, 120
   -Life, Adolescent, 111
   of lost loved one, 187
   manifest content, 112, 117, 120
   nature of, 109
   Non-Constructive, 112–13
   object, mouse as, 186
   -*Pattern,* 112 ff.
      in dependency and hostility, 114
      in dreams, 116
      recurrence of, 117
      systematized, 112
   Primary Repression and, 111, 363, 373
   psychologic flight and, 119
   Repression maintenance and, 114, 120
   resistance in therapy and, 118
   Restitution as meaningful theme, 396
   retreat and, 119
   romantic, 115
   sexual and aggressive urges and, 110,
      114 ff.
   Somatic Conversion and, 113
   Splitting-in-, 115, 488
   substitute gratifications, 112, 114
   -*System,* 113 ff.
   Unconscious, universal in childhood,
      110–11, 120
   -*Undoing,* in child, 442, 443
   Unhealthful, 113, 114, 120
   wish fulfillment in, 112
Fashion changes, *Mass Identification*
   and, 145
Father relationship, *Sexual-Object Dis-*
   placement and, 89
Fatigue, 114, 170, 332, 340, 342, 409
   Emotional, Regression and dependency
      conflict and, 340
   overwhelming in Schizophrenic Reac-
      tion, 409
   parental attitudes toward, 170

Fatigue (con't.)
  State, 114, 342
    regressive trends in, 342
Faulty Identification, 135
Fear, 21, 168, 187, 210, 242, 462
  compensation for, 21
  externalized in phobia, 462
  Fantasy of oral pregnancy and, 187
  freedom, from mother and, 168
  King David Reaction (KDR) and, 242
  response to external danger, 210
Feelings inverted, 183
Feelings of unreality, Depersonalization
  as, 103
Femininity, *Secondary Appeal in Adver-*
  tising (SAAC) and, 149
Fenichel, 76, 178, 190
  ego splitting theory in neurosis, 76
  on Identification, 178
  Introjection distinguished from Incor-
    poration, 190
Field, Eugene, 77
Figurative
  digestion, Incorporation as, 166
  Incorporation, mother as subject for,
    165, 168
  ingestion, Incorporation as, 165
  Introjection, 188
  into literal, 30, 47, 52
    conversion manifestations, 30, 47
    Figures of speech as, 52, 188
Figures
  entertainment, *Mass Identification* and,
    145
  Public, -Identification (PFI), 159
  of speech, 52, 166
Fire Drill, 469–71
  as preparation for emergencies, 470
  response pattern as, 470
  tie-in with Identification, 471
Fire, psychic, 470
First Line of Psychic Defense, 49, 358,
  378
  in Conversion, 49
  dynamisms represent, 358
Fixation, 334 ff., 353
  Permanent, 335, 337, 353
  Semi-Permanent, 335 ff., 353
Flaubert, Gustave, Madame Bovary's
  fantasies and, 115
Flesh pleasures, Reversal and, 487
Flight, psychologic, 43, 95, 105, 119, 331
  Dissociation and Dissociative Stages
    as, 95, 105
  Fantasy as, 119
  Motor Conversion and, 43
  Regression as, 331
Flight-to-the-Physical, Conversion as, 11
Forgetting, automatic, 378

Forgiveness, 448, 451
  Absolution and, 448
  Atonement-Penance and, 451
Formation
  Characterologic, Reaction Formation,
    281
  Compromise, 41, 333, 454–55
    Partial, 454
    Unsuccessful, 454
  delusion, in Denial, 73, 77
  Reaction, 279 ff. See also *Reaction
    Formation.*
  symptom, failure of defenses and, 10
Fortune, conflicts and, 398
FP. See *Fantastic Person.*
Fragmental Dissociation, Fainting as,
  464
Free association, 377–78, 416
  analytic therapy and, 377
  dream interpretation and, 416
Freud, Sigmund, 30, 33, 194, 361–63,
  379, 427
  Conversion concept and, 30
  Repression concept and, 361–62
  term of inversion used as dissimulation
    of hostile affect, 194
Freudian inversion, 194
Friendliness feigned, *Social Inversion*
  and, 195
Friends, Group Compathy and, 140
Frustration
  Displacement of, 86
  Internalization of objects and, 176
FSPC (*Functional-Structural Progression
  Concept*), 10, 52
Fugue States, 95 ff., 477
*Functional-Structural Progression Con-
  cept, primary, secondary* and
    tertiary changes in, 10, 52
Function
  Dissociation of, 96
  Idealization, 125
  intended, of dynamisms, 212
Functional expression of conflict in Phy-
  siologic Conversion, 50
Functioning, emergency, *Deferment* and,
  456
Funeral plans, Omission Denial and, 79

Gain, 31, 36, 49, 52, 125, 266
  absence of, in *Eleemosynary Rationali-
    zation,* 266
  Conversion symptoms, 36, 49
  endogain, 31, 49, 52, 86, 125
  epigain, 36, 45, 49, 52
  illusory, 32
Gardening, *Rechannelization* and, 309
Gauge, Regression-, 337, 345, 354
  in emotional illness, 337

Gauge (con't.)
neurotic vs. psychotic reaction and, 345
GE (*Gratification Enhancement*), 114–15, 120
Generalization, 460, 471 ff.
Anti-Authority, 473
Attitudinal, 473
Defensive Layering Concept (DLC) and, 472
definition of, 471
as *Emotional Diffusion,* 471, 472, 473
Extension and, 460, 471
Personal Yardstick and, 474
women, of feelings to include all, 472
General Symbol, 413, 415, 422
conveys wide meaning, 413
no limit to formation, 422
required in communication, 415
Genital stage, 329
Genocide, *Social Rationalization* and, 268
Gifts, Restitution and, 395
Glory, Basking in Reflected-, 144, 158
Goal(s), 377
blocked, *Rechannelization* and, 299
Devaluation, 259–60
direction, 112, 303
-Inversion, 201, 205
psychotherapeutic, 377
substitution of, 405, 410
unobtainable
downgraded through *Retrospective Devaluation,* 484
replaced through Substitution, 402
Gracious living, *Secondary Appeal in Advertising* and, 149
"Grandfather's Clock," 77
Grandiose Projection, major subtype of *Psychotic Projection,* 230, 232, 234
Grandiosity in paranoid reaction, 231–32
Gratification
Dependency, 347, 348–49
of disowned interests, 148
-Enhancement, 114, 115, 120
in impulsions and perversions, 115
in *Sexual Fantasy-System,* 114
Fantasy and, 110, 114, 115
neurotic, 198, 200, 252
Inversion and, 198
Rationalization and, 200
partial, Fantasy and, 110
patterns, Denial and, 79
readoption of infantile modes and, 322
Regression to era of most, 331
sexual, Fantasy and, 115–16, 120
splitting, 115–16, 121, 488
substitute, in Fantasy, 112

Gratification (con't.)
Substitutive, *Vicarious Identification* and, 151–52, 159
Great Imitator, Conversion as, 43–44
Gregariousness, 150
Grief, 165
Grief-Stricken Denial, 78, 82
Group(s), 19–20, 26, 139, 150–51, 160, 268–69
Compathy, 139, 140
Compensation, 19–20, 26
Identification, 150, 151, 160
contributing factors, 150
Rationalizations in, 151
motives leading to Social Rationalization, 268–69
Guidepost Dream, 417–19, 422
initial attitudes toward therapy and, 196, 418, 419
special value in therapy, 417, 422
Guilt, 9, 178, 263, 386, 429–30
abortion and, Undoing after, 433
absolved through *Absolution,* 448
Childhood Undoing and, 428, 432
Denial as defense, 69
disclaimed, 100–01
Dream-of-Regret reflects, 396, 399
Fantasy of oral pregnancy and, 187
feelings, 114, 274, 391, 397, 439
absolved through Rationalization, 274
blasphemous thoughts, *Symbolic Undoing* and, 439
Fantasy-Pattern and, 114
neurotically exaggerated, 391
parental disapproval, earlier, relation to, 169
success and, Restitution easing, 397
Restitutive-Behavior for, 391
Group Dynamisms, 387, 449, 450, 483–84
Absolution, 450
Atonement-Penance, 450
Restitution, 387
Retribution, 483
Undoing, 450
Introjection satisfying, 190
King David Reaction (KDR) and, 242
masturbation and, 407
paranoid delusions and, 69
Projection of, in *King David's Anger,* 243
prominent effects invoking restitutive endeavors, 390, 398
reparative endeavors for, 398
Restitution assuaging, 387
Social Restitution, 394
sexual, 452–53
social pressure and, 398
Spurious Confessions and, 147

Guilt (con't.)
   Suspended Reaction follows, 397, 399
   washed away in *Symbolic Undoing*, 440
   widespread, emotional conflicts and, 440
Gustave Flaubert, 115
"Guys and Dolls," emotional into physical miseries in, 47

Hair, *Atonement-Penance* and, 453
"Halfway house," Reaction Formation as, 290
Hallucinations, 57, 69, 102, 114, 186, 222, 230, 449
   Absolution and, 448–49
   Denial and, 57, 69
   from dissociated segments of psyche, 102
   Fantasy and, 114
   Projection and, 22, 232
Hamlet, 124, 240
   King David's Anger and, 240
   Literary Idealization and, 124
Handicap, Denial as, 75
Hand-in-Glove Concept, 171
Handwashing compulsion, 430, 440
   as intended Undoing, 430
   as *Symbolic Undoing*, 440
Handwriting change, *Partial Introjection* and, 188
Hangover Paradox, 431, 442
Hartmann, Eduard von, 362
Hatred
   disowned through *Displaced Complex*, 91
   diverted through Substitution, 403
   experienced as coming from external person, 183
   of self, Projection of, in *King David Reaction*, 239
Hazard
   in Idealization, 127
   Personal Invulnerability in, 478
Headaches
   Conversion, 35, 51, 340
   Denial of past events and, 63
   fear suppression and, 47
Health. See also *Emotional health.*
   parental attitudes and, 170
Heartache, *affect-equivalent* and, 47
Hemiparesis, Compromise Formation and, 41
Herbart, Johann F., 361
Herd instinct, 150
Hero worship, 126, 127
   Fantastic Person and, 126
   Shattered Ideal and, 127
Heterosexual Stage in adulthood, 329

Higher Order Defenses (H.O. dynamisms; H.O. ego defenses; H.O. mental mechanisms), 12–14, 256, 313, 315, 401
   Absolution as, 448
   compensation as, 13
   definition of, 12
   Identification as, 135
   Intellectualization as, 13, 476
   Introjection as, 182
   Neuroses, 14
   Projection, 13
   Rationalization as, 13, 251
   Rechannelization as, 13, 297, 311
   Restitution as, 13, 387
   Retribution as, 483
   Retrospective Devaluation as, 484
   Substitution as, 483
Higher Order Neuroses, 14
Historical perspective, *Eleemosynary Rationalization* in, 267
Historical Validation, 248, 267, 281, 316, 378
   King David Reaction and, 240
   Projection and, 226
   Rechannelization and, 301
   Repression and, 361
HOD. See *Higher Order Dynamisms.*
Holy, misdeeds regarded as, 267
Homeostasis, 213
Homosexuality
   Attraction-Inversion in, 196
   conversion, 39
   intrusions about, Replacement of, 483
   latent, *King David Reaction* and, 245
   obsessive preoccupation with, 406
   Projection of, 233
   Reaction Formation against, 291
   Repression, *Rechannelization* and, 306
   Reversal and, 488
   as *Sexual Inversion*, 194
Honesty
   inconsistent, Restitution and, 389
   super, as overcompensation, 25
Hostility, 91, 167, 184, 409, 435, 487
   Conversion into headaches, 30
   Displacement of, to *Convenient Target*, 88
   Fantasy-Pattern of, 114
   to father, Fantasies and, 118
   instructor toward students, Rationalization of, 273
   Introjection and, 186
   Inversion, 195, 204
   Reaction Formation and, 282, 284, 292
   Replacement and, 480, 483
   Repression of
      Acute Anxiety Attack and, 376
      Reaction Formation and, 284
   transference, Fantasies and, 118–19

Hostility (con't.)
underlying, Projection of, 222
underscored, repetitive telephoning and, 437
to women, sexual relations and, 432–33
Housewife
Identification with movie star and, 146
pseudoepileptic, *Behavioral* Conversion and, 40
Sensory Conversion and, 45
Humor, 80, 457
Denial-of-Death and, 80
Devaluation and, 457
Hungarians, *Underdog Identification* and, 157
HVC. See *Historical Validation.*
Hygeiaphrontis, 170, 436
Counterirritant Substitution in, 406
Identification in *symptom choice,* 156
Personal Invulnerability Defense and, 478
Personality, 342
Pessimistic, 479
phobic, 463–64
regressive implications, 339, 342
Somatic Preoccupation in, 343
Hypertrophy
Characterologic, *Principle of,* 18, 26
of ego defenses
character and functional neurosis and, 217
contributing to pathology, 183, 211
effects of, ego destruction and, 96
Functional-Structural Progression and, 10, 52
psychic, Fantasy and, 113
Hypnosis
Dissociative Reactions and, 98
Rationalization and, 253, 256, 275
Regression levels and, 341
Hypochondriasis, 184, 342
Hypothesis, Attention, 9

Iceberg Analogy, Fantasy and, 109, 117
Id, 91, 252, 256, 303, 454–55
gratification of inner needs, 256
Intrapsychic Reversal of repressed impulses, 288
Rechannelization of drives, 303. See also Instinctual drives.
and superego, ego as mediator, 454–55
ID (*Impact Deferment*), 457
Ideal, 125 ff.
Object-, 127 ff.
Relationship-, 128, 131
Shattered-, 125, 127, 130
unacceptable aspects of, 125
Unobtainable-, 127

Idealization, 80, 123 ff., 188, 263, 274–75, 458
Characterologic, 130, 131
definition of, 123
Denial and, in *Marital Idealization,* 80, 129
Distortion similar to, 458
emotional overestimation as alternative term, 123
endogain of, 125
Fantastic Person and, 125, 130
Impossible Standard and *Unobtainable Ideal,* 126
Internal Psychologic Functions, 125
legends and, 263
Literary, 124, 130
Marital, 80, 128, 129, 131
National, 128, 131
Object-, 127–28, 130–31
Oedipal, 124, 125, 130
aggressive drives and, 125
resolution of Oedipal conflicts, and, 124
Parental, 124, 125
Partial Introjection and, 188
relation of
to Rationalization, 128, 274–75
instinctual processes and, 274–75
overvalued personal possession and, 128
to *Soterial formation,* 128
self-defeat of, 125
Social, 128, 131
Substitute, 129, 131
Teen-Age, 127, 130
Idealized
image, surrender of, 127, 130
object, 125
person, 125, 126, 130
becomes *Fantastic Person,* 126, 130
placed on pedestal, 125
Ideation, affect divorced from
through Dissociation, 106
through *Isolation,* 476
Identification, 133 ff., 273
Actor, 136, 158
Acute Anxiety Attack and, 376. See also *Recapitulation, Psychologic.*
Affective, compathy as alternate term for, 136 ff., 158
Aggressor, 159
Bad, as socially non-constructive, 148, 159
Basking-in-Reflected Glory and, 144, 158
Central, 136, 140, 158
Characterologic, 134, 142, 143, 159
attributes acquired through, 134
conscious trait adoption and, 142
personality development and, 143

Identification (con't.)
 Childhood, 159
 Compathic, in dramas or novels, 137,
  140, 160
 conscious, as imitation, 135
 Criminal, 146–47, 159
  Spurious Confession and, 146–47,
   159
 definition of, 135
 Emotional Alliance, alternative term
  for, 133, 135, 158
 Emotional, term for *compathy* and
  Affective Identification, 137 ff.,
  150
 Faulty, 135
 Fire Drill and, 471
 Group, 150–51
  an important security operation, 151
 as *Higher Order Dynamism*, 135
 Idealization and, 125
 Incorporation and, 165, 169–70
 Individual, 133 ff.
 Instinctual Diversion restriction, 303
 Internalization and, 178
 Interpersonal, 153 ff.
  clarified in psychotherapy, 154
  major effects, 153, 159
  Rule of Impression Priority applies,
   152, 154, 159
  succeeds *Parental Identification*, 155
 with introject, psychosis and, 186
 King David Reaction and, 237, 241,
  242
  as major dynamism, 237
  Projection and, 242
 limited capacity for, 303
 love-object, 96
 Mannerism, 141–42, 158
 Mass, communication media and, 144–
  45, 159
 Military-Unit, 149, 150, 159
 Misidentification, 135, 159, 160
 operation of, therapy and, 154
 Parental, 148, 155–56, 159, 160
  succeeded by Interpersonal Identification, 155
 Partial Introjection and, 188
 Personal Yardstick and, 146, 152–53,
  159
 plays major role
  in emotional health, 135
  in popularity of legends, 263
 Predecessor, 140, 141, 158
  personality development and, 140,
   158
  serves social purpose, 141
 Projection and, 146, 222
  distinguished from, 146
  kindly attitudes and, 222

Identification (con't.)
 Projective, 136–38, 141, 158, 222
  occupying another's shoes and, 222
  rapport, sympatico, sympathy and
   empathy as categories of, 137–
   38
 Psychotic, 156–57, 159, 160
 Public-Figure, 144–45, 159
 raison d'être of ego defense, 133, 151
  Blake on, 133
  unconscious gain equating, 151
 rapport established, 137
 Rechannelization and, 303
 Secondary Appeal in Advertising, 149,
  159
 Symptom, 46, 50, 51, 156, 160, 190
  Conversion Reaction and, 46, 50, 51
  Hygeiaphrontis (hypochondriasis),
   156
 tacit, in advertising, *Primary* and *Sec-
  ondary Appeal*, 149, 159
 Underdog, 157–58, 160
 Vicarious, 152, 159
 Vocational, 145, 159
 with *Wrong Doer*, secret wishes and,
  147, 159
Ignorance, Unwitting, 489
Illness, 62, 73 ff., 457
 Deficit, 23, 26
 Denial, 62, 73–75, 82, 457
  cancer and, 73
  Devaluation a way station, 457
  terminal illness and, 74
 emotions as bases, 216
 Regression, 329–30, 353. See also
  *Symptom-Compathy; Symptom
  Identification;* PRR.
 terminal, 74, 77
Illusion-of-Continued-Living, 76–77, 78,
  82
Illusory
 aim of Denial, 76
 gain, 113, 266
  Eleemosynary Rechannelization and,
   266
  Unhealthful Fantasy and, 113
Image, idealized, surrender of, 127, 130
Imitation
 conscious Identification, 135
 deliberate copying, 141
Imitator, Great, 44
Impact, emotional, 102, 457
 Affect Dissociation and, 102
 Deferment of, 457
"Important" people, *Reflected-Glory* and,
  144
Impossible Standard, 126
Impotence, 22, 305, 433
 Behavioral Undoing Cycle and, 433

Impotence (con't.)
Compensation for, through powerful motors, 22
Excessive Rechannelization and, 305
Impression-Priority, Rule of, 154, 159
definition of, 145
earlier impressions and interpersonal relationships, 152, 237
Substitute Idealization and, 129
Impropriety, Denial of, 65, 84
Improvement Rechannelization, 310–12, 317
maturation during therapy, 312
prognosis and, 310, 317
psychosis and, 311
Impulses
aggressive, Introjection and, 186
expressed, as *body language,* 43
hidden, 375
ignorance maintained, 39
repressed, Conversion and, 43
reversed, *Reaction Formation* and, 288
sexual, 43, 299–300, 316
defended against, 43
Rechannelization and, 299–300, 316
violent, *Criminal Identification* and, 147
voyeuristic, 243–44
Impulsions, *Gratification Enhancements* and, 115
Inattention, *Unwitting Ignorance* and, 489
Incest, *Sexual-Object Displacement* and, 89, 489
Incomplete
Compartmentalization, 454, 468
Dynamism Defense, 22, 28
Introjection, 187–88
Rechannelization, 310, 316
Repressions, 377
Sublimation, 310, 316
Symptom Defense, anxiety and, 22, 44, 55
Inconsistency, emotional, Compartmentalization and, 454
Incorporation, 69, 163 ff., 175
Conflict Indicator (CI) and, 170
criteria for, 166
Engulfment Concept and, 170–72, 253, 258
marital and *parental,* 171
Identification and, 165, 170
implied recognition, in figures of speech, 166
importance of
diathesis of Conversion Personality, 69, 170
personality development and, 168
superego development and, 166
Infantile, 166

Incorporation (con't.)
Internalization, in similarity of problems, 175
knowledge and, 172
Literal, 164–65
cannibalism, 164–65
infant suckling of food, 164
Lower Order defense, 163
oral, 164, 165, 166
Painful reality, defense against, 172
Parental, 168, 169–70
constructive, 168
personal standards and, 169
Psychic Ingestion and *Assimilation,* alternate terms for, 163, 166
Psychotic, 170
Regression to, 166, 170
rivalry and hostility in children and, 167
Incorporative Learning, 172
Increasing Complexity of Dreams, Law of, 418–19, 422
Increasing-Complexity Principle, 325, 352
Indicator, Regressive-, undue pressure and, 326, 353
Indicators, Conflict, 38, 170, 325, 327, 330
Acute Forms of Conversion Behavior, 38
incorporative trends and, 170
mild Regressions of childhood, 325, 327, 330
Specific Emotional Hazards of Childhood, 327
Indifference
Excessive Rechannelization and, 304–05
Paranoid, 103, 230–31
Diffuse, Projection, 230, 231
impending destructive events and, 103, 234
Relationship-Replacement and, 482
Individual
Compathy, 139, 158
Psychology, Adler and, 25
Symbol, 413, 415, 422
significance of individual, 413, 415
Symbolization and, 422
Ineffective Rationalization, 284, 397, 399
Ineffective Rechannelization, 310, 317
Ineffectual Compromise Formation, 454
Ineffectual (or Judas) Confession, 429, 442, 444
Infant, oral incorporative attitude normal for, 166
Infantile
Incorporation, 166
patterns, *Massive* or *Complete Regressions* and, 345
Period, 329

Inferiority
    Complex, 25–26
    subjectively evaluated, 17 ff.
Ingestion
    Figurative, Literal Incorporation and,
        165
    Literal, 165
    Psychic, as term for Incorporation,
        163, 166
Inhibition
    of actions, 38–39
    overprotectiveness and, 459
    Socio-Sexual Dilemma and, 72
Inquisition, *Eleemosynary Rationalization*
        and, 267
Insecurity, 41. See also *Security.*
Insight, 118, 202, 212, 242, 408
    complex elucidation, 242
    deficiency, depression and, 202
    Fantasy and, 118
    self-understanding and, 169–70
    sought, as goal of therapy, 212
Instinct
    moral judgment of, 298
    reversal, Reaction Formation and, 288
Instinctual, 188, 287, 296 ff., 379
    Diversion, Rechannelization (Sublima-
        tion) as term for, 296 ff., 316
    drives
        ego dissociative effects, 213
        expression through *Rechanneliza-*
            tion, 297, 298, 308–9
        threatening Repression, 272
        Victorian Repression of, 314
    impulses, Reaction Formation and,
        287
    interest in dirt, 288
    material, comprising *Primary Repres-*
        sion, 363
    vicissitudes, 315
Insulation, Psychologic, 490
Insurance program, *Omission Denial* and,
        80
Integration of ego, Dissociation and, 96,
        105, 217, 488. See also *Ego;*
        Synthesis.
Integrity, ego, 96, 105–6, 183, 213, 333
Intellectualization, 13, 274, 474–76
    Characterologic, 475
    as *Higher Order dynamism,* 476
    Rationalization akin to, 274, 475
    Rechannelization akin to, 475
    Repression reenforced, 476
    Resistance-, in therapy, 475
    -Respite in intensive therapy, 475
Intellectualized Retreat from interper-
        sonal relationships, 476
Intelligence, 45, 93–94, 145, 218
    correlation of, with ego defenses, 214,
        215

Intelligence (con't.)
    Illness Denial and, 73–74
    limitations, emotional illness and, 215–
        16
    Somatic Conversion and, 45
    Vocational Identification and, 145
Intensive psychotherapy. See also *Analy-*
        sis.
    Interpersonal Identification and, 154
    Scapegoat Reaction and, 48
Intercourse, sexual
    fantasied, insight and, 118
    forbidden, *Replacement* and, 483
Interest Absorption defense (Attention
        Absorption d.), 460
Interest
    deflected through Diversion
        sexual, 305–6
        withdrawal in Hygeiaphrontis, 342
Internal compromise, 251 ff. See also
        Compromise Formation.
Internalization, 69, 174 ff.
    attitudinal, 174, 178, 179
    Characterologic, 174–75, 179
    Identification and Projection similarity
        to, 178
    of image, hallucinations and, 69
    Incorporation and Introjection akin to,
        176
    as *Major* or *senior dynamism,* 174
    nature and definition of, 174
    personality development and, 176
    postural attitudes taken over, 176–77
    superego and, 177
    in *Triad of "taking in" Ego Defenses,*
        174
Interpersonal. See also *Relationship(s).*
    Identification, 153–54, 159
        major effects of, 153, 159
        succeeds *Parental Identification,* 155
    Projection, Vicious Circle and, 229,
        234
    relationships
        Hand-in-Glove Concept, 171
        Impression Priority Rule, 152
        Intellectualized Retreat, 476
        Interpersonal Identification, 153
        Personal Yardstick and, 153
        Undoing, 441–43
        vicarious experience in, 151
    Restitution, 390, 392, 398
        amends for wrongs on another, 390
        comprising *Minor,* 398
        sought in any relationship, 392
Interpretation
    dream, 416, 419
        condensation, convergence and sym-
            bolism in, 416
        disadvantageous, if premature, 419

Interpretation (con't.)
  premature, *Resistance-Undoing* and,
    437
  Tenet of Variable-, 420
Intrapsychic
  conflict, 16
  Reversal, Reaction Formation as, 288,
    293
  transference, alternate term for Dis-
    placement, 86
Introject, 182 ff.
  depressive-, object-person in, 183–84,
    190
  as object figuratively taken in, 182–83,
    191
  oral, 186–87, 189, 191
  primordial, 189, 191
  symptom-, 185–86, 190
Introjection, 68, 176, 181 ff., 221
  definition of, 181–82
  Denial and, 68, 69, 187
  Depression and, 182–84, 190
  as *Higher Order dynamism,* 182
  Identification with object, 186
  Incomplete (or Partial), 187–88, 191
  Internalization, 176
  Major Distinguishing Features of, 182
  in marriage, love instinct and, 188
  Partial (or Incomplete), 187–88, 191
  product of conception as oral, 186–87,
    191
  Projection converse of, 182, 183, 190,
    222
  Psychodynamics of, 189
  Psychotic, poorly or only partially con-
    cealed, 186, 190
  Regression leading to earlier, 189–90
  Scapegoat Reaction and, 182
  substitute target and, 182
  suicide and, 184, 190
  superego development and, 189, 191
  Symptom-, 184 ff., 190
  in *Triad of "taking in" Ego Defenses,*
    190
  Visceral Masochism and, 185
Introversion, Withdrawal and, 490
Inversion, 8, 65, 193 ff., 294, 431
  Affect, 145, 204, 401
  Attitude, 201, 205
  Attraction, sexual urges and, 196, 204
  Character trait development and, 200
  Characterologic, 198, 200, 205
  definition of, 194
  delineation criteria and, 203
  Denial relationship to, 65
  Depressive Personality and, 200–01
  Ego-Enhancing, 200, 205
  Distortions produced by, 199, 204

Inversion (con't.)
  Emotional Reversal, as alternate term,
    193, 203
  Engulfment Concept and, 195
  of exhibitionism, in *Positive King
    David Reaction,* 247
  Expiative Undoing and, 442
  Goal-, blocked, 201, 205
  Hostility-, 195, 204
  Memory-, White-Washing Operation
    and, 197, 204
  as mental mechanism, 8
  Mood-, 201–3, 205
    depression into elation, 201
    insight deficient in, 202–3
    major in extent, 202
  Positive Affect, 195, 196, 204
  Rationalization and, 200
  Reaction Formation and, 203, 205,
    289
  Resistance-, defends *neurotic status
    quo,* 198–99, 205
  Retrospective Devaluation akin to, 197
  Reversal and, 205, 486
  Secondary Defense Concept in, 199,
    205
  as *secondary elaboration* and reen-
    forcement of Repression or De-
    nial, 195–96, 204
  Sexual, 194
  of sleep habits, 193
  Social, 194–95, 204
  Standards-, sexual behavior and, 197,
    204
  symbiosis, emotional, with *Undoing,*
    204
Inverted feelings, 183, 194–95, 204
Invulnerability, Personal, 60, 63, 478–
    79
  Concept of, Denial supporting, 60, 63
  effectiveness enhanced by, 478
  hygeiaphrontis converse of, 478
  Investment, Libidinal, 305, 317
  self viewed as indestructible, 478–79
IPR *(Impression-Priority Rule),* 145,
    152, 154, 159, 237
IR (Intellectualized Retreat), 476
ISD *(Incomplete Symptom Defense),* 22,
    44, 55
Isolation, 199, 476–77, 479, 488
  of affect component of *Emotional-Ob-
    ject Amalgam,* 476
  Dissociation akin to, 477
  negative transference and, 199
  Repression relaxed by, 477
  Splitting and, 488

Janet, Pierre, dissociation introduced as
    term by, 96, 106, 362

Janet Concept, alternate term for Personality Dissociation, 96, 106, 362

Jealousy, 81, 245, 487

Denial of, 81

subconscious, *Negative King David Reaction* and, 245

Jews, slaughtering of, condoned through *Collective* or *Social Rationalization* and, 268

Joining, Group Identification and, 150

Judas Confession, alternate term for *Ineffectual Confession,* 429, 442, 444

Instinctual Diversion restriction, 303

Collective Rationalization and, 256, 268–69, 276

Rationalization going beyond, 263

Unconscious, as major intrapsychic function, and alternate term for Rationalization, 251 ff.

widespread, 276

KDA. See *King David's Anger.*

KDR. See *King David Reaction.*

Kinetic-Energy Principle (KEP), 312, 360, 373, 374

definition of, 360

Repression maintenance and, 312, 373, 374

King David Reaction (KDR), 222, 225, 236 ff., 275, 301

attractions inexplicable in, 236

combination of dynamisms in, 237

definition of, 238

Denial operative in, 237, 244

Identification and, 241

literary instances of, in Shakespeare, 240–41, 248

Hamlet's reaction to Claudius, 240–41

Historical Validation, 240, 248

Nathan device, 240

masochism and self-defeat in, 246, 247

Mirror-Defense Concept and, 246

Narcissus Reaction in, 246, 248

Nathan's Parable in, 236

Negative, 238–39, 241, 243–44, 248

anger marking, 238. See also *King David's Anger.*

definition of, 239

Identification and Projection stimulating, 241

rejection of others and, 243

violence fostered, 244

Personal Yardstick misleading in, 246–47

King David Reaction (con't.)

Positive, 238, 245–47

definition of, as *Royal Affection* or *Love,* 238

exhibitionism in, 247

latent homosexuality in, 245, 246

masochistic pattern in, 247

profanity criticized in, 225

Projection in, 222

Rule of Impression Priority (RIP) and, 237, 248

Scapegoat Reaction and, 238, 249

self-appraisal projected, 236, 239, 241, 248

therapeutic elucidation of, 242

King David's Anger, 238 ff., 248

behavior influenced by, 244

elucidation of, 242

Identification and Projection leading to, 241

as *Negative King David Reaction,* 239

in overcompensation of combat hero, 242

in physician's disgust toward strangers, 243

as Projection of intolerable self-picture, 239

in Shakespeare's Hamlet, 240

Kissing, adolescent fears of, 187

Klein, Melanie, 76, 111, 177, 189

Denial-in-Fantasy study, 76, 111

infant introjects described by, 189

superego of child observed by, 177

Knowledge, in Incorporative Learning, 172

Korsakoff's syndrome, 24

La belle indifférence, 41, 45, 69, 103, 305

in *Behavioral Conversion,* 41

disinterest in *Excessive Rechannelization* and, 305

Paranoid Indifference and, 103

in Somatic Conversion, 45

first noticed by Charcot, 69

La Grippe as affect equivalent, 47

Lamb, Parable of the Ewe, 236, 248

Language, 33, 37, 42, 51, 419

Autonomic, 32, 54

behavioral, conversion of conflict and, 33, 37, 42

body, 33, 52

conversion, 31, 33, 51

physiologic, 33

preverbal, 33, 51

psychologic, 33

somatic, 31

symbolic, Tenet of Variable-Interpretation in, 419

Latent
Content, 112, 117, 417–18
in dreams, *Multiple Symbolization* in, 417–18
of Fantasy, Manifest Content and, 112, 117, 120
object of hostility, father as, 119
Period (also Latent Phase), 313, 329
Eight Major Stages of Man, 329
Sublimation (*Rechannelization*) reaching peak in, 313
Law
career, *Rechannelization* and, 308
civil, *Absolution* in, 448
criminal, *Enforced Restitution* and, 389
enforcement officials, aware of *Spurious Confessions,* 147
of increasing Complexity of Dreams, 418–19, 422
of Maturation (or *Maturity*); Fixation and Regression as interruptions to *Tidal-Progression* in, 335, 353
process of, *Public Restitution* and, 398
Proportional Ego-Response, Regression and, 322, 352
of Scientific Determinism, 393
Talion, 399
of Universal Affect, 99, 366–67, 379
definition, Repression and, 366–67
objects' emotional charge and, 379
Lawyer
Marital Engulfment and, 171
Symptom-Replacement of cough with backache and, 480
Vocational Rechannelization of maternal instincts and, 308
Layering, Concept of Defensive-, 391, 395, 399, 472
Leaning over backward, Reaction Formation as, 293
Learning, 145, 148, 159, 166, 172, 489
Bad Identifications and, 148
Incorporative, level of, 172
Unwitting Ignorance and, 489
viewed incorporatively, 166
Vocational Identification and, 145
Legacy Restitution, 397–98, 399
Lesson-Function, Fantasy, 116, 120
Liberal father, Reaction Formation against, 286
Libidinal-Investment in Therapy, 304–5, 317
Libido, 125, 298–99, 304–5, 317
Life course, *Characterologic Identification* and, 142–43, 146
Life work, *Vocational Identification* and, 145

LITP (*Libidinal Investment in Therapy, Principle of*), 304–5, 317
Literal
Incorporation, 164–65
of aphrodisiac, 165
cannibalism as, 164–65
infant suckling of food as, 164
Ingestion, alternate term for *Literal Incorporation,* 165
"Little Boy Blue," *Denial-of-Death* in, 77
Literary, 124, 301–2, 361
Idealization, 124
references, 301–2, 361
HVC
Plutarch's Lives, 61
Szu-Ma Chien, 302
Uriah Heep, 281
"Little Boy Blue," 77
Projection (Duchess of Malfi), 225
Rationalization
Aesop, 260
Robin Hood, 263
to Shakespeare, 24, 240, 440
Living, Illusion-of-Continued-, 76–77, 78, 82
Logic, Denial of, 199
Longevity, insured, *literal incorporation* and, 165
Loneliness, *Isolation* and, 477
Loss
Antidotal Substitution and, 407, 410
Denial of, in SEHC, 71
Love
affairs, *Sexual-Object Displacement* and, 89
daydreams and, 114–15
emotion of, *King David Reaction* and, 239
instinct, 188
lost, *Relationship-Displacement* and, 481
-object, *Replacement* of, Idealization and, 125
Denial and, 127
Lover retained through Introjection, 187
Lower Order Defenses (*L.O. dynamisms; L.O.* mental mechanisms), 388, 421
Conversion, 30
definition of, 12
Denial, 57–58
Displacement, 86
Incorporation, 163
Regression, 321
Repression, 359
Symbolization, 414
Undoing, 427
Lower Order Neuroses, 14

LSD (lysergic acid diethyl amide), 98–100, 119
Dissociative Reactions and, 98–100
promotes Fantasies, 119

Machinist, *Acute Anxiety Attack* when Repression falters, 376
Major
Ego Defenses (also *M. dynamisms; M. mental mechanisms*), 6, 7
professional acceptance of, 6
tabulated, 7
Projection, 233
Rationalization, six types of, 256
Rechannelization, gardening as, 309, 316, 399
Regression, 321–22, 343, 344, 351
massive behavioral reversions as, 321–22
psychoses with, illustrated in schizophrenia, 344
Repression, 364–65, 379
categorized, 379
complete, of significant event, 364
Stages of Personality Development, 328–29
Making-Up-For Process, 321, 331, 352, 398
Restitution as, 387
Maladie du doute (Falret), 427
Maladjustment, marital, *Socio-Sexual Dilemma* and, 73, 82
Man, Eight Major Stages of His Development and Adulthood, 328
Manic-Depressive Personality, 71
Manic-depressive psychosis, Denial in, 57, 70, 201–2
Manifest content, 112, 117, 120, 417
in *Dream-Symbols*, 417
Fantasy and
acceptable conscious wishes, 117
cover for latent content, 112
Manifestation, regressive, Fantasy as, 109
Mannerism Identification, 141, 142, 158
Marijuana user, Fantasies characterizing, 119
Marital
barriers, prohibition of sexual feelings, 88
Engulfment, 170–71
acceptable, 171
severe psychopathology from, 170–71
extramarital experience, opposition denied, 79
Idealization, 128–29

Marital (con't.)
enhances prospects of marriage continuing, 128–29
supported by Denial, 129
maladjustment, *Socio-Sexual Dilemma* and, 73, 82
Marriage, 67, 72–73, 79, 82, 88, 129, 188
emotional maturity preferable in, 72
extramarital sexual experience, 79
failure of, *Antitherapeutic Denial* and, 21, 62
Idealization, Marital, 70, 128–29
Introjection, husband and wife becoming alike through, 188
Sexual-Object Displacement and, 88
Socio-Sexual Dilemma in, 72–73, 78
Masculinity, *Secondary Appeal in Advertising* (SAAC), 149
Masochism. See also *Self-punishment*.
crippling, self-defeating to center of parental conflict, 118
delusion contributes, 186
needs, 190, 247, 332
Introjection development and, 190
subserved in *Positive King David Reaction*, 247
symptom pain, in *Psychologic Recapitulation Route*, 332
pattern, *King David Reaction* and, 247
-sadism combinations, in *Marital Engulfment*, 171
Visceral, Symptom-Introjection and, 185
Masserman, Jules, on oral region in regression, 168
Mass communication media, 145
Mass Denial, 82
Mass Identification, 144–45
Massive Regression, 320, 344–45, 354
Regression-Gauge useful in, 345
Schizophrenic Reaction and, 344
Massive Repression, 379
Masturbation, 330, 407, 451, 483
Atonement for, 451
as *Conflict-Indicator* in childhood, 330
as *Counterirritant Substitution*, 407
forbidden, *Obsessive Replacement* for, 483
Material Devaluation, 256, 261
Material Rationalization, 256, 261, 276
Maternal desires thwarted, 307, 308
Maturation, 312, 335
-*Fixation* at college level, 335–37, 354
Improvement Sublimation and, 312
Law of, 335
Maturity, 72
emotional, *Personal Yardstick* and, 226
Law of, 335, 353

Maturity (con't.)
  Regressive Therapy and, 351
  Tidal-Progression of, 335, 346, 354,
      382, 480
    childhood development and, 324
    normal, albeit uneven, 328, 352
"Maud Muller," Dream-of-Regret and,
      396
MDC (Mirror-Defense Concept), 220,
      226, 227, 234, 246
Mechanisms
  behavioral, 489
  mental, 3 ff. See also Dynamism(s);
      Ego Defenses.
Mediation
  by ego, of superego, 31, 256
  unconscious, term for Compromise
      Formation, 454–55
Medical
  Renaissance, 33
  secretary, Fantasy in, 118
  students, hygeiaphrontic concerns of,
      as Symptom-Identification, 156
Memory, 69, 358, 364 ff.
  blocks, Minor Repressions and, 365
  confabulation for gaps, 24
  convenient, Repression and, 57, 81–82,
      371, 375, 380
  Denial and, personality development
      and, 57
  function of ego, Denial and, 76
  Electronics Analogy, 369, 379
  Emotional-Object-Amalgam   (EOA)
      and, 368, 379–80
  -Inversion, Retrospective Devaluation
      and, 197
  lapses, Secondary Repression and, 364–
      65
  loss, 71, 98, 358
    automatic, Repression as, 358
    intrapsychic endeavor of Denial
      and, 71
    result of Repression, 98
  Minor Repression, 365
  Personality Dissociation and, 96
  poor, Unwitting Ignorance and, 489
  Repression, implications of, 367
  Universal Affect and, 367
Mental
  abilities, not tied to emotional health,
      215–16
  faculties, restricted, 489
  Function Dissociation, 104 ff.
  health, Rechannelization and, 317
  illness: term conveys mistaken im-
      pression, 216
  Mechanisms, 3 ff. See also Dy-
      namism(s); Ego Defenses.

Mental (con't.)
  message conveyed by symptoms, 35
  synthesis, 96, 106
Meticulousness, Rechannelization and,
      303
Military, 149–50, 292–93, 328, 398, 459
  Conflict-Indicators and, 328
  Distortion of inner feelings and, 459
  Identification in, 149–50
  Overcorrectness, 292–93, 294
  Reaction Formation, 292–93, 294
  Restitution-by-Will, lethal explosives
      and, 398
  -Unit Identification (MUI), 149–50
Miner, Somatic Conversion in, 48
Minimal Conversion (or Social Conver-
      sion), 38
Minor
  Dynamisms, 6–7, 447 ff.
  Ego Defenses, listed and defined, 447 ff.
  Projections in everyday life, 229–30
  Rationalization, types of, 256
  Rechannelization, 316
  Regressions, 321–22, 324, 351
    not pathologically significant, 324
    patterned type of response and, 321
  Repressions, 365–66, 379
    categorized, 379
    memory block of anniversary, 366
    myriad memory lapses in everyday
      living, 365
  Restitutions, Interpersonal, 390, 398
  Sublimation, 316
Mirror
  Concept, Projection and, 234
  -Defense, 220, 226, 234, 246
    concept of Projection as, 226, 227
    Royal Love (KDR) and, 246
    term for Projection, 234
Misidentification, 135, 160
  adoption of conflicting traits and, 160
  faulty Identification and, 135
Mixed Regression, 323–24, 329, 352
Mobs, Group Compathy and, 140
Modern Aims of Therapy, 377
Money, 175, 198, 459
  Characterologic Inversion and, 198
  Internalization of parental attitudes
      and, 175
  overzealous drive for, 459
Mood-Inversion, 201–3
Moral judgments, instinctual drives and,
      298
Morale, Military-Unit Identification and,
      149
Moralistic attitudes about sex, 73
Morals
  influenced by prominent leaders, 145
  relaxed, Sexual Rationalization sup-
      porting, 269

Morphine addiction, 62
Mother, 63, 90
  Antitherapeutic Denial and, 62
  competition with daughter, 118
  Complex-Supportive Rationalization and, 258
  -daughter relationship, 171
  death of, 71
  Emotional Decompensation of, 333, 353
  Fantasy-Pattern and, 114
  figurative Incorporation and, 165, 168
  Introjection of, by infant, 189
  Parental Incorporation, 169
  Pattern in finances reversed, 486–87
  resentment toward, in *Attitude Reversal,* 486
  role of second, 42
Motivation, 109–10, 267
  Eleemosynary Rationalization and, 267
  unconscious, *Iceberg Analogy* and, 109–10
  understanding of, 6
Motive-Rationalization, 254, 256, 260–61, 276
  Residents' behavior represents, 260
Motives of groups, *Social Restitution* and, 268–69
Motor Conversion, 43, 45, 48, 51–52
  defends against possible action, 43
  follows wife's illness, 48
Motors, impotence and, 22
Movie
  Central Identification and, 140
  star, housewife and, 146
MR (Medical Renaissance), 33
MS (*Multiple Symbolization*), 417, 419
MUI (*Military-Unit Identification*), 149–50
Multiple
  Confessions, 146–47, 159
  Denial Concept, 77
  Personality, 94 ff., 477
  Rechannelization, 308–9, 316
  in *Denial-of-Death,* 78
  Sublimation, 308, 316
  Symbolization, 417, 419
Murder, 146–47, 268, 440, 485
  Eleemosynary Rationalization and, 268
  Multiple Confessions and, 146–47
  Retrospective Devaluation and, 485
  Undoing and, 440
Murderous impulse
  Isolation and, 477
  Substitution and, 403

Nail biting as *Conflict-Indicator,* 327
Name forgetting Repression and, 370, 372

Narcissism, meaning defined, 245–46, 248
Narcissistic Period, 245–46, 329
Narcissus
  derivation from Greek legend, 246
  Reaction, 245–46
Nathan
  Device, 240, 248
    King David's Anger and, 248
    Shakespeare's Hamlet and, 240
  Parable, Ewe Lamb, 236, 248
National, 12, 19–20, 60–61, 82, 128
  -Compensation, 12, 19–20, 26, 128
    National Idealization and, 20, 128
    national leaders and, 12
    prominent person and, 20
  -Denial, Ostrich Concept and, 60–61, 82
  -Idealization, Compensation and, 20, 128, 131
Need(s)
  dependency, 144, 331, 343, 347–48, 404, 409
  direct satisfaction through *Primary Appeal in Advertising,* 149, 159
  earlier unmet, fulfilled in Regression Treatment, 347–48, 354
  indirect satisfaction through *Secondary Appeal in Advertising* (SAAC) 149
  oral, 168
  sexuality, 482
  stimulated through *Secondary Appeal in Advertising,* 149
  unacceptable, Replacement of, through Substitution, 402
Negation, psychologic, Denial as, 57
Negative
  feelings, Projection of, toward brother, 229
  King David Reaction. See *King David Reaction, Negative.*
  Projection, 230–32, 234
  paranoid reaction and, 231
NEP. See *Never Enough Principle.*
Neurasthenia, regressive trends in, 342
  Dependency-Seeking Principle, Regression and, 338, 340
  conversion headaches and, 340
Neuroses, 300, 427, 436–7, 443
  exaggerated and overdeveloped defenses and, 9
  -Following-Trauma, 343
  Higher Order, 14
  Lower Order, 14
  Obsessive-Compulsive, 270, 343, 404, 406, 476
    repetitive symptoms in, 436–37
    telephoning, 437
    Undoing in, 427, 436–37, 443

Neuroses (con't.)
Repression role important self-defeating consequences, 9, 12
Symptom-, 31, 54
Neurotic
Acting Out, 38
Compromise Formation, 454
drives, success and, 216
gains, Rationalization and, 252
gratifications, Rationalization and, 200, 252
-Position
Balanced, 461–62
Paradox of, with defensively intended distance in therapy, 35
-Reactions, 11 ff., 199. See also under individual names.
Dissociation as, 95, 98
Higher Order, 14 ff.
Regression less significant in, 338, 354
Secondary Defenses of, 11
Symptom Identification in, 156
satisfactions, Denial and, in extramarital sexual experience, 79
status quo, Distortion and, 12, 199, 205, 346, 428, 461
Never Enough
-Principle, 391–92, 399, 471, 482
in pervasive adoption of *Fire Drill*, 471
in *Relationship-Replacement* of father, 482
Restitution and, 391–92, 399
-Spiral
Fire Drill and, 471
Restitution and, 399
Niagara Falls Analogy, 312–13, 317
Nietzsche, Repression and, 370
Nightmares as *Conflict-Indicators*, 327
Nobel Peace Awards as *Restitution-by-Will*, 397
Nonconstructive features of *Fantasies*, 112–13
Normalcy, 217
Normal Regressions in *Tidal-Progression*, 324, 352, 382
Notoriety sought through *Spurious Confession*, 147
Novels, *Central Identification* and, 136
Noyes, on Projection and Denial, 80

Obesity rationalized, 255
Object(s), 125 ff., 414–16
Amalgam, Emotional-, 192, 367–69, 379–80, 412, 422, 458, 476
assimilated through Incorporation, 165
Condensation Symbols and, 414
Distortion altering, 458
Fantasy-, mouse as, 186

Object(s) (con't.)
"good" and "bad," 135
-Idealization, 125, 127, 128, 130
external emotional supply, 125
personal possession as, 127
for Identification lacking, 143
introjected, 183, 192
latent, of hostility, father as, 119
love-, Denial of unpleasant qualities of, 127
phobic, 338–39, 404
Dilemma, 338–39
travel as, 404
relationships, 176, 190
Replacement by another object, 479–80, 482
Sexual-, Displacement, 89
Soterial Reactions, 125, 128, 326, 368, 414–15, 478–79, 483
splitting of affect toward, 488
substitute, 401
Scapegoat Reaction and, 87–88, 284, 301, 409
symbolic, *Condensation* and, 414, 421
-symbols in dreams, 416
Objectivity, explaining strength of feeling and, 237
Obsequiousness, Reaction Formation and, 281
Obsessional rituals, Undoing and, 281
Obsessive
Characterologic Reaction Formation and, 288
-Compulsive
Neuroses, 427, 436, 443
repetitive symptoms in *Tidal Undoing*, 436–37
Undoing operation in, 427, 443
Reactions, 342, 402, 406, 410, 475, 476, 483
Counterirritant-Substitution, 406–7, 410
Intellectualization, 475
Isolation, 476
regressive trends, 343
relief from, 406
ruminations, 483
Substitution, 402
Rituals, 436–37
symptoms, *Expiative Undoing* and, 431
concerns over grammar, 483
defenses, 402, 404, 406–8
Personality, 73, 303, 475
Intellectualization and, 475
supermoralistic attitudes in, 73
traits, Reaction Formation and *Rechannelization* and, 303
Rationalization and, 270
Replacements for unacceptable feelings, 483

Obsessive (con't.)
rumination, 404, 406
Counterirritant Substitution and, 406
as repetitive thought, 404
traits, *Rechannelization* and, 303
Obstinacy, obsessive, anal era and, 303
Occupation, symbolism in, 305
Oedipal, 124, 125, 130, 241, 329
aggression, Hamlet's, 241
Idealization, 124, 125, 130
Period, 329
Omission
Denial in re: insurance and wills, 79, 80, 82
Undoing Dream and, 435
Omnipotent feelings, Denial and, 69
Operation, White-Washing (WWO), *Memory Inversion* in, 197, 204
Opposite, Reaction of the, as term for Reaction Formation, 279 ff., 284, 289, 293
Opposite, reversal into the, 486–88
Oral
era, 163 ff., 189, 328–29
primordial introjects and, 189
Erotic Phase, 329
Incorporation, 164
incorporative attitude normal for infant, 166
Introject, 186, 191
pregnancy and, 186–87, 191
vomiting and, 191
needs, 168
Period establishing literal incorporative pattern, 165
Phase, 329
pregnancy, Fantasy of, from kissing, 187
Stage
Infantile Period, 329
Incorporation in personality development and, 167
Orality in earliest interpersonal relatedness, 164, 173
Orator, *conscious Compensation* in, 24
Order, *Attention-Focus Substitution* and, 407
Orderliness, 288, 303
attitude symptom, 288
as obsessive trait, 303
as Reaction Formation, 288
Organ inferiority, 25
Organic pathology, FSPC consequence, 10
Organization, 150, 266
Eleemosynary Rationalization and, 266
Group Identification and, 150
Ostrich Concept, 60–62, 81, 489–90
Denial can be national, 60

Ostrich Concept (con't.)
Unwitting Ignorance, 489
Withdrawal and, 490
Ostrich Defense, as term for Denial, 56 ff.
Overactivity, sexual, 25
Overcompensation, 18, 21, 27, 243, 289 ff.
combat performance and, 243
progressive pathology and, 18
Reaction Formation as, 290, 292
military overcorrectness, 292
timidity, 290
for timidity, in lawyer, 21, 290, 480
Overconcern-with-Health, 156, 342–43, 478
Hygeiaphrontis as term for, 156
Personal Invulnerability as converse of, 478
Overconditioning, *Sexual Denial* and, 72
Overdependency of patients, 347
Overdeterminism, 88, 456, 477–78
Overdetermination, 88, 455
psychic, in Condensation, 455
Scapegoat Reaction and, 88
Overestimation, as term for Idealization, 123
Overextension in Repression, 360, 374, 375, 380
derepression with *Kinetic-Energy Principle* and, 374
overinhibition of psychic data, 380
psychopathology and, 360, 375
Overvaluation
Idealization and, 123 ff.
of personal possession, 128
of speaking ability through *Denial-for Confidence,* 59

Pain, 30, 176–77, 185
affect-equivalent and, 48
Conversion and, 52
Denial of, 64
emotional, combatting a function of ego defenses, 9
of interpersonal relationship avoided, 476
psychic
defense against, 4, 62, 101, 210
detachment from, 101
recapitulation via *Psychologic Recapitulation Route,* 332
Parable of Ewe Lamb, King David Reaction and, 236, 248
Parable, Nathan's, 236
Paradox
Hangover, Undoing and, 431, 442
of Neurotic Position, 35, 54
Paralysis, conversion, 30, 36–37, 40 ff., 48

Paraldehyde, in lieu of alcohol in *Regressive Treatment,* 350
Paranoid
  conditions, Denial and, 69
  Indifference, 103, 230, 231, 234, 305
    Diffuse, Projection, 230–31
    ideation, 103
    la belle indifférence and, in *Somatic Conversion,* 234
  reaction, *Negative Projection* and, 231
Paraplegia, childhood, 34
Parent(s), 64, 71, 104, 151
  conflict with, 118
  death, loss denied, 71
  Denial of interest in being, 64
  Depersonalization, 104
  drives of, *Vocational Rechannelization* and, 307
  encouragement of sexual inhibitions, 72–73
  Engulfment, 170–71
    cyclic depressions and, 171
    subtle operation of, 170
  Familial Rationalization and, 256, 269–70, 276
  Idealization, 124, 125
    anti-Oedipal bases, 124
    tabulated, 125
  Identification, adoption of disapproved aspects and, 148–49, 159
  Incorporation, 168, 169
    constructive, 168
    emotional crippling and, 169
  pressures, Identification and, 155
  Reaction Formation and, 285–86, 293–94
    sexual taboos and, 287
  Regressive-Indicator for, 327
  standards of, *Contra-Parent Reaction Formation* against, 285, 293
  -surrogate, 177
  vicariously living through child, 151
Paresis, *Phobic-Hygeiaphrontis* and, 339
Partial
  Compromise Formation, 454
  Introjection, 187–88, 191
    Identification and Idealization and, 188
    source of emotional difficulty, 187
  Rechannelizations, 308–9, 316
  Regression, 321, 323–24
  Repression, 379
  Sublimation, 308, 316
Particularization, 471, 473
  Emotional Diffusion and, 473
  Generalization and, 471
Part Reactions, Conversion and, 50
Paternal relationship, Replacement with destructive alliances, 482

Pathogenic Vicious Circle, 10, 14
Pathologic Regressions, 337, 353
Patriotic evil actions, *Eleemosynary Rationalization* and, 267
Patterns, Fantasy-, 112 ff., 120
  analogous to emotional symptoms, 113
  evolved
    in adolescence, 112
    in dependency and hostility, 114
Pedestal, *Idealization* and, 125
Peg Concept, Rationalization and, 254
Penance, 450 ff.
Perception, 76, 117, 464
  as ego function, 76
  inaccessible in latent content of Fantasy, 117
  shut off, through *Fainting,* 464
Period, Latent, 329
  Puberty, 329
Perfectionism, 407–8
Permanent-Fixation, 335–36, 337, 353
  disinterest in therapy and, 336
  personality progress encountering emotional opposition through, 335
Persecution, 69, 231, 301
  Denial in delusional aspects of paranoid, 69
  Projection and, 231
  Rechannelization and, 301
Person, Fantastic, 125–26, 130
Personal
  Compensation, attitudes and behavior reflecting, 18–19, 26
  -Feeling Displacement, 87, 92
  Invulnerability, 60, 63, 478–79
    Denial supporting, 60, 63
    Hygeiaphrontis and, 478
    soteria similar to, 479
    view of self, 478–79
  standards, *Parental Incorporation* and, 169
  -Tragedy Rechannelization, 300, 302, 316
    great undertakings initiated through, 300, 316
    Szu-Ma Chien illustrating, 302
  Yardstick (PY), 159, 246–47
    Bases for Application, 153
    Concept, in Identification, 146
    Generalization of attitudes and, 474
    Impression Priority and, 152
    King David Reaction and, 246
    Projection as earliest, 223, 233
    as universal measuring device, 226
Personality
  Alternating, 95, 98
    Dissociative Reactions and, 98
    psychologic flight and, 95

Personality (con't.)
  Conversion, 44–45, 69, 170, 340
    Denial employed, 69
    Incorporation and, 170
    Regression potential and, 340
    traits revealed, 45
  Depressive, 71, 200
    Denial employed, 71
    traits influenced through Inversion,
      200
  development, 95–97, 302–4, 334–35,
      379
    Characterologic Identification and,
      143
    Childhood Identification and, 135
    Fixation and, 334
    Identification in, 143
    Incorporation in, 166
    Internalization in, 176
    major stages of, 328–29
    Reaction Formation in, 282
    Rechannelization in, 302–3
  Dissociation, 95–97, 106
    dissociative phenomena considered
      under, 95
    Janet Concept, 96
    Self-Defense Concept and, 97
  Manic-Depressive, 71
  Obsessive, 73, 303, 475
    Intellectualization and, 475
    supermoralistic attitudes, 73
    traits, Reaction Formation and Re-
      channelization and, 303
  Split, 102
  synthesis, Dissociation and, 95
Perversions, Gratification Enhancements
    in, 115
Pessimism
  as attitude-symptom, 470
  Fire Drill and, 470–71, 487
Pessimistic Hygeiaphrontis, 479
PFI (Public Figure Identification), 144–
    45, 159
Phallic Stage, 329
Phantasia, 109 ff.
Phantasy. See Fantasy.
Pharmacologic Dissociations, 100
Phases, Oral
  Erotic, 329
  Incorporative, 164
  Sadistic, 328
Phenomena in Overdeterminism, 477
Phobia, 221, 404, 460–61, 463–64, 478–
    79, 480
  Displacement and Substitution and,
    404
  Externalization of, 221
  soteria and, 478
Phobic
  defense, Substitution operating with
    Displacement in, 404

Phobic (con't.)
  Dilemma, fear object secretly desired,
      338–39
  Displacement, 86, 91
  -Extension, 404, 460
  Hygeiaphrontis, Extension in, 463–64
  object, 404, 460–61
    Extension and, 460
    travel as, 404
  Reactions, 50, 478–79
    Dependency-Seeking Principle, 338–
      39
    Displacement and, 86, 91, 463
    diffuse, in childhood, 463
    psychodynamics, six major points in,
      404–5
    Substitution and, 402
    Symbiotic-Substitution and, 402
  Regression, repressed dependency needs
      and, 338–39
Phrase, Undoing, as repetitive activity,
    434, 443
Physical disease, Denial and, 73
Physician, 104, 243, 409
  Depersonalization and painful news,
    104
  rejects others, through Negative King
      David Reaction, 243
  substitute target, 409
Physicians and medicine treated humor-
    ously, 457
Physical, Flight-to-the, 11, 14
Physiologic Conversion, 31, 51, 185
  Conversion Reaction and, 31
  functional symptoms and, 51
Physiologic Language, 33
PI. See Personal Invulnerability.
Pilfering, Isolation and, 477
Pilot, Idealization by Denial and, 80
Pious Restitution, 394, 399
Play, child using Denial in, 57
Plays, Central Identification and, 136
Pleasure principle, Denial and, 75
"Pleasures of the flesh," Sexual Reversal
    and, 487
Plutarch's Lives, 61
Political
  figures, Basking-in-Reflected Glory and,
    144
  Reversal of parent's views, 286, 293,
    295
Position, dependent, Identification and,
    46–47
  neurotic, 35
Positive
  Affect Inversion, external expression
      and, 195, 196, 204
  King David Reaction. See King David
      Reaction, Positive.
Possession, overvalued, 128
Posthypnotic Rationalization, 253, 256

Posthypnotic suggestion, 253–54, 362
Postponement, emotional, as term for *Deferment,* 456
Postural attitudes, pain and, 176–77
Power, 20, 26, 144, 310
Compensation, 20, 23, 26
secret desire for, 144
struggle with mother, 310
Powerlessness, hobby of cars and, 22
Prayer, *Symbolic Undoing* and, 439
Predecessor Identification, 140–41, 158
Pregnancy, 64, 70, 73, 186, 195
Denial of, 70
false, 195
illegitimate, 73
Oral Introject and, 186
Reversal of attitudes and, 64
Prejudice, 124, 178, 216, 454, 474
Compartmentalization and, 454
Generalization and, 474
Internalization of camp counselor's, 178
melts, 214
unwarranted, toward emotionally ill, 216
Premature interpretation, 419, 437
dream, disadvantageous, 419
Resistance-Undoing and, 437
Preoccupation, 343, 406
obsessive, with homosexuality, 406
somatic, in *Hygeiaphrontis,* 343
Preservation of symptoms, *Secondary Defense* and, 11
Pressure, parental, Identification and, 155
Prestige, *Eleemosynary Rationalization* and, 267
Preventive Rechannelization, 310, 317
Preventive Sublimation, 310, 317
Preverbal Language, 33
Primal Displacement, 91–92
Primal Repression, 363, 379
Primary
Appeal in Advertising, 149, 159
changes in *Functional-Structural Progression,* 52
defenses, 10, 16, 271
character traits and neuroses and, 10
symptoms of emotional illness as, 271
Delusion, Secondary Delusion defending, 270, 277
dynamism, 7
ego defenses, 6–7
Gain, Endogain as, 49
mental mechanism, 7
Repressions, 12, 111, 363–64, 373
early instinctual psychic material comprising, 363
general reaction of undeveloped ego and, 373
Unconscious Fantasies and, 111

Prime dynamism, ego defense, or mental mechanism, 7–8
Primitive dynamisms, 12–13
listing of, 13
Lower Order of defenses as, 12
Primitive preverbal language, 33
Primitive psychologic defenses, 12 ff.
Primordial
defense, Repression as, 363
introjects, oral era and, 189, 191
rejection, Projection and, 223
Principle
Characterologic Hypertrophy, 18, 26
Dependency-Seeking, 331, 338, 340, 354
Regression and, 338, 340
Direct Proportion of Symptom-Prominence to (its) Secondary Defense, 11, 14
Flight-to-the-Physical, 11, 14
Increasing-Complexity, 325, 352, 481
Intellectualization-Respite, 475
Kinetic-Energy, 312, 360, 373, 374, 379
definition of, 360
Repression maintenance and, 312, 373, 374, 379
Libidinal-Investment in Therapy, 304–5, 317
Making-up-for-, 321, 331, 352
Never Enough, 391–92, 399, 471, 482
Overextension, in Repression, 360
Kinetic-Energy Principle and, 374
overinhibition of psychic data and, 380
psychopathology and, 360, 375
Self-Esteem Maintenance in therapy, Conversion Reaction and, 33
Scientific Determinism, Repression and, 371
Principles, dynamic, 5
of *Symptom-Prominence to its Secondary Defense,* 11
Priority, emotional, 145, 152, 178, 237, 248
Prisoner Processing, 268
Profanity, criticism of, 225
Professor, Identification with, 143
Prognosis, *Regression-Gauge* and, 337
Prognostic Rechannelization, 310, 317
Progression
Functional-Structural, 10, 52
of *Maturity Concept,* 324, 328, 353
in Therapy, *Tidal-,* 324, 328, 346, 354
Projection, 68–69, 220 ff.
of affect, typical, 222
of anger in *Grandiose Projection,* 232
antecedents of, *primordial rejection* as, 223
blind-spots about self, 224–25, 233

Projection (con't.)
BTEH and, 266
definition of, 220
Denial and, 68–69, 80, 223
Diffuse, 230, 234
Duchess of Malfi as literary instance,
225
Fantastic Person and, 221, 233
Grandiose, 230, 231–32, 234
guilt and, in paranoid conditions, 69
homosexual feelings and, 233
Identification differing from, 146
Internalization and, 178
Interpersonal, 222–23, 227–29, 234
Introjection and, 183, 186, 222
King David Reaction and, 22, 225,
227, 237, 238, 244
Denial and, 244
external vs. personal, 225
Repression, Identification, Rationali-
zation and, 222
secondary elaboration of, 238
King David's Anger and, 242–43
Major and *Minor,* 228 ff.
Mirror-Defense in, 220 ff.
Negative, 229–31, 234
Paranoid Indifference and, 230–31
Personal Yardstick and, 223, 226, 233
infant impulses and, 223
universal measuring device and, 153–
54, 159, 226, 233, 246
Primordial Denial and, 223
Projection and, 226
Psychotic, 230 ff.
Repression maintained through, 228
responsibility for gangrenous foot,
227–28
Projective Identification, 136–38, 158,
222
emotional sharing and, 136
Empathy and, 137–38
kindly attitudes and, 222
level of affectivity of, 137–38
Rapport and Sympatico, 137
Sympathy, 137
Projective Vicious Circle, 221–23, 228–
29, 233
Fantastic Person and, 221
self-critical feelings, 228
self-defeating aspects, 222–23
Prominence inviting Identification, 144–45
Promiscuity denied, 79, 80
Proportional Ego-Response Law, 322, 352
Protection
of self, *Devaluation* and, 457
soterial object as source of, 415
Protective intent of overconditioning in
Sexual Denial, 72
Proxy, Restitution-by-, 395, 399

PRR. See *Psychologic Recapitulation
Route.*
Prudishness, Reaction Formation and,
280
Pseudoconvulsions, 39
Pseudoepilepsy, *Behavioral Conversion*
and, 40–41
Psyche, 31, 314
Psychiatry
descriptive, 4, 14
dynamic, 4 ff.
responses of skepticism and defensive
reactions to concepts of, 314–
15
Psychic
assimilation, 163, 166
compromises, *Rechannelization* and,
300, 315. See also *Compromise
Formation.*
Defense, 29, 96, 358, 378
First Line of, 49, 358, 378
Conversion and, 49
Repression and, 378
integration and synthesis and, 96
energy, *Niagara Falls Analogy* and,
312–13, 360, 373, 379
Erasure, as term for Undoing, 426
Fire, 470–71
hypertrophy, Fantasy and, 113
Ingestion, as term for Incorporation,
163 ff.
pain, avoidance of, 4, 62, 101, 210
Denial and, 62
elaboration of defenses and, 4, 210
evolvement of psychosis and, 101
remission of sins, *Absolution* and, 448
requital, as term for *Retribution,*
Psychoanalysis, 49, 79, 90, 100, 224, 252,
312. See also *Analysis; Psychodynamics; Psychotherapy; Treatment;* and individual case illustrations.
Psychodynamics, 5, 183, 189, 317, 375,
405, 463. See also comments
concerning individual ego defenses, dynamics.
building blocks, 5 ff.
Externalization and, 463
Introjection and, 183, 189
Phobic Reactions and, 405
Psychologic
alopecia as *Atonement-Penance,* 452–
53
Alternative, as term for Substitution,
401
blindness, 224, 371, 380
as *convenient memory,* 371
nonawareness of self-aspects and,
380

Psychologic (con't.)
  Projection of disowned self-aspects and, 224
  blind-spots, 223 ff.
  blocking, 69, 96, 369, 457, 464, 489
  Conversion, 31, 32, 51
  Disavowal, as term for Denial, 56
  Erasure, as term for Undoing, 427, 442
  flight, 95, 105, 119, 331
    Dissociation and, 95, 105
    Fantasy as, 119
    Regression as, 331
  homeostasis, 213
  Insulation, as term for Withdrawal, 490
  Recapitulation Route, 353, 376. See also *Emotional Recapitulation; Illness-Regression; Symptom-Compathy; Symptom Identification.*
    in *Conversion Regression,* 340–41
    earlier era fits ego's needs in Regression, 331, 332
  Retreat
    distinguished from Withdrawal, 490
    as term for Regression, 321, 351
Psychopathologic sequence: anxiety; dynamism; hypertrophy or failure; emotional illness, 211. See also FSPC.
Psychopathology, 218, 374
  exaggeration and overdevelopment of defenses and, 10
  Fantasy-System and, 113
  Idealization and, 125
  Introjection and, 189–90
  Marital Engulfment and, 171
  Repression exaggerated in, 375
  Symptom-Extension and, 461
  Symptom-Introjection in, 185–86, 190
  Unhealthful Fantasies and, 113
Psychosexual development, 328–29
  Major Stages of, 328–29
  Tidal-Progression of Maturation and, 328, 335, 346
Psychosis, 57, 101, 103, 232, 339–40, 490
  absence of appropriate affect through Dissociation, 103
  Dissociated Psychotic-Survival, 101
  manic-depressive, Denial in, 57
  reality distorted through Projection, 232
  retreat into, as protection, 101
Psychotherapist, empathy and, 138
Psychotherapy, 5 ff., 19, 33 ff., 79 ff., 144, 252
  Association Convergence in, 456
  Conversion Reaction in, 48–49

Psychotherapy (con't.)
  Denial of sexual promiscuity in, 79
  derepression deliberately fostered in, 375
  as educational process, 212
  empathy important in, 138
  Improvement-Sublimation in, 312
  insight important in, 212
  Intellectualization in, 475
  Interpersonal Identification in, 154
  Libidinal Investment in, 305, 317
  Rationalization in, 252
  self-defeating aspects, 9, 12
  Sexual Rationalization in, 252
  status quo guarded through *Secondary Defense,* 12
  understanding of ego defenses vital, 218. See also individual cases.
Psychotic
  dissociation in *Dissociated Psychotic-Survival* (DSP), 101 ff.
  episode, Denial of reality and, 70
  Identification, delusion and, 157, 159, 160
  illness, *Major Regression* in, 344
  Incorporation, delusion in, 170
  Introjection, Identification and, 186, 190
  manifestations after Denial and Projection of guilt, 69
  Projection, Diffuse, Paranoid Indifference and, 230, 234
  Reactions
    Absolution, hallucinations and, 448–49
    Identification, 157
    Regression in, 323, 344, 345, 348
      Attitudinal and Behavioral, 323
      Complete or *Massive,* 344–45, 351, 354
      Schizophrenia and, 345
      Treatment, 348
    self-defeating forms of Dissociation, 101
  Regression, 344–46
  status quo, Schizophrenia and, 490
  -Survival Dissociated, 101, 106, 490
    retreat into psychosis, nature's protection as, 101
    Withdrawal as *psychologic retreat,* 490
PTR (*Personal-Tragedy Rechannelization*), 300–302, 316
Public
  Denial, 60, 61, 82
    potential catastrophe, 61
    in Seoul, Korea, 60
  -Figure Enhancement follows from *National Compensation,* 26
  -Figure Identification, 144–45, 159

Public (con't.)
  Restitution, two subdivisions of, 392,
    398
Punishment, 451 ff.
  Atonement-Penance and, 451
  Disciplinary-Regression and, 325–26
  need for, Introjection and, 190
  Retribution and, 483–84
  self-, 125, 448, 453, 483
  -Undoing Cycle, 430, 442
Punitive superego, 449
PVC (*Projective Vicious Circle*), 221,
    223, 229, 233
PY or PYC. See *Personal Yardstick.*

Rage
  reaction in KDR, 244
  Rechannelization diverting, 244, 301,
    404
Raison d'être, 133, 413. See also *En-
    dogain.*
  of Identification, 133
  of symbols, 413
Rank, Otto, "birth trauma" theory, 364
Rape, 477
Rapport, *Projective Identification* and,
    137, 158
Rationalization, 250 ff.
  Alcoholic, 24, 67, 256, 262, 271, 277
    Compensation and, 24
    Denial of problem, 67
    in habituation, 271
    self-deception in therapy, 262
  anxiety and, 264
  bases for, 254
  Behavioral, 256, 262–64, 276
  Characterologic, 254, 256, 272, 273,
    277
    attitudes and behavior influenced by,
      273
    as contempt for learning, 254
    Motive-Rationalization as, 272
  Collective, 256, 268, 276
  Complex-Supportive, Exploitation in,
    256, 258, 276
  compromises between id and superego,
    252
  confabulation as, 24
  conscious, to evade responsibility, 264
  definition of, 251
  Denial operates with, in *emotional
    symbiosis,* 64, 65, 262, 273
    hampering personality traits, 262
    impropriety, 65
    sterility, 64
  Devaluation as term for a major func-
    tion of, 256, 275
  Distortion and *emotional symbiosis*
    with, 459

Rationalization (con't.)
  dynamics, 272
  Ego-Enhancing Inversion and, 200
  Ego-Maintaining, 256–57, 258, 275
  Eleemosynary, 256, 265 ff., 276
    as "anything goes," in name of
      charity, 265
    selflessness promoted, 266
    throughout history, 267–68
  in emotional illness, 271
  Familial, equal treatment of children
    and, 256, 269–70, 276
  of fondness, latent homosexuality and,
    246
  Goal Devaluation and, 256, 259, 275
  Group Identification and, 151
  as *Higher Order dynamism,* 13, 251
  Ineffective, leads to *Restitution-in-
    Abeyance,* 397, 399
  Intellectualization akin to, 475
  King David Reaction and, 237, 275
  literary figures represented by Robin
    Hood, 263
  Major, types of, 256
  Material, 256, 261, 276
  Minor, types of, 256 ff.
  Motive-, 254, 256, 260, 276
    in psychiatric resident, 260–61
    socially acceptable, 254, 276
  motives for ego and, 259
  neurotic gains protected, 252
  Object-Ideal related to, 128
  Peg Concept illustrated, 254
  Posthypnotic, 253, 256, 275
  Recognition-Deferment, 256–58, 275
  relationship to other ego defenses, 274
  school failure and, 263–64
  Secondary Delusion supporting Pri-
    mary Delusion, 270
  secondary elaboration and, 251
  Sexual, 256, 269, 276
  Social (or Collective), 256, 268–69,
    276
  Sour-Grapes, 256, 260, 275, 484
    Aesop's fable explaining, 260
    Retrospective Devaluation and, 484
  standards and behavior reconciliation,
    252, 274
  Standards-Inversion assisted, 197–98
  Symptom-Defensive, 256, 271, 276
    Secondary Defense and, 271
    supporting symptoms and character
      defenses, 272
  types listed, 256
  weight reduction failure and, 255
RD (*Retrospective Devaluation*), 197,
    484–86
Reaction. See also individual entries for
    various types.
  Conversion, 31, 41, 48, 103, 420

Reaction (con't.)
  Depressive, 183–84, 202, 215, 342, 407
  Dissociative, 50, 94, 95, 98, 100
  -Extension, 461
  Hygeiaphrontic, 406
  King David, 222, 225, 236 ff.
  Narcissus, 245, 246, 248
  Neurotic, 11, 95, 98, 156, 199, 338, 354
  Obsessive-Compulsive, 343, 402, 406, 410, 475, 476, 483
  of the opposite, 280, 284, 289, 291, 293
  paranoid, *Negative Projection* in, 231
  Part, Conversion as, 50
  Phobic, 50, 86, 91, 338–39, 402, 404–5, 463
  Psychotic, 101, 157, 323, 344, 345, 348, 448–49
  rage, 244
  Scapegoat, 87, 93, 182, 273, 284, 301–02, 409, 456, 478, 480
  Schizophrenic, 230, 348, 409, 449, 490
  Suspended, 397, 399
  -of-the-Whole, Dissociation as, 50, 55
Reaction Formation, 8, 20, 203, 279 ff.
  Behavioral, 281, 282, 293, 295
  Characterologic, 282, 283
    as overcompensation for timidity, 290
    as *secondary elaboration* of Repression, 280, 284, 293, 294
    successful, in development of, *attitude symptoms,* 284, 288, 293
    obsessive orderliness and cleanliness, 288
    Scapegoat Reaction and, 284
  characterologic development as consequence, 280, 292
  characterologic evolvement through, 280, 293
  Contra-Parent, 285–86, 293
    Political Reversal as, 286
  definition of, 279
  dynamics, 287
  emotional allergy to conflict and turmoil and, 282–83, 293
  Intrapsychic Reversal of repressed impulses from id, 288
  leaning over backward, 293
  literary instance of, Uriah Heep, *Historical Validation* and, 281
  as mental mechanism, 8, 279
  Military, 292–93, 294
  nature of, 279
  as noun naming resultant characterologic formations, 281
  other ego defenses and, 289–91
    Compensation and, 20, 289, 290
    Inversion and, 203, 205, 289
    Rechannelization and, 283, 290

Reaction Formation (con't.)
  Repression and Denial and, 284, 290–91
  Parental, 286–87, 293–94
    of sexual taboos, 287
    as *Standards-Reenforcement,* 286, 293–94
    as *reaction of the opposite,* 280, 284
  Rechannelization and, social benefits and, 283
  Social, 281–82, 293
  Symptomatic, 291, 293
Reality, 80, 113, 114, 119, 120, 232, 489
  Denial of, in children's games, 80
  Distortion of, through Projection, 232
  retreat through Fantasy, 112, 119, 120
  unconscious retreat through Withdrawal, 389
  unreal feelings, 95, 103. See also *Depersonalization.*
  withdrawal from, through *Unhealthful Fantasy,* 113
Reassurance in *hygeiaphrontic dread,* 464
Rebound from lost love, 125, 481
  Idealization and, 125
  Relationship-Replacement and, 481
Recall, 367, 369
  Emotional-Object Amalgam and, 369
  Universal Affect Law (UAL) and, 367
Recapitulation, 331. See also *Psychologic Recapitulation Route; Symptom-Compathy; Symptom Identification.*
  Emotional, 353
  Identification and, 376
  Psychologic, Route, 331, 340, 353, 376. See also *Illness-Regression; Symptom Identification.*
  in *Conversion Regression,* 340–41
  earlier era fits ego's needs in Regression, 331, 332
  relationship, 129
Rechannelization, 296 ff.
  Aggression, 299, 316
  Avocational, 308–10, 316
  Characterologic, 302–3, 316
  Complete, 307–9, 316
  Constructive, "Philosophy of War" as example, 299, 302
  Contributory, 310, 317
  definition of, 299
  dynamics, 312
  -en-Therapy, 311, 317
  Excessive, of sexual drives, 304, 316
  as *Higher Order (senior)* defense, 297, 311, 317
  Historical Validation (AVC) and, 301–02, 316
  Identification and, 303

Rechannelization (con't.)
  Improvement, 310–12
    maturation in therapy and, 312
    prognostic significance, 310–12, 317
    in psychosis, 311
  Incomplete, 310, 316, 317
  Ineffective, 284, 310, 317
  Instinctual Diversion, as term for, 296, 297, 316
  instinctual drives, external expression and, 298
  Intellectualization akin to, 475
  Libidinal-Investment and, 304–5, 317
  maintenance of health and, 317
  Major, gardening as, 308, 309, 316
  Minor, 316
  most socially valuable defense, 297
  Multiple, 309, 316
  nature of, 296
  Niagara Falls Analogy and, 312–13
  obsessive and, 303
  Partial, success limited in, 308–9, 316, 317
  Personal-Tragedy, great undertakings initiated, 300–01, 316
  personality development and, 302, 304, 313, 316
  Preventive, 310, 317
  Prognostic, 310–12, 317
  as psychic compromise, 300, 315
  psychic energy of, *Kinetic-Energy Principle* and, 312, 317
  Reaction Formation
    as "halfway house," 290
    in social benefits, 283
  Sexual, 299, 304, 305, 316
  special therapeutic techniques, 307
  Sublimation, as term for, 296
  Substitution similar to, 317, 403
  Successful, 307, 316
  Symbolization and, 305, 422
  Therapeutic, 310–12
  Vocational, 303 ff., 316
    exhibitionism in acting, 306
    homosexuality and, 306
    parental drives thwarted, 307–8
    into law career, 308
    professional activities and, 303–4
    sexual energies diverted through, 304
    symbolism in occupation, 305
Recognition-Deferment Rationalization, 256–57, 275
  in loss of affection, 257
Recognition, *Eleemosynary Rationalization* and, 267
Reconciliation between standards and behavior, 252, 274, 276
Recriminations transposed in depression, through Introjection, 184

Reenforcement
  of Denial, 64
  Restitutive, 389, 399
  Standards-, 286, 293–94
Reflected-Glory, Basking in, 144, 158
Regression, 319 ff.
  Adult, 328
  attempts to maintain ego integrity, 333
  Attitudinal, 322, 323, 352
  Basic Trend Toward Emotional Health applies, 347, 354
  Behavioral, 322–24, 330, 345–46, 352
    assessment of, as *Regression-Gauge,* 345–46
    in childhood, 324
    knowledge of carcinoma leading to, 330
    in psychotic reaction, 323
    readoption of infantile modes of gratification, 322
  Childhood, 324, 325, 328, 352–53
    not necessarily pathologic, 324
    reaction to new baby, 325
    Tidal-Progression of Maturity Concept, 324
  Complete, 344–45, 354
  Conflict-Indicators, 325, 327, 330, 353
    return to earlier era of adjustment, 325, 352
    in stress consequent to situational interpersonal change, 327
    symbolism and significance of, 330
  Conversion, 50–51, 340, 353, 354
    basic to Conversion Reaction, 50–51
    dependency conflict and, 340–41
    Regression takes place readily, 340, 353
  decompensation and, 333, 353
  definition of, 320
  delusion and, 339
  Dependency-Seeking Principle (DSP) 331, 338 ff., 353
    in Conversion, 340
    in Delusion and Depression, 339, 342
    in Fatigue States, 342
    in *Hygeiaphrontis,* 339, 342–43
    in hypnosis, 341
    in *Neuroses-Following-Trauma,* 343
    in Phobic Reactions, 338, 339
    Vicious Circle of Self-Defeat applies, 342
  in Depression, 339, 342
  Directional-Tenet of, 320, 323, 351
    to earlier, less mature level of adjustment, 320, 351
    in *Major Regression,* 323
  Directly-Proportional Ego-Response, Law of, 322–23, 352
  Disciplinary, in childhood, 325–26, 352

Regression (con't.)
dynamics of, 329
Ego Retreat, as alternate term for, 319, 343, 351
Emotional Fatigue and, 340–41
Extension contributing to, 462
external emotional supplies and, 347
Fantasy representing, 110, 113, 119, 120
Fixation and, 334, 335, 352
-Gauge, 337, 345, 354
   in delineating neurotic from psychotic reaction, 345
   five different aspects of emotional illness and, 337, 353
hallucinations and, 69
Hypnotic, 341
Illness-, 329, 330, 353
   carcinoma and, 330
   major illness or surgery and, 329
Increasing-Complexity Principle and, 325, 352
Introjection and, 166, 189
levels of, in hypnosis, 341
as *Lower Order* defense, 321
Major, 321–22, 334, 344, 351
   as massive behavioral reversion, 321, 351
   overwhelming stress and, 334
   psychotic illness and, 344
Making-up-for Principle, 321, 331, 352, 354
Massive (or *Complete*), 344–45, 351, 354
Maturity, Law of, 335, 352
Minor, 321, 326, 334, 351
Mixed, 324, 329, 352
multiplication of dependency needs and, 331
nature of, 320
Neuroses-Following-Trauma and, 343
Normal, 324, 352
Obsessive-Compulsive, 343
Partial, 323, 352
Pathologic, 337–38, 353
Phobic, DSP operative in, 338–39
present in all emotional illness, 337
to primitive mode of perception in hallucinations, 69
Proportional Ego-Response Law in, 322, 352
psychic-emotional withdrawal as alternate term, 320
as *psychologic flight,* 331
Psychologic Recapitulation Route and, 331, 340, 352, 354
   of childhood illness, 332
   determines character, for and locale of symptoms, 352

Regression (con't.)
   earlier physical pain or symptoms and, 331
   Somatic Conversions and, 340
psychosexual development and, 328
psychosis and, 323, 345, 348, 351
as recapitulation, emotional, 333, 352, 353
   decompensation and, 333, 352
   of earlier manifestations, 353
Resistance-, as *Secondary Defense,* 346, 352, 354
-Retreat, 333
-Sans-Withdrawal in *schizophrenia,* 490
schizophrenia and, 344–45, 490
Sexual, 330
Temporary, 343, 353
Tidal-Progression in, 346, 352, 354
Total, 323, 334, 344, 351
in Traumatic Neuroses, 343
Treatment, 347, 348, 354
   dependency needs purposely gratified, 347, 354
   in psychotic reaction, 348
Ultimate-Dependency Goal Concept, 322, 338, 352
Unhealthful Fantasy and, 113
Vicious Circle of Self-Defeat applies, 342, 354
Withdrawal distinguished from, 351, 490
Regressive
behavior in child, 326
implications in *Hygeiaphrontis,* 339
Incorporation in adult, 170
-Indicator in attitudes and behavior, 326, 353
manifestations, Fantasy as, 109
Therapy, 349, 350, 351, 354
   freedom from responsibility and maximum support in, 350
   maturity fostered through, 351
   Regression encouraged, 349
Regret, Dream-of-, guilt and, 396, 399
Rejection, 63, 222, 223, 242, 243
minimal acquaintance and, 243
   in mother, 63
   Negative King David Reaction and, 243
primordial, 223
Projection of hostile feelings and, 222
Relationship(s)
Compartmentalization, 454
Hand-in-Glove Concept, 171
-Ideals, 128, 131
interpersonal, 153, 154, 164. See also *Interpersonal.*
   earlier person influencing new acquaintance, 154
Identification and, 153

Relationship (s) (con't.)
    orality as primordial type, 164
    Personal Yardstick and, 153
    sexual, 432–33, 441. See also *Sexual.*
  new, 152, 154, 159
  recapitulation, 129
  -*Replacement,* 479 ff.
    conscious level, 479
    destructive, with men, 482
    particularly applicable, 480
    with woman, alliance, 481
  strained, 89
  symbiotic, 46
  -*Undoing,* 441, 443
  unsuccessful, 126
Relative normalcy, 217
Religious
  doctrine, moral connotations of acts
    and, 448
  Identification, 128
  prejudice, Generalization and, 474
Remission, psychic, as term for Absolution, 448
Remodeling as Substitution, 403
Remorse, 432, 441
  motivates *Childhood Undoing,* 432
  Undoing of, in sexual relations, 441
Renaissance, 33, 267
  Eleemosynary Rationalization and, 267
  Medical, 33
Reparation, 386, 393, 395, 431, 441, 450
  endeavors at, through *Social Restitu-
    tion,* 393, 398
  gifts, in *Restitution-Via-Charity,* 395
  for hurts and injury through *Relation-
    ship-Undoing,* 441
  sought by ego through *Restitution,* 386
  unconscious, as term for *Restitution,*
    386
  for wrong doing through *Atonement-
    Penance,* 450
Repentance, 451
Replacement, 98, 125, 129, 403, 459,
  479 ff.
  Alternating Personality and, 98
  beliefs of alleged maltreatment and,
    230–31
  Displacement in phobias and, 479–80
  forbidden intercourse and, thoughts of,
    483
  Idealized Object and, 125
  Object-, 479–80, 482
  Relationship-, conscious level, 479,
    481–83
    in alliance with woman, 481
    destructive, with men, *Vicious Circle
      of Self-Defeat* and, 482
    Object-Replacement relates, 482–83
  Substitution, 402, 479, 482
    Idealization and, *rapid,* 129

Replacement (con't.)
  as one object replaces the other,
    402, 479
  similarity to original, 482
  Symptom-, of cough with backache,
    480–81
Representation, external, Substitution as
  an unconscious, 412
Repressed
  impulses, Conversion and, 43
  material, as goal of therapy, 374
  strivings, expression of, 360
Repression, 357 ff.
  Association-, 356 ff., 364–65, 378
  as automatic forgetting, 378
  Auxiliary, 360, 364–65, 375, 378–79
  character formation and, 373
  Conversion reenforcing, 31, 44
  definition of, 359
  Denial and, 59–60, 69, 80, 96, 359,
    374
    as adjunct, 80, 374
    as blocking of idea, 69
    close dynamic relationship, 59–60
    overlap of, 359
    symbolizes *Deferment* or Denial of
      something unpleasant, 96
  in Depressive Reaction, anger and, 184
  derepression and, *Acute Anxiety At-
    tack,* 374, 376
  desperate effort to maintain, 44
  Displacement and, 86
  Distortion toward nonawareness and,
    458
  dynamics, 372
  Electronic Analogy applies, 369, 379
  Emotional-Object Amalgam and, 367–
    69, 379
    definition of, 368
    memory and, 368–69
    Universal Affect in, 366, 367
  exaggerated in psychopathology, 375
  Fantasy and, 114, 120
    as ally, 120
    in maintenance of, 114
  Historical Validation in, 361–63, 370,
    378
    Bernheim, Janet, Breuer, and Freud,
      362–63
    Herbart, Schopenhauer, and Charcot,
      361
    Nietzsche and Darwin, 370
  hostile attitudes leading to Reaction
    Formation, 284
  Incomplete, 377, 380
  instinctual drives and, 272
  Intellectualization and, 476
  Inversion as secondary elaboration,
    204
  Isolation relaxing restrictive forces, 477

Repression (con't.)

Kinetic-Energy Principle (KEP) and, 312, 360, 373, 374, 379
application, 312
in *Principle of Overextension,* 374
psychic energy required, 360, 373, 379
in *King David Reaction,* 237
as *Lower Order* (or *primitive*) dynamism, 12, 359
Major, complete Repression as, 364–65, 379
Major Rechannelization and, 310
major role in emotional health and illness, 358, 372, 374, 378
derepression leading to therapy, 374
in *First Line of Psychic Defense,* 358, 378
precedes evolution of ego defenses, 372
Massive, 373, 379
in psychotic reactions, 379
success of, psychic-emotional make-up and, 373
Minor, 365–66, 379
of anniversary dates, 366
covers wide variety of items, 379
myriad memory lapses and, 365
neurosis and, 375
Overextension Principle and, 360, 374–75, 380
exaggerated Repression, 375
Kinetic-Energy Principle applies, 360
more data than necessary expressed, 380
Primal Displacement comparable to, in early life, 91
Primary, 12, 111, 363–64, 373, 379
instinctual material and, 363, 379
undeveloped early ego and, 373
as primordial defense, 363
Projection and, 228
psychologic blindness and convenient memory, 371, 380
psychologic endeavors of, 198
Rechannelization and, 315
Secondary, 363–64, 379
once-conscious data and, 363–64
Primary Repressions and, 379
in *Sexual-Object Displacement,* not complete, 89
suppression distinguished from, 361
Symbolization facilitating, 416
Total, 379
Universal Affect, Law of, 366, 367, 379
bound to object as emotional charge, 366, 379
implication in memory, 367

Requital, Psychic, as term for *Retribution,* 483–84
Resemblance, unrecognized, leading to negative *King David Reaction,* 241
Resentment, 116, 229, 408, 409, 486
checked, by *Fantasy-Lesson Function,* 116
toward mother, Reversal of attitudes and, 486
recognition, 229
Substitution expressing, 408, 409
family doctor as target, 409
masochism and, 408
Resistance, 11, 48–49, 118. See also *Secondary Defense Concept.*
apathy as, 196
Denial, in alcoholism, 67
dream interpretation, premature, 419
exaggerated ego defenses as, 10
Excessive Rechannelization and, 305
Fantasy and, 73–74, 120
-Intellectualization as, 475
-Inversion, 198, 199
attitude and behavior interpretation, 198
negative transference and, 199
Regression, as *Symptom-Defensive Rationalization,* 271, 346
-Undoing, 437, 443
of previous therapeutic interpretation, 437
Universal Affect Law (UAL), 367
Resolution, conflict
Sexual Denial evolves, 71–72
ultimate aim of Denial, 71, 79
Respite, Principle of Intellectualization in therapy, 475
Response pattern, *Fire Drill* as, 470
Responsibility, 81, 100, 227, 264
conscious *Rationalization* to evade, 264
Denial of, even if secretly admitted, 81
Dissociation of, 100–01
Projection of, for gangrenous foot, 227
Restitution, 13, 386 ff., 430, 440
-in-Abeyance, 396–97, 399
embezzlement as basis, 397
Suspended Reaction Concept applies, 396, 399
Atonement-Penance and, 388, 398
for bad checks, 104
Business, 396, 399
-Via-Charity, in character analysis, 395, 399. See also *Defensive Layering.*
Conscious, 388–89, 398
Criminal, 393, 398
definition of, 387
in dreams, as *Dream-Regret,* 396, 399

Restitution (con't.)
  Enforced, 389, 392, 393, 399
    criminal law and, 389
    as subtype of *Public Restitution,*
      392, 399
  Guilt Group Dynamisms and, 387
  as *Higher Order* defense, 387
  Interpersonal, 390–92, 398
    development of *Restitutive-Behavior*
      and, 390–92, 399
    Never-Enough Principle and, 391–
      92, 399
  Legacy, 397, 399
    bequests and, 397
    Restitution-by-Will, alternate term
      for, 399
  as *Making-up-for Process,* alternate
    term for, 387
  Minor, 390, 398
  nature of, 386
  Never-Enough Principle, or Spiral, in
    endeavors, 391–92, 399
  Pious, church contributions and, 394,
    399
  -by-Proxy, 395, 399
  Public, includes subtypes of *Voluntary*
    and *Enforced,* 392, 398
  Social, 393–94, 399
  superego pressure and, 398
  Token, 392, 393, 399
    for embezzlement, 397
    as *Voluntary Restitution,* 392, 399
  types of, 390
  Voluntary, as subtype of *Public Resti-
    tution,* 392, 399
  Undoing and, 388, 398, 430, 440
    as *Criminal Reparation,* 430
    human sacrifices represent, 440
    more primitive than *Restitution,*
      388, 398
Restitutive-Behavior, 390–91, 398
  exaggerated guilt feelings and, 391
Restitutive Reenforcements, inner needs
  and, 389, 393, 399
Restitutive Spiral, 391
Restriction of mental faculties through
  Unwitting Ignorance, 489
Retaliation, dread of, *Hostility-Inversion*
  and, 195
Retreat, 320, 475, 476
  Ego-, as term for Regression, 319, 333,
    351
  emotional-psychic, as term for With-
    drawal, 489
  Intellectualized-, 476
  psychologic, 321, 351
  from reality, Fantasy and, 114, 119,
    120
    Unhealthful Fantasy and, 114

Retreat (con't.)
  Regression-, 333, 353
    Directional-Tenet of, 320
  welcome, Intellectualization as, 475
Retribution, 242–43, 483–84
  Guilt Group of Dynamisms and, 483
  psychic requital as term for, 483
  punishment of self and others ob-
    served, 483–84
  suicide and, 484
Retrospective Denial, 197
Retrospective Devaluation, 197, 484–86
  Compensation as basis, 485
  Depersonalization and, 485–86
  Distortion and, 486
  downgraded emotional feeling and, 484
  Falsification and, 486
  as *Higher Order Dynamism,* 484
  murder plans and, 485
  Sour Grapes Rationalization similar
    to, 484
  suicide and, 484
Retrospective Falsification, akin to *Ret-
  rospective Devaluation,* 486
Revenge in *Fantasy-Lesson Function,* 116
Reversal, 65, 205, 285 ff., 408, 486 ff.
  Characterologic, mother's pattern in
    handling finances and, 486–87
  Contra-Parent Reaction Formation
    and, 285
  Denial and, 65
  emotional, 193, 203, 486
    Inversion and Reaction Formation
      as types of, 203
    as term for Inversion, 193, 486
  homosexuality and, 488
  Intrapsychic, Reaction Formation and,
    203
  Mood-Inversion and, 201
  of outer facade in *King David Reac-
    tion,* 247
  in phobia of vomiting, 339
  Political, of John Roosevelt, 286, 293,
    295
  pregnancy attitudes and, 64
  Reaction Formation and, 289
  Sexual, 72, 73, 487
Revulsion, *Attraction-Inversion* and, 196
RF. See *Reaction Formation.*
RG. See *Regression-Gauge.*
RI (*Regressive-Indicator*), 326, 353
Righteous Indignation, 7
Riots, *Group Compathy* and, 140
Rituals, 437, 439, 443
  Compulsive, *Symbolic Undoing* and,
    439, 443
  Obsessional, Undoing as unwitting aim
    of, 437
Rivalry, 167

Role, second mother, *Behavioral Conversion* and, 42
Romance, *Sexual-Fantasy System* and daydreams, 114
Romantic Fantasy as substitute sexual gratification, 115
Roosevelt, Theodore, *Conscious Compensation* and, 25
Route, *Psychologic Recapitulation*, 332, 340, 341, 353, 376
Royal Affection, as term for positive *King David Reaction*, 238 ff.
Royal Anger, as term for negative *King David Reaction*, 238 ff., 248
Royal Love, as term for positive *King David Reaction*, 238, 246
   unwittingness as requirement, 246
Rule of Impression Priority, 145, 152–53, 159, 178, 237, 248
   definition of, 145
   Internalization of attitudes and, 178
   interpersonal relationships and, 152
   King David Reaction and, 237
Rule, Surgery-in-Abeyance (SIAR), 48
Russian treatment of Hungarians, *Underdog Identification* and, 157

SAAC (*Secondary Appeal in Advertising Concept*), 149, 159
Sadistic Phase, Anal and Oral, 329
Sadness shared in *Group Compathy*, 140
Sales stimulated via SAAC, 149
Salesmen, *Illusion-of-Continued Living* and, 76
Satisfactions, 79, 151, 159, 164
   infant, through suckling, 164
   neurotic, through sexual promiscuity, 79
   Substitute, through Fantasy, 402
   Vicarious, 151, 159
   Substitutive-Gratifications follow, 159
"Saving face," *Ego-Enhancing Inversion* and, 200
Scapegoat Reaction, 90, 92, 248, 316
   Characterologic Rationalization with, 273
   Convergence in, 456
   Displacement to substitute object led to by, 87–88
   family doctor as *substitute target*, 409
   girl as victim of, 284
   Introjection as variation, 182
   King David Reaction and, 238
   overdeterminism in, 478
   replacement in, 480
   Substitution in, 409–10
   Szu-Ma Chien illustrations
      Historical Validation, 301

Scapegoat Reaction (con't.)
   Personal-Tragedy Rechannelization, 302
Schizophrenia, 102, 106, 232, 344, 345, 490
   Bleuler's Dissociation as term for, 102, 106
   Massive Regression in, 344
   paranoid delusion in, 232
   Psychotic Regression in, 345
Schizophrenic
   Dissociation, alternately *Bleuler's Dissociation*, 102–3, 106
   Reaction, 102, 222, 230, 348, 409, 490
   Dissociation, 102
   Paranoid Indifference in, 230
   Regression-Sans-Withdrawal, 490
   Regression Treatment, 348
   Scapegoat Reaction and, 409
School teacher, 41, 87, 90
   Behavioral Conversion, 41
   Personal-Feeling Displacement, 87
   Scapegoat Reaction, 90
Scientific Determinism, Law of, 371, 380, 393
   "chance" explained by, in *Public Restitution*, 393
   in Repression, 371
SD. See *Secondary Defense*.
Second mother role, 41–42
Secondary
   Appeal in Advertising, 149, 159
   changes in *Functional-Structural Progression*, 52
   Defense, Concept of, 14, 197, 213, 218, 332, 353, 438, 443
   in defense of ego defenses, 211
   definition of, 11
   "epilepsy" as, in alcoholism, 67–68
   Excessive Rechannelization and, 304–5
   in gain
      of Conversion symptoms, 36, 49
      of Rationalizations, 277
   Resistance, 10
      -Intellectualization, 475
      -Inversion, 199
      -Regression, 346
   Supporting Delusion, 270, 277
   Symptom-Defensive Rationalization, 271
   Undoing as resistant phenomena in therapy, 437
Delusion, 270, 277
elaboration, 213, 218, 238
   other ego defenses supported by Rationalization, 251
   of Reaction Formation, Repression and, 280, 293–94

Secondary (con't.)
of Repression and Denial, Inversion
representing, 195–96, 204
mental mechanisms, 7
Repressions, 364, 379
encountered in treatment, 379
once-conscious material and, 364
Secretary, 45, 244, 391
rage and, in *King David Reaction,* 244
Restitutive-Behavior, guilt and, 391
Sensory Conversion, 45
Security
anxiety relief and, 213
maturity in "outgrowing" *Conflict-In-dicators,* 327
Military-Unit Identification promoting, 150
operation, *Group Identification* and, 150–51
Soteria and, 125, 414, 415
Ultimate-Dependency Goal of Regression and, 322
unwittingly sought through Identification, 134
Seeker, Celebrity-, Reflected Glory and, 144, 158
SEHA (*Specific Emotional Hazards of Adulthood*), 327, 476
SEHC (*Specific Emotional Hazards of Childhood*), 71, 327
Selective inattention, *Unwitting Ignorance* and, 489
Self
absorption, Fantasy and, 109
-Aggrandizing Substitution, 402, 410
-appraisal, 227, 236, 237, 239, 241
inexplicable attraction and repulsions result, 236
King David Reaction and, 237, 239, 241, 248
blind-spots about, 224–25, 380
-condemnation, *substitute target* and, 228
-critical feelings, *Projective Vicious Circle* and, 228
-deception, 68, 251, 262
Denial of alcoholism and, 68
Rationalization and, 251, 262
-defeat, 12
Atonement-Penance and, 451
consequence of ego defenses, 9
Dissociation and, 101
Fire Drill operation and, 471
Idealization and, 125–27
Impossible Standard leading to, 126, 130
Projection of disowned affect and, 222
Projective Vicious Circle and, 228

Self-defeat (con't.)
Vicious Circle of, 21, 41, 336, 342, 482
Behavioral Conversions and, Compensation and, 21, 41
in *Hygeiaphrontic Personality,* 342
in *Maturation-Fixation* at college level, 335–36
in *Relationship-Displacement,* 482
-Defense Concept, 97, 104, 106, 108
Depersonalization and, 104
Dynamism Elaboration and, 97, 106, 108
Unconscious Identification and, 157–58
-deprecatory attitudes, *depressive-introject* and, 183
-discipline, parents and, 155
-enhancement, *Aggrandizing Distortion* and, 458
-esteem, 116, 237
Compensation and, 25
enhanced, 214
low, 243, 284
attitude-symptom and, 284
King David's Anger and, 243
Maintenance Principle, 33, 52
preservation through Denial, 66
Rationalization and, 259, 264, 273
built up and maintained, 259, 273
level of, revealed, 264
-estimation, *King David Reaction* and, 237
-hatred, *King David Reaction* and, 239
ideal concept of, 272
-picture, 64, 200, 205, 209
Denial in maintaining, 64
Ego-Enhancing Inversion and, 200
praise, 42
-protection, *Devaluation* and, 457
-punishment, 31, 185
Absolution and, 448
Atonement-Penance, alopecia in, 452
Identification in, 148
Retribution and, 483
Shattered-Ideal and, 125
-recrimination in depression, 184
Selflessness, *Eleemosynary Rationalization* and, 266
SEMT (*Self-Esteem Maintenance in Therapy*), 33, 52
Senescence, 329
Senior Dynamisms (*Senior Ego Defense* or *Senior Mental Mechanism*), also *Major, Primary* or *Prime,* 7, 317, 321
Rechannelization and, 321

Senior Dynamisms (con't.)
  Regression and, 321
  tabulated, 7
Sensory Conversion
  anesthesia and, 45
  dissociated sensation, 97
  includes sensation disturbances, 44–
    45, 51
Sensory loss, non-correspondence with
    nerve supply in Conversion, 44
Sensory perception, cutaneous dissocia-
    tion compared to *Affect*-Disso-
    ciation, 97
Sensuality
  Socio-Sexual Dilemma and, 73
  suppressed in Victorian Era, 314
Seoul, Korea, widespread Denial in, 60
Sequence, psychopathologic: anxiety; dy-
    namism; hypertrophy or failure;
    emotional illness, 211
  Conversion and, 51
Sex, 287, 302, 331, 401, 433, 483
Sex appeal in advertising, 149
Sex play, pedophilic, 200
Sexual
  adjustment, handicapping, 441
  attitudes, 73, 197, 204
    inverted, 197, 204
    reversal, 73
  behavior, 79, 89, 197–98
    compulsive, *Sexual-Object Displace-
    ment* and, 89
    neurotic satisfactions and, conse-
      quences denied, 79
    Standards-Inversion and, 197
  Compensation, as term for *Don Juan-
    ism,* 21
  Denial, 71–72
  drives, 245, 280, 299, 304, 312, 316
    disowned through *King David Re-
    action,* 245
    Excessive Rechannelization, 304,
      316
    Improvement Sublimation, 312
    Reaction Formation against, 280
    Rechannelization and healthful ex-
      pression of, 299
  energy, *Rechannelization* and, 299
  experience, 79, 139, 463
    compathy prominent, 139
    extramarital, Denial of consequences
      of, 79
    Phobic Hygeiaphrontis and, 463
  expression, *Sexual-Object Displace-
    ment* and, 88
  Fantasy-System, 114, 115–16, 120
    allows gratification, 115–16, 120
    love and romance as subjects, 114

Sexual (con't.)
  gratification, Fantasy and, 115–16, 120
    Splitting-in-, 115–16, 121, 488
  guilt, *Atonement-Penance* and, 452
  impulses, Conversion and, 43
  inhibitions, *Socio-Sexual Dilemma* and,
    72–73
  interest, 305, 306
    absent in *Rechannelization* of homo-
      sexual drives, 306
    minimal in *Excessive Rechanneliza-
    tion,* 305
  intercourse, thoughts replaced, 483
  inversion, homosexuality and, 194
  -*Object Displacement,* 88, 89
    follows serious conflict, 88
    original object replaced, 89
  overactivity, Compensation and, 25
  prowess, 165
  Rationalization in World War II, 256,
    269, 276
  Rechannelization in accepting intoler-
    able impulses, 299–300, 316
  relations, Undoing and, 432–33, 441
    guilt in *Behavioral Undoing Cycle,*
      432–33
    in *Relationship-Undoing,* 441
  Reversal of pleasurable into aversion,
    487
  -*Social Dilemma,* 72–73, 82, 115
  taboos, *Parental Reaction Formation*
    and, 287
  Undoing, 443
  urges, 110, 125
    disowned through *Idealization,* 125
    partially discharged through Fantasy,
      110
Sexuality, need for, *Relationship-Dis-
    placement* and, 482
Shakespeare, 124, 240, 440
  Literary Idealization and, 124
  Nathan device used by, 240
  Undoing operation in Macbeth, 440
Shattered Ideal, 125, 127, 130
  as former object, 127, 130
  self-punishment and, 125
  in *Teen-age Idealization,* 127
Shoplifting, *Identification with Wrong-
    doer* and, 148
SIA (*Surgery-in-Abeyance Rule*), 48
Sibling, *Mild Regressions* and, 324
Side-by-Side Dissociation, 96, 98, 105,
    106
  allows concurrent activities to be pur-
    sued, 105, 106
  in Dissociative Reactions, 98
  two or more parts of the mind operate
    independently, 96
Significance, 457, 484
  Devaluation reducing, 457

Significance (con't.)
  Retrospective Devaluation downgrading, 484
Similarities, unrecognized, underlying KDR, 239
Simpatico as type of Projective Identification, 137
"Sinfulness of pleasures of the flesh," 487
Sins, Absolution and, 448
Sleep, 77, 98, 193, 409, 436
  Denial-of-Death and, 77
  escape into dependency and, 409
  euphemism for death, 77
  habits, Inversion of, 193
  -talking, Undoing and, 436
  -walking, Undoing and, 436
Slip of the tongue, ambivalence in therapy and, 409
Smoking, Replacement with sweets and, 481
Social
  benefits, Rechannelization and, 283, 297
  Conversion, 38 ff.
  -Idealization, groups of people and, 128, 131
  -Inversion, dissimulation and, 194–95
  pressure, Restitution through guilt and, 398
  purpose subserved through Predecessor Identification, 141
  Rationalization, 256, 268–69, 276
    groups share in, 268–69
    widespread justification and, 276
  Reaction Formation, 281–82, 293
  Restitution, 393–94, 399
    to assuage guilt, 394
    society benefits, 399
    society, or a segment of it, attempts generalized endeavors, 303–4
  status, Secondary Appeal in Advertising and, 149
  Undoing, offense or compliment and, 438, 443
  value, 141, 297
    Identification and, 141
    Rechannelization and, 297
Society, limitations imposed by 210
Socio-Sexual Dilemma, 72–73, 82, 115
  in adjustment, 72
  Fantasy-System and, 115–16
  major current in today's society, 73
Solace, Childhood Regression and, 325
Somatic Conversion, 31 ff., 42 ff., 69, 113, 340, 354, 361
  in childhood, 34
    paraplegia and, 34
  as Conversion-Escape, 48
  epigain, 49

Somatic Conversion (con't.)
  expresses emotional conflict, 50
  Fantasy and, 113
  gross motor and sensory changes, 42 ff.
  la belle indifférence in, 45, 69
    first described by Charcot, 69
    in sensory loss and paralysis, 45
  as part of Concept of Conversion Reactions, 31
  pseudoepileptic Behavioral Conversion and, 41
  regressive features in, 340, 354
  as sensory loss and partial paralysis, 45
  symptoms of, hypnosis and, 42 ff., 361
Somatic language, 31
Somatic preoccupation in Hygeiaphrontis, dependency and, 343
Somnambulism, 69, 95, 98
  Denial and, 69
  Dissociation and, 95, 98
Sophistication, 215, 419
  correlation to type of defense evolved, 215
  Increasing Complexity of Dreams and, 419
Soteria, 125, 128, 326, 414–15, 478–79, 483
  blanket serves as, in Disciplinary-Regression, 326
  Personal Invulnerability similar to, 479
  phobia as converse of, 125
  formation, Object-Ideal and, 128
  object: comfort, security, protection and, 415
  Reactions, neurotic associations and, 368, 414, 415
Sour-Grapes Rationalization, 256, 260, 275, 484
  Aesop's fable of "Fox and Grapes" and, 260
  Retrospective Devaluation and, 484
Speaking ability, Denial-for-Confidence and, 59
Specific Emotional Hazards
  of Adulthood, 327, 476
  of childhood, 71, 327
    Conflict-Indicators, 327
    in Denial of loss, 71
Speech, Mannerism Identification and, 142
Spiral, 221, 391, 399, 431, 442, 471.
    See also Circle, Vicious; Cycle; Vicious Circle.
  Never-Enough, 399, 471
    Fire Drill, 471
    Restitution, 399
  Restitutive, 391

Spiral (con't.)
  Undoing, expiation and, 431, 442
  vicious, Fantastic Person and, 221
Split personality, 102
Splitting, 76, 97, 102, 115–16, 488
  Affect Dissociation and, 97
  Denial and, 488
  Dissociative, 95, 99, 102, 105, 115, 488
  of ego, 76
  -in-Fantasy, sexual gratification and, 115–16, 121, 488
  -off process, 97, 102
    in *Bleuler's Dissociation,* 102
    in *Self-Defense Concept* in Dissociation, 97
Spurious Confession, 146–47, 159
SR. See *Scapegoat Reaction.*
SSD (*Socio-Sexual Dilemma*), 72–73, 82, 115
Stability, 211
Stage(s)
  Anal, 329
  Genital, 329
  of Personality Development, 328–29
Standard(s), 102, 126, 155, 197, 204, 286
  Identification and, 155
  Impossible, 126, 130
    -Inversion, sex and, 197, 204
  personal, 169
  -Reenforcement, through *parental Reaction Foundation,* 286, 293–94
  taken in, 174
State, 98, 105, 114
  Dissociative, as major route for *psychologic flight,* 105
  Emotional Fatigue, Fantasy- Pattern and, 114
  Fugue as type of *Dissociative* Reaction, 98
Stature, compensation for small, 19
Status
  epilepticus, 40
  held up for admiration in SAAC, 149
  seeking in *Group Identification,* 150
Status quo, 12, 199, 346, 461, 490
  characterologic, in *Trait Balance,* 199, 272, 346, 461–62
  of existing psychologic defenses, 12
  neurotic, 12, 199, 205, 346, 428, 461
    in *Inversion* of therapist's role, 199
    in *Resistance-Regression,* 346
  psychotic, through *Schizophrenic Reaction,* 490
Sterility, Denial of, 64
Stress, 322–23, 331, 478
  Personal Invulnerability and, 478
  Regression and, 322–23, 331
Strivings seek expression, 360

Structural Progression, Functional (FSPC), 10
Student, 39, 72, 81, 100, 222, 253
  conversion pseudoconvulsions and, 39
  Denial of jealousy and, 81
  Dissociation of responsibility and, 100
  overconditioning in *Sexual Denial,* 72
  Projection of hostility and, 222
  Rationalizes behavior under hypnosis, 253
Styles, *Mass Identification* and, 145
Sublimation, 394. See also *Rechannelization.*
  alternate term for *Rechannelization* and *Instinctual Diversion,* 296
  Avocational, 304, 308–10, 316
  emotional health and, 317
  -en-Therapy, term similar to *Improvement Rechannelization,* 311, 317
  Excessive, 304, 305, 317
  Improvement, 310–11, 312, 317
  Incomplete, 310, 316
  origins of term, 297
  Partial, 308, 316
  Prognostic, 310, 317
  superego evolvement and, 313
Subservience, *attitude-symptom* and, 284–85
Substitute
  -Idealization leading to *Relationship-Replacement,* 129, 131
  object, 87, 401
    in *Scapegoat Reaction,* 87
    Substitution operation and, 401
  target, Introjection and, 183. See also *Scapegoat Reaction.*
Substitution, 401 ff.
  Activity, aggressive drives and, 402–3, 410
  Antidotal, hurt or loss made up by, 407, 410
  Attention-Focus, 403–4, 407, 410
    disturbing interests and, 403–4
    as more acceptable, 407
  Counterirritant, 406–7, 410
    in Obsessive-Compulsive Reactions, 406–7, 410
  definition of, 402
  Denial and, in alcoholism, 67, 403
  Displacement and, 89, 90, 402, 404–5
    emotional symbiosis and, 89–90
    Phobic defense and, 404–5
    forms *Symbiotic-Substitution* in Phobic Reactions, 402, 410
  in *Emotional Diffusion,* more general target and, 473
  as *Higher Order Dynamism,* 401, 410
  Idealization and, 129
  nature of, 404

Substitution (con't.)
   Obsessive-Compulsive and Phobic Re-
      actions and, 402
   operation apparent in therapy, 408–10
   Rechannelization and, 317, 403, 405,
      410
      aims and goals, 405, 410
      as requisite to, 317
      similarity of operation and conse-
         quences, 403
   Replacement and, 479, 482
      at times almost identical, 479
      at times differs, as object replaced
         is similar to original, 482
   resentment expression and, 408–9
   resolution of conflict, as endeavor at,
      405
   Scapegoat Reaction and, 409–10
   Self-Aggrandizing, 402, 410
      Compensation akin to, 402
      mediocre achievements and, 402,
         410
   Symbiotic-, Displacement and, in
      Phobic Reactions, 402, 410
Substitutive living in *Vicarious Identifi-
   cation*, 151
Substitutive Gratification, 151, 152, 159
   serving useful and constructive pur-
      poses, 159
   Vicarious Identification and, 151, 152
Substitutive satisfactions, Fantasy and,
   402
Success, guilt and *Restitution* and, 397
Successful Rechannelization, 307, 316
Suggestion
   Conversion Personality and, 46
   post-hypnotic, 253
Suicide, 184, 202, 339–40, 448, 484
   Absolution and, attempts at, 448
   Introjection and, 184
   Retribution in, 484
   Retrospective Devaluation of attempt,
      484
   rumination in Depressive Reaction,
      Mood-Inversion and, 202
   verge of, *Phobic Hygeiaphrontis* and,
      339
Superego, 31, 91, 148, 166, 195, 252,
   454–55. See also *Conscience*.
   demands mediated by ego through
      Rationalization, 256
   Denial of, in extramarital sexual ex-
      perience, 79
   development, contributed to by
      Idealization, 125
      Incorporation, 168
      Internalization, 177
      Introjection, 189
   as Divine Providence in *Retribution*,
      483

Superego (con't.)
   elaboration, 313, 328–29, 448
      Absolution evolvement and, 448
   in Oedipal Period, 328–29
      Sublimation (*Rechannelization*) con-
         current to, 313
   exacts toll in *Standards-Inversion* in
      sexual behavior, 197- 98
   ideal concept of self evolved, 272
   overzealous, 148
   pressure, leads to efforts at *Restitution*,
      398
   punitive, in *Schizophrenic Reaction*,
      449
   Rechannelization (Sublimation) con-
      current with, 313
   Restitutive-Behavior motivated, 391
   Subverted in splitting-off process, 97
Supplies, emotional, 125, 132
Support, maximal, in *Bowen's Regressive
   Therapy*, 349–51
   in alcoholism, 350
Supporting Delusion as secondary de-
      fense, 270, 277
Suppression, 12, 378
   of aggression consciously effortful,
      283
   definition of, 12
   of fears, 35, 47
   of obsessive preoccupation with homo-
      sexuality, 406
   Repression distinguished from, 361
   in Victorian Era, 314
Surgery, *Illness Regression* and, 329
Surgery-in-Abeyance Rule, Conversion
      Reactions and, 48
Surprises, unpleasant, *Pessimistic Hy-
      geiaphrontis* and, 479
Surrogate, parental, 177
Survival, Dissociated Psychotic-, 101–2,
   106
Suspended Reaction, from guilt and
      Restitution-in-Abeyance, 397,
      399
Swallowing disorder as symbolic symp-
   tom, 420
Sweets as *Replacement* for smoking, 481
Symbiosis, emotional, between dynamisms
   Displacement and Substitution, 89
   Idealization and Identification, 125
   Inversion and Undoing, 204
   Rationalization and *Distortion*, 459
   Undoing and Denial, 437
Symbiotic relationship, 46
Symbiotic Substitution, conjoint opera-
      tion of Displacement in, in
      Phobic Reactions, 402, 410
Symbol(s), 413 ff.
   Childhood, 421
   communication requiring, 415

Symbol(s) (con't.)
  Condensation, 414, 421, 455
    in dreams and symptomatology, 421
    several objects represented, 414, 455
  Dream-, 416–17, 422
  in *Emotional-Object Amalgam,* 412
  General, 413, 415, 422
    culturally evolved, 422
    similar meanings to most people conveyed, 413
    widely recognized, 415
  Individual, 413, 415, 422
    as human resource, 415
    wide acceptance not required, 413
  overdetermined, 478
  raison d'être, 413
  Symptom-, Concept of, 420, 421
Symbolic
  meaning
    alopecia in *Atonement-Penance,* 452
    in Conversion Reaction, 416, 420
  objects as security in *Soterial Reactions,* 368, 414–15
  -Undoing, 439, 440, 443
    Compulsive Rituals, as in handwashing, 440–41
    prayers representing, 439
Symbolism, 305, 314, 408, 413, 455
  Condensation important, 455
  occupational choice and, 305
  Substitution in therapy and, 408
Symbolization, 412 ff., 456
  Childhood, 421
  Condensation, as external object, 414, 421
  Convergence and, 456
  Conversion Reactions and, 416, 420
  definition of, 414
  displacement of emotional charge from original object in, 420
  distortion achieved, 421
  in dreams, 416 ff.
    Guidepost Dreams in therapy, 417–19, 422
    Increasing Complexity, Law of, 418–19, 422
    Three basic factors in interpretation, 416
    Variable Interpretation, Tenet of, 417, 419–20, 422
  Emotional-Object Amalgam and, 412, 421, 422
    affect attached to new object, 412
    symbol comprises EOA, 421, 422
  General and *Individual,* 413, 415, 422
  as *Lower Order* dynamism, 414
  Multiple, in dreams, 417, 422
  Phobic Reactions and, 415
  Rechannelization and, 422

Symbolization (con't.)
  Repression facilitated, 416
  Soterial Reactions and, 414, 415
Sympathy, 136–37, 158, 179
  definition of, 137
  for father, Internalization of his attitudes and, 179
  as *Projective Identification,* 136–37
Sympatico, 137, 158
Symptom(s), 10, 30, 43, 374, 420, 436, 478
  as *affect equivalent,* pain and, 48
  Attitude, 284, 285, 288, 293, 470, 490
    low self-esteem and, 284
    in Reaction Formation, 284, 288, 293
    subservience, 285
    Withdrawal and, 284–85, 293, 490
  -Choice, 46, 51, 420
    Identification in, 46, 51
    symbolism in, in Conversion Reaction, 420
  -Compathy, Identification and Conversion following, 46
  Compromise Formations ineffectual, 454
  Conversion, Fainting as, 43
  conveying message, 36
  defend against action, 39
  Defense, Incomplete, anxiety and, 44
  -Defensive Rationalization, 256, 271, 276
  Denial, 73, 82
  as disguised expression of hidden impulses, 375
  elaboration, Conversion, 51
  emotional, can be symbols, 420
  evolvement, incomplete Repression and, 377
  Extension, 461
  formation, 10, 30, 290
    Conversion and, 30
    as new defense, 10
    Reaction Formation and, 290
  Identification, 46, 50, 51, 156, 160, 190. See also *Recapitulation.*
    in Conversion, 46
    in symptom choice of *Hygeiaphrontis,* 156, 190
  -Introjection, 185–86, 190
    results in *Symptom-Introject,* 185
    significant in psychopathology, 185–86, 190
  Kinetic-Energy Principle and, as derepression, 374
  language as nonverbal communication, 36
  neurosis, Conversion as, 31
  obsessive-compulsive, *Expiative Undoing* in, 431

Symptom (*s*) (con't.)
  Overdeterminism and, 478
  -Prominence, 11
  recapitulations in Regression, 332, 340,
    352, 354
  repetitive in Compulsion-Neuroses,
    436–37, 443
  -Replacement, 479
    of cough with backache, 480–81
  Somatic Conversion, 42 ff.
  -Symbol Concept, 420, 421
  Transparency Theory of, 36, 52
Symptomatic Reaction Formation, 291,
  293
Symptomatology, 310, 414
  Condensation Symbol evident, 414
  Ineffective Rechannelizations and, 310
Synthesis, 95–96, 105, 183. See also In-
  tegration.
  ego, promoted by psychic defenses, 96,
    209 ff., 214
  Introjection and Projection and, 189,
    223
  personality, Dissociation distinct from,
    95
System, Fantasy, 113, 114–16, 120
  Sexual, 114–16, 120
Szu-Ma Chien, as instance of *Personal-
  Tragedy Rechannelization*, 301–
  2

Taboos, sexual, *Parental Reaction Forma-
  tion* and, 287
Talion Law, abandoned for *Public Resti-
  tution*, 399
Target, 87–88, 91, 248, 409, 410, 480
  Convenient, 87–88, 90–91
    in Displacement of anger, 91
    in evolvement of *Displaced Com-
      plex*, 90–91
    in *Scapegoat Reaction*, 87–88
  Replacement, for hostility, 480
  substitute, 182, 248, 409, 410, 473
    family physician as, 410
    general in Emotional Diffusion, 473
    Introjection and, 183
    in *King David Reaction*, 248
    resentment expressed, 409
Teacher, 46, 145, 202, 227, 483
  Conversion through *Symptom Com-
    pathy*, 46
  Mood-Inversion in Depressive Reac-
    tion, 202
  Projection in *Mirror Defense*, 227
  Replacement used, 483
  Vocational Identification, 145
Tears, suppressed, 35
Teen-age Idealization, followed by *Shat-
  tered Ideal*, 127, 130

Teen-agers affected by *Bad Identification*,
  148
Telephoning, repetitive, 437
Television, *Central Identification* and,
  136
Temporary Regression, Somatic Preoccupation and, 343
Tenet-of-Regression, Directional, 320,
  323, 351
Tenet of Variable-Interpretation, 417,
  419, 420, 422
  definition of, 420
  in dreams, 417
  in symbolism of psychoses, 419
Terminal disease, *Illness-Denial* and *De-
  nial-of-Death* in, 74, 75, 77
Tertiary changes in *Functional-Structural
  Progression*, 52
Theory of Transparency, 36, 52
  Therapeutic community, *Regression*
    and, 348
  elucidation, 223, 233, 242
    of *King David Reaction*, 242
    of *Projection of disowned feelings*, 223,
      233
  Progress, Tidal Progression Concept
    in, 346, 352
  Rechannelization and, 307, 310–11
Therapy, 169, 377
  of adolescent fears of kissing, 187
  of alopecia, as *Atonement-Penance*,
    453
  Attitudinal-Generalization against au-
    thority, 473
  Attraction-Inversion, in homosexuality,
    196
  Bowen's Regressive, 348 ff.
    in alcoholism, 350
    needs gratified and maturity fostered
      in, 351
    positively regressive approach, 348
    therapeutic community meets needs
      of developmental level, 349
  Conversion-in-, headaches and, 35, 51
  Denial and, 59–60, 67
    -for-Confidence, 59–60
    insoluble in alcoholism, 67
  derepression essential in, 376
  Dissociation in, 100, 103
  Distortion and *Inversion*, 199
  dream analysis beneficial, 417–19
    Guidepost Dreams, 417–19
    symbols in, 417
  as educational process, 311
  elucidation and *Partial Introjection*,
    188
    Personal-Feeling Displacement, 87
    Restitution-in-Abeyance, 397
    Sexual-Fantasy System, 115

Therapy (con't.)
 Fantasy and, 116, 118–20
  aids, when constructively used, 120
  elucidation of *Fantasy-Lesson Function,* 116
  of intercourse leads to therapy, 118
  as resistance, 118–19
 free association in, 378
 goals of, repressed material and, 374
 Identification with Wrongdoer, 147
 initial attitudes toward, revealed in *Guidepost Dream,* 419
 Intellectualization-Respite in, 475
 intensive, *Sexual Rationalization* and, 269
 Isolation of affect, from death wishes, 477
 Libidinal Investment Principle in, 304, 317
 maturation during, 312
 Parental Identification and, 149
 Parental Incorporation and, 170
 Rechannelization, 307, 311, 317
 Regression, 337, 346
  -Gauge, for prognosis, 337
  Resistance-, as *Secondary Defense,* 346
 resistance to, 11, 305
  Excessive Rechannelization and, 305
  Secondary Defense and, 11. See also *Secondary Defense.*
 Schizophrenic Reaction, 348
 Self-Esteem Principle in, 33
 session, *Basking in Reflected-Glory* dream and, 144
 sexual adjustment handicapped, in *Relationship-Undoing,* 441
 Sexual-Object Displacement, 89
 Standards-Inversion in sexual behavior, 198
 Sublimation-en-, 311–12, 317
 Substitution evident, 408–10
  family doctor target, 409
  resentment expression allowed, 408
 Symptom-Introjection, 185
 Tidal-Progression Concept in, 346, 354
 Undoing revealed, 441, 443
  intolerable drives and, 443
  sexual relations as means of, 441
Third party route, 450
Threatening events, *Devaluation* downgrading, 457
Threats, 60, 61, 479
 Denial dismissing danger, 60
 Personal Invulnerability forestalling, 479
Thumbsucking, 91, 330
 Conflict-Indicator, 330

Thumbsucking (con't.)
 dismissal vs. *Public Denial,* 61
 Primal Displacement and, 91
Tidal
 Mass Identification, 145
 -Progression, Concept
  of Maturation, 328, 335, 346
  of Maturity, Normal Regression and, 324, 352, 353
  of Therapeutic Progress, 346, 354, 356
 Undoing, 436–37, 439, 443
  as back and forth process, 443
  in Obsessive-Compulsive Neuroses, 436–37, 439
  repetitive prayers, 439
  repetitive telephoning, 437
Timidity, overcompensation for, 290
Tiger's whiskers as asphrodisiac, 165
Token Restitution, 392, 397, 399
 Restitution-in-Abeyance and, 397
 unexpected remittances for past deficiencies and, 392
Total Regression, 323–24, 334
Total Repression, 379
TPM (*Tidal-Progression of Maturity*), 324, 328, 352
TPT (*Tidal-Progression of Treatment*), 346, 353, 356
Trait(s), 144, 148
 Celebrity-Seeker adopting, 141
 characterologic change through Identification, 141
 Parental Identification and, 148
Transference, 86, 119, 170, 199
 of hostility, in Fantasies, 118–19
 Incorporation in, 170
 intrapsychic, as term for Displacement, 86
 negative, *Inversion* of therapist's role and, 199
Transgressions, undone in Restitution, 440
Translations into literal, affect equivalents represent, 47
Transmutation of conflict, Conversion and, 30
Transparency Theory, 30, 36, 52
 Conversion Reactions and, 52
 symptom unable to survive elucidation, 30
Trauma
 Behavioral Conversion follows, 39–40
 Personal Invulnerability Defense Concept in, 60, 478–79
Traumatic Encephalopathy, 98
Treatment, 111, 242, 347–48, 350, 354, 437. See also *Therapy.*
 of *Denial-in-Fantasy* by Klein, 111
 elucidation of *King David Reaction* helpful, 242

Treatment (con't.)
  insulin subshock, *Regression* and, 350
  Regression, early unmet needs and, 347–48, 354
  Psychotic Reaction and, 348
  Resistance-Undoing and, 437
Trend Toward Emotional Health, Concept of, 34, 347
Triad of "taking in" Ego Defenses, 163
  Incorporation, 163
  Internalization, 174
  Introjection, 181
Tribal Extension, 461
Turnabout, emotional, as term for *Reversal,* 486
TVT (*Tenet of Variable Interpretation*), 417, 419, 420, 422

UAL (*Universal Affect Law*), 97, 99, 366–67
UDG (*Ultimate-Dependency-Goal Concept*), 322, 338, 352
UI (*Unwitting Ignorance*), 489
Ultimate-Dependency-Goal Concept, 322, 338, 352
Unconscious, 110–11, 120, 357, 362, 458
  arbitration, 454
  assignment to, as term for Repression, 357 ff.
  Atonement, 388, 450 ff.
  disguise, as term for *Distortion,* 458
  existence proved by Breuer, 362
  Fantasy, 110–11, 120
    never entered awareness, 120
    Primary Repressions and, 110–11
  justification, 24, 250 ff.
Understanding, 212, 216, 218, 489
  needed with emotionally ill, 212, 216, 218
  slow, *Unwitting Ignorance* and, 489
Undifferentiated Dissociation, Amorphous Dissociation as, 95
Unobtainable Ideal, 126
Underdog Identification, 157, 160
Undoing, 167, 204, 388, 402, 426 ff.
  Attitudinal, 443
  Behavioral-, Cycle, unwitting operation of, 429, 432–33, 443
  childhood, guilt motivating, 167, 432, 443
  Confession-, Cycle, 429, 442
  Confession-Discrepancy, 428, 442
  Criminal-, -in-fact and *-by-wish,* 430, 442
  Cycle Concept, 429–30, 431–32, 442–43
  definition of, 427–28
  Denial and, symbiosis and, 437

Undoing (con't.)
  Dream, 435–36, 443
    -of-Erasure, 435–36, 443
    as wish fulfillment, 435, 443
  dynamics, 439
  Expiative, 204, 402, 431, 442
    emotional symbiosis between *Inversion* and Undoing, 204, 402, 442
    Obsessive-Compulsive Neuroses and, 427, 431
  Fantasy, by child, 442, 443
  guilt over abortion and, 433
  Hangover Paradox, alcoholism and, 431, 442
  incomplete, in *Ineffectual* (or *Judas*) *Confession,* 429, 442
  as *Lower Order* dynamism, 427
  as *Major Ego Defense,* 427, 442
  nature of, 426
  Phrase, 434, 443
  psychic erasure, as term for, 426, 427
  Punishment-, Cycle, crime and, 430, 442
  Relationship-, 441, 443
  Resistance-, as *Secondary Defense,* 437, 443
  Restitution and, 388, 430, 440
    more primitive, 388
    for transgressions by families, nations and groups, 40
  Sexual, 443
  similar to *Atonement-Penance,* 430
  Social, 438, 443
  Spiral, 431, 442
  Symbolic, 439–40, 443
    handwashing as, 440
    prayers as, 439
  Tidal, 436–37, 439, 443
    back and forth process, 443
    repetitive symptoms, in Obsessive-Compulsive Neuroses, 436
  type of, in sleepwalking and sleeptalking, 436
Unfamiliar, *Devaluation* and, 457
Unhealthful Fantasy, 113
Universal Affect, Law of, 97, 99, 366–67, 379
  Affect Dissociation and, 97
  objects' emotional charge and, 379
  Repression and, 366–67
Unobtainable devalued
  through Rationalization, 261
  in Retrospective Devaluation, 484
Unobtainable Ideal Concept, 127, 130
Unreal feelings, 95, 103
  Depersonalization representing, 103
  Dissociative Reactions and, 95
Unsuccessful Compromise Formation, 454

Unwitting Ignorance, 489
Urges, Idealization and, 110, 125
U.S. Treasury, *Token Restitution* and, 393

Validation, Historical, 226, 240, 301, 316, 378
Values, *Characterologic Internalization* and, 175
Variable-Interpretation, Tenet of, 417, 419, 420, 422
  definition of, 420
  in dreams, 417
  in symbolism of psychoses, 419
VCS. See *Vicious Circle of Self-Defeat.*
Verbal facility, *Incomplete Compartmentalization* and, 454, 468
Verdrängung, 361
Veterinarian, *Impossible Standard* and, 126
Vicarious
  experience through *compathy,* 140
  Identification, 151, 152, 159
    role, 151
    Substitutive Gratifications and, satisfactions, 151. See also *Engulfment.*
Vice, 254, 291
  Crusades, Reaction Formations and, 291
  unconscious interest in, Rationalization by reformer and, 254
Vicious Circle
  Pathogenic Concept of, 10
  Projective, 221, 222–23, 228–29, 233
    fantastic person and, 221
    self-critical feelings, 228
    self-defeating aspects, 222–23
  of Self-Defeat, 10, 21, 41, 336, 342, 354, 482
    Behavioral Conversions and, 21, 41
    in *Hygeiaphrontic Personality,* 342
    in *Maturation-Fixation* at college level, 335–36
    in *Relationship-Replacement,* 482
Vicissitudes, 303, 304, 315, 321
  of drives, 304
  of instincts, emotional illness in Victorian Era and, 315
  of living, regressive manifestations and, 321
Victorian Era, sensual and sexual suppression in, 314
Violence
  Fantasy-Lesson Function checking, 116
  fostered through Projection and Denial, 244
  repressed impulses for, leading to *Criminal Identification,* 147

Vocal inflections, *Characterologic Identification* and, 143
Vocation(s)
  Compensation and, 22
  Identification, learning and, 145, 149
  Reaction Formation and, 283
  Rechannelizations, 303 ff., 316
    exhibitionism into acting, 306
    homosexuality and, 306
    parental drives thwarted and, 307–8
    in law career, 308
    professional activities contributed to in varying degree, 303–4
    sexual energies and, 304
    symbolism in choice of, 305
  Sublimation, 303–4, 305, 316
Vogue, Cultural, Concept of, 215
Voluntary Restitution as subtype of *Public Restitution,* 392, 399
Vomiting, 191, 339
  phobia of, dependency strivings and, 339
  in pregnancy, *Oral Introjection* and, 191
Voyeurism repressed in *King David Reaction,* 243
Vulnerability
  increased as self-defeat of Idealization, 125
  Personal Invulnerability Defense Concept, 478–79
  Reversal defending against, 488

Warning, regressive manifestations indicating, 327
Wartime operations, 328, 478
  Conflict-Indicators from psychologic pressures, 328
  Personal Invulnerability, and 478
Weight, 118, 255, 459
  leads to entering therapy, 118
  loss, *Distortion* and, 459
  reduction, lack of, rationalized, 25
White-Washing Operation (WWO), *Memory-Inversion* as type of, 197, 204
Wife as *convenient target,* 91
Will, Restitution-by-, 389, 397–98
Wills, unmade, as *Omission Denial* of death, 80
Wish
  Criminals-by-, 430
  fulfillment
    substitute, through Fantasy, 112
    Undoing Dream in, 435, 443
Wishful thinking, Repression and, 371
Withdrawal, 113, 489–91
  as *Attitudinal Symptom,* 490
  as *Behavioral Mechanism,* 489

Withdrawal (con't.)
Depressive, the social and, 184
Dissociated Psychotic-Survival and, 101, 490
emotional psychic retreat as alternate term for, 489
Fantasy representing, 110, 113, 120
Unhealthful Fantasy, 113
in *Hygeiaphrontis,* 342
Introversion as manifestation of, 490
in major *Mood-Inversion,* 202
Ostrich Concept similar to, 490
from reality, 113
Regression and, 320, 490
psychic-emotional, dependency and, 320
Regression-Sans-Withdrawal, 490
in Schizophrenia, 345, 490

Worship, Hero, 127, 130
Writing, *Dissociation of Automaticity* and, 98
Wrongdoer, Identification with, 147
WWO (*White-Washing Operation*), 197, 204

Yardstick, Concept of Personal (PY), 152, 159
Bases for Application, 153
Generalization of attitudes and, 474
in Identification, 146
in *King David Reaction,* misleading in, 246
Projection as earliest, 223, 233
Rule of Impression Priority in, 152
as universal measuring device, 226